THE HANDBOOK OF CHINESE PSYCHOLOGY

THE HANDBOOK OF CHINESE PSYCHOLOGY

Edited by
MICHAEL HARRIS BOND

HONG KONG
OXFORD UNIVERSITY PRESS
OXFORD   NEW YORK

Oxford University Press

Oxford New York
Athens Auckland Bangkok Bogota
Bombay Buenos Aires Calcutta Cape Town
Dar es Salaam Delhi Florence Hong Kong Istanbul
Karachi Kuala Lumpur Madras Madrid Melbourne
Mexico City Nairobi Paris Singapore
Taipei Tokyo Toronto

and associated companies in
Berlin Ibadan

Oxford is a trade mark of Oxford University Press

First published 1996
This impression (lowest digit)
3 5 7 9 10 8 6 4 2

Published in the United States
by Oxford University Press, New York

British Library Cataloguing in Publication Data
available

Library of Congress Cataloging-in-Publication Data

Handbook of Chinese psychology /edited by Michael Harris Bond.
p. cm.
Includes bibliographical references and index.
ISBN 0-19-586598-7
1. Chinese —Psychology. 2. National characteristics, Chinese.
I. Bond, Michael Harris, 1944–
DS721 . H254 1996
155.8'951—dc20

Printed in Hong Kong
Published by Oxford University Press (China) Ltd
18/F Warwick House, Taikoo Place, 979 King's Road, Quarry Bay, Hong Kong

Foreword: Psychology Moves East

Almost all contemporary psychology is based on data obtained from the swiftly decreasing 6 per cent of humanity that lives in North America, north of the Rio Grande. Yet more than 20 per cent of all humans are Chinese. To the extent that Chinese data are different from Western data, psychology reflects distortions of reality. Many of these distortions will be corrected in this volume.

The coverage is broad. It ranges:
(a) from abstract, basic psychology, such as perception and motivation, to concrete, applied psychology, such as the appropriate methods of psychotherapy for Chinese populations or the attributes of Chinese consumers;
(b) from universal, *etic* processes — such as universals of values and human behaviour — to *emic*, Chinese values — such as those discovered by the Chinese Cultural Connection (1987);
(c) and from historical reviews to analyses of the way modernity impinges on the Chinese.

In the West, many phenomena are understood very narrowly, because their study has used only Western data. In this volume some of these phenomena are placed in a broader framework. For example, the connection between written and spoken language is understood in the West only in the case of words that have alphabetic-phonetic components. But since the Chinese use logographs, Chinese studies of these connections open a new dimension for the understanding of the links between written and spoken language.

The range of coverage in this *Handbook* is impressive. People of Chinese ethnic backgrounds are found in different ecologies, facing pressures towards acculturation into social environments that vary in their level of modernization, and hence have different cultural attributes. This volume examines the social identities that emerge in such widely different environments. The indigenous conceptions of the person, the way they develop, and the possible implications of different conceptions are examined. For example, Lau Sing suggests that there are relationships between self-concepts and delinquency rates. Socialization that emphasizes parental control, restriction, protection, nurturance, and discipline (David Wu) may well be linked to the low delinquency rates and the high levels of academic achievement often found among Chinese populations. Others suggest links between linguistic socialization and reading comprehension. Learning that is responsive to the social context may be linked to excellent school achievement. Yet too much emphasis on such collectivist child rearing and values such as filial piety may results in low levels of cognitive complexity and high levels of cognitive rigidity (David Ho).

Studies of attributions and beliefs provide rich dimensions for the analysis of the way cognitions are linked to functioning in Chinese social environments. High levels of tested intelligence (Jimmy Chan) may be associated — to a greater extent than is the case in the West — with the overlearning of some cognitive elements in the Chinese social environment. Thus, Western standardizations of some tests may be completely inappropriate for the measurement of some of these traits.

The emergence of Chinese conceptions of morality that are more socio-centric and less ego-centric provide yet another opportunity to broaden Western-derived models.

Turning to social interaction, we find in this volume discussions of communication, personal relationships, leadership, and decision-making. The collectivist-hierarchical qualities of Chinese culture are reflected in many aspects of these processes and are mentioned explicitly by many of the authors of the corresponding chapters. More specifically, deferring to decisions taken by authorities, for example, seems more typical of Chinese than Western samples (Yates and Lee).

The etic constructs of collectivism and individualism are reflected in many of these discussions. Chinese collectivism has some unique attributes, but other cultures have much to learn from it. Collectivism, in general, has many strengths and some weaknesses. For example, it predisposes towards norm-congruent behaviours and discourages delinquency and crime. On the other hand, it limits the effectiveness of individual behaviour in broad public contexts, such as in political life. A full understanding of these relationships will enrich many aspects of psychology and provide applications of great value. For example, the greater social support received by individuals during life crises in collectivist cultures, relative to what happens in individualistic cultures, can result in lower levels of stress. Low stress, other things being equal, results in lower incidence of cardiovascular disease and enhances the immune system, so that there is also a lower incidence of infectious diseases. Such broad influences of culture on behaviour may well constitute the frontiers of the psychological research in the next century. Data from Chinese populations, especially now that some segments of Chinese society match the standards of living in Europe, will provide invaluable clues toward a better understanding of such relationships.

To take another example, while all humans have access to both collectivistic and individualistic cognitions, and use them to construct their social relationships, collectivists have more complex collectivist cognitive elements and are more likely to sample them in social interaction. This tendency has the effect of increasing the probability of harmony-seeking, interpersonal relationships among in-group members, but also increases the probability of distrustful or even hostile behaviours towards those who are perceived as belonging to outgroups. Such sampling of cognitive elements has broad implications for self-concept formation, and the sampling of the attitudes, beliefs, norms, and values that determine social behaviour. What we learn from the Chinese in this domain is likely to be much more relevant to our understanding of social behaviour in traditional cultures, and in parts of Asia, Africa, the Pacific, and Latin America where collectivism is widely found, than what we learn from American undergraduates.

The authors selected for this *Handbook* are the top experts on each of the topics. The match between topic and author is extraordinarily good, because, in many cases, the author has written on the same topic on previous occasions, and thus can expand previous theoretical statements in this volume. Also, they represent both the older generation of psychologists, such as Yang Kuo-shu and Harold Stevenson, and the new up-and-coming psychologists like Leung Kwok and C. Harry Hui.

In sum, psychology will be much richer, broader, and more comprehensive because of this volume.

HARRY C. TRIANDIS
University of Illinois
Urbana-Champaign
Spring 1994

Preface

Easier to describe a thing than to do it!

Shang Shu

In 1986, Oxford University Press published *The Psychology of the Chinese People*. This book was an edited collection of six chapters, constituting what was then state-of-the-art knowledge about Chinese psychological functioning. By the spring of 1992, this book was into its sixth printing and had sold more than 6,500 copies. Evidently, there was a considerable demand for the information and insights it was providing.

This demand reflected the growing prominence of the Pacific Rim in international trade, a trade which helped to fuel an increase in psychological research about Chinese people. *The Psychology of the Chinese People* had helped greatly to stimulate and to guide such research, but was slowly being overtaken by intellectual developments. By April 1992, I thought that the time may have arrived to consider a reprise. However, because so much more research was now available, it was clear that the 1986 work would need to be enlarged to handbook status.

Consequently, I then approached old friends and trusted colleagues in the area of Chinese psychology for advice. I requested their nominees for who should write chapters about topics in Chinese psychology where there was sufficient empirical data to justify coverage. Indeed, I also wanted to know what topics should be covered. I indicated that I was particularly keen to involve younger Chinese psychologists who had the necessary competence.

Part of that necessary competence involved professional-level skill in using English. Much of our research base is written in English and the *Handbook* would be published in English. In addition, skill in reading Chinese or in accessing such skill was necessary, since much necessary material has been published in that language.

With my colleagues' feedback and these considerations in mind, I compiled a list of topics and approached authors to write the chapters. I indicated that the process would include a conference to be held at the Chinese University of Hong Kong in May 1994. There, the combined expertise of all the *Handbook* authors could be focused on enriching each of the chapters. Final submissions would then be made by the end of December 1994, and the draft submitted to the judicious care of our publisher.

You now hold in your hands the fruit of this planning, writing, and mutual review. Throughout this lengthy process, my colleagues and administrative staff in the department of psychology at the Chinese University of Hong Kong have supported me with their flexibility, thoughtfulness, enthusiasm, and sacrifice of time. The university also provided me with a resource-rich, unfettered, task-oriented environment in which to work. Its students are among the best in the world; teaching and learning from them for 21 years has inspired me to believe that the psychological story of the Chinese people needs to be told to the world. And finally, the professionalism and competence of the staff at Oxford University Press enhanced the final quality of this *Handbook*, as it has our previous publications together. I thank you all heartily, each and every one, and, as my Chinese friends often say, 'sincerely apologize for any inconvenience caused'.

Listen to the words,
but observe the actions

Chinese adage

MICHAEL HARRIS BOND
Hong Kong
May 1995

Contents

Tables and Figures

LIST OF TABLES

LIST OF FIGURES

Contributors

(in alphabetical order)

John Balla
Faculty of Health Sciences
University of Sydney, Australia

Geoffrey H. Blowers
University of Hong Kong

Michael Harris Bond
Chinese University of Hong Kong

Jimmy Chan
University of Hong Kong

Hsuan-Chih Chen
Chinese University of Hong Kong

Fanny M. Cheung
Chinese University of Hong Kong

Paul T. Costa, Jr
Gerontology Research Center
National Institute of Health, USA

Kathleen S. Crittenden
Department of Sociology
University of Illinois, USA

Karen K. Dion
University of Toronto, Canada

Kenneth L. Dion
University of Toronto, Canada

Juris G. Draguns
Pennsylvania State University, USA

Solvig Ekblad
National Institute for Psychosocial Factors and Health, Sweden

Norman H. Freeman
University of Bristol, England

William K. Gabrenya, Jr
Florida Institute of Technology, USA

Ge Gao
Department of Communication Studies
San Jose State University, USA

Robin Goodwin
University of Bristol, England

Lyn Gow
Faculty of Art and Social Sciences
University of Sydney, Australia

William Gudykunst
Department of Speech Communication
California State University at Fullerton, USA

Gustav M. Habermann
Massey University, New Zealand

Kit Tai Hau
Faculty of Education
Chinese University of Hong Kong

David Y. F. Ho
University of Hong Kong

Sophie Hsia
Department of English
City University of Hong Kong

Jong-Tsun Huang
National Taiwan University

C. Harry Hui
University of Hong Kong

Kwang-Kuo Hwang
National Taiwan University

David Kember
Educational Technology Unit
Hong Kong Polytechnic University

Ju-Whei Lee
Chung Yuan Christian University, Taiwan

Peter W. H. Lee
Department of Psychiatry
University of Hong Kong

Shin-ying Lee
Center for Human Growth and Development
University of Michigan, USA

Che Kan Leong
Department for the Education of Exceptional Children
University of Saskatchewan, Canada

Patrick W. L. Leung
Chinese University of Hong Kong

Kwok Leung
Chinese University of Hong Kong

In-mao Liu
National Chung Cheng University, Taiwan

Robert R. McCrae
Gerontology Research Center
National Institute of Health, USA

Veronica Pearson
Department of Social Work and Social Administration
University of Hong Kong

Michael R. Phillips
Hui Long Gan Hospital, Beijing, China

James A. Russell
University of British Columbia, Canada

Peter B. Smith
University of Sussex, England

Harold W. Stevenson
University of Michigan, USA

Chen K. Tan
University of Hong Kong

Catherine So-kum Tang
Chinese University of Hong Kong

Stella Ting-Toomey
Department of Speech Communication
California State University at Fullerton, USA

David K. Tse
Faculty of Business Administration
City University of Hong Kong

Zhong-Ming Wang
Hangzhou University, China

David Y. H. Wu
Department of Anthropology
Chinese University of Hong Kong

Jei-tun Wu
National Taiwan University

Kuo-Shu Yang
National Taiwan University

J. Frank Yates
University of Michigan, USA

Michelle S. M. Yik
University of British Columbia, Canada

An-Bang Yu
Academia Sinica, Taiwan

Where not otherwise indicated, contributors are members of their university's
Department of Psychology.

Introduction

Michael Harris Bond

> By blending the breath of the sun and the shade
> True harmony comes into the world
>
> *Tao Te Ching, Poem 42*

This Handbook signals a coming-of-age for the psychological study of Chinese people. Over the past three decades a ground swell of research activity has been gathering momentum, so that numerous, identifiable pockets of knowledge are now plainly visible to informed scholars. This increase was initiated by overseas Chinese in North America, carried forward by psychologists in the colonial institutions of Hong Kong, given indigenous flavour and energy by Taiwanese psychologists trained mostly in North America, and is now being passed on to mainland Chinese psychologists through professional contacts with foreign colleagues, both Chinese and non-Chinese.

As a consequence of this energetic scholarship, the discipline of psychology now has a counterweight to the dominance of the field by the West. Chinese culture has the necessary age, coherence, and difference from Western traditions to provide a litmus test to the presumptions of universality that tend to characterize psychology done in the mainstream. If a construct or process is universal, then Chinese human beings should give evidence of its validity. Such generalizing research must be done to ground our discipline on firmer bedrock.

A Chinese cultural context, however, can provide more: If the doing of psychology is itself a cultural product, then the topics, the emphases, the concepts, the methodologies, and the theories of our discipline can be fertilized by growing in 'foreign' soil. Many chapters in this Handbook bear witness to the productive influence of work developed in, what is for psychology, an atypical cultural context.

Nurturing such synergy is no easy task. Historically, the science of psychology originated in the West and many psychologists working in Chinese societies were trained in the West. If 'the eye cannot see its own lashes', to quote a Chinese adage, how then can psychologists escape the prison of their pasts to discover novelty in Chinese culture? This challenge goes to the heart of our discipline, raising the question of how to promote intellectual self-transcendence and creativity. In practical terms, it is being addressed at the individual level by psychologists who experiment with novel subject populations, research methodologies, measurement tools, and interpretive strategies in order to allow Chinese social reality to speak in its own voice.

At the organizational level, it has and is being addressed by the formation of an association based in Taiwan which promotes indigenous Chinese social science. There is a potential danger here, of course, in the exclusive use of Chinese culture to build a truly universal understanding of man, since an emphasis on what is unique in Chinese behaviour may blind us to what can be related to findings elsewhere. As Andrew Nathan puts it, 'A culture's uniqueness or non-uniqueness is not a characteristic of the culture itself, but of the way its attributes are conceptualized' (p. 931). So, for example, Yu presents socially oriented achievement motivation (in his chapter) as a collectivist variant of achievement. McCrae, Costa, and Yik, however, assume a universal stance towards personality variation in their chapter. They might well argue that social-oriented achievement motivation is more economically conceptualized as a blend of the culture-general Achievement Striving and Compliance facets of Conscientiousness and Agreeableness, respectively. In the chapters that follow, this conceptual tension between distinctiveness and commonality ebbs and flows. It is a necessary tide, however, in more fully humanizing the discipline of psychology. This Handbook is a contribution towards such a development.

It begins with a historical overview by Blowers which provides one analysis of the context out of which our knowledge base has sprung. Social science is a reflexive human enterprise whose origins shape its development and, some would say, limit its claims to objectivity, comprehensiveness, and even truth. We may be more sanguine on this point. Nonetheless, such a chapter is essential reading as fascinating, provocative background for understanding the present content of Chinese psychology.

That content is by and large covered in the next 29 chapters that follow the historical overview. The chapters are organized traditionally from perception and cognition, through developmental and personality, to social, organizational, and clinical psychology. Within each broad section, the more basic research is presented first, followed by chapters describing work on applications.

These content chapters are rounded out by Yang's, which addresses the impact of societal modernization on Chinese psychological functioning. This is essential reading, for it considers the question of whether a handbook on Chinese psychology is an exercise in futility. Some would argue that the forces of modernization are inexorably pushing humanity towards a homogenized future where cultural differences will disappear. Yang disagrees. More importantly, he provides both theoretical rationale and empirical support to suggest where cross-cultural convergence will and will not occur.

The resulting 31 chapters vary in many respects other than in their areas of coverage. Some, like Ekblad's on ecological psychology, involve the extension of recent psychological concerns into Chinese culture; others, like Huang's on visual perception, involve well established areas, indeed. Some chapters, like Cheung's on the assessment of psychopathology, provide a detailed historical survey; others, like Crittenden's on causal attributions, provide a refined conceptual analysis. Chen's, on reading, is informed by extensive, empirical documentation; Tse's on consumer behaviour is more speculative. Bond's discussion of values emphasizes measurement procedures, while Phillips and Pearson's on coping emphasizes asking the right questions. Some, like Ho's on filial piety, focus on indigenous concepts; others, like McCrae, Costa, and Yik's on personality structure, focus on universal aspects.

Ultimately, such variation reflects the predilection of the authors combined with the size of the database and the richness of the extant theory. The availability of data and theory also explains why the coverage may appear uneven at first blush. There are, for example, four chapters on language. This richness arises from the Chinese use of idiographic script and tonal speech. In both these respects Chinese language differs from those in the West. Western psychologists have conducted a host of studies on subjects socialized to a phonetic script and atonal speech, and so a picture window of opportunity exists to do research on Chinese persons who may evidence distinctive processes for language acquisition and processing. Furthermore, Chinese bilinguals who use both types of language forms then become a human laboratory for cultural synergy. Not surprisingly, these unique affordances provided by Chinese culture have been exploited by psychologists. The coverage of this Handbook generally mirrors the relative level of research activity in the various areas of Chinese psychology.

Inevitably, there is some overlap. The Chinese concept of *yuan* (fatedness), the focus on achievement, the concept of hierarchy, and so forth receive repeated mention in various chapters. This is understandable: Chinese culture is a kaleidoscope whose different behavioural manifestations reflect different permutations of the same conceptual elements. The editors have attempted to remove repetitious material, but such editing is always a judgement call. If we have erred, it is on the side of overlap, so as to ensure that each chapter could stand independently of the rest.

For, each chapter addresses a varied readership who may select only one, or a few, chapters to read. Although this Handbook is addressed to a scholarly audience, the topic of Chinese psychology interfaces with many disciplines in addition to psychology. Psychiatrists will profit from Dragun's chapter on psychopathology, architects from Ekblad's on ecological psychology, government policy planners from the Dions' on immigration, political scientists from Smith and Wang's on leadership, educators from Gow et al.'s on approaches to learning, English-language teachers from Leong and Hsia's on Chinese learning English as a second language, travellers from Gao et al.'s on communication, international negotiators from Yates and Lee's on decision-making, and businesspersons from Tse's on consumer behaviour. The possibilities are endless; Chinese culture is a vast repository!

Psychologists will find their scientific imaginations stretched and any lurking complacencies challenged. For, the emergence of a viable, vibrant Chinese psychology allows us to assay our discipline's legacy to date. How universal are our past findings? In what way will Chinese results force us to expand our theoretical nets? What areas of behaviour could provide litmus tests of current ideas in the mainstream of psychological practice? How can Chinese psychological reality broaden our conception of what it is to be human? This Handbook will be a worthy investment of its authors' energy and resources if it assists us all to address these issues more energetically.

The volume is offered as a steppingstone towards a more dynamic, more comprehensive, more insightful psychology of the Chinese people. It is also offered as a herald for the psychologies of other cultural groups whose traditions hold promise of further synergizing our discipline. Most important, it is offered to you as a person who will help realize these important goals.

All men have been created to carry forward
an ever-advancing civilization

Baha'u'llah

Chapter 1

■

The Prospects for a Chinese Psychology

Geoffrey H. Blowers

Chinese psychology, in some senses of the term, is as old as the civilization that has fostered it. One can see in the teachings of Confucius, Mencius, Lao Zi, and their followers, philosophies which deal with the concepts of humanity, development, and appropriate forms of conduct (Mote, 1967). But the common and diverse views of man contained within them did not have an impact upon, nor explicitly inform, the modern Western discipline until 1978, when Chinese psychologists, in the wake of another political upheaval, took it upon themselves to link modern psychology to their own historical and philosophical past (Gao, 1985; Zhao, Lin, and Zhang, 1989).

Since it was introduced into China at the turn of the century, psychology has followed a difficult path to arrive at its current standing. Its development has been buffeted by enormous political upheavals, and these interruptions have had a very strong and very mixed influence. Chinese psychology, or rather, psychology in China, thereby stands as an acute example of a discipline peculiarly sensitive to ideological influence.

For a variety of reasons, psychology was seen from the beginning of its importation to be a foreign discipline, initially Americo-European, later Marxist, and later still, Soviet. In the second decade of the People's Republic of China (PRC) it became progressively Maoist in outlook, only to be outlawed subsequently as a bourgeois discipline (Munro, 1977). It then re-emerged, with a broadened scope and aims, as China once again became receptive to ideas from inside and outside the culture. Ironically, this re-opening has come just at the time when a highly inflationary economy is luring many younger academics and graduate students out of the universities and into the commercial sectors.

It is also clear, from even a casual perusal of the growing research literature, that modern accounts of 'Chinese psychology' render the term ambiguous. This ambiguity lies deeply rooted in the variety of ways psychologists, in both the East and West, have come to see the subject and is a succinct indication of its current state. No longer considered a unified and coherent discipline in some Western quarters, psychology, in Sigmund Koch's formulation (Koch, 1993), has given way to psychological studies, separate and parallel activities arising largely as a result of the crisis of confidence over what are the subject's aims, objects, and modes of enquiry. At issue are the means for establishing the validity of its findings and determining their truth value, as well as the social, political, cultural, and sexual identifications from which different researchers report their findings.

Partly as a reaction to this development, and partly in ignorance of it, many Western and some Chinese psychologists are continuing to seek universal concepts for understanding mental phenomena and have sought validation by employing non-Western subjects for their research studies. Here, the employment of Chinese subjects in Western research studies has become the sole and sufficient criterion for classifying them as studies in Chinese psychology. This development has extended the original understanding of the term as encompassing something indigenous to the Chinese population and prompts a reexamination of the question of what a Chinese psychology might be.

WHAT IS CHINESE PSYCHOLOGY?

Broadly defined, Chinese psychology is but one form of indigenous psychology. In the introduction to *Indigenous Psychologies: The Anthropology of the Self,* Heelas (1981) defines indigenous psychology as the perspective whose claims are generally accepted, in contrast to what he calls specialist psychologies which enjoy credibility among minorities, usually academics and professionals. Indigenous, in this sense, is the study of grass-roots thinking, the everyday, the commonplace, as ingrained among inhabitants of a community and a culture.

Defining the term more closely will quickly get us into trouble, for the metaphysical assumptions which underlie different indigenous psychologies show the enormous variation in their possibilities. As Heelas says,

indigenous psychologies differ with respect to…inner/outer, conscious/unconscious, internal control [will]/external control [fate or destiny], hot/cold, reason/emotion, up/down, public/private, unitary self/fragmented self, and…[the] subjective/objective distinction (p. 10–11).

These distinctions highlight the different ways we come to understand ourselves. They are in part bound up with the belief systems of the socio-cultural milieu we inhabit. Across a wide spectrum, indigenous psychologies help regulate and articulate personality judgements, behaviours, and emotional responses. They also play a central role in how suffering, emotional disturbances, and pain are handled, mediating between an animal nature and the outside world.

The sense here is of indigenous as local, thereby rendering the project for an indigenous Chinese psychology as the making explicit of what is implicit in the minds of ordinary Chinese folk: the articulation of the processes shaping personality, emotion, and behaviour—both normal and abnormal as culturally defined. When taken seriously this understanding has much to tell us about actual psychological processes.

In a variant of this sense, however, indigenous can also be taken to mean *national*—the institutionalized discipline informed and structured by the history and politics of a nation. When this is so, not only the discipline's subject matter but also its methods may come under scrutiny of the guardians of political correctness. Relevant questions to be raised in this context might explore why one area of psychology is relatively underdeveloped in China and another emphasized, or why some methods enjoy prominence at certain times in the country's history while at other times they fall from grace. More specifically, we may ask why personality theory is not much stressed in China, and why there is a marked preference for testing and experimental psychology. Why has it been necessary to debate the importance of taking account of the class position of subjects? Why has there been an idealization of the dialectically materialistic approach (Lee and Petzold, 1987; Petzold, 1984)?

Even to talk of China and Chinese psychology we have to be clear whether we are referring to mainland China, Taiwan, Hong Kong, or elsewhere. We can, of course, assume that the studies done within these regions as a whole constitute, by dint of their geographical location and the ethnicity of their participants, a de facto indigenous psychology. But this would be to dismiss the enormous historical and socio-political differences between these regions and to extend the meaning of the term to include any research studies in the psychological sphere involving ethnic Chinese as subjects.

A more recent sense of indigenous psychology as brought to the Chinese is the application of Western psychological methods to study culturally specific practices such as calligraphy, acupuncture, *qigong* (Wang, 1989), and even the Chinese language itself (Chen and Tzeng, 1992). The metaphysical assumptions which lie behind these practices shape the culture's health beliefs, aesthetic preferences, and other attributes, and generally frame the way it is perceived by its inhabitants. Each of these practices is a potentially fruitful area in which to work, although the terms and conditions of their study have sometimes led to a tendency for the term *indigenous* to imply 'Chinese only' psychology—one which is seen not only to lie outside Western experience, but also to be beyond its critical boundaries. It is noteworthy that in the more recent attempts to study indigenous concepts from indigenous viewpoints (for example, Yang, 1993), there has been little enthusiasm for the reporting of them to the English-speaking world at large.

This exclusion, if adopted as policy, would indeed be unfortunate, for it undermines the rationale for studying indigenous psychologies in the first place: that each culture makes a unique contribution to the general study of mind. Compounding these viewpoints is the long-running debate over whether culturally isolated practices should be studied using a conventional cross-cultural set of methods, given that these have been developed in cultures other than those which are usually the objects of study (for example, Berry, 1989; Jahoda, 1977). These methods and the belief systems which inform them are on the agenda of those involved in the study of indigenous Chinese psychology, for they highlight a conflict over intention, often expressed as a debate over cultural versus universal features of mind. The conundrum has been well expressed by Lock:

When one proposes some basic universal dimensions from one cultural perspective and finds an apparent fit of other cultural systems to these dimensions, one has not proposed universals at all. Rather, one has constructed a translation and classificatory system which enables one to gain some understanding of an alien culture by locating elements of their systems within the hermeneutic circle of one's own (1981, p. 184).

While many traditionalists in the discipline would not share this understanding, it does clarify the pro-indigenous case. Those who would advocate the study of universal features of mind are, from this viewpoint, already engaged in the proclamation of an indigenized psychology. It is the hallmark of those cultures which celebrate the centrality of the individual in society, and whose authoritative, dominant, intellectual mode champions the cause of rationality over superstition. Its origins lie in the European Enlightenment.

We should be reminded, however, that in spite of the distinctions in meaning which can be wrestled from the phrase 'indigenous Chinese psychology' there have been few studies which have attempted to research psychological questions from solely these standpoints. The reasons have more to do with the historical forces which have come to shape the discipline in and outside China, and these are examined next.

PSYCHOLOGY COMES TO CHINA

Problems of Translation

In the few narratives outlining the coming of Western psychology to China, the starting date usually cited is 1899, the year in which Joseph Haven's *Mental Philosophy* first appeared in the country in translation. The book's appearance in Chinese was the outcome of a need felt for it by its translator based upon his own teaching of it, in English, to Chinese students for many years previously. Y. K. Yen (Yan Yongjin), under the sponsorship of the American church mission in Shanghai, studied at Kenyon College, in Ohio, where he acquired an enthusiasm for the philosophy of the mind. He subsequently taught the subject in church schools in China as part of a general moral education program (Kodama, 1991).

Haven's book was not only the first psychology text to be translated, it was also the first to encounter the difficulty of translating psychology into the Chinese language—of finding appropriate equivalent terms which would not distort the original meanings. Having no prior Chinese translation for the term *psychology,* Yen chose three characters not previously conjoined, *xinlingxue* (心靈學), a combination which translates back into English as 'pneumatology', the study of spirit, a far remove from the contemporary understanding of psychology! His choice of the character *ling* (靈), for spirit, may have been informed by his reading of Aristotle's *De Anima* and Bain's journal, *Mind.* It may also be that the theme of Haven's book, that behaviour is a derivative of the soul, and the fact that in Chinese culture the soul is considered a primary element of mind and nature, exhausted all other possible interpretations (Zhao, 1983).

In any event, by the time of the appearance in China of the next prominent Western psychology text, Harald Hoffding's *Outline of Psychology,* the term for psychology, probably relying on the Japanese translation, had become *xinlixue* (心理學), *li* (理) replacing *lin*, though not removing the problems of ambiguous meanings (Blowers, 1991). While the modern simple back-translation renders this phrase as 'knowledge of the heart', both *xin* and *li* have long histories of meaning, including, from the time of Mencius, ethical principles of conduct arising out of competing views on human nature—from the Confucian ethic of intrinsic goodness, to a belief in the heart's propensity for evil most fully expressed in the writings of Xun Zi (荀子) (Creel, 1954). The heart–mind performed a natural evaluative role. While this activity included the making of sensory distinctions, all evaluations would appear to be made in accordance with how one should act in relation to others. These understandings have generally framed the Chinese intellectual outlook, as other commentators have noted (see, for example, Munro, 1969, 1977; Petzold, 1987). They also help to explain why, traditionally, there has been no sophisticated philosophical or psychological system of mind, and why it is necessary to distinguish conscious from unconscious thought.

This beginning, then, marks two developments for Western psychology into China: the selective borrowing of a psychological literature for utilitarian purposes, rather than for a general philosophical orientation, and the reshaping of its meaning through the difficulties of translation. Western psychology was introduced to aid instruction for moral guidance, as most of the teachings came through Church-sponsored organizations of various religious persuasions. Teaching about the mind was not so much to understand its workings per se as to foster the notion of a healthy mind which would instigate correct patterns of behaviour. This understanding was entirely in keeping with Confucian doctrines and served the general pedagogical purpose of the time. In selecting texts with concepts for which there were no Chinese equivalents, decisions were arbitrarily taken to coin new terms by borrowing Chinese characters with similar, but by no means identical, semantic features. Translation of texts thus marked the beginning of an indigenizing process common to many foreign subjects, which only became apparent after the trickle of translated academic books at the end of the nineteenth century turned into a flood in the early part of the twentieth.

The Initial Impetus

The advent of the May Fourth Movement in 1919 brought forth a challenge to the Confucian political structure, as a strong student movement sought to overthrow the feudal system with which China had been saddled for centuries and to re-evaluate traditional thinking. As many commentators have remarked (see, for example, Chow, 1964; Franke, 1967; Israel, 1966; Pepper, 1978), since the 1911 revolution, student-led movements had campaigned vigorously for improvements to society based upon the twin, mythic giants of science and democracy (known at the time as 'Mr Science' and 'Mr Democracy'). These were thought to hold the key to the West's superiority over China and would serve to liberate the nation from a feudal past based upon superstition. The attention paid to Western science in the 1920s spread the seeds for China's receptiveness to many Western subjects, and led to their becoming disciplines taught in institutions of higher education. Psychology was one such discipline.

Early Institutional Developments

The first psychology laboratory in China was established at Peking National University in 1917, under the urging of the democratic reformer Cai Yuanpei, who had studied under Wilhelm Wundt in Leipzig (Petzold, 1987). Many of the intellectuals of this period had studied abroad in Europe or America, and many of the first generation of Chinese psychologists were American-trained. The first psychology department was opened at Southeastern University in Nanjing in 1920. Within ten years other departments had opened at universities in Canton, Shanghai, Qinqhua, Amoy, and Tientsin (Chou, 1927, 1932). By 1928 the Institute of Psychology had been founded within the Chinese Academy of Sciences. A Chinese Psychological Society was formally established in 1921 and the following year began publishing *The Chinese Journal of Psychology*, whose main emphasis reflected the contemporary mainstream of psychology in the West in which many of the Chinese students educated abroad had been steeped. The outlook was primarily behaviouristic, and educational testing and measurement formed a large part of the body's initial concerns (Chou, 1927). Between 1922 and 1940 some 370 books on psychology were published in China (Pan, Chen, Wang, and Chen, 1980).

These developments did not pose any threat to fundamental values, since they were seen as tools in the service of the greater good of society. The behaviourism and functionalism which the American-educated students brought back to China could be accommodated within the new pragmatic view of the need for Western science, even if their essentially deterministic conceptions could, arguably, be seen as a challenge to Confucian notions of mind. This leniency was not accorded to psychoanalysis, however. Here Chinese intellectuals trod warily through some of the more radical aspects of the theory as they attempted to exalt Freud for the purposes of education and social reform. Some translations of Freud resulted in layers of censorship introduced by his translators in order to downplay what they took to be his pansexualism and to make his ideas more palatable. Oedipal theory, for example, was subverted into a social theory of family conformity (Blowers, 1994).

By the end of the 1920s and the early 1930s, not only universities but also many teacher colleges were instructing their pupils in the ideas of Freud, Watson, McDougall, Piaget, Lewin, and Kohler using translated texts and critical essays (Bauer and Hwang, 1982). Unfortunately, these did not aid the modernization of the country in the way the student movement hoped (see Pye, 1992, for a lucid account of this period).

The war against the Japanese at the end of the 1930s and the political upheavals that accompanied the Communist revolution brought developments in psychology to a halt. Institutions teaching the subject or engaged in psychological research were closed down or evacuated. The Chinese Psychological Society suspended practically all its activities including publication (Lee and Petzold, 1987).

PSYCHOLOGY IN THE PEOPLE'S REPUBLIC

Redefining the Discipline

Following the founding of the People's Republic in 1949, a broad program of socialist reform was ushered in. At this time it was widely held that psychology, based as it was upon Western ideas, would need to be revised to fit better into the new social and political milieu. Like other intellectuals, psychologists had to study Marxist philosophy, and their discipline had to be practised in accordance with two principles: that psychological phenomena are a product or function of the brain, and that mind is a reflection of outer reality. These were drawn from Lenin's theory of reflection expressed in his *Materialism and Empirio-criticism* and Mao Zedong's *On Contradiction* and *On Practice* (Ching, 1980). Soviet psychology had to be studied, and Western psychology, in its various schools, had to be critically examined for its failings (Lee and Petzold, 1987).

The year 1949 thus brought a halt to the teaching and practice of Western psychology on the Mainland (Chin and Chin, 1969). In that period most of the allowable textbooks in psychology were translations from the Russian (Petzold, 1984). Russian educationalists came to China in the early 1950s to teach in Beijing, advocating a new foundation for the acquisition of knowledge. Inspired by the work of Vygotsky, Luria, and Leont'ev, dialectical materialism became the central philosophy underlying all permissible psychology. From this position consciousness was an historically and developmentally formed mental product so that its objects could not be thought of as separate from the reflection process (*fanshe* 反射) which brings them into being. This contrasted with certain idealist tendencies in Western psychology which were predicated upon a separation of subject and object, or mental image and objective reality.

An effect of this position was to introduce a new term for consciousness, *zijue neng dongli* (自覺能動力)—active consciousness—which is formed out of the activities of people in society undertaking concrete actions. Mental processes, it was argued, could not be studied apart from the contexts in which they occur. Consciousness was seen as the supreme force governing human behaviour unchallenged by (and therefore granting no status to) competing forces such as the preconscious or unconscious. It was capable of self-reflection, that is, awareness of its own changes, and by all of its activities it increased its knowledge, this process of growth being known as *renshi* (認識)—recognition. Ding Zuan (Ting Tsang), the secretary of the Chinese Psychological Society, re-formed in 1955, said in an article published one year after the society's re-establishment that there was little room within this framework for Freud's 'mysterious sexual drives' (Ding, 1956). Paradoxically, psychotherapy, a direct offshoot of Freud's theory, gained respectability only when its theoretical justification was presented in Pavlov's system of an ordering of reflexes responding to verbal stimuli.

In spite of the tendency to theorize all psychological activity in terms of Pavlovian reductionism, Chinese psychologists, following the re-opening of the psychological society, fought for their own views. This was made possible in the brief period of the One Hundred Flowers Movement of 1957, during which the Communist Party invited criticism from intellectuals. It was during this period that psychologists questioned the status of much reductionist psychology, arguing that it was becoming divorced from reality (Zhao, 1989) and should have a practical or applied component. This led many psychologists to give up laboratory work and to seek applications for their work in factories, hospitals, and schools.

Early Suppression

However, this period of open debate and questioning was quickly counteracted in the Anti-rightist or Criticism Movement which followed in August 1958. Psychology was banned as 'bourgeois pseudo-science' and many psychologists were persecuted.

The political justification for this suppression was explained as follows: by concentrating on the biological foundations of behaviour and the experimental isolation of variables, psychologists were guilty of abstracting entities from their social context. By so doing, psychology remained too 'academic' and therefore played into the hands of class enemies of the state. By failing to take account of the social nature of the subject (as the study of consciousness, psychology was class bound), psychologists essentially dehumanized the class nature of their activities. This line of thinking, quite unfounded, denied the possibility of any common or universal features of the mind that were worthwhile objects of study.

Following the failure of the Great Leap Forward, in 1959–60, these criticisms were stopped, and discussions among psychologists led to an integration of the viewpoints of psychology as both a natural and social science (Cao, 1959). In the early 1960s, educational and developmental psychology became the most productive areas of the discipline, so that by 1963, at the first annual meeting of the Chinese Psychological Society, they comprised over three-quarters of the 203 papers presented. Other papers were also in the applied areas of personnel and clinical psychology.

Later Suppression

This hiatus of productivity was short-lived, as attacks on the discipline soon came from students and young cadres engaged in the Cultural Revolution. Following a general line taken by Mao, the country's youth was encouraged in anarchic activities against the more progressive elements of the Communist Party, which had been content to accede a certain autonomy to intellectuals (whom Mao believed would lead the country to failure). Attacks on many academic disciplines occurred. Psychology was a particular target of a leading figure in the party, Yao Wenyuan. In an editorial written under a pseudonym in *Renmin Ribao* (The People's Daily), Minister of Propaganda Yao attacked an article, written by Chen Li and Wang Ansheng, on colour and form preferences in children for much the same reasons that had motivated outbursts during the earlier Criticism Movement: the experiments were abstracted from the lived realities of people, in actual social contexts, and therefore were not legitimate objectives of research. Because of Yao's influential position, his editorial fuelled the flames of a growing attack on the discipline as a whole, forcing it to be completely shut down by 1966, with the banning of psychology books and journals and the ceasing of its teaching in universities and research institutes.

Rehabilitation

However, at the Third Plenary session of the Chinese Communist Party Congress in 1978 the discipline was once again made respectable. The first meeting of the Chinese Psychological Society held during this period elected Pan Shu—who had served in the role prior to the Cultural Revolution—as its president. With another of his generation of scholars, Gao Juefu, Pan was invited to write histories of Chinese and Western psychology (Gao, 1985; Gao and Pan, 1983). Also at the meeting were many opportunities for the denunciation of the previous injustices perpetrated by Yao Wenyuan, which were led by Chen Li himself (Blowers, in press [*World Psychology*], Chen and Wang, 1981; Petzold, 1987). In this more favourable post-Mao climate, psychologists were called upon to contribute to the modernization program as China, once again, became receptive to the West. Intellectuals of various persuasions began visiting the country's institutions of learning, and exchanges began to be encouraged.

The Outlook

The prospects for the development of psychology in China, however, are far from rosy. To begin with, there is the enormous gap in continuity of education created by the ten-year closing of the university doors, resulting in the loss of intellectual development for a whole generation of actual and potential students. In addition, there are only nine universities throughout the whole of China where a student can receive a degree in psychology, although it is taught in many of China's 'normal' universities, or teacher-training institutes, as a subject allied to education. In the practical spheres of education, health, and industry, there is still much demand for the subject matter. But the store of local data is weak as a result of the many political disruptions of research activities.

Dialogue with Western psychological authorities continues, through visits and reciprocal arrangements for study periods. Since 1980, China has been a member of the International Union of Psychological Science (IUPS). However, the development of an appropriate theoretical perspective for Chinese psychology has yet to emerge. If one takes an historical perspective on psychology in China, and on psychological research by Chinese in other regions, one fact seems clear: While much present-day Western psychology is welcomed for its utilitarian value, there is little evidence that the metaphysical assumptions of its rigid determinism (as seen in radical behaviourism and psychoanalysis) and its individualism (in personality and intellectual assessment) are embraced in any fundamental way by Chinese people. Western psychology, seemingly, provides skills training that helps society solve a myriad of problems in child development, health, and industry, but remains in the service of an authoritarian collectivist culture. This appears to be all the more reason, therefore, for the Chinese themselves to develop a specifically Chinese framework for future study (Pan, 1980). Whether this framework will ultimately materialize will depend upon, among other things, the number of students that China is willing to accommodate for university training in the discipline and the opportunities for postgraduate research in its institutes.

Two unfortunate trends militate against any immediate prospects for expansion. In the present inflationary economy, graduates and young teachers are leaving the universities in droves, lured by the financial opportunities promised by joint-venture businesses. An equal number are seeking study in the United States and elsewhere with a view not only to obtaining a higher degree but to securing residence in their host countries for employment purposes. These opportunities are granted to only a relatively few in each case, but they highlight an underlying dissatisfaction that a mobilization of those remaining within the discipline is unlikely to eradicate.

PSYCHOLOGY IN OTHER CHINESE REGIONS

Institutional Developments

By contrast to the situation in mainland China, Taiwan, Hong Kong, and even Singapore have made great strides in the development of their psychological studies, even though the discipline, in each of these regions, arose from humble, colonial beginnings in the period before the Second World War. In Taiwan under Japanese rule, psychology was taught in Japanese in the department of literature at Taipei Imperial (now National Taiwan) University. That legacy was richly endowed with many hundreds of translations and secondary sources written in Japanese on Western psychological topics. Japanese psychology in the 1930s and 1940s was dominated by the gestalt school, with the result that the early stages of experimental research in Taiwan were concerned with problems of perception.

In Hong Kong under the British, psychology was taught at the University of Hong Kong in English in the faculty of arts, as an adjunct to philosophy. It remained there until the annexation of those departments in 1967, when the faculty of social sciences was formed. In Taiwan, psychology's emergence from the department of literature came in 1949 when, following the declaration of the Republic of China on Taiwan by Chiang Kai-shek and the implementation of Mandarin as the medium of instruction, it became a separate department housed in the faculty of sciences. In Taiwan and Hong Kong, each department, once separated, made great strides in its development; shortly thereafter other departments at other institutions in these regions sprang up (Blowers, 1987; Hsu, 1987).

Singapore does not, as yet, have a separate psychology department at either of its universities. Psychology is taught at present in the National University of Singapore within the department of social work and psychology. However, in the areas of mental and educational assessment, it finds application in the mental health, educational, and military sectors. This development offers possibilities for growth although not, seemingly, within the academic sphere, where large-scale misconceptions about the subject still abound among the population at large (Long, 1987).

The Investment in Research

Economic growth from the 1950s onwards made for closer ties to Britain in Hong Kong's and Singapore's cases, and to America in the instance of Taiwan, with curricula tailored to each educational tradition. These changes affected the kind of psychology that was taught and the psychological problems investigated. In each location the general, intellectually liberal climate that prevailed at the tertiary level enabled many exchanges with overseas academics and the fostering of closer intellectual ties. Research activity flourished.

Of significance was the formation in Hong Kong in 1972 of the International Association for Cross-cultural Psychology (IACCP), an organization devoted to the testing of hypotheses in different cultures, in all aspects of the discipline, using samples of Western (usually American) subjects as a baseline for cross-cultural comparison. An outgrowth of this endeavour was the gathering in 1986 of research data in several areas in social psychology, psychopathology, language, and personality, among others, into a single edited volume entitled *The Psychology of the Chinese People* (Bond, 1986). The authors included were all established researchers in their respective fields and had carried out many studies using Chinese subjects, although none of the scholars involved came from mainland China originally.

Virtually all of the experimental research which has used Chinese subjects, be they from the Mainland, Taiwan, Hong Kong, or elsewhere, and which is written in English, has been conveniently abstracted in a useful volume by Ho, Spinks, and Yeung (1989). More detailed summaries of specialized aspects of the discipline can be found in the present volume.

While the scope of their compilation was extensive, Ho, Spinks, and Yeung noted that many of the papers they abstracted were poorly written, methodologically unsound, and lacked insight or theoretical rigour. They attributed these weaknesses to the blind copying by Chinese psychologists of Western studies and the inadequacy of the steps taken to ensure impartial peer review and editorial responsibility in Chinese journals. At the same time they commented favourably upon the conference on sinicization held in Taiwan in 1980 at which criticisms were voiced about the continued use of Western models for the study of psychological processes in the Chinese (Yang and Wen, 1982). Similar conclusions were reached by Hsu in his review of psychological research in Taiwan up to 1982 (Hsu, 1987). Hsu commented that while Taiwan may advocate a policy of sinicization, with its emphasis upon Chinese traditions and culture, the country's psychologists have remained adamant in their adherence to the 'empirical stance, to objective data, and to the operational definition of concepts'. He concluded, 'Thus the results of any such policy [will] be limited to changes in *content*, without innovation in basic concepts and methods' (p. 135).

Whether this position enhances or inhibits the development of a specifically Chinese psychological theory, or contributes to research in Chinese sociocultural phenomena, remains to be seen. It does, however, encapsulate a widely held attitude, that psychology is science, akin to the natural sciences, even if the study of its subject matter, its 'objects', may not be undertaken independently of the manner in which they are conceived. This view has been profoundly challenged in the West, and the future of any psychological studies, perceived as indigenous or otherwise, will depend upon the extent to which communities of psychologists meet this challenge.

THE POST-MODERN TURN

In the last fifteen years or so, psychology in the West has taken a self-critical turn. An earlier generation of psychologists in the thrall of Kuhn's *The Structure of Scientific Revolution* (1970) had debated the consequences of whether areas of their own discipline were paradigmatic or pre-paradigmatic science. What was generally not at issue, however, were the rules to be adopted for determining what counted as legitimate forms of enquiry, valid data, or appropriate method. Appeals to universal certainty were justified in the name of unprejudiced observation, tried and tested. While abstractions from data were always on shaky ground and liable to sudden replacement, the means of deciding upon the truth of any abstraction invoked the cardinal rules of the game. Psychology was science, and science proceeded by the empirical methods of operationalism, hypothesis testing, and the prioritizing of observation over theory.

Increasingly, however, the notion of truth has come to be seen not as a foundation of knowledge but as a perspective, and therefore as a product of social exchange built, as Gergen (1992) eloquently argues, into systems of communication and relationship. From this it follows that 'what passes as knowledge within the sciences may properly be seen as the result of social processes within the culture of science' (p. 21). The discourses of science, far from transparently revealing an already available subject matter, are, in tandem with other discourses, narratives, employing a variety of rhetorical devices for persuading us about the world. As such, they resonate with the valuational biases of their authors and with the literary forms and styles of the historical and cultural moment of their genesis.

The earlier view, namely, the presumption of the independence of objects from the means of their description, can only be upheld by masking its metaphysical and ideological commitments. For example, the notion that there are universal properties of mind only maintains credibility at the expense of leaving unchallenged the 'peculiarly Western ontology of the person' (Gergen, 1992, p. 24), for not all cultures attribute cognitive processes to persons. This universalist fiction promotes the idea of a person as a private decision maker in charge of his or her own fate. Enquiries into the social realm remind us that our languages are a product of interaction, not isolation, and that our ways of speaking about minds are precisely that: culturally endorsed ways of speaking.

The focus of much new-look psychology in the West has turned the emphasis to discourse and its analysis, and to the social construction of our knowledge base. This development has two important implications. The first is that it will no longer be legitimate to prioritize some methods over others, since the notion that methods are linked to truth claims is unwarranted and misleading; the goal is no longer a claim to truth but to the exploration of a perspective and all that is entailed in it. The second is that, if cultural specificity is to become the central feature of study, the search for universals will have to be (temporarily) abandoned. There have already been hints in the literature that the search for understanding at the cultural level should precede any judgements of transcultural understanding, especially in the rash fitting of data to overarching theory where the fit is often far from smooth (Gabrenya and Hwang, this volume; Jahoda, 1992, 1994; Ongel and Smith, 1994). Understanding in this context would then have to take account of the social, political, and historical forces that shape cultural phenomena, and would cast the psychologist in the role of cultural critic—a human, rather than a natural, scientist.

THE FUTURE FOR CHINESE PSYCHOLOGY

In spite of this challenge, it may be that Hsu's (1987) forecast, described above, will prevail. Chinese psychologists, following fundamental cultural imperatives, have been interested in the pursuit of knowledge more for its relation to conduct and action than for the elaboration of specific forms of analytical self-reflection (Munro, 1967, 1977). This agenda has probably contributed to the tendency to see psychology as an applied discipline and to evaluate it only with respect to its utility: in education, as an adjunct to teacher training; in industrial sectors, as a spur to productivity; and in the medical sphere, as a preliminary to clinical diagnosis (although this latter use is still relatively rare).

In some areas of the discipline, notably social psychology, the justification for pursuing indigenous lines of research is strong given the cultural influence over social processes. In areas more traditionally aligned to natural sciences, for example experimental and cognitive psychology, Chinese psychologists are likely to continue imitating their Western counterparts. Funding for experimentally based projects continues from China itself and from grants abroad. Given how funding is often tied to academic exchanges among those with mutual interests, there will likely be a tendency to develop more studies in partnership with psychologists in the West, and therefore to strengthen more traditional areas of the discipline. These financial considerations will continue to affect Chinese psychologists both in and outside of China.

Some factors are also likely to influence the possibility of an indigenous psychology emerging in the near future. Given the propensity to see the worth of the discipline for its applications, many students and young academics weighing their future prospects see professional development not as a lifelong commitment but as a job opportunity, one among many. As such, psychologists in the workplace compete alongside other workers. With the differential salary structure weighted heavily against any work with academic leanings, in China itself the choice of occupation for many young graduates will be a simple economic one.

Beyond these economic constraints, there are problems raised by the writing of research reports and papers in one's second language of English, an activity which is necessary for the advancement of the discipline in the international community, as well as for the academic promotion of each individual scholar. This requirement poses an added strain, since one's standard will have to be good enough to pass muster in the editorial offices of leading overseas journals. But since writing academic psychology can be seen as the exhibition of one's latest conjectures, it poses a problem for those exceptionally concerned about negative evaluations. A typical solution to this problem leads many to adopt an ultra conventional style of writing as seen, for example, in the format of the experimental report, with its attention to technical detail at the expense of conjecture and reflection, and its often 'variable vague' view of the behaviour of its studies' participants (Billig, 1994). This solution encourages a movement away from a more conjectural writing about one's own culture and its influences.

However, from this standpoint one can also see how some researchers will be driven, either through poor English, or more positively, through zeal and commitment, to write about cultural experience in the language of that culture, Chinese. In so doing there might arise the need to borrow terms derived from Western psychology, and therefore to deal with the problems posed by translation as mentioned earlier. Moreover, the borrowing of terms cuts both ways, as Western psychologists may begin to show interest in translating Chinese texts into English in order to learn more about the social processes that are uniquely Chinese.

Against the, albeit slim, possibility of the emergence of a Chinese cultural view of psychology must be countered the impact of the cross-cultural psychology movement, which has been slow to meet this challenge. Retaining for the most part a modernist view of the discipline as a progressively evolving natural science, it has continued to pursue cultural enquiry by referencing measures of cultural difference with respect to criteria culled from primarily North American, university student populations. With its emphasis on quantitative differences with respect to reference group criteria, and its reliance on cultural stereotypes to explain those differences (often in *post hoc* fashion), 'Chinese psychology' uses these strategies to become, almost by definition, nothing other than the employment of Chinese subjects in (any) comparative psychological studies. Such research activity proliferates, even if most of its cultural content has been confined to pan-cultural abstractions (for example, individualism versus collectivism). This kind of work is undergoing critical re-evaluation even from adherents to this movement (Jahoda, 1994; Ongel and Smith, 1994), and it is to be hoped that this re-evaluation will encourage a widening of perspective and critique.

Unless and until psychology curricula in tertiary institutes in the West include evaluation of the knowledge base as a core activity, and cultural critique and interpretative stance become the accepted tools of the trade, Chinese psychologists are likely to continue to emulate what they see as the still dominant positivist mode of mainstream Western psychology. But as this brief historical excursion into China's relations with the discipline has shown, a distinctive Chinese view informing the discipline is unlikely to be forthcoming in the near future. Unlikely, that is, unless Chinese psychologists grow sufficiently confident to challenge their own long-held assumptions about the ways of doing psychology, and Western psychologists become overwhelmingly post-modern in outlook and begin to encourage Chinese psychologists in similar ways.

NOTES

An earlier version of this chapter was presented at the International Conference on Chinese Psychology held at the Chinese University of Hong Kong, 31 May–2 June 1994. This work was supported by funds from the Department of Psychology and the Conference and Research Grants Committee of the University of Hong Kong. I am grateful to Chan Wing-man for her help in compiling and translating material for this chapter.

Chapter 2

Visual Perception in Chinese People

Jong-Tsun Huang

The term *visual perception* refers to all experiences caused by stimulation of the visual modality. It usually describes the perception of an object's form, colour, motion, depth, and configural organization. The stimuli which trigger a series of visual experiences in a human observer may be composed of surrounding natural objects or presented artefacts (for example, printed materials and paintings). These perceptual attributes are analysed and integrated by the visual pathway and its delicate neural circuitry. For the literate, perception of linguistic materials involves detection, discrimination, and recognition, activities which are quite similar to those required in perceiving surrounding natural objects. One of the main linguistic functions, moreover, is to adopt artificial symbols to denote or even connote the perception of natural objects. Miller and Johnson-Laird (1976, p. 590) speculated that the basic division of the English verbs of vision (for example, see/look, or equivalently, *kan/kanjian* in Chinese) reflects a common feature of universal human attempts to communicate about visual experience.

The whole of visual experience is primarily a coherent percept entailed through the processing of sense data, taking into account the data's interaction with the observer's subjective interpretations of it. Some researchers believe that varieties of experience in observing the same event may emerge due to perceivers' specific environments or their different cultural origins. The Sapir–Whorf hypothesis of cultural relativity argues that the language a person speaks controls the ideas that person can have (Whorf, 1956). Intrigued by this hypothesis, many investigators have searched out the relationship between language and general perceptual abilities. It is thus a relevant issue within this tradition to see if a Chinese way of perceiving visual scenes might be different from its Western counterpart.

Hoosain (1986) conducted the first systematic review concerning the perceptual processes of the Chinese. He looked first at some of the more basic aspects of visual perception, including acuity of vision, coding of colours, direction of scanning, and eye movements in reading. After reviewing the relevant literature, he found no suggestion of any racially unique perceptual characteristics in acuity of perception, colour coding, direction of scanning, or eye-movement patterns. Concerning cultural influence on visual illusion or a scriptal effect on perceptual processing, the results were not as clearly negative. Discussion of that topic will be deferred to a later section of this chapter. The present article reviews selective Chinese studies, among others, concerning the basis of visual perception, perception of nonverbal information, and perception of verbal information.

Ancient Chinese scientists and artists made keen observations concerning phenomena of visual perception. The phenomena of the moon illusion (the apparent change in the size of the moon as it moves across the earth's horizon), apparent motion within a pre-modern cinema construction, aerial and linear perspectives, form perception, and the superposition principle in distance perception were all considered. Some of these studies constitute the earliest observations in the history of science. A particular emphasis has also been given to the visual information processing mechanism used for recognizing Chinese characters. In this paper, an analysis of the historical development of Chinese orthographic categories and its lack of grapheme–morpheme correspondence rules is first undertaken, followed by a cognitive interpretation of Chinese character processing. It is hoped that a discussion from basic visual function to perception of nonverbal information and finally to perception of verbal information might eventually reveal a pattern of uniquely Chinese ways of perceiving.

AN HISTORICAL INTRODUCTION

Light, Vision, and the Brain

Our modern world is predominantly visual, and the nature of sight and the structure of the organ of vision rank among the foremost subjects with which the minds of thinking persons have been occupied since the dawn of recorded history (Polyak, 1941). The importance of the brain in perception was appreciated very early, as for example by Plato, although some thinkers of his time proposed the heart as the sentient core. Plato developed an emanation theory of vision, according to which an inner fire gave rise to visual rays shooting outward from the eye in the direction of a perceived object. No vision, however, occurred in the total absence of light, and so Plato was forced also to propose the existence of outer rays of light that were supposed to interact somehow with the visual rays (Boynton, 1979).

The father of scientific medicine, Hippocrates, had already acquired a vast knowledge of the anatomy and physiology of the brain. The brain was then considered the substrate of nervous action and intelligence. Dissection was practiced by the Greeks and the gross anatomy of the eye was explored by post-Greek scholars. Mankind's greatest acquisition of important knowledge about the anatomy of the eye came after the second century AD through the dissection of animals (Le Grand, 1975).

Euclid's *Optics* (written about 300 BC) is the earliest treatise devoted to the mechanics of vision. The argument of the book rests on the supposition that through a medium of even density we see in straight lines. Based on the analysis of visual angle, Euclid demonstrated that objects of equal size unequally distant appear unequal, the ones lying nearer the eye always appearing larger. Euclid also found that parallel lines, when seen from a distance, appear not to be equally distant from one another. This is a close precursor of the modern view of perspective (Pirenne, 1975).

In the sixteenth and seventeenth centuries AD, great progress was made in anatomical studies of the visual pathway and of the relationship between geometrical optics and image formation. In 1604 the astronomer Johannes Kepler first documented the formation of the retinal image on the strangely curved inner surface of the human eyeball, the first significant finding in the history of vision study. Some years later, Rene Descartes proposed that animal spirits move along tubes in the optic nerves from a given point on the retina to a corresponding point on a topographical representation of the retina produced in the brain. His proposal anticipates a modern discovery of this connection. Further studies identified the blind spot in 1668, and photoreceptors were verified in 1835. In the nineteenth century John Muller proposed that it is the nerve signal rather than light itself that stimulates the brain. Soon afterwards, knowledge about the nature of light and the physiology of vision expanded greatly, paving the way for active research into visual psychophysics and visual neurophysiology at the turn of this century.

However, due to a lack of scientific exchange between China and the West, the philosopher Fang Yizhi (d. 1671) could begin in the late Ming dynasty to suggest that human intelligence is solely determined by the clarity of fluid content in the brain. In the eighteenth century, during the Qing dynasty, Wang Jinren proposed that spiritual essence resides in the brain and not in the heart. This lengthy interruption in the exploration of the functional role of the brain seems to explain most fully why the investigation of an eye–brain connection was not undertaken by Chinese science, despite that tradition's early formulation of physical principles regarding image formation.

Optics and the Eye–Brain Connection

In China, the discovery of the effect of the angle of vision on the perception of object size was made in the fourteenth century, during the late Song dynasty (Wang and Horng, 1984, p. 211-12), quite a bit later than the contribution of Euclidean optics. Similarly, Cheng Fuguan in 1847 published the first systematic Chinese study of geometrical optics, *A Personal Perspective on Mirror Reflection and Image Formation* (Lo, 1993), more than 240 years after Kepler presented his treatise on retinal image formation.

However, many investigations of optical and visual phenomena undertaken in China deserve recognition for their pioneering status. Mo Zi (478–392 BC) experimentally verified the nature of rectilinear light propagation, reflection, and image formation in both planar and spherical lenses. He also found the principle of pinhole image formation and the formation of shadows through object occlusion (Wang and Horng, 1984, p. 108–22). His speculation that human eyes perceive because of the light of the torch, instead of via an emanation from the eyes, appeared earlier than did Plato's emanation theory.

During the Tang dynasty, more than 1300 years ago, observation of rainbow formation through raindrop reflection of incident sunlight was first published, a suggestion that appeared earlier than Francis Bacon's similar argument. Genuine understanding of spectral decomposition was introduced by Chang Fuxi in 1853, about 150 years later than the first publication of Newton's Optics.

To explain why the eye–brain connection was not better understood by Chinese scientists, despite that tradition's early knowledge of optics, we need to examine then-prevailing conceptions of the brain and its workings. Ancient

Chinese medicine is quite complex and its precepts are very much tied to metaphysical notions. Belief in the concept of *zangfu*, a general schematic designation of the internal organs, was widespread in China in early times (Finger, 1994). The doctrine of *zangfu* appears in the *Huangdi Neijing*, a collection of ancient beliefs. Fragments of the *Huangdi Neijing* can be traced back to 475 BC, but it has been revised many times throughout its long history.

Zangfu looks upon the heart as the most important organ, because it houses the spirit and is filled with blood. The heart, along with all the other *zang* (including the lungs, kidneys, liver, and spleen), was believed to be involved in mental activity. The brain, on the other hand, was believed to be composed of marrow and is classified in the doctrine as a peculiar *fu*, an auxiliary organ, the main ones of which were involved with digestion. The *Huangdi Neijing* asserts that the eyes are connected to the brain; from this formulation it concludes that if evil invades the eyes, it will also invade the brain (Finger, 1994). Obviously, this is a spurious treatment of the eye–brain connection, since it does not consider the brain as a central information processor and does not confine the eye to its sole function as a light reception device.

Early Observation of the Moon Illusion

The moon over the horizon appears to be larger than the moon high in the sky. This difference in the perception of the size of the moon is illusory, as there is no difference in the physical stimulus produced by the moon at different elevations above the horizon. Scientific study of the moon illusion is as old as science itself, originating during the period 600 to 300 BC, when philosophers in ancient Greece began to propose natural, rather than supernatural, explanations of the world (Plug and Ross, 1989).

An early, pre-scientific reference to the moon illusion occurs in a Chinese manuscript of possibly the first or second century AD. The author is claimed to be Lie Zi, a philosopher said to have lived during the fourth century BC. The document relates a probably apocryphal story about the philosopher Confucius, who found two boys arguing about the distance of the sun. One said that the sun was much larger at sunrise than at noon and must therefore be closer to us in the morning. The other answered that the sun is much hotter at noon and must therefore be closer to us in the middle of the day. Confucius was unable to solve the problem.

This story indicates that, like the moon illusion, the sun illusion was well known in China at that time. The sun illusion was adopted by Gao Hung (AD 283–343) to argue against the beliefs that celestial bodies when setting move in a straight line to an infinite distance and that they are created anew each day (Ho, 1966, p. 57). Gao Hung argued, 'If it is said that the sun can no longer be seen because it has gone a very great distance from us, then when the sun sets, on its way towards the north, its size should diminish. But on the contrary the sun becomes larger at sunset. This is far from being proof that the sun is moving further away when it sets.' This argument is very similar to what Ptolemy had proposed a century or two earlier (Plug and Ross, 1989, p. 8).

Investigations of factors influencing the moon illusion continued for centuries (Boring, 1950). The possible influence of the moist atmosphere surrounding the earth (involving refraction theory), the postural position of the observer, the observer's eye elevation or aerial perspective (with the effect of a higher density of atmosphere near the horizon), the presence of a flat or an elliptical sky, intervening objects between the observer and the horizon, and the proximity of the moon to the visible horizon, among others, were all suggested during sometimes heated debate. The Chinese, although they had observed the phenomenon very early compared to their Western counterparts, contributed little to the discussion of influencing factors, irrespective of its mathematical and astronomical sophistication.

Perceptual Aspects of Early Chinese Paintings

Some insights concerning artistic expressions of human perception were suggested in treatises on early Chinese paintings. One such essay reminded the painter that 'distant men have no eyes, distant trees have no branches, and distant water has no ripples' (Gombrich, 1969, p. 222; Liu, 1994, p. 61). This may be seen as the ancient version of a modern theory detailing low spatial frequency resolution due to viewing from a great distance and an observer's reduced contrast sensitivity function.

At times the argument on form perception in art neared the absurd. A standard Qing-era textbook on painting, *The Mustard Seed Garden Manual of Painting* (AD 1679–1701), stated: 'One should know well the whole form of the bird. Birds are born from eggs. And their forms resemble eggs, with head, tail, wings, and feet added' (Gombrich, 1969, p. 163). In developing the form of the bird from the egg the artist followed the way of nature. This guideline seems to demonstrate an obvious fallacy of origin, although the instruction may be quite practical for guiding a beginning artist.

The expression of the relative distance from the viewer of objects on the canvas is one of the most important criteria used for evaluating the developmental maturity of a painting. The space-building role of superposition in Chinese landscape painting is well known. The relative location of mountain peaks or clouds is established visually by overlaps (Arnheim, 1974). Liu (1994, p. 55) points out that occlusion as a depth cue had been used on wall paintings as early as the Qin dynasty (221–207 BC). Placement lower in the painting denotes a nearer object, while occlusion in the upper part of a painting denotes a more distant object.

It is rare in ancient Chinese paintings to express distance relationships by means of object size (that is, larger images to indicate closer objects and smaller ones for more distant objects). Instead, the size of the image of a person usually expresses his or her placement in the hierarchy of status in the society. A more prestigious person occupies a larger portion of the canvas, irrespective of his or her distance from the viewer.

Euclid is commonly credited with discovering the rudimentary concept of linear perspective. Leonardo da Vinci made it popular in the West during the fifteenth century in the expression of depth cues for painting. While aerial perspective was widely practised in Chinese painting after the Song dynasty, Liu (1994) suggests curiously that the notion of linear perspective might have been employed by the painter Zhong Bing (AD 375-443) before the Song era and one thousand years earlier than Albrecht Dürer's use of the technique in the West. Its practice in Chinese painting, however, was not fully realized until the Qing dynasty. Descriptive geometry or perspective was first introduced in 1729 by Nian Xiyao (Shen, 1991). Lan Shining (1688–1766) was the first painter in China to use linear perspective, which was at that time incongruent with Chinese artistic doctrine for depicting parallel lines.

The practice of perspective flourished in Western paintings after the Renaissance. After hundreds of years of development, the artist's mastery of light, shadow, colour, and their interactions may be said to have reached its peak in the nineteenth-century style termed Impressionism. A combination of these technical achievements has helped artists to produce patterns on canvas or paper that can act as surrogates for a three-dimensional and colourful world. Although ancient Chinese painters practised superposition techniques frequently, and a notion of perspective was suggested quite early in their works, the use of other artistic techniques in combination with the subtle representation of light and perspective was rare.

A further aspect of perception is motion. Modern motion pictures consist of a succession of static pictures; motion pictures with sound are usually projected at a rate of 24 frames per second, relying on a frequency of the viewer's change of vision that is just outside the range of detectable flicker.

The attempt to make pictures that move is an ancient one. It has long been recognized that space and time can be reconstructed through multiple images (Hochberg and Brooks, 1978). The Chinese practice of creating a rudimentary motion picture was in vogue as early as during the Tang dynasty (AD 618–907). The Galloping Horse Lantern, invented in that era, was a device for such entertainment. Silhouettes of a horse were made and pasted on to a lantern. Candles heated the air and caused the silhouettes to rotate at a relatively constant speed, giving the impression of a vivid, galloping horse. Unfortunately, the practical creation of the device was all that was achieved during that time, and no further scientific enquiries were made.

CULTURE AND VISUAL PERCEPTION

Cross-cultural comparison of visual perception started in the study of illusory phenomena. Exploring this topic, Segall, Campbell, and Herskovits (1963, 1966) made a systematic investigation of susceptibility to geometric illusions in persons from different cultures. Their research suggested what is termed the carpentered-environment hypothesis: that visual illusions occur because habits of perceptual inference are transferred from the spatial environment to line drawings. In short, they found that the magnitude of the Müller–Lyer illusion ($\updownarrow$ — although the shafts of both arrows are of equal length, the one with the outgoing heads looks longer) was greater for people living in environments containing more rectangular objects and living spaces than for people in non-carpentered environments. Dawson, Young, and Choi (1973) compared the illusion susceptibility of Hong Kong Chinese samples with Americans and Australian Aboriginal Arunta desert-dwellers. In studies testing the Müller–Lyer illusion, the American subjects were most susceptible, an expected outcome if we consider their environment to be the most carpentered. The Chinese were intermediate in their response, and the open-desert-dwellers least susceptible.

With respect to the horizontal/vertical illusion ($\perp$ – the vertical line looks longer than the horizontal one, though they are in fact of equal length), which tests the interpretation of vertical lines as greatly shortened but extending into space in an environment such as a desert or sea, the Arunta sample showed the greatest degree of illusion. The Arunta interpreted the vertical lines as longer than the horizontal lines (Hoosain, 1986), as would be predicted by the carpentered-environment hypothesis. However, the Hong Kong Chinese sample showed less susceptibility than did the American one, and this was attributed to the more closed environment of the crowded city of Hong Kong. In such an environment there is not much opportunity for seeing lines extended into very distant space.

Interesting as the carpentered-environment hypothesis may be, further studies were not congruent with the above findings. A retinal-anatomy hypothesis was later suggested as an alternative explanation (Bornstein, 1973). One form of this hypothesis is that increased pigmentation (in some cultures) produces decreased image contrast on the retina. This, in turn, produces more veridical perception of the illusion-eliciting figure. However, the account of cultural differences in visual perception by hypotheses of these sorts was eventually a failure (Pick and Pick, 1978). A major difficulty was that cultures vary in a multitude of ways, so that identifying the critical dimension is often logically or practically impossible.

After reviewing the literature concerning Chinese visual acuity, directional scanning, eye movement, and actual colour perception, Hoosain (1986) found that the visual perception of the Chinese was not substantially different from that of any other people. He concluded that, irrespective of racial or cultural differences, human beings share a common biological endowment such that most subjects in different cultures prefer, for example, directional scanning from top to bottom and from left to right. Further evidence on these matters will be addressed in the following sections.

Chinese Cognition through Colour Naming

When certain colours are more easily and more frequently taken to label objects existing in the world, they are called focal colours. Focal colours appear to be salient for children as young as four months of age and are important in the establishment of colour-name labels. Some authors thus argue that the internal colour space is the same worldwide (Davidoff, 1991). The universality of the colour space suggests that its organization has a neurophysiological basis, with that basis presumably derived from opponent and interactional processes at the lateral geniculate nucleus (in the thalamus), V1 (visual cortical area 1), and V4 along the visual pathway (Zeki, 1993). However, findings indicate that the final organization of the internal colour space does not correspond to the neurophysiology of colour vision. Moreover, to some extent, the organization of the internal colour space is flexible and may be altered by experience (Davidoff, 1991).

Berlin and Kay (1969) studied colour vocabularies in almost 100 languages; naming tests were carried out in 20 languages, and evaluation of linguistic publications in 78 others. They discovered that the development of colour terms follows a clear sequence (as shown in Figure 2.1). The referents for the basic colour terms of all languages appear to be drawn from a set of 11 universal perceptual categories, and these categories tend to become encoded in the history of a given language in a partially fixed order. Phylogenetic development of colour names in language evolution proceeds first from perceiving spectrum amplitude, then recognizing its chromatic decomposition but not colour saturation. There appears to be no evidence to indicate that differences in complexity of basic colour lexicons between one language and another reflect perceptual differences between the speakers of those languages. Primitive peoples do not necessarily perceive colour differently from those in more advanced civilizations. The whole spectrum can be divided completely even by two or three achromatic colour terms. No physical or physiological explanation for the apparently greater perceptual salience of these particular eleven colour stimuli can be found, nor for their relative ordering.

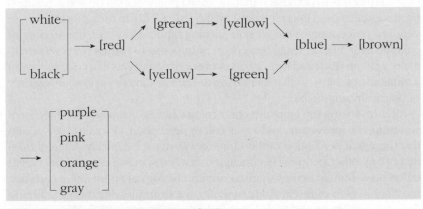

Figure 2.1   Developmental Sequence of Colour Terms

Bornstein (1973) has integrated the evidence supporting the hypothesis that cultural differences in colour naming reflect physiologically based differences in colour vision. He has found that differences in colour-naming systems might occur because of differences in sensitivity at the blue end of the spectrum. Therefore, blues and greens would be strongly absorbed, resulting in a corresponding insensitivity to these colours. However, the argument was not conclusive (Pick and Pick, 1978), as was stated previously. Huang and Huang (1994) found that the perception of illusory colour among Chinese observers does not show any difference from that of Western subjects. Boundary completion and filling-in processes are modulated in the same way by depth information to assure the emergence of illusory colour.

The temptation to give a physiological explanation is very natural. By 1880 the scholarly world was aware of certain facts relating to the differences in colour nomenclature of different languages. There was general agreement that earlier stages of European languages and the languages of contemporary primitives contain fewer basic colour terms than do the modern European languages. Gladstone (1858) and Geiger (1880) believed that the observed lexical development of colour nomenclature must be based on the physiological development of perceptual abilities. Nearly a century later, Berlin and Kay (1969) pointed out that understanding of this general topic could not grow until it was realized that perceptual abilities and colour naming behaviour may vary independently.

It is often argued that language and perception interact, and that when separate sensory experiences exist, these labels make discriminations easier. In other words, the Lakuti tribe for example, who have only a single term for blue and green, may see the two colours as being more similar to each other than do English speakers, who have separate words for these stimuli (Whorf, 1956). The suggestion that different language terms for colours indicate different perceptual abilities has been presented in many different forms.

Robertson (1967) suggested that an evolutionary development has occurred both in the colour-perceiving ability of humans and in the colour terms encoded in each language. He suggested that the first discriminations were between red and green, and that the discrimination ability for yellow evolved later, and finally that for blue. He analysed a number of ancient languages and found such evolutionary trends. One might conclude from such evidence that the ancient Greeks were relatively weak in their ability to perceive colour in that their language had a small set of colour names.

Actually, when the ability of individuals to match, discriminate, or produce colours (rather than just to name them) is measured directly, the picture changes. It has been found that the number of colour names in a language does not affect the ability to make such discriminations (Berlin and Kay, 1969). For example, there is question whether spectral sensitivities of Chinese eyes fit the standard luminosity curve, set by the Commission Internationale de l'Eclairage (CIE), in responding to spectral wavelength ($V(\lambda)$). His study (as cited in Brown, 1981, p. 9) has shown that they do.

Berlin and Kay (1969) suggested that colour lexicons with few terms tend to occur in association with relatively simple cultures and simple technologies, while colour lexicons with many terms tend to occur in association with complex cultures and complex technologies. They identified seven evolutionary stages for the development of basic colour terms. They placed all the languages of highly industrialized European and Asian peoples at stage VII, while all the languages they located at the early stages (I, II, and III) are spoken by people with small populations and limited technology, located in isolated areas. They treated Mandarin Chinese (Putonghua) as an example of stage V and identified Cantonese as stage VII. This classification is inconsistent with the generally accepted view of the formation of Chinese civilization and its cultural diffusion, given that Cantonese is a local dialect, while Mandarin is the more literary language. In addition, the two spoken languages share the same logographic script.

Berlin and Kay also classified Japanese and Korean as at stage VII, even though the two languages use many Chinese loan words for colour naming (a point acknowledged by Berlin and Kay). The unexpected classification of Mandarin may be due to synchronical differences within the study (that is, cross-sectional and regional changes of colour terms at a given time). Historical reconstruction may provide a different interpretation of diachronical (historical and evolutionary) linguistic changes. For example, the great Qing-dynasty novel *Dream of the Red Chamber* contains at least 100 colour names (not restricted to single morphemes). Therefore, the assertion of Mandarin as a stage V language must be wrong on diachronic grounds. Even on the basis of synchronic speech domains, Berlin and Kay have admitted that their classification of Mandarin may be problematical and that more data would be needed for fuller clarification. It may be argued, therefore, that Mandarin would be better scored at stage VII in their study.

Another cognitive aspect of colour information processing deserves mention. Although evidence for the effects of colour on emotional states are weak, the affective meanings attached to specific colours may vary across cultures according to different conventions or interpretations (Davidoff, 1991). For example, white dominates in Chinese funeral settings, while black prevails for Western funerals. The meaning attached to colour may also vary diachronically: green, for example, was reserved for the brave and noble before the Han dynasty (206 BC–AD 220) but later came to be regarded as an ignoble colour (Hsing, 1991).

Chinese Language and Its Perceptual Processing

The genesis and evolution of the Chinese logographic script follows a clear sequence from pictographs to ideographs to phonographs to phonetic compounds. Phonetic compounds are composed of a phonetic radical and a semantic stem (for example, when the phonetic for 'horse' is combined with the signific for 'woman', we have *mà* which means 'mother'). Phonetic compounds evolved at the time when messages were still inscribed on oracle bones (Li, 1992). Phonetic compounds account for almost 80 per cent of the present-day Chinese language.

The earliest Chinese writing still in existence dates back some 3,500 years. Chinese orthography is in use today, although there have been profound stylistic changes in the course of its historical development. The earliest Chinese writings yet discovered are incisions in ox bone and tortoise shell. Most of these inscriptions appear to have been oracular, dealing either with political or religious events or with weather or warfare. More than 100,000 inscribed pieces have been found; of the 2,000 to 3,000 characters on these shells and bones, about half can be read today (Wang, 1973).

Kang (1992) documented the linguistic origins of a wide selection of Chinese characters. These characters describe the form and meaning of human faces from different profiles, body components, production in agriculture, natural phenomena, and life events, among others. However, diachronic representation of the script does not necessarily reflect the language behaviour of current users. Synchronically, it is important to ask how form, sound, and meaning are encoded and how they are represented in the mental lexicon of present-day Chinese people.

THE NATURE AND LOCUS OF THE CHINESE MENTAL LEXICON

Through a series of positron emission tomography (PET) studies on healthy brains, some interesting results have been obtained (Petersen, Fox, Posner, Mintun, and Raichle, 1988; Petersen, Fox, Snyder, and Raichle, 1990; Raichle, 1994). A left inferior frontal area (Brodmann's area 47) has been identified that almost certainly participates in processing for semantic association. Moreover, if subjects are allowed a few minutes of practice on the task of generating verbs using a noun–verb association task, they become relaxed and proficient after 15 minutes of practice. This activity completely changes the neural circuits recruited (Raichle, 1994), with the circuits responsible for noun repetition (simply reading out loud) now generating the verbs. This finding is reminiscent of what is involved in changing an action from voluntary to involuntary by repeated practice.

The notion of a mental lexicon emphasizes the figurative handshake between stored triplets (a phonological–syntactic–semantic compound) and incoming information. Is the left inferior frontal area a most probable locus for storing the mental lexicon? Petersen and his colleagues (1988, 1990) suggested that the left hemisphere may be the locus of lexical representation in normal subjects. They found increased activation in extrastriate regions of the left hemisphere when subjects read words or pseudo-words, relative to the activation produced in the same subjects by reading random letter strings. Furthermore, these effects were not observed in the right hemisphere. Mazoyer et al. (1993) carried out a study to compare the brain areas that are activated when subjects listen to stories spoken in their mother tongue and in a foreign language. In right-handed male subjects listening to their native language, the activity was distributed across the temporal and frontal areas of the left hemisphere. In contrast, when these subjects listened to a story in a foreign language, both hemispheres were activated to the same extent, mostly in the superior temporal gyri. These results suggest that the left hemisphere may become attuned to process utterances in one's own language and not in a foreign language. They might also suggest that the left hemisphere initially processes any language and gradually becomes specialized for the maternal language (Mehler, Dupoux, Pallier, and Dehaene-Lambertz, 1994).

This speculation should not, however, be considered as a total rejection of any involvement by the right hemisphere in lexical processing. Reuter-Lorenz and Baynes (1992) observed the role of the right hemisphere in language processing on a callosotomy (split-brain) patient, J. W. They found that the right hemisphere may have an independent visual lexicon and may provide an alternate, though less efficient, route to reading. It may suggest that J. W. achieved a slow but still successful lexical access by adopting a letter-by-letter processing strategy.

To propose a dominant role of the left hemisphere on normal lexical processing does have merit in its own right. A triplet representation in the mental lexicon thus needs not be split into both hemispheres for effective storage. Such a design seems to exemplify an efficiency principle that serves in rapidly activating a familiar lexical entry. It can also prevent the formidable effort or transmission loss which might occur in the process of massively commuting across the corpus callosum through connecting fibers to retrieve and integrate necessary triplet ingredients from both hemispheres.

Contribution of Frontal Cortex in Lexical Processing

Is the frontal cortex a locus for conducting semantic association? In addressing this question, we will limit our discussion to the domain of visual information processing. Almost 30 visual areas have been identified in the cerebral cortex of the macaque monkey. The anterior part of the TE (one of the major regions of the inferior temporal cortex, located on the ventral part of the temporal lobe) projects more to various structures outside the visual cortex (for example, to areas 35 and 36, and to the prefrontal cortex) than from the areas at earlier stages (Tanaka, 1993). Most cells in the TE require moderately complex features for their activation. These critical features are more complex than orientation, size, colour, and simple texture, which are known to be extracted and represented by cells in the visual cortical area V1 (Fujita, Tanaka, Ito, and Cheng, 1992). It is also believed that the TE can store representations for various kinds of visual stimuli. It is thus not surprising if a modality-specific word form is discovered to be completed and represented in the TE.

Suppose the TE could be considered as the exit station in the vision module and that picture information would be completed in the TE. The picture-superiority effect (a superiority of pictures to words in free recall and recognition; see Crowder, 1976) would suggest a higher centre beyond the TE to process further linguistic information. It is therefore plausible to believe that linguistic materials must await further processing after leaving the TE for various structures outside the visual cortex.

Crick and Koch (1990) have suggested that neural computations on an attended object and the consequent visual awareness (upon completion of the perceptual binding of distinct stimulus attributes) are expressed by phase-locked, 40Hz oscillations (neuron firing) across many cortical regions. In the vision module, for example, visual areas along the occipitotemporal cortical pathway (for 'what' information in object vision) or the occipitoparietal cortical pathway (for 'where' information in spatial vision) may provide a base for such operation (Ungerleider and Haxby, 1994). Feedback signals may spread to interact between cortical levels in the module through horizontal lateral interaction across cortical layers (Wiesel and Gilbert, 1989) or through top-down diffuse feedback connections (Nakayama and Shimojo, 1990). Effective feedback induces synchronous oscillations, and these oscillations then spread to other neighboring regions (for example, to the frontal cortex). Some of these peripheral activities may correspond to what is considered the 'meaning' of the percept. Beyond the vision module, top-down effects may originate in the frontal cortex. Such top-down effects might modify saliency characteristics of incoming stimuli (from the TE) and be responsible for adjusting the size of the attentional spotlight (Crick and Koch, 1990). These speculations together with the findings of Petersen et al. (1988) indicate that the frontal cortex may be one of the best loci to serve the needs of establishing a mental lexicon.

The questions remains, can this assertion of a locus for the mental lexicon in the left inferior prefrontal area be generalized to non-alphabetic scripts, especially for a Chinese linguistic processor? Although two-character Chinese words are often equated in function as English words, one might suspect that the prevailing incidence of two-character words in Chinese will signify different perceptual consequences. However, Tzeng, Hung, Cotton, and Wang (1979) have shown a similar pattern in comparison with lateralization studies using English materials. They found that the naming response of a single Chinese character manifested a left visual field (LVF) superiority effect, whereas the naming or lexical decision time for two-character words showed a right visual field (RVF) superiority effect.

It might be argued that a single character is processed in a holistic, gestalt manner, while a two-character word is analysed sequentially and analytically. If the sequential order between characters were to be processed so that a two-character word could be correctly recognized, then an RVF superiority effect in the two-character word recognition might be attributable to a finer temporal resolving power in the left hemisphere. Such a finer cerebral function would, in turn, provide the opportunity for better sequential coding. Following these findings, Tzeng and Hung (in press) have proposed that a time-based neuronal mechanism might lateralize the left hemisphere as a linguistic processor; such a temporal code could be implemented neurophysiologically. Libet, Wright, Feinstein, and Pearl (1979) proposed a 'timing signal' for indexing temporal order. The primary evoked potential in the cortex 10 to 20 milliseconds after peripheral stimulation was proposed to be crucial for representing event sequences. These timing signals might be better utilized by the left hemisphere, since finer temporal resolution is performed in this half of the brain.

The process of indexing the flow of utterances in acquiring a maternal language is essentially the same from our early childhood, irrespective of whether the maternal language is alphabetic or logographic. Therefore, Chinese language processing might also be lateralized in the left hemisphere for a native speaker (see Mazoyer et al., 1993; Mehler et al., 1994). Tzeng and Hung have observed that Chinese language processing (at least for recognition of complex characters, with two or more elements) is largely lateralized in the left hemisphere, not only in speech but also in stroke writing. This localization may be due to a sequential graphomotoric coding property which makes stroke writing lateralized in the left hemisphere. As to whether the locus of the Chinese mental lexicon is in the frontal area, there is no clear evidence at present.

Structure and Dynamics of the Chinese Mental Lexicon

To explore the structure and dynamics of this process, Marslen-Wilson, Tyler, Waksler, and Older (1994) adopted a cross-modal immediate repetition priming task in which the subject hears a spoken prime and immediately sees a visual probe that is related in some way to the prime. For example, an auditory prime *happiness* might be followed by the visual probe *happy*. The subject is asked to make a lexical-decision response to this probe which is the stem of a derivationally suffixed or prefixed word. The rationale behind this arrangement is as follows: If the access of a derived form *happiness* involves access to its stem *happy*, then this relationship should affect an immediate response to the stem when it is itself presented as a probe stimulus. The researchers claimed that suffix- and prefix-derived words and their stems prime each other through shared morphemes in the lexical entry. Morphologically complex and semantically transparent words were represented at the level of the lexical entry in decomposed morphemic form. This was independent of phonological transparency, suggesting that morphemic representations are phonologically abstract.

Due to a lack of inflectional morphology in the Chinese language, it is difficult to replicate the arrangement used in the experiments of Marslen-Wilson et al. In addition, other complications impinge on the preparation of comparable experimental materials. Some morphologically related pairs, such as *successful* and *successor*, are unrelated in the Chinese language not only semantically but morphologically. The stem of a derivationally suffixed word in Chinese orthographic or phonemic form is often a proper subset of the morphologically complex word. For example, in the pair *happy* + *di*, *di* is served as an adverb modifier for an adjective. In other instances, a stem is identical with its derived form, as the example *punishment* and *punish* shows. Therefore, a priming effect may sometimes be easily obtained by the mechanism of strict overlapping, without recourse to the morphological decomposition process occurring in inflectional morphology. Nevertheless, the logic that Marslen-Wilson et al. have convincingly demonstrated in their experiments is worth serious verification in relation to logographic scripts.

A supposition that the mental lexicon is stem-based leads us to question how lexical entries are stacked in the lexicon. There is ample evidence concerning the existence of a modality effect in alphabetic language processing studies. The term *modality effect* refers to typical findings in immediate free or serial recall to the effect that the last few items in the list are better recalled if the presentation modality was auditory rather than visual. Recently, the auditory superiority effect in a long-term recognition memory task has been reported (Conway and Gathercole, 1987). However, Penny (1989) showed that visual presentation produced better performance than did auditory presentation for one-syllable, common English words in the delayed free recall and delayed recognition test. For a logographic script, the superior long-term recall through visual presentation (a reversed long-term modality effect) has been consistently found with Chinese logographs (Liu, Zhu, and Wu, 1992). To discount an interpretation relying on scriptal difference to explain such effects, Liu et al. suggested a frequency explanation. One set of Chinese words is experienced more frequently in print than in speech, while another is experienced more frequently in speech than in print. A larger visual superiority effect may be obtained from the former than from the latter.

Construction of a model of the structure of a mental lexicon, with special reference to Chinese character recognition, is possible by considering the common mechanisms underlying these findings. The dynamics of a particular mental lexicon, or how a single entry in the mental lexicon is accessed, can then be explored. Discussion of these points is beyond the scope of the present article; interested readers are referred to Huang (1994).

CONCLUDING REMARKS

Hoosain (1986) comprehensively reviewed the studies concerning the basic perceptual processes of the Chinese. He found no suggestion of significant, racially unique perceptual characteristics in most cross-cultural studies of basic perceptual abilities. The present article, after reviewing selective studies concerning basic visual perception, perception of nonverbal information, and perception of verbal information, echoes these findings. However, the scarcity of relevant studies in this respect does not support a hasty conclusion. There is still a need for a range of psychophysical experiments to justify the assertion that Chinese perceptual abilities are truly indistinguishable from those of other peoples (see also Tzeng and Hung, this volume).

A final issue which concerns us is the connection between a model of the Chinese mental lexicon and the visual perception of verbal information. Properties such as the structure and the dynamics of a typical Chinese mental lexicon should be further explored. We cannot yet truly understand how the visual experiences of incoming linguistic materials are accessed for a search of meaning. Through future research efforts, it is hoped that we may get a clearer picture of visual perception with reference to low-level and high-level information processing in Chinese people.

Chapter 3

Chinese Lexical Access

Jei-tun Wu and In-mao Liu

When we comprehend a sentence, we seem to arrive at its meaning by a process of construction. That is, we build the meaning of the sentence by processing each component word within the context in which the sentence is experienced. However, the process of comprehending a single word is quite different. Only when we succeed in contacting a stored representation of the word is it said to be comprehended. The term lexical access has been used to refer to the complete processing sequence whereby a subject gains access from an orthographic encoding of a word to its stored properties, such as its meanings, syntactic properties, and pronunciation(s).

In the context of studying the frequency effect, however, lexical access has been used to refer to lexical identification, the process of contacting a stored word form without necessarily contacting other word properties. The lexical processing of spoken words was overlooked, and included only when it was necessary to throw light on visual lexical processing.

Two tasks have generally been used as tests for measuring the time of lexical access, although some other methods, such as the technique of threshold measurement and the method of measuring eye movements, have also been used. The first of the two primary tests, known as the lexical decision task, was developed by Rubenstein, Garfield, and Millikan (1970). The subject in this type of experiment is exposed to a letter string (a sequence of letters, such as 'tiger' or 'siger') and is asked to decide as quickly as possible whether or not it comprises an English word. The time taken by the subject to make this decision is called the lexical decision time.

Lexical decision times can be measured also in readings of Chinese words. A complication involved in such testing is the construction of Chinese 'nonwords'. Although Huang and Liu (1978) estimated that more than 60 per cent of Chinese words consist of two characters, out of the most frequently used 500 words obtained from a count by Liu, Chuang, and Wang (1975), single-character words themselves constituted more than 60 per cent. Many of the most frequently used Chinese words consist of single characters, whereas many less frequently used words take the form of two characters. To address this difference, most studies have either constructed 'non-characters' (pseudo-characters) to study Chinese lexical access involving single-character words or 'two-character non-words' to study lexical access involving two-character words.

In the second most frequently used test for studying lexical access, the naming task, the subject is presented with a word and asked to name it aloud as quickly as possible. By means of a voice-operated relay, the time from the presentation of an item to the onset of the subject's vocalization can be measured. One problem presented by the naming task in the study of many languages is that naming times are likely to underestimate lexical access times: a word may be pronounced by observing the rules for spelling and sound correspondences without contacting a stored representation of the word. Although this situation prevails in naming an alphabetic word, such a situation does not exist in naming a Chinese character, because a character is pronounceable only if it is a part of the language. In other words, without contacting a stored representation of a character, the subject is unable to pronounce it correctly. It will be seen in this chapter that this feature of the Chinese language makes the study of Chinese lexical access unique in some respects.

LEXICAL ACCESS AND FREQUENCY EFFECTS

Waley (1978) studied a large sample of words using the lexical decision task with an aim to determine which properties of words had the strongest influence on speed of response. He came to the conclusion that frequency of occurrence was by far the most potent variable. The finding that subjects respond faster to high-frequency than to low-frequency words has been well confirmed. If a word appears more than fifty times per million words of readings, it is generally considered as a high-frequency word. On the other hand, if a word appears less than three times per million words of readings, it is certainly a low-frequency word. Most models of word recognition account for the frequency effect by locating it in the process of lexical access (Morton, 1969). A decade ago Balota and Chumbley (1984, 1985) came to challenge this view. In the following, let us consider their challenge and how it generated subsequent research. We close this section by describing how this problem is resolved in studies of Chinese orthography.

Balota and Chumbley's Challenge and Subsequent Research

Balota and Chumbley (1984) found that the time required to classify a word as a member of a particular semantic category was not significantly affected by the frequency of occurrence of that word. They reasoned that lexical access must be involved in the semantic classification task. Therefore, Balota and Chumbley argued that decision processes having little to do with lexical access exaggerate the word-frequency effect which had been reliably obtained by studies using the lexical decision task. In experiments using the naming task, decision processes are nearly absent in this type of test. Balota and Chumbley (1985) reasoned that the frequency effect in naming may be localized at the encoding of a word, its production, or both. By using the technique of a delayed naming procedure, they showed that the frequency effect in naming is localized at the production stage and is not to be attributed to lexical access (the encoding stage). These findings are critical in that they cast doubt on one of the most important findings in psychology, the effect of experience on behavior. A study by McCann and Besner (1987) on pseudohomophones seems to support Balota and Chumbley's view.

In a subsequent study, when the subjects were required to classify words as belonging to one of two very large and general categories, either 'human' or 'inanimate', Monsell, Doyle, and Haggard (1989) obtained a strong frequency effect. A further study by McRae, Jared, and Seidenberg (1990) showed that, when the stimuli were equated in terms of articulatory properties, the large frequency effects obtained in immediate naming were eliminated at the longest delay intervals. Taft and Russell (1992) were also able to obtain a frequency effect in the naming of pseudohomophones, when they controlled for orthographic factors that McCann and Besner (1987) had ignored.

Results of the studies by Monsell, Doyle, and Haggard (1989), McRae, Jared, and Seidenberg (1990), and Taft and Russell (1992) are, however, inconclusive. This is because, first, the decision component in lexical decision-making was never isolated and, second, it is not known to what extent any subject relied on a sub-lexical route to arrive at a word's pronunciation, applying general knowledge of grapheme–sound correspondences to word fragments. It will be clear from the following section that these two problems cannot be resolved in studies involving alphabetic orthographies.

Studies with Chinese Orthography

In the early 1970s there was no useful character frequency account yet available for research with Chinese logographs. Therefore, Yeh and Liu (1972) used meaningfulness as a variable to stand for frequency of occurrence in studying its relation to the recognition threshold. It was well documented that there is a close relationship between frequency and meaningfulness. Among other results, they found that meaningfulness is inversely related to recognition threshold. In other words, high-frequency characters are recognized faster than are low-frequency words.

Seidenberg (1985) classified Chinese characters into phonograms and non-phonograms and attempted to study the effect of frequency on the naming task. Frequency was determined on the basis of subjects' ratings. Although not clearly specified, it can be inferred from Seidenberg's examples that phonograms stood for those characters whose pronunciation was the same as that of their phonetic components, without considering intonations. Therefore, phonograms may be considered as 'regular characters' and non-phonograms as 'exceptions'. He found the typical interaction of frequency with regularity obtained in studies with English orthography, that is, regularity effects (faster reaction times for regular words compared to exceptions) are larger in low-frequency words and are small or nonexistent in high-frequency words (see also Waters and Seidenberg, 1985).

Shu and Zhang (1987) divided Chinese characters into three frequency categories: high, medium, and low. Using the naming task, they not only obtained support for the frequency by regularity interaction but also the frequency by consistency interaction. Consistent characters are those that contain the same phonetic component and are pronounced uniquely (consistently), and inconsistent characters are those that contain the same phonetic component but are pronounced inconsistently. The consistency effect was first observed with English words by Glushko (1979). More recently Hue (1992) obtained the consistency effect, as well as the frequency by regularity effect, with Chinese logographs in studies using the naming task.

Resolving the Issue of Locating the Frequency Effect

Character-sound correspondences

One characteristic feature of character-sound correspondences in Chinese may affect the relative size of the frequency effects in naming and lexical decision-making. In alphabetic orthographies, there is usually only a very limited number of letters, for instance fewer than 30, in the alphabet. The number of letters to serve as cues for sounds is, therefore, limited in alphabetic orthographies. When a non-alphabetic orthography such as Chinese logographs is considered, the situation is quite different. Although about 80 per cent of Chinese characters are formed by compounding sound-cuing phonetics and meaning-conveying radicals, the relationship between phonetics and sounds in actual characters is not unambiguous.

Liu (1994) devised a procedure by which the predictability of a sound from its script component can be calculated for any language. When this calculation procedure is applied to samples of Chinese characters and English words, the predictabilities were found to be much larger for the latter than for the former. One implication of this finding is that the naming latency should be much slower for low-frequency Chinese characters than for low-frequency alphabetic words. For a high-frequency item, it is well established that a subject is not likely to rely on the rule system for its pronunciation. By defining the differences between the mean latencies for high-frequency and low-frequency words as frequency effects then, we predict that the frequency effect in naming should be larger for Chinese characters than for alphabetic words. This line of argument is well supported by the findings of Hue (1992) and Seidenberg (1985).

Closely related to the characteristic of ambiguous grapheme–sound correspondences in Chinese is a demonstration by Perfetti and Zhang (1991) that there is no prelexical phonology in the Chinese language. Although this conclusion may be too strong to apply to all Chinese characters, it is certainly true that the naming of Chinese characters is achieved via a lexical route. In other words, without recognizing a stimulus as a character, it cannot be pronounced.

Isolation of the post-lexical decision component

Since the naming of Chinese characters is always achieved by contacting their stored representations, the decision component in lexical decision-making can be easily isolated by introducing it into the naming task. In the lexical–decision naming task, pseudo-characters as well as true characters are presented. Since a pseudo-character has no pronunciation, the subject is to say aloud 'jia' (literally, 'false'; meaning a pseudo-character) when one is presented. The naming of a character in the lexical–decision naming task involves a decision component, while it does not in the conventional naming task. The lexical-route view guarantees that the naming of a character follows character recognition in both tasks. Therefore, the decision component can be directly estimated by comparing the mean naming times obtained from both tasks. Precisely this type of study was conducted by Liu, Chou, and Wu (1993). It was found that a decision time of about 100 ms is involved in naming a high-frequency character.

Once the decision component in lexical decision-making can be estimated, all other components involved in lexical decision-making and naming can also be estimated. A normal lexical decision time of 450 ms for a high-frequency character is analysed to comprise: a) about 50 ms for the stimulus to be registered in the brain, b) about 110 ms to decide which key to press, c) another 200 ms to execute a motor response, and d) another 70 to 110 ms to encode the word (the lexical access time). The lexical access time so estimated is in good agreement with what is concluded from eye-movement studies (Rayner and Pollatsek, 1989). Moreover, the theoretical scheme for this estimation is compatible with parallel distributed processing models (for example, Seidenberg and McClelland, 1989) that do not assume the existence of a lexicon.

In conclusion, by capitalizing on some distinctive surface features of Chinese logographs, it has been possible to unravel the components of the frequency effects in lexical decision-making and naming that have plagued investigators of alphabetic orthographies.

LEXICAL ACCESS AND CONTEXT EFFECTS

Words are rarely accessed in isolation. The reading of a word or words frequently aids in our access of those that follow. For instance, if a word is presented a second time for lexical decision during an experiment, it has been found to produce a more rapid and accurate response (Scarborough, Cortese, and Scarborough, 1977). This is called the repetition effect, and it has been proposed also as the basis for the frequency effect. This effect belongs to a class of effects known as priming effects. Other major examples of priming effects (or context effects) are produced by a manipulation of the context in which the test item occurs.

Phonological Priming Effects

According to one notion (Coltheart, 1978), in order to access a word, one must first recode the orthographic stimulus in terms of a code that represents the speech segments involved in the pronunciation of the word. Rubenstein, Lewis, and Rubenstein (1971) early demonstrated that a non-word such as *brane*, which sounds the same as *brain*, took longer to reject than did a nonword which did not sound the same as a particular word. However, this finding cannot constitute evidence for phonological recoding, because the experiment demonstrated only that pronunciation is determined before the final decision has been reached, not that the pronunciation must be determined before access can be attempted.

Both Hsieh (1982) and Cheng (1992) investigated phonological processes in reading Chinese characters in a lexical decision task. Their test required their subjects to judge on each trial whether or not a visual target, preceded by a visual priming cue, was a legitimate Chinese character. They manipulated the visual and phonological similarities between the cue and the target, and the asynchrony between the onset of the cue and that of the target. They found that lexical decision times were faster when preceded by homophonic priming characters than when preceded by phonologically dissimilar ones.

Zhang and Shu (1989) also studied the phonological priming effect on character recognition, and obtained the phonological priming effect in the naming task. They manipulated the frequency of the target characters and found that the priming effect tended to be larger for low-frequency than for high-frequency characters, resulting in a smaller frequency effect in the priming condition.

Semantic Priming Effects

Meyer and Schvaneveldt (1971) found that lexical decision times for a target word such as *butter* were faster if this word followed another word that was related to it in meaning, such as *bread*, compared with a control condition in which it followed a completely unrelated word, such as *book*.

Studying Chinese orthography, Peng and Tan (1987) also obtained support for the semantic priming effect when they manipulated both frequency of target characters and strength of associative relationships between priming and target items. They observed a stronger priming effect for low-frequency targets than for high-frequency targets when an associative relationship was present than when it was absent. These findings were replicated in a further study by Tan and Peng (1989).

Character Recognition in the Context of Words

Reicher (1969) first demonstrated that a letter is recognized faster and more accurately if it is presented as part of a word than if it is presented alone or as part of a non-word. This phenomenon is known as the word superiority effect. Working with Chinese logographs, Cheng (1981) compared the accuracy with which a briefly presented target character could be identified in a two-character word or non-word. A non-word consisted of two characters that do not form a word when combined. He found that a character was better identified when embedded in a word context than when embedded in a non-word context. Performance was also better for high-frequency words than for low-frequency words. This word superiority effect was replicated by Mattingly and Xu (1993) using a slightly different procedure.

Since most characters can be also used as words, Liu (1988) reasoned that what Cheng (1981) had demonstrated was the compound-word superiority effect. Therefore, he attempted to study a naming analogue of the compound-word superiority effect. The subjects voiced first-position or second-position characters in two-character words, two-character non-words, or in isolation, or voiced first-position, second position, or third-position characters in three-character words, three-character non-words, or in isolation. It was found that characters were named faster in word contexts than in non-word contexts. However, characters were not named faster in word contexts than in isolation.

Liu's (1988) study also included an experiment in which bilingual subjects in Hong Kong named first-position or second-position constituents in English compound words, compound non-words, or in isolation. A naming version of the compound-word superiority effect was obtained for English, since the subjects named constituent words faster in compound-word contexts than in compound non-word contexts or in isolation. However, since Chinese characters were not named faster in word contexts than in isolation, the word superiority effect obtained in English was not obtained in Chinese.

Liu (1988) proposed an explanation of why a naming version of the word superiority effect was not obtained in Chinese but was obtained in English. He noted that in Chinese there is not as effective a computational procedure as is found in English for arriving at a correct pronunciation for each Chinese word, because the success rate of using a phonetic component to predict a character's pronunciation is estimated to be very low (Zhou, 1978). Therefore, in arriving at a correct pronunciation for each word or character, an English speaker can rely on a small set of letter cues, while a Chinese speaker has to search through a less restricted number of character-sound correspondences. This implies that there is not only a facilitative effect on naming characters that results from the word context but also an interference effect due to the processing of the word context. The processing of the word context taxes the limited resources available for naming Chinese characters, because the subject has to search through a less restricted number of character-sound correspondences. In the case of naming a constituent in the English compound-word context, the processing of the context information taxes limited resources less, because a simpler set of grapheme–sound correspondences is available and so the interference effect is less likely to be observed.

If this analysis is correct, then it may be predicted that the hypothesized interference effect can be observed only in the naming task but not in the identification or lexical decision task.

ACTIVATION OF VARIOUS TYPES OF INFORMATION IN LEXICAL ACCESS

Since the term *lexical access* is used in an inconsistent manner by different authors, Monsell, Doyle, and Haggard (1989) defined *lexical identification* as a process in which one finds the best match for the input among the many word forms stored in a mental lexicon. On the other hand, they used the term *lexical transcoding* to refer to the generation of a code in the semantic or phonological domain from input in the orthographic domain. Lexical identification is supposed to activate learned phonological, semantic, and other properties required to perform tasks such as reading aloud, semantic categorization, and normal comprehension. This section is concerned with the lexical transcoding aspect of lexical access, and specifically deals with the time course of when and how phonological and semantic information is activated in Chinese lexical access.

Activation of Phonological Information

Working with alphabetic orthographies, many investigators (for example, Perfetti, Bell, and Delaney, 1988) have come to the conclusion that automatic phonological processes occur prior to complete word identification. With respect to Chinese characters, Perfetti and Zhang (1991) conducted a series of masking and priming experiments and found evidence that there is no pre-lexical phonology involved in the identification of characters. They used the backward masking paradigm as follows: a typical trial sequence in this type of experiment consists of a brief exposure to the word target, a pseudo-word mask of brief exposure, and a pattern mask exposed until the next trial, serving also as a fixation area. In work with English words (Perfetti et al., 1988), the target word is in lower case and the masking pseudo-word in upper case. The following sequences represent a trial with a 'phonemic mask': late — LAIT — XXXX; a trial with a 'graphemic mask': late — LART — XXXX; and a trial with a 'control mask': late — DOSK — XXXX. The main results found in studies with English orthography are that relative to control masks, more targets are reported with graphemic masks, and relative to graphemic masks, more targets are reported with phonemic masks. The phonemic mask reduction effect reflects the activation of phonemes of the target prior to its identification, indicating pre-lexical phonological activation.

The picture is different for Chinese orthography. In the masking experiment by Perfetti and Zhang (1991), their Chinese subjects identified characters briefly exposed then masked by a homophonic, graphic, semantic, or neutral character mask. The target character was presented at the subject's threshold for 50 per cent identification. They found no phonemic mask reduction effect and no semantic mask reduction effect, with identification rates of 40 to 50 per cent for both conditions as well as for controls. Thus, there is no reliable evidence of pre-lexical phonology in Chinese.

Activation of Semantic Information

Although activation of semantic attributes may occur before identification of a word form (lexical identification), specification of a word's meaning that is sufficiently precise for normal comprehension is generally assumed to be dependent on unique identification (Marslen-Wilson, 1987). Using a variant of the semantic categorization task, Liu, Zhu, and Wu (1992) attempted to test the direct-image hypothesis for accounting for the visual superiority effect obtained with Chinese logographs. The direct-image hypothesis refers to a widespread view that Chinese logographs map more directly onto meaning than do alphabetic words (see Aaronson and Ferres, 1986). The visual superiority effect, or reverse long-term modality effect, refers to the superiority of the visual over other modalities obtained for pre-recency items. Recency items refer to several times (3 or 4 items) in the last positions of the list. Pre-recency items naturally refer to all other items that are presented in the beginning and middle positions. In the following, we briefly describe how the problem of the visual superiority effect arose and how the direct-image hypothesis and other hypotheses were tested.

In McGinnies's (1965) study of persuasion through printed versus spoken communication, he found that Japanese subjects were more apt to be persuaded by printed than by spoken messages, contrary to findings frequently obtained with Western subjects (Hovland, 1954). Since Japanese script includes Chinese characters, McGinnies reasoned that the visual superiority effect in persuasion may be due to script differences. Turnage and McGinnies

(1973), therefore, manipulated the input modality of the stimulus presentation and found that Chinese subjects learn a list of two-character words more quickly when it is presented visually, whereas American subjects learn the list more quickly when it is presented as an auditory input.

If Chinese logographs give rise directly to images or are more like pictures, then the visual presentation superiority of Chinese logographs follows, because the superiority of pictures to words in free recall and recognition is well documented (see Crowder, 1976). According to the direct-image hypothesis, if Chinese logographs give rise directly to images, they will be coded both verbally and 'imaginally' in Paivio's dual coding framework (1971). Since alphabetic words are assumed to be coded verbally and, to a lesser extent, in images, an added image trace should result in better memory for Chinese logographs than for alphabetic words, if they are presented visually.

In undertaking to study these questions, Liu et al. (1992) first chose a set each of Chinese pictograms and phonograms and translated them into English words. A dominant meaning component of each item was determined by testing with a group of subjects. For example, *water* was given as a dominant meaning component of *river*. Another group of subjects was then tested in a variant of the semantic categorization task in which the subjects were timed in deciding whether a target item (in either Chinese or English) contained a dominant meaning component (also in either Chinese or English) presented as a prime two seconds prior to the target. It was found that reaction times were not faster to pictograms than to phonograms, nor faster to Chinese than to English targets. However, reaction times were faster for English primes than for Chinese primes. The latter finding is consistent with the observation that when words are used more frequently they tend to acquire more meanings (Johnson-Laird, 1983; Miller, 1951). In a further experiment, it was shown that reaction times were faster to pictures than to Chinese characters, although they were not faster to pictograms than to phonograms as was previously believed. Thus, even Chinese pictograms can be coded only indirectly to give rise to images.

It has also been believed that Chinese characters are more distinctive in shape or more discriminable than are alphabetic words (forming the discriminability hypothesis). Finally, Chinese characters have been considered to facilitate recall through their graphic features that classify Chinese characters into categories (the graphic-feature hypothesis). A series of experiments did not support either of these two hypotheses. More convincing evidence against these hypotheses came from a series of experiments in which the visual superiority effect was also obtained with English words, when tested with Chinese subjects.

Further experiments (Liu et al., 1992; Zhu, Liu, Shieh, and Fan, 1992) showed that the visual superiority effect can be accounted for by the relative strength of two types of frequency: of a verbal item as it appears in print, and of a verbal item as it appears in speech. Visual frequency is responsible for the availability of visual traces, and auditory frequency is responsible for the availability of auditory traces. Whenever there is a large discrepancy between visual and auditory frequencies in favor of the former, the visual presentation superiority effect is likely to obtain.

The Stroop Effect

Cattell (1886) early observed that objects and colours took longer to name aloud than the corresponding words took to read aloud. It took half a century before Stroop (1935) hit upon the idea of combining colours and words in compound stimuli where the word was incongruent with the ink colour. The Stroop interference effect generally refers to the finding that subjects are consistently slower in naming the ink colours of words printed in different colour names (e.g., *green* in red ink) than in naming control stimuli (e.g., a row of Xs in red ink).

Language-specific interpretation.

Language differences in the Stroop effect were first investigated by Dalrymple-Alford (1968) and Preston and Lambert (1969). For a comparison involving the Chinese language, Biederman and Tsao (1979) found a greater interference effect for Chinese subjects in a Chinese-version colour-naming task than for American subjects in an English version. Their explanation was that, since the perception of colours and the processing of characters are presumed to be functions located in the right hemisphere, they might be competing for the same perceptual capacity of the hemisphere.

Biederman and Tsao's (1979) language-specific hypothesis, that the Stroop interference effect is generally larger when Chinese characters are presented to the right hemisphere than when they are presented to the left hemisphere, received support from Hatta (1981), Morikawa (1981), and Tsao, Wu, and Feustel (1981). Smith and Kirsner (1982), however, obtained more symmetrical data using Chinese–English and French–English bilinguals. This issue, therefore, remains to be resolved.

Intra- and inter-language interferences.

Working with bilingual speakers, Preston and Lambert (1969) found a large Stroop interference whether the ink colours were named in the same language as the distracting words presented or in the bilinguals' other language. Dyer (1971) observed that English monolinguals naming colours in English manifested maximal interference when the words were in English and decreasing interference as the similarity of the irrelevant words to English declined. Working with diverse languages of Chinese–English and Japanese–English, Fang, Tzeng, and Alva (1981) confirmed that the ratio of inter-language to intra-language interference was reduced as language similarity decreased. They hypothesized that this reduction reflected the difference in the demand on the same central processor due to orthographic similarity.

In a more recent study, Lee, Wee, Tzeng, and Hung (1992) attempted to examine inter- and intra-language Stroop effects with Chinese, Malay, and Indian children in Singapore who were bilingual in English and their mother tongue. With this wide range of orthographic variations, these investigators hoped to replicate Biederman and Tsao's (1979) finding that Chinese characters produced more interference than did English words for these more balanced Chinese–English bilingual children. Moreover, they expected the reduction in the inter-language interference to be greatest for the Chinese–

English cases, less for the Tamil–English, and much less for Malay–English cases. It was found that the Chinese characters did not produce more interference than did the English words and that the reduction in inter-language interference was the same for all three bilingual groups. They suggested that the speed of decoding colour words and the speed of generating colour names may combine to determine the magnitude of the Stroop effect.

Although the effect of language similarity on the reduction of inter-language interference was not replicated (Lee et al., 1992), the variable of proficiency in one language over another may be important. Magiste (1984) observed a changing pattern with the development of the individual's second language. She used German–Swedish bilinguals (native German speakers) as subjects on the basis of their familiarity with Swedish in terms of length of residence in Sweden (1 to 16 years). She found that German-dominant subjects experienced more Stroop interference from German words when responding in both German and Swedish and that Swedish words caused more interference for Swedish-dominant subjects.

In testing Magiste's (1984) proficiency hypothesis, Chen and Ho (1986) had Chinese–English bilingual individuals, in educational grades 2, 4, 8, and 10 and at the tertiary level, name in Chinese or English the colours of patches and Chinese and English words that were incongruent colour names. They observed a developmental shift from greater between-language interference to greater within-language interference when English was the response language, supporting the proficiency hypothesis. However, their subjects at all levels of English proficiency showed greater within- than between-language interference when responding in their primary language, Chinese. Although the latter finding is on the surface incompatible with the proficiency hypothesis, it is understandable because, unlike Magiste's subjects, Chen and Ho's subjects continued to use Chinese as their primary language on most occasions.

MORPHOLOGICAL DECOMPOSITION IN LEXICAL ACCESS

With respect to how words are represented in the mental lexicon, a question of interest is whether words are represented in their intact forms or in decomposed forms. There is considerable evidence with English that morphological analysis takes place when the stem morphemes are non-words (e.g. 'vive' in revive) as when they are words (e.g. 'just' in unjust) (see Stanners, Neiser, and Painton, 1979; Taft, 1979).

Although it is easy to define a 'word' in an alphabetic orthography, it is relatively difficult in Chinese. In the ancient literature almost every character functions as a word. In modern times, however, many idea units are expressed in two characters. There is no dispute about the lexical status of such two-character words as 'old-master', although there is a question as to whether some two-character words are lexicalized. Therefore, there are one-character words as well as two-character or three-character words in Chinese. In this sense, Chinese two-character words provide ideal materials for studying the problems associated with morphological decomposition.

Coordinative versus Modifier Compounds

In designing their research, Zhang and Peng (1992) selected two types of two-character words: coordinative words and modifier words. The latter were formed by adjective–noun combinations. With word frequency kept constant, Zhang and Peng manipulated component character frequency and found faster lexical decision times for coordinative words with high-frequency component characters irrespective of whether the words occupied the first or second position. This finding supports the decomposition hypothesis in lexical access. In the case of modifier words, frequency of the second character was again significant. The research failed, however, to identify a significant effect for the first character, although the results were in the direction predicted by the decomposition hypothesis. They concluded that Chinese words are accessed through individual characters and that morphological structure has a role in the representation of characters in the lexicon.

Taft, Huang, and Zhu (1993) selected two-character words with their component characters that varied orthogonally in individual character frequencies (high-high, high-low, low-high, and low-low), while the mean frequencies for the four types of two-character words were equated. They found that, although high-high words were faster than high-low and low-high words, low-low words were as fast as high-high words in lexical decision times. Note that there were no low-low words in the Zhang and Peng (1992) study. When the frequency of the first (second) characters was varied, the mean frequencies of the second (first) characters were always high.

Binding Words

In the study by Taft et al. (1993), the lexical decision times were as fast for low-low words as high-high words. They reasoned that this is because their low-low words were highly predictable from one character to another in the sense that they were nearly the only words to contain their first character in the first position and nearly the only words to contain their second character in the second position. They called such words 'binding words'. However, in their second experiment they found no difference in lexical decision times for binding words and non-binding words.

The reason why Taft et al. (1993) did not obtain a significant difference in lexical decision times for binding and non-binding words could be due to the small number of words sampled. The notion of predictability invoked for explaining no difference between high-high and low-low words is compatible with the concept of context. Since one character is highly predictable for another character in a binding word, the encoding of one character naturally functions as the context not only for retrieving another character but also for retrieving the stored representation of the binding word. On the other hand, since each character in an high-high word is of high frequency, it tends to appear with other characters. Therefore, the strength of intra-word connection will be much lower than would be expected from absolute word frequencies.

CONCLUSION

All experimental studies of Chinese lexical access may be easily understood in terms of an interplay between two types of variables: structural and experiential. With respect to the word frequency effect, the effect of experience is obvious. It was shown that the decision component in lexical decision times can be isolated by noting characteristic grapheme–sound correspondences in Chinese, whereby it was possible to unravel components of the frequency effects in lexical decision and naming.

As for the problems associated with context effects in lexical access, it is again not difficult to see the effect of experience; context effects generally refer not to the effect of word frequency but to the effect of frequency in experiencing a unit larger than a word, such as the word *nurse* being related to the word *doctor*.

There is no exception for those studies concerned with activation of various types of information in lexical access. In the case of the visual superiority effect, the structural variable may occur as a result of a variation in Chinese dialects, producing a large discrepancy between visual and auditory frequencies of word usage. In those studies involving the Stroop effect, for instance, more and more investigators have come to consider proficiency and automaticity as the important variables in producing the observed results.

Finally, if we consider morphological decomposition in lexical access, the effect of component character frequency again reflects the influence of past experience. The interplay between this experiential factor and those structural variables, such as coordinative versus modifier words and binding words, may continue to attract future investigations.

Chapter 4

Chinese Reading and Comprehension:
A Cognitive Psychology Perspective

Hsuan-Chih Chen

'昔者倉頡作書，而天雨粟，鬼夜哭。'
劉安〈淮南子 · 本經訓〉(ca 150 BC)

And so to completely analyse what we do when we read would almost
be the acme of a psychologist's achievements, for it would be to describe
very many of the most intricate workings of the human mind, as well as to
unravel the tangled story of the most remarkable specific performance
that civilization has learned in all its history.

E. B. Huey (1908)

The evolution of written language is a stupendous achievement of human
intellectual activity. Through its use, we not only can document events occurring in daily life but can also transcribe complex, abstract, and very transient
human thoughts and emotions into precise and concrete records, which can
be kept and used without the limits of space, time, or our memory. Each individual's thinking and feelings can thus be accumulated to form the collective
wisdom of all humanity. The civilizing of people then becomes a rapid, automatic process. By the same means, each person is no longer merely an isolated
individual; once he or she has been successfully trained as a literate, that person can in principle be connected with other people across time and space and
has access to the knowledge and experiences of others. It is therefore appropriate to say that the invention and use of written language mark the advent of
real civilization and have brought about great changes in the human life experience.

Across the world there are many varieties of written languages. Various
orthographies differ in their solutions to the problem of representing meanings
in written forms. Most European languages, for example, adopt an alphabetic
writing system in which the solution developed is to use the written language
to represent the spoken one. There are, however, other writing systems (for
example, Chinese orthography) that have been developed following a logographic principle (that is, one in which symbols mainly and directly encode
meaning). Because various orthographies are constructed on distinct principles and present linguistic information in diverse forms, it is by no means self-
evident that the same cognitive processes are activated to recognize and
comprehend information written in the different orthographies. Thus, it is
important and useful to carry out reading research across languages, because it

can reveal both universal and orthography-specific processes associated with the reading of different writing systems, which in turn can help to build a genuinely comprehensive theory of how people read and comprehend written information.

Written Chinese has a number of unique and important properties and is probably the most widely used written language on earth (Chen, 1992). Most reading research, however, has been conducted on European languages with alphabetic writing systems, and only a relatively small amount has involved the Chinese language. How do readers comprehend written Chinese? Can the specific properties of the language affect its corresponding processes in reading and comprehension? If so, how? These are the questions addressed in this chapter.

The section that follows presents first an analysis of the visual spatial layout of written Chinese and discusses how visual information is extracted from the printed page. The succeeding section is on the processing of Chinese characters and describes some of the main work that has been done to understand how characters are recognized and understood (both in isolation and in context). The chapter then turns to what is known about the processing of words and the time course of lexical, syntactic, and semantic processing in reading Chinese text. The chapter concludes that the unique properties of the language may have important implications in cognitive processes involved in Chinese reading and comprehension.

VISUAL ENCODING

Readers do not often realize how heavily they rely for comprehension on visual spatial information embedded in the printed page and gained during reading. For example, try to read the following sentence:
tHiSsEnTeNcEiSdIfFiCuLtToReAd.

The preceding sentence presents a problem for the reader for two reasons: words in written English are conventionally divided by spaces, but these important cues are not available in the above sentence; and the letters here are in alternating cases, thus the visual cues are incongruous. In addition to spacing and case, there are other visual spatial cues in English, just as there are in many other alphabetic orthographies. For instance, words that are segmented by spaces differ in length (for example, *a* versus *professionalism*) and in height (for example, *by* versus *as*).

There is ample evidence in the literature to show that the spatial layout factors mentioned above can affect reading performance and/or its related processes in alphabetic systems. For example, it has been established that word reading time increases directly with the length of the word (Haberlandt and Graesser, 1985; Just, Carpenter, and Woolley, 1982). The movement of the eyes is influenced by the length of the word to the right of fixation: a longer eye movement tends to be formed (or executed) when the subsequent word is long rather than short (O'Regan, 1979; Rayner, 1979). Furthermore, manipulating the nature of inter-word spacing in printed text (by replacing inter-word spaces from the text with arbitrary symbols, adding many more spaces between words, or simply removing them completely) can affect reading comprehension in general and the processing of individual words in particular (Healy and Drewnowski, 1983; Patberg and Yonas, 1978).

Moreover, the readability of text and strategies of reading can be influenced by the display format of the text (Chan and Chen, 1991; Chen, 1986; Chen and Chan, 1990; Chen, Chan, and Tsoi, 1988; Chen and Healy, in press; Chen, Healy, Bourne, 1985; Chen and Tsoi, 1988; Juola, 1988; Magliano, Graesser, Eymard, Haberlandt, and Gholson, 1993; Spaai and Chen, 1992). For example, one common way of presenting continuous text on computer displays and other electronic display devices is the moving method, in which text is horizontally advanced in jumps of one or several characters at a time from right to left along a single line on the display screen. Research investigating the readability of moving text has shown that, in contrast to the conventional use of the moving format, text presented in small jump lengths of one character at a time was read slower and less efficiently than that presented in larger jumps of five or more characters (Chen and Tsoi, 1988), and that giving readers control over the text display rate not only did not enhance reading performance but disrupted it in some occasions (Chen and Chan, 1990; Chen et al., 1988).

In contrast to the effects described above, the physical layout of written Chinese is strikingly different from that of alphabetic systems such as that of English. To illustrate, Figure 4.1 presents a short, quantized Chinese passage and a corresponding passage in English. (The quantization procedure substitutes fine detail in each character or letter space for the more global spatial information in the area.)

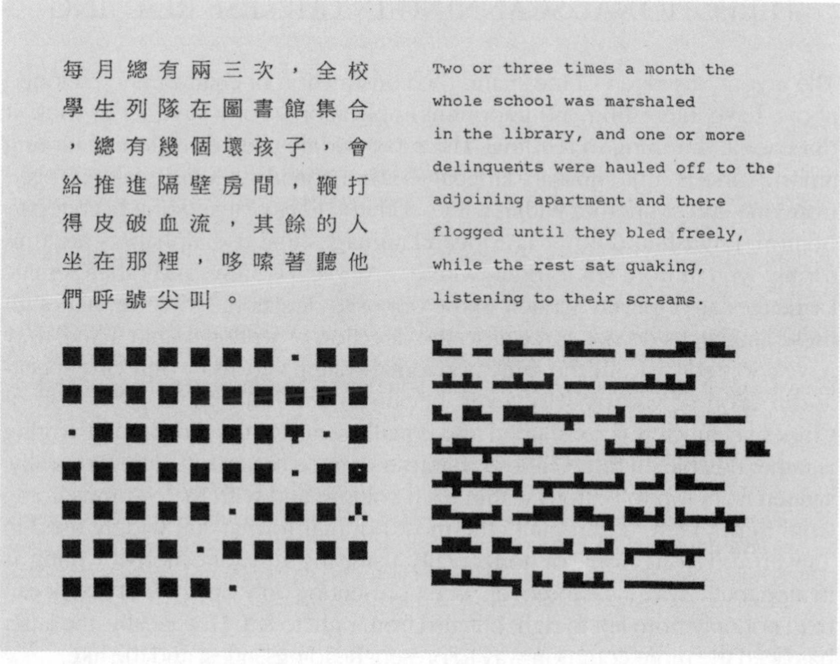

每 月 總 有 兩 三 次 ， 全 校
學 生 列 隊 在 圖 書 館 集 合
， 總 有 幾 個 壞 孩 子 ， 會
給 推 進 隔 壁 房 間 ， 鞭 打
得 皮 破 血 流 ， 其 餘 的 人
坐 在 那 裡 ， 哆 嗦 著 聽 他
們 呼 號 尖 叫 。

Two or three times a month the
whole school was marshaled
in the library, and one or more
delinquents were hauled off to the
adjoining apartment and there
flogged until they bled freely,
while the rest sat quaking,
listening to their screams.

Figure 4.1 A Quantized Chinese Passage, its Corresponding English Version, and the Original Texts.

As can be seen from the figure, the Chinese passage is constructed by arrays of equally spaced, box-shaped elements called characters. As all characters take a constant square space in print, the characters themselves provide no cue to indicate the overall organization of the print. Thus, Chinese characters can be arranged freely either by columns or by rows. It is not obvious whether a given Chinese passage is organized in columns or in rows unless some sort of proximity cue such as bigger or smaller spacing between columns and rows is built in. The English text, on the other hand, is formed by strings of words of various shapes and lengths. In fact, it is fairly clear that the text is arranged horizontally, because the units that are segmented by spaces differ mainly along the horizontal dimension. Taken together, despite being very symmetrical and artistic, the layout of written Chinese actually provides few spatial cues to its readers as compared with those available in alphabetic systems.

Before moving on to discuss the implications of the layout of written Chinese on visual encoding, let us take a closer look at the construction of individual characters. The basic elements in constructing Chinese characters are strokes. Strokes can be used to compose either radicals or simple characters, both of which can be taken to form compound characters in a recursive way within a prescribed box-form region. Since both the number of strokes (they can range from 1 to about 30) and the manner of construction (there are more than 15 diverse patterns; see, for examples, Huang and Wang, 1992) of an individual character can vary to a great extent, a large variety of characters can be assembled, and the potential complexity of a character can thus be very high.

DIRECTIONAL SCANNING IN CHINESE READING

The layout of written Chinese and the construction of characters mentioned above have interesting and important implications. For a start, let us look at directional scanning in reading. The most widely used direction of writing among various contemporary languages is horizontal, with materials arranged from one end to another within a line, with the lines of text going from top to bottom. English and other European languages that use alphabets are uniformly written from left to right, whereas Arabic, Hebrew, and other Semitic languages are typically written in the opposite direction. However, although these languages do not agree as to the direction of writing within a line, they have adopted basically the same horizontal system and allow only one specific direction of writing. However, because of the unique construction of Chinese characters (box-shaped and equally spaced), the direction of writing is rather flexible. In fact, Chinese characters can be organized either vertically, written from top to bottom within each column and with the columns going from right to left, traditionally the most popular format still widely used in Taiwan and Hong Kong, or horizontally, using the same direction of writing as in alphabetic systems. Moreover, when presenting only one row of text, it can read not only from left to right but also from right to left. Historically, the latter has been the more common way to present headings, titles, and the like.

It appears that the flexibility of Chinese orthography in the direction of its writing can be related meaningfully to patterns of directional scanning in reading. For instance, in the first half of the twentieth century, Chinese was pre-dominantly written down the vertical dimension, and a vertical over horizontal advantage was typically found during that period in studies with Chinese stim-uli, using various procedures such as reading, recall, and/or symbol detection (see, for example, Chen and Carr, 1926; Shen, 1927). In the latter half of the century, however, the horizontal format has also been commonly used to print Chinese, especially in mainland China. As modern Chinese readers are consid-erably adapted to both vertical and horizontal reading, it comes as no surprise that an advantage for the vertical arrangement has not usually been found in recent studies investigating the possible effects of the direction of print on naming or visual acuity with Chinese stimuli (Chen and Chen, 1988; Chen, 1981; Freeman, 1980). Chen and Chen (1988) further demonstrated that first-grade Chinese students in Hong Kong who had little experience in reading materials presented horizontally showed faster naming responses for vertical rather than horizontal scanning, whereas subjects who had had several years of experience in horizontal reading (samples of fifth graders and tertiary-level students), the vertical-over-horizontal advantage disappeared (in fact, a hori-zontal over vertical advantage in reading Chinese text was found for tertiary students in speed reading). These results thus indicate that directional scan-ning can indeed be influenced by reading experience.

HOW IS VISUAL INFORMATION EXTRACTED FROM PRINTED CHINESE?

Although only a few studies have investigated the pattern of eye movements of Chinese readers, a typical finding is that they use relatively small, voluntary eye movements called saccades during reading (the average saccade length is less than two characters; Shen, 1927; Stern, 1978). Because the majority of Chinese words are formed by two characters (about 75 per cent, according to Yu, Zhang, Jing, Peng, Zhang, and Simon, 1985), the average saccade length seems less in Chinese than in English (it is about a word and a half in English; Rayner and Pollatsek, 1989). Indeed, when patterns of reading eye movement in Chinese and English were compared, Peng, Orchard, and Stern (1983) report-ed that Chinese readers made many more saccades per line than did English readers (see Stern, 1978, for the same finding). Similarly, when the saccade length was measured in visual angle, Sun, Morita, and Stark (1985) found that the average saccade length for Chinese readers was about 15 per cent smaller than that for English readers.

Furthermore, another aspect of the eye movements of Chinese readers is interesting to note. In conventional reading with alphabetic materials, readers extract useful visual information from a printed page by executing a series of eye fixations spaced by saccades. This method of acquiring visual information differs from another method called 'pursuit movements', which are usually observed when the eyes are tracking a moving target. In pursuit movements, the eyes can move smoothly and extract visual information constantly. In read-ing English or other alphabetic text, only saccadic movements have been observed, but a different pattern of results has been reported in reading written

Chinese. Shen (1927) reported that eye movements in reading vertically arranged Chinese text had a tendency to glide into a pattern of pursuit-like movements. Likewise, more than 50 years later, Stern (1978) found that Chinese readers reading horizontally printed Chinese text showed the pursuit pattern of eye movements; one of his subjects revealed this pattern frequently, whereas the others displayed it only occasionally.

The evidence available seems to indicate that readers do not always display a saccadic pattern of eye movement while reading Chinese text and that, when they do, they tend to make smaller and more regular saccades than do readers of alphabetic systems like English. Although at present systematic studies have not yet been undertaken to conclusively determine whether visual information is indeed extracted in such ways during the reading of Chinese, two unique factors in the layout of written Chinese are worth mentioning here. The first is the informational density of the text. It is known that informational density is related to the reader's saccade length in reading of both Chinese and English texts (that is, saccade length decreases as the text becomes more difficult; Peng et al., 1983; Rayner and Pollatsek, 1989). It is also known that when a Chinese passage is translated into English, or vice versa, the Chinese version typically takes up less space than does its English equivalent (for a clear example of this effect, refer to Figure 4.1). There are at least three reasons for this difference: in the amount of visual information given per character, Chinese characters are generally more complex than alphabetic ones, as measured by the number of strokes or line segments in the character; in construction and physical length, whereas alphabetic words can have a great variation of length, most Chinese words are formed by one or two characters (about 95 per cent; Sun et al., 1985); and, finally, unlike in many alphabetic systems, various forms of syntactic information (for example, inflectional markings and intrasentential concordance rules) are usually absent in the Chinese text itself, and are instead carried by the context as a whole. Consequently, Chinese sentences often comprise fewer characters and fewer words than do their English equivalents. The informational density, hence, is greater in Chinese than in an alphabetic system like English.

The second factor concerns parafoveal information available in the layout of written Chinese. Text written in an alphabetic system consists of word strings with spaces between individual words. Various alphabetic words differ in form, in height, and in length. Thus, a great deal of parafoveal information is available to guide saccades and to provide a partial preview of the words not being fixated. Written Chinese, however, is formed by strings of lexical morphemes called characters. Different characters are constructed by varying a relatively large amount of visual detail and by adjustment of how their components are organized within the same, square-form area. The box-shaped characters so constructed are usually equally spaced within the text.

The obvious effect of all these features is that relatively little parafoveal information is available to the reader of Chinese. It has been shown that movement of the eyes, shown in saccade length and fixation position, can be influenced by parafoveal information like spacing and word length to the right of fixation (O'Regan, 1979; Pollatsek and Rayner, 1982; Rayner and Pollatsek, 1981). Thus, it is plausible that, because the parafoveal information is rather opaque in written Chinese, readers of Chinese tend to make smaller and more regular saccades than do readers of alphabetic systems. Furthermore, it has been suggested that under certain circumstances, the relatively small and regular saccades that have typically been observed in the reading of Chinese may glide into a pattern of smooth pursuit-like movements, especially when the proficiency of the reader, the readability of the text, and the reader's familiarity with the topic are all very high, and the purpose of the reading is to extract the general meaning rather than the specific details of the text (e.g., Hoosain, 1991). These speculations, however, need to be verified systematically in future research.

In summary, we have seen that readers of Chinese seem capable of displaying unique patterns of eye movements and directional scanning. This may have its basis in the important differences of the layout of written Chinese from that of alphabetic systems. The evidence available seems to suggest that both directional scanning and information extraction from a printed page can be affected by the physical layout of the written language. However, because only a very few studies have addressed these issues, future research is needed to explore more systematically the influences of layout variables on information extraction during the reading of such a unique written language as Chinese.

THE PROCESSING OF CHARACTERS

Distinct Orthographic Units in Written Chinese

Among various research topics in Chinese reading, processing of characters is the most extensively studied, not only because Chinese characters are distinct orthographic units of the language well known to and widely used by the Chinese people, but also because they have a number of unique properties. To begin, let us look at major structural properties of Chinese characters that are particularly revealing of the spatial layout of written Chinese.

Written Chinese, as mentioned above, is invariably formed by evenly spaced, box-like elements called characters. Because characters are made up of strokes and components in a constant, square-shaped area, they can have a relatively high complexity of construction. Different characters vary in number of strokes (for example, '一', meaning 'one', is made up of one stroke; '鬱', 'unhappy', 29 strokes) and in manner of construction ('柑', 'tangerine', is formed by combining two simple characters '木' and '甘' horizontally, but '某', 'unspecified', is constructed by joining the same two characters vertically). These properties suggest that the Chinese character is suitable as a basic perceptual unit that serves the reading of Chinese in a way not unlike the role of words in alphabetic reading. For instance, Healy (1976) carried out reading experiments in English in which she asked her subjects to read a passage for comprehension and to detect every case of a target letter while reading. The results showed that subjects made many more detection errors on correctly spelled words than on misspelled words, presumably because correct words, especially those of high familiarity, were more likely to be recognized as single units, whereas rare or misspelled words were read in terms of smaller units (for similar results and discussions, see Healy and Drewnowski, 1983; Healy,

Oliver, and McNamara, 1987). Consistent with this word inferiority effect, Chen (1984) demonstrated a character inferiority effect in Chinese reading by using a component detection task: more detection errors were found when a target component was embedded in genuine characters than in misconstructed characters. Chen (1984, 1986) further reported that the character inferiority effect was vulnerable to manipulations of perceptual environments such as the size of text display (using a 1-character or 10-character window to show the text), but it was not sensitive to conceptual manipulations such as context (showing either the original text or a scrambled version of the text in which the order of the characters was randomized). These results indicate that in reading Chinese text, characters serve as important perceptual units which may function as encoding units similar to those of alphabetic words.

Linguistic Properties of Chinese Characters

Various orthographies differ in their solutions to the problem of representing meaning in written forms. In alphabetic writing systems, for instance, symbols are made to correspond more or less to elementary units in speech, that is, phonemes. Chinese characters, however, typically represent basic units of meaning, that is, morphemes. One advantage of using such a logographic orthography, as opposed to a sound-based writing system, is that the same script can be used to represent different spoken languages. This is a crucial advantage especially for the Chinese, who are comprised of a large population spread over a wide geographical area and speaking a large number of dialects, many of which are not mutually intelligible (Li and Thompson, 1981). Moreover, Chinese characters are typically monosyllabic: because the number of characters used regularly is only about 4600 (Liu, Chuang, and Wang, 1975), and the number of possible syllables is only about 400 (Cheng, 1982), there is a good deal of homophony in the Chinese language.

Although Chinese characters generally represent lexical morphemes, many of them may in principle provide some clue to pronunciation. In fact, a substantial number of Chinese characters (about 82 percent, according to Zhou, 1978) consist of complex characters formed of two components, one of which, sometimes called the signific or radical, provides a graphically distinctive, categorical cue to the meaning; the other component, called the phonetic, may cue in an all-or-none fashion the pronunciation of the character as a whole. However, the phonetic parts in these complex characters are basically themselves characters having their own pronunciation (thus providing phonetic cues) and different meanings (their meanings being typically different from the meanings of the complex characters in which they are embedded). For example, 馬, ma, meaning 'horse', is the phonetic in the character 罵, ma, 'to scold', but is the radical in the character 駕, jia, 'to ride' or 'to drive'. In addition, these phonetic components do not always provide constant and reliable cues to the pronunciation. Some may serve as phonetics in some complex characters, but as radicals in others. Also, over the whole distribution of character types, the percentage of complex characters in which the phonetic components provide the correct pronunciation is only about 39 per cent (Zhou, 1978) and is less than 35 per cent for high- and medium-frequency complex characters (Perfetti,

Zhang, and Berent, 1992). Note that these estimations were only made on the basis of Mandarin Chinese, and there are many other Chinese dialects (in fact, Mandarin is only one of the seven major dialect groups in Chinese). In other words, even though the phonetic component in a compound character provides a valid cue for pronunciation in Mandarin, this may not be the case in other dialects. For example, 包 is a valid cue for 抱 in Mandarin, because both are pronounced with the same segments as *bao*, but they are pronounced as *baau* and *po* in Cantonese. Thus, it is reasonable to conclude that, as compared with many alphabetic writing systems, the script–speech relationship in written Chinese is highly opaque.

COGNITIVE PROCESSING OF CHARACTERS

Given that Chinese characters are logographic in nature and that written Chinese has a high degree of homophony and a generally poor symbol-to-sound correspondence, it is not clear whether the same kind of cognitive processes (for example, activation and processing of graphemic, phonological, and semantic information) that have often been observed in word recognition using alphabetic systems will also occur in character recognition using Chinese. This issue has attracted much interest of research over the years (see Besner and Hilderbrandt, 1987; Chen, 1992; Chen, Flores d'Arcais, and Cheung, in press; Chen and Juola, 1982; Chen and Tsoi, 1990; Flores d'Arcais, 1992; Hung and Tzeng, 1981; Peng, Guo, and Zhang, 1985; Perfetti and Zhang, 1991; Seidenberg, 1985; Taft and Chen, 1992; Wydell, Patterson, and Humphreys, 1993).

To determine whether the same mental procedures or strategies are involved in the processing of Chinese and alphabetic materials, let us examine subjects' performance in two widely used lexical tasks: naming aloud and lexical decision. When examining subjects' performance in these two tasks using alphabetic materials, two results are typically found: naming is usually faster than lexical decision, and the magnitude of the word frequency effect is generally larger in the lexical decision task than in the naming task (Forster and Chambers, 1973; Frederiksen and Kroll, 1976; Katz and Feldman, 1983). This pattern of result has been found with such alphabetic systems as English (the most widely studied alphabetic script) and Serbo-Croatian (a shallow alphabetic orthography in which the phonemes of the spoken word are represented by the graphic items in a direct and unequivocal manner). The most striking observation is that a similar pattern of result with only minor differences can also be found with Hebrew (a deep alphabetic orthography in which the spelling-to-sound ambiguity is relatively high); in this case although naming is no longer faster than is lexical decision, the word frequency effect is still larger in lexical decision than in naming (see, for example, Frost, Katz, and Bentin, 1987). A very different picture is shown, however, when Chinese characters are used as stimuli: naming is almost always slower than lexical decision, and the word frequency effect is larger in the naming task (Wu, Chou, and Liu, 1993).

Note that the mentioned differences between the results of naming and lexical decision using Chinese and alphabetic materials are obtained from comparisons between groups. Since different groups of subjects might have different personal and social characteristics, the possibility therefore exists that it was not the orthography factor *per se* which caused the difference between results using different materials. More direct evidence that suggests that reading different orthographies may activate different lexical processes comes from a study (Chen and Tsoi, 1990) in which English monolinguals were asked to name logographic symbols (for example, + and -) and corresponding words in English (*plus* and *minus*), whereas Chinese-English bilinguals participated in both the Chinese and English versions of the task. The naming of calculation symbols and of characters in Chinese was equally fast for the bilinguals, whereas symbol-naming in English was slower than word-naming in English for both the monolingual and bilingual subjects. Moreover, when Chinese–English bilinguals were required to respond in their second language, English, they showed a similar pattern of response as that found for native English subjects, clearly indicating that different recognition processes, at least in terms of name retrieval, are involved in reading non-alphabetic Chinese and alphabetic English. The difference between results with Chinese and English stimuli, according to Chen and Tsoi, is probably due to the fact that the spoken name of alphabetic words, unlike that for calculation symbols or many of the Chinese characters, can be readily derived from their orthography.

PHONOLOGICAL PROCESSES IN RECOGNIZING CHINESE CHARACTERS

The research reviewed above leads to the suggestion that recognition of Chinese characters is not mediated by phonological coding, which, at least in principle, is possible with alphabetic orthography. It is instead possible that once the meaning of a character is recognized (or even before that point), its corresponding phonological information can be activated using the whole character, the phonetic component in the character (if it is a compound character, and if the component provides valid information), or both (if possible) to help retrieve the name (for relevant discussion, see Bertelson, Chen, Tseng, Ko, and de Gelder, in press). The proposition that character recognition is not mediated by phonological coding has received some empirical support. For example, Perfetti, Bell, and Delaney (1988) adopted a backward masking procedure (to display very briefly three items successively: the first one served as the target, the second as the mask, and the last a pattern mask) to study phonological activation of an English word before it reaches identification. The results showed that relative to a control condition (for example, a target *rate* followed by a neutral mask *busk*), more targets were correctly reported when the second item was homophonic to the target (*rait* and *rate*, respectively). These results have been taken as evidence for the idea that pre-lexical phonological activation exists in word recognition for English. However, when a similar study was carried out in Chinese, Perfetti and Zhang (1991) did not obtain evidence for phonological activation before lexical access in reading Chinese characters, although they found phonological effects with a standard priming procedure in both the identification and naming tasks.

It is interesting to note that, while there are studies that have shown phonological effects in recognition of Chinese characters (Cheng and Shih, 1988; Fang, Horng, and Tzeng, 1986; Flores d'Arcais, 1992; Lam, Perfetti, and Bell, 1991; Perfetti and Zhang, 1991; Seidenberg, 1985; Tan, Hoosain, and Peng, in press), these studies have typically adopted such tasks as naming, identification, or homophony decision in which a character's name is required or can be helpful. Although phonological effects have also been shown in other studies using the lexical decision task and Chinese characters as stimuli (for example, Cheng, 1992; Cheng and Shih, 1988), it is not clear whether these necessarily provide evidence concerning phonological activation in semantic access. Lexical decisions are vulnerable to the composition of the lexical and nonlexical items in question, and can sometimes be made on the basis of the orthographic or phonological familiarity of the stimuli before meaning has been activated (see Balota and Chumbly, 1984; Waters and Seidenberg, 1985). Therefore, it is not clear whether the phonological effects found in the studies reviewed above can be generalized beyond the tasks under which those effects were shown, or whether the effects are related to the specific properties of the tasks used.

The studies discussed above cannot answer the question whether phonological activation occurs routinely and necessarily as part of character recognition. This critical question needs to be addressed in situations in which the meaning of a character has to be consulted to make a response and the phonological information of the character is not needed for the task, as is the case in a semantic-decision task. This question has been investigated in a recent study by Chen et al. (in press) using a semantic categorization task, similar to the paradigm used to study word recognition in English. In English, Van Orden and his colleagues (for example, Van Orden, 1987; Van Orden, Johnston, and Hale, 1988) have used a categorization task in which subjects were given a category name (for example, *flower*) and have been asked to decide whether a subsequently presented target word (for example, *rose*) is a member of the category. They found that their subjects made more categorization errors and spent more time on homophone foils than on spelling controls (for example, category: FLOWER; exemplar: *rose*; homophone foil: *rows*; spelling control: *snobs*), indicating an automatic and independent activation of phonological information in the activity of recognizing English words.

In the study by Chen et al. (in press), however, subjects' reaction times and error rates showed clear effects of graphemic interference (that is, the subjects made more errors and produced longer categorization latencies on graphemically similar foils than on the corresponding controls), while no effect of phonological interference was found with homophonic foils in two experiments with Cantonese-speaking subjects. A similar finding of the absence of a homophonic effect in the semantic categorization task has been reported independently by Leek, Weekes, and Chen (in press) in research with Mandarin-speaking subjects. However, unlike the two semantic studies reviewed above, a study by Perfetti and Zhang (in press) has recently demonstrated small but nevertheless significant effects of homophonic manipulations in a synonym task in which subjects had to make synonym judgements in regard to pairs of successively presented characters. In these experiments, the first character in each pair of stimuli was presented in an exposure of short duration between 80 and 300 ms, and the second character was displayed after the first and remained in view for a relatively longer period or until the subject responded. The results showed homophonic interference in both false positive synonym judgement errors (the effects in error rate were about 6.6 per cent and 2.3 per cent in two experiments) and decision latencies (the effects were about 46 ms and 18 ms). It is interesting to note that although Perfetti and Zhang found reliable homophonic effects using a synonym decision task, the magnitude of the effects is small compared to similar effects with alphabetic materials (for example, the size of homophonic effect in error rate in the study by Van Orden was generally larger than 15 per cent on average and that in reaction times was about 160 ms). Taken together, the absence of phonological effects (or the relatively weak effect of phonological interference) in the studies of Chinese semantic tasks reviewed above stands in contrast with the results of testing in English, indicating that distinctive processes of phonological activation are probably involved in semantic processing of individual lexical items written in different orthographies.

Another point in the research mentioned above deserves our attention. A widely held model in lexical processing is the dual-route approach (see, for example, Carr and Pollatsek, 1985; Coltheart, 1978; Forster and Chambers, 1973; Patterson and Morton, 1985; Seidenberg and McClelland, 1989; Shallice, Warrington, and McCarthy, 1983). The basic assumption of this approach is that there are two major pathways by which the meaning of a lexical item can be accessed, the direct visual route and the phonologically mediated route. A number of studies have demonstrated the use of the phonological route in lexical access for alphabetic systems (for example, Seidenberg, 1985; Van Orden, 1987).

However, in lexical research with alphabetic materials, the direct access from orthography to meaning has typically been assumed as a default route whenever a phonological manipulation fails to produce a notable effect on lexical performance. This kind of evidence can thus only be considered as indirect. The reason that there is only indirect evidence for the direct visual route in research on alphabetic word recognition is that visual and phonological properties of an alphabetic word are closely related and thus cannot be completely unconfounded, whereas a similar confounding is usually absent in Chinese (for relevant discussions, see Chen and Juola, 1982). Hence, the Chinese writing system provides a unique opportunity to demonstrate the existence of the direct access from orthography to meaning. In fact, the presence of graphic similarity effects in the semantic processing of Chinese characters reviewed above (for example, in Chen et al., in press) provides clear evidence for the direct visual route to lexical access.

CONTEXT DEPENDENCY/SEMANTIC PROPERTIES OF CHINESE CHARACTERS

In major alphabetic writing systems, perceptual units that are clearly marked by spaces in the text are usually also basic functional units in sentence formation. This, however, is not the case in Chinese, at least not in contemporary Chinese. Although, as discussed earlier, Chinese characters are distinct orthographic units, they generally represent lexical morphemes rather than syntactic words. In fact, most characters simply do not possess the kind of syntactic and semantic independence and integrity that alphabetic words do.

To discuss the semantic properties of Chinese characters, let us first look at the relationship between the character and the word. A Chinese word can include one or more characters. Although in classical Chinese words were usually monosyllabic (that is, there was a very large number of single-character words), modern Chinese words are often comprised of more than one character. In addition, even though there is still a considerable number of Chinese characters that can be independently used as words in text, they can almost always join other characters to form multiple-character words with distinctively different meanings. For example, 生 is a single-character word in the following sentence: 她生了一個男孩, meaning 'she gave birth to a boy', but it can also join other characters to form such different words as (生長) meaning 'to grow', 生意 (business), 生氣 (angry), 畜生 (beast), 生分 (distant), 生命 (life), 花生 (peanut), 衞生 (health), 發生 (to happen), 接線生 (operator), and 陌生人 (stranger), among others. Thus, the meaning of a Chinese character can be relatively shifting and ambiguous, especially if the character is included in a large number of different words. Such a situation is not uncommon; in fact, on the basis of a Chinese corpus of about one million words (Liu, Chuang, and Wang, 1975), Cheng (1982) reported that the 125 most commonly used characters accounted for 50 per cent of the whole corpus, and the next 293 characters account for another 25 per cent. Using a similar corpus, Wu and Liu (1988) reported that the average number of different words that can be constructed using each of the 240 highest frequency characters is about 100. These calculations indicate that Chinese characters can often be associated with several different meanings and that context is critical in determining the meaning of the character.

As we have seen, the meaning of a Chinese character can be highly context-dependent, and the activation and processing of a character's phonological information can be contaminated by the problems of poor symbol-to-sound correspondence and substantial homophony. On the other hand, the graphic aspects of each character are distinctive in comparison with its phonological and semantic aspects. This probably explains why the results of a number of previous studies (Chen and Juola, 1982; Peng et al., 1985) that compared the efficiency of recognition and memory of graphemic, phonological, and semantic information of Chinese characters suggest that graphemic representation and processing plays the prominent role among the three dimensions of lexical coding in Chinese. In contrast, there is evidence to show that visual representation plays a less important role for English words than do phonological and semantic representations (Chen and Juola, 1982).

To sum up, evidence in the literature indicates that there are general principals (for example, that the preferred code for verbal information in working memory is probably the phonological one as proposed by Tzeng, Hung, and Wang, 1977, among others) that can be applied to the processing of lexical items from different writing systems (for relevant discussion, see Liu, Zhu, and Wu, 1992). However, studies show as well that script differences can indeed affect relevant lexical processing and memory (Chen et al., in press; Chen and Ho, 1986; Chen and Juola, 1982; Chen and Tsoi, 1990; Frost et al., 1987; Kimura, 1984; Peng et al., 1985; Simpson and Kang, 1994). In the processing of Chinese characters, we have seen that unique properties of the character have interesting and important implications for the activation and processing of various sorts of lexical information (graphemic, phonological, and semantic). However, characters are typically morphemes, and morphemes and words are different linguistic units. In the following sections I shall therefore discuss issues related to processing of Chinese words in reading Chinese text.

THE PROCESSING OF WORDS

In alphabetic writing systems such as English, words are clearly separated by spaces, whereas morphemic boundaries are not usually marked. This characteristic is probably related to the finding that skilled readers of alphabetic languages typically have a clear concept about what a word is. For instance, if asked, native English speakers can effortlessly count the number of words in a given sentence, and the result of counting will be consistent among different readers. A distinctively different picture can be seen in Chinese, where words can be made up of one or more characters. In Chinese text, characters are indicated by spaces, and phrases and sentences are indicated by punctuation markers like commas and periods, but word boundaries are not marked by extra spacing or punctuation. Hence, word identification in reading Chinese is not a simple and straightforward matter, even for skilled readers of the language. For instance, the sentence 這些花生長得多麼好呀 is ambiguous, because 花 can be used independently to mean 'flower(s)', but it can also join its following character 生 to mean 'peanut(s)'. Likewise, 長 means 'to grow', but it can also be used together with its preceding character 生 without changing its meaning. Thus, the sentence can be interpreted as, 'How wonderfully these flowers are growing' or as, 'How wonderfully these peanuts are growing'. Furthermore, the concept of the word has a substantial degree of fluidity to ordinary Chinese people. Hoosain (1992), for example, investigated Chinese speakers' conceptions of the word by asking skilled Chinese readers to segment sentences into constituent words. The results showed that there was considerable disagreement concerning what were word boundaries, even in very simple sentences.

PSYCHOLOGICAL REALITY OF THE WORD IN CHINESE

Given that Chinese words are not explicitly marked in text and that Chinese readers have vague ideas about the concept of the word, it is sensible to consider the psychological reality of the word in reading and comprehension of Chinese. In the following sections, let us examine some studies that provide indications of the processing role of the word in Chinese.

Chen and Au Yeung (1993) reported an experiment which was carried out to investigate the cognitive processes involved in reading Chinese texts. They measured subjects' reading time for individual characters, using a subject-paced, sequential display technique, as an on-line indicator of comprehension processes (for information about this paradigm, see Chen, 1992). The character reading times so collected were analysed in multiple regression analyses to identify regression effects at various textual levels. Character reading times significantly increased with the number of characters in a word when characters formed words of new concepts in the text and at the boundaries of a word. That is, several word-level variables had a significant impact on the character reading times after the effects of other variables (for example, characters, sentences, and texts) had been statistically partialed out (for similar findings, see Chen, 1992). These findings indicate that despite being loosely defined, the word as an important linguistic unit does play a unique role in processing Chinese text for comprehension.

Further evidence for the view that the Chinese word plays a distinctive role in Chinese reading was provided by Chen (1987). In this study, subjects were asked to read Chinese sentences and to perform a character detection task (to respond to the occurrence of a given character in reading a sentence). The results showed a clear word superiority effect: response latencies were significantly longer and detection errors were larger when a target character was embedded in a non-word rather than in a word context. A similar finding, that a target character was identified more readily as part of a word than a non-word, has been reported by Cheng (1981) using a tachistoscopic presentation procedure in which only one two-character item was briefly displayed in each trial and subjects were given a forced-choice task. The word superiority effects for two-character words demonstrated in these studies indicate clearly that there are mental representations corresponding to the word in the mind of Chinese readers.

In contrast to the word superiority effect just discussed, Chen (1984, 1986) used a component detection task and demonstrated a character inferiority effect in reading Chinese text when component detection was disrupted by familiar character contexts. This character inferiority effect, together with the word superiority effects (Chen, 1987) previously discussed, provides valuable information about the processing roles of characters and words in reading Chinese text: Chinese characters not only serve as prominent units of encoding during reading for comprehension but that they also contribute to the overall comprehension analysis. If they themselves are single-character words, they serve as basic processing units in syntactic and semantic analyses; when they serve as part of a multiple-character word, especially if their meaning relates to the concept of the word, they help the identification of that word. On the other hand, because they are not explicitly marked in text, words themselves are not likely to serve as important encoding units, as is the case for Chinese characters or alphabetic words in reading. However, Chinese words can in principle play an important role in further comprehension processes, such as parsing and semantic analysis.

Further evidence for the psychological reality of the Chinese word can be derived from studies using a lexical decision task. For instance, Hung, Tzeng, and Chen (1993) compared possible effects of character frequency in lexical decision-making with two types of two-character words (idiomatic and compound) as stimuli. Many multiple-character words in Chinese are compound words; the meaning of a compound word is generally related to the meaning of its component characters (for example, 飛機 is a compound of 'fly' and 'machine' meaning 'airplane'). For idiomatic words, however, there is no apparent semantic connection between the meaning of the word and the meaning of its constituents (風流 is a compound of 'wind' and 'flow' meaning 'amorous'); only very few multiple-character words are of this type (Li and Thompson, 1981). Hung, Tzeng, and Chen found a significant character frequency effect in lexical decisions for compound words, but none for idiomatic ones, although a reliable word frequency effect was found for both types of the words. These results indicate that different types of Chinese words may activate distinct recognition processes, and that some words, especially idiomatic words, are processed as a single psychological unit.

HOW DO PROPERTIES OF WORDS AFFECT READING STRATEGIES IN CHINESE?

Another notable property of Chinese words is that they do not generally have inherently marked lexical categories and inflectional indicators of the number, gender, and case for nouns or the tense and aspect for verbs, as is the case in English and other alphabetic languages (see Li and Thompson, 1981; Wang, 1973). Further, intra-sentence concordance rules, such as subject–verb agreement, are also absent in Chinese. As a matter of fact, various forms of syntactic and semantic information are not usually carried by individual words in Chinese, but are carried by the sentential context as a whole. On the contrary, although various alphabetic languages differ to some extent in terms of their morphological complexity, words in alphabetic systems typically have inflectional markings to indicate a considerable range of grammatical attributes. Thus, unlike words in alphabetic languages, Chinese words do not have clearly marked boundaries, neither do they generally contain explicitly marked syntactic information. These features have led Chen (1992) to propose that in extracting relevant information from individual words, readers of Chinese may use a more diffused, context-dependent strategy, whereas readers of English may rely on a more focused, word-dependent strategy. This hypothesis has been verified in two lines of research as reviewed in the following.

The first line of research (Chen, 1992; Chen and Au Yeung, 1993) was carried out using a multiple regression approach to relate on-line measures of comprehension processes, such as character reading times, to various properties of the characters. The basic assumption behind this approach is that readers perform various analyses at different levels (character, word, sentence, and text) during reading for comprehension. Thus, variables at each of these levels work as a whole to influence the reader's cognitive load and manifest at character or word reading times. The multiple regression technique has been fruitfully used by other researchers to analyse reading times for various linguistic units in English (see Just and Carpenter, 1980; Haberlandt and Graesser, 1985). A typical finding in these studies that is particularly relevant to our present discussion is that word-level predictor variables, such as word length and word frequency, show robust effects on word reading times, regardless of which type of data collection procedure is used (for example, eye-monitoring or self-paced computer display). In addition, the magnitudes of word-level effects are usually comparable with those seen at the sentence level. Experiments with reading in Chinese (Chen, 1992; Chen and Au Yeung, 1993), however, have demonstrated that the basic properties of characters (for example, complexity and frequency) and those of words (for example, length and frequency) do not generally show reliable effects on character reading times. In fact, among variables at various character and word levels, only one (the new argument noun: nouns that introduce a person, object, location, or concept in the text for the first time) has consistently shown in various experiments a significant impact on character reading times. Furthermore, some sentence-level variables, such as the end of clause boundaries and the number of new argument nouns in the sentence, have consistently had robust effects on character reading times; their effects were usually stronger than those produced by other levels of textual variables. These results indicate that Chinese readers seem to engage more heavily in operations at the sentence level than analyses at character or word level, whereas readers of English tend to pay comparable attention to both the word and sentence levels of processing.

The experiments reviewed above adopted a correlational approach to investigate comprehension processes involved in reading Chinese texts. The second line of studies (Chen, 1992, in press) used an experimental approach to examine reading strategies in Chinese. The basic manipulation in these experiments was to change a critical word in a short text so that various combinations of lexical, syntactic, and semantic information were violated (these violations can be produced by replacing a genuine word with a non-word, making changes in syntactic category, or substituting a semantically anomalous but syntactically appropriate word for the original word). Patterns of disruptions caused by different violations were compared to reflect the time course of extracting and using lexical, syntactic, and semantic information from individual words during reading for comprehension.

This paradigm was originally developed by Danks and his colleagues to study comprehension processes in oral reading (Danks, Bohn, and Fears, 1983). In their study, native English speakers were asked to perform oral reading tasks, and their oral production times were scored. In general, the results showed that lexical, syntactic, and semantic violations all produced immediate disruptions at the specific position where those violations were introduced (the critical word position) in oral reading performance. The results also showed that both syntactic and semantic violations created comparable disruption effects, but that lexical violations produced a larger effect.

The violation paradigm of Danks et al. has been shown to be equally effective in studying comprehension in a silent reading condition where character or word viewing times, rather than oral reading protocols, were measured. Chen (1992), for example, in research with English-language materials, successfully replicated the major findings of the study by Danks and his colleagues using a modified, visual reading task rather than the oral reading one. However, very different patterns of results were found when a similar procedure was used in a Chinese version of the task. For instance, Chen (in press) reported that various types of violations resulted in very different disruption profiles in Chinese. The most notable finding is the relative positioning resulting from each type of violation: the disruption effects created by the lexical violations without exception appeared much earlier than did those produced by other types of violations (semantic and syntactic). These results stand in strong contrast with those found in studies with alphabetic materials (for example, Chen, 1992; Danks et al., 1983; Danks and Kurcz, 1984), indicating that the time course of lexical, syntactic, and semantic processing is very different in the course of reading text written in different languages. Chen (1992), for example, argued that in English lexical information as well as syntactic and semantic information can all be extracted and used without delay in comprehension analyses, because violating any one of the three types of linguistic information patterns yields a disruption of reading performance at the same location. The results in Chinese, however, indicate that lexical, syntactic, and semantic information of individual Chinese words does not become available simultaneously, probably because in Chinese (a non-inflective language) different sorts of syntactic and semantic information (for example, genders, numbers, tenses, and cases) are generally not marked by the word itself, but often need to be inferred from such attributes of sentential context as word order (the target word's sequential relation to other words; for empirical evidence and discussion, see Chen, 1994). Moreover, the Chinese results do not support the delayed comprehension hypothesis proposed by Aaronson and Ferres (1986) which states that Chinese readers may postpone the semantic and syntactic analyses until reaching the end of sentence boundaries, because Chinese words are not well defined and lack clear explicit marking. Rather, the findings discussed previously suggest syntactic and semantic operations can be conducted relatively on-line in reading Chinese text.

Another result from the study by Chen (in press) deserves our attention. In this research, different types of critical words produced very different disruption curves. There were in total four types of critical words in the study, including nouns, classifiers, and two types of prepositions (the object marker, 把, and the passive marker, 被, used to construct special word orders such as subject-object-verb and object-subject-verb, respectively). The most notable difference among the disruptive effects produced by various types of critical words was the relative positioning of the disruption curves resulting from semantic violation (inserting an anomaly) as well as from syntactic/semantic violation (inserting a syntactically incorrect and semantically anomalous word). When nouns were used as the critical words, the disruptive effect produced by the purely semantic violation appeared earlier than those created by the combined syntactic/semantic violations, indicating that although nouns play a prominent role in both the semantic and syntactic analyses, the emphasis is on the semantic. When the critical words were classifiers, however, both the semantic and syntactic/semantic violations yielded compatible patterns of disruption, suggesting that classifiers contribute equally to both types of operations in the process of reading Chinese. Furthermore, when using prepositions as the critical words, the syntactic/semantic violations resulted in strong and long-lasting disruptive effects, whereas the semantic violation did not produce a reliable disruption until the end of the sentence boundary was reached. This finding confirms the notion that prepositions play a more important role in the syntactic analysis than in the semantic analysis. Together, these results clearly suggest that although the time course of lexical, syntactic, and semantic processing in reading Chinese is very different from that in alphabetic systems such as English and other European languages. Chinese readers are sensitive to the linguistic properties of different types of words and can use them properly in a timely, if not immediate, fashion.

To summarize, despite their ambiguity and lack of explicit marking and inflections, Chinese words are used as important processing units for syntactic and semantic analyses, just as words in alphabetic systems are used. However, we have also seen that Chinese readers, unlike readers of alphabetic languages, need to perform such additional operations as word segmentation and to utilize a reading strategy relying more heavily on context and less on individual words. It appears that readers are sensitive to the differences in the cognitive demands imposed by different orthographic and linguistic structures in reading comprehension and that they adapt their processing strategies to meet the cognitive demands of the orthography.

CONCLUSIONS

There has been substantial progress over the past several decades in understanding the processes behind reading and comprehension. Most research in this field, however, has been conducted using materials in English, and only a small amount has been addressed other alphabetic languages or non-alphabetic systems like Chinese. This bias presents a serious problem for the development of a general theory of reading, because it does not account for the processing roles played by orthographic and linguistic properties not found in English. Fortunately, the recognition and correction of this bias has recently accelerated. In fact, systematic study of reading in an increasing variety of languages and writing systems has been carried forward over the past decade.

The present chapter has attempted to review relevant issues and research in order to explore some of the psychological implications arising from major properties of Chinese orthography. Up to this point, the results from research have suggested that unique characteristics of the Chinese writing system can affect processing strategies used in reading Chinese text. This conclusion, however, should be considered as tentative, because systematic study of Chinese reading and comprehension has only just begun. If results continue to support the plausibility that language-specific properties can affect related reading and comprehension processes, then some revision of the reading theory developed on the basis of one and/or a small group of closely related languages is in order. It is hoped that the review and discussion provided here has served to clarify some of the issues concerning processes involved in Chinese reading and comprehension and will promote the search for both universal and orthography-specific processes associated with the reading of different written languages.

ACKNOWLEDGMENTS

This work was supported by Earmarked Grants CUHK2/92H and CUH153/94H to the author from the Research Grants Council of Hong Kong. I am grateful to Ovid Tzeng and Daisy Hung; their original work on Chinese writing system inspired me greatly. I also thank my colleagues In-Mao Liu, Rumjahn Hoosain, Marcus Taft, Ino Flores d'Arcais, and Paul Bertelson, who notably affected my thinking about language processing in Chinese.

Chapter 5

Cross-linguistic Constraints on Chinese Students Learning English

Che Kan Leong and Sophie Hsia

We begin this chapter by delimiting several parameters for our discussion. The first is the notion of cross-linguistic constraints which are exerted by students' knowledge of their first language (in this case, Chinese) when using a second language (in this case, English). Theorists of language learning (Bialystok, 1991; Kellerman and Sharwood Smith, 1986; Selinker, 1972; Sharwood Smith, 1991) have proposed a 'theory of interlanguage' to explain how these linguistic constraints work. The general notion is that a successive reorganization of psychological and linguistic processes (development of a series of systematic 'interlanguages') is required among second-language learners to approximate the skills of native language users in mastery of the target second language. Bialystok and Sharwood Smith emphasize the interaction of knowledge systems and control processes as the crux of inter-language or cross-linguistic influences in second-language learning.

For much of this chapter, we use the term *language* to refer mainly to the writing system, or orthography, which is a representation of the spoken language. We explore some of the psycholinguistic factors affecting Chinese students, especially university students, learning (reading) English as a second or target language. We discuss their English-language performance within a framework of componential analyses of reading with emphasis on the interaction of phonology, morphology, syntax, and semantics. The theory of prototypes, or 'best-fit' effects, explains our findings in the realm of segmentation and stress-like syllabification phonetic analyses and sentence grammaticality. This functionalist language framework, with its analyses of the coalition and competition of different linguistic cues, is seen as important for the understanding of Chinese students learning English.

RELATING WRITING SYSTEMS TO LANGUAGE

Current literature on linguistic analyses, as well as psychological studies of English as an alphabetic or segmental system and of Chinese as a morphemic orthography, emphasize the productivity of these systems (Mattingly, 1985). The term *productivity* refers to the systematized methods of transcribing new or possible lexical items, including possible but non-occurring words. It has been found that to a large extent phonological and morphological structure constrains orthography. Phonological units are largely phonemes, syllables (*morae* for the Japanese *kana*), and sub-syllabic units such as onsets and rimes (initials and finals for Chinese). In the case of English, the term *morphological structure* refers to morphemes, inflection, and derivation (including compounding). While the passage from script to sound differs in the English and Chinese languages, it may be said that the underlying mapping mechanisms between these orthographies and their linguistic structures reflect broad phonological constraints. One source for this claim comes from analysis of the historical development of the Chinese writing system with reference to the phonological information inherent in Chinese characters (DeFrancis, 1989; Wang, 1973, 1981). DeFrancis suggests that a purely logographic system, as Chinese is often reputed to be, does not function efficiently in reading and that a well-developed orthography is speech-based, even though linguistic representation and units of mapping or transcription may vary across orthographies.

Another source for the claim of recovering phonological information from the basically morphemic Chinese orthography derives from psychological or psycholinguistic studies. Tzeng and his associates were among the earliest researchers to show that phonetic recoding in reading Chinese is needed at times at the working memory stage to aid text comprehension (Hung and Tzeng, 1981; Tzeng, Hung, and Wang, 1977; Tzeng and Wang, 1983). Their current research programs address the ways that different linguistic cues in Chinese (orthographic, phonological, and semantic) interact to activate phonetic recoding (Hung, Tzeng, and Tzeng, 1992).

In a series of experiments using the backward masking paradigm in reading Chinese by Chinese subjects, Perfetti and his colleagues (Lam, Perfetti, and Bell, 1991; Perfetti and Zhang, 1991; Perfetti, Zhang, and Berent, 1992) have also found evidence of phonological activation in identifying Chinese characters. Perfetti et al. (1992, p. 241) are careful in suggesting that the phonology in the Chinese experiments is a 'component of identification' and will 'accompany lexical access but not precede it' in a 'retrieval process'. The probabilistic nature of the retrieval and 'the principle that writing systems constrain the level at which phonology is activated and not *whether* it is activated seems to hold, when considering the contrast between alphabetic and logographic systems' (Perfetti et al., 1992, p. 241, original emphasis).

To summarize the discussion of the psycholinguistic analyses of the alphabetic English and morphemic Chinese writing systems, current psychological studies suggest some generalized phonological activation in the identification of lexical items (words or characters) according to the transparency or opacity of the orthography. The segmental and more transparent English, as compared with the morphemic and more opaque Chinese, encourages a different, and probably a faster, time course in the phonological processing of lexical items. This time course, or chronometric aspect, in phonological mediation has been shown to relate more to low-frequency English words and Chinese characters (Seidenberg, 1985; Shu and Zhang, 1987), with low-frequency English words showing larger effects (Van Orden, 1987). Evidence for the relative time course, however, is less clear in accessing phonology and the meaning of 'exact', as compared with 'fuzzy', semantic characters in a recent study by Tan, Hoosain, and Peng (1995). Seidenberg (1992) discusses the computing of orthographic and phonological codes in a connectionist approach and suggests a 'division of labor between component processes in a multi-route system' with orthographic depth being one of these factors (p. 113). Thus, the evidence indicates that there are similar mechanisms active in reading English and Chinese, modulated by the segmental and morphemic nature of these two orthographies.

A FRAMEWORK FOR STUDYING CHINESE STUDENTS LEARNING ENGLISH

From that necessarily succinct discussion of the analytic reading of English and Chinese lexical items, one concludes that the apparently disparate segmental and phonemically-based English and the morphemic Chinese orthographies would need to be learned in both a modular, or 'vertical', and a 'horizontal' manner (for explication of these concepts, see Holender, 1991; Liberman, 1992). We discuss below the general thinking that has guided our study of native Chinese (Cantonese-speaking) university students learning English as a second language. We would like to think that this framework may apply generally to Chinese students learning English both for communicative purposes and as a vehicle for their thought processes.

Assumptions of Performance Proficiency

In attempting to gain some insight into the learning of English by adult Chinese students in Hong Kong, we make several assumptions based on the research literature. We assume that late bilinguals, as with the college subjects in our study, have a coordinating organization of their two language systems (Chinese as L1 or native language, English as L2 or target language). The differentiation between compound and coordinating language systems is not discrete but is instead ranged along a continuum (Hamers and Blanc, 1989), with possible differences in cognitive organization or representation. The nature and task demand of the linguistic materials to be learnt, the overall learning environment, and the cultural milieu also contribute to the learning of the target language.

Functional Language Performance

We consider as reasonable MacNamara's (1967) notion that a bilingual is someone with a minimum competence in one of these four language dimensions: listening, speaking, reading, or writing in a language other than their mother tongue. The term competence here should not be interpreted in the formal linguistic sense. The focus should be on actual language performance, rather than on abstract competence in second-language learners (see Bates and MacWhinney, 1989; MacWhinney, 1987). This emphasis on linguistic performance in L2 learners may be compared with Chomsky's (1986) notion of implicit and explicit knowledge. For example, native language users may cogitate implicitly and bring to the explicit level of cognition the different agentive roles of 'John' in the sentence pair 'John is easy to see' and 'John is eager to go', or the grammaticality of the sentence 'The door opened', where a recipient or patient becomes the subject with an intransitive verb. Some second-language learners may have difficulty in distinguishing between the roles of 'John' or the relations among the valencies of English verbs.

Adult Second-language Learners with Reference to Chinese Students

Furthermore, adult learners, compared with children, come to learn a second language with a fairly well established mastery of their spoken and written first language. This mastery of L1, combined with cognitive, social, and psychological factors, may assist in the learning of the new language. Conversely, there may also be some discontinuity in the new learning if specific language uses require different processing components or skills. This is particularly so in the phonological domain, as there may be different speech processing mechanisms (Marslen-Wilson and Tyler, 1980) which require neuromuscular and vocal tract maturation and reorganization for native-like perception and production (Locke, 1983). In addition, there are many confounding factors, including developmental variables, L2 input environment, and motivational and affective aspects that inhibit native-like target-language pronunciations (Flege, 1987). While adult learners may 'fossilize' in their L2 language learning (Selinker, 1972), they do not necessarily do so from missing out on the critical period of learning; this hypothesis on its own is not sufficient to explain their target-language performance (Flege, 1987).

Experimental evidence of cross-linguistic constraints on Chinese learners of English phonology comes from psycho-acoustic studies by Flege, McCutcheon, and Smith (1987). Flege et al. examined the acoustic, temporal, and aerodynamic parameters distinguishing the production of /p/ and /b/ in English word final positions (for example, in 'heep, heeb', 'hip, hib', and 'hop, hob'): the duration of labial closure, the duration of voicing, and the peak oral air pressure in native Chinese adults (Mandarin- or Putonghua-speaking) and Chinese children, compared with native English adults and children.

One of the main findings of the Flege et al. study is that the duration of voicing in the closure interval of /b/ is in the predicted direction of: English adults > English children > Chinese children > Chinese adults (without assuming equal distancing in this implicational hierarchy). Flege et al. suggest that because Mandarin/Putonghua Chinese lacks voiced stops in word final positions, the Chinese adults are perceived to devoice the stop consonants /b/, /d/, and /g/. These adults may be implicitly aware of the voicing difference between /p/ and /b/ but may not be able to access this implicit knowledge to bring it to the explicit level. Compared with the Chinese children in the study, the Chinese adults made less effective use of perceptual inputs associated with stop consonants, perhaps because they did not enlarge sufficiently the supraglottal cavity to sustain voicing, or had not learnt to do so. Flege et al. point to the need for experience in listening to, and uttering, English stops; they argue for high-quality language training in general (see also Flege and Fletcher, 1992).

A summary of the basic assumptions underpinning our notion of how Chinese students, especially adults, learn English, with reference to our study outlined below, needs to take note of the L1 linguistic, cognitive, and other factors that may impinge on L2 learning. It requires flexibility in the notion of fluency or proficiency in English, and to accept that different language uses require different component processing skills and at different levels of performance in a goodness-of-fit approach (Bialystok, 1991). Furthermore, research into second language learning must take into account the interaction of the grammatical components of phonology, morphology, syntax, semantics, and pragmatics (Gass, 1987).

A Componential Analysis Approach

We derive our theoretical framework from the componential analysis of verbal ability (Hunt, Lunneborg, and Lewis, 1975) and especially the knowledge-based and procedure-based reading of English (Carr and Levy, 1990; Frederiksen, 1981, 1982), and from the two-phase, two-cohort study by Leong of nearly 300 Canadian children within this framework (1988, 1992). This latter developmental study has found some evidence for the differential effects of phonological, morphological, and sentential processing on reading performance in English; the data generally fit the framework well as tested with linear structural equation modelling.

Very briefly, the componential framework is an 'attempt to identify a set of functionally defined information-processing systems or components, which in interaction with one another accomplish the more complex performance—in this case, reading with comprehension' (Frederiksen, 1982, p. 125). Typically, reaction times (RT) are used to provide fine-grained measures of such basic subskills as differentiating words from non-words (lexical decision tasks), or naming words quickly and accurately (vocalization tasks). In addition, the information-processing activities may be hierarchically arranged, but the initiation of 'higher-order' operations does not necessarily depend on the completion of 'lower-order' operations in the hierarchy. These higher- or lower-order tasks operate in an orderly cascade system, allowing outputs from one particular level (for example, word processing) to feed into adjacent levels (for example, sentence processing) and also into distant levels. It is the time course of the processing of the components that is particularly important and there are quite large individual differences within it.

A STUDY WITH CHINESE STUDENTS

Encouraged by the apparent efficacy of the componential approach in understanding the processing and reading of language, we recently carried out a study to examine the component language or reading skills of some 80 Cantonese-speaking, Chinese university students (about twenty years old) learning English as a second language. For space reasons, we will report on only those aspects of the project relevant to accessing English language and text. One part of the project deals with phonological processing among these adult students along the lines of analysing phonological and morphological components and extending our earlier work (Hsia, 1992; Leong, 1992). The other part centres on sentence processing for sentential comprehension, also from the componential analysis framework.

Phonological and Morphological Processing

Subjects and Tasks

The study of the phonological and morphological processing of English used 82 Cantonese-speaking Chinese subjects completing their first year of English studies at the City University of Hong Kong. The hypothesis to be tested was that students in the Putonghua language (PL) subgroup (n = 24) receiving Putonghua segmental analysis training should perform better in phonological processing tasks than would their counterparts in the Cantonese language (CL) subgroup (n = 58) not receiving such training. It should be noted that tonal languages such as Putonghua Chinese, with its four classical tones, and Cantonese Chinese, with its nine variant tones, carry phonemic significance (Leong, 1986; Wong, 1968). If native speakers of English find it difficult to identify and use tones in Putonghua or Mandarin (Chiang, 1979), it is also not always easy for Cantonese speakers to master what appears to be a cognate tonal system in Putonghua (Leung, 1978).

At the outset of the project, all of the target and control students were given reading comprehension tests in English and digit span tests (backward and forward) in English and Chinese to assess their reading level and short-term memory span. There was no difference in the performance in these tasks between the two language training subgroups.

To test the hypothesis of phonetic representation within the phonological grammar of English (Chomsky and Halle, 1968), all 82 subjects were given a number of tasks. Of direct relevance here were these main processing tasks:

a) Vocalizing or naming 20 words (EW) (for example, *crystal, stadium*) and 20 pronounceable non-words (ENW) (e.g., *padony, blundin*) constructed after the BOSS morphemic principle (Taft, 1988), as modified by Leong (1992). The tape-recorded reading of these lexical items by the subjects was compared with 'prototypic' readings by native speakers of English for such phonetic cues as allophonic variations, stress patterns, and sonority of consonants to arrive at an accuracy index (see Hsia, 1994, for details).

b) Segmental analysis of initial consonants (ESEGIC) and final consonants (ESEGFC) of 16 English pseudo-words of the kind (C)CVC(C) (for example, *shaps, krums*).

c) Segmental analysis of initial Cantonese consonants (CSEGIC) in 25 Chinese characters with Cantonese phonemes considered in positions of flux, such as liquids and nasals /l/ and /n/, the velar stop /k/, the velar /h/, reduction of /g/ in the consonant cluster of /gw/, and the glottalization of the velar nasal /n/.

d) English stress-type dictation tasks with 30 items (for example, *malice, relish*) for stress on first syllable-like units (EDICT1) and another 30 items (for example, *sarong, emerge*) for stress on second syllable-like units (EDICT2) adapted from Treiman and Danis (1988) and along the lines of Hsia's (1992) study. Each word stress type consisted of 30 bigrams presented auditorily with liquids, nasals, fricatives, and stops as intervocalic consonants. The intent was to study the subjects' ability to represent intervocalic consonants such as liquids and nasals in phonological syllabification (see Hsia, 1994, for details).

Summary results and discussion.

Without going into too much detail, it may be said that statistical analyses comparing the performance of the PL subgroup with training in Putonghua segmental analysis and the CL subgroup without such training showed significant differences, task for task, with the exception of the English segmentation task for final consonants (ESEGFC). The means and standard deviations for the tasks by the subgroups are shown in Figure 5.1. The task differences could not be due to differential levels of reading, since the two subgroups did not differ in their reading comprehension of English; nor could the differences be due to different memory span, since the subgroups did not differ in their digit forward and backward span tasks in either Cantonese or English. While there may be other factors at work, cognitive, motivational, and linguistic (orthographic and phonological), we put forward the very tentative suggestion that the learning of Putonghua and segmental training promote the learning of phonological and phonetic principles inherent in English. The non-significant difference in the English segmentation task for final consonants might be due to the tendency for Chinese speakers to devoice word final stops in English (that is, *rig* may be pronounced *rick*) (Eckman, 1981; Flege, McCutcheon, and Smith, 1987). We further conjecture (Hsia, 1994, 1994) that phonological and phonetic training leading to better performance in aspects of the English phonological domain, as found in this study, may help these readers in their learning of English in general.

Sentence Acceptability

Subjects and Task

As discussed earlier, the sentence pattern task (elaborated on in the two-phase, two-cohort study of Leong [1988, 1992]), used 22 pairs of parallel acceptable and anomalous sentences to study the automatic processing in the classroom of 'functional' English grammar by 87 Chinese university students. Some examples of sentence-pairs used were: 12a) 'Anne ran the home' and 12b) *'Home was run by Anne', to assess passive construction; and 16a) 'I bought some fruit', 16b) *'He visited some Rockies', 18a) 'A Mr. Bobby Orr wanted to see you', and 18b) *'Some Bobby Orr wanted to see you; *Some Bobby Orr won the [hockey] game', to assess mass or count nouns. The sentences, which read at about grade 5 level, were generated one at a time at random at the rate of 200 milliseconds per word on a microcomputer screen. The subjects were required to make accurate and rapid YES/NO responses to the grammatical acceptability of these sentences by pressing the relevant keys. The latency in milliseconds for the correct answers was taken as an index of the efficiency of the subject's automatic processing of functional English grammar.

Summary results and discussion

The 87 subjects were trichotomized into 37 above-average, 26 average, and 24 below-average readers on the basis of a reading comprehension test administered prior to the sentence pattern task. After adjusting for outliers, the RT measures for the correct scores were subjected to a 3 (reading group) by 2

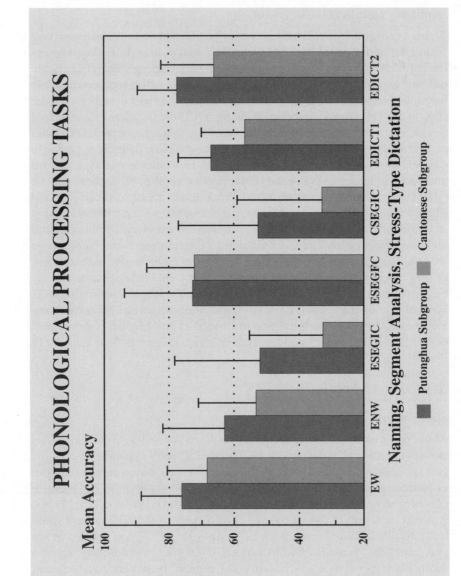

Figure 5.1 Performance (mean accuracy scores and standard deviations) of Putonghua (PT) and Cantonese (CT) language subgroups of university students in phonological processing tasks: Naming of English words (EW); of pronounceable English nonwords (ENW); segmental analysis of initial English consonants (ESEGIC), and of final English consonants (ESEGFC); segmental analysis of initial Cantonese consonants (CSEGIC); English stress-type dictation for stress on first syllable-like units (EDICT1), and for stress on second syllable-like units (EDICT2).

(grammaticality) analysis of variance. There was no difference in the performance of the three reading subgroups in accuracy scores. There was, however, a significant difference in their response time to the two levels of grammaticality (acceptable or anomalous sentences)(F [1, 84] = 5.09, p <.05.). The means and standard deviations of the latency scores for the group of 87 Chinese students are shown in Figure 5.2.

It should be noted that there are considerable individual differences. Furthermore, careful inspection of the accuracy scores of the subjects shows that for 10 of the 44 items the accuracy ratio between acceptable and anomalous sentences was equivocal, raising questions about the efficient processing of fairly simple syntactical constructions by these adult learners. The anomalous sentences shown earlier (12b, 16b, 18b) were rejected as grammatically unacceptable or anomalous by only about 44 per cent of the subjects. In other words, an equal or greater proportion of the 87 students accepted the grammaticality of these (and about 7 other) statements.

These observations raise questions about both accuracy and automaticity in the processing of simple English sentences in terms of word-order parameters by these Chinese university students. Could it be that they reorganize their lexical, syntactic, and semantic subskills in English through successive stages or 'interlanguages'? Could there be some interference, or what Corder (1981) calls 'intercession', from their native Chinese language in the communicative and cognitive processes of learning English? Could their comprehension of grammatical categories of sentence acceptability be better explained by the kind of prototype theory within cross-linguistic settings as set out in Bates and MacWhinney's competition model (Bates and MacWhinney, 1982; MacWhinney, 1987, 1992; MacWhinney and Bates, 1989)?

GENERAL DISCUSSION AND IMPLICATIONS

Multi-components and Multi-levels of Language Processing

In a review chapter on cross-language transfer in bilingual reading, Durgunoglu and Hancin (1992) emphasize a componential analysis approach similar to that of Leong (1988, 1992) and Carr and Levy (1990). Durgunoglu and Hancin suggest that there is a need to isolate the components of reading processes and to investigate the nature of cross-linguistic transfer in particular, and bilingual cognition in general. Support for this line of thinking comes from research into the psychology of second-language learning. Bialystok (1991) emphasizes interacting subskills or subcomponents in her analysis of linguistic knowledge and the control of linguistic processing in second-language learning. Specific language uses require specific skill levels in different processing components or subcomponents; second-language learners may develop proficiency for their specific needs (for example, in technical writing), while their ability in other components may be less well developed (Bialystok, 1991, 1991). In her investigation of bilingual sentence processing within the framework of the competition model (Bates and MacWhinney, 1982; MacWhinney, 1987, 1992; MacWhinney and Bates, 1989), Gass (1987) emphasizes the inter-

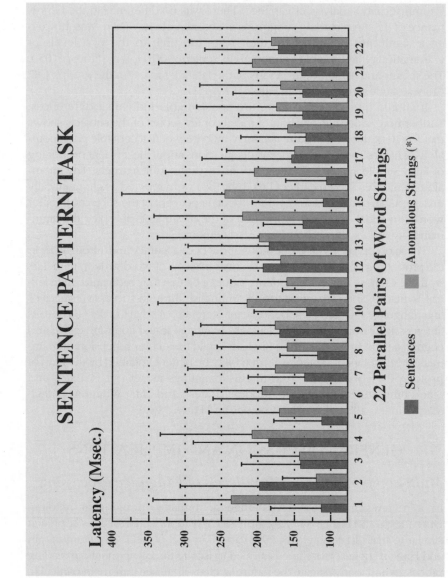

Figure 5.2 Performance (mean latency scores in milliseconds and standard deviations) of 87 university students in grammaticality task with 22 parallel pairs of acceptable and anomalous English sentences.

acting effects of syntax, semantics, and pragmatics in a prototypic or 'best fit' approach to help learners to acquire knowledge of the second language.

Prototypic or 'Best Fit' Effects in Language Processing

Psychological study of prototypes derives from the work of Rosch (1978), who emphasizes that they be considered as constraints and not as determinants of models of representation. Grossly simplifying the matter, one might say that the presence of prototypes or prototypic effects suggests an asymmetry of categories, where one member is regarded as more basic than the other and where the less basic member assumes a default value when only one member of the category occurs (Lakoff, 1987). Essential characteristics of prototypes are the category structure of central tendency, core to peripheral membership categories with attendant 'fuzziness', 'family' resemblance, goodness-of-fit, and the relative weights of the categories. While much of the research undertaken thus far deals with semantic prototypes, the prototype model provides a powerful and parsimonious framework to describe and explain phonological and sentential processing and the progression from less-acceptable to more-acceptable formal systems in 'interlanguage' processing.

Phonological Processing Component

The prototypic or categorical concept of two members in opposition, with one member carrying an element lacking in the other, can be traced to the work on markedness and unmarkedness in phonology by Trubetzkoy (1936). For example, voicing in /b/, /d/, and /g/ is marked, while the minimum contrastive voiceless elements /p/, /t/, and /k/ are unmarked. Voiced and voiceless consonants show an asymmetry both in the sound systems of the English language and in articulation, where voiced consonants are intervocalically more natural than voiceless consonants. This prototypicality effect suggests that certain phonetic structures are more easily learned than are others. The marked options usually include the unmarked one; the reverse is not true. The notion of typological markedness has been invoked by Eckman (1981) to explain the difficulty of his Mandarin-speaking Chinese subjects in pronouncing English word final-voiced obstruents. Psycho-acoustic studies by Flege, McCutcheon, and Smith (1987) have shown that Chinese adults find it difficult to distinguish voiceless /p/, /t/, and /k/ from voiced /b/, /d/, and /g/, and are not effective in implementing /b/, /d/, /g/ sounds.

Our study of segmentation and stress pattern analyses with the 82 Chinese students was also motivated by the general notion of prototypical effects or 'best fits' of Bates and McWhinney (1982). The phonetic analyses are rooted in findings that demonstrate that English is characterized by a stress-based rhythm (Cutler and Butterfield, 1992; Cutler, Mehler, Norris, and Segui, 1989), and that intervocalic rhythms are a function of phonetic categories (Treiman and Danis, 1988). Through their training in Putonghua segmental analysis, the PL subgroup achieved greater accuracy than did the CL subgroup in the phonetic details of all but one of the segmentation and stress-like syllabification tasks. These phonetic realizations, more than those of particular phonemes, seem to be one source of individual variation in adult Chinese students' learning of English.

The need to differentiate and categorize input speech signals is much more important in bilinguals than in monolinguals. In a thoughtful discussion of the phonological and phonetic processing of bilinguals, Watson (1991) decries the treatment of phonology as the 'Cinderella of bilingual studies' and suggests that with the heightened interest in speech perception, it is high time that the Cinderella phonology be invited to the bilingualism ball to the accompaniment of 'phonetic technology'. If the invitation is slow in coming, as predicted by Watson, the 'prince charming' should be received in the guise of a much fuller understanding of target L2 phonological systems as a whole. Learning the segments of a particular L2 phonological system involves not only understanding phonetic realizations and their representation, but also the constraints of suprasegmental (prosodic and rhythmic) conditions (James, 1986).

Word-order Parameters

The sentence pattern task was designed to examine the Chinese university students' judgement of the grammaticality of English sentences as a function of the rigidity or flexibility ('leakage') of canonical elements of subject-verb-object (SVO), subject-object-verb (SOV), and verb-subject-object (VSO) formulations. The results of the test show considerable individual variation in efficiency, as indexed by the millisecond reaction times with which the 87 Chinese university subjects judged the grammaticality of 22 parallel pairs of sentences and the rather 'fuzzy' discriminability of some of the sentence dyads. The variability and fuzziness encountered are slightly puzzling, as all the sentences were at about the grade 5 to 6 reading level for English-speaking children.

Relevant to our purpose is a study by Gass (1987), as seen within the prototype theory of Rosch (1978) and the functionalist language framework of Bates and MacWhinney (1982), MacWhinney (1987, 1989), and MacWhinney and Bates (1989). Gass (1987) investigated the interaction of syntax, semantics, and pragmatics in comprehending English sentences by adult native speakers of Italian, a language more sensitive to semantics than is the mainly SVO word-order syntax usually found in English. She discusses the ordering within a language typology and the 'best-fit' approach to language comprehension. Sentence interpretation is conceptualized as a function of the distance between a prototypic core and the peripheral boundaries (her examples treat 'He is *walking* to the store *now*' as being more central in time progression than is 'John is *flying* to New York *tomorrow*', which is seen as being more peripheral). The placement of prototypical instances from centre to periphery is further constrained by the degree of coalition or conflict between different linguistic categories of syntax, semantics, and pragmatics and the cues within them. Second-language learners will need to learn the ordering of these linguistic elements and their relative importance in order to gain mastery over the language.

Comprehending Chinese Sentences and Possible Intercession

For the comprehension of Chinese sentences, some evidence suggests that native Chinese adult speakers rely more on lexical–semantic than on syntactic cues in processing canonical Chinese sentence schema (Miao, 1981). Could this be one possible reason why the 87 students found the grammaticality of a number of the English sentences rather fuzzy? Could they be using lexical meaning and these semantics strategies to interpret the grammaticality of such sentences as: 9b) *'The runner turned the road off', 12b) *'Home was run by Anne', 16b) *'He visited some Rockies', and several others, which were all judged as acceptable about 40 per cent of the time? These are very tentative and speculative extrapolations, but these issues are worth exploring. This kind of simple transfer or 'functional restructuring' of syntactic patterns from native to target languages would not guarantee acceptable usage (MacWhinney, 1992), as can be seen from our results.

To return to the early Miao (1981) study, it should be noted that Chinese is generally considered to be topic-prominent, in that the focus or the sentence topic (what the sentence is about) is placed first, whether or not it is the grammatical subject, verb, or object (Chang, 1992; Chao, 1968; Li and Thompson, 1981; Li, Bates, Liu, and MacWhinney, 1992). This context dependency in a gradual diachronic drift may allow Chinese sentences to accept SVO or SOV orders, in comparison with the largely SVO order found in English. Li (1975) and Li and Thompson (1981) argue from their discourse analyses that the gradual diachronic drift from SVO to SOV may result from grammaticalization of serial verb constructions and that the SOV order may be a special status of Mandarin or Putonghua Chinese (Li and Thompson, 1981). There is, however, some question as to whether or not verb reduplication and reanalysis of the reduplicated verb may constitute strong support for the SVO to SOV shift from the evolution of prepositions from classic to Mandarin Chinese discourse (Huang, 1978). There are also suggestions by Sun and Givón (1985) from their text-based quantified study of written and spoken Mandarin that Chinese is synchronically a rather typical SVO language.

Integrating Language Cues Interactively

Miao reports that a more recent study (Miao and Zhu, 1992) has shown that Chinese people's comprehension of a sentence depends on both word order and meaning and that there are complex relations between the two. Miao and Zhu suggest that semantic strategy is more powerful than word order strategy for Chinese adults and for Chinese children (except for those from ages five to seven) in comprehending simple sentences. Chang (1992) further states that when word order contradicts meaning, Chinese children, more often than will Chinese adults, will likely follow canonical schemata from word order in interpreting simple sentences. They are, however, more likely to resort to extra-linguistic cues as they become older.

In two recent studies, one off-line and one on-line, Li, Bates, Liu, and MacWhinney (1992) have refined the prototypic Miao (1981) study. In this research, they systematically varied the language cues of word order, animacy, and the grammatical markers of *ba* and the passive *bei* to investigate Putonghua-speaking Chinese adults' interpretation of simple spoken Chinese sentences. Their results confirm the stronger effect of animacy over word order, as well as the significant interaction between animacy and word order. Furthermore, they demonstrate a strong second-noun effect not found by Miao (1981). Li et al. (1992, p. 229) state that Chinese speakers 'make use of almost all possible [linguistic] cues and integrate them interactively in identifying the functional roles of different linguistic constituents.'

The more recent, more refined sentence processsing studies by Miao and Zhu (1992) and by Li, Bates, Liu, and MacWhinney (1992), among others, all point to the coalition and competition of lexical–semantic and syntactic grammatical categories as providing fine-grained ways to understand psycholinguistic development in Chinese people in their unilingual or cross-linguistic learning. We should be reminded that Li and Thompson (1981, p. 26, emphasis added) are cautious in stating that 'Mandarin *may* be undergoing a change from SVO to an SOV word order'. These authors assert that it is difficult to answer the question of the basic word order of Mandarin Chinese, because sentence elements interact with other features of language, such as the notion of topic and the expression of pre-verbal and post-verbal directionality.

Backward Transfer or Intercession

In a 'diglossic' (Ferguson, 1959) society such as Hong Kong, where English remains the lingua franca for international trade and official usage (as of writing), and Chinese is the language used in the home and the community at large, a backward transfer from L2 English to L1 Chinese is noticeable. There may even be a 'triglossic' effect ranging from English to Cantonese Chinese with Putonghua Chinese in an intermediate position, now that this common language is in the ascendancy (T'sou, 1989). The influence of this 'superposed variety' (the preferred term of Ferguson [1959], rather than the usual 'high' or 'low' diglossic classification) results in some deleterious effects on the 'purity' of Chinese.

The more noticeable Anglicizing 'degradation' of the Chinese language occurs in new or borrowed terms from English, which act through some minor sound or meaning changes in ways almost analogous with the coining of loan words from foreign vocabulary in the Japanese *katakana*. No less 'invidious' are the effects of English word order parameters on the topic-prominent Chinese syntax. Some areas of Anglicized 'degradation' of Chinese sentences include: the addition of a redundant subject when the verb–object pairing is made clear by context; overly elaborate sentences more typical of English; the use of auxiliary verbs to distinguish hypotheses and counterfactuals; passive rather than active voice to denote both pleasant and unpleasant events (where the passive voice is confined to descriptions of unpleasantness in Chinese); and inappropriate application of empty morphemes or characters and conjunctions.

These lexical and syntactic cross-linguistic constraints from English to Chinese present interesting issues for sociolinguistic and corpus linguistic research. The backward transfer or intercession from L2 to L1 is a neglected but needed area of psycholinguistic investigation. The notion of coalition and competition of lexical–semantic and syntactic language categories can be further harnessed for this purpose, as advocated by Liu, Bates, and Li (1992).

Coalition and Competition of Language Cues

It is appropriate to conclude the discussion of sentence processing (in Chinese and/or English), and this chapter as a whole, with further examination of the prototype theory, and especially the competition model, as a powerful framework for understanding cross-linguistic learning. This examination will be necessarily brief. In-depth explications of the competition model and its empirical studies of sentence processing in different languages are provided in the volume by MacWhinney and Bates (1989), a book chapter by MacWhinney (1992), and in the special issue of *Applied Psycholinguistics* devoted to the competition model and bilingualism (Snow and Locke, 1987), among other locations. Additionally, the application of the model to examine sentence processing strategies in Chinese is found in research papers by Liu, Bates, and Li (1992), Li, Bates, and MacWhinney (1993), and relevant chapters in Chen and Tzeng (1992).

In the early version of their competition model, Bates and MacWhinney (1982, p. 214, original emphasis) stated that 'the prototype model could be expanded to describe peaceful coexistence and competition between semantic *and* pragmatic factors, for example, agent and topic as categories underlying subject phenomena. This approach would provide a good fit not only to facts about English, but to psycholinguistic studies of different language types.' In essence, the model is predicated on a functionalist approach to grammar in that the focus is on real-time language performance by real people in real situations, rather than on language competence in idealized situations. This approach accords with interactive models of performance when different information sources interact.

Cross-linguistic data have supported an evolving refinement of the competition model that now covers these major themes: a) the cognitive basis of language universals and typologies (language similarities and differences); b) functional grammar as providing explanations for fluid and robust form-function mapping in language; c) biology as subserving language functions (as in aphasia); and d) validation with the use of maximum likelihood estimation of the strength and validity of lexical–semantic and syntactic language cues (MacWhinney and Bates, 1989). The highest level of the functionalist approach to grammar is a 'theory about the nature of *intermediate* structures in the representation of grammatical knowledge' (Bates and MacWhinney, 1982, p. 188, original emphasis). The structures linking linguistic elements and categories in coalition and competition explain real-time language processing by bilinguals in their intercession from L1 to L2, their imperfect acquisition of L2, the backward transfer from L2 to L1, or a mix of these processes. The use of the connectionist networks to formalize the competition model (MacWhinney and Bates, 1989) should be seen as a novel way of representing knowledge from the initial state of the system, through the system input, to the capacity of the system to learn. It could thus be argued that connectionism, as utilized in the competition model, might bridge the 'great divide' of learnability and parsability of a grammar in building a theory of knowledge of language processing (Seidenberg, 1993).

SUMMARY

In a field where theory-based, empirically verifiable research and learning deserve more attention, we have attempted to provide a framework for the component analyses of language and reading in cross-linguistic studies, with emphasis on those for Chinese students learning English. Areas of phonological and phonetic processing and sentential comprehension are some of the components to be further investigated. The notion of the coalition and competition of language cues, with estimation of their strength and validity by use of rigorous statistical methods such as linear structural equation modelling provides for further experimentation. As this chapter goes to press, we have encountered a review paper by Koda (1994) on second-language reading, in which she also emphasizes basic skill development, the role of prototypicality, and the interplay among universal linguistic principles in the L1 and L2 language systems. There is still much to explore in subcomponent processes and the intercession between first and second languages in bilingual speakers.

Chapter 6

Linguistic Socialization:
A Chinese Perspective

Norman H. Freeman and Gustav M. Habermann

The speakers of any given natural language do not habitually use all the constructions and lexemes that the language system provides. Children come both to exploit the generativity of their natural language and to curb it: as Hymes (1983, p. xiii) noted, 'That is the heart of cultural reproduction through speech: the process by which children find order in the speech around them, and the process by which a social order is renewed'. In short, along with a language, a culture is acquired. The mutual dependence of language variation and its use to define a social situation is the focus for the study of linguistic socialization (Fasold, 1984).

Presumably, the earliest stages of becoming a Chinese speaker are similar to those of any other language community. To infants of 2 months of age, Mandarin 'motherese' resembles other motherese (Grieser and Kuhl, 1988), although prosodic exaggeration may be somewhat less than in English (Papousek, Papousek, and Symmes, 1991). Cantonese speech addressed to infants is more attractive to infants of 4.5 months of age than is Cantonese speech addressed to an adult (Werker, Pegg, and McLeod, in press).

It is difficult to formulate precise models of subsequent linguistic socialization. The history of research on the topic is marked by an understandable tendency of researchers to veer between analyses of language and analyses of culture in an attempt to impose order on the borderland topic of how 'conversational competence' is both a product and a tool of acculturation.

An intriguing study by Yang and Chiu (1988) exemplifies the type of open question that one encounters. It has often been reported that Chinese people score higher than do people in the United States on 'lie tests'. Does being Chinese encourage lying in some sense or in some context (see Bond, 1991; Gao, Ting-Toomey, and Gudykunst, this volume)? Lying is a central topic of linguistic socialization, a case where 'language is not simply responsive to the social activity...; it is the social activity', to borrow the formulation of Schieffelin and Ochs (1986, p. 3). A lie test score is calculated on the basis of the subjects' pattern of assent to statements about themselves that contain frequency words (for example, 'I often gossip' and 'I sometimes gossip'). The pattern of such answers can reveal self-contradictions (interpreted as 'lying' about oneself). Yang and Chiu (1988), however, have showed that Chinese lexemes that quantify frequency are quite ambiguous: some of the apparent self-contradiction may result from the failure of the Chinese subjects to discriminate between frequency terms, thus departing from test administrators' scaling assumptions (it is not known how much of the variance may be accounted for in this way). It is common for many types of quantifiers to be elided, so that the distinction between 'I wrote a letter' and 'I wrote some letters' may be lexicalized or 'may be equally well left unexpressed' (Lyons, 1968, p. 283). Yang and Chiu recommend a tactic for Chinese test construction, and then immediately add that 'the functional equivalence…may still be complicated by the Chinese subjects' possible inclination to commit humility self-presentation'.

That point is precisely where a linguistic socialization analysis would begin. Do Chinese quantifiers become more fuzzy when embedded in self-presentation statements than when in other social-relation statements? Do Chinese communities actually exploit fuzziness in natural-language quantifiers for self-concealment (Young, 1994) in the service of modesty? Fundamentally, do Chinese frequency- quantifiers display anything like the order of complexity of semantic constraints that apply in English (see Stump, 1981)? Repeatedly, one finds in the literature open questions such as these concerning just those issues for which sociolinguistics needs additional information to support a judgement.

Our survey of the literature reveals a field of research that takes one only to the threshold of modelling. The data found are in the nature of markers that approach the substance of linguistic socialization from one end or the other. We make no apology for presenting open questions in this chapter. Indeed, a prime purpose is to draw the attention of researchers to a golden opportunity. Following our statement of the questions we find as yet unresolved, we describe three approaches to linguistic socialization and then focus our concern on social labelling. The aim is to explicate how constraints on individual terms of address became nested within a pan-Sinitic campaign towards standardization, a campaign of varying success, itself nested within a global language-rectification movement. The global movement was highly prescriptive about rules of language use, amplifying the inherent prescriptive aspect of language change to which Haas (1982) drew attention.

APPROACHES TO LINGUISTIC SOCIALIZATION

The terms *linguistic socialization* and *language socialization* have increasingly come to refer to a dazzling variety of processes (Berko Gleason, 1988; Ochs, 1990, 1991; Ochs and Schieffelin, 1979; Schieffelin, 1987). Even at a basic conceptual level, linguistic socialization is Janus-faced. This duality is described concisely as 'socialization through the use of language and socialization to use language' (Schieffelin and Ochs, 1986, p. 163).

Lock (1980) identified three main consequences of social interaction for language development: 'it inducts the child into the specific social world he has been born into', 'it brings him to an agreed and socially shared perception of that world', and 'it…creates the meanings for his actions that will underlie his later development of language' (p. 2). Chomskyan nativism continues to generate fertile acquisition research, especially in the acquisition of syntax (for Sinitic studies, see Chien and Lust, 1983, 1985; Lee, 1991; Lust and Chien, 1984;

Lust, Chien, and Mangione, 1983). Many investigators of language development in the past decade are, however, more comfortable with an interactionist view:

> interactionists…assume that many factors (e.g., social, linguistic, maturational/biological, cognitive, etc.) affect the course of development and that these factors are mutually dependent upon, interact with, and modify one another. Not only may cognitive or social factors modify language acquisition, but language acquisition will in turn modify the development of cognitive and social skills (Bohannon and Warren-Leubecker, 1989, p. 181).

For the present purposes, it is sufficient to distinguish three broad, interactionist categories.

Linguistic Socialization as Development of Communicative Competence

Early characterizations of communicative competence (Hymes, 1967) focused on the set of internal conditions that enable an individual to use language appropriately in real-life, communicative situations. More recently, communicative competence has been viewed as 'a synthesis of knowledge of basic grammatical principles, knowledge of how language is used in social contexts to perform communicative functions, and knowledge of how utterances and communicative functions can be combined according to the principles of discourse' (Canale and Swain, 1980, p. 20; see also Verhoeven and Vermeer, 1992).

Communicative competence is construed in opposition to Chomskyan linguistic competence (McCarthy, 1973). A generative grammar as originally and typically proposed does not attend to contexts of sentence use. It is not meant to describe the particular human competence that is manifested in the control of situational and interpersonal appropriateness.

Contextual sensitivity is apparently even more important for users of the minimal-syntax family of Sinitic languages than for users of syntax-rich languages such as English (Aaronson and Ferres, 1986). Context may be viewed as a set of constraints and resources external to the person, complementing internal constraints and resources. The latter can usefully be regarded as setting relative costs and benefits for members of any given language community.

Thus it has been proposed as a testable hypothesis by Hunt and Agnoli (1991) that the absence of a subjunctive mood in Chinese has the effect that the relative cognitive on-line cost of counterfactual reasoning is greater in Chinese than it is in English. Positive evidence on this point would suggest that Sinitic linguistic socialization encourages relatively less counterfactual reasoning about people than does Anglo socialization. This hypothesis is a performance proposition and not a competence one, a question of norms not of rules. It has been demonstrated that Chinese adults and children show no deficits in counterfactual reasoning from a Chinese text (Au, 1983; L. G. Liu, 1985), and it should be straightforward to probe for start-up and on-line costs. In short, researchers are starting to view Chinese language socialization in terms of the use of internal and external resources that induction into the language structure makes available.

Turning now to socialization to use language, a genre well researched in middle-class Anglo-Saxon environments is that of dialogical and group conversation. Conversational competence here involves knowing and utilizing rules of how to contribute to a conversation, turn-taking, introducing and changing topics, and politeness routines (Berko Gleason, Perlmann, and Greif, 1984; Berko Gleason and Weintraub, 1976; Greif and Berko Gleason, 1980). Such a characterization of communicative competence is not sufficient to clarify the concept of linguistic socialization (Habermas, 1970, 1987). To sharpen the definition, one still has to explicate what entities qualify as 'agents of a society' and how an 'influence of a societal agent on an individual' is to be formulated. Particular approaches to linguistic socialization give rather different answers to these questions.

Approaches differ, for instance, in whether parents are to be viewed as agents of society in the same way as are large organizations (education systems, the military, law enforcement agencies, the media, and so on). Goodwin and Tang (this volume) highlight the traditional Chinese reliance on the concept of the family as a basic societal unit. Further, the nature of the socializing influence by agents of society can be conceptualized in dissimilar ways. For some researchers, the prototypical example of a socializing influence would be planned, purposive—often coercive and institutionalized—action. A simple case occurs when a child is explicitly told by a parent or teacher what to say in a given social or interpersonal context and is expected to repeat the utterance verbatim (Ochs, 1986). Chinese pedagogy is often viewed as an exemplar of formal methods. For other researchers, unplanned, unintended, and non-institutionalized influence, such as the spontaneous behaviour of parents and peers, would qualify as socializing influence. These distinctions are important in analysing linguistic socialization in political systems like that of the People's Republic of China, where formal indoctrination (Snook, 1972) and familial socialization, planned intervention, and unintended practice can militate against each other.

Linguistic Socialization as Societal Transmission and Structural Reproduction

A second approach classifies language and language use as a tool or medium of a power-related transmission and reproduction machinery (Bernstein, 1971, 1990). In this view, the prime function of socialization would be the management of knowledge in individuals and in social groups, and the reproduction of social relations and the stratification in society at large. The approach intends to elucidate how 'class relations generate, distribute, and legitimate distinctive forms of communication' (Ribeiro Pedro, 1981, p. 69). The approach concentrates more on 'socialization through language' than 'socialization to use language'.

Bernsteinians assume that social relations and stratification in society are manifested in and preserved by two different mechanisms of dominance: power and control. Power relations affect practices of boundary-setting between categories. Categories may be strongly discriminated and insulated, each having a distinctive specialization (a 'strong' classification). Categories may, in other settings, be less discriminated or specialized (a 'weak' classification). Societal power relations create, legitimize, maintain, or modify assemblies of inter-categorial boundaries. Examples relevant to linguistic socialization are categories of gender as expressed in sexist or non-sexist language, or categories of roles in a formal education system. A cross-comparison of Chinese and English stereotype labelling has been offered by Hoffman, Lau, and Johnson (1986).

Control relations pertain to the social relations in the context of which socialization takes place, especially relations of knowledge and information transmission, acquisition, and evaluation. The setting of a social frame of control is conceptualized as a continuum ranging from what can be called 'strong' to 'weak' framing. Under conditions of strong framing, the transmitter (for example, the parent or educator) explicitly regulates communicative practices. Regulation extends to interactional patterns: the relationship tends to lack equity. The acquirer (for example, a child or student) can only minimally influence communicative practice. With weak framing, both the transmitter and the acquirer have control over regulating the flow of communication: the relationship is more egalitarian. In a system with strong classification and strong framing, communicative practices can socialize individuals into either dominance-laden, asymmetric relationships (at a micro level) or, as Bernstein believes, to massive educational and/or employment failure of individuals.

The original formulations of this model have been superseded by new theorizing that involves even more abstract concepts (Bernstein, 1990). However, the concerns continue to provoke studies on linguistic socialization. Educationalists value Bernstein's concepts, as they clarify discourse data stemming from classroom discourse (see, for example, Milroy and Milroy, 1985).

The more or less radically Marxist frameworks in which research has been conducted in the People's Republic of China, as well as governmental projects of large-scale language education and planning, seem unintentionally to have been based on assumptions similar to those of Bernstein. This conclusion applies particularly to the relationships of language use, linguistic socialization, and social stratification.

Linguistic Socialization as Constructing, Maintaining, and Modifying Social Representations

A contemporary set of research approaches views the nature of linguistic socialization as being substantially wider—and often deeper—than simply a process conducive to communicative competence (even if the latter is liberally defined). More thoroughly influenced by the paradigms of present-day cognitive science than are the two described above, this approach attempts to map the system of mental representations (Von Cranach, Doise, and Mugny, 1992) established, maintained, and altered by socialization processes. Under the assumption that socialization is a process of creating (social) representations in the individual's permanent memory, linguistic socialization appears as a process of building a system of representations through the linguistic medium. Language socialization is seen as a process establishing and structuring individuals' inferential capacities.

Inspired by social representation theories (Moscovici, 1976; 1988; Farr and Moscovici, 1984) these researchers define social knowledge at both the individual and social levels (Von Cranach, 1992). As Wegner (1986) explains, 'other people can be locations of external storage for the individual...; (the) interdependence produces a knowledge holding system that is larger and more complex than either of the individuals' own memory systems' (p. 189). Socialization can be seen as a series of interactions between a system of social representations in the group and a system of social representations in the individual.

The social psychology of language has recently specified the linguistic character of some social representations. The linguistic category model (Fiedler, 1978; Fiedler and Semin, 1988; Semin and Fiedler, 1992) empirically substantiates a semantic system involving at least four categories of verbal and adjectival forms distinguished along a number of explicitly stated dimensions. The choice of descriptors instantiating a category by a communicator is found to heavily affect the causal attribution of interpersonal actions, stereotyping, impression formation, and other crucial processes that modify the system of social representations. Semin and Fiedler have showed that a relatively simple semantic taxonomy accounts for 'relationships between outgroup impression formation and discrimination against outgroups', as well as resolving 'conflicts in traditional actor–observer and egocentric bias explanations of attribution' (Applegate, 1993, p. 1077).

Through socialization, individuals learn to use linguistic descriptors belonging to certain categories. Once used, the descriptors allow and invite wideranging inferences about the interpersonal and social character of events described, and at least partly determine the social knowledge constructed (for Chinese data, see Bond and King, 1985; Yang and Bond, 1990).

HOW SHALL A PERSON BE CALLED?

A system of linguistically marked terms signals the role of the family in Chinese socialization. The functional significance of the terms can be analysed at each of the levels briefly reviewed in the preceding section. The justification offered for the terms is usually the promotion of good relationships: so marked is traditional Chinese interest in the topic that a common sense 'relationology' has developed, labelled by Chiao (1982) *kuanhsisueh* (*guanxi xue*).

Linguistic socialization as the term is used here describes socialization for traditional beliefs and values which many authors consider significant in describing the historically persistent core of Chinese culture (Bond, this volume; Ho, 1981; Leung, this volume; Wilson, 1970, 1974; Yang, this volume). The semantics of various terms, the structure of semantic sub-domains and networks (like those relating to kinship) as well as observations of peculiar uses of language, like the naming of children, conducting of spiritual rites, good wishes, lucky words (Sung, 1979; cf. Bond and Venus, 1991) and insults (Chang, 1979; Bond, Wan, Leung, and Giacalone, 1985), constitute indirect evidence.

In the Confucian tradition, types of asymmetric interpersonal relationships had an outstanding role in maintaining peace in society. The Wu Lun (five cardinal relationships, Bond, 1991)—those between sovereign and subject, father and son, elder and younger brother, husband and wife, and senior and junior friend—are inherently unequal. As Bond and Hwang (1986, p. 216) wrote, 'the senior member was accorded a wide range of prerogatives and authority with respect to the junior'.

Three of these exemplary patterns of authority are intra-familial, and so the role of family socialization to follow authority is clear. Another aspect of expected and required intra-familial attitudes is often called 'lineage solidarity'. It involves respect and active helping, in addition to or in lieu of love, among members of an extended family. Filial piety applies, in a more abstract way, to ancestors with whom an individual has never been in personal contact.

While in the West respect for ancestors is often displayed in the naming of children, Chinese beliefs documented for more than 2000 years command that the names of the most respected ancestors should not be mentioned: 'people will not choose names for their children which contain the same characters or characters which are homophonous with their forefathers' names' (Chang, 1979, p. 233). The constraint against using homophonous names is not peculiar to social labelling. Homophony plays a role in an enormous variety of social practices and popular customs. The custom of eating seaweed of the type called *fat choi* (*faatchoi*) at Cantonese New Year is explained by the near-homophony with 'to strike it rich' (Chang, 1979, p. 233). A similar explanation is offered for the Cantonese custom of offering mandarin fruit (homophonous with 'gold') to guests.

We are not here concerned with the origin of each of these customs, but only with the notable characteristic of Sinitic languages that they are salient to their speakers and formative in the speakers' representations of the customs. Homophony is a powerful general force in linguistic socialization, and makes it possible to discern the strongest links between what Chinese people say, what they explicitly represent, and what they do. Current oral tradition among the minority Yi people credits Mao Zedong with ordering a change from the pejorative *yi* (barbarian) to the homophonous, auspicious *yi* (fine cooking pot) for their group name (Harrell, 1989).

Linguistically, family names are 'passed along according to a system of patri-lineage, and men of the same family names are considered offspring of the same ancestors' (Chang, 1979, p. 221). Claiming certain family names entails wide-ranging psychological consequences if not societal privileges, at least for men. Having merely the same family name (a coincidence far more frequent in Chinese groups than in European or North American) triggers 'feelings of affinity' toward one another as (supposed) blood relatives. Names which are considered those of families with the largest membership or prosperity confer positive self-concept to the bearer irrespective of personal merits. It may well not be stretching the limits of an account to say that naming sustains a phenomenon of 'agglutinating clanship' in Chinese societies.

Familial authority and solidarity are linguistically expressed in the highly differentiated and lexicalized kinship networks of any Sinitic language. One study (Harrell, 1989) has shown an association between socio-economic integration into Han society and kinship terminology among two groups (Nuosu Yi and Lipuo Yi); more studies are needed along these lines. Chang (1979) cites work from Hokkien (Fujian province), listing 141 different relations, more than 100 of which are distinctively lexicalized as kinship reference terms. At least half of the relations also imply a required, distinctive address term. While superiors and seniors should be addressed by exact kin terms, inferiors and juniors are more often addressed by given names, showing a linguistically marked power differential. The process of becoming a native Chinese speaker in Fujian province involves internalizing a vast conceptual structure of kinship relations and patterns of appropriate conversational address, along with the appropriate compliments and insults that attend such classification.

The categorial segregation of gender and male chauvinism are values which are almost certainly socialized through language use. Primary evidence waits to be seen, but practices of naming children provide some data on the subject (Chang, 1979). Married-out girls add their husbands' family names to their own (although Chang claims that only the maiden names of these wives are remembered by their offspring after their death). Concerning given names, boys are never given female names (unlike in Spanish or French), and neutral names (comparable to, in the West, Robin, Lesley/Leslie, and Frances/Francis) are traditionally eschewed.

Has party policy in mainland China replaced traditional patterns with more egalitarian relationships and patterns of language use? After 1949, rules and habits promoted by linguistic socialization, at least in the public sphere, changed significantly on the Mainland. In particular, during the era at the heart of the Great Proletarian Cultural Revolution (from 1966 to 1969) and the consequent educational revolution, students were encouraged to ignore their teachers' and superiors' authority and to pursue conversations on a more equal basis (Lehmann, 1975). The following examination of this sub-domain of communicative competence, rules of address, invites caution in assessing the long-term efficiency of these changes, a consideration to which we shall return.

In 'the glorious revolutionary tradition of democracy and equality' (Fang and Heng, 1983, p. 499), generations were socialized by the education system in mainland China to use address terms like *tongzhi* (Tang, 1975; Scotton and Zhu, 1981). *Tongzhi* is the Chinese variant of the Russian *tovarisc*, meaning someone who shares communist aspirations (*tong*, 'the same', *zhi*, 'aspiration'). It was intended to eliminate deferential and dominance-laden address terms and to promote egalitarian discourse.

Lehmann (1975) and Scotton and Zhu (1983) cite traditional terms that were intended for elimination (honorifics like *xiansheng* [Mister], *taitai* [Madam], *xiaojie* [Miss], as well as special addresses at both poles of the status hierarchy like *laoban* [proprietor], *nong fu* [peasant], *che fu* [driver], and *ku li* [coolie worker]). At least some communists regarded classical honorifics when applied to them as insults. 'No young man would like to be called *xiansheng*. I remember when I was addressed in this way in 1960 by a(n)...elderly peasant, I felt quite hurt. ...I was a highly class-conscious revolutionary comrade!' (Ju, 1991, p. 388). In addition to the introduction of *tongzhi* as an address term, new compounds involving *yuan* (member) and *ren* (human being) were introduced. The formation of the new compounds can be viewed as natural to

Chinese in the sense that the language generally relies heavily on classifiers, where English deploys them only sparingly.

Surface patterns involving address terms, however, changed dramatically within 10 years of their official introduction. The frequency of occurrence of many traditional address terms dropped, while *tongzhi* and others were used by people in all walks of society, including those who were not members of the Communist Party (Vogel, 1965). Perhaps through sheer repetition and semantic satiation, *tongzhi* soon lost its original reference to Party members (or non-members committed to the cause) and came to mean 'person' (Fincher, 1973), a phenomenon also documented in other communist systems.

Does this imply that discourse and underlying attitudes became more egalitarian? Two studies of address rules have showed that this was hardly the case (Fang and Heng, 1983; Scotton and Zhu, 1983). Results from the early 1980s corroborate four observed patterns of address.

First, many Communist Party and government officials in the People's Republic were embarrassed by being simply addressed as *tongzhi* and required more complex addresses of the type

Surname or Full name + Rank + *tongzhi*

(for example, Liu shu-ji tongzhi [Secretary Comrade Liu]), where the 'rank' element identifies status. In addressing numerous officials of the party-state, *tongzhi* was not even required, as shown by the pattern

Surname or Full name + Official title

(for example, Lin zhuren [Director Lin] and Hu buzhang [Minister Hu]). Second, non-prohibited terms carrying more local flavour were conjoined with *tongzhi* to produce widely expected and accepted forms of address. To quote a telling example from Fang and Heng (1983), Chinese 'leading officials' who are 'on guard against the tendency of being divorced from the masses' did not invite being addressed by official rank or title. Instead, they favoured combinations with the words *lao* (old) and *xiao* (little). A resulting address pattern is

Lao + Surname + *tongzhi.*

Superiors irrespective of age were addressed by the *lao* combination, while they tended to address subordinates by the *xiao* combination. In this way, one non-egalitarian address system appeared to alternate with another.

Third, in some key relationships, like those in the formal education system, the new terms were never adopted. Fang and Heng (1983) reported that *jiaoyuan tongzhi* (comrade teacher) was found in textbooks printed in China for external use, but 'has never been used in the Chinese context' (p. 496).

Finally, Scotton and Zhu (1983) distinguished between marked and unmarked uses of *tongzhi*. In the case of marked use by superiors towards inferiors, *tongzhi* was selected to make power more salient in the relationship, and to further limit the addressee's individual power base by reminding him or her of an ideologically defined relation to the 'people as a whole'. Conversely, when *tongzhi* was used by inferiors towards superiors, it was intended as 'a negotiation to decrease social distance' by making 'solidarity as co-members of the people the most salient'. As one notes, this analysis takes for granted that strong pre-formed superiority relationships continue to exist and to determine conversation patterns (especially in public and official settings).

There is evidence that the address patterns observed in the 1980s may not characterize relations in today's China. Following the introduction of a controlled market economy and the influx of selected products of Western culture and science, the 'mental outlook of the people has changed. ...The bourgeoisie is not as bad as it was painted to be; capitalist society is not as crisis-ridden as some people imagined' (Ju, 1991, p. 390). As a general trend, the use of *tongzhi* has decreased and has become restricted almost entirely to Communist Party members (Liu, 1994). Terms like *shifu* (master worker, as distinct from an apprentice) and *shouzhang* (leading official, commanding officer) have been devalued (Ju, 1991) and lost most of their ideological connotation: 'Wherever you go in China...you will hear farmer-peddlers shifu-ing nearly everyone, be the customer a man or woman, a government cadre or an army officer, a college teacher or an undergraduate' (p. 389). *Xiansheng* and *xiaojie* are again becoming popular and may lose their potential derogatory shade:

> To those people whose thinking has undergone a complete about-face in the short period of two or three decades, ...formerly shunned titles have acquired...complimentary connotations: to be a xiansheng is to be rich and handsome; to be a xiaojie, instead of being a girl with bourgeois family origins...is to be young and beautiful; ...a laoban is no longer...'an exploiter of employees' but a successful businessperson and enterpreneur, possibly a 'red millionaire' (Ju, 1991, p. 390).

It is reported that Communist Party secretaries of enterprises now prefer to be called *laoban* rather than *tongzhi* (Ju, 1991).

Little is known about dialogical and group conversational patterns and rules that prevail in the many particular situations found in Chinese communities worldwide. There has been a lack of research regarding unicity or universality of these patterns among Chinese communities and in Chinese versus non-Chinese societies. One point of departure for more serious research into patterns of socialization for communicative competence could be the determination of the elements and targets of such competence, the pragmatic rules of language use in various Chinese settings of interchange. Examples of research settings are intra-familial conversation with one or more generations present, classroom dialogue among peers as well as between students and teachers, official and business negotiations, discourse in leisure and sports contexts, and so on. The rule systems to be described for each of the genres and contexts may involve turn-taking, introduction of new topics, interpersonal clarification of meanings, repairs of violations, and similar strategies.

When such pragmatic rule systems have been described and compared across Chinese cultures, the question emerges of how and when individuals are socialized to use them. What is the relative weight of various channels and means of socialization in establishing these patterns?

Terms of address constitute a minimal segment of the larger sphere of interpersonal communication. Even within this segment, however, there are unresearched topics. Which sub-processes of socialization determine changes of address systems and honorifics in various Chinese societies? Do familial and institutional influences work in concert or contradict each other in different Chinese contexts? How do the values inherent in honorifics fit into the general pattern of values promoted by socializing practices in various Chinese societies?

In a recent book, Young (1994) presents a painstaking analysis of communicative self-effacement based on naturalistic observation of dialogues (in Hong Kong and Taiwan) and subsequent clarificatory interviews with native Chinese respondents. The findings reveal the value systems, role relationships, and interpersonal dynamics in which address patterns are embedded, point to their socializing origins, and explain metamorphoses within them. They also shed some light on tendencies which appear to be universal in the Sinitic world, irrespective of government systems. As Young writes, 'Chinese communicative rituals require a constant attendance to hierarchical status and...social deference: markers of respect must be articulated and meaningful ritual action personalized. ...[Rituals] cater to a bone-deep sense of social harmony and interdependency that inspires people to seek possibilities for mutual engagement and joint action' (p. 137).

Dialogues between unequal participants, like the talk on purely business-related topics between a salesman at a Taiwan television company and his immediate superior, are cited as evidence of communicative conflicts typically triggered by Chinese language socialization. In strategies of persuasion, 'assigning a non-face-threatening intention to the communication is essential' (Young, 1994, p. 139). Subordinates tend to use 'subtle displays of hesitant reserve, willing humility, and negotiable openmindedness that signal [their] reluctance to impose' (ibid.). Introducing a solution to a business problem straightforwardly by verbal means runs counter to 'a Chinese aesthetic preference to leaving it implicit' (p. 149). It is perceived to be 'out of a subordinate's province to make a suggestion to someone senior' (p. 150). Rather, subordinates 'conspicuously recognize [the superior's] presence and power and the hierarchical relationship' (p. 154). Humbling oneself through deferential and respectful behaviour represents 'a conscientious effort to make cooperation a basic frame of reference; it signals a willingness for personal accommodation and possibilities of mutual adjustment' (Young, 1994, p. 155).

It appears that socialization for these communicative options may be rooted in ancient canons of *li*, a term which may be interpreted as 'rites', 'propriety', 'decorum', or 'manners'. *Li* was 'a body of norms, conventions, and mores which influenced all secular and sacred aspects of social living in traditional China' (Young, 1994, p. 7). *Li* unites harmony and diversity. However, it presents 'individual expression, individual recognition and individual fulfillment to be of secondary importance' (p. 10) and promotes collectivistic conduct. The character for *li* originally symbolized sacrifice.

The communication patterns just described can also promote a practice which fits Snook's criterion: 'A person indoctrinates P... if he teaches with the intention that the pupil or pupils believe P regardless of the evidence' (Snook, 1972, p. 154). The next section will describe a few processes of mass socialization in the People's Republic of China.

A SOCIALIZATION EXPERIMENT WITH ONE BILLION SUBJECTS

The agenda of promoting *tongzhi* was nested within a broad 'experiment' of profound social impact on language, which, *mutatis mutandis*, continues today. The language modification campaign formulated by the Communist Party in 1955 was to serve a number of larger political goals, especially the reduction of inter-ethnic and inter-regional differences within mainland China (Zheng, 1952; Wang, 1956). The history of the campaign has been documented by Cheng (1973). It was resolved that a common language, Putonghua, should be defined and made the language used by people over the whole of the country. Execution of the campaign began early in 1956 by 'forceful measures...promulgated by the highest governmental...authority, ...the State Council' (Chen, 1973, p. 706).

Prescription is an integral part of the life of most languages (Haas, 1982), and the idea of a standardized Chinese lingua franca was not new. Linguistic unification movements had existed decades before the Second World War (Chao, 1976; Fang, 1965; Hsia, 1956; Mills, 1956). However, it is the recent campaign for Putonghua that has made the unification issue central in the linguistic socialization of millions of Chinese. The direction of efforts has also changed. Putonghua is not meant to be identical with pre-communist Mandarin, and in an important sense should be (re-)learned by Mandarin speakers. As Chen (1973) put it, 'the State Council's 'Directions' contain the overall guiding principles. ...Ideologically, it attempts to dissociate the new program from all earlier language reform movements'.

It is not possible to understand the Putonghua program without reference to the political role of language use. As declared by one Communist-era minister of education, *pu-tong* is to be taken to mean 'universality' (*pu*) and 'common possession' (*tong*) of the language (Chen, 1973, p. 707). The grammar of Putonghua is based on Northern Han dialects, its phonetics on a Beijing pronunciation. The most difficult task in fixing a standard is to delineate a vocabulary. Authorities originally intended the lexis of Putonghua to be based on modern colloquial Chinese literature. However, they wished to avoid setting a diglossic standard, remote from the language of everyday life (Lehmann, 1975). The language of Mao Zedong's works was initially set as the supreme example; further, it was equated with the 'language of the workers and peasants'. People were pressed to learn texts verbatim (Chen, 1973). The unsurprising lack of explicit rules for generalizing forms of language from texts to everyday social contexts led to confusion and ambiguity over 'correct' forms of speech.

Can the introduction of Putonghua be conducive to a rapid elimination of traditional Sinitic languages and dialects? Most authors doubt that such an elimination is possible. Regionality and local roots are by tradition highly respected by most Chinese. As Chang (1979) stressed in connection with minorities in Singapore, regional origin or descendence is a salient category affecting many forms of social behaviour and thinking. As the activities of regional 'friendship associations' in many Chinese communities (including those in North America) show, this 'agglutinating clan' factor has a greater priority than a similar one in modern societies of the West. Even within a Chinese context, people tend to prefer those with similar origins, sharing their particular language or dialect, having concerns about the same affairs in their homelands in the narrower sense. Regionality is also associated with factual or supposed familial ties. As a result, individuals are highly reluctant to abandon their local language or dialect.

In 1958, Chou Enlai reported to the Chinese People's Political Consultative Conference that 'our promotion of Putonghua aims at the removal of the barriers among the dialects but not at the suppression or destruction of the dialects. ...Dialects will stay for a long time' (Chou, 1958, p. 6). However, another party representative taking part in the 1955 conferences asserted that 'the promotion of Putonghua will naturally reduce the use of the dialects' (Chen, 1973, p. 708).

A delegation of American linguists visiting mainland China concluded that the 'practical position' of the Committee on Language Reform was that 'dialects cannot be abolished by administrative order' (Lehmann, 1975). A similar position was observed ten years later with the committee reportedly announcing 'because of the variety of languages in China, everyone is required to speak the common language. The policy is not to replace one's own dialect but to become bilingual in one's own language and...Putonghua' (Mei, 1984, p. 78; see also Homel and Palij, 1987). Nevertheless, the persistence and range of efforts in spreading Putonghua qualifies the experiment in the People's Republic as one of the strongest linguistic campaigns ever attempted by a political system. There has even been a spread of this initiative into Hong Kong, where Putonghua has prudently been on offer as an optional subject in late primary and early secondary classes since 1988.

The Communist Party on the Mainland also used the complementary route: socialization of Mandarin-speaking cadres in other Han languages which are mutually unintelligible with Mandarin. Similar bi-directional policies had been followed in the Soviet Union.

Interestingly, linguistic socialization processes in a society as different from mainland China as Singapore also move toward use of a common language for Chinese ethnic groups. In Singapore, Mandarin is increasingly spoken of as the Chinese lingua franca. Kuo (1979) quoted frequencies from the 1957 census and from a 1972 survey suggesting that speakers of Sinitic languages (Hokkien, Teochew, Cantonese, Hainanese, Hakka, and Foochow [Fujianese], in greatest numbers) were able to understand Mandarin in much larger proportions during the 1970s than even 15 years before. Although in Singapore Mandarin Chinese is one of the official languages, and 'Chinese' is declared to be the mother tongue of the Chinese community, the encouragement to use Mandarin cannot easily be compared to the force of socialization in the Mainland. Rather, the spread of Mandarin appears to reflect the wish for easier communication among the various Chinese groups in the republic (Kuo, 1979). Hokkien has also played a role as an inter-Sinitic communication medium in Singapore.

Due to the scarcity of rigorous empirical investigations of these subjects, there are many unresolved issues. Some key questions address the learning of Putonghua as a first or second language, asking, What are the tendencies of the present and immediate past in the proportions of Sinitic languages learned as first and second languages in various Chinese communities? On the Mainland, how many children are actually taught Putonghua as a first language? And, what are the degrees of Putonghua mastery across various language districts, and why?

Other questions address mother tongues: Are there differences in choosing the familial language of socialization instead of that of the formal education system (or other societal agencies)? How widespread is bilingualism involving a Sinitic 'mother tongue' in the family and another Sinitic language (for example, Putonghua) in various states and regions?

A group of questions explores parents' choices of a language of socialization, asking, Which are the main psychological determinants of parents' choosing one medium over the other?

Yet others ask what are the consequences of language choices for the individuals. Does socialization secure competence (including communicative and conversational competence) in the given languages? What is the structure of attitudes toward various Sinitic languages among Chinese youth (especially those socialized in the Mainland)? And does coercion bring about negative attitudes toward Putonghua or acquiescence toward it?

CONCLUSION

This chapter has concentrated on a few central issues. It begins with the belief that the study of linguistic socialization flourishes on what linguistics proper ignores: that language is used by speakers to define a social situation (Fasold, 1984). A theory of communication is essential to research on conversational competence, but in itself a theory of communication is not sufficient: research has come to deploy as well a theory of society. When one attempts to assess the current state of knowledge at the places where communication and social forces are interdependent, one encounters the historic vitality of Chinese cultures. D'Andrade (1990, p. 67) wrote, 'culture consists of learned and shared systems of meaning and understanding, communicated primarily by means of natural language'. To which one needs to add 'and shaped powerfully by natural language'.

ACKNOWLEDGEMENT

The authors are greatly indebted to Julie K. Bunnell, Che Kan Leong, Simon M. Leung, In-mao Liu, and Andrew J. Lock for comments and advice. Errors that remain are our own.

Chapter 7

Chinese Intelligence

Jimmy Chan

Researchers in Western countries, for example, Hunt (1961), Thomson (1966), Wiseman (1967), Butcher (1968), Dockrell (1970), Plomin (1988), Brody (1992), and Anderson (1992), among many others, have carried out a great deal of systematic work on the topic of intelligence. The contributions of Hans Eysenck, Arthur Jensen, and Philip Vernon to the study of mental abilities and to mental testing in the past three decades are particularly useful in understanding the concept of intelligence as it is perceived in the Western world. Their work is also significant in cross-cultural studies and has particular relevance to the Chinese context. In China, however, comparatively little empirical work has been done in this area of knowledge, although the concept of intelligence has deep roots in Chinese civilization dating back almost 2,500 years.

This chapter will discuss the effects of historical background, education system, and family influence in the development of intelligence in Chinese individuals. The adaptation of modern Western mental tests to Chinese communities will be reviewed. Sex differences in intelligence among Chinese will be examined in terms of academic achievements and intellectual abilities. Finally, an account of the major findings from cross-cultural research will be given to shed light on the nature of Chinese intelligence when compared with that found in the West.

HISTORICAL BACKGROUND

The concept of intelligence has been firmly rooted in China for about 2,500 years and was clearly articulated during the time of the philosopher and scholar Confucius (Fung 1983). The ideographic Chinese characters first invented by Cang Kie (倉頡) 4,600 years ago are very revealing; those for 'intelligence' give important clues to the understanding of mental ability. Because the Chinese and English languages are fundamentally different in structure and in their written forms, the different concepts of intelligence may be seen to be fundamentally characteristic as well, as will be demonstrated below.

In Chinese, a bright child is often labelled as *congming* (聰明), having wisdom, meaning that he has two good sense organs for receiving remote information through sound and light. The character *cong* (聰) tells that the ears are acute and can thus receive and analyse information accurately, whereas the character *ming* (明) denotes that the eyes are sensitive to any external objects (whether stationary or moving) under the light of both the sun and the moon.

Thus, listening and seeing are considered to be two important components of becoming intelligent. Touching, tasting, and smelling by making direct contact with the skin, the tongue, and the nose respectively are considered to be comparatively less important in understanding the external world. It is interesting to note that a deaf person is described as suffering from a loss of *cong*, and a blind person as suffering from a loss of *ming*, implying that he or she has lost one of the important means for becoming intelligent (Chan, 1991).

Equivalent terms for *congming* are *congying* (聰穎) and *congmin* (聰敏). The characters *ying* (穎) and *min* (敏) mean 'top' and 'quick' respectively, thus signifying that intelligence relates to a top brain and a quick mind. The term opposite to *congming* is *yuchun* (愚蠢), *yu* (愚) meaning 'corner of the mind' and *chun* (蠢) meaning 'stupid as two spring worms', a low-level form of animal life.

Other Chinese words for intelligence are *zhili* (智力) and *zhineng* (智能), which equal having the strength, power, or ability (high or low) to know. The character *zhi* (智) itself denotes knowing (知) the sun (日). In ancient times, the sun was so mystifying and distant that very little was known about it, and it was therefore believed that it was extremely difficult to understand. If a person knew the sun, he or she must have exceptional ability. Further, the character *zhi* (知) means having a mouth (口) as quick as an arrow (矢).

Another Chinese term for intelligence is *zhihui* (智慧), the character *hui* (慧) meaning 'to have a lightning heart or a fast mind' (as quick as a *huixing* 彗星 or fast-moving comet). All these words reveal vividly an ancient conception of intelligence relating to brightness and quickness of the mind, with information obtained by the ears and the eyes.

Confucius categorized people into three types, namely, superior (上), medium (中), and inferior (下). Other ancient commentators considered people to be *tiancai* (天才, talented or made of heaven's material), *rencai* (人才, ordinary or made of man's material), and *yongcai* (庸才, mediocre or made of fool's material). In the ancient *Han Shu* (漢書) written about 2,200 years ago, people were divided into nine classes according to their levels of intelligence, namely, 'top top', 'top middle', 'top bottom', 'middle top', 'middle middle', 'middle bottom', 'bottom top', 'bottom middle', and 'bottom bottom'. Moreover, a genius was said to possess the devil's supernatural ability (*guicai*, 鬼才). Ancient Chinese scholars described people as 'early developers' and 'late developers', terms now often used by psychologists. These concepts correspond rather closely with those used in modern psychology to separate the sheep from the goats by using the scores of intelligence tests.

A great teacher as well as a philosopher, Confucius advocated that all people should be taught irrespective of their abilities (*you jiao wu lei*, 有教無類) and that all people should be educated according to their abilities (*yin cai shi jiao*, 因材施教). These ideas are in perfect agreement with the modern concepts of 'human rights' in receiving education, and 'individual differences' in providing suitable types of education for the mentally challenged and the intellectually gifted.

It was concluded in ancient China that intelligence must be built on a foundation and could not develop from a vacuum, and thus it was believed that 'people can only know through learning and are not born with knowledge' (學

而知之，焉有生而知之). This assumption laid the basis for the concept of interaction between heredity and environment through the use of the five human senses in order to understand the environment. Further, ancient Chinese believed that everyone had his or her *zhuanchang*(專長), or specific ability, in addition to their *tianzi* (天資), or general ability. The term *tianzi* refers to the mental resources given by heaven, whereas *zhuanchang* describes the results of learning through training and education. This distinction appears to coincide neatly with the modern concept of 'inborn' and 'acquired' characteristics of intelligence and the modern theory of general plus specific factors, as advocated by Vernon (1965) and many other psychologists.

It is important to note that ancient Chinese scholars accepted intelligence as an attribute born with us and an original gift from heaven. Hence, the concept of heaven is often included in terms for intelligence: *tiancai*(天才), *tianzi*(天資), and *tianfu*(天賦), translated as 'ability emanating from heaven', 'resource coming from heaven', and 'endowment bestowed upon us by heaven', respectively, are some examples. An intelligent person is often described as someone being *de tian du hou*(得天獨厚), 'getting a uniquely big share from heaven'. The Chinese concept of intelligence has long been connected with heaven and genetic endowment, which is taken to be more generous for some people than for others. This ancient assumption is generally in agreement with the estimate of 80 per cent hereditary influence on intelligence that is accepted by many contemporary psychometricians, such as Eysenck (1979, 1982) and Jensen (1980, 1981).

Chinese ideas of intelligence also relate to the central Confucian concept of *ren*, describing a type of kindness between two persons. Confucius considered that *zhizhe li ren*(智者利仁), the intelligent people would be able to facilitate *ren* (仁); *wei zhi yan de ren* (未智焉得仁), people without intelligence could not achieve *ren*; and *zhizhe bu huo* (智者不惑), an intelligent person would not be perplexed. The link between intelligence and morality has been regarded as being of great importance (see also Bond, 1979), as the success of the society relies on the work of intelligent people who also know the right things to do in order to develop a harmonious social climate.

THE CHINESE EDUCATION SYSTEM

Education in ancient China placed great emphasis on examinations in the selection of mandarin officials for the public service. The *keju*(科舉) examination held every three years aimed to find nationwide the top scholar, *zhuangyuan*(狀元), the second-place scholar, *bangyan*(榜眼), and the third-place scholar, *tanhua* (探花). The system was greatly valued by the public, since it was an open competition between males, and success in the examinations led to status and wealth and even to a marriage with a princess in ancient times. The examination papers were set to test primarily the abilities of the candidates' memories in reciting classical works, although testing their power of poetic composition was also used. In other words, creative thinking, concept formation, information processing, and decision-making abilities were not given prominent attention. These emphases may have exercised a profound effect on the development of certain facets of intelligence in the Chinese people.

Traditionally, Chinese society has valued scholars more highly than it has members of other occupations, namely, farmers, workers, merchants, and soldiers, which have been ranked in this order of significance. As a result, the examination-oriented education system has continued up to the present day and has dominated schools and universities both in mainland China and in Hong Kong, Taiwan, and Singapore, highly competitive societies made up largely of Chinese people. Students in Hong Kong tend to study only material which will help them to achieve better results in public examinations, and the acquisition of other life skills tends to be neglected. Moreover, parents in Hong Kong tend to be practically oriented, wanting their children to be successful in getting a well-paid job through obtaining a place in a renowned university. Teachers in Hong Kong are forced to cater to the needs of the students and parents, and they often regret that their educational ideals in developing students' potential are not fostered.

Examination results have received much of the emphasis within the education system. Effort has been concentrated to achieve the learning 'product' (what the answer is) rather than to understand the learning 'process' (how the answer is obtained). Problem-solving and creative thinking have not been encouraged or fostered and hence the strength of Chinese intelligence may have been handicapped in these important areas. Originality, fluency, and flexibility have not been given due emphasis in the education system, as reflected in the research results of the Educational Research Establishment (active from 1964 to 1994) in Hong Kong. The long-standing tradition stressing memorization and the regurgitation of factual knowledge at examinations has been criticized by many psychologists and educators (see Chan, 1969, 1970, and 1972) for stultifying the proper and healthy development of a critical mind charged to analyse and solve problems.

FAMILY INFLUENCES

The development of the child's intelligence has been agreed by various psychologists generally to be a three-fold process, based in the family, the school, and the society. The family has been identified by many psychologists to be the single dominating environmental factor affecting the growth and development of the mental abilities of children. Chan (1972, 1975, 1977, 1979, 1980, 1981) has carried out systematic research into the effects of both physical and psychological aspects of the home environment, focusing particularly on the effects of parent–child and teacher–child interactions (see Andry, 1960; Chan, 1972, 1989) on the development of various psychological attributes of children, including their intellectual and academic performance. For both father and mother, parent–child interaction factors, yielded by principal component analysis followed by varimax rotation, were found to be 'treatment', 'teaching', and 'discipline'. The treatment factor covers two important components, namely, 'concerned' and 'restrictive'; the teaching factor includes 'democratic' and 'demanding'; whereas the discipline factor comprises 'rational' and 'auto-

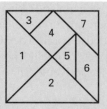

(a) Designed in Song Dynasty (960-1279)

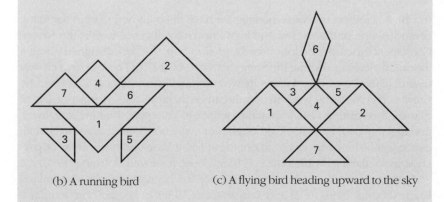

(b) A running bird   (c) A flying bird heading upward to the sky

Figure 7.1 Chinese Seven-Coincidence Board (七巧板)

cratic'. It was empirically found that the home behaviour of parents and children can be described adequately by these three interaction factors, since 'treatment', 'teaching', and 'discipline' in effect deal with all aspects of life: the conative (affective feeling and emotion), cognitive (intellectual knowledge and skills), and behavioural (attitude, interest, motivation, popularity, and personality) domains.

As far as cognitive elements are concerned, the parent–child interaction factors have been noted to have significant relationships with one another. Certain important factors for the enhancement of children's intellectual development were identified as 'father concerned', 'father restrictive', 'mother restrictive', and 'mother autocratic', that is, more concerned and less restrictive fathers and less restrictive but more autocratic mothers were both found to be more effective than their opposites as far as academic performance is concerned. Also, as pointed out by Chan (1972), contrary to a common belief parental 'democratic' teaching appears to be unfavourable to the acquisition of numerical and verbal–numerical skills. Apparently, in Hong Kong an appropriate amount of parental pressure is conducive to the development of certain intellectual abilities in accordance with school requirements.

It is of interest to note that on the whole, parental 'treatment' rather than 'teaching' and 'discipline' seems more influential for a child's intellectual development (Chan, 1972). In other words, emotional relationships such as warmth and closeness between parents and their children are paramount. This may have an important bearing on marriage guidance and family counselling in

Hong Kong and possibly also in mainland China and Taiwan where the family structure and home atmosphere are fundamentally the same. However, more specific research work is needed to confirm details of parental influence on the development of different aspects of intelligence in Hong Kong and China at large, so that appropriate advice and remedial work can be formulated accordingly.

INTELLIGENCE TESTING

In China, attempts to assess intelligence have been known to exist for many centuries; one of the earliest and best-known intelligence tests is the Seven-Coincidence Board (wisdom boards, *gi giao ban*, 七巧板), designed about a thousand years ago during the Song dynasty (960-1279). These boards closely resemble the Form Board items in Western intelligence tests as described by Cronbach (1969). The wisdom boards can be manipulated to form a variety of figures, thus testing visual–spatial perception, divergent thinking, creativity, and ingenuity (cf. Lin, 1980), although they were not devised as formal intelligence tests. The early development of mental testing and other areas of psychology in mainland China since 1910 has been reviewed by Ching (1980).

Systematic work on Chinese intelligence has been carried out in mainland China (Zhang, 1988, 1992) and Taiwan (Hse, 1971). In Hong Kong, standardization of the Raven's Progressive Matrices tests was completed by Chan (1983, 1984). Various American intelligence tests, including the Wechsler Intelligence Scales for Children (WISC) and the Torrance Test of Creative Thinking, have been adapted and used in mainland China, Taiwan, and Singapore (Chan and Vernon, 1988). Creativity, as one aspect of intelligence, has also been targeted in the recent selection of gifted and talented children for 'special' education in Hong Kong (see Dunn, Zhang, and Ripple, 1988). This early identification is believed in a number of Chinese communities to be important for the provision and preparation of future pillars of society.

Chan (1970) constructed and validated the first intelligence test developed in Hong Kong, which consists of three subtests, namely, verbal, numerical, and nonverbal (arranged in repeated cycles), for the use of senior secondary students aged 19 years in counselling, selection, and placement. This pioneering work in Hong Kong is significant in the sense that it was the first attempt to assess Chinese intelligence empirically by employing multiple-choice items in a Western test format. This test has now become a standard instrument for reference by research workers in Hong Kong.

Various types of ability and aptitude tests have been constructed and standardized in Hong Kong by the Educational Research Establishment over the past thirty years. Overseas mental tests which have been adapted for local use include the Raven's Progressive Matrices tests (Coloured, Standard, and Advanced versions for primary, secondary, and tertiary students respectively) and the Wechsler Intelligence Scales for Children (translated and adapted in Hong Kong), which have been found quite useful in identifying learning difficulties among schoolchildren, although results indicate that they may still be culturally biased to some degree. Research evidence is available to substantiate the claim that they largely serve the purpose of testing the intellectual levels of Chinese children in Hong Kong (Chan, 1987). The information obtained from intelligence testing in schools can be properly utilized in teaching, for example, in determining under- and over-achievers and determining possible causes, and can lead to remedial measures, such as assigning a particular curriculum developed by psychologists to suit the child's ability and for the benefit of the child (Chan, 1989, 1992).

As the Raven's tests are simple to administer in groups and to score manually, they are used extensively both for remedial and research purposes (Chan, 1974, 1984, 1995). However, the value of the Raven's scores has been considered to be rather limited because of the nonverbal content of the tests, and hence another group of intelligence tests, the Alice Heim Tests (AH4 and AH5)(Heim, 1970, 1971) has been administered either in their original forms or in translated versions to obtain information concerning the two other dimensions of intelligence, verbal and numerical abilities, which are considered to have greater educational and academic value (Chan, 1970) under local norms. The other intelligence tests commonly employed in clinical situations are the Wechsler Intelligence Scales for Children and the Wechsler Adult Intelligence Scales (WAIS). These, however, are individual tests, time-consuming and requiring special training and skill for their administration and interpretation.

Other overseas intelligence tests used by Hong Kong psychologists in various situations for specific purposes include the Stanford–Binet Intelligence Scale (Form L-M), the Merrill–Palmer Scale of Mental Tests, the Leiter International Performance Test, the Columbia Mental Maturity Scale, the Bayley Scales of Infant Development, the Cattell Infant Intelligence Scale, the Griffiths Mental Development Scale, the Cattell Culture-fair Intelligence Test, and the British Ability Scales. Regrettably, the nature of these tests has not been fully explored from the local perspective. Their value in the Hong Kong context is therefore an open question (Chan, 1976), as they have not been scientifically translated, adapted, and standardized for use by Chinese, they are seen to be Western-oriented and culture-specific, and many of their items are unfamiliar to Chinese subjects.

In recent years, for cross-cultural comparison and other purposes, it has been found necessary to develop intelligence tests that are not dependent on learning effects and cultural influences. Jensen (1980) and Chan, Eysenck, and Lynn (1991) carried out a number of visual reaction-time experiments, and Poon, Yu, and Chan (1986) started work on auditory reaction time experiments in Hong Kong. It has generally been found that brighter children, as assessed by the culture-fair Raven's tests, have shorter reaction times. These methods of measuring intelligence have been shown to provide new channels for achieving accuracy in the estimation of intellectual ability, irrespective of cultural, family, educational, and other intervening variables (Jensen, 1994).

While psychologists have been looking for universality in intelligence (Liu, 1993), indigenous aspects of intelligence, particularly those existing in two such widely contrasting cultures as the Chinese and the Western, cannot be neglected. In any case 'intelligence' seems capable of being divided into various components, emerging as 'factors' when factor analysed (see Vandenberg,

1959; Vernon, 1965). Research suggests that, for example, the reason that engineers score highly on intelligence tests is mainly due to a seemingly specific factor of space-perception (see Chan and Vernon, 1988; Vernon, 1969, 1980). Altogether this brings up the discussion again of general versus specific factors, leading to the identification of various kinds of displayed intelligence (Vernon, 1969). Furthermore, some researchers, Furneaux, for instance (Eysenck, 1982), found that intelligence has at least three main components: speed, accuracy, and persistence.

As early as 1959, Vandenberg found that five congruent factors could be readily identified in his studies of Chinese and American university students: spatial, verbal, numerical, memory, and perceptual speed. He concluded that cultural influences play a role in the process leading to the formation of the abilities underlying some of these factors, but that at least several potentialities exist in the adult neurophysiological organization that are independent of one another and, to some extent, independent of the particular kind of cultural, linguistic, and educational background of the subject tested. In a similar study on South American students, Vandenberg (1967) found high congruence on the factors of native language, verbal, memory, spatial, and perceptual speed, and lower congruence on the factors of numerical and rote memory. Thus, his findings suggest that the same major dimensions of ability operate in two or more cultures, making cross-cultural comparisons legitimate and possible. So, for example, Lesser, Fifer, and Clark (1965) found that Chinese subjects consistently showed higher functioning than did their American counterparts when concepts or abilities involving space, form, or shape were being assessed. The superior performance in space perception would possibly be due to extensive practice in reading and writing Chinese characters (see also Chan, 1976).

SEX DIFFERENCES

In addressing differences between the genders in measures of intelligence, it should be pointed out that the emphasis on patriarchy within the family structure in China, although less pronounced now than in the past, may have had a far-reaching effect. Educational opportunities and the intellectual development of females has been severely constrained, and up to recent times women still played only a minor role in most Chinese communities. A common saying in ancient Chinese culture reads, 'It is a virtue for women not to have talent' (女子無才便是德), implying that intelligence in women may be a handicap. Ignorance and submissiveness were all that was required of a good wife or a good mother. Naturally, this view no longer holds as strongly in modern society, where both sexes contribute to the economy and welfare of the family.

One might ask, however, if test results indicate that girls are less intelligent than boys. Generally, there are no sex differences in the intelligence scores measured by the Raven's Progressive Matrices tests (Chan, 1983, 1986; Zhang and Wang, 1989), although at the ages of 9, 15, and 16 years boys in Hong Kong are found to test more highly than do girls, and for the age group 40–49 years old in mainland China, men have a higher mean score than do women. Generally, it is not necessary to separate the Raven's norms for the two sexes

(Chan, 1989), a conclusion which is in line with the single norms used for both the British and Australian populations.

In Taiwan, Hse (1971) found that boys performed better than did girls on Raven's Coloured Progressive Matrices Test in primary schools, and the sex difference increased significantly from Primary 1 to Primary 3. However, when the Raven's Standard Progressive Matrices test was administered to Secondary 1 students, no sex differences were found. He gave the following explanations for this change. Until Primary 1, boys are superior to girls in their reasoning and concept-formation power, but the girls catch up later; the differences disappear when the subjects reach the age of Secondary 1. This implies that girls are intellectually later developers at the formative years than are boys. In addition, after primary schooling, a greater proportion of boys continue with their secondary education and this group includes the less able ones. A smaller proportion of girls enter secondary school and hence the less bright drop out. Together, such conditions would work to even out the early sex differences found by testing.

Recently, Dai and Lynn (1994) found from WISC results that Chinese boys in mainland China have higher verbal and visual–spatial abilities, whereas girls are superior in memory. They point out that the high level of cross-cultural consistency in such sex differences in the United States, Scotland, and China lends support to the possibility that these differences may have a biological basis.

In Hong Kong, it has been found that boys tend to do better in public examinations in the science subjects of biology, chemistry, physics, and mathematics, whereas girls tend to do better in the arts subjects of Chinese, English, history, and geography (Chan, 1989). Boys tend to excel in the science-related university degree examinations, whereas girls tend to perform better in the arts-related university degree examinations. These findings may well have direct relevance to the genders' respective intellectual abilities or may reflect their corresponding inclination or social role expectations.

Chan (1984, 1986) found that girls in Hong Kong are consistently superior to boys in both Chinese and English language and in reading scores at each of the three age groups from 9 to 11 years, thus confirming many overseas findings (for example, Jensen, 1981, and Vernon, 1982) except those for cultures, including African and Eskimo groups, which show either no difference or boys scoring better on verbal tests. Greater sex differences in favour of girls were found in English (a foreign language) than in Chinese (a mother tongue), showing that girls may learn a foreign language more easily than do boys. This finding may indicate that girls have better intellectual ability than boys in language (see also Chan, 1989; Vernon, 1982).

Furthermore, it was found by Chan (1984, 1986) that sex differences in language abilities became more significant from Primary 1 (aged 6 years) to Primary 4–6 (aged 9–11), and then to Secondary 3 (aged 14), indicating a wider gap as the children grow older, that is, after longer exposure to the educational environment. This finding contrasts with WISC results from mainland China that indicate no tendency for sex differences regarding verbal ability to increase with age, although there was a striking increase in the boys' visual–spatial advantage, starting from age 11, and there was a corresponding increase with age in the girls' advantage on memory (Dai and Lynn, 1994).

Although it is quite clear that certain sex characteristics are determined genetically by the sex chromosomes (XX for females and XY for males), such as physical build and physiological phenomena, it is not certain whether mental and psychological attributes such as intellectual abilities are genetically determined for both sexes. In the absence at present of convincing evidence, sex differences in intelligence, as well as other general and specific abilities, can best be explained in terms of external factors, such as those related to home, school, and society with respect to particular educational and cultural values and practices.

The mental and psychological make-up of a person is the product of interactions among these factors which affect the two sexes differently. Hence, gender differences in academic achievement and ability could be due to external influences and particularly the social factors in Chinese culture which inhibit or facilitate the development of certain aspects of intelligence. They may not reflect the true innate mental faculty of the two sexes. In other words, the external sex differences could be mistakenly taken to be entirely genetic in origin. Given the same environment, cultural emphasis, educational goals, and sex roles, these apparent sex differences would no doubt become less apparent, as is seen in other countries (see Jensen, 1981).

CONCEPTIONS OF INTELLIGENCE

Many methods have been tried to explore people's conceptions of intelligence. For example, Chen, Braithwaite, and Huang (1982) regarded the items on an intelligence test as functioning like different dimensions which characterize the domain of human intelligence. It was believed that by asking a person to rate each item's relevance to the measure of intelligence, it would be possible to find out how closely each item resembles that person's ideal of the concept. They argued that basic perceptual and cognitive skills are dimensions commonly accepted by all people of our intellectual domain and that individual differences may be expressed not in terms of what skills different individuals have but in terms of how much of each skill each person has.

Furthermore, Chen, Braithwaite, and Huang (1982) found that the Stanford–Binet and Wechsler Adult Intelligence Scales provided strong cross-cultural generalizability in the sense that the perceived relevance of the subtests had a similar structure across cultures. Their results showed that Chinese and Australians agreed on the relative importance of intellectual skills, with spatial-mechanical (nonverbal) skill being the most important, language (verbal) the next most important, and memory (retrieval of information) the least important. It is interesting to note that the Chinese regarded items requiring rote memory as being easier than did the Australians. This reflects a common understanding of the effects of the type of education system, styles of parental emphasis, and cultural pressures that Chinese children have undergone in their early formative years since ancient times.

Later, Chen and Chen (1988) studied the conceptions of intelligence of two groups of Chinese university students in Hong Kong with different secondary experience, namely, being taught in the medium of Chinese and English respectively. The students were asked to rate items from intelligence tests in terms of their relevance to measuring intelligence. Analysis of the results revealed two major factors, nonverbal and verbal reasoning skills, and three minor ones, social, numerical, and retrieval skills. Nonverbal reasoning skills were rated equally relevant by the two groups and were considered the most relevant skills to measuring intelligence. This strongly supports the rationale of adopting Raven's Progressive Matrices tests, which are being widely used in Hong Kong, mainland China, and Taiwan. The group educated in Chinese tended to rate verbal reasoning skills to be less relevant than did the group educated in English. These findings were attributed by Chen and Chen (1988) to the mental effort involved in solving each type of task and to the differences in the medium of instruction.

On the other hand, Fang and Keats (1987) studied the effects of social and cultural background on the conception of intelligence. Chinese and Australian subjects were asked to describe the general ability, cognitive ability, and personality of an intelligent child or adult and then to rate the characteristics suggested for each category. Substantial differences between the two groups were found in the prioritizing of characteristics for cognitive ability but not for general ability and personality. This outcome is understandable in view of the differential cognitive emphases inherent in the intellectual requirements of the two cultural systems (see Gow, Balla, Kember, and Hau, this volume; Stevenson and Lee, this volume).

CROSS-CULTURAL COMPARISONS OF INTELLIGENCE

The work of Sternberg and Gardner (1982) is important for pointing out that general intelligence can be understood componentially as deriving in part from the execution of general components in information processing behaviour. Sternberg (1988) acknowledges the considerable difficulty of achieving a measurement of intelligence that is cross-culturally fair. He rightly points out that there are cross-cultural universals, not in the domain of measurement but in the domain of theory, and there is a clear distinction between the measurement of intelligence and the theory that generates that measurement.

It should be specially noted that 'effective intelligence' in different parts of the world may well be different when measured, because this represents the outcome of interaction with different conditions of the measurement situation, cultural environment, education systems, and family upbringing. In view of the large Chinese territory itself and the wide distribution of the Chinese people in different parts of the world, it is not surprising to find differences in levels of specific intelligence factors within the Chinese race. It is also expected that the differences would be as large as, if not larger than, those between races, as demonstrated by Vernon (1980, 1982) in his studies on Chinese samples in Canada and the United States.

It is appropriate here to point out for historical background that Hong Kong, with its indigenous Chinese population much merged since 1949 with emigrants from mainland China, is a unique place where Eastern and Western cultures constantly and actively interact. The territory is very close to China itself and will revert to Chinese sovereignty on 1 July 1997. Hong Kong is increasingly influenced by China both politically and economically; one might expect that it soon will be influenced by philosophical and ideological formulations as well. In view of these impending changes, and the likelihood of consequent changes in curriculum contents, teaching methodology, examination orientation, selection criteria, and society structure, a different emphasis in the territory on intellectual development might be expected. Turning to the case of Taiwan, as communication between mainland China and the island increases, the main concerns in intellectual development through education and training are expected to become more similar between the two regions.

Raven's Progressive Matrices

Chinese intelligence has been empirically studied in Hong Kong, mainland China, Taiwan, Singapore, and the United States. Results for the Chinese peoples have been compared with British, American, and Malaysian subjects using Raven's Progressive Matrices, which is highly weighted on psychometric 'g', the factor common to many tests of intelligence. These tests are generally considered by psychometricians to be culture-fair, though not necessarily culture-free, instruments for research investigations of this kind. It has been consistently and universally found that the Chinese score more highly as a group on these tests, suggesting that they are superior to their Western (and also Malaysian) counterparts in the nonverbal abilities required to solve a diagrammatic type of intellectual items. Statistical evidence is overwhelming in the research work of Vernon in Canada (1965, 1966, 1969, 1979, 1982, and 1983), Eysenck in England (1979, 1980, 1982, 1983), Jensen in the United States (1980, 1981, 1994), Phua in Singapore (1976), and Chan in Hong Kong (1974, 1976, 1989).

The norms of Raven's Standard Progressive Matrices Test for groups aged between 5.5 and 15.5 years were established in Hong Kong by Chan (1989) in 1968, 1977, 1980, and 1982, using representative samples of kindergarten, primary, and secondary pupils. When the norm values for Hong Kong are compared with those of the British (established in 1960) and Australia (established in 1958), the Hong Kong norms are consistently higher than those of the other two groups. Chan and Lynn (1989) studied representative samples of 6-year-old Chinese pupils in 1981, 1983, and 1984, respectively, and established their Raven's Coloured Progressive Matrices Test norms, which again are much higher than the British norm (Raven and Raven, 1989). As regards the Raven's Advanced Progressive Matrices Test, research results in Hong Kong have been analysed by Li (1986) and compared with overseas values. It was found that Chinese performed better than did the British and New Zealanders at the same age. Clearly, the Chinese in Hong Kong are found superior to their counterparts in Western countries in all the Raven's Progressive Matrices tests.

Chan (1986) found that the Chinese students in Hong Kong are superior in their Raven's Standard Progressive Matrices test scores to their Western counterparts in Hong Kong. Attempts have been made by Chan (1972) to account for the differences. It has been postulated that the way Chinese scan diagrams may have helped them to arrive at the correct answers more easily, and the high motivation of the Chinese in doing the test would undoubtedly drive them to score higher. Chen (1981) studied the direction scanning of visual displays among the Chinese; this skill, based on the Chinese experience with ideographs, certainly has an important bearing on how the Chinese adapt to analysing the Raven's items.

Phua (1976) found that Chinese pupils in Singapore aged 14 years old scored better than did Malaysians in the Raven's Standard Progressive Matrices Test. The means for the two groups were found to be 47.8 and 41.9 in favour of the Chinese. This difference was attributed by Phua to higher motivation for school learning among the Chinese.

Evidence has accumulated to suggest that the mean IQ of Asians in the United States and in the countries of the Pacific Basin are higher than those of Caucasians in Britain and the United States. Lynn, Pagliari, and Chan (1988) found that the mean IQ of age groups in Hong Kong from 6.5 to 13.5 years old is approximately 108 in relation to a mean of 100 for Caucasians in Britain and the United States. Chan and Lynn (1989) found that 6-year-old Chinese children in Hong Kong obtained a mean IQ of 116 on the Raven's Coloured Progressive Matrices Test as compared to a range of 95–102 among natives of the countries of Australia, Czechoslovakia, Germany, Romania, Britain, and the United States. Lynn (1991) reported that studies of the intelligence of Asians in Japan, Hong Kong, Taiwan, Singapore, and the United States have shown slightly higher mean IQs than those of Britain and the United States. In 1989, results became available from a standardization of Raven's Standard Progressive Matrices test for a sample of 5,108 individuals in mainland China (Zhang and Whang, 1989). These results indicate that Chinese aged 6 to 15 years old obtain a mean IQ of 102.1 in relation to the American standard of 100.

On the other hand, Chan, Eysenck, and Lynn (1991) and Lynn, Chan, and Eysenck (1991), in studies of reaction times and intelligence in Chinese and British children reported that Hong Kong children had a higher IQ and faster reaction times than did British children. They suggested that the difference in mean IQ scores between Hong Kong and British children has a neurological basis. More recently, Jensen and Whang (1993, 1994) reported a difference of 5 IQ points in favour of Chinese-Americans, when the Raven's Standard Progressive Matrices Test was administered to 584 Anglo-American children and 167 Chinese-American children all aged about 11 years. Once again it was confirmed that Asians scored significantly higher than Caucasians on the Raven's Standard Progressive Matrices Test. All these empirical results show that the Chinese are superior in measurement by the Raven's tests to their counterparts in the West. Results to the contrary have not yet been reported.

Cattell Scores

Similar intelligence test results in favour of the Chinese were also reported in Taiwan. Rodd (1959) gave a battery of tests, including Cattell's Culture-fair Intelligence Test, to native Taiwanese and mainland Chinese students in

Taiwan, and found that the 16-year-old group obtained mean IQs of 104 (for Taiwanese) and 106 (for Chinese) and the 15-year-old group averaged 114 and 117, respectively. The British and American mean is 100.

Primary Mental Abilities Scores

Lynn, Pagliari, and Chan (1988) gave both Western and Chinese samples in Hong Kong the space relations and perceptual speed scales from the Primary Mental Abilities (PMA) Test; the subjects were also asked to write down the names of as many animals as they could think of in two minutes. Values for spatial and perceptual speed were found to be substantially higher in the Chinese sample. Chinese children, however, were found to be relatively weak on word fluency. The pattern of abilities of Hong Kong Chinese children is broadly similar to that obtained from other Asian populations (see also Lesser, Fifer, and Clark, 1965).

Creativity Scores

Ripple (1989) studied divergent thinking abilities and found that Westerners scored higher in fluency (that is, the greater production of ideas per unit time) than did Hong Kong Chinese. Dunn, Zhang, and Ripple (1988) studied the performance of Chinese and American subjects on creativity tests and found that the Chinese subjects performed better in convergent recognition tasks, whereas the American subjects were more successful in divergent tasks, such as 'fluency' and 'flexibility'.

Possible reasons for lower fluency scores among Chinese samples include the presence among the Chinese children of 'respect for seniors', as proposed by Liu, (1986) and 'family discipline', as pointed out by Bond (1991). In other words, it appears that parent–child interaction plays a significant part in shaping the ways children are trained to think, as reported by Chan (1972).

Mathematics, Aesthetics, and Perception Scores

On the basis of a cross-cultural study by Stigler, Lee, Lucker, and Stevenson (1982) of mathematics performance in Japan, Taiwan, and the United States, Stevenson, Lee, and Stigler (1986), and Stevenson, Chen, and Lee (1993) discovered that American elementary school students in 1990 lagged behind their Chinese and Japanese peers to as great a degree as they had ten years before. Stevenson, Stigler, Lee, Lucker, Kitamura, and Hsu (1985) found similarities in the level, variability, and structure of cognitive abilities among the three cultures, Japanese, Chinese, and American. However, Chinese children were found to surpass Japanese and American children in reading scores, and both Chinese and Japanese children obtained higher scores in mathematics than did the American children. The researchers suggested that the high achievement of Chinese and Japanese children could not be attributed to higher intellectual abilities, but must be related to their experience at home and at school (see Stevenson and Lee, this volume).

Chan, Eysenck, and Gotz (1980) studied aesthetic tastes and talents among Hong Kong, English, and Japanese samples; their results suggested considerable similarity between the three groups. Gordon, Zukas, and Chan (1982) conducted a cross-cultural study on the perception of schematic faces as a form of visual or nonverbal evaluation and also found similar responses in Hong Kong, British, and Zambian samples of students.

SUMMING UP

While the superior performance of Chinese samples in the Raven's Progressive Matrices tests has been explained to be genetic in nature by psychologists in the field, such as Eysenck, Jensen, and Lynn, influences of the environment and upbringing cannot be entirely ruled out. It has been suggested that learning of the pictorial Chinese language characters may have a profound effect on the development of Chinese intelligence, particularly on nonverbal tests such as the Raven's (Chan, 1972). On the question of why Chinese-Americans also excel in Raven's tests, one likely supposition is that Chinese families in the United States have maintained at home their Chinese traditions, family values, and expectations of upbringing, even though their children are no longer required to master Chinese pictographs.

Chan and Vernon (1988) summarized the individual differences among the peoples of China and concluded that the superior educational, and especially nonverbal and mathematical, achievements of overseas Chinese is not readily explained by genetic theories. It is, however, conceivable that a biological factor underlies the consistent capacity of Chinese to score more highly on visual–spatial and mathematics tests, and in the visual arts, than on verbal tests. Therefore, it seems that, apart from possible temperamental differences, the most likely explanation of Chinese achievement must surely lie in values. Focus is given to the traditional Chinese emphasis on academic excellence and on child-rearing practices that include a vigorous parental promotion of academic pursuit in their children (see also Leung, Lau, and Lam, 1995).

FUTURE DIRECTIONS FOR RESEARCH

In view of the long tradition, cultural background, and heritage of the Chinese people, as well as their wide dispersal throughout the world, more research work at individual, national, and international levels should now be launched to study the specific aspects of Chinese intelligence. More indigenous intelligence tests, taking into account what the Chinese consider to be intelligent behaviour, need to be specially constructed and validated for use by particular groups of Chinese people.

Intelligence testing has grown increasingly important, expanding in scope to meet the demands of guidance and counselling professionals in educational and clinical settings, and selection and placement activities in personnel management and industrial settings in the private sector, particularly in response to the recent economic boom in China. As a large market for these tests can be expected to develop, in view of the recent opening up of mainland China and the expanding need for skilled human resources in the region, more psychologists should be trained for this important task.

Resources within the People's Republic of China should be pooled to establish a National Central Psychological Testing Bureau in mainland China or elsewhere, where test production and distribution and the control of test users can be supervised. The proposed bureau could work closely with various psychological societies comprised largely of Chinese psychologists, for example, the Chinese Psychological Society in Beijing, the Shaanxi Psychological Society in Xi'an, the Chinese Psychological Association in Taipei, the Hong Kong Psychological Society, and the Singapore Psychological Society, as well as the Chinese Academy of Sciences in Beijing. It is expected that such a joint venture promoting common efforts would contribute significantly to the understanding of the nature of Chinese intelligence.

Chinese intelligence, as measured by Western-style tests and items, may not fully reflect the mental faculties of the Chinese people, who have different cultural values and systems. It appears that these differences have encouraged the development of certain specific areas of reasoning and thinking abilities (Chan, 1991). On the frontiers of research, the construction and validation of indigenous intelligence tests are essential for the better understanding of the Chinese ways of conceptualization, as well as approaches to solving problems.

Bearing in mind that Chinese score lower in cross-cultural comparisons on creativity (particularly fluency) and on verbal items, instead of merely suggesting genetic or environmental reasons for consistently better results among Chinese samples, intensive effort is needed to identify the specific factors which account for their higher scores on most Western intelligence tests. In addition, in view of conflicting results found in different contexts, sex differences in measurements of overall intelligence and related abilities need to be further investigated in order to confirm the areas of superiority, if any, of one sex over the other. Perhaps in addition to representative sample studies, it is worthwhile to use more factor or component analysis, step-wise multiple regression analysis, and multivariate covariance analysis models to control the independent variables by statistical methods. The relative importance of the various possible factors contributing to cultural and sex differences in intelligence among the Chinese can then be identified, thus helping to explain the phenomenon found in so many separate studies throughout the world that favours Chinese intelligence.

Chapter 8

The Learning Approaches of Chinese People: A Function of Socialization Processes and the Context of Learning?

Lyn Gow, John Balla, David Kember, and Kit Tai Hau

There is ample anecdotal evidence which paints a stereotypical picture of the passive Chinese student relying heavily on rote learning and having a non-critical and non-analytical approach to the information learnt. Such attitudes and characteristics are not consistent with a self-managed style of learning. However, seemingly contradictory evidence indicates that Asian students are 'very good' (see Stevenson, this volume), a phrase typically used to mean that they are achievement-oriented and academically successful. When enrolled in courses overseas, they often perform particularly well compared to local students.

In this chapter, we challenge the stereotype that Chinese students have a marked predilection towards reproductive learning approaches and suggest that, as elsewhere, approaches to learning tasks are more a function of the learning environment than of inherent characteristics. We provide evidence from cross-sectional and longitudinal studies of Chinese people using both quantitative and qualitative analytic techniques. Case studies of Chinese people are documented and discussed. We draw the conclusion that the Chinese approach to learning is contextually bound and intrinsically related to achievement motivation. The case is argued that the Chinese tendency to use rote-learning approaches is a function of socialization processes and the learning context.

The chapter begins with a brief description of approaches to learning, followed by a discussion of various sociocultural influences and contextual factors that may affect Chinese students in the ways they learn. Some of the elements addressed are a tendency to cultivate a strong achieving approach (for example, in the Chinese attitude towards education, and in teachers' emphasis on academic performance) and issues that may induce students to memorize (such as authoritarian parents and teachers and the student's inadequacy in the language of instruction). This description is followed by a review of the results from collaborative projects and longitudinal studies, as well as those from related research on Chinese students' approaches to learning. It is argued that many of the contradictory anecdotes on the learning approaches of Asian students result from a confusion between observations of memorizing with understanding and of memorizing for the reproducing of information. There is also marked evidence that students adopt superficial approaches in response to their perceptions of the requirements of the learning environment (for example, assessment), and yet that they are capable of adopting a deep approach if that is what the curriculum appears to warrant.

APPROACHES TO LEARNING

The study of student approaches to learning stems primarily from the work of Biggs (1979), Entwistle and Ramsden (1983), Marton and Saljo (1976), and Pask (1976). Three types of approaches, surface, deep, and achieving, have generally been used.

Types of Approaches

The surface approach to learning is based on extrinsic motivation: the student sees learning as a means towards some end, such as obtaining a better job or simply keeping out of trouble. In such cases, the student needs to balance avoiding failure against working too hard. The strategy employed is to limit one's attention to essentials, reproducible through rote learning. The student focuses on concrete and literal aspects in the learning task, such as the actual words used, rather than on their wider meaning. The components of the task are thus seen as unrelated to each other or to other tasks. Affectively, the student avoids personal meanings the task might have, tends to resent the time taken by the task, but worries about failing.

The deep approach to learning is based on an interest in the subject matter addressed by the task and aims to maximize understanding so that curiosity is satisfied. The student is personally involved and focuses on underlying meaning or meanings rather than on the literal aspects of the subject. The task's components are integrated with each other. The student adopting a deep approach reads widely, discusses with others, theorizes about the subject, and relates what is learned to other areas of interest and other applications. Affectively, the student feels challenged and engaged.

The achieving approach to learning is based on a particular form of extrinsic motive: the ego-enhancement that comes out of visibly achieving, indicated particularly through receipt of high grades for the work. The related strategies refer to organizing time, working space, and syllabus coverage in the most efficient way. A student is competitive about obtaining high grades, sees it as important to be self-disciplined, neat, and systematic, and plans ahead, allocating time to tasks in proportion to their 'importance'. Affectively, the student is motivated by the feelings of satisfaction that come from success in studies and from his or her potential for future achievement.

It is believed that a predominantly surface approach is generally incompatible with the aims of education, particularly in higher education, whereas a predominantly deep approach seems to be consistent with the general goals of higher education (see, for example, Baird, 1988). More recently, it has been hypothesized that more successful students will tend to switch strategically among approaches according to the requirements of the task at hand. We argue that the appropriate matching of study approach to task demand is more critical for success in higher education than is the unilateral adoption of a particular approach. This is an area requiring additional research.

In the measurement of students' approaches, two questionnaires have been developed relatively independently: the Study Process Questionnaire (SPQ), with the Learning Process Questionnaire (LPQ), its shorter version for school students, developed by Biggs (1987); and the Approaches to Study Inventory (ASI), developed by Entwistle and Ramsden (1983). For the former, norms are available for Australia (Biggs, 1987) and Hong Kong (Biggs, 1992). The internal structure of the SPQ has been examined (Balla, Stokes, and Stafford, 1991; Kember and Gow, 1991; Watkins, Hattie, and Astilla, 1986) and its applications to Chinese students have been found generally satisfactory (for example, Balla, Stokes and Stafford, 1991, 1992).

The SPQ, the LPQ, and the ASI all have scales for deep and surface approaches to learning. The SPQ and LPQ have been used extensively in the Asian region since their author moved to Hong Kong and arranged for their translation into Chinese. Now that its cultural relevance has been established and norms compiled, this pair is likely to remain the preferred option for the region. However, there has been some use of the ASI in Asia, and its wider range of additional scales has proven useful in the discovery that memorization and understanding can occur together (Kember and Gow, 1990; 1991), a topic which is discussed later in this chapter.

Influential Factors on Students' Approaches

The approach adopted by students depends on both the sociocultural setting as well as the school milieu. Students' approaches reflect not only their own attitudes, habits, abilities, and personality, but also the demands made by the learning environment (Biggs, 1987; Chow, Gow, and Kember, 1989; Gow and Kember, 1990; Kember and Gow, 1989). Each student normally has a preference for a particular approach to learning but will modify or abandon that approach if, in his or her judgement, an alternative approach is more suited to the learning context. Course syllabi, teaching, and assessment all place constraints on the student and affect the approach to learning taken, depending on how the student views the demands of the course.

Students are more likely to adopt a surface approach to learning if they perceive that there is an excessive amount of material to be learnt, a lack of choice over content and methods of study, and that the assessment system requires the reiteration of information. On the other hand, students are more likely to develop a deep approach if they are given time for contemplation and discussion with other learners, and if their examinations probe for the understanding of principles rather than the reproduction of facts and procedures (Biggs, 1987).

CULTIVATING A HIGH ACHIEVEMENT MOTIVE AND STRATEGY FOR LEARNING

Traditional Chinese cultural values relating to education have influenced parent, student, and teacher goals and approaches in ways which seem to cultivate a high achievement motive and strategies for learning.

The Chinese Attitude Towards Education

Education has a high status among traditional Chinese values; children are taught that all jobs are low in status, except study, which is the highest (*wan ban jia xia pin, wei you dushu gao*). Education is believed to be important not so much as a ladder up the social hierarchy, but as training towards the better development of the whole person (Ho, 1981; Mordkowitz and Ginsburg, 1987).

The importance of education among Chinese is also reflected in empirical cross-cultural studies examining student and parent attitudes, whether demonstrated at home or overseas. It was found that Chinese children at all grades liked school in general more than did their Western counterparts (Chen, 1989; Sui, 1992). When asked to list their wishes, Chinese children mentioned education-related items (such as books, stationery, grades, future educational aspirations, and knowledge), where American children mentioned a more diverse range (money, toys, pets, and fantasy items, for example). As reflected in their wishes, the Chinese children perceived education as their most pressing task. Chen concluded that Chinese children had incorporated traditional beliefs on the value of education. Further, Ghuman and Wong (1989), interviewing 34 Chinese families in Manchester, in the United Kingdom, found that the parents valued education highly, would like more homework for their children, and preferred a stricter regime in the schools.

In Mordkowitz and Ginsburg's (1987) interviews with 15 Asian-American students (of Chinese, Japanese, and Korean descent), they found a reciprocity between the parents' love and the children's hard work in school. The parents showed their love by providing the best possible opportunities for learning, while the children tried to return love by doing their best in school. The children's academic striving was driven by the recognition of the sacrifices made by their parents.

The strong emphasis on education makes Chinese students believe that academic study is a central and important task to be accomplished. They work hard and generally attribute their academic performance more to their effort than to ability (Hau and Salili, 1990, 1991). They learn as much as they can in school so as to fulfil their duties towards their parents. Thus, Chinese students' strong achievement orientation partly reflects the value of education in the culture.

Teachers' Emphasis on Academic Performance

The function of education in selecting for future occupations has a great influence on the teaching practices seen in Hong Kong. As pointed out by Morris (1983):

> The role of education as the primary source of social mobility and socio-economic status contributes to an instrumentalism which is manifested in the perceived importance and influence of public examinations and in a pedagogic style which functions primarily to provide pupils with the information necessary to pass the relevant examinations (p. 81).

Consequently, Hong Kong teachers have an appropriately high concern for the academic performance of their students. In Morris' (1983) study, teachers were given the names of three of their pupils and were asked to put together two students who were in some respect the most alike. He found that Hong Kong teachers most often used the criteria stupid–intelligent (50 per cent of matches), lazy–hardworking (13 per cent), and unresponsive–responsive (12 per cent). This was in marked contrast with teachers in the United Kingdom, who used constructs related to a pupil's personality, work habits, and classroom behaviour. Morris concluded that Hong Kong teachers classified and judged their pupils predominantly in terms of their academic performance.

While it is difficult to make a direct comparison of the strictness and use of approval between Chinese and Western teachers, Chinese parents and teachers are usually strict in their demands. They set high standards of excellence, irrespective of the students' actual ability level. As it is difficult for the children to meet such high standards, they seldom earn praise for their performance. In a comparative study between Chinese students in Taiwan and American children in the United States, McDaniel and Soong (1981) found that Chinese students were more fearful of tests and were less confident in their school skills than were the American children. However, all the Chinese students rejected the idea that they hated school, whereas a comparatively larger number of American children accepted such a notion.

The teachers' emphasis on academic achievement, it seems, would produce a stronger achievement approach among students. However, whether students are so conscious of their achievement that they become surface-oriented in their learning is a supposition yet to be examined.

The Goals of Teachers

The teaching style and perceived goals in education of the instructor are also influential in shaping a student's approach to learning. Gow, Kember, and Sivan (1992) conducted semi-structured interviews with 39 members of the lecturing staff at a polytechnic in Hong Kong. They found a mismatch between the lecturers' own perceived goals in higher education and their actual teaching practices in class. Lecturers believed that higher education should encourage problem-solving and independent learning. However, when it came to the main goal of their course, preparation for a specific profession and training in specific job-related skills stood out as the primary, and at times the only, goals.

From this study, Gow and Kember (1993) developed a questionnaire of 46 items, which identified two orientations towards teaching: knowledge transmission and learning facilitation. The orientations are composed of five and four scales, respectively. Through both intuitive thinking and by examining models of teaching and learning, they developed the hypothesis that of the two orientations the teachers' learning facilitation orientation would be more likely to produce desirable learning outcomes in students. The knowledge transmission orientation appears to assume that what is transmitted is received as sent, an assumption which current teaching models are said to reject. The student seems to be neglected in the information transmission process, being regarded as a passive receiver.

This hypothesis was examined with academic staff and students from a total of 15 departments in two polytechnics in Hong Kong (Kember and Gow, 1994). It was found that the lecturers' knowledge transmission orientation correlated negatively with a change in the students' deep learning approaches. That is, in departments that emphasized high knowledge transmission (for example, stress on the imparting of information, or tests of knowledge of a subject), the students' deep approach to learning was discouraged and would drop in prominence as students progressed in their studies. On the other hand, departments with a propensity towards learning facilitation (for example, giving the emphasis to problem-solving and interactive teaching) tended to promote the use of the achieving approach and to discourage the adoption of a surface approach by their students.

Although tertiary-level teachers generally believe that the cultivation of deep and achieving motives and strategies are important, the actual teaching practices used in the classroom do not always reflect such a perspective. Thus, the extent and direction of influence from such factors on students' approaches to learning may vary from teacher to teacher and from subject to subject.

INFLUENCES ON LEARNING APPROACHES

Many factors potentially influence the approach adopted by Chinese people when they are involved in learning. We will discuss three that have emerged from our analysis of the literature: Chinese child-rearing practices, a pyramidal education system, and the language of instruction.

Chinese Child-rearing Practices

One distinctive feature of the patrilineal-descent family system in Chinese culture has been the centrality of the relationship between parents and their children, rather than that between the husband and wife. Filial piety (*xiao*) and submission to one's parents or elders are strongly emphasized (see Ho, this volume). Children are instructed to be obedient to their elders, irrespective of whether the demands or requests at times seem unreasonable. Foolish filial piety (*yu xiao*—acts to fulfil one's duties in filial piety but considered to be foolish or stupid by others (for example, sacrificing one's life for parents)—is a virtue said to be admired and followed. Thus, it could be expected that Chinese students would take their teachers' words as golden principles which could not be challenged. It would also be understandable, therefore, that teachers would be respected by Chinese students as authority figures second only to their parents (Siu, 1992).

The space in this chapter does not permit a detailed account of Chinese child-rearing practices (see Wu, this volume). Ho (1989), however, has identified two important characteristics of it in his review of socialization in contemporary China, namely, authoritarian moralism (versus a democratic–psychological orientation) and collectivism (versus individualism). The former characteristic stresses impulse control (rather than expression), whereas the latter involves interdependence (rather than autonomy) and conformism (rather than unique individuation). Ho and Yu (1974) have also shown that authoritarianism and filial piety, although they may appear to be distinct constructs, are in actuality positively related.

The demands and expectations of Chinese parents are high. In a study that compared child-rearing practices among Chinese living in Taiwan, Chinese-Americans who had emigrated from Taiwan, and Anglo-American parents, Chiu (1987) found that Chinese parents tended to have higher ratings than did American parents on parental control and emphasis on achievement. Chinese mothers were found to be more restrictive and controlling than were Chinese-American or Anglo-American mothers.

Chinese parents are also harsh with their children, particularly when they feel that the child is old enough to be responsible for his or her own behaviour (Ho, 1981, 1989). Nevertheless, Chinese children are given independence at an age comparatively older than children in the West. Feldman and Rosenthal (1991) asked students in grades 10 and 11 from Hong Kong, Australia, and the United States to complete questionnaires that asked the age at which they expected to achieve behavioural autonomy. In general, they found that Chinese youths in Hong Kong had later expectations for autonomy, and placed a lower value on individualism, outward success, and individual competence. However, Chinese students placed a higher value on traditional, pro-social, and well-socialized outcomes.

The strong emphasis on filial piety and obedience to authority, together with strict demands from parents and teachers, make Chinese students receptive towards education. Students do not challenge the teachers' authoritative role. This assertion was confirmed in a longitudinal study of a cohort of tertiary-level students across six courses of study (see Balla, Stokes, and Stafford, 1991). It was observed that responses to an item grouping alternatively labelled to submission to authority or 'maintaining face' remained stable throughout the course of study, even though curriculum objectives clearly expected students to become less submissive during the course of their studies. In such a learning process, students tend to seek constant approval and confirmation from their teachers, paying particular attention to what should be reproduced (Houghton, 1991) thus reducing opportunities to lose face.

The Pyramidal Education System

Success in education has traditionally been used in Chinese society as a means of selection for further educational and career opportunities. The pyramidal education systems existing today in Hong Kong, Taiwan, and Singapore, which provide a context in which students, parents, and teachers are continually focused on progression with fewer and fewer students achieving the next higher level, can be seen as quite consistent with traditional Chinese culture and values.

Historically, only a small proportion of students progressed to the top of the pyramid (in this case, tertiary study). As recently as 1981, for example, 5 per cent of the relevant age cohort in Hong Kong could hope to enter a tertiary institution. Changes in government priorities have resulted in these percentages increasing dramatically in Hong Kong, Singapore, and Taiwan. Roberts (1992) reported that in 1991, 18 per cent of the 17–20-year-old age group in

Hong Kong could enter tertiary institutions (diploma, high diploma, and other first-degree courses), and the Hong Kong Government plans to increase the number of first-year, first-degree places to about 15,000 in 1995, approximately 18 per cent of the relevant age group. While the proportion of tertiary places is growing rapidly (with a perception of reduced competition for places), the competition among students for entrance to the more preferred courses of study or more preferred universities will most likely remain.

Parallel to a pyramidal education system is an examination approach which has resulted in a great number of public examinations. In the past, a scarcity of places in higher education in Hong Kong, with a great disparity in quality among schools of the same level, has meant that a person's examination results have been paramount in determining which future options are open to them. Commonly, a student in Hong Kong may go through as many as eight sets of competitive examinations in his or her school years. The examinations measure readiness to enter schools at various educational levels, namely, kindergarten, G.1, G.6, G.9, G.11, the Chinese University of Hong Kong (G.12), the University of Hong Kong (G.13), and overseas universities (these tests are, for example, the General Certificate Examination, the Test of English as a Foreign Language, or the Scholastic Aptitude Test). In addition to the above-mentioned public or competitive examinations, most schools have full-scale examinations at least twice a year, and formal or informal tests at regular intervals (monthly or even weekly).

In Hong Kong, the pressure for success in examinations is so great that some educators are concerned about the detrimental effects of examinations on students' social development. Education in Hong Kong has been described as predominantly a highly utilitarian means to economic and vocational ends. Academic success is so strongly emphasized that the cost is at times seen in less personal development and a lower sense of personal fulfilment for most Hong Kong students (Llewellyn, Hancock, Kirst, and Roeloffs, 1982). In recent years, due to the increase in the amount of resources allocated to education, the competition for subsidized places has been very much alleviated. Examinations originally used for sieving students to subsidized places have lost their function. Moreover, public and competitive written examinations are now replaced by internal school assessment (for example, at G.9) and informal interviews (for example, for entry into G.1). All these measures represent attempts to reduce the possible detrimental effects that public examinations may have on students.

Nevertheless, success in examinations and general academic success can be seen as widely accepted acts of aggregation (that is, acts that contribute to the rite of passage or movement from one status to another; see Gow and Balla, 1994). In this case, general academic success results in the movement of the child to the achievement of a new status exemplified by a successful career. One crucial element of an act of aggregation is that it be commonly accepted and celebrated by the student, teacher, and parents. This seems to be the case in Chinese culture, where progress in education is highly valued. Thus, students, as well as their parents, remain very concerned with their performance in all examinations, particularly those involving public competition.

In view of the keen competition for better education opportunities, and the significance of public examinations, students adopt an approach to study which increases their chances of success. It seems that Chinese students have found that rote memorization of facts prior to examinations has been quite successful. This is not to say that they do not have an underlying understanding as well. That understanding may be well developed but stored in the medium of their first language. Unfortunately, this thesis is difficult to test in Hong Kong, where assessment requirements of the majority of courses offered at the tertiary level still require English language (see Balla, 1991, 1992).

Language of Instruction: An Impediment to Understanding?

In most elementary schools in Hong Kong, students learn English as a second language. There is an abrupt switch, however, at the secondary level, where most schools use English as the medium of instruction for all subjects except Chinese. The problem arises that the majority of students do not have sufficient competence in English to learn the subjects' content through this second language. Although English is used quite widely in the commercial sector, particularly for document preparation, the language is seldom used at home or in social life. A recent study of tertiary students using a diary methodology clearly demonstrated that students used English predominantly within the context of education (Pennington, Balla, and Detarami, 1992). The use of English is so restricted in Hong Kong that it may be characterized as an auxiliary, rather than a second, language (Luke and Richards, 1981).

Richards, Tung, and Ng (1992) reported that only 5 per cent of secondary school teachers believe that teachers should never use Cantonese in English classes. The majority of these teachers agreed that Cantonese could be used to explain difficult terms. Thus, in actuality, teachers choose to switch back and forth between English and Chinese during lessons, particularly when explaining new and abstract concepts (Johnson, 1983; Richards, Tung, and Ng, 1992). Such 'code switching' has been criticized as one of the main causes leading to the decline in English standards (Richards, Tung, and Ng, 1992). At the tertiary level, English is used more frequently because it is the official language of instruction, English reference materials are more easily accessible, the specific technical terms (particularly in subjects such as science or engineering) do not have Chinese equivalents, or the instructors do not speak Chinese.

Nevertheless, the degree of the use of English by instructors varies considerably, as is evidenced by a study undertaken at the City Polytechnic of Hong Kong (Balla, 1992). A certain degree of code switching in teaching has been reported (for example, Gow, Kember, and Chow, 1991), and students employ a range of coping mechanisms including glossing, translations, and peer support (Walters and Balla, 1992).

In the 1981 review of the Hong Kong education system, overseas consultants commented that language instruction tended to 'crowd out' other curricula, and that the time devoted to language was much greater than in countries which were officially monolingual (Llewellyn, Hancock, Kirst, and Roeloffs, 1982). The experts argued that, due to a lack of competence in English, the students' mode of learning was seriously hampered as well. They explained that, as most students were unable to master English at the level of proficiency required for intricate thinking, they could only revert to rote memorization. Cooper (1980) wrote in criticism, 'The child is reduced to memorization by rote, both of what is said in class, and what is written in books' (pp. 40–1).

It is understandable that if students have only a few words at their command to express their thoughts, at best they can only regurgitate verbatim either from notes taken during lessons or language found in textbooks (Llewellyn, Hancock, Kirst, and Roeloffs, 1982). Such learning through a second language may affect students' learning strategies or approaches to learning. A student who is struggling to understand the language is more likely to try to remember small sections which have been deciphered, rather than to seek a global understanding of assigned readings. Similarly, in writing tasks, a student who is weak in that language is more likely to rely on verbatim reproduction than on original expression. Students weaker in English will adopt a range of coping mechanisms, including concentration on deciphering the rhetorical aspects of text, and thus are less likely to conceptualize the underlying meaning.

Such a relationship between students' ability in English and their approaches to learning was confirmed in Gow, Kember, and Chow's 1991 study with tertiary students. It was found that those with low ability in English were more likely to adopt a surface strategy in their learning, whereas deep motivation was related to high English ability. English-language ability (where English is an auxiliary language) can perhaps be seen as a prerequisite to employ a deep approach, if the course is in the English language. Students with limited English-language ability may find it difficult to progress beyond a surface strategy. On the other hand, students with a sufficient command of English to employ a deep approach may not do so if they have not learnt an appropriate orientation or have been discouraged to do so by the learning environment.

If students' approaches are impaired by their inadequate English, it is logical to expect a shift in their approach as the language of instruction changes when they go to secondary school. This result was in fact observed in Biggs' (1991) study with Primary 6 (Chinese teaching) and Secondary 1 (mixed medium) students in Hong Kong. For the top 20 per cent of students with better English, their approaches did not change in the transition. However, for the other students, there was a moving towards surface approaches, which was described as a development of learning pathology (Biggs, 1991).

Related studies in other Asian countries have revealed similar trends. In Watkins, Biggs, and Regmi's (1991) studies with Hong Kong and Nepalese university students, it was found that students' lower confidence in English was associated with more surface and less deep approaches. The less confident students in both countries relied more on rote learning without trying to understand the material. In another study with younger (age 14 to 16 years) Filipino and Nepalese students, Watkins, Regmi, and Astilla (1991) found that the academically more successful students had deeper and stronger achievement approaches. However, little evidence was found that these students were more prone to rote learning than were Australians in the same age group.

EMPIRICAL FINDINGS

The general belief that Chinese students have a strong achievement approach to learning was confirmed, for example, in Kember and Gow's 1991 study comparing students from Hong Kong and Australia. They reported that Hong Kong students register higher in an achieving approach than do Australian students, suggesting that Hong Kong students are keener and more competitive. In another study with high school students in Singapore (Chang, 1989), it was also found that an achieving approach ranked top for most of the four subjects (English, Chinese, mathematics, and science) across different educational levels.

Evidence also indicates that the higher education system in Hong Kong has not succeeded in promoting the deep and achieving approaches which are necessary building blocks for independent thinking. In a series of cross-sectional and longitudinal studies with polytechnic students in Hong Kong (Balla, Stokes, and Stafford, 1991; Gow and Kember, 1990; Gow, Kember, and Cooper, 1994), it was found that deep motivation, achieving strategy (manifested in good study skills), enthusiasm, interest in study, and competitive drive all declined from the first to the final year, accompanied by a narrowing of the focus of study over the three-year period. Increasingly, students restricted their studies to what was specifically set out in the curriculum, as they thought it was unnecessary to demonstrate any additional learning. This outcome might be seen as a response to perceived course demands. Garner (1990) poses a convincing argument that, if primitive routines are seen to get the job done, it is unnecessary to continue more acceptable and yet more time-consuming study patterns.

The trends in primary and secondary education are less obvious and consistent. In a study with students in grades 7, 10, and 12, Biggs (1989) found that G.7 students were less rote-oriented than were the others. Sex-related differences showed that girls had a tendency to increase in the use of a surface approach from G.7 to G.12, whereas boys had the highest surface approach at G.10, and gradually returned to the G.7 level by G.12. No clear trend could be identified for the deep approach scores. Concerning the achieving motive, a steady increase throughout secondary school was found in both sexes.

Students became more surface-oriented upon going to secondary school. Biggs (1990) found that students' surface motive and strategy scores increased from primary to secondary school, in both sexes and in both government and English Foundation schools (staffed largely by expatriates and offering a British curriculum to competent English speakers). The change appeared to be greater in the government sector, where the medium of instruction changes from mainly Chinese to predominantly English after primary school. There is no language change in the English Foundation schools; the changes registered in learning styles were less pronounced.

Thus, at the present stage, it cannot be argued that the decline in deep approach is unique to Chinese students or to tertiary education in Hong Kong. Findings of similar trends have been reported in other cultures (for example, Australian students in Biggs, 1987). These results may be seen as a symptom of widespread weaknesses in tertiary education across the globe.

Given the influence of contextual factors, in particular the use of a second language as the medium of instruction and in general the teaching styles employed, one may expect that Chinese students with an inadequate grasp of language would focus on specific words and reproduce them when tested. The students would measure higher in a surface approach and lower in a deep approach as compared with students in other countries. Surprisingly, this speculation has not been unanimously supported in other research (Biggs, 1989, 1990; Chan et al., 1991).

Gow, Kember, and Cooper (1994) compared students from various departments in a polytechnic in Hong Kong with those in colleges of advanced education in Australia. The stereotype that Hong Kong students relied more on rote learning and were less self-managing was not supported by their findings. Overall, the Hong Kong students had somewhat lower scores on the surface approach scales than did Australian students. Biggs (1989, 1990) has suggested that Chinese students might first translate the content from English into Chinese, then work on the concepts in Chinese, and finally translate the results back into English. The 1994 study found that students assimilated the material not as words in English but rather as content meaning in Chinese, a deep rather than surface process.

MEMORIZATION AND UNDERSTANDING

There are apparent contradictions between the anecdotal evidence of Chinese students' rote learning and the empirical Study Process Questionnaire (SPQ) data which compares them favourably with students elsewhere. There is also a discrepancy between the anecdotal evidence and the academic performance of Chinese students when comparison with others becomes possible. A significant part of this apparent contradiction can be explained in terms of a different relationship between memorization and understanding in Chinese students as is seen in Western students.

Researchers from a Western perspective have tended to see memorization as purely a surface learning approach. Those attempting to memorize information are portrayed as making no attempt to understand the material, but merely as attempting to commit it to memory until it can be regurgitated in an examination. This is the classic description of a surface approach.

When Chinese students were observed attempting to memorize material, it was widely assumed that they were employing the surface approach. However, several researchers have recently reported evidence which suggests that some Chinese students combine attempts to memorize and to understand material. In other words, the students may not in fact be employing a surface approach, because their intention is to understand rather than merely to reproduce without understanding. Yet, because they have been observed memorizing material, their strategy has been equated with rote-learning that makes no attempt at understanding.

The first to advance this hypothesis were Kember and Gow (1990), who described a 'narrow orientation' which was characterized by the students systematically working through material section by section, attempting to first understand and then to memorize what they had learnt. This approach to

study was graphically illustrated by a quotation from an interview with a typical student:

> I read in detail section by section. If I find any difficulties I try my best to solve the
> problem before I go on to the next section. …If you don't memorize important
> ideas when you come across them, then you will be stuck when you go on. You
> must memorize and then go on—understand, memorize, and then go on,
> understand, memorize, and then go on. That is my way of studying (Kember
> and Gow, 1990, p. 361).

The evidence for the narrow orientation comes in part from analysis of
interviews with students. The above quotation is characteristic of statements
indicating this approach. There was confirmatory evidence from factor analysis of results from the Aproaches to Study Inventory (ASI). The first factor to
appear included both operation learning and improvidence, which characterize a narrow, systematic, and, in the extreme, even blinkered approach to
study. This factor appeared more prominently here than it had in previous
studies with Western students.

Kember and Gow went on to suggest two possible reasons for the adoption
of this narrow approach. Firstly, it could arise because the students had limited
ability in English comprehension and so studied in a systematic, linear manner,
deciphering each section as they went along. Evidence for this suggestion
comes from significant negative correlations between sub-scales in the narrow
orientation factor of the ASI and a measure of English ability. Secondly, the
approach could arise because of the cultural influences discussed above.

The adoption of a narrow approach may lead to a positive rather than negative relation between surface and deep approach scores. Actually, Tang
(1991) interpreted higher than usual correlations between deep and surface
approach scores as evidence of deep memorizing. Her interpretation, aided by
interview comments, was that students set out with the intention to use a deep
approach but found course assessment required them to reproduce defined
bodies of knowledge. Hence, they set out to understand the material and then
learnt it by heart for the examinations.

Teachers can distinguish memorization with understanding. Marton,
Dall'Alba, and Kung (1994) interviewed 20 teacher educators from mainland
China, asking about their interpretation of learning, memorizing, and understanding. The researchers concluded that the teachers distinguished mechanical memorization from memorization with understanding. They also found
evidence of both memorization of what had been understood and enhancing
memorization through understanding.

Watkins (1994) interpreted interviews with Hong Kong secondary school
students as showing a sequence of four developmental stages:

> Stage 1: The intention is to achieve through reproduction, with a rote learning
> strategy.
> Stage 2: There is an intention to achieve through rote learning important things.
> Stage 3: The intention then is achievement through reproduction, but after first
> understanding the material.
> Stage 4: The intention is understanding and achievement by combining under-
> standing and memorization.

Biggs (1994) believes that much of the anecdotal evidence concerning Asian students and the apparent paradox of research results about them is based upon misperceptions by Western observers. Researchers have observed Asian classrooms and noticed relatively passive students engaged in repetitive learning actions. The Western observers have assumed that the intention is mechanical learning without meaning. In fact, as the above researchers also concluded, the repetitive processes may not exclude a search for meaning and understanding.

A learning approach that combines understanding and memorization is clearly not a surface approach. What is not clear at this stage is how effective this relatively passive form of learning is for developing qualities like critical thinking, novel problem-solving, and independent learning. It is possible that they are less effective than would be a deep approach, as originally defined, which demands an active engagement of material determined by the students themselves to be of interest and relevance.

CHANGING THE TEACHING ENVIRONMENT

While surface learning is not as prevalent among Chinese learners as many casual observers appear to think, there remains the evidence cited above of classroom practices which act to discourage a deep approach. Gow and Kember (1990) and Kember and Gow (1991) provide evidence that deep and achieving approach scores on the SPQ tend to drop as students proceed through a course of tertiary study. The decline has been attributed to aspects of the learning environment such as excessive workloads, didactic teaching styles, courses concentrating on knowledge acquisition, and assessment demanding reproduction of information. While the levels of surface learning are perhaps not as high as casual observers might think, in many cases the teaching environment does tend to encourage students to employ a surface approach normally inconsistent with course goals.

It is possible, however, to change the teaching environment so that more desirable study approaches are encouraged. An approach to educational development which has been explored in Hong Kong is educational action research projects. In these projects, teams of academics work to investigate aspects of their teaching and courses which are of concern or interest to them. Projects go through cycles of planning, action, observation, and reflection to implement and refine teaching initiatives. Projects can be supported by educational developers acting as critical friends. A rationale for action research projects as a form of academic staff development and as a means of improving the quality of teaching and learning is provided by Kember and Gow (1992).

Educational action research projects have become quite prominent within the higher education sector in Hong Kong (see, for example, Au Yeung, Gow, and Sivan, 1992; McKay, Gow, and Kember, 1991; Sivan, Leung, Gow, and Kember, 1991). Kember and Kelly (1993) and Kember, Gow, and Balla (1993) give brief descriptions of a range of projects. These encompass initiatives like the following: introducing learning activities, replacing lectures with self-study booklets, optimizing the student workload, developing teaching skills through peer observation, and reflective writing.

CONCLUSION

Examining the learning approaches of Chinese students has proved to be an interesting exercise in cross-cultural psychology. The interest arose in response to anecdotal evidence, mostly from Western observers, that indicated that Chinese students appear to learn by rote more often than do their Western counterparts. In spite of this apparent predilection towards undesirable study approaches, though, they are often high achievers in academic performance when compared to students socialized in different academic and cultural environments.

This apparent paradox has been investigated by means of student interviews and instruments designed to measure learning approaches, initially of Western students. What has emerged is a finding that the learning approaches of Chinese students cannot be adequately described by the deep/surface dichotomy. The major distinction is that many Chinese students combine memorizing with an attempt to understand. This approach is distinct from a surface approach, in which a student has no interest or intention of discovering underlying meaning.

What is common to Western and Chinese education is that the learning environment does influence the study approach adopted by the students. Unfortunately, it seems all too common in both East and West that, contrary to stated goals, teaching practices and courses induce students towards reproductive forms of learning. There has, however, been some success in transforming courses with action research projects. This amelioration has been seen to occur in many cultural settings.

The bulk of the research into learning approaches of Chinese students has taken place in Hong Kong. There has been as yet very little research in Chinese communities outside Hong Kong, such as in Taiwan, Singapore, and the People's Republic of China. However, there have been a number of studies which have used the SPQ or the ASI in other countries in the Asian region, including the Philippines and Nepal, or in other non-Western countries (see, for example, Meyer and Parsons, 1989; Watkins and Adebowale, 1992). In each case it was shown through factor analysis that the constructs were applicable as intended in the original design of the instrument. Given the diversity of settings in which these instruments have now been tested, there seems little reason to doubt the wide, if not universal, applicability of the constructs of deep, surface, and achieving approaches.

What is less clear at this point in time is the generalizability of the more recent discovery that memorization could co-exist with understanding in Chinese students. Again, the majority of the research has taken place in Hong Kong. The work of Marton, Dall'Allba, and Kung (1994), which provides supporting results, studied teacher educators from mainland China. Therefore, it seems probable at this stage that the phenomenon of memorizing with understanding is applicable to Chinese students generally and is not confined to those in Hong Kong. More work in other areas is needed, however, before this claim can be made with greater certainty.

Chapter 9

The Academic Achievement of Chinese Students

Harold W. Stevenson and Shin-ying Lee

Investigating the academic achievement of Chinese students is a daunting task. We are immediately faced with the question of which groups of Chinese we should consider. Should we include children of the peasants of Hunan along with students in urban Beijing? Should we compare Chinese students in mainland China with those in Taiwan, Hong Kong, Singapore, Canada, Australia, Great Britain, and the United States? Must we look at new immigrants as well as at third- and fourth-generation Chinese? Is it necessary to contrast Chinese students in the 1990s with their counterparts 25 years before, when the Mainland was in the midst of the Cultural Revolution? We quickly realize that it is perilous to make generalizations over such a widely dispersed, diverse population, especially since the research literature deals nearly solely with urban Chinese, primarily in Beijing, Hong Kong, Taipei, and several metropolitan areas in the United States. The failure to include representative samples of families in other locations is an obvious limitation of every study we will describe. Scholarly interest in the academic achievement of Chinese and other East Asian students, however, is a recent phenomenon. As a consequence, huge holes exist in many aspects of our knowledge about the topic.

As we describe the achievement of Chinese students, we must keep in mind not only that we are dealing exclusively with urban students; we must also recognize, as Bond (1991) has noted, that children's achievement is defined by Chinese primarily in terms of academic achievement. Achievements in social, personal, athletic, or aesthetic realms are considered to be subsidiary to the major goal of academic advancement.

We must also remember that motivation for academic achievement in Chinese societies is multiply determined. There is always the recognition that education brings increased opportunities for economic and social advancement (Sue and Okazaki, 1990), but there is a third important factor. Behind the commitment to academic achievement is the assumption that education provides an avenue through which one can advance as a moral person (Munro, 1969). This emphasis on moral development has a long history in Chinese thought but has no clear counterpart in the West.

COMPARATIVE STUDIES OF ACADEMIC ACHIEVEMENT

The major interest in comparative research on academic achievement has been felt in three areas of study: mathematics, reading, and science.

Mathematics has been the primary focus of much of the recent activity, while reading and science have been explored much less frequently. Part of the reason for this imbalance is that it is much easier to devise acceptable tests in mathematics, a subject for which there is a universal language and for which the curricula in different countries are much more similar to each other than is the case for either reading or science.

Studies involving Chinese students have been of two types. Some have explored the performance of Chinese students studying in Chinese settings, while others have compared the performance of Chinese immigrant groups with that of other groups residing in the same location. We will discuss each type of study in our exploration of the subject.

Mathematics

Until Chinese students began participating in international studies of academic achievement, it was not clear how competitive their performance might be. It quickly became apparent, however, that they were among the strongest contenders for top place among industrialized societies in their knowledge of mathematics. Although mainland China was not included in either the First or Second International Mathematics Study, students from Hong Kong did participate in the second study. Among the 15 nations and regions represented, Hong Kong twelfth-graders ranked first or tied for first place in advanced algebra, elementary functions/calculus, and geometry. Performance at the eighth-grade level was less outstanding; the Hong Kong students' average scores were often near the middle of the range for 20 participating countries (Garden, 1987). However, in the Second International Assessment of Educational Progress, an international comparison involving 19 countries, 13-year-olds from mainland China and Taiwan were the top-ranking groups (Lapointe, Mead, and Askew, 1992; Liu, 1992).

The relative standing of Chinese students in within-country comparisons is equally impressive. In these studies the Chinese immigrant groups have received higher scores than have other minority groups and have scored higher than non-minority members of the population as well. Scores of Chinese-Americans, for example, have been consistently higher than those of Americans from other ethnic or racial groups (see, for example, Hsia, 1988; Wong, 1990). Similar results have been obtained with Chinese immigrant groups in other countries, including Canada (Kwok and Lytton, 1993), the Netherlands (Pieke, 1991), Great Britain (Taylor, 1987), and Australia (Rosenthal and Feldman, 1991).

Almost all of the studies of mathematics achievement have compared the performance of Chinese children from late elementary school through high school. However, in order to determine the impact of schooling and socialization on mathematics achievement, it is also necessary to examine the performance of children at earlier ages. In our cross-cultural research in Taipei and Minneapolis, for example, we included students from kindergarten through high school (Stevenson, Chen, and Lee, 1993; Stevenson, Lee, and Graham, 1993; Stevenson, Lee, and Stigler, 1986). For these studies we constructed mathematics achievement tests on the basis of detailed analyses of students' textbooks. Only items represented in the curricula of all participating locations were included in the tests. As a further means of ensuring fairness we tested representative samples of the full range of students from each of the metropolitan areas, including students from some of the best schools and from schools that were less successful.

The distributions of mathematics scores obtained by the students appear in Figure 9.1, which summarizes the results for over 5,000 participants. Chinese kindergarten children performed reasonably well, but their understanding of and ability to apply mathematical concepts were actually lower than those of American children. Chinese children's performance improved rapidly, however, after they entered elementary school. By the fifth grade they were clearly superior to the American students. At eleventh grade the Chinese students' scores take the form of a bimodal distribution. This is readily explained by the recognition that there are two types of high schools in Taiwan, regular high schools and technical–vocational high schools. The lower portion of the curve primarily represents the scores of students from the latter type of school and the upper portion, the scores of students from regular high schools. Even so, the average score of the technical–vocational students was above that of the American high school students.

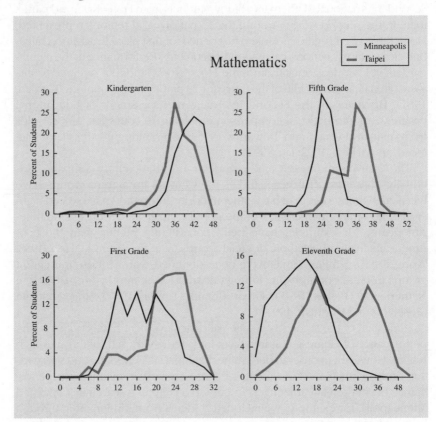

Figure 9.1 The distributions of mathematics scores of kindergarten, first-, fifth-, and eleventh-grade students in Taipei and Minneapolis.

The degree of Chinese superiority in mathematics is illustrated even more dramatically by the percentage of Chinese students at each grade level who received scores at or below the mean for their American peers. During kindergarten, 87 per cent of the Chinese students received scores at or below the American mean. After the children entered elementary school, much smaller percentages of the Chinese students in Taipei received scores that low: 20 per cent at first grade, 6 per cent at fifth grade, and 16 per cent at eleventh grade. Because attendance at elementary school is compulsory and the drop-out rate of high school students is low in both cities, possible bias from differential attendance at school in the two locations is minimal.

It is sometimes suggested that the average scores of Chinese students are higher than those of American students because the least able American students pull down the American average. Proponents of this view argue that the better American students are competitive with the better Chinese students. As is evident in Figure 9.1, however, the distributions of scores after kindergarten offer no evidence to support this argument.

A further indication of the superiority of the Chinese students' performance on mathematics tests was found in another study in which separate analyses were conducted for the top scorers in each city (Stevenson, Chen, and Lee, 1993). The top 10 per cent of Taipei students received significantly higher scores than did the top 10 per cent of the students in Minneapolis.

Evidence of the superior performance of Chinese students at the upper levels of competence has also been reported by Stanley (1989), who studied the most outstanding of many thousands of American students who had taken the mathematics portion of the Scholastic Aptitude Test. Students of Chinese ethnic origin were over-represented among the highest-scoring group; 22 per cent of those receiving the highest scores were of Asian, and primarily Chinese, ancestry.

Another interpretation that has sometimes been suggested by both Chinese and Westerners for the superiority of Chinese children in achievement tests in mathematics is that Chinese and other East Asian students perform well on items dependent upon rote learning, but are less competent in applying what they have learned on items involving problem-solving and creativity. A simple reply to this suggestion is seen in the results we obtained for fifth- and eleventh-graders in Taipei and Minneapolis (Stevenson and Lee, 1990). The test given to fifth-graders included both computation and word problems. Chinese children were just as adept at solving word problems as they were at solving computation problems. In the test constructed for high school students, items could be divided into those that involved arithmetic, algebra, geometry, trigonometry, and advanced mathematics. Chinese eleventh-graders maintained their superiority in all five categories.

We made a more detailed analysis of children's mathematics ability in another study by constructing ten tests that tapped different aspects of mathematical knowledge (Stigler, Lee, and Stevenson, 1990). Comparisons of students in Taipei and Chicago revealed no differences at the first-grade level, but by the fifth grade Chinese children surpassed American children, not only in computation and word problems, but also in their understanding of mathematical concepts, estimation, geometry, and mental calculation. Only in reading graphs and tables, visualization, and mental folding problems were the scores of the two groups of children similar to each other. Thus, although Chinese children may be good at calculation problems that rely on rote learning, they are also able to apply what they know about mathematics to more complex situations.

Reading

Comparative studies of children's reading ability are more difficult to conduct than are studies of mathematics. Reading in different cultures involves different writing systems, grammars, and vocabularies. Nevertheless, if tests are constructed on the basis of careful analyses of the grammatical structure, content, and vocabulary included in the children's textbooks, reasonably comparable versions of tests can be developed for young readers in Chinese and English.

Before comparing scores, it is important to mention an advantage held by children learning to read an alphabetic language. Readers of English have the advantage of being able to sound out words; children learning to read Chinese are deprived of such cues. Although some minimal information about meaning and pronunciation can be obtained from the components of some Chinese characters, children typically must be taught both aspects of each character. The fairest comparisons of reading ability, therefore, should involve only words that have been included in the children's textbooks at or below the child's grade level. With these steps taken, the difference measured between Chinese and American students' reading skill is not so large as is the case for mathematics, but Chinese children exceed American children in both reading vocabulary and comprehension (Lee, Stigler, and Stevenson, 1986; Stevenson and Stigler, 1992). Elementary school students in both Taipei and Beijing achieved a higher level of competency in reading words that were contained in their curricula than did American children (Lee, Uttal, and Chen, in press).

Science

Still more difficult to evaluate is students' mastery of science, but one index of the degree of mastery of scientific concepts is the representation of various groups of students in national and international science competitions. For example, in the Westinghouse Science Talent Search conducted in the United States, students of Chinese descent have been over-represented in relation to their presence in the population at large. Of the 40 finalists in 1994, 8 were Chinese-Americans. Of the 200 finalists from 1990 through 1994, 45 were Chinese-Americans (Science Service, 1994). These figures are especially impressive when one realizes that Chinese-Americans constitute less than 1 per cent of the US population.

Chinese students are also strongly represented in international science competitions. Since 1985, when mainland China began participating in the international science Olympiads, Chinese participants have captured many gold medals in physics, chemistry, and information sciences. In the International Chemistry Olympiad in 1993, 5 of the top 19 students were Chinese. Between 1990 and 1993, the top 61 students included 17 Chinese (American Chemical Society, 1993).

In comparisons of achievement test scores, Chinese students have been among the top performers. In the Second International Assessment of Educational Progress, students from Taiwan ranked second after Korea in science achievement among the 19 participating countries (Lapointe, et al., 1992).

Summary

Other studies could be invoked for support, but the conclusion suggested is the same whether one considers mathematics, reading, or science. There is compelling evidence of superior academic achievement by Chinese students. Moreover, positive findings are not limited to results from achievement tests but appear in other forms as well. Hsia (1988) has described other indices of success in her comprehensive discussion of Asian-Americans. Siu (1992), in another review of Chinese-American educational achievement, has summarized these indices in the following manner:

> The consistent finding is that Asian Americans start school earlier, stay in school longer, drop out less often, have larger percentages of high school graduates, are over-represented in gifted student programs, and under-represented in programs for learning disabled, manifest fewer disciplinary problems, and are better prepared for college than candidates overall (p. 5).

There is one caution, however, in over-generalizing from the studies that have been reported. One primary limitation to the findings, aside from the restriction of the subjects to urban populations, is that they do not necessarily pertain to Chinese adults in the United States or other countries. For example, Kwong (1987) has pointed out that 71 per cent of the Chinese-Americans residing in New York City's Chinatown at the time of the study had no high school diploma and 25 per cent lived below the poverty line. Members of these families tended to be manual and service workers, occupations much below those of the high-income professionals who have immigrated mainly from Taiwan and Hong Kong and who already possessed high levels of education before arriving in the United States. Moreover, in mainland China the illiteracy rate currently stands at around 16 per cent (Xie, 1992), and each year only one-third of the cohort receives more than a ninth-grade education (State Education Commission, 1992).

EXPLAINING HIGH LEVELS OF ACHIEVEMENT

Establishing that students from Chinese families have high levels of academic achievement is only a first step. Understanding why this should be the case is much more complicated. Families, schools, and cultural beliefs all play a part in children's academic successes and failures. Even though we are very far from a complete understanding, we can identify some of the factors that seem to play a central role.

Intelligence

One common explanation of the success of Chinese students is that they may simply be smarter than their peers in other countries (see Chan, this volume).

As early as the 1920s, educational psychologists discussed this possibility (Sandiford, and Kerr, 1926). Later, Vernon (1982) pursued this argument and looked for evidence to support a genetic interpretation for superior intelligence of the Chinese. The evidence was equivocal. The representativeness of the samples involved, the size of the samples, and the types of tests used made it difficult to summon convincing support for such a view.

Perhaps the most consistent advocate for an interpretation of Asian academic success in terms of genetic factors is Richard Lynn, an Irish psychologist who argues not only for genetically determined differences in intelligence, but also for 'the possibility that Asians have some genetic predisposition for working hard for long-term goals' (Lynn, 1991, p. 875). While it may be true, as is reported in studies by Vernon and Lynn, that some of the samples of Chinese children and adolescents received higher IQ scores than did representative samples of students in other countries, there is no clear evidence that the IQ scores of *comparable* samples of students, say from both urban and rural areas in China and in the United States, would differ.

The only study of which we are aware that has attempted to organize comparable groups of Chinese and American students and to create a culture-fair test similar to an IQ test is one that we conducted in Taipei and Minneapolis (Stevenson, Stigler, Lee, Lucker, Kitamura, and Hsu, 1985). Ten subtests of the types found in the Wechsler Intelligence Scale for Children and the Thurstone Primary Mental Abilities Battery and containing items judged by both Chinese and Americans to be applicable to their cultures were included in a study of first- and fifth-graders.

Chinese first-graders surpassed their American peers on only one subtest, memory for digits. In contrast, American first-graders surpassed their Chinese counterparts on six subtests, involving matching line drawings, remembering patterns of sounds, remembering strings of words, carrying out instructions involving spatial relations, recalling details of a short story, defining words, and answering questions about general information. Tests of coding, spatial relations, and remembering strings of words did not differentiate the two groups at either grade. By the fifth grade the two groups obtained equivalent scores on seven of the ten tests. Chinese children continued to receive higher scores on memory for digits, but received lower scores on matching line drawings and remembering patterns of sounds.

One of the subtests included in most tests of intelligence addresses possession of general information. This subtest taps the child's knowledge of common, everyday phenomena, such as why we need to put stamps on letters when we mail them, why people cannot live under water, what is needed for a plant to grow, and the difference between a rock and a fossil. Answers to these questions are not necessarily taught in school, but presumably depend on information children have acquired from their everyday experiences. This subtest correlates at a high level with overall IQ scores and is thought to be one of the most reliable indicators of cognitive ability of all the types of subtests in IQ tests.

Figure 9.2 indicates little evidence in support of superior performance in general information on the part of the Chinese children. In fact, in kindergarten the difference favors the American children. By the eleventh grade, the performance of the two groups is very similar. These data are of interest, not only in pointing out the similarity of scores at the higher grade levels on representative cognitive tasks, but also in revealing the large gap in general information on the part of young Chinese children.

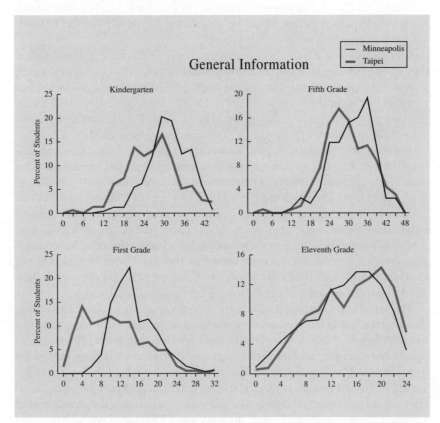

Figure 9.2 The distributions of general information scores of kindergarten, first-, fifth-, and eleventh-grade students in Taipei and Minneapolis.

The few data that exist, where the tests are culturally fair and where care has been taken to ensure that the samples are as comparable as possible, point to similarity in intellectual functioning of Chinese and American students after they enter school. If we reject the hypothesis that cross-cultural differences in academic achievement of Chinese and American students can be explained by reference to innate differences in intellectual functioning, we must turn to other factors for an explanation. One prime factor may be found in children's everyday experiences.

Everyday Experiences

The everyday experiences of Chinese children differ greatly from those of American children, especially in the amounts of out-of-school time they devote to their studies. These differences reflect, in part, contrasting cultural conceptions of child development and education. Chinese identify two phases of childhood: an early period of innocence, followed by a period of reason (Ho, 1986). The innocence that exists during the preschool years defines a time for indulgence by adults, a time when children should have freedom and opportunities for exploration. Partly because Chinese parents assume that learning about academic matters should occur at school, they see little reason to provide experiences that would be stimulating cognitively or to try to teach subject matter during the preschool years.

Innocence ends when children enter school. At this time, parents define their child's primary task as that of doing well in school. Children are expected to study, and parents expect to assume responsibility for creating a home environment that is conducive to academic achievement. Whenever possible, children are provided with a desk and workbooks. Parents make few demands of their children that are unrelated to schoolwork (Stevenson and Lee, 1990).

We interpret the relatively poor showing of kindergarten-age Chinese children on tests tapping intellectual and academic abilities to parental attitudes about early cognitive stimulation (Stevenson, Lee, and Graham, 1993). During the kindergarten year, for example, only 40 per cent of Chinese mothers—in contrast to 91 per cent of American mothers—report reading to their children either daily or several times each week. Only half as many Chinese as American mothers say they or their husbands had taken their children on outings to movies, museums, sporting events, or the zoo. Fewer Chinese (49 per cent) than American mothers (66 per cent) say they had tried to teach their child the alphabet or the phonetic writing system used in Taiwan.

The rapid improvement in Chinese children's levels of achievement during and after the first grade appears to be attributable, in part, to the great amounts of time Chinese children spend on their studies (see Fuligni and Stevenson, in press). For example, we found that high school students in Taipei, compared to students in Minneapolis, were at school longer each day (an average of 9.2 versus 7.3 hours) and each week (50 versus 36 hours). When the amounts of after-school time spent studying, taking lessons, and reading for pleasure were summed, the average for Chinese students was 25.5 hours a week, compared to 15.4 hours for American students. In Taipei, 36 per cent of high school students were enrolled in after-school academic classes, compared to 3 per cent in Minneapolis. The Chinese students spent more time in their studies than did the American students, but they also spent less time socializing after school with their friends, and fewer had dates, or engaged in athletics, or worked at out-of-school jobs.

Differences in the amount of time spent studying and reading for pleasure were evident as early as the elementary school years (Stevenson and Lee, 1990). Similar findings were obtained for Asian-American students, who spent significantly more time studying than did other ethnic groups in the United States (Chen and Stevenson, in press). The greater devotion to studying places Chinese students at an early and continuing advantage in terms of opportunities for learning and practice related to school work.

Motivation for Education

The willingness to devote large amounts of time to academic pursuits is an indication of the high motivation Chinese students have for doing well in school. As mentioned earlier, their motivation is derived from the time-honoured Chinese emphasis on education as the most effective avenue to social and economic advancement and for the improvement of the person. In traditional Chinese society there were four classes of people: scholars, farmers, labourers, and merchants. Scholars were highly respected and Chinese parents dreamed of having a scholar in the family. This is illustrated in an old saying, 'Whatever occupation one chose to be, it would not be as honourable as being a learned person.'

One became a scholar in ancient China by gaining an education and being successful in examinations. As long ago as 1100 BC, procedures were instituted for attracting the most able citizens to the civil service by selecting persons who demonstrated knowledge not only of music, archery, horsemanship, and the rites and ceremonies of private and public life, but also of writing and mathematics (Zhang, 1988). Since the Sui dynasty nearly 1500 years ago, examinations were maintained as a national testing and selection system for the civil service. Scholars from all over China gathered in the capital for examinations that determined who would be chosen for these positions. Proficiency in remembering and interpreting Confucian classics was emphasized, but the candidates also wrote essays, composed poetry, completed classic sentences with missing words, and, in a test much like some contemporary tests of intelligence, selected words and phrases with similar and opposite meanings. A very small percentage of the candidates were successful in gaining appointments (O'Neill, 1987), but this small chance of success did not discourage attempts in light of the possibility of attaining extremely desirable rewards.

The importance of scholarship persists in Chinese public service today. In Taiwan, for example, of the 39 current cabinet members, 31 have advanced college degrees: 27 have Doctorates and 4 have Master's degrees (Yang, 1993). There are indications that the influence of this goal may be weakening in mainland China as opportunities increase for achieving social and economic status through entrepreneurial activities rather than through scholarship.

Competition to advance to successively higher levels of schooling is something of which contemporary Chinese students, parents, and teachers are well aware. Motivation is strong even though students know that the probability of gaining such an education is low. In Beijing, 86 per cent of the high school students we studied said they would like to graduate from college or have a graduate degree. This occurred despite the fact that only about 40 per cent of junior high school graduates enter high school and among these, only about 20 per cent are able to gain admission to institutions of higher education (State Education Commission, 1992). Currently no more than 3 per cent of the youngsters from any one cohort are admitted to colleges and universities.

In Taipei, where only 49 per cent of high school graduates were able to pass the college entrance examination in 1990 (Ministry of Education, 1991), 83 per cent of the high school students interviewed said they hoped to obtain a university education. Even in rural Taiwan, where parents are labourers with little education, 90 per cent of the junior high school students said they want to go to college (Liu, 1985).

Aspirations for more education can be traced in part to the fact that nearly all children in mainland China, Taiwan, and most other locations in which

Chinese live attend elementary school. In 1991, for example, 98 per cent of the school-age children in mainland China were enrolled in elementary schools (State Education Commission, 1992). Evidence of strong motivation for education among young children was manifested in the following situation (Stevenson, 1992). We said to large numbers of fifth-graders in Beijing, 'Let's say there is a wizard who will let you make a wish about anything you want. What would you wish?' The children's most frequent wishes fell into four categories: money; material objects, such as toys or pets; fantasy, such as wanting to be sent to the moon; and educational aspirations, such as doing well in school or going to college. Nearly 70 per cent of the Chinese children's spontaneous wishes, but only 10 per cent of those of American children in Chicago, dealt with education. Few Chinese children mentioned money or fantasy and only 10 per cent said they wished the wizard would bring them things.

The importance of school in the lives of Chinese children was also evident when we asked elementary school children in Beijing what they thought about on their way to school. The vast majority (81 per cent) mentioned topics related to school. School occupied the thoughts of fewer Chicago children (60 per cent). What else did the American children think about? Movies, games, food, snacks, lunch, treats, and socializing.

Social Orientation in Academic Achievement

Behind the individual's striving for academic success, and beyond any effort to seek recognition for themselves, is the image of the larger value their success would have for their family and society (see Yu, this volume). The consequences of failure, as well as of success, are similarly magnified by the individuals' identification with their families and the larger society. Just as success enhances the family's status, the consequences of poor performance include not only a loss of status and prestige for the individual, but a far more critical loss of family 'face'. The student seeks to avoid at all costs the stigma and shame that would accompany a loss of face (Stigler, Smith, and Mao, 1985).

In describing these two orientations, Hsu (1985) considered two aspects of the self: *da wo* (the greater self) and *xiao wo* (the smaller self). The greater self is oriented to family and society, rather than to the individual, and is viewed as the dominant force in the motivation of Chinese students for academic success. Yang and Yue have made a similar distinction by dividing achievement motivation into that which is socially oriented and that which is individually motivated (Yang and Yu, 1989; Yu and Yang, 1987). In Chinese societies, where the orientation is assumed to be toward the larger group, a student's motivation to do well in school is assumed to be based on societal values or parental expectations, rather than simply on a desire for self-advancement.

Environmentalism

Chinese have long placed great emphasis on the influence of the environment on behavior. Liu (1987) characterizes this position by describing the writings of Mo Zi, who 'considered human nature as white silk and said, "It will become green if dyed in dark green, and yellow if dyed yellow. When the dye is changed it will change accordingly."' Another well-known parable is that of the mother of the philosopher Mencius (Meng Zi), who changed her residence three times in order to ensure that her son was living with good neighbors.

Munro (1969, p. 9) describes why living in a good environment has such potentially profound effects on young persons:

> The Chinese theory of learning assumes that people are innately capable of learning from models. This learning can occur unintentionally, through the unconscious imitation of those around one; thus it is important to choose one's neighbors well. Or it can occur intentionally, through the purposive attempt to duplicate the attitude and conduct of a teacher, scholar–official, or ancestor. For the Confucians, model emulation was not just one way of learning; it was by far the most efficient way, and one could inculcate any virtuous behavior in people by presenting the right model.

In an attempt to inculcate proper attitudes about studying or to promote certain socially desired characteristics, efforts have been made to select child models. For example, every schoolchild in mainland China knows the story of Lei Feng, a young soldier who exemplified the diligence, loyalty, and thoughtfulness to which all students are expected to aspire.

Individual Differences

Despite their strong adherence to an environmental explanation of behavior, Chinese philosophers do not fail to consider the fact that people differ, both physically and psychologically, in their innate endowments. Rather than viewing these differences in endowment as potentially restrictive forces, however, they are seen primarily as aspects of human beings about which one must be aware in planning such things as a child's educational experiences.

It is generally assumed that all children possess the necessary capacity for advancement to higher levels of development, including advancement in school, but that some have the capacity to progress more rapidly than others. The slow bird, says the Chinese proverb, must start out early. This optimistic view of human development is a residual of Confucian precepts which emphasize the malleability of human beings (Munro, 1977). People are considered to be like clay, capable of being moulded by the environments in which they live. If the environment is supportive, healthy development is likely; progress is more difficult in less wholesome environments. Experience, rather than innate endowment, is believed to bear major responsibility for creating the vast diversity that exists among human beings. Book 17 of the Analects summarizes the Confucian position on individual differences in this way: 'By nature, near together; by practice, far apart.'

The Importance of Effort

Establishing a healthy, nurturing environment is one component of the Chinese formula for academic success, but a second important element is the degree to which children are willing to work hard. From age-old stories about how the roughest piece of iron can be transformed into a sharp needle through daily polishing, to the maxim of the Maoist era, 'Study hard and make progress every day,' Chinese children have been exhorted to dedicate themselves wholeheartedly to their studies.

Chinese parents and teachers assume that children will be more willing to work hard if they and other adults point to the virtues of hard work than if they emphasize the potentially restrictive effects of differences in innate ability. When innate ability is stressed, bright children may believe they are so bright that they do not need to work hard. Children who learn more slowly may come to believe that working hard has little likelihood of leading to success.

There is ample evidence that Chinese children, their parents, and teachers adhere to this credo. Chan (1992), for example, studied elementary school children in Hong Kong and their mothers. When asked to rate eight attributes that might contribute to academic success, including effort, ability, difficulty of the task, help from home, luck, method of studying, interest, and help from teachers, both children and their mothers gave the highest ratings to effort. This was the case for low- as well as high-achieving children as defined by their grade point averages.

Chinese parents attempt to reinforce the importance of effort by helping their young children with their school work. Mothers of first-graders we studied in Beijing said they helped their child an average of seven hours a week. Mothers in Taipei helped their child an average of seven and a half hours. Involvement in their child's school work did not continue at an equally intense level during subsequent years, but mothers of fifth-graders in the two cities still helped their children a reported four and one-half and five hours a week, respectively.

Although Chinese people emphasize the role of effort in promoting academic achievement, the degree to which they adhere to this view may differ, depending upon whether they live in a totally Chinese society or in a society that places less emphasis on the utility of hard work (Chen and Stevenson, in press; Yamauchi and Li, 1993). There is also evidence that the Chinese interpretation of the relation between ability and effort may differ from that found in other societies. Several recent studies illustrate these points (see also Crittenden, this volume).

Hess, Chang, and McDevitt (1987) asked mothers of high achievers and of less successful children to consider five factors that might explain their child's performance in mathematics: natural ability, effort, training in school, training at home, and luck. Mothers of less successful children gave the greatest emphasis to lack of effort, whether they were Beijing or Chinese-American mothers. Even so, Beijing mothers were much more likely than Chinese-American mothers to make this judgement. Both groups gave the greatest emphasis to school training in explaining the performance of successful children. Children responded in the same fashion as their mothers, indicating successful transmission of the parents' values to their children.

The interpretation of the relation between ability and effort differs between Chinese and Westerners, as Salili and Hau (1994) have recently demonstrated. Students from the first through tenth grades were read four scenarios involving easy and difficult problems that led either to success (praise from the teacher) or failure (correction by the teacher). Students were asked to rate the level of effort and ability expended by the children described in the scenarios. Ratings for effort and ability by the Chinese students were positively related at all grade levels; that is, children who were described as working hardest were also considered to be the most able. For American students at the higher grade levels the relation was strongly negative, implying that those who worked hard lacked ability.

The findings suggest that Chinese, unlike American students, believe that working hard not only leads to success, but also increases one's ability. This view provides the best of all possible situations: success is dependent upon hard work and hard work reduces or eliminates any constraints imposed by differences in ability.

Standards

In view of the outstanding performance of Chinese children in international competitions, surprisingly few Chinese parents express high degrees of satisfaction with their children's academic achievement. Only 13 per cent of our sample of Beijing mothers thought their child was doing 'very well' in mathematics. Less than half of the Chinese parents were satisfied with their children's academic performance and at least one out of five was dissatisfied.

One interpretation of the low levels of satisfaction of the Chinese parents is that they hold high standards for their children's academic achievement. Support for this interpretation was seen in the following situation (Stevenson, Chen, and Lee, 1993). Mothers were told, 'Let's say that your child took a math test for his or her grade level with a maximum of 100 points. The average score was 70. What score do you think your child would get?' After answering this question the parent was asked, 'What is the least number of points you would be satisfied with?' The average score predicted by Chinese mothers described children who were above average. When asked what score they would be satisfied with, however, the mothers had higher aspirations; the average with which they would be satisfied was in the high 80s. American mothers included in this study also expected their children would obtain high scores, but in contrast with the Chinese mothers they said they would be satisfied with the scores they expected their children would obtain.

These results give us further insight into the high motivation of Chinese students to do well in school. If children believe that their parents are not satisfied with their performance, they assume they are expected to work harder. Whatever their level of achievement, Chinese children face the constant incentive from their parents to surpass their previous performance or, if they already are among the top students, to work hard to maintain this status.

Reaction to High Emphasis on Education

The strong emphasis on education is not without its critics. Many Chinese parents, teachers, and students criticize what they consider excessive pressure to do well in school. A recent issue of a Hong Kong newspaper, for example, reported that 'very young children are being turned into robots, slaves to an oppressive, regimented system which values rote-learning and memorizing more than creativity' (Turay, 1994).

The same complaints are heard so frequently throughout East Asia that it has become a stereotypic description of the typical student. When, however, researchers have investigated the attitudes and behavior of Chinese students, they find little support for this stereotype. Biggs (1991) and Chan (1990), for example, have found little support for the charge that Chinese students display rigid adherence to rote learning. Rather, the type of response was a function of what was being asked. If they were asked questions about matters the respondent in a situation had not experienced or had not had time to respond to, they answered more superficially. If they were asked to analyse situations with which the respondent had experience, they answered at a deeper, analytic level. Further evidence contradicting the description of Chinese students as rote learners appeared in the data cited above that indicates the high proficiency of Chinese students, not only in computation, but also in solving word problems and in demonstrating a clear understanding of mathematical concepts and operations (see also Gow, Balla, Kember, and Hau, this volume).

In addition, complaints are heard about how pressure for achievement results in various types of psychological maladjustment on the part of students. Such a scenario is not indicated by the results of interviews with teachers and mothers or from questionnaires given to high school students.

We asked Chinese and American first-grade teachers about their pupils' physical symptoms of tension. Chinese teachers reported less frequent complaints of stomach-aches, headaches, fatigue, and not wanting to go to school than did American teachers (Stevenson, 1992). We then asked them to estimate how many out of 100 children would be likely to display various types of behavior during their early days in school. Fewer Chinese than American children were considered to be disorganized (12 per cent versus 33 per cent) and to have trouble following directions (11 per cent versus 33 per cent). Only one-sixth as many Chinese as American children were estimated to display nervousness in class (2 per cent versus 13 per cent). When we asked mothers to rate psychological characteristics of their children, Chinese mothers described children who appeared happier, more obedient, and more self-confident than did the American mothers.

These data portray children who are calm, with few symptoms of tension, committed to their school work, and generally well adjusted in school. Getting an education may be considered the Chinese child's primary obligation, but because getting an education is a common norm, school work appears to be not a source of great worry and concern.

In another study, over 3,000 high school students in Taipei and Minneapolis were asked about the frequency with which they experienced stress, depressed moods, academic anxiety, aggression, and somatic complaints (Crystal, Chen, Fuligni, Stevenson, Hsu, Ko, Kitamura, and Kimura, 1994). The overall picture was one of similar levels of psychological adjustment among Chinese and American students. Although some statistically significant differences were found, cross-cultural differences in the frequency of complaints were small. Chinese students reported less stress, lower academic anxiety, and fewer aggressive feelings than did their American counterparts, but did report higher frequencies of depressed moods and somatic complaints. High academic achievement as assessed by a test of mathematics was generally not associated with psychological maladjustment.

Significant effects were found for two variables: degree of parental satisfaction and parental expectations. On all five indices of maladjustment—stress, depressed moods, academic anxiety, aggression, and somatic complaints—Chinese students who perceived their parents as having low satisfaction with their performance reported higher levels of maladjustment than did those who perceived that their parents were very satisfied. Similarly, Chinese students' perceptions of their parents' expectations for their academic achievement were highly related to their psychological well-being. Students reporting high parental expectations tended to show greater psychological distress than did those reporting low parental expectations. This was the case for all measures except for feelings of depression.

The finding that Chinese students reported higher frequencies of depressed mood and of psychosomatic disturbance is in line with the results of numerous other studies (for example, Cheung, 1986; Draguns, this volume; Yamamoto, 1985). Nevertheless, the results suggest that high levels of academic achievement can be attained without necessarily increasing students' reports of psychological problems. This appears to be especially true in the Chinese culture, where the importance of education is so strongly emphasized. Hard work done at home and at school in pursuit of a socially accepted goal may be difficult, but it does not necessarily lead to a high incidence of stress, anxiety, or other psychological problems.

Opportunities for Education

Although education was historically the privilege of a very small percentage of the Chinese population, there is a great deal of concern in contemporary Chinese societies about providing equal opportunities for education. In Taiwan, for example, many studies have compared the academic achievement of Chinese students from families of different socio-economic status. As has been found in Western studies, the level of parental education was significantly related to children's school performance and the likelihood of entering a university (for example, Chien, 1984; Huang, 1974; Huang, 1978; Huang and Liu , 1983; Ma, 1985; Zhang, 1977). Much of the literature in Chinese on academic achievement is devoted to discussions of this problem, and how the government and schools might help to offer more equal opportunities to students whose parents are not equipped to help them with their school work or to provide the kinds of experiences after school that are conducive to academic achievement.

The government of mainland China attempted to eliminate these inequities during the Cultural Revolution of 1966–76 by admitting to universities only persons recommended by their fellow workers. This practice proved to be a failure and was abandoned, for the persons admitted to the universities were often ill-prepared for university classes. Soon after the end of the Cultural Revolution the policy was reversed. Now mainland Chinese, like the Chinese in Hong Kong, Taiwan, and other places, must compete for entrance to higher education through examinations.

The Influence of Schooling

The findings we have described are indicative of the strong cultural emphasis on schooling that exists among Chinese. Although, as we have seen, Chinese children attending schools in many parts of the world excel in their academic achievement, there are some special features of Chinese schools that should be noted.

Moral education is a recurrent theme in Chinese discussions of education generally. During the Cultural Revolution and even today, Chinese define the purpose of education as to advance moral, intellectual, and physical development, with moral development always cited first. Currently, aesthetic development has been added to this trio of goals in mainland China, and social development has been added as a fourth component in Taiwan.

School plays a central role in the lives of Chinese children and youths. School is often portrayed as a big family, where teachers are like parents and students are like brothers and sisters. It is, therefore, a place not only for learning but also for social interaction. Frequent social opportunities arise during the time the students spend walking to school and during recesses that follow each 45- or 50-minute class period. Lunch periods are at least an hour in length and students remain after school for sports, clubs, extracurricular classes, and for studying together. Perhaps because of their experiences of greater opportunities for social expression, elementary school children in Beijing responded more favourably to questions about their life at school than did children in Chicago (Stevenson, 1992).

According to their mothers, Chinese children were eager to go to school in the morning, talked positively about their teachers, came home from school happy, and said they could not wait for their vacations to end. We asked the children how well they liked school, and then how well they liked reading and mathematics. Chinese children gave significantly more positive answers than did the American children when the ratings dealt with school and mathematics. They did not express a greater fondness than did the American children for reading, perhaps because they are constantly faced with the need to learn new Chinese characters. The importance of school life for high school students is reflected in the fact that school-related activities and issues were the most frequently mentioned topics when we asked the students about the source of their happiness, pride, and worries.

Teachers we have observed in classrooms of mainland China and Taiwan bring a remarkable level of dedication, enthusiasm, vigor, and knowledge to their teaching. They are intensely motivated to fulfil a role highly regarded by society, and devote long hours and great effort to this task. They arrive at school early in the morning and leave late in the afternoon. In contrast to the situation that exists in Western countries, they are not required to teach during the majority of the time they are in school. In Beijing, for example, elementary school teachers typically teach only three or four classes a day; at high schools, they teach only two. This situation leaves the teachers ample time to work together in preparing lessons, meet individually with children who are having difficulty, correct papers, and conduct other duties.

Elementary teachers attempt to assume the role of guide rather than that of lecturer. The image of a knowledgeable person who leads children through their lessons is in marked contrast to that of a stern task-master who dominates the classroom and is the primary source of all information and arbiter of what is correct. Chinese teachers may have displayed such characteristics in earlier eras, but teachers today are much more likely to call upon students to provide answers and then to ask other students to evaluate these answers. By constantly seeking students' responses, Chinese teachers are able to elicit a high degree of attention and involvement on the part of students (Stevenson and Lee, in press). The situation changes somewhat in junior high school and high school, where the teachers are faced with the need to cover large amounts of information. High school students remain involved in their lessons, but their involvement seems more dependent upon the teachers' authoritative knowledge and the students' awareness of their need to pass college entrance examinations than upon their teachers' compelling style of teaching.

With the rapid economic development of East Asia, Chinese schools are bound to change. At present the schools are able, for the most part, to attract highly capable individuals to the teaching profession. Whether this will continue when opportunities expand for other professional or entrepreneurial activities is unclear. What is evident, however, is that the high levels of academic achievement attained by students in Chinese societies is attributable in part to the remarkable skill of their teachers.

CURRENT STATUS OF THE RESEARCH

One of the difficulties in reviewing the literature on the academic achievement of Chinese children is that the topic is so large. Although studies have been reported by researchers from many parts of the world, these have dealt with different aspects of achievement, included different populations, and employed different research methods. While the results have been remarkably consistent, the research is somehat patchy, consisting of bits of information about a great many topics.

It is especially surprising in view of its importance that so few studies in the Chinese literature have dealt with the correlates of academic achievement. When such studies have been reported, they have explored areas covered in the Western literature: the impact of socioeconomic status, achievement motivation, attributions about achievement, personality characteristics, and expectations of parents and teachers. Topics such as moral education, gender differences, political socialization, and other issues of special interest to Chinese society have received little attention.

Part of the explanation of why a more coherent literature does not exist lies in the very complex nature of trying to understand the bases and consequences of academic achievement by nearly one-fourth of the world's population. The literature is bound to grow, however, for the topic is one of great interest to both industrialized and developing nations. As each country strives to maintain or improve its status in a global economy, the need for knowledge about how to improve education assumes great economic, as well as social, importance.

From what we have learned so far, we know that successful academic achievement depends strongly on attitudes and beliefs about the nature of individual differences. In contrast to a pessimistic view that the degree of success depends upon some pattern of innate abilities, the strong environmental views of the Chinese point to what can be accomplished when there is a shared belief that education is of prime importance in human development, that all children are capable of learning, and that, through diligence and hard work on the part of students, parents, and teachers, high levels of academic achievement by all normal children is possible.

Chapter 10

■

Chinese Childhood Socialization

David Y. H. Wu

This chapter engages in a psycho-cultural discussion of child development in Chinese culture. Focusing on individuals, psychologists often examine individual capacities and variations in child development according to pan-species assumptions. In contrast, anthropologists, although incorporating psychological approaches in their study of child development, have paid more attention to cultural environmental influences, such as socio-economic conditions of a specific population, ideologies of child rearing in a local culture, parental behaviours in child care in a selected society, and comparative studies of cultural variations in these aspects based on accumulated knowledge of childhood socialization in different societies or populations. This paper presents a discussion of Chinese cultural assumptions about child development and child-rearing practices among Chinese parents in the Chinese homeland and in communities overseas.

Childhood socialization, how parents rear their children and how children learn to become acceptable members of a society, is perhaps the most conservative or persistent part of a culture. Traditional values and practices in child rearing often persist, unless the society undergoes lengthy and critical changes in its fundamental social structure and cultural system (LeVine, 1982). Continuity through time of an established, culturally appropriate way of socialization is especially evident, as this paper shall describe, in a literate civilization such as that of the Chinese, with an uninterrupted cultural history of several thousands of years. The present paper will address the issue of what is an acceptable Chinese way of socializing children and what kind of adults Chinese socialization aims to produce. We shall examine this issue from both a historical approach and an anthropological comparison of Chinese in different locations today.

THE CONFUCIAN TRADITION OF PARENTAL EDUCATION

A cultural model of child care and child education has great influence on the societal level of childhood socialization. We shall begin by explaining the origin of indigenous conceptions about the person and childhood in Chinese culture.

Through the past two thousand years, Chinese scholars and political authorities have maintained a clear idea about the concept of the child, the meaning of childhood, and the function of family education for the young. These ideas were first stated in essays by Confucian scholars, who proposed and argued for the important role adult family members should assume in early childhood education. Several essays, such as the *Di zi zhi* (Duties of children) and the *Ji jiu pian* (Crash essay on guidance), written as early as the first century BC, were considered exemplary pieces and were frequently quoted by later scholars. By the time of the Ming (1368–1644) and Qing (1644–1911) dynasties, many neo-Confucian scholars were writing short essays in plain language to guide parents in providing their children with proper discipline and educational instruction at home (the *San zi jing* is one example; see Giles, 1964, for a translation in English). These elements were seen as necessary in the preparation of children to become competent human beings (*ren,* 人)(Saari, 1989). In this view, a person by nature does not become an acceptable human being unless educated through deliberate efforts. The emphasis is placed both on parental responsibility for instruction and the child's responsibility for learning about the way of becoming human, or *zuoren* (做人). By the sixteenth century Confucian scholars proposed increased restrictions on children. There were more than a dozen texts to advise parents on child rearing which correlated disease etiology with a lack of moral cultivation among parents and a lack of effective moral teaching for their young children (Dardess, 1991, p. 75).

Environmentalist Theories of Child Development

One of the most basic assumptions of the Confucian scholar is built on the belief that a child's disposition derives from environmental influences. A child's disposition, it is believed, begins to develop before birth and during gestation, a condition which suggests the need for 'womb education', or *tai-jiao*. Headland (1914, p. 109–11) translates the concept as 'gastatony education', while Dardess (1991, p. 75) refers to it as 'placental instruction'. 'When a woman marries and becomes pregnant she is put into the school of "gestatony education", if such it may be called, in order that she may be able to impart to the child a proper disposition before it is born' (Headland, 1914, p. 109). 'If she is affected by good things the child will be good, if by bad things the child will be bad' (p. 111). The pregnant woman seeks to shape the character of the coming child by restricting her activities: avoiding bitter or spicy foods, and listening to refined music and elevated moral discourse (Dardess, 1991, p. 75). After the child is born, parents must provide the correct environment for raising it. Often cited and recited for parents is the exemplary story of a good mother who sought the best neighbourhood for raising her child. The story called *Mengmu San Qian* (Mencius' mother moves three times) was first mentioned in Liu Xiang's (77–6BC) *Lei Nu Zhuan* (Biographies of virtuous women)(Zhang, 1993, p. 169).

The process of learning to become human, according to Confucian theorists, must begin early enough in the family to lay the foundation for the child to become a future adult of proper manners and moral tenets. The ancient Chinese theories of child development emphasize the formation of habits of correct behaviour without a trace of deliberate teaching or coercion. Some scholars advocated that parents must avoid verbal abuse or physical punishment in raising a child. Cited in *Hanshi Waizhuan* is the following: 'Do not curse a son when he reaches adulthood. Do not beat a son when he is a young child' (Zhang, 1993, p. 146).

Models and Strategies of Traditional Child Rearing

Teaching by example was and still is an important principle of childhood socialization. In Chinese culture, a schoolteacher is expected to set the standards of personal morality (Meyer, 1988, p. 37). Parents, however, are considered a child's first teachers, and they must model exemplary behaviour to set a life-long foundation for the child (Luo, 1987).

Chinese parents interviewed during our research, whether in mainland China or overseas, made frequent reference to teaching by example, *yi shen zuo ze*(以身作則), as an essential element for a successful education. Parents may also take dramatic actions and cite symbolic examples, such as in the story of *Menmu Duanzhi* (Mencius's mother broke the shuttle from the loom) to teach children (see Giles, 1964, p. 8). In this story, Mencius's mother cut her almost-complete weaving on the loom while lecturing him for truancy. Mencius was so frightened at his mother's determination and the meaning of destroying her work in mid-course that he studied diligently day and night, eventually becoming a leading scholar.

Training of Affective Control

Early training in the control of affective display is part of the education in good manners for young children. *Yanshi Jiaxun* (Yan's family teaching), by Yan Zhidui (AD 531–91), emphasizes training a child from infancy to learn to interpret adults' facial expressions and to act according to parental wishes. Yan explains his own childhood by saying, 'Our family has always emphasized strictness in teaching children. When I was a young child at home, we [following two older brothers] walked properly and took every step delicately, spoke gently and calmly, and showed great reverence and fear [in front of parents and elders], as if we were approaching the emperor at the court' (Zhang, 1993, p. 249). Yan's twenty essays on family education set a model for later Confucian scholars in writings aimed at members of one's own family or clan.

The Confucian families of the gentry placed great emphasis on composed, reverential behaviour and on the restriction of physical activities among children. Many texts on family education written after the fourteenth century emphasize that the parent should teach the children 'no leaping, arguing, joking, slouching, or using vulgar language' (Dardess, 1991, p. 79). Chen Dexiu's (1178–1235) often-reprinted *Jiaozi Zhai Guai* (Regulations for the studio where I teach my sons) specifies how children should be taught to sit, stand, walk, speak, bow, recite, and write. For instance, 'The little ones are exhorted always to walk slowly with the arms held within the sleeves, with no waving of the arms or jumping' (Dardess, 1991, p. 79). Another set of Confucian family rules lists no fewer than fifteen stipulations governing the child's control of his facial expressions, his bodily postures, and his speech. This underscores an important aspect of socialization in traditional Chinese culture: to train a person to be *bugou yanxiao* (不苟言笑), to never reveal his or her thoughts and feelings.

Chinese parents were pressured to instill solemnity and self-control early on in their children. A Chinese living in the United States, Lee Yan Phou, remarked, 'The Chinese boy at sixteen is as grave and staid as an American grandfather. ...All violent exercise is discouraged, and a boy is taught that the more dignified and grave his deportment, the greater approbation he will receive from his elders' (Dardess, p. 79). Dardess correlates this emphasis in child training with the preservation of authority in Chinese society. Some neo-Confucian scholars had no tolerance for children spending time playing. Friends, it was said, 'must not gang together to make jokes, laugh, or cavort' (Dardess, 1991, p. 76). Xu Xiangqing (1479–1557) wrote, 'The child must constantly be taught not to engage in silly behaviour' (quoted in Dardess, 1991, p. 77).

On Dongshi

The argument among Confucian scholars concerning the age at which a child is old enough to be punished is based on the assumed developmental stages of a person's capacity for moral reasoning: called *dongshi* (understanding things)(see also Ho, 1986). This Confucian concept had a profound impact on folk epistemology about children's conscious intentions and interpretations of active parental teaching. Han Ying wrote in the first century BC, 'When the son reaches the age of *dongshi* (reason), the father must be serious and proper in his speech and way of living in order to teach his son' (Zhang, 1993, p. 145). Sima Guang (AD 1019–86), another famed Confucian scholar whose *Jia fan* (Family examples) was often cited, wrote, 'As soon as the child can eat by himself, he must be taught to eat with his right hand. Family discipline must begin as soon as the child can talk and begin to know things. By the age of six, teaching of numbers and names of things must begin' (Zhang, 1993, p. 353). Cheng Jing and Cheng Yi (brothers and eleventh-century Confucian scholars) wrote, 'People in ancient times discipline their children as soon as they can eat and talk' (Zhang, 1993, p. 367).

Mentioned in Dardess's (1991) paper is a seventeenth-century scholar, Jiang Yi (1631–87), who reiterated the strategy of earlier writers by emphasizing that filial devotion (*xiao*) must be taught to toddlers as soon as they can talk and walk; toddlers must learn to address elders properly and to pay daily respect to grandparents. 'The family regulations are such that as soon as a child begins to understand, he is not only taught to obey, but also loses his freedom of action' (Yan Phou Lee, 1861, quoted in Dardess, p. 77). Dardess, however, does not acknowledge that Yan Zhidui had specified an even earlier teaching of infants, as soon as they begin to be aware of adults' emotional states, to distinguish pleasure from anger. Once the children become accustomed to adults' commands and 'act or stop on demand', which should be achieved when the child is very young, then no corporal punishment is necessary. Yan quoted a common proverb saying, 'To educate a daughter-in-law, one must begin on the first day of marriage; to educate a child, one must begin with infancy'. Pang Shangpeng (c. 1524–81), a Cantonese scholar–official who wrote *Pangshi*

Jiashun (The Pang family instruction), 'laid it down that boys from the age of five will no longer be permitted to act as they please' (Dardess, 1991, p. 77).

China has produced a number of specific theories of psychological development. Lu Shiyi (AD 1611–72) developed a theory of memorization for young children and espoused early teaching, starting at the age of four, in order to take advantage of an innate capacity for memorization in childhood (Dardess, 1991, p. 81). Lu believed that the method of educating children beginning at the age of eight or nine that was advocated by Zhu Xi (c. AD 1130–1200) in his classic *Xiaoxue* (Teaching for children) began too late for the child to learn effectively. According to Lu, a man by the age of fifteen will develop the capacity of *wu* (悟), or understanding, and therefore should be pushed harder in learning the classics as preparation for the national examination. As recommended by Confucian scholars, if a young scholar had not succeeded in passing the local examination by the age of 25, then he would be forced to remain a farmer for life.

Spoiling the Child

Drowning with love, or parents allowing their affection for their children to interfere with their disciplinary responsibilities, is an important topic exercising the mind of educators and parents in contemporary China. The earliest reference to *ni'ai* (spoiling) appeared in Lin Pu's writing one thousand years ago. Lin remarks, 'These days many scholar–officials are criticized for their misbehaved children. This is an example of drowning with love and the parents have to suffer the consequences (such as being cursed by others for their children's behaviour)' (Zhang, 1993, p. 329).

The legacy of these Confucian teachings on childhood socialization still carries significant weight in contemporary Chinese societies. In two respects we can indicate how Chinese parents are still subject to these ancient teachings. First, during the early years of the People's Republic of China (PRC), authorities condemned Confucian teachings as feudal practices. With the opening up of China in the 1980s, however, Communist educators began to re-emphasize the relevance of these ancient texts for education in socialist China. Several essays on the value of ancient texts about child rearing appeared in leading academic journals. These include Shen's (1981) analysis of *Ji jiu pian*, Wang Jing's (1986) study of Zhu Xi, and Wang Bingzhao's (1984) essay on the 'critical and selective adaptation of ancient moral education'. In Taiwan, a comprehensive thesis on *Di zi zhi* by Feng (1986) echoed mainland Chinese concerns about family education for young children. Furthermore, Chinese educators boldly advocated the positive value of filial piety (Yan, 1985) as a folk (proletarian) legacy of moral education and argued for the relevance in socialist China of traditional Confucian texts on moral education (see Luo, 1987).

Secondly, despite official denouncement of ancient Confucian teachings during the early years of the People's Republic, and in spite of rapid socio-economic change, Chinese parents today manifest strong beliefs in these ancient teachings and practice accordingly in raising their children. This observation is supported by research findings to be explicated in the last section of the present paper.

CONTEMPORARY CHINESE CONCEPTIONS OF SOCIALIZATION

The second part of our discussion is focused on a literature review of recent research on the theme of Chinese socialization and findings reported in the Chinese world as well as in the Western world.

In 1986 an encyclopedic review of literature on Chinese socialization was provided by David Y. F. Ho in the collected volume *The Psychology of the Chinese People* (Bond, 1986). Characteristic Chinese socialization was described as including training for obedience, for proper conduct, for impulse control, and for the acceptance of social obligations, while a relative lack of emphasis is given to independence, assertiveness, and creativity. In a later article, Ho (1989) argued that continuity with traditional patterns of Chinese socialization is still evident in contemporary Chinese societies, although there are geographical variations in child-rearing practices.

Ho's chapter nearly exhausted the relevant publications prior to 1985 in both Chinese and English by scholars of anthropology, education, and psychology. Since the mid-1980s few references of academic work on Chinese socialization can be added to Ho's review of Chinese socialization, as there has been little new research reported on this subject. A search into diverse sources, including *Chinese Patterns of Behavior: A Sourcebook of Psychological and Psychiatric Studies* (Ho, Spinks, and Yeung, 1989), which contains more than 1,000 entries from Chinese and Western publications, yields only a few dozen references that give some indirect information about Chinese socialization in Taiwan, China, and overseas. Most studies of the topic included in this source concerned children's behaviour in kindergartens or elementary schools that reveals possible results of Chinese patterns of socialization. Another area of recent literature of Chinese socialization concerns the single-child policy, its consequences on children's behaviour, and preliminary research results on the rearing of single children in the People's Republic of China. The relevant references may be summarized as follows.

Reports on socialization in Taiwan based on psychological tests continue to focus on learning skills and achievement in school (Burton, 1986; Chen and Utal, 1988; Chalip, 1986; Farris, 1988; Lummis and Stevenson 1990; Stevenson, 1987, 1990; Winner, 1989). In kindergartens and elementary schools, Chinese children were found to be less aggressive (Ekblad, 1988), to be more cooperative in a group (Chiu, 1987, 1989), to be trained in concentration to accomplish a task in learning mathematics (Stevenson, 1987, 1990) or painting (Gardner, 1989; Winner, 1989), to be subject to more pronounced gender-role differentiation (Farris 1988; Lummis and Stevenson, 1990; Wang and Xreedon, 1989), and to receive deliberate training in honouring the collective (Wu, 1994).

One aspect of socialization in Taiwan and in the Taiwanese immigrant communities in the United States was reported in the finding that Chinese parents are still more restrictive or authoritarian than are their American counterparts (Chiu, 1987, 1989). Similar findings were also reported from mainland China, supporting the impression in the West about the restrictiveness of Chinese child rearing (Ekblad, 1986; Tobin, Wu, and Davidson, 1989).

Since the opening up of China to visits by foreign scholars in the late 1970s, Western psychologists and educational specialists have discussed the issues involved with how the Chinese raise a communist child (Baum and Baum, 1979; Honig, 1978; Kwong, 1985; Ptraka and Wilfried, 1989; Press, 1987; Roberta, 1985; Wu, 1985). The 1980s saw a growing interest among Chinese and Western experts of childhood socialization or child development on the single-child issue (Hare-Mustin and Hare, 1986; Ho, 1989; Wu 1985, 1994). Beginning in the early 1980s, there emerged in the PRC a nationwide concern about undesirable behaviour by single children due to parental leniency. Early papers by Chinese psychologists and psychiatrists confirmed official and public fears that single children were being spoiled (Tao and Chiu 1985; Jiao, Ji, and Jing, 1986). However, research on patterns of child rearing conducted under the direction of foreign scholars have yielded impressive results that deny any statistically significant differences between the behaviour of single children and children with siblings in the PRC (Wu, 1991). No distinctions can be recorded in children's behavioural patterns in schools (Falbo and Poston, 1988, 1989; Polit and Falbo, 1988; Poston and Yu, 1985). As one research group wrote:

> Despite the existence of hundreds of scientific studies demonstrating that the personality and other outcomes of only children are very similar to those of children with siblings, the only-child stereotype persists in the West. We expect that the little emperor stereotype will persist in China, despite the results reported here (Falbo and Poston, 1988, p. 16).

In an attempt to gain a more insightful understanding of the above issues, foreign scholars recently have begun to pay attention to issues of cultural discourse—how the members of the society think about, share, and debate views of social processes—on the ideology of Chinese socialization (see Wu, 1995). While a number of foreign scholars have traced the historical development of child-rearing theories from the writings of early Chinese intellectuals (Dardess, 1991; Davin, 1991; Saari, 1989), Chinese scholars in China, mostly coming from research backgrounds in history and literature, have begun to compile, edit, and publish ancient texts to instruct parents about the proper ways of rearing their children according to Confucian teachings. At least a dozen of these edited volumes have been published privately and by non-governmental publishers (see, for example, Tang and Sui, 1991; Zhang, 1993). There appears to be a demand for this type of book, as is demonstrated by the printing of 12,000 copies of Tang and Sui's (1991) 1,700-page book on family education.

Given this background for the historical development of dominant ideologies about socialization in China, it is not surprising to discover that the basic ideology and substance of Confucian teachings regarding early childhood socialization are still very much evident in today's China (see Tobin, Wu, and Davidson, 1989; Wu, 1995; Wu and Xue, 1995). Davin (1991) regards the national concern about single-child socialization as a 'moral panic about the "Little Emperors" and "Little Empresses"'. She believes that contemporary China's obsessive search for the right way to educate its children reflects a much more general and historically continuing uncertainty felt by Chinese parents about educating their young. Both Dardess (1991, p. 88) and Wu (1994) have taken the view that socialization in the kindergartens of Mao's China, by emphasizing discipline and learning while discouraging free play, perhaps evidences the continuation of Confucian ways in socializing children: training them to know their proper place in the society.

A COMPARATIVE STUDY OF PARENTAL ATTITUDES TOWARD CHINESE WAYS OF CHILD SOCIALIZATION

The third part of this paper discusses whether there is a shared Chinese cultural identity that is reflected in the way contemporary child socialization is carried out by Chinese located in different parts of the world. Do Chinese in mainland China today teach their children values different from those taught by parents in Taiwan? In spite of geographic separation and ideological differences, do Chinese in the Homeland (that is, mainland China and Taiwan) share commonalities with overseas Chinese in methods of child training?

Between 1991 and 1993 six research teams conducted research in Shanghai, southern Taiwan, Bangkok, Singapore, Honolulu, and Los Angeles. Three types of research methods were applied: videotaping of selected families of a target child's daily routines, reflexive ethnography on three central issues by interviewing thousands of parents of 5-year-old children, and a questionnaire survey (including some 40 questions) that addressed parental attitudes toward child rearing and discipline.

Here we will discuss the first part of the research in which parents first watched videotapes (one local , one from outside the community) that showed daily routines of family life centered on a target child (each tape was condensed to 20 minutes). The parents commented in writing on the same set of three questions: What makes a child an ideal child?, What are the traits of good parents?, and What constitute good methods of family education for young children? We shall describe findings from Shanghai, southern Taiwan, and Singapore.

Shanghai

Characteristics of Shanghai parental attitudes on child rearing are drawn from a survey of 600 households, representing a random sample drawn from 120 street or neighbourhood wards. The list by rank order of the leading answers to the question concerning what is a good child (*hao xiaohai* 好小孩) is grouped as follows. The most often cited indicated good moral character (answers such as: loves others, is group-oriented and cooperative, respects elders, has good manners, and is obedient and, hence, demonstrates *dongshi*, an understanding of adults' desires). The second most often cited characteristic was intelligence (answers such as: is eager to study in school and to do homework at home, is smart, and is a quick learner). The third most cited indicator was obedience (answers such as: obeys the rules, loves to help with chores, and is self-reliant, not depending on parents for dressing, washing, and studying). The fourth most cited was showing good health, and the fifth was that the child has a good personality (answers such as: is lively, active, autonomous, persevering, confident, and brave).

On what is a good parent (or ideal parents), the most often cited type was one who is responsible about his or her child receiving a good education, who is conscientious about his or her child's schooling and achievement, who is able to coach his or her child at home and is responsible in disciplining the child, who loves the child in such a manner as to become the child's *liangshi yiyou* (良師益友, good teacher and good companion). The second most often cited type was one who behaves oneself so as to set a good model for the child. The third most cited type was one who looks after his or her family's needs and keeps the members in harmony.

Regarding the goal of child training in the family, the leading answers were, first, to carry out moral education for the children, especially in teaching honesty and bravery. The second most often cited was to coach the child to study and become knowledgeable and intelligent. The third most often cited characteristic was to enrich the child's good personality or character, allowing the child to develop a healthy mind and body, and abilities and interests in manual skills. The fourth most cited characteristic was to complement and support the school by ensuring that the child does homework (even as young as at the age of five years).

Other characteristics of a parent's attitudes toward childhood socialization were noted and are worthy of mention here. These findings are summarized from a community survey of an additional 500 parents drawn from three neighbourhood kindergartens operated by the Shanghai municipal government in three street wards. Parents of both sexes report that they believe that boys and girls should receive equal levels of education, a departure from traditional Chinese attitudes on the subject. On disciplinary measures, mothers expect to discipline boys more severely than do fathers. This also varies from the traditional thinking that a severe father does not spare the rod in order to produce a filial son (*xiaozi*)(see Ho, 1974). It was discovered that mothers use methods of verbal threatening more frequently with boys than with girls. This finding conforms to other studies of socialization in Taiwan and Hong Kong, where mothers are taking a more active and decisive role in disciplining children, as extended families grow more distant and the prevalence of nuclear families increases (see Ho, 1984).

Apparently, new values have emerged with the advent of a generation of parents of single children. Parents of both sexes opposed the traditional idea that when parents discipline the child, he or she should obey and should not talk back. This new tolerance of assertive children seems to be the consequence of rearing a single child, as the indulging parents become soft when facing their demanding, domineering, and defiant child.

Other traditional ways of parenting among young Shanghai parents were found in their attitudes that 'praising children is harmful to children's development' and 'if a child fails in school, the entire family is ashamed'. Still other traditional attitudes manifested during the study include a disagreement with the statements that 'a child who always gets his way will have a better future than one who is *zhonghou laoshi* (忠厚老實, honest and considerate)' and 'parents should train children not to be bullied or yielding to others'. Concerning the last two points, the researchers suspect that parents answered the survey questions in this way to demonstrate that they submit to these values in support of the socialist collective spirit. The parents may not act accordingly in their actual behaviour.

The traditionally conservative Chinese attitude toward sexuality was shown in the young Shanghai parents' endorsement of the statement that 'parents should not display intimacy in the presence of their child'. An overwhelming 94 per cent of the fathers and 86 per cent of mothers agreed with this statement. The parents reasoned that they must provide a healthy environment for child rearing and if parents do not behave (what in the West means intimacy becomes obscene behaviour in China), it would be detrimental to their child's healthy growth. It is not, therefore, surprising to learn that more than half of the parents surveyed are opposed to the idea that they need to educate their older child to learn about dating the opposite sex.

Southern Taiwan

A total of 2,151 parents participated in two community surveys in southern Taiwan. On the three key questions of socialization, the Taiwanese parents also maintain strong traditions. On the goals of socialization, a majority of the parents are in agreement on the following points.

First, moulding a child's character to fulfill moral teaching is the main goal of socialization at home. Parents should teach desirable values, including respect for elders and identification with Chinese culture (including patriotism). It is also regarded as important to teach a child manners and that they should obey rules. Children should learn to 'become human' (*zuoren*). Taiwanese parents expect children to achieve in school and eventually to graduate from college. Most of the parents do not agree that children should be assertive, as they value a loving parent–child relationship.

The results from southern Taiwan contrast with the Shanghai results in interpretations of how parents should behave in rearing their children. The responses indicate that both parents should show loving, tender care to children, a view that disagrees with the ancient Confucian maxim that a father must be strict and not approachable (*yan* 嚴), while a mother must be kind and gentle (*ci* 慈). A high percentage of the Taiwanese parents agree that a child should have his or her say in matters that affect them. Parents must keep their promises to children, and parents must apologize to children if they are wrong. Another new attitude is the idea that parents must make time to be with their children. This development may reflect the fact that, in a growing number of Taiwanese families, both parents are working and rarely spend time with children.

An important departure from tradition, and a contrast with the views of the parents in Shanghai, is found in the area of sexual behaviour. Most of the Taiwanese parents (more so among mothers) agree on embracing and kissing their children to show love. More than 60 per cent of mothers believe that it is all right to show intimacy with their spouse, in actions such as embracing, in front of their own children.

Some new trends have developed in the methods of socialization in Taiwan. A high percentage of parents are against strict disciplinary measures. They also do not believe that parents are always right. They are particularly against the use of corporal punishment. On the other hand, Taiwanese parents are found to be conservative in other areas. In order to maintain harmonious relations with others, such as neighbors, most parents strongly disagree that 'when your own child is bullied, you should complain to other child's parents'. Another new aspect of the training of children is to teach them to beware of strangers. This concern certainly reflects the increasing degree of urbanization and anxiety about crime against children. (In Taiwan in the late 1980s and early 1990s, there were dozens of reported kidnappings of children to extort money from their parents.) The Taiwanese parents' responses indicate a changing attitude regarding individualism. A child's failure in school used to bring shame to his or her entire family, but a majority of the parents surveyed believe that it should not reflect on the family.

Singapore

Parents of students in fifteen kindergartens in Singapore were involved in a community survey, for which 542 Chinese parents returned questionnnaires to the researchers (about 50 per cent used an English questionnaire, with the other half using a Chinese version). Singaporean parents were found to be more conservative or traditional in many aspects of childhood socialization than are parents in either Taiwan or Shanghai (see also Schwartz, 1994). On the goals of socialization, the top ranking answers were, first, education for children, second, maintenance of Chinese identity, and third, assertiveness. (In a group discussion, some parents made the point that, to maintain Chinese identity, they teach their children when grown up not to marry a person who is not of Chinese descent.)

The Singaporean parents took the position that they are more Westernized, citing that they allow their children to be assertive. The evidence observed, however, indicates that these parents are unaware of the extent to which they retain many traditional Chinese values in the areas of family education, moral education, and the teaching about interpersonal relations. The presence of English as a dominant lingua franca and a Western outlook prevalent in the society may have contributed to the Singaporeans' self-image of being Westernized.

Parents in Singapore believe in the importance of discipline in early childhood. Among the respondents, 65 per cent of the parents agree that 'when parents discipline their child, the child should obey and not be allowed to talk back'. In order to discipline a child effectively, many parents admit to having sometimes threatened the child, such as reporting them to a teacher or a policeman.

Shared with the Shanghai respondents is the feeling of helplessness in being parents today. Several mothers revealed their ambivalence in disciplining their children. Although Singaporean parents report that they depend less on physical punishment than do parents on the Mainland, they profess to not entirely dismissing corporal punishment in creating a filial son. Shared with the Taiwanese parents is a new concern about safety and the teaching of children to be wary of strangers. A child must be taught to show respect for adults, and elderly people in particular. Saying polite phrases, parents believe, represents an old, and still valued, Asian tradition.

Childhood socialization among the Chinese in Singapore also shows the resiliency of conservative traditions, as exemplified in parental teachings about male–female relationships. Some 58 per cent of the surveyed parents agreed that it is not proper for parents to show intimacy in front of their children. Traditionally, Chinese parents do not praise their children for their behaviour or achievements, an attitude still endorsed by Singaporean Chinese parents.

CONCLUSION

By comparing parents' approaches to socialization in China, Taiwan, and Singapore, we realize that today's Chinese parents, despite geographical separation and ideological differences, still share many basic values and practices. They pay attention to training children to develop a moral character, such as respecting elders, cooperating, and maintaining harmonious social relations. They help and push children to achieve in school, and expect adults to set examples for children to emulate. The young parents today may not be harsh disciplinarians, but they still expect children to obey, to act on parents' commands.

Furthermore, our research teams report that Chinese parents in Honolulu and Los Angeles (some second- or third-generation Chinese-Americans) maintain the traditional value of demanding children to obey and respect their elders (see Wu and Xue, 1995). Our research findings from Los Angeles are especially important, for they involve two groups of parents, ethnic Chinese and European-Americans. Analysis of the evidence, answers to 37 survey questions, was particularly directed at testing both the subjects' 'acculturation' to American culture and their 'maintenance' of Chinese traditions. Despite sharing some general values on child rearing with their European-American counterparts, the Chinese parents' approach to socialization remains quite different from that of the other group. Our researchers discovered that in Los Angeles, there is not a great deal of acculturation of child-rearing attitudes among Chinese-Americans. The parents report that they value doing well for one's family, and adhere to parental strictness and discipline that support parents' rights and position of authority.

These comparative studies strengthen a common belief that Chinese traditions have an enduring historical and cultural continuity (see Bond, 1988; Hsu, 1981; Wu and Tseng, 1985). Bond's observation makes an important point: 'One aspect of values that may be relatively more salient from the Chinese tradition is, of course, the value of tradition itself' (1988, p. 1010). Our research on socialization among descendants of Chinese emigrants shows that overseas Chinese are concerned to retain some basic elements of Chinese culture and, like their forefathers in the Confucian tradition, believe that childhood socialization is the key to maintaining Chinese identity.

Traditional Chinese conceptions of childhood and prescribed socialization for young children prevail in the modern world. We have drawn from historical sources, from contemporary psychological research, and from comparative studies of Chinese socialization to identify the characteristic patterns of socialization that have been and still are practiced in Chinese societies.

Chapter 11

Filial Piety and Its Psychological Consequences

David Y. F. Ho

Confucian filial piety provides an example of culturally defined intergenerational relationships *par excellence*. Although some of its component ideas (obedience, for example) are shared by other cultures, filial piety surpasses all other ethics in its historical continuity, the proportion of humanity under its governance, and the encompassing and imperative nature of its precepts. The attributes of intergenerational relationships governed by filial piety are structural, enduring, and invariable across situations within Chinese culture. They may be generalized to apply to authority relationships beyond the family, and they are thus potent determinants of not only intergenerational but also superior–subordinate interactions.

For centuries, filial piety has served as a guiding principle governing general Chinese patterns of socialization, as well as specific rules of intergenerational conduct, applicable throughout the length of one's life span (D. Y. F. Ho, 1987). It prescribes how children should behave towards their parents, living or dead, as well as towards their ancestors. It makes stringent demands: that one should provide for the material and mental well-being of one's aged parents, perform ceremonial duties of ancestral worship, take care to avoid harm to one's body, ensure the continuity of the family line, and in general conduct oneself so as to bring honour and avoid disgrace to the family name.

Filial piety justifies absolute parental authority over children and, by extension, the authority of those senior in generational rank over those junior in rank. The veneration of the aged, for which Chinese society has long been renowned, also owes its ethical basis to filial piety. Filial obligations, both material and spiritual, are overriding in importance, rigidly prescribed, and are binding from the time one is considered old enough to be disciplined to the end of one's life.

To be sure, the Confucian classics do not advocate *yu xiao* (foolish filial piety), such as blind obedience to one's parents. On the contrary, it is a filial obligation to remonstrate with them, with unfailing patience, when questions of unrighteous conduct on the part of parents arise. Nevertheless, rebellion or outright defiance against parental authority, except under the most unusual circumstances, can in no way be condoned. In real life, the pressure to submit to parental demands, backed by the weight of cultural tradition, typically leaves one with little choice but to accede. It is thus important to recognize that, as a cornerstone of Confucianism, filial piety goes far beyond the requirement that one merely obey and honour one's parents. This point is critical to the discussion of conceptual and methodological issues that follows.

Scholars have long recognized the central importance of filial piety as the basic ethic governing intergenerational and, by extension, interpersonal relationships in Chinese society. For the most part, however, they have shown little interest in studying filial piety from a psychological perspective. One reason for this lack of interest is academic compartmentalization. Traditionally, sinology is a discipline dominated by historians, philologists, and philosophers, who have largely ignored the behavioural science literature on Chinese society. Another reason is that psychological research on filial piety began only recently. Not until the 1970s did empirical studies appear in the psychological literature.

That the psychological study of filial piety should have seen such a belated beginning is deplorable, as it is indispensable for a deeper understanding of the instrumental role that filial piety plays in shaping personality, social behaviour, and socio-political institutions. The knowledge derived from psychological research can no longer be ignored if sinology is to be invigorated by the cross-disciplinary fertilization of ideas. Beyond the reach of sinology proper, the study of filial piety also contributes to a body of knowledge about the cultural definition of intergenerational relationships, of crucial importance to understanding the transmission of culture from one generation to the next. Viewed in this light, the growing volume of psychological research on filial piety in recent years is an encouraging development.

The present chapter is an attempt to assess the current status of psychological research on filial piety. We review the research literature and endeavor to integrate findings into a coherent body of knowledge, paying particular attention to the influence of filial piety on parental attitudes, child training, personality formation, and cognitive functioning. The wider implications for socio-political processes are also explored. A central theme is that internal psychological and external socio-political processes, both rooted in filial piety, are mutually reinforcing. Two theoretical constructs, authoritarian moralism and cognitive conservatism, serve as conceptual linkages between cultural values and psychological functioning. Finally, we will discuss the cross-cultural significance of research on filial piety.

REVIEW OF THE LITERATURE

We turn first to a discussion of approaches to the measurement of filial piety, before reviewing research findings grouped according to the following headings: determinants of filial attitudes, continuities and departures from tradition, and filial attitudes and filial behaviour.

Approaches to Measurement

A survey of empirical studies reveals two broad approaches to the measurement of filial piety, each addressed to different research questions.

Use of moral dilemmas to study filial cognition

The first approach to measurement, prompted by Kohlberg's theory of moral development, uses stories of filial piety involving moral dilemmas to study filial cognition. One advantage of this approach is that it enables the researcher to study the processes of moral reasoning involved in the excercise of filial piety. Lee (1974) delineated five stages of development in filial cognition, wherein filial piety is respectively regarded as: first, giving material benefits to parents or ancestors; then, any behaviour beneficial to parents or ancestors, with an understanding that emotional or spiritual support is more important than material support; recognition that filial piety is instrumental in realizing parent–child relationships based on mutual expectations regarding caring, love, and obedience; recognition that it is instrumental to realizing ideal relationships founded on mutual caring and love, not merely to maintain harmony within the family; and finally, that filial piety is the most suitable route for Chinese people to actualize their ethical ideals. The results showed that age correlated highly (.70) with the stages of filial cognition. Lee's stages of filial cognition correlated highly (.70) with Piaget's stages of cognitive development; the partial correlation was .49, with age being controlled. Lee contends that Piaget's stages are necessary, but not sufficient, conditions for the development of filial cognition. For example, he argues, the stage of formal operations must be reached for the last two stages of filial cognition to emerge.

Yeh and Yang (1989, 1990) proposed a conceptual framework for analyzing filial behaviour, comprising six elements: the actor, usually a son or daughter; normative principles followed by the actor; the object of interaction, usually a parent; instigating or motivational factors; relational attributes (for example, unequal–unidirectional versus equal–bidirectional) of the actor–object dyad; and the goals of filial actions (material versus spiritual). Yeh and Yang (1989) reported that, with increasing age, filial cognition tends to shift: from other-regulated to self-regulated normative principles, from filial acts directed toward parents or ancestors to those directed toward a larger domain of objects (for example, one's country and society), from inequality–unidirectionality to equality–bidirectionality, and from material to spiritual goals. These changes occur at about the time when children enter senior middle school (equivalent to grades 10 to 12). Additionally, older children tend to be less absolutist and do not rely on a single bipolar dimension (such as filial–unfilial) in their judgements of filiality.

The studies by Lee (1974) and Yeh and Yang (1989, 1990) illustrate the great variability with which individuals construe what it means to be filial. As expected, the moral maturity of that construal is a function of cognitive development. The question arises, however, if we can still regard aspects of the more mature construals by older children as Confucian. To construe the parent–child dyad as an equal relationship, for instance, clearly deviates from the Confucian tradition—and probably from most other cultural traditions.

Psychometric measures of filial attitudes

The second approach to measuring filial piety relies on the development of scales or questionnaires as instruments to measure attitudes or beliefs toward filial piety. Typically this approach has been used when the object is to investigate the determinants, psychological implications or correlates (for example, personality traits) of filial attitudes, to compare the strength of filial attitudes among various groups, or to measure changes in filial attitudes between generations.

Following a psychometric approach, Y. F. Ho and Lee (1974) developed the Filial Piety Scale as a measure of traditional filial attitudes rooted in Confucianism. Subsequently, using modified versions of this scale, researchers investigated the effect of parents' filial attitudes on their children's cognitive performance (Boey, 1976), the extent of change in the strength of filial attitudes between generations (D. Y. F. Ho and Kang, 1984), filial piety and its relations to family care for the elderly (Yeung, 1989), family–matrimonial traditionalism (D. Y. F. Ho, Hong, and Chiu, 1989), and child training, authoritarian moralism, and cognitive conservatism (D. Y. F. Ho, 1994). D. Y. F. Ho (1993) assembled, analysed, and integrated available data collected with the Filial Piety Scale on the determinants and correlates of filial attitudes. The data support the claim that the scale is a suitable instrument for research, with sufficient reliability and validity.

From a methodological point of view, developing a measure of traditional filial piety, such as the Filial Piety Scale, has strategic importance for research. It enables researchers to gauge the direction, extent, and momentum of change within a geopolitical location, as well as variation across locations. This is important because continuities with and departures from tradition may differ widely as a function of location. There are undeniable variations among mainland China, Taiwan, Hong Kong, and overseas Chinese communities, representing divergent departures from tradition. No assumption should be made that traditionalism is necessarily the opposite of modernism (see Yang, this volume). Traditional and modern filial attitudes may coexist and may be better represented on more than one continuum.

Determinants of Filial Attitudes

The determinants of attitudes toward traditional filial piety were systematically investigated by D. Y. F. Ho (1993). In the results of that study, education emerges as the most potent predictor, and one which is negatively related to filial attitudes. Other determinants, with rather small effect sizes, are sex, age, membership of a subgroup within the culture, and exposure to Western and Christian influences. Women, older people, and people in Taiwan tend to affirm filial attitudes more strongly than do men, younger people, and people in Hong Kong respectively. Exposure to Western, and especially Christian, influences is associated with a weakening, though rather mild, of filial attitudes. Family structure and sibship variables have no predictive power. Similar results have been reported by D. Y. F. Ho et al. (1989).

Of great theoretical import is the finding that attitudes toward filial piety are more strongly held among people, both young and old, with a lower socio-economic status, and in both Hong Kong and Taiwan (D. Y. F. Ho, 1993; D. Y. F. Ho et al., 1989). This pattern contrasts diametrically with that in traditional Chinese society, where members of the scholar–gentry were expected to be models of filiality. If indeed values held more strongly by low-status than by high-status people tend to wane in time, we may expect a decline of traditional filial piety. The association of filial attitudes with lower socio-economic status is in line with a general pattern linking the endorsement of conformity-obedience values to lower socio-economic status in different societies (Kohn, Naoi, Schoenbach, Schooler, and Slomczynski, 1990).

Continuities and Departures from Tradition

Undoubtedly, filial beliefs and actions among contemporary Chinese differ from those of their forebears. Nevertheless, the significance of filial piety, so deeply rooted in Chinese society, remains evident. Some studies suggest that filial piety, although not unchallenged or unchanged, remains a durable ethic in Taiwan (Hwang, 1977; E. S. H. Yu, 1974), in Singapore (Thomas, 1989), and among Chinese immigrants in the United States (Lin, 1985). A study of word-frequency counts (Liu, Chuang, and Wang, 1975) gives an illustration of how pervasive the ethic of filial piety remains in Taiwan. The investigators sampled printed passages containing one million words from newspapers, magazines, works of fiction and nonfiction, primary and secondary school textbooks, and non-educational reading materials. The frequency count of Chinese compound words that include the roots filial, loyal, and official far exceeded those of English words related to the same three roots, based on counts included in the teacher's word book by Thorndike and Lorge (1944).

However, there is evidence that filial piety is on the decline and no longer commands the same degree of absolute observance it once did (D. Y. F. Ho, 1993; D. Y. F. Ho, Hong, and Chiu, 1989; D. Y. F. Ho and Kang, 1984). Some core filial obligations (for example, ancestral worship and repaying one's indebtedness to parents) continue to be affirmed. Other filial demands (such as absolute obedience and subjugation of individual needs and interests to those of parents) tend to be negated. This finding is consistent with patterns reported by Hwang (1977) and Chuang and Yang (1990). The most direct evidence pointing to a decline of filial piety, which is measurable even between only two generations, may be found in the study by D. Y. F. Ho and Kang (1984).

The apparent inconsistency in empirical results may arise from differences in the ways in which filial piety is defined and measured. D. Y. F. Ho and his associates used the Filial Piety Scale to measure traditional filial attitudes. In Hwang's (1977) study, a questionnaire was used to survey filial attitudes among students in Taiwan. He found that the students overwhelmingly responded in the affirmative to the question: 'In modern society, how necessary is it for children to be filial toward their parents?' This result is hardly surprising, simply because Chinese children are expected to be filial sons and daughters. However, when the same students were asked to list specific aspects of filiality they regarded as 'incompatible with modern life, hard to put into practice, and most disagreeable to myself personally', the most frequently listed included those essential to traditional prescriptions (for example, absolute obedience, continuation of the family line, and living together with one's parents). Clearly, to say that one would remain filial toward one's parents does not necessarily imply that one would want to act so in the traditional sense.

Filial Attitudes and Filial Behaviour

A related question concerns the extent to which filial attitudes are reflected in filial behaviour, the distance between what one believes ought to be done and what one in fact does or intends to do. L. C. Yu (1983) reported that the level of filial behaviour did not correspond to that of filial belief among Chinese-Americans. D. Y. F. Ho (1990) reported that filial attitudes were significantly correlated (at the .05 level) with the Traditional Behavior Index, a self-reported measure of traditional behaviour. However, the magnitude of the correlations was rather small (around .25 for two samples of subjects from Hong Kong and Taiwan). An item analysis showed that correlations with filial attitudes were generally no higher for items pertaining to filial behaviour (for example, ancestral worship and remembering parents' birthdays or dates of death) than for other items of traditional behaviour (such as observing formalities during Chinese New Year). That filial attitudes may not translate into filial behaviour was driven home by another result obtained: a group of young male offenders in Hong Kong, by and large, said that they subscribed to the precepts of filial piety. Each had been convicted and was serving a sentence in an institution for juvenile delinquents, thus bringing disgrace to his family, a decidedly unfilial behaviour in Chinese society.

D. Y. F. Ho (1990, see also 1993) compared the filial attitudes and filial behaviours of a traditional and a non-traditional group of Hong Kong secondary school students. As expected, the traditional group showed much stronger filial attitudes than did the non-traditional group. However, an item analysis of the Traditional Behavior Index revealed no significant differences in filial behaviour between the two groups. Such results suggest that differences in filial attitudes may not be reflected in actual differences in behaviour.

Yeung (1989) reported that elderly people in Hong Kong held attitudes toward filial piety that were negatively correlated with measures of the medical care, social support, and psychological support they received. The author suggested that those holding stronger filial attitudes tended to have higher expectations of support from their family members, and would hence experience greater disappointment when their expectations were not met. Indeed, a negative correlation was found between filial attitudes and self-reported life satisfaction. Yeung's study reveals the strain of societal changes in Hong Kong: it is ironic that the more strongly the elderly hold onto traditional filial values, the less likely they are to find life satisfactory.

Chuang and Yang (1990) attempted to measure the distance between filial belief and filial behaviour in Taiwan. Filial belief was regarded as an attitudinal component, measured by the degree to which respondents agreed that various aspects of filial piety ought to be observed. Filial behaviour was a self-reported measure of the degree to which one had actually observed them. Filial beliefs that were still strongly held included remembering and worshipping one's deceased parents, minimizing parents' worries, bringing glory to one's parents, and treating one's parents with respectful propriety. Staying close to serve one's parents, continuing the family line, and obedience were less strongly held. The extent to which filial beliefs were reported to be actually observed varied according to how strongly they were held. For filial beliefs that were strongly held, mean scores tended to be higher than were those for filial behaviour; the reverse was found for filial beliefs that were less strongly held. Thus, the distance between belief and behaviour varied according to the particular beliefs concerned.

In sum, the research results reviewed point to two broad generalizations, both of which reinforce the view that filial piety no longer commands absolute observance as it did in the past. First, the extent to which traditional filial attitudes are reflected in actual behaviour seems rather limited. Second, present-day Chinese are becoming selective in their filial beliefs and actions.

THEORETICAL CONSTRUCTS AND CROSS-CULTURAL CONSIDERATIONS

Two constructs, *authoritarian moralism* and *cognitive conservatism*, serve as linkages between filial piety as a Confucian value external to the individual and the corresponding psychological functioning internal to the individual (D. Y. F. Ho, 1994).

Authoritarian Moralism

D. Y. F. Ho (1993, 1994) argues that authoritarian moralism is a central characteristic of Chinese patterns of socialization guided by filial piety. This construct embodies two salient features of Confucian societies: a hierarchical ranking of authority in the family, in educational, and in socio-political institutions and a pervasive application of moral precepts as the primary standard against which people are judged.

The absolute authority of parents and teachers is both a symptom and a cause of authoritarianism. Moralism puts overriding emphasis on the development of moral character through education. It predisposes parents to be moralistic, rather than psychologically oriented: to treat their children in terms of whether their conduct meets some external moral criteria, rather than in terms of sensitivity to their internal needs, feelings, and aspirations. Children are to be transformed into adults who exercise impulse control, behave properly, and fulfill their obligations—above all, filial obligations (D. Y. F. Ho, 1987).

Data assembled by D. Y. F. Ho (1994; see also Boey, 1976) show that attitudes toward filial piety tend to be moderately associated with traditional parental attitudes and child training: overcontrol, overprotection, and harshness; placement of emphasis on proper behaviour; and neglect, even inhibition, of the expressing of opinions, of independence, and of self-mastery, creativity, and all-around personal development in the child. They support the view that filial piety underlies socialization characterized by authoritarian moralism, putting the accent on obedience and indebtedness to parents, not self-fulfillment, on impulse control, not self-expression, and on moral correctness, not psychological sensitivity.

Such a pattern of socialization is in line with the demands of Confucian societies. The emphasis on internal impulse control prepares children to meet the strong demands of external social control. The insistence on obedience at home prepares children to function in the hierarchical social order later in life. Not surprisingly, the Filial Piety Scale is found to be correlated with measures of traditional Chinese attitudes pertaining to authority relations, status distinctions, and politics (D. Y. F. Ho, 1993). That is, filial attitudes are closely associated with views of a socio-political order predicated on hierarchical authority relations, sharp social-status distinctions, and faith in the moral character of the leader rather than in institutions, the rule of law, and political participation. Thus, filial piety is instrumental to the definition of authority relations not only within but also beyond the family.

Clinical observations of the reactions of Chinese children to absolute parental authority reveal typical patterns: emotional distancing from parents, especially the father; a generalized tendency to fear authority figures; a tendency to adopt silence, negativism, or passive resistance as a behavioural style in dealing with authority's demands; a tendency to turn aggression inward; and a dissociation between affect and roles. D. Y. F. Ho (1987) suggests that affect–role dissociation is a psychological mechanism in response to filial prescriptions. The mechanism makes it possible for children to remain filial sons and daughters, while performing their acts of filiality with emotional detachment.

Of all human relationships, that between father and son is the most important in the Confucian social fabric. Tu (1985) explains that the father–son relationship is 'absolutely binding' (p. 237); it 'provides a context and an instrumentality for self-cultivation' (p. 248) and spiritual development. Tu is aware of the assault on Confucian values by Chinese intellectuals since the turn of the present century, and seems to be concerned with defending Confucianism against this assault. He concerns himself exclusively with the ethical question of what ought to be, and completely ignores the scientific question of what is. He makes no reference to the relevant behavioural science literature. After reviewing the empirical evidence, D. Y. F. Ho (1987) concludes that the Chinese father–son relationship tends to be marked by affective distance, perhaps even tension and antagonism.

Thus a basic contradiction is addressed: psychological distance rather than closeness has been found to characterize the relationship idealized by Confucians. At rock bottom, this is a contradiction between cultural prescription and the psychological reaction to it. Until most recently, it has not been addressed, let alone recognized, in the culture. Filial piety itself acts to repress awareness of the contradiction, and in this sense engenders cultural blindspots.

Cognitive Conservatism

Cognitive conservatism is a psychological construct described by Greenwald (1980) that refers to a disposition to preserve existing knowledge structures. Greenwald argues for a conception of the ego as an organization of knowledge, characterized by three cognitive biases: egocentricity (self as the focus of knowledge), beneffectance (perception of responsibility for desired, but not undesired, outcomes), and cognitive conservatism (resistance to cognitive change). His psychological portrait of what he calls the totalitarian ego bears a striking correspondence to the portrayal of totalitarian political systems by political scientists.

Research results are summating to an impressive body of evidence that implicates filial piety in the development of cognitive conservatism. Boey (1976; see also D. Y. F. Ho, 1994) administered a battery of psychological tests measuring rigidity and cognitive complexity to college students in Hong Kong. It was found that the students' own attitudes toward filial piety were not correlated with any of the tests. However, the subject's father's attitude toward filial piety was positively correlated with some of the child's scores on tests of rigidity, and both the father's and mother's attitudes toward filial piety were negatively correlated with some of the child's scores on tests of cognitive complexity. The consistency of results was striking: in all instances, correlations with tests of rigidity (ranging from -.19 to -.65) were negative, and correlations with tests of cognitive complexity (ranging from .14 to .49) were positive. These results have causal implications, because it is reasonable to assume that parents are instrumental in the development of children, rather than the other way around. They provide the strongest evidence yet that parental attitudes toward filial piety have an adverse effect on cognitive development.

Data assembled by D. Y. F. Ho (1994, see also 1993) indicate that people holding filial attitudes tend to adopt a passive, uncritical, and uncreative orientation toward learning; to hold fatalistic, superstitious, and stereotyped beliefs; and to be authoritarian, dogmatic, and conformist—a constellation of attributes pointing toward cognitive conservatism. They are also more likely to engage in superstitious practices, such as consulting an almanac or fortune-tellers in making decisions (D. Y. F. Ho, 1990).

D. Y. F. Ho (1993, see also 1994) reported that filial attitudes are strongly associated with traditionalism and culturocentrism. Both constructs express a conservative ideology. Traditionalism reinforces what D. Y. F. Ho calls 'orientation toward the past' or 'past orientation', both culturally and psychologically. Chinese people refer to their forebears as 'the people ahead' and future generations yet unborn as 'the people behind'. The moral implication is that we are to follow the footsteps of our forebears. Psychologically speaking, the past is in front of us and the future behind us, directly opposite to the Western conception. Culturocentrism refers to a world-view based on a firm belief in the permanence, centrality, and perhaps even superiority of one's culture in comparison with others.

Taken together, the evidence supports a conclusion that Chinese patterns of socialization that are guided by filial piety are biased toward the development of cognitive conservatism. It also establishes a linkage between external cultural values and internal individual cognition: cognitive conservatism operating within the individual mirrors the ideological conservatism of Confucianism governing human relationships and social institutions. In short, filial piety underlies both ideological and cognitive conservatism.

The causal sequence through which Chinese culture exerts its influence on individual cognition may be conceptualized as follows: filial piety constitutes the ideological basis for parental attitudes, which translate into child-training practices and, more generally, socialization patterns characterized by authoritarian moralism. In turn, these patterns exert their influence on cognitive development.

Cross-cultural Considerations

Cross-cultural studies of filial piety are virtually nonexistent. One obvious reason is that filial piety is indigenous to China. It is an emic concept to which there is no real conceptual equivalent, to my knowledge, in non-Confucian cultures. Accordingly, an endorsement of filial piety cannot be equated with an endorsement of filial values that are common to other cultures, such as submission to parental authority. Rather, the definition of intergenerational relationships based on filial piety assumes a culture-specific, and rather extreme, form. Nevertheless, research has established an empirical base for linking filial piety to authoritarian moralism and cognitive conservatism, constructs that have an etic significance. Such a linkage suggests that components of filial piety shared by other cultures and their psychological correlates require cross-cultural study.

Filial piety was included as 1 of 40 items in the Chinese Culture Connection (1987), a survey of Chinese values in 22 countries around the world. One methodological difficulty encountered in this study was that the filial piety item (translated into English) was presented as: 'filial piety (obedience to parents, respect for parents, honouring of ancestors, financial support of parents)'. The expressions within the parentheses were regarded as synonyms for the main term. Certainly, the item contains some key components of filial piety; however, as I have taken pains to point out, filial piety is an encompassing ethic, much more than what the item expresses. This methodological point should be borne in mind particularly when research on filial piety is conducted outside Confucian cultural contexts.

The filial piety item was found to be negatively related both to the factor Integration in an ecological or culture-level factor analysis (Chinese Culture Connection, 1987), and to the bipolar factor Social Integration versus Cultural Inwardness in an individual-level factor analysis (Bond, 1988). This result implies that key components of filial piety are negatively related to 'pro-social virtues that enhance cohesiveness with others in general', and are among those virtues concerning 'loyalty to more narrowly defined groups (family, culture) along with their defining habits and customs' (Bond, 1988, p. 1011). Such an implication would be unsettling to Confucians, who have always regarded the maintenance of harmony within the family as a basis for attaining wider social harmony.

It is also instructive to place the association of filial piety with traditionalism and culturocentrism, an intracultural finding in Ho's (1993) study, in the context of cross-cultural research. Given the argument above about cognitive conservatism, a similar conflation of constructs may be found in other cultures as well. Indeed, Bond (1988) finds that the filial piety item is associated with 'respect for tradition' and 'a sense of cultural superiority' in his multicultural study. This result supports the contention of a universal linkage between submission to parental authority, a key component of filial piety, and cognitive conservatism.

More recently, in a study of university students in Hong Kong, E. F. K. Ho (1994) reports that filial piety has a high loading on Agreeableness and, to a lesser extent, Conscientiousness, two of the 'Big Five' personality factors (McCrae and John, 1992). This result is difficult to interpret for both methodological and theoretical reasons. To begin with, the author provides no theoretical reasoning or explanation for the result obtained. Filial piety (more precisely, filial behaviour) was measured by a factor comprising only five items, hardly adequate in terms of content validity; its reliability was modest (.65). It was among 4 'indigenous' factors, together with 30 'imported' facets comprising the Big Five factors, included in a factor analysis. The aim was to determine if the indigenous factors could be incorporated into the five-factor model of personality. Because no new factor emerged, the author concluded that the five-factor model provided a 'defensible and conservative interpretation' of the result obtained.

This conclusion is unwarranted, however. The indigenous factors would be dwarfed merely on account of their numeric disproportion to the imported facets, and be easily absorbed into the Big Five factor structure. More importantly, the facets within imported factors were correlated, but the factors themselves were orthogonal and hence uncorrelated. (Data on the intercorrelations among indigenous factors are not provided.) Thus, the result of the factor analysis could be nothing more than a mathematical artefact that has no clear psychological meaning, especially if the intercorrelations among indigenous factors are low. These considerations invite a further study of the linkages between filial piety and imported personality factors.

CONCLUSION

Two salient impressions emerge from the literature review and discussion above. First, traditional filial piety is on the decline, as can be seen in the change in filial attitudes between generations, the negative relation between the strength of filial attitudes and socio-economic status, and the reduced extent to which filial precepts command observance. This decline signifies a radical change in the Chinese definition of intergenerational relationships, leading to a liberalization of traditional constraints on the development of individuality. Authority relations between generations are altered, necessitating new approaches to the resolution of intergenerational conflicts (cf. D. Y. F. Ho, 1987).

Second, the research evidence consistently points to negative psychological consequences of filial piety from a contemporary perspective on human development. Authoritarian-moralistic personalities, having been inculcated with filial precepts in childhood, would find it congenial to function in authoritarian institutions. Similarly, cognitive conservatism is adaptive to living in a society governed by a conservative ideology. The internal psychological and the external socio-political processes go hand in hand. Thus, the psychological research on filial piety compels us to be cognizant of the ancient cultural root that frustrates democratization in modern China. It now demands rightful attention from scholars of Chinese culture and society.

NOTES

The author gratefully acknowledges the financial support for the preparation of the present chapter from the University of Hong Kong.

Chapter 12

∎

Emotion Among the Chinese

James A. Russell and Michelle S. M. Yik

Observers both inside and outside the culture have speculated about the emotions of the Chinese. What in their emotional lives do the Chinese people share with all other human beings and what is unique to the Chinese? How do Chinese people understand emotion? Certain emotions have been said to have universal facial expressions, universal physiological signatures, and universal subjective feelings. Have these hypotheses been verified in Chinese samples? Concepts such as anxiety, depression, and romantic love have been said to be alien or even missing from the Chinese understanding of emotion. Could that be so?

In this chapter, we seek to explore such questions and to review those writings on Chinese emotions that are available to researchers. Unfortunately, the amount of evidence collected and the breadth of discussion of the topic is discouragingly small. Our emphasis here is thus placed on raising questions and suggesting topics for further study.

Before we begin the discussion, we should make explicit our own supposition that an emotion is not a thing but a process consisting of a sequence of components. Emotion is the pattern among the components rather than a component in and of itself. In this chapter, we begin with the delineation of the components that constitute an emotional episode. Specifically, we consider the situational antecedents of emotion, its cognitive antecedents, the facial and vocal expression of emotion, the physiological or somatic component, emotional behaviour in a social context, and the influence of emotion on subsequent cognitive performance. Finally, the last section is devoted to the indigenous Chinese conceptualization of emotion.

EMOTIONAL EPISODES

Situational Antecedents of Emotion

What brings pride in one culture might bring shame in another. Foods or behaviours found delightful in one culture might be considered disgusting in another. Borke and Su (1972) and Borke (1973) found that Chinese and American children sometimes associate different emotions (represented by stylized facial expressions) with a given situation. General principles on this matter have not emerged, however, and recent efforts have searched for cognitive mediators that might account for systematic differences in the antecedents of emotion.

Cognitive Mediators

Many writers on emotion argue that what appears to be the 'same' antecedent event need not be the same psychologically, in that it can be construed differently by different people or at different times or places. Cultural differences in the antecedents of emotion might therefore suggest differences in how events are construed, and differences in how an event is construed would suggest cultural differences in the emotional reaction to that event. Attribution theory (Stipek, Weiner, and Li, 1989) and appraisal theory (Mauro, Sato, and Tucker, 1992) attempt to describe the cognitive links that mediate between an antecedent event and the emotional reaction to that event.

Stipek et al. (1989) suggested the possibility of cultural differences in the attributional links between events and emotions on just such grounds. Consider, for example, the emotion of pride. The Chinese counterpart to the word pride (*jiaoao*) has the connotation of *hubris*, and Chinese were found to be less likely than were Americans to judge pride as an emotion that they would like to experience (Sommers, 1984). Chinese subjects who made self-enhancing (pride-related) attributions following success on a task have been found to be less well liked than were subjects who made self-effacing attributions (Bond, Leung, and Wan, 1982). Stipek et al. (1989) therefore anticipated that these cultural differences in the value of pride would have implications for attribution-emotion linkages for Chinese: 'Unlike Americans, for whom pride is a prominent emotion that is linked with high ability ascriptions in achievement contexts, ...Chinese may not experience or may tend to deny experiencing pride. Or, given the often reported cultural value of sacrificing personal gains for the good of society, ...Chinese may only report experiencing pride for achievements that benefit others' (p. 110).

Stipek and her colleagues (1989) conducted a series of studies examining the relationship between emotions and attributions in mainland China and the United States. In one study, subjects were asked to describe situations that would make someone feel pride (*jiaoao*), as well as anger (*shengqi*), guilt (*neijiu*), pity (*kelian*), and shame (*diulian*). Results for pride did not show what had been anticipated: More Americans (82 per cent) than Chinese (29 per cent) spontaneously referred to effort as an antecedent to feeling pride, although, as expected, significantly more Americans (92 per cent) than Chinese (77 per cent) referred to personal achievements in their descriptions of pride-evoking events. It may be that Americans saw effort as above and beyond the call of duty, and therefore something to be proud of, whereas the Chinese saw effort as an obligation to the group. The authors did not find evidence for the stereotype of Chinese as emphasizing effort over ability as a cause of achievements or as de-emphasizing personal achievement. We speculate that this result might be unique to their subjects, who were young and educated, and that a different result might occur with more traditional Chinese subjects (see Yang, this volume).

More generally, Stipek et al. (1989) found that the main tenets of attribution theory generalized well to the Chinese. For example, construal of someone as lacking ability elicits pity, construal of that person as lacking effort elicits anger, and construal of that person as a victim of one's own failure elicits guilt. In

short, Chinese and American subjects produced a very similar pattern in attribution–emotion linkages (see also Crittendan, this volume).

Mauro et al. (1992) approached the study of cognitive mediators from the
perspective of appraisal theory. Subjects in Hong Kong, Japan, mainland
China, and the United States recalled one emotion episode of a type specified
by the experimenter (16 emotion terms were used). The subject then rated the
eliciting antecedent event on scales thought to tap dimensions of cognitive
appraisal. The same dimensions of appraisal emerged from multivariate analyses within each sample. The correlations obtained among the appraisal dimensions themselves also suggested no differences among these four groups.

Mauro and his colleagues (1992) also explored possible differences in the
associations between emotions and each dimension of appraisal. On the more
primitive dimensions—pleasantness, certainty, attention, ability to cope, con-
duciveness to goal—no differences among the four groups were found. On
three more cognitively complex dimensions, however—anticipated effort,
control, and responsibility—significant differences between country samples
were observed. Of these, appraisal of control over events was responsible for
most of the cultural differences. Compared with Americans, the Chinese were
more likely to take pride in events that they perceived to be beyond their control and to perceive that other people are the cause of acts that make them sad.
Americans took more pride in their own actions and felt sadder in circumstances beyond anyone's control.

To summarize, firm evidence has not been found that would clearly show
any situations in which Chinese react to an event with dramatically different
emotions than would be observed with members of another ethnic group. The
available evidence suggests more similarities than differences in the
antecedents of emotion, a conclusion consonant with evidence from other cultures (Boucher and Brandt, 1981; Scherer, Wallbott, and Summerfield, 1986).
Moreover, the cognitive processes that intervene between eliciting events and
emotional reactions seem remarkably similar as well. Perhaps differences
might become more apparent when research has moved beyond the more
'basic' emotions to more cultural-specific ones, and from more 'basic' appraisal
and attribution dimensions to more complex ones.

Facial and Vocal Expression of Emotion

Some writers have emphasized pan-cultural facial and vocal expressions of
'basic' emotions that are universally recognized (Ekman et al., 1987; Izard,
1977), whereas others have argued that different cultures may have somewhat
different ways of expressing at least some emotions (Klineberg, 1938).

In a typical study, subjects are shown a photograph of a facial expression
reported to be of a certain emotion and asked to name that emotion. Table 12.1
shows representative results from one such study. The figures shown are
called 'recognition' scores, the percentage of subjects who agree with the
experimenter's prediction. The first column of Table 12.1 shows the target
emotion. The second column shows results from a method used frequently in
research on facial expression. Respondents saw photographs of posed facial
expressions, which had been highly selected to achieve consensus on one

Table 12.1   Recognition Scores (in percentages) for Facial Expressions
of Emotion

Emotion condition	Forced-choice labelling of posed expressions of Chinese adults[a]	Free-labelling of spontaneous expressions of Chinese babies[b]
happiness	100.0	100.0
surprise	80.0	72.5
sadness	76.7	35.0
anger	96.7	20.0
fear	50.0	32.5
disgust	66,7	10.0

Note   Figures given are percentage of respondents who agreed with the
predicted label on that photograph with the highest degree of recognition.
[a]Wang and Meng (1986), $n = 30$.
[b]Meng, Yan, and Meng (1985), $n = 40$.

specific emotion. They were then asked to select their response from a short
list of emotion words. The results seem to suggest two conclusions. First, as
found in other cultures, Chinese respondents obtained recognition scores far
greater than chance. Second, recognition varied with type of expression:
recognition scores for happiness were high, whereas those for fear and disgust
were moderate. Recently, the method used in these and similar studies (for
example, Chan, 1985; Ekman, et al., 1987) has been criticized as insensitive to
cultural differences and capable of overestimating the degree of consensus on
which emotion is expressed by a given face (Russell, 1994).

The third column of Table 12.1 shows results from a potentially more sensitive method: free-labelling of the photographs of spontaneous facial expressions. Meng, Yan, and Meng (1985) produced their own stimulus photographs
of facial expressions by eliciting emotions in ten mainland Chinese babies
(with a mean age of 15.6 months). Happiness, for example, was elicited by
allowing the baby to play with a toy; disgust was elicited by the smell of vine-
gar. Fifteen photographs of the babies were then selected and shown to 40 college students, who were allowed to choose their own emotion label. Only the
expression of happiness achieved the degree of agreement seen in studies of
posed expressions.

The intracultural study conducted by Meng and her colleagues provides
researchers with materials for interesting cross-cultural comparisons originating in the East. For example, Meng et al.'s (1985) photographs were subsequently shown to Canadian, Hong Kong Chinese, and Japanese respondents
(Yik, Meng, and Russell, 1994). Overall, results were similar to those of Meng et
al., although a significant cross-cultural difference was observed in responses
to the 'surprise' and the 'sadness' expressions. Furthermore, because the photographs were of Chinese babies, Chinese judges might be expected to yield
the highest recognition scores. In fact, the trend was in the opposite direction.
Chinese consistently scored lower than did either Canadian or Japanese
respondents. This difference might reflect cultural differences in how emotions are labelled or conceptualized; Canadians achieved 'higher' scores

because the scoring key originated in the West and the 'correct' emotion labels were thus closer to the Canadians' conceptualization of emotion.

The notion that there might be both similarities and differences in expression is reinforced by several other studies. In undertaking their studies, Borke and Su (1972) and Borke (1973) first wrote stories that described antecedents of emotions. The stories were based on interviews with kindergarteners, and only those types of antecedents mentioned by both American and Chinese kindergarteners were selected. Some of the stories were written to convey just one of four emotions (happiness, fear, sadness, or anger); other stories were written to be more ambiguous. Chinese and American children in the second grade were then asked to match the stories with line drawings of facial expressions. For the less ambiguous stories, Chinese and American children gave similar responses overall, although the percentage matching the prediction varied significantly with the culture of the subject for 13 of the 29 stories. The most salient difference was that Chinese children were less likely than Americans to match a 'sad' face with a 'sad' story. For the ambiguous stories, however, a clear difference due to culture emerged. In 5 of 9 stories, Chinese children were significantly less likely to select the 'sad' face, and were more likely to select the 'angry' face, than were the American children. The authors suggest that the cultural differences might be attributed to cultural variation in child-rearing practices, in which American children are trained to be more tolerant of feeling sad (rather than feeling angry) in response to frustration.

Klineberg (1938) cited passages from Chinese writings to suggest both universal and culture-specific aspects of expression. He added the proposition that 'photographs illustrating these [Chinese-specific] literary expressions are judged more easily by Chinese than by American subjects' (p. 520). Unfortunately, he provided no details of these data, and the hypothesis has not been pursued, an area that clearly needs further research.

Vocal expression, as well, shows both universality and room for cultural differences. Van Bezooijen, Otto, and Heenan (1983) asked Dutch, Taiwanese, and Japanese subjects to guess which one of ten emotions was expressed by Dutch speakers reading a standard phrase in a way that would convey a specified emotion. Recognition scores from Taiwanese and Japanese were greater than chance, but lower than those from the Dutch subjects. Analysis of the 'confusions' suggested that a dimension of activation might account for the differences across cultures.

To summarize, studies of facial and vocal expression of emotion have provided apparent support for the universality hypothesis, but they have at the same time given indications of the existence of cultural differences. Unfortunately, just what the differences are, how and when they arise, and how extensive they are remain to be explored. Fortunately, indigenous Chinese stimulus materials are becoming available and they are being used both in intracultural and cross-cultural studies. Further intracultural studies are needed to explore recognition of suggested culture-specific facial actions. Further cross-cultural studies are then needed to differentiate universal from culture-specific aspects of emotional expression. Moreover, the recognition studies reviewed here concern the *capacity* to attribute emotions to expression under specific experimental conditions. Results do not indicate how emotions are expressed, nor what expressions are recognized, in everyday life. Much research remains to be done on the occurrence and recognition of emotional expression in non-experimental contexts.

Emotional Behaviour in a Social Context

Many outside observers agree that Chinese emotional behaviour provides an interesting contrast with Western emotional behaviour, but they do not agree on how or why the difference occurs. According to Klineberg (1938), Chinese believe emotion to be dangerous, value moderation in all matters, and emphasize social harmony over individual expression. As a consequence, emotional behaviour is normatively moderate or is suppressed altogether. From his study of psychiatric disorders, Kleinman (1986) came to a similar conclusion. Wu (1982) pointed out that in traditional Chinese medicine, extreme emotions are thought to cause illness.

Potter (1988) provides a quite different analysis of Chinese emotional behaviour: emotions, she says, are less relevant in China than they are in the West. Like minor aches and pains, emotions are best ignored. They do not achieve social ends and are not needed to legitimate social relationships. Harmful emotions can therefore be discouraged; other emotions can be allowed full expression but ignored. Potter undertook her study in villages in mainland China and indeed found open expression of emotion there, although she acknowledges that her Chinese informants insisted, 'How I feel doesn't matter' (p. 187). According to her results, the villagers did not expect emotional expressiveness to help in achieving an end. They believed that anger would not help repeal an unpopular policy or make a travel permit available to them. In short, expression of emotion was neither efficacious nor dangerous to social relations. Open expression of anger at an unpopular policy was not punished, although disobeying the policy would have been. Similarly, the open expression of sorrow was not stigmatized, but it did not elicit public sympathy either. Expressions of sorrow did not elicit any valued response, and sharing of emotion was not a sign of intimacy between individuals.

Potter argued that in China, social order, social relationships, and social behaviour do not require an emotional basis. In the West, for example, love is thought to be the proper basis of the relationship between husband and wife and between father and son. In Potter's village, love was not required for a successful marriage or for filial piety. Marriages were arranged between persons from different villages, with no opportunity for love to develop before the union. Love between two persons in the same village could therefore only bring harm. A father who expressed affection for a son was thought to invite a breakdown of the proper respect and obedience owed the elder by the younger. Rather than affirming the social structure, love was seen to endanger it. When legal reform in 1953 and 1981 changed the basis of marriage, Potter argued, it did not make the basis love.

Potter (1988) emphasized the lack of romantic love in mainland China and concluded, '...romantic love is a culturally alien concept in China' (p. 200); instead, '...marriage choice is ideally based on what are called "good feelings"' (p. 201). A person with good feelings toward another is willing to work and sacrifice on behalf of that person. 'Good feelings' represents unconditional responsibility and altruism. One informant in Potter's village said, 'We Chinese show our feelings for one another in our work, not with words' (p. 205). In support of Potter's analysis, Chu (1985) has argued that marriage in early China emphasized *men tang hu tui* (status comparability between two families of the couple), and concluded that 'the criterion of romantic love did not seem to figure in most people's minds' (p. 264). Such Chinese behaviour has been interpreted by some scholars (for example, Beach and Tesser, 1988; Grant, 1976) as indicating that the Chinese do not experience romantic love (see also Goodwin and Tang, this volume).

The lack of romantic love among Chinese has been disputed by Jankowiak (1993). In his study of Hohhot, the capital of the Inner Mongolian Autonomous Region, Jankowiak found romantic love as the theme of films and magazines. Young men and women date and *tan liang ai* (falling in love). Jankowiak (1993) has also pointed out that 'romantic love in China is not the product of Westernization nor an artifact of communist ideology. ...It existed well before the founding of the Han dynasty, and, in some cases, actually thrived in the face of powerful parental opposition' (p. 221).

In comparing the two accounts, one must recognize that Potter studied village life in rural China, whereas Jankowiak studied urban life in Inner Mongolia. However, their accounts are not incompatible in that Potter acknowledged the existence of romantic love in the village but emphasized the opposition to it. Potter acknowledged that opposition has existed but emphasized its waning. Much research remains to document how emotional behaviour is regulated among the Chinese and the consequences of such regulation. Can romantic love be regulated out of existence, at least in some historical circumstances? Or can it be brought into existence by certain historical circumstances? Both historical and contemporaneous studies are needed to address such questions.

Physiological Correlates and Somatization

In our review of literature, we could find no evidence linking specific emotions to specific physiological events. So, here is a clear need for research. Nevertheless, in China, perhaps even more so than in the West, emotions are clearly thought to be associated with physiological events. Many observers have made the claim that Chinese 'somatize' their emotions (see Draguns, this volume).

The term *somatization* refers to the experiencing of bodily, or somatic, symptoms in place of an emotion. Bodily symptoms commonly experienced include headaches, backaches, insomnia, and loss of appetite. From a Western perspective, the Chinese pattern of reaction might be thought of as 'somatizing' the emotion. Alternatively, the Western pattern could be thought of as 'psychologizing' the emotion. Each pattern is a culturally established response to a single organismic event. As Ots (1990) suggested, '...the Chinese have a less restricted bodily perception and thus serve as an example of a different bodily awareness. Chinese are culturally trained to "listen" within their body' (p. 26).

One consequence of the association of somatization with the Chinese is that Chinese have been accused of having a lack of psychological awareness (Cheung, 1982, 1985, 1986; Kleinman, 1977; Kleinman and Kleinman, 1985; Tseng, 1975). Other researchers, however, have argued that somatization is not equal to the lack of psychologization and that these two phenomena could coexist (Chang, 1985; Cheung, 1985; Wu, 1982). As will be discussed later in this chapter, the Chinese language contains a rich vocabulary of emotion-related words (Kwong and Wong, 1981). Wu (1982) suggested that how an emotion is expressed depends on the situation. Following on this point, Kleinman (1980) noted that physical (but not emotional) complaints induce social support in Chinese societies. Cheung, Lau, and Waldmann (1981) found that, although patients complained of somatic problems, they would admit to psychological or emotional problems when asked directly about them.

The Influence of Emotion on Cognitive Performance

Meng and her colleagues reported an important series of studies on the influence of emotion on cognitive performance. They specifically studied babies aged 16–18 months (Meng and Campos, 1984; Meng, Wang, Liu, and Lin, 1988). The baby to be studied was first placed in an emotion-arousing situation. For example, happiness was elicited by allowing the baby to play games with its mother. Distress was elicited by separating the baby from its mother. After the emotion manipulation, various tasks, such as finding a toy, were given to the subject. The results show that the quality of cognitive performance is a linear function of the valence (hedonic quality) of the emotional state, although with a slight reversal at extremely high happiness. Performance is thus optimal in a moderately pleasant emotional state. This effect of emotion on performance might be mediated by changes in heart rate, since the measurement of the heart rate was seen to follow a similar curve.

THE INDIGENOUS CHINESE CONCEPTION OF EMOTION

To import a concept from one culture into another has been criticized as the 'imposed-etic' approach to research (Berry, 1969). For example, a researcher translates an 'anxiety' scale from English into Chinese, administers the new scale to a Chinese sample, and then makes inferences about the anxiety of the Chinese people. This procedure presupposes the universal, or etic, status of the concept of anxiety. In this section, we examine the status of anxiety, emotion, and other such concepts for Chinese people. More generally, we seek to explore the indigenous everyday conception of emotion found in Chinese culture. Even if emotion *per se* were found to be entirely universal, different groups might conceptualize that universal reality differently, much as different peoples have different conceptions of disease or of the solar system. To explore these issues, we examine the Chinese lexicon, Chinese metaphors for emotion, and ancient and modern Chinese ideas about emotion and its role in disease and medicine.

The Emotion Lexicon

Analysis of the Chinese lexicon can help reveal the concepts available to Chinese speakers through which they categorize the emotions they witness or experience. Although concepts can exist that are not lexicalized in a single word, the presence of a word implies the existence of the concept it expresses. Comparison of the Chinese emotion lexicon with that of another language can therefore suggest similarities and differences in conceptualization of emotion. This perspective on the conceptualization of emotion raises a number of difficult questions: What is the set of emotion-denoting words in the Chinese language? Is there a structure implicit in the domain of emotions? Can such Chinese words be adequately translated into English? In addition to the theoretical implications of answers to such questions, there are practical implications as well. Can emotion questionnaires or hypotheses arising from scientific theories of emotion be translated between, for example, Chinese and English, without changes of meaning?

What is the set of emotion-denoting words?

A precise analysis of these issues requires an identification of the full set of words that denote emotion in Chinese. Immediately, however, problems arise. First, there is no consensus on just what set of words we are talking about. Does the English word *emotion* specify that domain? There are two similar but not completely synonymous Chinese terms, *qingxu* and *qinggan*, that have been translated as 'emotion' (see Table 12.2). Second, there is no agreement on how many words in Chinese refer to an emotion. Shaver, Wu, and Schwartz (1992) began with 204 emotion-denoting words culled by Shelly Wu from a Chinese dictionary, 110 of which were rated as good examples of emotion. Boucher (1979) estimated that there were 750 emotion-denoting words in Chinese. Hama, Matsuyama, and Lin (1986) found 2,915 words or phrases for emotions, 500 of which were rated as highly related to emotion. On the other hand, Yu (1994) found only 88 words freely listed as examples of emotion (*qingxu*) by at least two subjects in a sample of 200 students in mainland China. Yu's result suggests that the working vocabulary of readily available terms may be only one-tenth of the full set of words potentially available. Not only are the number of emotion words in dispute, but the lists of emotion words from different investigators do not agree well. For example, only 15 of Yu's (1994) 88 words, and more surprisingly, only 47 of Hama, Matsuyama, and Lin's (1986) 500 words appeared on Shaver, Wu, and Schwartz's (1992) list of 110.

Difficulties encountered in delimiting the domain of emotion-denoting words are consistent with the position that the boundaries around concepts such as emotion (or *qingxu*) are fuzzy rather than sharp (Russell, 1991). The category of emotion possesses an internal structure such that some types of emotion are prototypical, clear cases; other types are less easily identified, and some are very much open to debate. Membership in the category of emotion is graded rather than either/or, and no sharp boundary separates emotion from not-emotion.

Structure

Another question that arises is how to describe the set of relations that exist among the various emotional concepts. In searching for the structure implicit in the Chinese lexicon for emotion, different researchers have begun with different sets of emotion words, have obtained somewhat different measures of the similarity between words, and then have analysed the results using different techniques.

Russell (1983) began with the least-adequate sample of 28 emotion-related words (derived from a study in English simply through translation by a fluent bilingual). Subjects were Chinese-speaking residents of Canada and provided an indirect measure of similarity (through a sorting procedure). Multidimensional scaling resulted in a two-dimensional circumplex in which emotion-related words fell roughly in a circle in a space with axes interpretable as pleasure–displeasure and arousal–sleepiness. Despite these humble beginnings, the circumplex has turned out to be robust across changes in method. For example, a similar result was obtained from Hong Kong Chinese in a study in which emotion words were bypassed altogether by using emotional facial expressions shown in photographs (Russell, Lewicka, and Niit, 1987). Chan (1985) obtained a result he likened to the circumplex from a multidimensional scaling solution of ratings from Hong Kong Chinese subjects who were asked to judge the similarity of facial expressions of different emotions. Chan's second axis, however, was interpreted as degree of control, rather than as Russell's (1983) degree of arousal. Mauro et al. (1992) found support for the pleasure and arousal dimensions when correlations among affect ratings of remembered emotional incidents were subjected to multidimensional scaling. They also found that emotional incidents varied along a third dimension, which they called 'direction' (whether the subject's focus of attention is directed inward at the self or outward toward the environment).

None of the results obtained by these studies implies that emotional structure can be captured by only two or three dimensions: it has been found that the pleasure and arousal dimensions are necessary but not sufficient to describe the structure of emotional concepts. What further dimensions might be found can be anticipated on the basis of studies in English: beyond pleasure and arousal, the dimensions supported through the use of factor analysis or multidimensional scaling seem to describe the cognitive processing of the emotional antecedent (Russell, 1978). As already described, Mauro et al. (1992) found a basic similarity in such dimensions for Chinese and other languages, although with the suggestion that as more complex dimensions are examined, more cultural or language differences might be found.

Hama, Matsuyama, and Lin (1986) provided a different hypothesis on the structure of emotion. As described above, they began with 500 emotion words. A sample of 40 Taiwanese then judged the relevance of each word to 17 emotion anchors preselected by the authors themselves. The profile of relevance scores were used to derive a measure of similarity for all possible pairs of the 500 emotion words. This similarity matrix was then factor analysed, and eight factors were extracted. Five were bipolar: joy–sadness, friendliness–antagonism, emotional stability–neuroticism, carefulness–carelessness, and pride–humility. The last three factors were unipolar: anger, hope, and fear.

Shaver et al. (1992) began with the set of 110 words described above. A sample of 104 university students in Beijing grouped the words by similarity. The pairwise similarity matrix was submitted to hierarchical cluster analysis. The result was interpreted as indicating six basic emotions: happiness, hate/anger, sadness, sad love, fear, and shame. This result bore a rough resemblance to hierarchical structures found in English and other Western languages, but the more surprising aspect was the differences. Shaver et al. had used the same procedure to provide a hierarchical representation of the English emotion lexicon. In English, there were three positive categories (joy, love, and surprise) and three negative (fear, anger, sadness). The Chinese results had but one positive cluster, happiness. There was no surprise cluster (the only emotion word related to surprise in their list was *xi chu wang wai* [surprise and happiness] which fell in the happiness cluster). Love was a negative emotion—'sad love'—exemplified by *chiqing* (infatuation), *dan xiangsi* (unrequited love), *yousi* (remote concern), and *lianlian bu she* (attachment). Chinese had five negative clusters, including shame, which had not appeared as a separate cluster in English. Moreover, the placement of individual terms into even the common clusters differed between English and Chinese.

To summarize, when dimensions of emotion words are sought, Chinese yields at least two dimensions very similar to those obtained in other languages, a result consistent with the general pattern seen across many languages and cultures (Russell, 1991). Broad bipolar dimensions interpretable as pleasure–displeasure and arousal–sleepiness appear to be pan-cultural. Similarly, Chinese sort emotions into broad positive and negative clusters. On the other hand, the attempt to find more fine-grained clusters of emotional concepts and to arrange them in a hierarchy appears to reveal a system somewhat similar to English but somewhat unique to the Chinese. Clusters of sad-love and shame in particular are more elaborated in Chinese. If we extrapolate from the general trend observed so far, we can anticipate that differences between Chinese and other conceptions of emotion will be revealed only by a fine-grained analysis. The more detailed the analysis, the more differences will be revealed.

Translation for emotion-related terms

The English word *anger,* the Chinese word *nu,* and the Japanese word *okotteiru* have been used as translations for one another. However, to what extent is any particular word such as *anger* really translatable? Are *anger* and *nu* equivalent? Let us begin our discussion by asking whether specific translations are reliable.

Table 12.2 shows 95 Chinese emotion-related words translated to or from English in 18 studies in our reference list. Of these, 66 were found in only one study, and the translation has not therefore been replicated. The remaining 29, however, allow us to examine the replicability of translation across studies. Only 5 translations were found where a one-to-one correspondence between Chinese and English had been replicated; they are *zhending* (calmness), *shuiyi* (sleepiness), *jingqi* (surprise), *neijiu* (guilt), and *xingqu* (interest). For

Table 12.2 Translation of Emotion Terms

Terms in Chinese	Terms in English	Sources
qinggan	emotion	l
qingxu	emotion	b, e, f, h, l, n, q
	feelings	e
jingqi	surprise	h, k, n
jidong	excitement	j, k, p, q
	excitement and thrill	l
xingqu	interest	f, n
deyi	pride	q
jiaoao	pride	m
gaoxing	gladness	k
	happiness	q
huanle	joy	e
kuaile	happiness	j, k
	happiness and joy	l
	joy	q
xingfu	happiness	e, p
yukuai	happiness	f, g, h
	pleasure	q
	joy	n
pingjing	peace	q
zhending	calmness	j, k
shuiyi	sleepiness	j, k
ailian	caring about face	c
bishi	to despise	q
buhaoyisi	embarrassment	c, o
buyaolian	shame	o
cankui	shame	l, o
diulian	shame	m, o
jianjie	embarrassment	q
nao xiu cheng nu	shame and rage	l
wuchi	shame	o
xiuchi	shame	e, l
xiufen	shame and resentment	l
	losing face	c
xiukui	shame	l
xiuqie	diffidence	l
	shame/shyness	n
xiu xiu lian	shame on you	c
haixiu	shyness	q
zibei	inferiority	q
houhui	regret	l
fujiu	guilt and regret	l
neijiu	guilt	e, m, n, q
duji	jealousy	e
jidu	jealousy	l, p, q
xianmu	envy	q
yanfen	boredom	q
men	anguish	a
	boredom	j

Table 12.2   *(Cont'd)*

Terms in Chinese	Terms in English	Sources
kumen	anguish	a
aishang	sadness	n
beiai	sadness	a, j
	misery	k
	grief	l
beishang	sadness	e, h, p, q
kunao	distress	j
nanguo	misery	j
youchou	sadness	a
	worry and depression	l
	worry and sadness	p
youshang	sadness and worry	l
tongku	distress	g
	pain and agony	p
bugaoxing	unhappiness	p
bukuaile	unhappiness	a, e, k, l
jusang	depression and sadness	p
shiyi	depression	j
yayi	depression	e
yiyu	depression	q, r
youyu	depression	a
danxin	worry	e
danyou	worry	p, q
jiaoju	worry and anxiety	l
jiaolu	anxiety	e, q, r
	worry	l
youlu	worry	l
taoyan	disgust	p
yanwu	disgust	h, k, q, n
	dislike and disgust	l
fen	annoyance	a
fannao	vexation	l, p
	annoyance	a
naonu	irritated	e
fennu	anger	e, f, h, n, q
	mad	k
gongfen	righteous anger	i
nu	anger	j, k
shengqi	anger	l, m
haipa	fear	e, l, q
jupa	fear	f, h
konghuang	fear and panic	l
kongju	fear	l, n
jing	afraid	j
	scared	k
kongpa	afraid	k

Table 12.2   *(Cont'd)*

Note   Chinese words were written in pinyin romanization.
[a]Chan (1990). [b]Chen, Meng, and Lin (1990). [c]Fung (1994). [d]Kipnis (1993). [e]Liang (1993). [f]Liu, Meng, and Lu (1990). [g]Meng and Campos (1984). [h]Meng, Yan, and Meng (1985). [i]Potter (1988). [j]Russell (1983). [k]Russell, and Sato (in press). [l]Shaver, Wu and Schwartz (1992). [m]Stipek, Weiner, and Li (1989). [n]Wang and Meng (1986). [o]Wilson (1981). [p]Wu, and Shaver (1993). [q]Yu (1994), [r]Zhang (1991).

Xu, and Shen, 1986). Of course, word association, semantic differential ratings, and Davitz's (1969) list may not be definitive assessments of meaning. The cautious researcher, however, can no longer assume that emotion words in different languages can be translated in a one-to-one fashion. The translation–back-translation method can succeed in obtaining the best available translation, which still might not be exact.

An alternative approach to testing equivalence of meaning is to examine the referents of words. Two words, to be equivalent, must refer to the same events. Equivalence of reference is thus a necessary but not a sufficient condition of equivalence of the concepts expressed by the words. In a small study, Russell and Sato (1995) used 14 facial expressions (representing an effort to sample broadly from the range of possible emotional states) as an external, pan-cultural manifestation of emotion. Reference is considered a matter of degree, and the membership in a category labelled by an emotion word is graded. Subjects in different cultures were asked to judge how well each face shown served as an expression of X, where X was one of the emotion words. Thus, for each word a profile was created by the degree to which it was said to refer to various emotions as represented by the facial expressions. The similarity between any two words, regardless of language, was indexed by the correlation between their profiles. Synonyms within a language yielded high correlations (.80 or above). In a test of alleged translations across Chinese, English, and Japanese, 12 of the 14 translations into Japanese yielded high correlations (.76 to .99). Two problematic cases in Japanese were revealed by low correlations across languages (as low as -.04). All 14 Chinese translations bore high enough correlations with English (.72 to .97).

Translation equivalence is an assumption in nearly all cross-cultural studies and in attempts to discuss the emotional lives and conceptions of different people. It is unfortunate, therefore, that so little attention has been devoted to this issue. The preliminary results obtained by Russell and Sato (in press) are encouraging, but provide only a weak test of equivalence of meaning, a test that can supplement the back-translation procedure by screening poor translations. Attempts to provide fuller examinations of meaning are few in number but tend to argue against translation equivalence (Chan, 1990; Imada, 1989; Imada, Kujime, and Narita, 1994; Tanaka-Matsumi and Marsella, 1977; Wierzbicka, 1986).

Hypercognition and Hypocognition of Emotion

Some aspects of the Chinese lexicon for emotion can be described through use of Levy's (1973) distinction between hypercognition and hypocognition in language. The distinction recognizes that one language might provide a large set of related concepts for a particular type of emotion (hypercognition), whereas another language might provide few or no concepts (hypocognition). For example, the Tahitian language hypercognizes anger; it provides 42 different words that refer to some type of anger. In contrast, the same language hypocognizes sadness; it provides no words for sadness. Sad feelings—if that is the appropriate designation—are described through more general terms, such as feeling bad or troubled.

Hypocognition

One sign of hypocognition is a lack of vocabulary items. Some observers have claimed that certain concepts are named in English but are missing from Chinese. Cheng (1977, p. 151) found no exact translation in Chinese for the term *anxiety*, although *jiaolu* (tension and worry) appears to be a common translation (see Table 12.2). Marsella's (1981) review concluded that there was no word for depression among many non-Western cultural groups, including Chinese. As is made evident in Table 12.2, the term *depression* has been translated into three additional Chinese terms (*shiyi, yayi,* and *yiyu*), but these too capture only the mood aspect of the concept. Apparently, there is no lexical entry in the Chinese language for depression; as in the case of sadness in Tahitian, depression is described through more general Chinese terms or with more than one Chinese word. This difference is consonant with Marsella's (1981) conclusion that '"depression" apparently assumes completely different meanings and consequences as a function of the culture in which it occurs' (p. 261).

Hypercognition

The term *shame* appears to be hypercognized in the Chinese language relative to English. Shame has been recognized as an elaborate and important emotion in Chinese culture by many scholars (Hu, 1944; Chu, 1972; Marsella, Murray, and Golden, 1974; Wilson, 1980, 1981). Chu (1972) concluded that 'Chinese society is a shame society' (p. 115). Wilson (1981) defined a verbal scale of shame in Chinese, ranging from the least to the most intense feelings: *xinli bushufu* (unease), *buhaoyisi* (embarrassment), *diulian* (shame, losing face), *cankui* (deep shame), and *wuchi* or *buyaolian* (extreme shame). In Chinese, there are terms for the combination of shame with other emotions, such as *nao xiu cheng nu* (shame and anger), *xiufen* (shame and anger), and *xiuchi* (humiliation). Marsella et al. (1974) noted that shame is often used as a social control technique in Asian societies. They speculated that Asian groups might, therefore, be better able to read somatic cues associated with shame and experience shame more readily (p. 323).

In Fung's (1994) longitudinal study of socialization among Chinese children in Taiwan, parents reported that their preschool children understood shame by the age of 2.5 years. The children already had a vocabulary of shame including *buhaoyisi* (embarrassing), *diulian* (losing face), and *haixiu* (shy). This finding is consistent with Shaver et al.'s (1992) estimate that 95 per cent of 2.5- to 3-year-old mainland Chinese children understood *xiu* (shame or shyness).

In contrast, only 10 per cent of American children of the same age understood the term *ashamed* and 16.7 per cent *embarrassed*.

The abundance of shame-related words is also evident in Shaver et al.'s (1992) list of 110 Chinese emotion words extracted from their sorting study with Chinese adult respondents. The Chinese words *xiukui, xiufen, nao xiu cheng nu, xiuchi, xiuqie*, and *cankui* represent different kinds of shame-related emotions among Chinese. The authors mention that Chinese-English dictionaries translated all these words as 'shame', or a combination of shame with other emotions, and it seemed that there were no more specific English alternatives within the domain of shame-related terms. Similarly, Wang (1994) explored the structure and content of shame-related terms among mainland Chinese adults. She searched the dictionary and asked native Chinese speakers for shame-related words. She also asked 50 respondents to judge the accuracy of each candidate term. The rating procedure resulted in 113 shame-related words in Chinese.

The data reviewed in this section were intracultural; no comparison data from another culture or language were gathered. More precise, intercultural comparisons would be required for a clear demonstration of hypocognition or hypercognition. Nevertheless, the data reviewed above suggest that such differences do exist.

Metaphors

Lakoff and Kövecses (1987) and Kövecses (1995) have argued that concepts in general and emotion concepts in particular are understood in terms of metaphors, which are conceptual in nature and are part of the meaning of the terms. Two emotion words in different languages, such as *anger* in English and *nu* in Chinese, are considered to be equivalent only if their underlying metaphors are the same.

King (1989) and Kövecses (1995) argued that the Chinese concept *nu* and the English concept *anger* share the common metaphor of a pressurized container. For example, we have in English 'He was filled with anger' and 'Don't get a hernia!' (examples taken from Kövecses, 1995); and we have *man qiang nu huo* (to have one's body cavities full of angry fire) in Chinese (an example taken from King, 1989). However, this general metaphor seems to be elaborated in different ways in different languages (Kövecses, 1995). In English, anger is understood in terms of a series of metaphors not found in Chinese: 'angry behaviour is an aggressive animal', 'anger is an opponent', and 'anger is a dangerous animal' (King, 1989).

This line of argument adds further complication to the process of translation across languages. Even if we obtain a one-to-one Chinese–English translation replicable across different studies, we need still to consider the equivalence of their full conceptual structure, some of which is metaphorical.

Chinese Writings

Assumptions about emotion are embedded in ancient Chinese writings, in traditional Chinese medicine, and in current medical practice. Study of such texts and practice therefore reveals something of these assumptions.

Idiographs

Chinese characters (idiographs) are often composed of parts (radicals), which can reveal something of the character's origin. Many emotion-related Chinese characters, such as *nu* (anger), *kong* (fear), and *bei* (sorrow), include a radical (心、忄) which means 'heart'. The *Tongyong Hanying Cidian* (General Chinese–English dictionary) lists 81 emotion-related words. Of these, which include the heart radical, 51 are commonly used in Chinese writing. This evidence indicates that grouping together the various emotions into an implicit category is a very ancient practice.

Basic emotions in ancient writings

Chinese tradition points to certain emotions as a basic (Chen, 1963). However, different texts provide a slightly different number and different types of basic emotions (see Table 12.3). *Huangdi Neijing*, a compilation of ancient beliefs, listed five. *Zuo Zhuan* listed six. And *Li Ji* listed seven. There are three different versions of the seven emotions (*qiqing*) in different texts. Only *xi* (joy) and *nu* (anger) appear on all the lists.

Table 12.3   Five versions of the 'Basic Emotions'

'Five'	'Six'		'Seven'		
Neijing	Zuo Zhuan	Daoism	Confucianism	Buddhism	English translation
xi	xi	xi	xi	xi	joy
nu	nu	nu	nu	nu	anger
bei	ai	bei	ai		sorrow
kong		kong	ju	ju	fear
you		you		you	worry
	wu		wu	zeng	hate
			ai	ai	love
			yu	yu	desire
	hao				like
	le				happiness
		jing			fright
		si			longing

Note   The 'basic' emotions are presented in pinyin and in English translation. The seven emotions stated in *Li Ji* correspond with those of Confucianism. The *ai* glossed as *sorrow* is written in pinyin in the same way as the *ai* glossed as *love*, but the pronunciation and Chinese characters differ.

The ideas of the ancient texts are still evident in everyday thought through many frequently cited proverbs, such as *you lu cheng ji* (worrying makes you sick) and *le ji sheng bei* (extreme happiness produces sorrow). Even if the ancient texts disagree to a point, most modern Chinese are familiar with such proverbs as *qi qing zhi bing* (seven emotions that induce disease) and *ren you qiqing liuyu* (man has seven emotions and six desires). But, do they know just what those seven emotions are? When 50 educated Hong Kong Chinese adults were asked to list the *qiqing*, no consensus was reached regarding the seven (see Table 12.4). In fact, 56 different emotions (22 non-idiosyncratic and 34 idiosyncratic) were listed as making up the *qiqing*, and 10 of the 12 from Table 12.3 were listed by the respondents. A majority of respondents listed *nu, xi, ai* (sorrow/grief), and *le* (happiness). Many responses were related to 'feeling' (*qing*), such as terms describing a love relationship or friendship. This phenomenon can be attributed to the fact that the Chinese character *qing* could be interpreted either as emotion (*qingxu*) or as feeling (*ganqing*). These results suggest that the contribution of traditional texts to the modern understanding of emotion is limited.

Table 12.4 What are the *Qiqing* (Seven Emotions) in the Proverb *Ren You Qiqing Liuyu?*

Emotion (pinyin)	English translation	Percentage of occurrence
nu*	anger	68
xi*	joy	66 (68)
ai*	sorrow/grief	66
le*	happiness	64 (70)
ai*	love	42
wu*	dislike	38
aiqing	love relationship	30
youqing	friendship	30
hen	hate	26 (28)
qinqing	feeling with family	26
bei*	sorrow/sadness	14 (18)
yu*	desire	12
tongqing	feeling of sympathy	12
chou	sadness	8 (10)
yuan	resentment	6
fumu zhi qing	feeling with parents	6
liqing	feeling of separation	6
zeng*	hate	4 (6)
you*	worry	4
ganqing	feeling	4
xiongdi zimei zhi qing	feeling with siblings	4
ju*	fear	2 (8)

Note *n* = 50 Hong Kong Chinese adults enrolled in a college night class. The proverb *ren you qiqing liuyu* was quoted and subjects were asked to list the *qiqing*. A resulting 34 idiosyncratic terms were found; only nonidiosyncratic responses are listed. Emotion words marked with an asterisk are those listed in Table 12.3. Numbers in parentheses represent the percentage after synonyms were added to the respective categories. These synonyms were: *xiyue* added to *xi; kuaile, huan,* and *yukuai* to *le; hengqing* to *hen; beiai* and *beiqing* to *bei; chouqing* to *chou; kongju, pa,* and *jing* to *ju;* and *zenghen* to *zeng.*

Folk models of Chinese emotions

By analyzing *chengyu* (four-character traditional sayings or idioms) found in *Hanyu Chengyu Fenlei Cidian* (A Classified Dictionary of Chinese *Chengyu*), King (1989) investigated the ways in which Chinese conceptualize five emotions: *you* (worry), and *nu, kong, xi*, and *bei*. The *chengyu* revealed a conceptualization of each emotion that mostly, although not entirely, overlaps with its English counterpart. For example, *you* is thought of as a hot substance inside the body and a heavy burden caused by threats over which one has no control. *You* can be seen on the face (worry lines) and affects eating, sleeping, and the internal organs. *Kong* is a loss of soul, a coldness stemming from a bursting of the gall bladder (conversely, a large gall bladder leads to courage). *Xi*, too, is a fluid in a container, and it too can be seen in the face (via smiles, laughter, weeping, stretched brows, and the head raised up). *Xi* is caused by joining together, as in a wedding, just as *bei* is caused by separation. *Nu* is similar to worry and is thought of as a hot liquid or fire in a container, as an excess of the life spirit, *qi*. *Nu* interferes with mental functioning (producing incoherent thoughts) and health (producing dizziness, stomach-aches, and loss of appetite).

King (1989) found that each emotion word implies a folk model of that emotion. An example of the folk model for *bei* is given as follows:

1. There is a situation where Self is separated permanently from loved ones (parents, spouse, friend, etc.) in life or death.
2. Grief exists. Self experiences emotion in terms of intense physical pain and agitated behaviour. Also weight loss and loss of *qi*.
3. Self receives support of friends and relatives.
4. Self expresses grief through crying.
5. Grief gradually and slowly ceases to exist.

King (1989) concluded that metonymies (a part standing for the whole, such as a smile standing for happiness) play a more significant role than do metaphors in the Chinese conceptual structures of the five emotion concepts he studied. This emphasis on parts (such as crying and pain in sadness) is consistent with the Chinese focus on bodily manifestations of emotion known as 'somatization'.

King (1989) also found that *qi* plays an important role in the understanding of emotion (see also Lin, 1980). *Qi* is believed to be the energy flowing throughout the body, it originates in one's parents, as well as in food and air. *Qi* is believed to exist in all parts of the body, and its excess and deficiency in any part results in disease. In the *Huangdi Neijing*, the relationship between emotion and *qi* was stated as follows:

Nu ze qi shang (anger makes *qi* rise);
Xi ze qi huan (joy makes *qi* become slow);
Bei ze qi xiao (sorrow makes *qi* become weak);
Kong ze qi xia (fear makes *qi* descend);
Jing ze qi luan (fright makes *qi* become chaotic);
Si ze qi jie (contemplation makes *qi* obstructed).

Traditional Chinese medicine

Wu (1982) analysed ancient medical practice and found that the theory linked the symptoms, organs, and emotions. Chinese physicians who adhered to the

Huangdi Neijing applied the balance theory of emotion to the treatment of disease: to increase the positive force for the negative, and the negative for the positive. Physical symptoms were diagnosed according to the affected organ, the problematic emotion was inferred, and a strategy was devised to induce a counter-emotion. For example, a famed doctor Wen-chi cured an ailing king of his illness by insulting him, thereby risking his own life. The king had been diagnosed as suffering from excess of 'contemplation', the antidote to which was anger. Another doctor cured one patient by inducing joy. Another patient's disease was caused by excess joy; the cure was to frighten him sufficiently. The *Huangdi Neijing* delineated the relationship between five emotions and five organs as follows:

Nu shang gan, bei sheng nu (anger is injurious to the liver, but sorrow counteracts anger);

Xi shang xin, kong sheng xi (joy is injurious to the heart, but fear counteracts joy);

Si shang pi, nu sheng si (contemplation is injurious to the spleen, but anger counteracts contemplation);

You shang fei, xi sheng you (worry is injurious to the lungs, but joy counteracts worry);

Kong shang shen, si sheng kong (fear is injurious to the kidneys, but fear can be overcome by contemplation).

Using ancient medical texts to provide information concerning conceptions of emotion is a fascinating but difficult endeavour. As we have seen, various ancient documents list different numbers of basic emotions, although they share some common terms. Translation is also a persistent problem. Wu (1982) and Veith (1972), for example, provided quite different translations for *bei* and *you*: Wu used 'sorrow' and 'worry', whereas Veith used 'sympathy' and 'grief', respectively, for the two words. Nevertheless, the overall conception of emotions counteracting one another and of emotional imbalance leading to disease is clear. A further question is whether these ancient ideas bear on today's conception of emotion or medicine.

Current medical practice

Ots (1990) conducted a study at the Jiangsu Provincial Hospital of Traditional Chinese Medicine in an attempt to investigate the correspondence between emotions and bodily complaints in psychosomatic disorders. He found that each patient typically arrived with specific somatic rather than emotional or psychological complaints. The physician also avoided diagnosis in terms of mental problems or, translated literally, *xinli de wenti* (problems of the heart), to which a stigma is attached. Both patient and doctor preferred a somatic idiom. Nevertheless, somatic complaints were understood in partly emotional terms through the concept of *qi qing zhi bing*. Emotions are understood as causal factors, not as part of the disorder, and treatment is not primarily oriented toward emotional change but rather toward remedying somatic dysfunction. Remedies relied on herbs, food, and rituals rather than talk or insight.

Ots (1990) phrased the emotional interpretation of symptoms as using the body and its organs as metaphors for the emotions. For example, he found that the liver is a metaphor for anger, the heart for anxiety, and so forth. According to Ots, social norms prohibited patients from reacting aggressively. The resulting repression of anger was expressed by varying degrees of self-directed aggression described as 'liver-*yang* flaming up' and 'liver attacking the spleen'. In one case, the patient's aggressive facial expression helped in reaching a diagnosis. The heart is a metaphor for anxiety, and most of the 'heart' patients suffered from anxiety, uncertainty, and fear. Life events that suggested a threat or greater insecurity were the cause, such as an impending examination for university students or promotion to a new position for an employee. The spleen, he found, is a metaphor for depression. The spleen was involved when any emotionally affected disorder went untreated for a long period of time. Ots characterized those 'spleen' patients as depressed. The Chinese doctors did not, however, perhaps because these patients showed culturally desirable quiet and introverted demeanors. Kidney is a metaphor for decline in the vital essence and a decline of the reproductive forces, which occurs with aging. The Chinese doctors attributed kidney disorders to excessive sexual activity in men, and to childbirth and menopause in women. Fear and flight are supposed to injure the kidneys. Even so, Ots realized that most patients suffering from kidney disorders did not primarily suffer from fright. He concluded that the fright was culturally construed as acting through the distinct somatic network of the kidney.

CONCLUSION

Those seeking the universal aspects of emotion have often turned to China for their studies. Universal aspects undoubtedly exist, and our review documents an overall similarity between the emotional life and understanding of the Chinese people and that of other peoples. Still, the evidence has not demonstrated precisely what the universal elements of emotion are. Emotions are certainly caused by similar antecedent events, are mediated by similar appraisal and attributional processes, and are manifested in similar physiological and behavioural events. The way in which Chinese emotion is currently understood, and was traditionally understood as revealed in ancient texts, also resembles its Western counterpart.

Those seeking evidence for cultural differences in emotion have also turned to China for evidence. Claims of differences have sometimes been dramatic. However, claims of vast differences between Westerners and Chinese in their emotional life seem exaggerated at best. Anxiety, depression, and romantic love, for example, are not missing in Chinese, although differences exist between their expression in each culture. Traditional Chinese medicine does not, as has been claimed, lack a psychological component, although again differences exist between practices in the East and West.

Once we abandon the search for vast differences, we may begin to notice more subtle but still important contrasts. Although Chinese are as capable of romantic love as are Westerners, the social practices and personal experiences of couples in China has certainly taken its own form, especially in traditional rural areas. Although cognitive appraisal of emotional antecedents involves such simple dimensions as pleasantness, degree of certainty, and attention in both Chinese and Western groups, both the events that elicit emotion and other, more complex cognitive dimensions might vary between the two.

Although it is reasonable to assume that the biological processes of emotion are similar in Chinese and Western samples, no conclusive evidence has yet been offered on this question. Psychologists tend to assume that emotional experience (that is, the subjective, mental experience of emotion) is the same in all peoples, but again no evidence has yet been put forth to suggest a resolution of this question. Moreover, one line of reasoning suggests otherwise. If we think of emotional experience as similar to perceptual experience, then we can speculate that emotional experience depends on normative expectations and available concepts. That is, if emotional experience is meaningful in the same way that a percept is meaningful, then we can explore the conceptual assumptions that influence the meaning found in emotional events. Here we may begin to see important if subtle differences between Chinese and Western groups. The Chinese lexicon, Chinese idiom, and ancient Chinese texts suggest a system of concepts that are similar to but also different from the Western conceptualization of emotion.

We have tried here to summarize the weight of the evidence so far put forth in the debate between the universalist and the cultural relativist perspectives. It may be tempting to conclude precipitously that the similarities between cultures outweigh the differences. However, two cautions are in order. First, the trend in the research field is that the more fine-grained the analysis, the more differences tend to be found. Comparisons conducted so far have not all been fine-grained. Second, our conclusions on such matters are only as good as the evidence used to reach those conclusions, and there is much need for more and better evidence. Comparison groups were sometimes missing or haphazardly chosen. Some writings on this topic have been marred by implicit assumptions that then emerge in the conclusions. For example, emotional differences between a Chinese sample and another group need not be due to cultural differences; differences could be economic, historical, geographical, or even genetic. Similarity between a Chinese sample and another group need not be due to our common genetics; similarities could be due to shared elements of culture, economics, history, geography, or social practices (the proper choice of comparison groups should begin to sort out such possibilities). In some writings, universal 'basic' emotions are assumed to exist, and therefore judgements about such emotions, prompted, for example, by facial expressions, are classified as correct or incorrect and local concepts are ignored. In some writings, ancient prescriptions about emotions, such as *qi qing zhi bing*, are assumed to capture the everyday experience of emotion in contemporary Chinese. Evidence indicates that most of these have never read the ancient texts and cannot name the seven emotions.

Much of the evidence concerns what people *can* do, often in artificial circumstances. For example, Chinese people can match certain posed facial gestures to preselected emotion words with as much agreement as is seen in Western samples. This kind of study, however, does not tell us what facial movements actually occur, what emotions, if any, cause facial movements, or what emotion is typically inferred from facial movements in the circumstances of ordinary life. Evidence is at best anecdotal on such questions about what happens, in what intensity, and with what frequency, in the non-experimental world of ordinary people.

NOTES

Preparation of this chapter was facilitated by a grant from the Social Sciences and Humanities Research Council of Canada to the first author.

All transliterations are in hanyu pinyin. English translations were provided either by previous researchers or by Michelle Yik.

We thank Ben Chan, Heidi Fung, Steve Heine, David Ho, Patrick Leung, Steven So, and Paul Trapnell for their generous help in the preparation of this chapter.

Chapter 13

■

Universal Aspects of Chinese Personality Structure

Robert R. McCrae, Paul T. Costa, Jr, and Michelle S. M. Yik

Much the same range of variation and much the same personality types are to be found in all societies.... When one becomes sufficiently familiar with an alien culture and with the individuals who share it, one finds that these individuals are fundamentally the same as various people whom he has known in his own society.

Linton, 1945, pp. 128, 149

Homo sum; humani nil a me alienum puto
(I am a man; nothing human is foreign to me.)

Terence

During the first half of this century, many of the best minds in the social sciences—Sigmund Freud, Bronislaw Malinowski, John Dewey, Erich Fromm, Margaret Mead, and Henry Murray among them—focused on the relations between personality and culture (Barnouw, 1985; Singer, 1961). Was human nature universal or as diverse as the cultures in which it was shaped? Could cultures be characterized by a personality configuration inferred from their customs and institutions (Benedict, 1934)? Did all or most of the individuals in a culture mirror the personality traits of the culture as a whole (DuBois, 1944)? What social and psychological mechanisms explained the formation of personality and the perpetuation of culture (Erikson, 1950)?

Unfortunately, these questions were as difficult as they were fascinating, and the young science of personality psychology lacked the conceptual tools and assessment techniques needed to resolve them empirically. Theory was dominated by psychoanalysis, and virtually all cross-cultural personality assessments employed the Rorschach ink-blot test (see, for example, Abel and Hsu, 1949), an instrument of highly questionable utility even in the culture in which it was developed (Barnouw, 1985; Suinn and Oskamp, 1969). The result was a rapid disillusionment with the topic. During the 1960s, both anthropologists and personality psychologists turned from grand to mid-level theories, and in the 1970s personality psychology entered a period of crisis in which the validity of all its measures and the utility of its most basic concepts were widely called into question.

That period of crisis has now passed (Wiggins, 1992), and the time has perhaps come to return to the topic of culture and personality. This time, however, trait psychology has replaced psychoanalysis as the dominant theoretical paradigm in personality research (McCrae and Costa, in press), and

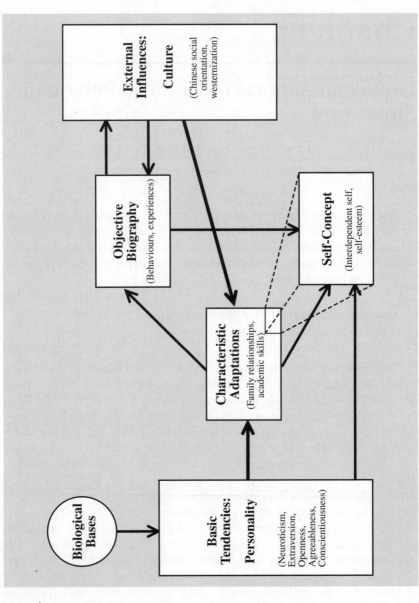

Figure 13.1 A Model of the Person, with categories of personality variables, examples of specific content, and arrows indicating the direction of major causal pathways. In this model, personality traits are biologically based tendencies; they interact with the external influences of culture to produce characteristic adaptations such as habits, attitudes, and vocational interests. The cumulative stream of behaviours and experiences forms the individual's objective biography. Adapted from McCrae and Costa (in press).

questionnaires have replaced inkblots as the preferred form of personality assessment. Perhaps most important, Western personality psychologists have begun to agree among themselves on an empirically based taxonomy of personality traits, the five-factor model (FFM)(Digman, 1990; McCrae, 1992). This model of personality structure has brought order to a chaotic field and systematized research on personality development, assessment, and stability (Deary and Matthews, 1993). Conceptually, empirically, and methodologically, trait psychology offers a radically new basis for studies of personality and culture.

The central conceptual shift in the new approach involves a distinction between personality traits and their overt manifestation. Classic theories viewed personality as a set of habits, values, and adaptations acquired through interactions with the culture, particularly in childhood (see, for example, Whiting and Child, 1953). Contemporary trait theory (McCrae and Costa, in press; Tellegen, 1991), informed by the findings of behaviour genetics (Eaves, Eysenck, and Martin, 1989; Loehlin, 1992), postulates that personality traits are endogenous dispositions in the individual that are expressed in culturally determined forms. This implies that personality is not the product of culture, but is instead an independent co-determiner of characteristic adaptations. The view that personality may be transcultural is consistent with new developments in evolutionary personality psychology (Buss, 1991) and the view that there are biologically based universals in human nature (Brown, 1991). We will return to this argument at the end of the chapter; our conclusion is anticipated by Figure 13.1, which shows a model of the person that might be used in studies of personality and culture.

Empirically, the growing consensus among Western personality psychologists on the adequacy of the FFM as a model of personality structure provides a promising basis for systematic cross-cultural comparisons. Cross-cultural psychologists, implicitly adopting a trait perspective, have translated and administered a wide range of personality trait measures (see Chen, 1983; Chiu, 1990). How can this literature be summarized? How can one be sure that important traits have not been overlooked? If the FFM is found to be a comprehensive model of personality traits across cultures, it can provide a unifying framework for answering these questions. That is, of course, a very big 'if', and much of this chapter will be devoted to an examination of data relevant to determining its usefulness.

Finally, the factor-analytic methodology employed in the development of the FFM provides a possible resolution to one of the most vexing questions in cross-cultural psychology: if personality traits are expressed in culturally-determined ways—if the same behaviour may have different meanings in different cultures and different behaviours may have the same meaning—how can one be sure that a translated scale measures the same trait? The pragmatic answer is that the equivalence of meaning must be demonstrated by an equivalence in psychological consequences which can be seen in a pattern of predictable correlates. Equivalence of meaning is essentially a matter of construct validity, inferred from convergent and discriminant correlations.

As it happens, factor analysis is ideally suited to provide a first test of convergent and discriminant validity, because it groups together variables that covary among themselves (convergent validity) and that are relatively independent of other variables (discriminant validity). When a single scale is translated, its meaning must be laboriously inferred from a pattern of correlations with external variables. If a set of scales with a known factor structure is translated, however, and if the same factor structure is seen in data from administrations of the new version, then it is likely that the original meanings have been retained. Just as the adequacy of a translation is judged from the similarity of the back-translation to the original, so the equivalence of a set of traits across cultures can be assessed by the cross-cultural replicability of the factor structure.

PERSONALITY STRUCTURE: THE FIVE-FACTOR MODEL

Most cross-cultural studies of personality ask whether two groups differ on the mean level of a trait. For example, Chiu (1990) administered a Chinese version of an American personality questionnaire to Taiwanese college students and concluded (among other things) that Chinese were higher in needs for deference, order, and endurance than were their American age peers. Such a design not only assumes that the Chinese and English versions of the test are strictly parallel forms (a dubious assumption); it also—and more fundamentally— assumes that traits identified in American populations can be meaningfully measured in Chinese individuals, that 'deference', 'order', and 'endurance' have exact counterparts in Chinese psychology. This is by no means necessarily so; it rests on the largely untested assumption of the universality of personality structure.

All human groups have a vocabulary for describing people in trait terms (Dixon, 1977), so the concept of traits must be considered a universal aspect of folk psychology. Members of every culture learn to describe themselves and others using such terms as 'talkative', 'timid', and 'diligent'. Scientific psychologists define personality traits as relatively enduring tendencies to show characteristic styles of acting and reacting across a range of situations. Traits are quasi-normally distributed, with a few individuals located at each extreme and most in the average range. Traits are abstract tendencies of the individual, but they are concretely manifested in habits, attitudes, patterns of interpersonal interaction, motives, interests, and so on (McCrae and Costa, 1990).

Natural languages vary in the richness of their vocabulary for describing personality, but trait terms are abundant in most languages. Norman (1967) listed 2,800 English trait descriptors; Yang and Lee (1971) examined a wide variety of printed sources including books and magazines and identified 557 widely used Chinese trait adjectives. In addition, personality theorists have proposed a host of other trait constructs, including introversion–extraversion (Jung, 1971), locus of control (Rotter, 1966), self-monitoring (Synder, 1974), sensation-seeking (Zuckerman, 1979), and needs for abasement, defendence, and succorance (Jackson, 1984). The sheer number of traits would make the systematic study of personality unmanageable were it not for the fact that there is considerable redundancy among terms, suggesting that a much smaller number of basic dimensions underlie the diversity of specific traits.

Since the 1930s psychologists have used factor analysis, a statistical technique for identifying clusters of co-varying variables that define a factor or dimension, to study personality traits. But different researchers began with different item pools, adopted different approaches to factoring, and came to different conclusions about how many factors were necessary to describe personality. Eysenck (1978) proposed three factors, Guilford (1959) ten, Cattell (1973) sixteen. The debate between proponents of these systems has continued for more than 40 years, undermining the credibility of factor analysis and making cross-cultural comparisons dubious. How could Western psychologists hope to interpret factors in the Chinese personality when they could not agree on how to interpret factors in American and English samples?

The resolution of the controversy on the number and nature of major factors (at least to the satisfaction of most trait psychologists) began with the lexical hypothesis, the idea that because personality is important in social interaction, every language will invent terms to describe important traits (John, Angleitner, and Ostendorf, 1988). Under the strong form of this hypothesis, natural-language dictionaries provide exhaustive enumerations of personality traits, and the factor structure of trait terms mirrors the phenotypic structure of personality. Tupes and Christal (1992), using a distillation of English-language trait adjectives, reported five recurrent factors which they labeled Surgency, Agreeableness, Dependability, Emotional Stability, and Culture.

Although lay terms provide one important perspective on personality, the strong form of the lexical hypothesis is probably not justified (McCrae, 1990): clinical and experimental personality psychologists have identified important individual differences that are not well-represented in natural languages (for example, thin boundaries; Hartmann, 1991). Factor-analytic studies, however, have shown that factors similar to those found in adjectives can be found in most theoretically based personality questionnaires (Goldberg, 1993). For example, Extraversion as measured by the Eysenck Personality Questionnaire (EPQ)(Eysenck and Eysenck, 1975) corresponds to Tupes and Christal's Surgency, and EPQ Neuroticism to the low pole of Emotional Stability. (Tupes and Christal's Dependability and Culture are now better known as Conscientiousness and Openness to Experience, respectively.)

Five broad factors are surely insufficient to exhaust important individual differences in personality. For each of the five factors, a number of more specific traits can be identified to provide a more fine-grained analysis of personality. The Revised NEO Personality Inventory (NEO-PI-R)(Costa and McCrae, 1992), an instrument designed to operationalize the FFM, measures six traits for each factor. Agreeableness, for example, is defined by scales that measure Trust, Straightforwardness, Altruism, Compliance, Modesty, and Tender-mindedness.

In American studies the FFM has proven to be extremely robust, with similar factors appearing in many different questionnaires, in males and females, in children, college students, and older adults, in self-reports and observer ratings (McCrae and Costa, 1990). But would the same five factors be found in other cultures? Language, after all, has a powerful effect on perception (Sapir, 1921); perhaps the FFM was only the result of social perception among English-speaking peoples. Lexical studies in Dutch and German (John, Goldberg, and

Angleitner, 1984; Ostendorf, 1990) have suggested that similar factors are to be found in all three of these Germanic languages. Research using the NEO-PI in Spanish (Silva, Avia, Sanz, and Grana, 1993) and Italian (Caprara, Barbaranelli, Borgogni, and Perugini, 1993) supported the structure in two Romance languages. Paunonen, Jackson, Trzebinski, and Forsterling (1992) found a similar five-factor structure in the scales of the Personality Research Form (PRF)(Jackson, 1984) in Canadian, Finnish, Polish, and German samples.

However, of these languages only Finnish is non-Indo-European, and so it might be argued that linguistic similarities among Indo-European languages account for the similarity of factor structures. Again, all these nations (including Finland) are historically and geographically a part of Europe, and the FFM might be regarded as a product of Western culture. Some reason to doubt its broader generality came from a study by Guthrie and Bennett (1971), who used Norman's (1963) adaptation of Tupes and Christal's instrument and replicated only four of the factors (Neuroticism, Extraversion, Agreeableness, and Conscientiousness) in a Philippine sample. Bond, Nakazato, and Shiraishi (1975) used the Norman instrument in a sample of Japanese undergraduates and clearly replicated the same four factors; the fifth factor, Culture/Openness, also emerged, but it was defined by only two of four intended variables.

Cross-cultural replications of the FFM are extraordinarily important both for an understanding of cultures and for an understanding of personality itself. It is only with respect to common dimensions that cultures can be quantitatively compared; the FFM (to the extent that it is replicable across cultures) could provide a meaningful basis for asking about cultural differences in personality. More fundamentally, invariance in personality structure would suggest that there are universal dimensions of individual differences and would reinforce the conclusion that personality traits are an inherent part of human nature.

CHINESE PERSONALITY STRUCTURE

Although China, like the West, has been a literate civilization for centuries, and although Hong Kong in particular is very much a modern city, there are profound cultural and linguistic differences between Chinese and Westerners. The psychological ramifications of these differences are explored in all the chapters in this Handbook, and it would probably surprise few of their authors if the Chinese were shown to have a distinctive personality structure. The handful of studies that have addressed this question, however, suggest more similarities than differences.

Imported Instruments

Much cross-cultural research has been conducted with translations of Western instruments, on the implicit assumption that the same dimensions of personality would be found in any culture. The Minnesota Multiphasic Personality Inventory (MMPI)(Hathaway and McKinley, 1983) had been used in Singapore for at least 20 years before Boey (1985) examined the equivalence of the Chinese and English versions. Using a sample of 65 bilingual Singapore Chinese, Boey administered English and Chinese versions of the MMPI one week apart. Correlations between the two sets of scales ranged from 0.56 to 0.91, with a median of 0.84. These data suggest that the two versions assessed very similar dimensions. Zou, Zhao, and Jiang (1989) administered the Chinese MMPI to 1,095 subjects in Beijing (including both normals and psychiatric patients) and factored the 13 clinical scales; results showed factors similar to those reported in American samples.

Chen (1983) examined the item structure of the Eysenck Personality Questionnaire (Eysenck and Eysenck, 1975) in Mainland China. He administered adaptations of the original 90 items plus nine indigenous items to 643 subjects in Beijing. Correlations between items and factors of the EPQ were examined within sex, and 85 items appeared to work as intended; most of the problematic items came from the Psychoticism scale, a scale frequently found to be weak in American studies as well (McCrae and Costa, 1985). A study by S. B. G. Eysenck and Chan (1982) replicated the four-factor structure of the EPQ in both adult and child versions, 'indicating that the major dimensions of personality were very similar in Hong Kong Chinese as in British subjects' (p. 153).

Two of the EPQ factors are Neuroticism and Extraversion, so these data provide some support for the hypothesis that the FFM might be recovered among Chinese subjects. More direct evidence was provided first by Bond (1979), who administered Norman's (1963) instrument (in English) to 192 Chinese university students to investigate dimensions of person perception. Subjects nominated other members of the group as being in the upper, middle, or lower third of their group on each trait. Factor analysis showed a clear replication of the Norman structure, with coefficients of factor congruence ranging from 0.85 to 0.95. The single variable (of 20) that was misplaced was *intellectual*, which loaded on the Conscientiousness factor—a common occurrence in American studies as well (McCrae and Costa, in press).

In 1990, Yang and Bond published a large-scale replication. In this study, the Norman scales were translated into Chinese, and 2,000 subjects in Taiwan were asked to describe two of six targets (father, mother, most familiar teacher, most familiar neighbor, most familiar same-sex friend, and self). In place of nominations, subjects employed a 7-point rating scale. Five factors were extracted and rotated, and the structure was recovered more or less adequately for all six targets. Factor loadings were reported for father, friend, and self; for each of these three targets 20 variables were factored, and in 49 of these 60 cases the variable loaded primarily on the intended factor, although there were numerous secondary loadings. The inclusion of self as a target moved this study beyond person perception to a study of self-rated personality.

A better test of the replicability of the FFM would employ more contemporary measures. Paunonen and his colleagues (1994) recently administered the PRF and a new, picture-based Nonverbal Personality Questionnaire to respondents in six cultures, including Hong Kong. Correlations between these two measures of Murray's needs showed modest validity, with coefficients ranging from 0.09 to 0.65 in the Hong Kong sample. The factor structure of the two instruments, however, was similar, and clearly reproduced the FFM.

Since 1990, Bond and his colleagues and students at the Chinese University of Hong Kong have collected data on a Chinese translation of the NEO-PI-R, a 240-item measure of the FFM. An initial version, revised after examination of a back-translation, was administered by Liu (1991) to 99 undergraduates at the Chinese University of Hong Kong, and by Luk and Bond (1993) to an additional 36 students. Item analyses using these data suggested possible problems with several items, and 15 were re-translated. The final version was administered by Ho (1994) to 217 undergraduates. By treating the 15 revised items as missing data in the first two data sets, a combined sample of 352 subjects (161 male, 191 female) was obtained. All subjects were from introductory psychology classes and completed the questionnaire in group sessions.

The internal consistencies of the scales in the final version were generally comparable to those found in American samples (Costa and McCrae, 1992). A clear exception was O6: Values, which had an alpha of 0.32 in the Chinese sample. This finding suggests that the particular social and moral attitudes that reflect Openness to Experience may differ in American and Chinese cultures, and that the construct might best be expressed with different items in a Chinese personality inventory. Coefficient alphas for the five global domain scales were 0.92, 0.85, 0.79, 0.82, and 0.91 for Neuroticism, Extraversion, Openness, Agreeableness, and Conscientiousness, respectively.

A factor analysis of the combined data provides direct evidence on the generalizability of the NEO-PI-R factor structure. A scree test suggested five factors and Table 13.1 reports factor loadings after varimax rotation. The results are an unequivocal replication: 29 of the 30 facets have their highest loading on the intended factor, and 28 of these are larger than 0.40. The pattern of secondary loadings is also similar to that found in American samples (Costa and McCrae, 1992), and coefficients of congruence are quite high for all five factors.

Table 13.1 Factor Analysis of Revised NEO Personality Inventory Facet Scales in Hong Kong Chinese Undergraduates

NEO-PI-R	Varimax-rotated Principal Component				
Facet	N	E	O	A	C
N1: Anxiety	**.83**	−.12	−.02	−.05	−.08
N2: Angry Hostility	**.65**	.12	−.03	−.38	−.12
N3: Depression	**.75**	−.24	−.03	−.02	−.27
N4: Self-consciousness	**.64**	−.31	−.11	−.04	−.13
N5: Impulsiveness	**.56**	.26	.12	−.17	−.38
N6: Vulnerability	**.74**	−.10	−.22	.10	−.34
E1: Warmth	−.02	**.66**	.09	**.49**	.06
E2: Gregariousness	−.03	**.67**	−.12	.22	−.12
E3: Assertiveness	−.13	**.66**	.08	−.15	.20
E4: Activity	.04	**.64**	−.07	−.03	**.41**

Table 13.1 *(Cont'd)*

NEO-PI-R	Varimax-rotated Principal Component				
Facet	N	E	O	A	C
E5: Excitement-seeking	.03	**.51**	.19	−.28	−.12
E6: Positive Emotions	−.23	**.60**	.18	.30	.03
O1: Fantasy	.13	.04	**.55**	−.15	−.31
O2: Aesthetics	.00	.11	**.67**	.27	−.05
O3: Feelings	**.50**	.23	**.56**	.06	.11
O4: Actions	−.21	.28	.29	−.09	−.28
O5: Ideas	−.15	−.10	**.61**	−.03	.32
O6: Values	−.17	.04	**.43**	.06	.03
A1: Trust	−.23	.18	.02	**.68**	.12
A2: Straightforwardness	−.07	−.23	.03	**.68**	.13
A3: Altruism	−.10	.29	.18	**.64**	.29
A4: Compliance	−.09	−.17	−.06	**.69**	−.08
A5: Modesty	.29	**-.46**	−.14	.32	−.15
A6: Tender-mindedness	.27	.19	.15	**.62**	.02
C1: Competence	−.39	.28	.16	−.14	**.65**
C2: Order	−.07	.05	.00	.07	**.73**
C3: Dutifulness	−.15	−.03	−.07	.28	**.69**
C4: Achievement-striving	−.03	.22	.07	.04	**.78**
C5: Self-discipline	−.30	.15	−.04	.14	**.78**
C6: Deliberation	−.29	−.19	.05	.04	**.69**
Congruence Coefficient	.97	.93	.92	.93	.97

Note n = 352. Loadings greater than .40 in absolute magnitude are given in bold-face. Congruence coefficients compare the factors with normative American data (Costa and McCrae, 1992).

One facet of Openness, O4: Actions, does not have a clear loading on any factor, which may indicate problems with the scale, a real difference in the nature of this dimension among Chinese, or simple sampling error. One facet of Agreeableness, A5: Modesty, has its primary loading on (low) Extraversion rather than on Agreeableness. Together with the large secondary loading of E1: Warmth on the Agreeableness factor, this suggests that the varimax rotation of these two factors is somewhat different in this sample than in the normative American sample. Such rotational variations are not uncommon even among American samples, and are due to the fact that the facets that define Extraversion and Agreeableness form an interpersonal circumplex (McCrae and Costa, 1989) rather than a simple structure. A minor adjustment to the rotation of these two factors would yield an even clearer replication (Costa, McCrae, Bond, and Paunonen, 1994).

Indigenous Approaches to Personality Structure

The data reviewed so far suggest that personality traits identified in Western populations can be measured in Chinese samples, and that they show the same five-factor structure. In this sense, the FFM can be said to summarize aspects of Chinese personality structure that are universal. However, cross-cultural psychologists have pointed out that many individuals—certainly including students at modern universities—have been influenced by both traditional and Western cultures, and can respond to different situations by either ethnic affirmation or cross-cultural accommodation (Bond and Yang, 1982). To the extent that completing Western personality questionnaires (even in translation) elicits cross-cultural accommodation, the studies reviewed so far may say more about Westernized Chinese personality structure than about traditional Chinese personality structure.

Further, the fact that the FFM can be replicated in Chinese samples does not necessarily mean that the model provides the most natural or useful way to describe personality in Chinese populations, nor does it imply that the five factors are fully comprehensive. Perhaps there are additional factors in the Chinese personality not found in the West, and perhaps these new factors are precisely the most important for understanding individual differences among Chinese (Yang, in press).

This argument in favour of indigenous, or emic (Berry, 1969), approaches has formed the basis for several attempts to measure personality from a distinctly Chinese perspective. Yang and Bond (1985) reported a study of factors derived from Chinese trait descriptive adjectives. They sampled 150 monopolar adjectives from Yang and Lee's (1971) pool of 557 Chinese personality-descriptive predicates commonly used in the Chinese language. Factor analyses were performed on ratings of six targets, and three bipolar factors appeared to be replicable; these they labeled Social orientation–Self-centeredness, Competency–Impotency, and Extraversion–Introversion. In a reanalysis of these data (Yang and Bond, 1990), five factors—the 'Chinese Big Five'— were identified: Social Orientation–Self-Centeredness, Competence–Impotence, Expressiveness–Conservativism, Self-Control–Impulsiveness, and Optimism–Neuroticism.

Lew (1985) examined the structure of Chinese personality by using the Multi-Factor Personality Inventory (MFPI), a Chinese instrument based on his observations of people from Asian and Western countries in Hong Kong and the United States, a review of the literature on Chinese character, and interviews with Chinese intellectuals (Yik and Bond, 1993). Lew's inventory contained many terms that cannot be found in Yang and Bond's (1990) item pool, including *subjective, democratic, passive,* and *overconcerned about 'face'.* There were 122 bipolar personality items in total. The subjects tested were 506 Taiwanese intellectuals. Eight factors were extracted from the self-ratings of the items: Weak morality–Strong morality, Neuroticism–Emotional stability, Extraversion–Introversion, Dominance–Humility, Open-mindedness–Authoritarianism, High conformity–Low conformity, Tender-mindedness–Tough-mindedness, and Reflectivity–Impulsiveness.

In 1987, Lew and Hau reported another study on the MFPI, in which data were collected from 2,476 Chinese intellectuals from Hong Kong, China, Taiwan, and the United States. Eleven factors were extracted from self-ratings, adding Adventurism–Cautiousness, Liberalism–Conservatism, and Idealism –Realism to the original eight.

P. C. Cheung, Conger, Hau, Lew, and Lau (1992) used the items of the MFPI in samples from mainland China, Hong Kong, the United States, and Taiwan to create a new instrument, the Multi-Trait Personality Inventory. About half the items were believed by the authors to reflect culture-specific traits; the remainder were thought to be universal. Factor analyses at the item level were inconclusive, so an item-clustering procedure was adopted, leading to the identification of 19 clusters. Factoring these item clusters lead to five replicable factors, labelled Outgoing–Withdrawn, Self Serving–Principled, Conforming–Non-conforming, Unstable–Stable, and Strict–Accepting. These factors appear to correspond to Extraversion, low Conscientiousness, low Openness, Neuroticism, and low Agreeableness, respectively, and the authors concluded that 'these factors resemble those in the Big Five [that is, FFM] theory' (p. 548).

Comparing Imported and Indigenous Factors

This survey of indigenous approaches to Chinese personality structure suggests that there may be three, five, eight, eleven, or nineteen factors—a situation that echoes the state of personality assessment in the West prior to the ascendance of the FFM. Is it possible that the alternative Chinese models can all be understood in terms of the FFM, just as many Western personality models have been (McCrae, 1989)? A series of studies suggests this may be the case.

Yang and Bond included Norman's factors as well as the Chinese Big Five in their 1990 study. All five Chinese factors were predictable from the Norman factors, with multiple Rs ranging from 0.46 to 0.69, although clear one-to-one correspondences were not found. Liu (1991) selected 46 items from Chinese questionnaires to represent indigenous aspects of Chinese personality. Subsequent item factor analysis by Ho (1994) suggested four factors: Job Confidence, Filial Piety, Authority Submission, and Neuroticism. A joint analysis of these four Chinese factors with the facets of the NEO-PI-R showed that they did not define unique factors. Instead, Neuroticism loaded on the NEO-PI-R Neuroticism factor, Filial Piety on Agreeableness, Authority Submission (negatively) on Openness, and Job Confidence on the NEO-PI-R Extraversion factor.

Yik and Bond (1993) created a culturally balanced person perception scale, the Sino-American Person Perception Scale (SAPPS), by analyzing imported adjectives measuring the FFM and indigenous adjectives taken from Yang and Bond (1990) and Lew (1985). In a joint analysis eight factors were extracted, labelled Emotional Stability–Neuroticism, Extraversion, Application, Openness to Experience, Assertiveness, Restraint, Helpfulness, and Intellect. Cheng, Cheng, Ng, and Yip (1991) correlated these scales with the Chinese NEO-PI-R domain scales, and a factor analysis of the 13 variables gave a clear five-factor solution: Neuroticism, Extraversion, and Openness scales from both instruments jointly defined three of the factors; SAPPS Helpfulness loaded on an Agreeableness factor, and the remaining SAPPS variables—Application, Restraint, Assertiveness, and Intellect—loaded on a factor defined by NEO-PI-R Conscientiousness (McCrae, 1994). These results suggest that the same five factors are found in Chinese as in American samples, although some aspects of personality (notably Conscientiousness) may be emphasized more in Chinese culture (Bond, 1994).

Further comparisons of indigenous and imported models of personality are of course needed, and at least two major efforts are in progress. F. M. Cheung and colleagues (in press) have painstakingly developed a new Chinese Personality Assessment Inventory (CPAI) intended to measure both normal personality traits and psychopathology from a distinctively Chinese perspective; and K. S. Yang (personal communication, 22 July 1994) has conducted a new survey of indigenous Chinese personality adjectives. Joint analyses of these measures with the NEO-PI-R will provide important evidence on the comprehensiveness of the FFM as a model of Chinese personality traits.

Predictive Validity of the Five-factor Model in Chinese

Factor analyses in themselves constitute only one step in the demonstration that the factors of the FFM adequately capture Chinese personality traits: an entire program of research on their construct validity is needed. A few steps have already been taken. Yik (1993) has shown consensual validation for the scales of the SAPPS by demonstrating significant agreement between self-reports and peer ratings. Luk and Bond (1993) found meaningful relations between NEO-PI-R scales and measures of values such as universalism and benevolence. Yik and Bond (1993) reported that Openness to Experience predicted both self-reported degree of Westernization and academic major. Luk and Bond (1992) showed that Extraversion, low Neuroticism, and especially Conscientiousness (measured as Application and Intellect on the SAPPS) were all independent predictors of global self-esteem, a finding replicated by Ho (1994) using the NEO-PI-R. All these data suggest that the dimensions of the FFM may be as important in Chinese psychology as they have proven to be in Western psychology.

MEAN LEVELS OF PERSONALITY TRAITS IN CHINESE STUDENTS

We argued earlier that the question of mean differences between cultures on personality traits could not properly be asked until it had been established that the same traits existed in both cultures. Having concluded that very similar personality traits can be measured in American and Chinese culture, we can proceed to a comparison of mean level differences.

Before doing so, however, a different but equally important set of cautions is needed. Mean level comparisons are appropriate across cultural groups if and only if the two versions of the test are strictly parallel—that is to say, if bilingual, bicultural individuals would obtain the same score on both versions of the test. This is a testable proposition (at least as regards bilingual subjects) and should ideally be considered a required step in the validation of any translated assessment device. Without this kind of evidence, any observed differences might be due to a host of variables other than population differences in personality traits.

For example, the items might be more or less extreme in translation than in the original language. An item like 'I sometimes feel sad', to which many subjects would assent, might be paraphrased in translation as 'I often feel depressed', which would be endorsed by far fewer. Even items with concrete behavioural content may have different implications in different cultures. 'I study at least three hours each night' would be an indication of extreme conscientiousness in American students, but not in Chinese.

In addition, personality measures almost invariably use self-reports, and there may be cultural differences in styles of self-presentation. Recalling the Confucian maxim that 'He who speaks without modesty will find it difficult to make his words good', Chinese respondents might be less eager to endorse such items as 'I am efficient and effective at my work' than would their equally conscientious American counterparts. Comparing self-reports with observer ratings could teach us something about Chinese styles of self-presentation, but only a few such studies have yet been conducted (Yik, 1993).

With these caveats in mind, Figure 13.2 displays mean levels of NEO-PI-R scores for Chinese men and women, plotted on profile sheets based on North American college student norms (Costa and McCrae, 1992). The five basic factors are shown on the left, followed by facet scales for each factor. Normed within sex, very similar profiles are seen for men and women. At the factor level, Chinese students are chiefly distinguished from Americans by their low Extraversion scores; they score in the low range on all six Extraversion facets. Interpersonally they are more distant and detached; temperamentally they are less excitable and emotional. This finding is consistent with a large body of research using Western measures of extraversion and sociability (see Yang, 1986, for a review).

Chinese students generally score within the average range on facets of the other four domains. The wide fluctuations within the Agreeableness domain can be understood at least in part in terms of differences in Extraversion.

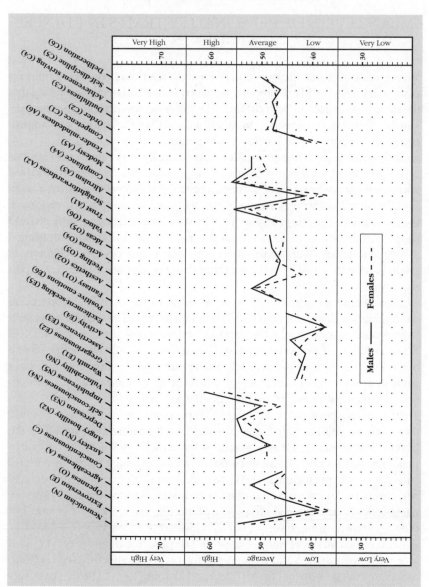

Figure 13.2 Mean levels of personality traits for male and female Hong Kong university students, standardized with reference to American college age normative data.

Profile form reproduced by special permission of the publisher from the Revised Neo Personality Inventory. Copyright 1978, 1985, 1989, 1992 by PAR, Inc. Further reproduction is prohibited without permission of PAR, Inc

Straightforwardness and Compliance are relatively introverted forms of Agreeableness, and Chinese students score high on these facets; they score low on Altruism, a relatively extraverted form of Agreeableness. Another explanation concerns the fact that Altruism involves generosity toward strangers, toward whom Chinese are customarily indifferent or even opportunistic (Yang, in press).

What is perhaps most remarkable about the profile is the lack of elevation on facets of Conscientiousness. Behaviourally, Chinese students appear to be far more conscientious than do their American counterparts, at least in regard to academics (Bond, 1991), but they describe themselves as merely average on Order, Dutifulness, Achievement Striving, Self-Discipline, and Deliberation, and distinctly low on Competence. This may be due to the use of other Chinese students—or ideal Chinese students—as a reference group, or to a self-effacing style of self-description. Combined, however, with high scores on N6: Vulnerability, it suggests a real insecurity about personal effectiveness which may be a response to heavy social pressures to succeed.

A comparison of standard deviations—measures of variability among individuals—in the Chinese and American samples shows small differences. Standardized using North American college-age norms and expressed as T-scores, the 30-facet scales have standard deviations ranging from 7.6 to 10.9 (median = 9.0) in the Chinese sample. Some Chinese score very high, some very low on all the traits measured. These data are consistent with Linton's (1945) observation that the same range of variation in personality traits is found in all societies.

PERSONALITY AND CULTURE RECONSIDERED

Within personality psychology, a return to the larger issues of personality and culture was made possible by a clearer understanding of personality trait structure. In anthropology a very different approach has been taken: 'The "person" re-emerged in cultural psychology as a "semiotic subject," for whom the historically acquired meaning of a situation or stimulus event is the major constraint on his or her response to it' (Shweder and Sullivan, 1990, p. 399). Briefly, this view holds that all human experience is culturally shaped: reality is perceived in terms of shared meanings that evoke a limited range of responses. The person is the agent who 'interprets' and responds to the 'text' of the world, and without culture there is neither person nor world.

From this perspective, all Chinese are alike insofar as they see the world in a uniquely Chinese way. It would not, for example, occur to most Americans to consider the spatial orientation of their house except perhaps in regard to energy efficiency. Many Chinese, however, take a keen interest in *feng shui*, seeing dangers and possibilities to which Americans are oblivious (Hornik, 1993). More profoundly, Chinese differ from Americans in their emphasis on interdependence rather than autonomy, a difference with effects on the self-concept, cognition, motivation, and emotion (Markus and Kitayama, 1991). This distinctively Chinese social orientation has been shaped by centuries of tradition (Yang, in press).

To radical semiotic cultural psychologists like Shweder and Sullivan (1990), the culture creates the personality, and all members of a culture must have very similar personalities, different from the personalities of members of other cultures. Benedict (1934) and DuBois (1944) had similarly hypothesized a 'modal personality' that would characterize all or most of the members of a culture. The empirical disconfirmation of that earlier hypothesis was a blow to the field of culture and personality, and the data on which Figure 13.2 is based, showing wide variation among Chinese respondents and generally modest differences between Chinese and American samples, might be taken as refutation of the radical semiotic position.

Yet surely Shweder and Sullivan (1990) raise an important point: given massive cultural differences, in what way can Chinese be said to share universal dimensions of individual differences in personality? In what respect is it meaningful to say that Chinese extraverts resemble American extraverts more than they do Chinese introverts?

McCrae and Costa (in press) have recently proposed a five-factor theory of personality that offers an explanation of this phenomenon. As Figure 13.1 illustrates, they distinguished several conceptually independent aspects of the person, including biologically based *basic tendencies,* abstract potentials of the individual including abilities and dispositions; *external influences* which provide the social environment in which individuals develop and act; *characteristic adaptations* such as language, skills, habits, goals, relationships, and, of particular importance, the *self-concept;* and the *objective biography,* what the individual does and experiences across a lifetime. Within this framework, personality traits are basic tendencies, culture (as experienced by the individual) is an external influence, and the semiotic subject is a set of characteristic adaptations.

McCrae and Costa (in press) postulated that characteristic adaptations interact with external influences over time to produce the objective biography—precisely the position taken by Shweder and Sullivan, who see acquired meanings as the determinants of behaviour. McCrae and Costa further postulated, however, that characteristic adaptations are themselves the product of the interaction of basic tendencies with external influences, of personality with culture. This simple premise, together with the further postulate that personality traits are endogenous, provides a new basis for studying personality and culture.

The Independence of Personality and Culture

The effects of culture on the individual's values, habits, tastes, beliefs, relationships, and goals are incalculable, yet to the question, 'How does culture affect personality?' McCrae and Costa (in press) offered the parsimonious if radical answer that it has no effect at all. They postulated that personality traits are endogenous, determined largely by genetics, and that personality and culture are independent contributors to the development of characteristic adaptations. This is, of course, an unproven premise, but it is an idea worth entertaining as a way of considering problems of culture and personality.

If culture has no effect on the development of personality traits, how can we account for mean level differences in trait scores across cultures? Why are

Chinese apparently more introverted than Americans? One explanation would be differences in the gene pool, an explanation that would be consistent with observed differences in infant temperament (Yang, 1986). In principle it would be possible to test this hypothesis by transcultural adoption studies, showing, for instance, that Chinese adoptees raised in Western families would remain more introverted than their Western adoptive siblings. In practice, such studies would probably not be feasible.

However, even if genetics accounts for some cross-cultural differences in personality test scores, it cannot hold the full explanation. There are historical changes within the same society and gene pool that also appear to affect personality; changes in behaviours due to Westernization are, in fact, a major concern for many Chinese (Bond, 1991).

But these effects are perhaps best regarded as cultural differences or changes in the *expression* of traits. Feldman (cited in Bond, 1991) conducted a study of parental restrictiveness in Hong Kong and in first- and second-generation Chinese immigrants to Australia and the United States, and found adaptations in norms about social activities. Chinese raised in the United States engaged in more social activities, but that does not necessarily mean that they became more extraverted. Instead, it might be interpreted to mean that the cultural norm for social behaviour had changed. Under this hypothesis, if monozygotic twins were raised separately in Hong Kong and the United States, the former would spend less time socializing outside the family than would the latter, but they would be equally extraverted, scoring at the same percentile within the local distribution.

The Interaction of Culture and Personality

The interpretation of group differences in terms of the phenotypic expression of traits implies that both personality and culture are involved in the formation of characteristic adaptations. This notion is in some respects trivially true. Extraverts in every culture are talkative, but they speak many different languages. Open individuals try new and foreign foods, but what is exotic in one cuisine—sea cucumber and chicken feet, cottage cheese and tossed salad—is common in another. Personality traits are necessarily expressed in behaviours, and the range of possible behaviours is largely determined by culture.

In other respects, the influence of culture may be more subtle. There may be quantitative shifts in similar behaviour. For example, extraverts are more emotionally expressive than are introverts, but Chinese culture tends to restrain the expression of feelings (Bond, 1993). Thus, an extraverted American may laugh twice as much as an equally extraverted Chinese. There may also be qualitative shifts in the phenotypic expression of traits. Anthropologists have been particularly interested in the expression of emotion in different cultures (Lutz and White, 1986), pointing out that what Westerners may regard as purely affective states are perceived in physiological terms by others. If Americans scoring highly in neuroticism have frequent spells of depression, Chinese scoring highly in neuroticism may report frequent feelings of discomfort in the heart (cf., Zheng, Xu, and Shen, 1986).

The fact that different cultures express the same traits differently does not mean that the relations between a trait and the characteristic adaptations it gives rise to are wholly arbitrary. Effort, for example, is a universal psychological process, and people who regularly exert great efforts to achieve goals are recognized (or stigmatized) as hard-working or ambitious in every culture. The goals toward which people work and the standards by which efforts are evaluated differ, but the basic phenomenon is recognizable. It is because of these underlying universals that cultural psychologists can 'document genuine differences without turning the other into an incomprehensible alien' (Shweder and Sullivan, 1993, p. 517).

The generalization that culture and personality jointly shape the characteristic adaptations of the individual omits a myriad of details about the psychological mechanisms by which individuals acquire and coordinate their plans, beliefs, skills, and roles; and about the cultural mechanisms by which values, knowledge, and social patterns are transmitted and maintained. It does, however, put the end result of all these mechanisms in perspective: the functioning adult in any viable culture has developed ways of living that are consistent with the requirements of the group and that also express his or her personality.

That dual function has often been ignored, with attention paid only to the group's requirements. Both anthropologists and psychologists have tended to depict cultures in modal terms: we say that Chinese tradition promotes social orientation, industriousness, and emotional restraint, and we somehow expect that all Chinese will show these traits. We fail to recognize that there is inevitably a distribution of behaviours around the modal goal that all cultures tolerate, a spectrum of possible behaviours. Individuals express their personality by finding their place on these spectra, by choosing the roles they wish to play or by interpreting their assigned roles in congenial ways. The cultural imperative of harmony within the family (Yang, in press) may preclude the direct expression of hostility there, but antagonism may be expressed indirectly (as Zhang Yimou's film *Raise the Red Lantern* vividly illustrates), and rudeness to strangers is not strongly prohibited. It is in such ways that individual differences in agreeableness versus antagonism might be expressed in Chinese societies.

Cultures differ in the extent to which they allow or facilitate expression of personality. Yang (in press) noted that Chinese culture is highly formalistic, with behaviour dictated by position in the family and society. Yet even in traditional China, individual differences in intelligence and diligence affected social mobility through the civil service examinations. It is worth recalling that culture is created by persons, and therefore just as every culture must deal with the universal human needs for food, information, and companionship, so every culture must provide ways of expressing individual differences in personality. This suggests a new agenda for cultural anthropologists, who need to explain not only how people are fed, instructed, and socialized, but also how they are allowed to express varying levels of neuroticism, extraversion, openness, agreeableness, and conscientiousness.

CONCLUSION

Anthropologists and cross-cultural psychologists naturally prefer to emphasize the differences they find in their populations of interest. There would, after all, be no reason for their disciplines if all people were in every respect alike. But it is also useful from time to time to put the differences in perspective and to note cross-cultural similarities (Hwang, 1982), the universal aspects of human nature that are so persuasively demonstrated when they are found in such alien environments.

Psychologists who have been taught to see the environment as the source of personality may be surprised by the uniformity of personality structure seen in this chapter. It should come as no surprise, however, to travellers or to anyone familiar with world literature. A modern reader can appreciate the *Epic of Gilgamesh*, Lady Murasaki's *Tale of Genji*, Icelandic sagas, and Pearl S. Buck's *The Good Earth* not only because those works treat universal human experiences like vengence, grief, and love, but also because their protagonists are characterized by familiar clusters of personality traits. Individual differences are ubiquitous, but it appears that the ways in which people differ are everywhere the same.

NOTES

The authors gratefully acknowledge the inspiration of Professor John H. Useem and helpful comments by J. Chan, J. R. Conrad, and K. S. Yang. Official contribution of the National Institutes of Health; not subject to copyright in the United States.

Chapter 14

Chinese Values

Michael Harris Bond

> Culture must include the explicit and systematic study of values and value systems viewed as observable, describable and comparable phenomena of nature (Alfred Kroeber and Clyde Kluckhohn, *Culture: A critical review of concepts and definitions*)

Just as dreams are 'the royal road to the unconscious' for many psychoanalysts, values have constituted the royal road to explaining cultural differences for many behavioural scientists. In consequence, a number of instruments for measuring values have been developed and administered to a variety of cultural groups over the past fifty years. The results of these comparisons have then been used to 'explain' a host of observed behaviours distinguishing members of the cultures whose values have been previously assessed (see, for example, Bond, Wan, Leung, and Giacalone, 1985).

Values continue to enjoy this position as a touchstone in cultural studies. Fortunately, over the last few decades, the quality of cross-cultural research on values has improved: samples are more comparable, instruments are more comprehensive, analyses are more sophisticated, and studies are more multicultural. Extending our range beyond the all-too-typical contrasts of one group against a group of American subjects, social scientists have been able to chart a wider geography of values, mapping cultural groups with respect to one another. By including a number of Chinese cultural groups in the same study, we have been able to discover those values which unite and distinguish these descendants from the Middle Kingdom. In consequence, simplistic, monolithic conceptions of Chinese values are being replaced by more highly differentiated ones, and Chinese societies are being grouped in terms of their value similarities together with some surprising neighbours.

This essay will examine the recent harvest of multicultural values studies. It will not recapitulate Yang's (1986) thorough integration of value studies prior to the 1980s. Nor will it consider most descriptive, bicultural contrasts of one culture's values with those of a Chinese culture; such limited studies are of interest only in so far as they illuminate the results of more syncretic, theoretically ambitious work.

We begin by considering a definition of values, expanding on key aspects of the definition. Measurement issues are covered next, including the basic contrast between culture-level and individual-level treatments of data. Results from these two approaches will be discussed with respect to the Chinese groups included and conclusions about the profile of Chinese values, if any, drawn.

THE CONSTRUCT OF VALUE AND ITS MEASUREMENT

Definitions

Kluckhohn (1951) examined a host of studies concerning the concept of value and produced this definition: 'A value is a conception, explicit or implicit, distinctive of an individual or a group, of the desirable which influences the selection from available modes, means and ends of actions' (p. 395). Kluckhohn's synthesis identified a number of features common to many discussions of value before and since. It will define the ambit of our concern in this chapter.

How to Measure Values

Types of measurement

A number of approaches have been taken in attempts to quantify Chinese values. Domino and Hannah (1987) content-analysed stories completed by their subjects; McClelland (1963) scored public school textbooks for themes related to power, affiliation and achievement; Watrous and Hsu (1963) collected responses to cards from the Thematic Apperception Test (TAT), assessing the resulting stories for a number of needs, such as dependence, aggression, and so forth. Self-report inventories have frequently been used and have varied in the simplicity of the stimuli to be rated: from complex value patterns, as in Yang and Chang's (1975) use of the Kluckhohn and Strodtbeck (1961) questionnaire or in Yang's (1972) use of the Morris (1956) Ways to Live survey, to words and their synonyms, as used in the surveys by the Chinese Culture Connection (1987) or by Ng et al. (1982).

One clear challenge is to integrate the results across these various measurement approaches (see, for example, Yang, 1986). This task is difficult because few studies empirically assess the convergence across such instruments for Chinese subjects. One such study (Yu, 1974) showed that TAT and self-report measures of achievement needs did not correlate. Further research is needed to link these various measures, especially now that self-report inventories measuring consciously held values are becoming so widely used (see Schwartz, 1992).

Individual values or groups of values?

Instruments in the study of values have been developed out of theory which specified certain important constructs (see, for example, Murray's 1938 theory of needs) or out of the author's judgement about which values were important (see, for example, Rokeach, 1973). These various values have often been individually measured without much attention being paid to their inter-relationships (see, for example, Lau, 1988).

More recently, value theory has been developed which pays careful attention to the dynamic interplay among different values (Schwartz, 1992). Overlap among psychologically similar values and opposition between psychologically dissimilar values thus come to assume theoretical importance. Sophisticated statistical techniques, like smallest space analysis (SSA), factor analysis, or cluster analysis, are deployed to group related values into domains, factors, or clusters. Empirical results are reported at the level of these group-ings. This integration has the statistical advantage of increasing reliability of measurement, and the intellectual advantage of reducing cognitive overload, for those trying to understand empirical results from multi-item questionnaires.

Metric equivalence?

The issue of grouping raises the spectre of equivalence in research on values. Cross-cultural studies require that those who import instruments or who make comparisons establish that the same concepts are being measured in the dif-ferent cultural groups concerned (see, for example, Poortinga, 1989). It is sim-ply not enough to assume that linguistically equivalent terms (words, statements, scenarios, and the like) are tapping the same constructs. Instead, it must be demonstrated that items presumed to group together do so in the same ways in all cultural groups being compared (see, for example, Elizur, Borg, Hunt, and Beck, 1991). Only then can comparisons be meaningfully made.

Metric equivalence can be established by demonstrating similarity in the network of relationships among the values being measured (see Schwartz, 1992, for a rare example of such careful assessment). This examination may employ coefficients of congruence, Cronbach alphas, domain overlap (from smallest space analysis), and so forth. When such a process is not undertaken, mistaken conclusions may be drawn. Lau (1992), for example, compared mainland, Hong Kong, and Singapore Chinese using the Rokeach Value Survey (RVS). He noted the high endorsement by mainland Chinese of 'a sense of accomplishment' and of the terms 'capable' and 'ambitious', and he con-cluded that mainland Chinese 'showed…some very clear individualistic con-cerns' (p. 364). Lau may have interpreted the evidence correctly (see also Katz, Juni, Shope, and Tang, 1993). Alternatively, however, these achievement val-ues may be linked for these subjects to the concept of family or national secu-rity, not to self-enhancement. If so, then the high endorsement of these values by mainland Chinese may instead reflect collectivist concerns, not individualis-tic dispositions. Because Lau did not first establish the metric equivalence of the values to be compared, we cannot accept his conclusions about the mean-ing of the differences he found.

Cultural response style

Individual values are measured by requiring the subject to respond in some way: by producing stories (for example, Domino and Hannah, 1987), by checking scales, and so forth. These responses are then scored in various ways: by the frequency of certain value themes in the stories, by the average level of scale endorsement across a value domain, and so forth. The problem is that persons of different cultures may respond differently in general to these methods of collecting data (see, for example, Hui and Triandis, 1989). People from one culture may, for example, be more fluent in producing *any* story than are people from another culture. Or, they may agree more about the importance of *any* value than do people from another culture. Such general response differences mean that, when any particular value endorsement is compared in the different cultures, a difference will appear. This difference may, however, only reflect differences in response styles across cultures.

Cross-cultural researchers have therefore developed a number of strategies for eliminating the potential influence of these response styles from their data, so that substantive differences in value endorsement across cultural groups may be detected. These corrections can only be made if a number of values are being measured in the same research. One can then examine the strength of a given value or value grouping relative to the other values or value groups being assessed. These relative strengths may then be compared across cultural groups whose overall response strengths have been equated.

Procedures used have included standardizing the scores for the various values within each subject (Bond, 1988) or equating the average score across the whole value survey for each cultural group (Schwartz, 1994). When such procedures have not been adopted in cross-cultural research (see, for example, Ng et al., 1982; Triandis et al., 1986), the results obtained must be checked for convergence against studies where cultural response styles have been controlled. Results may or may not differ (see, for example, Chinese Culture Connection, 1987).

Levels of Analysis: Individual or Cultural?

The issue of the proper level of analysis in the study of values has become important since the seminal work of Hofstede (1980). Hofstede's results continue to be misinterpreted because of widespread failure to heed his warnings about the ecological fallacy (1980, pp. 28–31). This conceptual error occurs when an index derived from a culture-level analysis is applied to individuals (for example, Ralston et al., 1993).

As larger, multicultural data sets are created, the potential for confusing the levels of analysis will increase (Scheuch, 1970). Such confusion will lead to incompatible results whenever individual-level analyses produce item correlations different from those produced by country-level item correlations, as with the Chinese Value Survey (CVS)(Chinese Culture Connection, 1987; Bond, 1988). We must be vigilant in order to avoid adding confusion to complexity.

Which level to use?

In common parlance we speak of individuals holding values, not of countries holding values. Of course, it is possible statistically to characterize the values of a country by averaging the scores given to a set of values by a representative sample of persons from that country. Various country value scores may then be factor-analysed and countries given factor scores (Chinese Culture Connection, 1987; Hofstede, 1980; Hofstede and Bond, 1984; Schwartz, 1994). These factor scores can then be related to country 'behaviours', such as levels of domestic violence, the economic growth rate, the degree of human rights observance, and so forth (see, for example, Bond, 1991). Conceptually, this approach is reminiscent of the 'dimensions of nations' project (Rummel, 1972) and yields a fascinating 'psychology of countries'.

The country-level approach does have the major advantage of side-stepping the need to establish metric equivalence among the values across cultural groups (Leung and Bond, 1989). Furthermore, some argue that it should produce results for values similar to those produced by the individual-level approach (Schwartz, 1994). There are, however, many examples in social science where the pattern of results change when one shifts the level of analysis away from the individual to larger units (Hofstede, 1980; Hofstede, Bond, and Luk, 1993; Leung 1989; Scheuch, 1970). For the time being, results will be considered separately for culture-level and individual-level studies of value.

Which Cultural Groups?

Depending on the ethnic composition of the sample, the data may or may not reflect the cultural diversity present in the country whose population is being assessed. Method sections must be carefully read to determine, for example, which Canadians, Anglophone or Francophone, are being compared with, say, which Malaysians, Malays or Chinese. This specification problem is less a concern with the Chinese societies studied, since the samples involved are either representative of their culture (as, for instance, in Singapore) or exclusively Chinese (as, for instance, Han Chinese in mainland China). Schwartz's (1992) work has set an exemplary standard for such research by precisely characterizing each sample's cultural heritage and not mixing ethnic samples from the same country.

CULTURE-LEVEL STUDIES OF VALUE

As Schwartz (1994) has maintained, 'The commonalities in the intentional and unintentional value socialization to which different members of society are exposed reflect the cultural emphases that support and maintain the social, economic, and political system of the society. The average of the value priorities of societal members reflects these commonalities of enculturation' (p. 92). Research reported in this section examines societal value emphases inferred from individual value responses that have been averaged across a comparable social group (teachers, students, employees of a given multinational corporation, and so on).

The Hofstede Project

In 1980 Hofstede published the classic *Culture's Consequences*, an exhaustive description of his analysis of 'work-related values' in 40 countries. The empirical core of this treatise was an analysis of the personnel survey conducted by IBM, a multinational corporation with operations in many countries. Part of that survey was a core of 32 items tapping perceptions (for example, employees are afraid to disagree with their superior), personal goals (for example, rate the importance of 'earnings'), behaviour intentions (such as, I intend to continue with this company for x years), and beliefs (such as, employees lose respect for a consultative manager). Responses to these 32 items (and others) were taken in the late 1960s from a stratified, standard sample of IBM employees in 74 countries. Forty of these countries, including Taiwan, Hong Kong, and Singapore, were selected for ecological factor analysis. Where appropriate, cultural response sets were controlled by standardizing responses.

Each country was represented by the average response of its sample to each of the 32 items. Input for the factor analysis was thus a 32 x 32 correlation matrix. Hofstede (1980) chose a three-factor solution accounting for 49 per cent of the variance and rotated these factors to orthogonal structure. The first factor was then subdivided into two separate dimensions, Individualism and Power Distance. Since they were extracted from the same factor, these dimensions are highly correlated (-.67), a fact that must be remembered in subsequent discussions. The other two dimensions were labelled Uncertainty Avoidance and Masculinity–Femininity. In a number of publications (for example, Hofstede, 1980, 1983, 1991; Hofstede and Bond, 1984, 1988), these dimensions have been thoroughly described and their correlates presented.

Locating the Chinese

Each of the original 40 countries was scored for each of the four dimensions. The four 'culture markers' produced were entered as inputs into a hierarchical cluster analysis in order to assess patterns of grouping among the countries. This clustering procedure groups countries on the basis of similarity, proceeding from smaller units of greatest similarity to larger units of lesser similarity, in a step-wise manner.

Singapore and Hong Kong join each other first and early in the linking progression (Hofstede, 1980). Taiwan joins Pakistan first and does not join the other Chinese pair until relatively late in the linkage process, by which time Singapore and Hong Kong have linked with India and the Philippines. When this group of four finally joins Taiwan, it has already linked with 19 other countries! These results indicate that Taiwan is clearly different from Hong Kong and Singapore with respect to Hofstede's value dimensions.

Hong Kong and Singapore are united in their high Power Distance, low Individualism, low Uncertainly Avoidance, and medium Masculinity ratings. Only when the Uncertainty Avoidance range is broadened to include medium levels can Taiwan link with them. By that broadening, however, the three Chinese cultures are also joined by India, the Philippines, and Thailand in what Hofstede labelled the 'less developed Asian' grouping. What is common to the three Chinese societies, however, is their high Power Distance, low Individualism, and moderate Masculinity ratings. These qualities, however, they share with Greece, Iran, and Turkey, along with Pakistan, Thailand, India, and the Philippines.

With respect to the United States, indeed to most Western countries except France, Chinese societies are higher in Power Distance and lower in Individualism. This finding confirms what earlier bicultural contrasts between American and Chinese subjects have consistently found using more focused value measures, for example, higher Chinese scores for deference and order, lower scores for dominance, abasement, and heterosexuality on the Edwards Personal Preference Scale (EPPS)(Yang, 1986, p. 110), but does so at a higher level of generality in values.

Of course, many other countries such as India are also high in Power Distance and low in Individualism relative to the United States. Thus, if we wish to 'explain' a Chinese–American difference as arising from cultural differences in Power Distance or in Individualism, the same results must also appear for an Indian–American comparison. So, for example, the Chinese score lower than do the Americans on EPPS aggression. However, the Indians score higher than do the Americans (Yang, 1986, p. 110). Thus, the Power Distance–Individualism construct is unlikely to be responsible for differences in this type of aggression. In such ways multicultural comparisons of the sort initiated by Hofstede (1980) allow social scientists to sharpen their explanatory precision by assessing patterns of convergence with results from other multicultural studies.

Commentary

Firstly, Hofstede separated Power Distance and Individualism by dividing his first factor. He did so for conceptual and theoretical reasons related to previous work in the social sciences. It must be remembered, however, that together Power Distance and Individualism (negatively) represent one empirical reality and probably correspond to the contrast Fiske (1991) has drawn between the social models of 'authority ranking' and 'market pricing'.

The literature on individualism has burgeoned (see, for example, Kim et al., 1994; Triandis, 1990). Most commentators present hierarchy as a feature of collectivism (Triandis, Brislin, and Hui, 1988). Had Hofstede not split Power Distance and Individualism, it might have reduced the tendency to reify these constructs as separate and have simplified our search for external correlates of the unified construct.

In respect to collectivism in this broader sense all three Chinese societies are similar, albeit with considerable company around the world. Mainland China was also assessed sometime after the Hofstede survey by Chong, Cragin, and Scherling (1983), who found it to be high in Power Distance and low in Individualism, as defined by Hofstede's items. Authority ranking within collectivism, as a common theme running through the value systems of these disparate Chinese societies, is compatible with many analyses of Chinese cultural dynamics (Bond, 1991; Pye, 1985; Stouver, 1974; Wilson, 1970).

Secondly, Hofstede's four dimensions were defined by a congeries of work goals, perceptions, preferences, and behaviour intentions. One might ask if indeed he has provided dimensions of values, work-related or otherwise. However, Hofstede and Bond (1984) assessed a subset of the original 40 countries using the Rokeach Value Survey (Ng et al., 1982). The value profiles of these countries on the RVS correlate very highly with country scores on the original Hofstede dimensions. Subsequent work with the Chinese Value Survey resulted in similar overlap with Hofstede's results (Chinese Culture Connection, 1987), so perhaps we can accept that Hofstede was in fact tapping into fundamental dimensions of value across countries even though he did not exclusively use value items to measure his constructs.

The Chinese Value Survey

The next multicultural analysis of culture-level data was performed by the Chinese Culture Connection (1987). These researchers administered a survey of 40 values adduced by Chinese social scientists as being of 'fundamental importance in Chinese culture'. Concepts like filial piety, humbleness, thrift, adaptability, moderation, and non-competitiveness were assessed. This deliberately ethnocentric collection was translated from Chinese and administered to undergraduate males and females in 22 countries.

Ecological factor analysis was run after the mean scores had been standardized within each country's 40 means. Four factors were extracted and labelled Integration, Confucian Work Dynamism, Human-heartedness, and Moral Discipline. Countries were then assigned four scores representing their average on the values which defined each factor. This country mapping made possible country comparisons and a search for external correlates.

Locating the Chinese

The three Chinese societies among the original 22 were Singapore, Taiwan, and Hong Kong. Relative to the rest of the 22 countries, they were low on Integration, high but scattered on Confucian Work Dynamism, scattered on Human-heartedness, and middling on Moral Discipline. In effect, these Chinese societies were similarly positioned on Integration and Moral Discipline, but more separated across the other two dimensions.

These differences among the three Chinese samples are underscored by the results of a hierarchical cluster analysis of the 22 countries. Results show Hong Kong and Taiwan linking early at the second step. They do not join Singapore, however, until the thirteenth step, by which time 18 of the 22 countries have been linked together.

Commentary

The Chinese Culture Connection (1987) showed that Integration and reversed Moral Discipline correlated with Hofstede's Individualism and reversed Power Distance. In fact, a second-order factor analysis showed all four (negative Integration, Moral Discipline, negative Individualism and Power Distance) forming a single factor. It is this common factor, labelled Collectivism, on which all three Chinese societies score consistently highly. The convergence across these two studies is impressive, given the difference in instruments used, time periods assessed, and subject populations measured.

Confucian Work Dynamism was identified as a factor unique to the Chinese value survey. It was defined by a subset of Confucian values with a uniquely Chinese flavour. This dimension positioned countries with scores that correlated .70 with economic growth over the 20 year period 1965–84. Recent reassessments of this correlation over the period 1965–90 and with the addition of data from China yields a correlation of .76. This finding is noteworthy because none of Hofstede's four dimensions produced country scores correlating with economic growth. Evidently, the use of an indigenous Chinese measure of values has added an important dimension to the social science literature (Hofstede, 1991, Ch. 7). West meets East and both are enhanced.

The Schwartz Value Survey

The most recent arrival to the expanding territory of multicultural value surveys is the team headed by Shalom Schwartz. Using a careful, incremental approach, Schwartz and Bilsky (1987, 1990) began with a thorough review of past work and a theoretical mapping statement of the value domain:

I derived a universal typology of the different contents of values by reasoning that values represent, in the form of conscious goals, three universal requirements of human existence to which all individuals and societies must be responsive: needs of individuals as biological organisms, requisites of coordinated social interaction, and survival and welfare needs of groups (Schwartz, 1994, p. 88).

Initially they adduced eight distinctive types of valuing based upon these three universal requirements. Subsequent work in 20 cultures (Schwartz, 1992) has led to modifications in the definitions and contents of the early types along with the addition of two new types. Schwartz (1992) used smallest space analysis (SSA) of data from the 20 cultures to derive metrically equivalent item groupings of values to measure these 10 domains in his culturally diverse samples.

In addition, Schwartz (1992) argued for a circumplex model to represent the dynamic relations of compatibility and conflict among the ten value domains. Initially, his reasoning was based upon the contrast between those types believed to serve individual interests, namely, hedonism, achievement, and self-direction, and those serving collective interests, namely, security, conformity, and tradition. Subsequent elaboration of hypotheses and empirical mapping of multicultural samples has led Schwartz to represent the 10 value types in a circumplex mode with the types progressing from Power to Security, Restrictive Conformity, Tradition, Benevolence, Universalism, Self-direction, Stimulation, Hedonism, Achievement, and returning finally to Power.

With this groundwork firmly in place, Schwartz (1994) turned to a culture-level analysis of his ever-growing data set. He selected those 45 value items with equivalent meanings in his 20-culture analysis. Each of his now 86 samples was represented by the average sample score on each of the 45 values and an SSA was run. Based upon his a priori hypotheses, interpretability of each region and replicability of the structure across different subsets of samples (teachers, students, workers), Schwartz identified seven culture-level value types. As before, these seven types were located in theoretically meaningful patterns of contiguity and opposition, corresponding to their closeness around the culture-level circumplex which follows the order listed below.

The Schwartz types

Given the sophistication of the Schwartz project, it seems important to briefly describe his seven culture-level types. For greater detail readers are referred to his paper (Schwartz, 1994):

1. *Conservatism* emphasizes stable in-group relations where the self has meaning as a part of a collectivity embedded within a traditional order.
2. *Harmony* emphasizes a protective, appreciative relationship to the world of nature.
3. *Egalitarian Commitment* emphasizes a transcendence of egocentric concerns by embracing an interpersonal morality and social principled-ness.
4. *Intellectual Autonomy* emphasizes cognitive freedoms.
5. *Affective Autonomy* emphasizes personal desires for stimulation and pleasure.

6. *Mastery* emphasizes energetic self-assertion to control the social and physical environments.

7. *Hierarchy* emphasizes power and ranking in social affairs and distribution of resources.

Locating the Chinese

Of Schwartz's (1994) 38 samples of teachers, six are Chinese. Those three from the People's Republic of China (from Hebei province and the cities of Shanghai and Guangzhou) produced such similar results that Schwartz considers them a unit. In characterizing these samples from China he comments:

> The mainland China samples are especially high on the importance attributed to Hierarchy and Mastery values, low on the importance of Egalitarian Commitment values, and average on the autonomy-conservatism dimension. These data suggest that China is not a prototypical 'collectivist' society, if collectivism refers to a conception of the person as deeply embedded in the collectivity without legitimate autonomous interests. The notion of China as a culture that legitimizes hierarchial differentiation is supported; and the major hallmark of this culture is an emphasis on entrepreneurship within highly regulated relationships... (Schwartz, 1994, p. 111).

If China is not prototypically collectivist (see also Lau, 1992), Singapore is: 'the sample from Singapore shows a profile that is closest to the pure Hofstede conception of collectivism, high in Conservatism and Hierarchy and low in Autonomy and Mastery' (Schwartz, 1994, p. 111). The other two Chinese samples, from Hong Kong and Taiwan, generally position themselves within the Singapore–China contrast.

In fact, these four Chinese societies present very different profiles. They fall within the same third of the 36-culture distribution only for the measure Hierarchy, where they all score high. A cluster analysis of these 36 (combining the Hebei, Shanghai, and Guanzhou samples into one China score) underlines the differences: Hong Kong first links with four Israeli groups; Singapore first links with Malaysia; Taiwan first links with Bulgaria (Turks); and China links first with Zimbabwe and Thailand. Hong Kong links with Singapore at the fifth cluster step, but only after they have joined with the four Israeli groups and Malaysia. China joins Singapore and Hong Kong only at the eighth cluster step, by which time Zimbabwe and Thailand have joined the cluster. Taiwan finally links up with its three Chinese compatriots at the second-to-last step in the clustering, a finding which underscores its distance from the other Chinese societies, as was seen in Hofstede's (1980, p. 334) earlier results.

American values were seen to be quite different from these results. All four Chinese societies are linked together before they join the group which includes the United States, and this union occurs only at the final step when all 36 cultures are finally connected. It is hardly surprising that bicultural American-Chinese comparisons continue to yield differences in values. What we do not learn from such bicultural contrasts, however, is which of these differences are common to *any* contrast between the United States and a Chinese society. For such purposes we need multicultural contrasts which include a number of Chinese societies.

Commentary

Schwartz's work has been theory-driven, rather than data-driven. Theoretical considerations have been balanced, however, by a thorough reading of the empirical work available, so that his value measure includes items that reflect many cultural traditions. In addition, results from many countries have been carefully assessed to establish adequate metric equivalence for the value items defining any given value type.

Consequently, it appears that Schwartz's value survey will become the standard measure against which other value instruments will be examined. As more and more cultural groups are administered the survey, the data set will become ever more comprehensive. The eventual consequence will be a value map for the world's cultures, a map which will empirically anchor discussions of value similarities and differences. This is an important development for a cross-cultural social *science* (Smith and Bond, 1993, Ch. 11).

Integrating Culture-level Studies

Multicultural surveys enable us to detect patterns among a number of countries and cultures instead of restricting our research to differences between an arbitrary pairing of two countries. The three surveys discussed in the following involved more than 20 countries, and each included at least three Chinese samples. Do these studies, with their wider perspective, reveal any constellation of values linking Chinese societies?

The first answer is negative. In none of the three studies do cluster analyses of the countries join the constituent Chinese societies early in the process. Two join early, but those two are Singapore and Hong Kong and such a result is achieved only twice, not in all three studies. In each case, all three Chinese cultures are linked together only after at least half of the other countries have joined them. Across the whole range of value dimensions measured, one cannot conclude that the values of Chinese societies are generally similar.

It is worth noting, however, that whatever the study and whatever the Chinese society, there are always selected dimensions on which all Chinese cultures are closely positioned: on Individualism and Power Distance for the Hofstede (1980) project; on Integration and Moral Discipline for the Chinese Culture Connection (1987); and on Hierarchy for the Schwartz (1994) survey. Might it be possible to identify dimensions of communality for Chinese societies across all three multicultural surveys?

A higher-order analysis

There are 12 countries common to the 53 units of Hofstede (1983), the 22 of the Chinese Culture Connection (1987), and the 36 of the Schwartz (1994) survey. Each of these 12 may be represented by 15 scores, four each from Hofstede and the Chinese Culture Connection and seven from Schwartz. These scores may be intercorrelated, and then factor-analysed in a preliminary examination of commonalities. By this means, these multicultural studies of value, using different measures on different types of population at different periods in history, may be compared.

A scree plot of the resulting eigenvalues reveals a final 'elbow' at the fourth. A varimax rotation of these four factors yields the following factor composition of items loading >.45:

Factor I

Egalitarian Commitment .95
Individualism .86
Integration .85
Intellectual Autonomy .63
Power Distance -.79
Conservativism -.80
Hierarchy -.97

This factor includes measures from all three studies and opposes universalistic, open values with traditional, authoritarian emphases. This contrast can be designated Individualism–Hierarchy. Of the 12 countries, Hong Kong, Taiwan, and Singapore rank eighth, ninth, and twelfth, respectively.

Factor II

Uncertainty Avoidance .89
Intellectual Autonomy .70
Harmony .69
Moral Discipline .57
Affective Autonomy .48

The results for Factor II indicate a strong emphasis on stability with a striving for individual freedoms grafted on to this theme. Together, the construct could be labelled Orderly Autonomy. Taiwan is fourth, Hong Kong, eleventh, and Singapore, twelfth on this dimension, indicating considerable Chinese divergence.

Factor III

Confucian Work Dynamism .74
Moral Discipline .68
Affective Autonomy -.73
Mastery -.73

In the results for Factor III, the focus on achievement and satisfaction is opposed by an emphasis on restraint and a long-term focus. We may designate this factor Discipline–Assertion. Hong Kong, Singapore, and Taiwan occupy the first, second, and third ranks on this dimension, followed immediately by Japan in the fourth position.

Factor IV

Masculinity .93
Human-heartedness .91
Mastery .48

In the results for Factor IV, we see a grouping where achievement-oriented concerns are emphasized. The puzzle is the positive loading of Human-heartedness on this factor, a puzzle that was noted by the Chinese Culture Connection (1987) in its discussion of the results. On this Achievement factor, Hong Kong is third, Singapore eighth, and Taiwan twelfth.

With only 12 cases, any conclusions made from these results must be regarded as tentative. They do, however, recommend themselves to our consideration in that the original three factors of Hofstede remain separate, Confucian Work Dynamism continues to define a factor separate from the Hofstede three (see also Chinese Cultural Connection, 1987), the polarities on Factors I and III are compatible with theoretical oppositions which have been discussed in the literature (in, for example, Schwartz, 1994) and, finally, the Schwartz value types for cultures locate themselves in plausible positions *vis-à-vis* the other dimensions.

For present purposes the results allow us to detect some valuable convergences in the value profiles of the three Chinese societies, Singapore, Taiwan, and Hong Kong. Relative to the other nine cultural units these Chinese cultural groups are high and are similar both in their Hierarchy and in their Discipline. These emphases appear to represent enduring features of Confucianism, so it is understandable that Japan is closely allied with Chinese societies on these two dimensions. The Confucian emphasis on hierarchy and discipline is found in the philosophical legacies of other cultures as well, so it would be of interest to examine results as the pool of common cultures grows across different multicultural studies of value (see, for example, Smith, Dugan, and Trompenaars, in press).

With respect to the other two dimensions, the three Chinese societies produce varied profiles, with different pairs allied but separate from the other. This variability is responsible for the finding that different Chinese societies fail to cluster together when all dimensions of variation are considered. It is to these other dimensions that one could turn to assess the influence of particular histories, ecologies, and social situations.

INDIVIDUAL-LEVEL STUDIES OF VALUE

Research reported in this section examines individual responses to the same value survey administered in many different countries. The data from the various cultural groups must first be treated to remove cultural response sets and then a procedure applied to ensure that comparisons are made using metrically equivalent values or value dimensions. Once these procedures are followed, then statistical tests may be run to assess whether the average respondent's value endorsement in any given country is significantly different from that given in any other country. Such tests are, of course, impossible in country-level studies of value where each country (or culture) is represented by only one score.

Unfortunately, these procedures have only recently begun to be applied. In addition, as of this writing, data from the Schwartz project is not yet available from the individual level of analysis. As a consequence, results from only three studies will be reported in this section.

The Chinese Value Survey

In 1988, Bond presented the individual-level analysis of the data collected by the Chinese Culture Connection. He followed a number of procedures to eliminate cultural response sets and to establish metric equivalence for the etic factors which resulted from the pooled factor analysis of more than 1,300 respondents.

Two factors emerged from the results:

> The first factor, Social Integration–Cultural Inwardness, is defined by two poles. The positive end consists of values which have a broadly integrative function. The target of this integration is unspecified, and so this value constellation is regarded as more universalistic and centrifugal in its thrust. The negative pole is inward looking, exalting the value of in-group traditions and identity, exerting a centripetal, collectivist pull on the individual.
>
> The second factor, Reputation–Morality, contrasts a concern for public prestige and status against a principled approach to life in society. Reputation relates to the domain of power, morality to those of maturity and restrictive conformity.
>
> (Schwartz and Bilsky, 1987) from Bond, 1991, p. 141

Using the defining values for each factor, Bond gave each individual from each of the 21 cultural groups two factor scores. These individual factor scores were compared across the groups. Differences in the average scores of university students from these countries were found at very high levels of statistical significance.

Locating the Chinese

Subsequent to Bond's 1988 article, data were obtained from the Philippines and from China. The average factor scores of individuals in these two countries were added to the original 21. The position of Chinese from China, Hong Kong, Singapore, and Taiwan could then be compared with those from the 19 other countries (Bond, 1991).

On the first factor, Singaporeans are in the eleventh position; Taiwanese in the twentieth, with the groups from Hong Kong and mainland China falling in between. On the second factor, mainland Chinese are in the thirteenth position, and the group from Hong Kong is in the twentieth position, with the Taiwanese and Singaporeans falling in between the two. One might conclude that the Chinese in this sampling tend to be moderate in Cultural Inwardness (that is, low in Social Integration) and moderate in Morality (low in Reputation). There is, however, considerable spread in the various Chinese scores.

A hierarchical cluster analysis puts this conclusion into multicultural context. Chinese from Taiwan and mainland China link at the first clustering step with Nigerians. Singaporeans link at the second step with Hong Kong Chinese, by which time they are joined by Filipinos, Poles, South Koreans, and Thais. When these four groups of Chinese join together, 10 other cultural groups join as well. It may be best to think of two groupings of Chinese at the individual level: the mainland Chinese and the Taiwanese, moderate in Cultural Inwardness and neutral in Reputation–Morality, and the Singaporeans and Hong Kong Chinese, neutral on Social Integration–Cultural Inwardness and moderate on Morality.

Commentary

Again, it is worth noting that on any bicultural Chinese–American comparison, significant differences would have been found. That same difference,
however, would be found in comparing many groups, for example, Filipinos
or Nigerians, with the Americans. When one casts a wider cultural net, there is
nothing uniquely Chinese about the values of Chinese *vis-à-vis* Americans. In
addition, the direction of difference between another group and the
Americans will differ depending on which Chinese group is chosen for comparison and on which dimension. For the contrast between Social Integration
and Cultural Integration, the Americans fall between the Taiwan–mainland
China and the Singapore–Hong Kong groupings. Again, the analysis alerts us
to the danger of bicultural comparisons where a particular group of Chinese is
used to represent all Chinese. The same caveat applies, of course, to using the
Americans alone to represent the Western position. The above cluster analysis
shows other Westerners (for example, West Germans and English) in separate
clusters which do not unite with the Americans until the final step in the linkage.

The Rokeach Value Survey

In 1982, Ng and his colleagues collected rating data from ten cultural groups
using an expanded version of the RVS. These data were then analysed using
discriminant analysis, but without eliminating cultural response sets.

This correction, plus others necessary for a pooled factor analysis (Leung
and Bond, 1989), were later made with nine of the original ten cultural groups
(Bond, 1988). A factor analysis yielded four etic dimensions of variation in values: Competence–Security, Personal Morality–Success, Social
Reliability–Beauty, and Political Harmony–Personal Sociability. Factor scores
were calculated for the average respondent from each of these nine cultural
groups on the four factors. As occurred in use of the Chinese Value Survey
(CVS), highly significant main effects for cultural group were seen when comparisons were made across the four RVS dimensions.

Locating the Chinese

Three groups of Chinese university students took part in the Ng et al. sample:
groups of Chinese from Taiwan, Hong Kong, and Malaysia. Overall, these
three groups were separated from one another on all four dimensions, came
no closer together than five positions, and paired only twice. It is also noteworthy that on all four dimensions, Western respondents from either Australia
or New Zealand occupied positions on the value dimensions between the
three Chinese groups of respondents. Westerners, it would seem, are different
from Chinese, but different in opposite ways, depending on which value
dimension is under scrutiny. So, for example, New Zealanders are lower in
emphasis on Competence than are Taiwanese, but higher in such emphasis
than are Malaysian Chinese. Both bicultural comparisons would be significant
and by themselves support interesting speculations on Chinese–Western differences (see, for example, Feather, 1986). Seen in a multicultural contrast,
however, it is evident that there is no singular Chinese position but rather

many, and the difference of any one group of Chinese respondents from any one group of Westerners can be in opposite directions depending on which Chinese–Western pair is selected for contrast.

Nevertheless, a hierarchical cluster analysis reveals some expected patterns. Two pairs link first: Australians with New Zealanders, and Hong Kong Chinese with Malaysian Chinese. This Chinese pair joins the Malaysians next, followed by the Taiwanese, to form a South-East Asian cluster. This relative distinctiveness of the Taiwan and the Hong Kong groups on the RVS is reminiscent of their separation on the CVS, noted above.

This South-East Asian cluster eventually merges with the Japanese–Bangladeshi–Indian cluster, and together they combine in the last step with the antipodean group. The basic Asian–Western contrast remains evident in the data, although it breaks down in places on closer inspection, just as the Chinese monolith does.

Commentary

The Ng et al. (1982) sample of countries was rather small and geographically confined. Furthermore, the RVS, like the CVS, is an incomplete survey of values (Braithwaite and Law, 1985) and is not theory-based. In consequence, it would seem premature to dwell too closely on the specifics of these particular findings.

The Triandis Study of 'Collectivism'

In 1986, Triandis and his colleagues used a 21-item attitude survey to measure various components hypothesized as part of the collectivism–individualism construct. The majority of the 21 items were value statements, as, for example, 'I like to live close to my friends', and so fall within our purview. They later collected responses from gender-balanced student samples in nine countries, including Hong Kong and the People's Republic of China (the Indian sample was from working men only). Contrary to typical practice, their sample of 10 countries included only three Western groups: from France, Poland, and the United States.

Data from these respondents were later factor-analysed (Triandis et al., 1993), using the Leung–Bond procedure (Leung and Bond, 1989). This technique eliminates cultural response sets and then pools all the data, so that etic factors may be extracted at the individual level from multicultural data sets.

In their eagerness to identify components of collectivism, Triandis et al. (1993) may have over-factored their matrix; some factors appear to be doublets and are composed of at least one item which is triple-loaded. For present purposes, it is worth considering only the first three factors which the authors claim to be 'strong etics', that is, found at both the individual and the cultural level. These three were labelled 1. Separation from In-groups, 2. Independence, and 3. Personal Competence. The average score for persons from each of the 10 cultures was calculated and visual comparisons made between them.

There appears to be some conceptual overlap between these etic factors and those identified by Bond (1988) using the CVS and the RVS. Separation from In-groups probably corresponds to to the factor Social Integration–Cultural Inwardness (negatively), Independence to Social Reliability–Beauty (negatively), and Personal Competence to Competence–Security. It may be concluded that Triandis et al. (1993) have measured different aspects of personality variation across cultures, even though they began with a single construct. Collectivism has been the Rorschach of cross-cultural theorizing and is freighted with considerable baggage. The Triandis et al. study will help sweep this Augean stable by identifying essential features of the construct at the individual level. Triandis has already begun this procedure by correlating his 21 items with the 56 items of Schwartz's value survey (Triandis et al., 1993, pp. 380–1). When this correlation is made multiculturally at the level of factors and types, we will have a sharper perspective on collectivism–individualism at the individual level.

Locating the Chinese

People from Hong Kong and mainland China were included in the Triandis et al. (1993) data set. These two groups represent very different economic and political cultures, despite their both being Chinese. Nevertheless, they are close together and low in both Separation from In-groups (see also Bond's 1988 results for Factor I, reported above) and Independence. This conclusion appears to be even stronger if one discards the non-comparable group of Indian working men. Only on Personal Competence do Chinese from Hong Kong and the Mainland diverge, with the Hong Kong group providing a low score and the mainland Chinese a high one.

Commentary

As with the CVS and the RVS, a Chinese–Western contrast would produce different results depending on which Chinese and which Western group were chosen, and on which value dimension was selected for comparison. On the factor of Independence, the Hong Kong Chinese rank higher than do the French, and the mainland Chinese rank lower than do the Americans; on Personal Competence, the mainland Chinese rank higher than do the Poles, and the Americans rank higher than do the Hong Kong Chinese. Only on the first factor, Separation from In-groups, do we find a consistent Chinese–Western split, with the Westerners ranking higher. We must clearly be more specific and discriminating in our discussion of Chinese values: we must begin asking the question, 'On which value dimension is which Chinese group different from which other group?'

Integrating the Three Studies

In this regard it would appear that there is some convergence across groups of Chinese in their endorsement of values relating to in-group identification. This finding contrasts with the commonly found Western emphasis on both detachment from in-groups and a connection with humanity as a wider in-group.

On other value dimensions there is divergence among the Chinese groups. Mainland Chinese and Taiwanese tend to group together, as do Chinese from Hong Kong, Singapore, and Malaysia. When one looks at comparisons across specific value dimensions, however, even these alliances break down.

SUMMARY

This essay has examined multicultural studies of value analysed at both the cultural and the individual levels. By focusing on multicultural studies, it has become possible to discover if any values are commonly endorsed by different Chinese societies and with which other cultural groups these value endorsements are shared. A number of conclusions may be drawn.

First, one may say that there is more similarity among Chinese at the cultural level than at the individual level of studies. This similarity is seen, however, only for certain dimensions of valuing, and not for the entire constellation of value dimensions. At the cultural level, Chinese societies may be characterized as high in hierarchy and very high in discipline; at the individual level, Chinese may be characterized as placing a high value on identification with their various in-groups. Across other dimensions there is considerable variation among the results for the Chinese groups, variation which further studies might indicate can be explained in terms of factors like economic modernization, colonial experience, and political structuring. It is clear at this point that there is no identifiable constellation of values common to all Chinese.

Secondly, these studies reveal considerable variation among so-called Western nations, with similarity confined to the broad value of individualism. The people of the United States cannot stand as representatives of a Western position any more than the citizens of any other Western country can. The standard approach which compares an American sample with a convenient Chinese sample consequently cannot tell us about Chinese–Western differences. When we scan cultural groups more comprehensively, these simplistic contrasts disintegrate. There is little justification for continuing the descriptive tradition of bicultural comparisons of values.

FUTURE DIRECTIONS

The past fifteen years have witnessed considerable progress in the cross-cultural study of values, but more remains to be done. First, samples need to be more varied and more representative, and to be surveyed using the same instrument. In this respect Schwartz has set an admirable standard by pushing for two types of sample from each of his collaborators around the world. By so doing he is able to confront the challenge that taking data from student samples distorts the value maps which result (see, for example, Schwartz, 1994). As similar, varied samples are assessed around the world, it will also be possible to assess universal relationships in the effects of social structure on value endorsement (see, for example, Kohn, Naoi, Schoenbach, Schooler, and Slomczynski, 1990).

Second, more effort must be expended in exploring the links between values and behaviour, both at the individual level (see, for example, Feather, 1988; Leung, Bond, and Schwartz, 1993) and at the cultural level (see Bond, 1991; Hofstede, 1980). Values, like personality traits, have an intrinsic fascination which may distract from examining their function in predicting human behaviour. Such an examination is the more difficult enterprise and one to which we must return before value studies sink under their own weight.

Third, the labour-saving strategy of using surveys of written values for assessing populations must be supplemented. Other multicultural approaches are possible, may provide access to less literate populations, and could yield different results worth exploring.

Fourth, in our rush to map the values world, we must not foreclose on indigenous contributions. Each culture has its unique storehouse of values, some of which are perceived as essential to a cultural group. These particular values may help social scientists contribute new dimensions of variation in values (see, for example, Chinese Culture Connection, 1987). They can be easily grafted onto existing value surveys and the relationship of a particular cultural heritage to existing concepts examined through correlation. Intellectual and cultural imperialism may thus be avoided.

Finally, longitudinal studies of value are needed. The important issues of modernization and convergence (see Yang, this volume) could thereby be assessed within and across Chinese societies. Personality approaches to this issue have been taken within Taiwanese culture (see Yang, 1986, pp. 148–60), but a multicultural approach would enable us to tease out societal trends.

NOTES

Portions of the empirical work reported in this chapter were supported by grants to the author from the Social Science and Educational Panel of the Chinese University of Hong Kong. Harry Triandis and Geert Hofstede made helpful comments on an earlier version.

Chapter 15

■

Ultimate Life Concerns, Self, and Chinese Achievement Motivation

An-Bang Yu

While wealth, fame, and longevity have long been seen by the Chinese as collective representations of individual achievement and familial glorification, virtue has always been considered the highest goal to be achieved by an individual in his or her moral performance. Thus, 'self' within a Chinese context has long connoted both 'family-self' and 'moral-self'. The merging of these two selves has been and still is the social and psychological basis underlying Chinese motivation for personal achievement. This chapter will elucidate the meaning of Chinese achievement motivation, and will clarify the differences between it and the concept of achievement motivation as constructed by Western researchers, especially D. C. McClelland and his followers.

Attempts to measure achievement motivation present several problems. The reliability and validity of projective measures, such as the Thematic Apperception Test (TAT), and self-report measures, such as the Edwards Personal Preference Scale (EPPS), have been questioned and criticized by many scholars (see, for example, Fineman, 1977; Ho, 1986; Murstein, 1963; Weinstein, 1969). McClelland (1980) has asserted that the use of self-report scales is couched in special instructional language which produces particular responses through directive stimuli. Self-report measures may also be called respondent measures of achievement attitudes or values, rather than tests of needs for achievement. On the other hand, projective tests such as the TAT obtain samples of an individual's actions or thinking under certain standard conditions; it is an operant measure that reflects desires or needs. According to McClelland, only projective tests can accurately measure an individual's need for achievement, but K. S. Yang (1986) argues that both can measure achievement need or motivation, albeit different kinds. Yang believes that self-report measures are better able to measure Chinese achievement motivation, while projective measures are better equipped for measuring Western achievement motivation.

McClelland, Koestner, and Weinberger (1989) have since modified their earlier position and asserted that traditional projective tests can, in fact, measure need for achievement (which they term *nAch*); they further state that the need for achievement is an implicit motive. On the other hand, they believe that self-report tests such as the Personality Research Form (PRF)(Jackson, 1974) measure self-attributed need for achievement (*sanAch*)— an explicit achievement motive existing on the conscious level. These two kinds of achievement motivation exercise different influences on achievement-related behaviour.

McClelland (1985) and Heckhausen and Halisch (1986) believe that the need for achievement is related to the incentive value of a given task or project. Koestner, Weinberger, and McClelland (1988), however, argue that a self-attributed need for achievement is stimulated by external social incentives, including external encouragement, expectations, and requirements.

If we look at what McClelland calls *nAch* and *sanAch*, we find that he is generally in agreement with Yang on the usefulness of self-report measures in Chinese contexts. Nonetheless, most of the existing literature on the origins and consequences of achievement motivation is open to challenge. It is difficult to determine whether the cross-cultural inconsistencies that have been found are due to genuine cultural differences in the nature of achievement motivation or are merely due to problems with the validity and reliability of the instruments involved.

It does appear to be the case that self-report scales are useful in measuring an individual's *nAch* in both individualist and collectivist societies, and one need not be restricted to using only projective measures to record these motivational constructs. What is critical is the type of theoretical conceptualization of achievement motivation used to develop a measurement tool. The achievement motivation theories and concepts developed by McClelland and his associates are the products of Western, middle-class society, and as such should not be used to measure the achievement motivation of people from collectivist, non-Western societies (A. B. Yu, 1990; A. B. Yu and Yang, 1994).

RESEARCH ON ACHIEVEMENT MOTIVATION IN CHINESE SOCIETIES

Most Chinese researchers have borrowed or adapted Western achievement motivation measurement instruments, and their choices have not necessarily been based on any specific theoretical orientation. As a result, 40 years of Chinese research on achievement motivation has produced a disorganized body of findings; almost no proposals have been made for an indigenous theory or model of achievement motivation, nor has much work been done on empirically verifying Western models. As of yet, no one has proposed an indigenous 'experience-near' (Geertz, 1984) concept upon which measurement instruments for Chinese achievement motivation could be based. For example, researchers such as C. M. Chu (1981), Y. Y. Hung (1982), and S. Y. Kuo (1973) used independently developed scales and questionnaires, as well as instruments adapted from Western models, to measure self-concept, self-attitude, and individual achievement motivation; the validity of these tools remains open to question (Cronbach and Meehl, 1955; Messick, 1980, 1981).

With a certain amount of overlap, Chinese research on achievement motivation can be divided into two periods: 1950–70 and post-1970. The earlier research was primarily carried out in Taiwan, and an important research focus was the use of Murray's (1943) Thematic Apperception Test (TAT) to explore the relationship between individual achievement needs and life adjustment (Ni, 1962). Besides being used to delineate deviance in the nature of achievement (Han, 1965, 1967, 1968), TAT figures and testing procedures were modified to establish its reliability and validity for use with both Chinese adults and children (Chu, 1955, 1968).

Since 1970, Chinese researchers have developed their own tools to measure Chinese achievement and achievement motivation. S. Y. Kuo's (1973) work, based on student achievement motivation questionnaires developed by Entwistle (1968), Hartley and Holt (1971), and Russell (1969), is the best-known and most widely used. His questionnaire consists of 50 yes–no items measuring scholastic achievement motivation, and its split-half reliability is a satisfactory .86 (Cheng and Yang, 1977; S. Y. Kuo, 1973, 1982, 1984). In addition, Li (1981), and J. J. Wu, Lin, and Lai (1978) adapted and used Helmreich and Spence's (1978) Work and Family Orientation Questionnaire (WOFO); W. C. Chang and Wong (1992) later used the WOFO structure for use with Singapore Chinese. Wang (1993) independently developed a set of projective figures (similar to the TAT) to measure achievement motivation among university students in mainland China. It should be noted that the development of these instruments was not based on any particular conceptualization of achievement motivation; instead, they were simply determined by the researcher's preference. In addition, many Chinese researchers before and after 1970 developed self-report questionnaires and scales, but rarely did they design projective instruments.

For convenience, researchers have generally used group testing to collect data on a large scale, primarily for researching student achievement motivation (about 80 per cent of all research subjects have been students). Since the external validity of studies on students has its limitations, the conclusions drawn from these studies are also limited in scope.

THEORIES AND MEASURES OF ACHIEVEMENT MOTIVATION IN THE WEST

The Nature of Western Achievement Motivation

In combination with extensive cross-cultural research, the scoring system developed by McClelland and his associates (1953, 1958), which most Western scholars have adopted, suggests that achievement motivation involves the following three suppositions: personal success is individual achievement, so individuals determine their own achievement goals; subjective judgement determines the degree of incentive value for any particular achievement; and subjective judgement also defines standards of excellence. These suppositions reflect the cultural values of middle-class Western societies (Kornadt, Eckensberger, and Emminghaus, 1980; Maehr, 1974, 1978). We might call this kind of achievement motivation self-oriented, person-oriented, or individual-oriented achievement motivation (IOAM).

IOAM describes an individual's motivation in terms of an internally determined goal or standard of excellence achieved through acts which contain a degree of uncertainty as to the outcome (K. S. Yang and Yu, 1988). A list of its five aspects may help one to better understand its special nature: achievement goals and standards of excellence are largely determined by the individual, as are the incentive values of the achievement goal and standard of excellence; each individual determines the behaviour needed to reach achievement goals, as well as the maintenance, continuation, and evaluation of such behaviour; the individual is the primary evaluator of his or her achievement performance; positive or negative reinforcement of achievement performance also comes from within the individual, including a sense of success or failure, self-satisfaction or self-contempt, and self-approval or self-criticism; and, finally, the overall characteristics of IOAM are strong self-instrumentality and functional autonomy (K. S. Yang and Yu, 1988).

A Critique of Western Achievement Motivation Theory

Many scholars (including McClelland) believe that achievement motivation is culturally universal and varies across cultures or societies in degree only. However, McClelland's (1961, 1963) findings of lower levels of achievement motivation in Brazilian, Japanese, and traditional Chinese societies do not hold up under closer scrutiny. For example, Maehr (1974, 1978), Maehr and Nicholls (1980), Serpell (1976), and Weiner (1980) have all pointed out that McClelland's model of 'culture => child training => personality => achieving society' overemphasizes the influences of personality and early social development on the formation of achievement motivation. Although McClelland (1965) pointed out the importance of social structure in his theoretical model, he did not conduct empirical studies on the relationship between social structure and achievement motivation. His assumption that achievement motivation is a stable personality factor, constant in different contexts and at different times, has also been criticized by Kornadt et al. (1980) and Maehr and Nicholls (1980). As K. S. Yang and Yu (1988) wrote concerning McClelland's failure to take the cultural environment into consideration:

> The most frequently leveled criticisms are that McClelland's framework neglects the importance of social and/or interpersonal factors as contextual conditions in defining the concept of achievement motivation, and that it does not do justice to achievement in culturally distinctive, non-Western societies, especially those with a collectivist orientation. ...McClelland's theory and method, because of their neglect of social-contextual factors, have obvious limitations even when applied intra-culturally. Their unsuitability is much more evident when they are adopted in cross-cultural research, especially in studies using subjects from Oriental societies such as China (including mainland China, Hong Kong, and Taiwan) and Japan. Previous research using people from the collectively oriented Chinese and Japanese societies has repeatedly attested to the fact that their achievement motivation patterns are strikingly different from those of Western peoples and cannot be adequately understood in terms of McClelland's highly individualistic concept of achievement motivation (pp. 2, 6).

De Vos (1968, 1973) claims that McClelland's theoretical limitations became obvious when his model was used to explain Japanese and Chinese achievement motivation. E. S. Yu (1974, 1980) was one of the first to observe that

McClelland's theory of individual achievement motivation was based on concepts of individualism. She concluded that achievement motivation scores derived from McClelland's TAT scoring system reflect an individual-oriented need and place emphasis on the pursuit of personal rather than collective-oriented achievement, since the TAT scores did not correlate significantly with filial piety or familism scales, both of which carry a collectivist orientation (see also Ho, 1986; Yu and Yang, 1994). Individual-oriented achievement motivation resembles what Veroff (1969, 1973, 1977) called 'autonomous achievement orientation', and what K. S. Yang (1982, 1986) and K. S. Yang and Liang (1973) defined as 'self-oriented achievement motivation', that is, achievement motivation based on internalized standards of excellence. This kind of achievement motivation is ability- and task-oriented (Maehr and Nicholls, 1980), and it resembles what Nicholls (1984) termed 'task-involvement achievement motive'. Jerath (1981) called this type 'intrinsic achievement motivation'.

CULTURE, SELF, AND ACHIEVEMENT MOTIVATION

If IOAM is just one form of achievement motivation, then McClelland's assertion of its universality is false, and the assumption that it alone can be used to measure Chinese achievement motivation is unsupportable. In order to understand Chinese achievement motivation, we must ask three questions: How does Chinese achievement motivation differ from IOAM? How does the Chinese self relate to Chinese achievement motivation? And what broader cultural significance does Chinese achievement motivation possess?

Ultimate Life Concerns of the Chinese

The unifying intellectual philosophy in the Chinese 'great tradition' is Confucianism. Confucianism already exercised considerable influence during the pre-Qin period (before 221 BC), and from the Han dynasty (206 BC–AD 220) on until recent decades, its legal status was assured. As a decisive force in Chinese intellectual tradition, Confucianism has always exerted a profound influence on ordinary people. Consequently, any path to understanding the Chinese concept of achievement must pass through a study of the Confucian version of ultimate life concerns and idealized life goals.

Confucianism's ultimate life concerns are based on the Wu Lun, the five cardinal relationships: the relations between ruler and minister, father and son, husband and wife, elder and younger brother, and older and younger friends. Confucianism is a humanistic philosophy centered around *ren* (the fundamental quality of being human, or benevolence), *yi* (righteousness), and *li* (ritual propriety). An ideal, highly ordered, and harmonious Confucian society relies on a virtuous ruler to establish ritual order, plus individuals to cultivate themselves in a lifelong effort to reach the highest possible spiritual plane (*tianren heyi*, the unity of heaven and man), and therefore become a sage or a perfectly realized man (K. K. Hwang, 1988, 1992; Liou, 1992; Mou, 1985). In the

Confucian sense, self-cultivation is a process of self-realization in which an individual must actualize both his a priori ethical ideal and innate sense of moral self-control.

The highest concern of Confucianism is attaining virtue (*lide*, establishing virtue), the highest form of achievement. Attaining virtue means 'to create and bequeath to posterity a model of behaviour' or 'to leave benevolence and grace for eternity'. Next in the Confucian achievement hierarchy are 'rendering meritorious service' (*ligong*, 'establishing deeds') and scholarship (*liyan*, 'establishing words'). Meritorious service involves saving those in distress, ridding the world of evil, and benefiting the world by good works. Scholarship, of course, means writing great works or contributing to traditional fields of knowledge. Together, virtue, meritorious service, and scholarship are known as the 'three permanencies' (*sanbuxiu lun*). It is important to note that traditional Confucians have viewed scholarly achievement as a last resort (Lin, 1992); as Feng wrote:

> Chinese philosophers mostly spoke of the way [*dao*] of internal sagehood and external kingship [*neisheng waiwang*]. 'Internal sagehood' implies the attainment of virtue; 'external kingship' implies the attainment of meritorious service. Their highest ideal was to possess the virtue of a sage and the accomplishment of a king—to be the so-called sage–ruler, which is parallel to Plato's philosopher–king. When it was impossible for them to attain the accomplishment of a king or to find an external manifestation of personal sagehood, then they turned to writing. Book-writing was therefore the most unfortunate thing for them. They wrote books only when everything else had failed (Feng, 1934, p. 9).

In contrast to the great tradition, the 'little tradition' includes the customs, habits, ideas, and values of ordinary Chinese people; Johnson, Nathan, and Rawski (1985) called it 'traditional Chinese popular culture'. While the Confucian great tradition reflects the idealized, abstract thought of the upper classes, the little tradition reflects the achievement values of ordinary Chinese, including wealth, emolument, official rank and respect, longevity, perpetuation of the family line, integrity, and ethics. Integrity and ethics are moral achievement values which indicate a high degree of self-cultivation, noble character and disposition, and moral conscience. The four types of popular Chinese achievement values—economic, reputational, biological, and moral—are the ultimate life concerns and achievement goals of most ordinary Chinese (A. B. Yu, 1994).

The Confucians strove to attain a convergence of life goals. The hierarchy of achievement in the Chinese great tradition has always consisted first of attaining virtue, followed by meritorious service and scholarship. However, in practice most intellectuals valued meritorious service above all else (Wen, 1989). Since pre-Qin times, Confucians have paid lip-service to attaining virtue but have actually striven for successful official careers or fame and reputation. Confucius, Mencius, and Xun Zi all directly addressed the importance of reputation in their writings (Lin, 1992). The *Classic of Filial Piety (Xiao Qin)*, one of the cornerstones of the traditional Confucian canon, defines filial piety as 'raising one's reputation in order to exalt one's parents' (*yangming xianqin*).

Wen (1989) has pointed out that the highest possible achievement goal in the pre-Qin era was to become emperor, with serving as a high official in central or regional government or becoming a member of the local gentry being honourable secondary goals. Becoming a landlord held the lowest achievement value. Holding an official position was the achievement goal of intellectuals, while becoming a landlord was an achievement goal for farmers and merchants.

For most people, the best way to achieve meritorious service was through the civil service examinations; only by entering the bureaucracy and achieving an official position could one win glory in politics or the military. If one succeeded in an official career, then wealth, emoluments, and fame followed, and individual or family status also rose. Achievement in an official career was not a complete actualization of an individual's potential, interest, or disposition, but rather the realization of honouring one's ancestors and glorifying one's parents. Only in this way was it possible for an individual's achievement to receive societal recognition and commendation.

Those unable to pass the civil service examinations had no other choice but to work or engage in trade to accumulate property, become landlords, and obtain wealth. However, after obtaining wealth, these individuals expended great effort in preparing their sons or younger brothers for the civil service examinations. Being a landlord or engaging in trade was viewed as a means to the goal of having a son or younger brother enter the imperial bureaucracy. The honour of an entire family depended on success in this manner (see C. N. Chen, 1987, for an analysis of officialdom in the late Ming and early Qing dynasties).

As neither intellectuals nor those from the lower ranks of society spent their entire lives pursuing self-cultivation (pursuing instead economic achievement in the form of wealth, emolument, and reputation, plus biological achievement in the form of longevity and the prolongation of the family line) there has always been a convergence of great and little tradition goals. Both idealized and popular achievement goals were centered on cultivating the self, promoting the interests of the family, ruling the state, and making the world more peaceful. Simultaneously, achievement goals involved such family or clan interests as glorification of family or ancestors, family-line prolongation, strengthening, and social status. Combined, these two types of achievement goals (of the great and little traditions) may be called family- and clan-oriented achievement goals. Clearly, Chinese achievement values and goals have a strong collective and social nature.

Self and Achievement Motivation

In Confucian thought, the role of the self is not to express and manifest itself (as in Western models), but to develop the internal moral self; this has always been expressed as 'conquering selfishness to restore ritual propriety'. Self-realization, as a process of internal self-development, is considered a gradual, regimented process (Abbott, 1970; Tu, 1985, 1992). While Western ideals emphasize an understanding of what the self is and how to control and master it, Confucianism stresses the remaking and reforming of the moral self in hope of realizing the ethical ideal of 'ultimate goodness' (*zhishan*)(S. H. Liu, 1987). Attaining these family- and clan-oriented achievement goals was the true measure of self-realization and the fulfillment of one's familial self. Ordinary Chinese people have pursued these social values with societal, clan, or familial characteristics, and these values have been (and still are) a great motivating force behind individual self-development. The formation, development, and completion of the moral and familial selves are the ultimate life concerns and life goals of Chinese; Chinese individuals are motivated to achieve not through a desire to externalize the kind of Western self upon which McClelland's IOAM is based, but through a desire to realize and merge their familial and moral selves.

Social-oriented Achievement Motivation

After studying junior high school students, E. S. Yu (1974) found that the TAT did not measure Chinese achievement motivation, but instead measured a kind of achievement motivation based on concepts of individualism. Consequently, Yu's TAT scores did not correlate significantly with self-report filial piety and familism achievement scores which reflect values highly stressed by Chinese (see also Ho, 1986; Yu and Yang, 1994). After analyzing the content of mainland Chinese children's stories, Blumenthal (1977) found that reaching collective goals was the primary form of achievement presented. In addition, Pusey (1977) further described Chinese aspirations as fulfilling family, social, and other significant group expectations.

In his comparison of differences between Americans and Chinese, F. L. K. Hsu (1981) wrote that the motivating force behind Chinese success primarily came from a concern for family and clan. De Vos (1973) argued that dutiful service to one's family and clan constituted Chinese achievement goals, and that individuals would pay any price for familial benefits. In addition, Kornadt et al. (1980) asserted that Chinese are taught from an early age to pursue group-related goals, and Wilson and Pusey (1982) stated that from the time they begin school, Chinese children are encouraged to pursue individual and group achievement in the name of group success. These findings suggest that individual success must be shared by other members of a group if the individual is to receive acceptance and recognition.

As K. S. Yang and Yu (1988) wrote, the content and characteristics of Chinese achievement motivation include the dynamic tendency to reach an externally determined goal or standard of excellence in a socially approved way—with a certain amount of uncertainty in the outcome. One can call this type of achievement motivation social-oriented achievement motivation (SOAM). SOAM has five primary characteristics: achievement goals or standards of excellence are set by significant others, a group, or society; achievement behaviour is also selected and determined by significant others, a group, or society (who, in addition, supervise and judge the maintenance, continuation, adjustment, and self-evaluation of SOAM achievement behaviour); outcome evaluation is made by significant others, a group, or society; final consequences, including praise or condemnation, acceptance or rejection, and promotion or demotion are determined by significant others, a group, or society; and the motivation dynamic reflects strong social instrumentality but weak functional autonomy, that is, SOAM's importance in social relations is much stronger than its functional use or practicality outside social groups (i.e. in job-related or economic activities). SOAM and IOAM concepts are summarized in Table 15.1.

Table 15.1   Summary of Two Varieties of Achievement Motivation

Aspect	Social-oriented Achievement Motivation (SOAM)	Individual-oriented Achievement Motivation (IOAM)
A. Achievement Goal	Goal or standard of excellence mainly defined by others in membership groups. Incentive value of attainment of goal or standard of excellence mainly determined in terms of membership groups' evaluation or value judgement.	Goal or standard of excellence mainly defined by self. Incentive value of goal attainment or standard of excellence mainly determined in terms of one's own evaluation or value judgement.
B. Achievement Behaviour	Actions or means necessary for goal attainment mainly approved by others or membership groups. Outside supervision, surveillance, or encouragement usually expected or required to maintain achievement behaviour in the right direction. Appraisal and change in achievement behaviour usually made after consulting others for opinions, suggestions, or directions. Dependence on others' or membership groups' halp in the pursuit of achievement. Achievement behaviour low in flexibility and responsiveness.	Actions or means necessary for goal attainment mainly determined by self. No outside supervision, surveillance, or encouragement expected or required to maintain achievement behaviour in the right direction. Appraisal and change in achievement behaviour usually made in accordance with one's own judgement. More reliance on one's own ability and effort in the pursuit of achievement. Achievement behaviour high in flxibility and responsiveness.

Table 15.1   *(Cont'd)*

Aspect	Social-oriented Achievement Motivation (SOAM)	Individual-oriented Achievement Motivation (IOAM)
C. Outcome Evaluation	Evaluation criteria mainly defined by others or membership groups, and therefore difficult for the actor to fully comprehend.	Criteria of evaluation mainly defined by self, and therefore easy for the actor to determine.
	Accomplishment mainly evaluated by others or membership groups.	Accomplishment mainly evaluated by self.
	Emphasis is on whether or not the outcome matches others' or membership groups' goal or standard.	Emphasis on whether or not outcome matches one's own goal or standard.
D. Final Consequence	Positive or negative reinforcements usually given by others or membership groups as a result of outcome evaluation.	Positive or negative reinforcements usually given by self as a result of outcome evaluation.
	Affects generated are other-oriented and able to influence one's social self positively or negatively.	Affects generated are self-oriented and able to influence one's personal self positively or negatively.
E. Overall Characteristics	Motivation high in social instrumentality. Motivation high in self-instrumentality.	Motivation low in functional autonomy. Motivation high in function autmy.
Source	K.S. Yang and Yu, 1988	

CONSTRUCT VALIDATION OF ACHIEVEMENT MOTIVATION IN CHINESE SOCIETIES

If it is true that IOAM is the dominant form of achievement motivation in individualist societies such as the United States, while SOAM is the predominant form in collectivist societies such as China, then IOAM and SOAM are conceptually independent but occasionally interactive psychological constructs. That is, individuals in any given society may react to both types of achievement motivation at the same time; what varies across peoples are the absolute and relative degrees of intensity for each type.

In addition, as collectivist societies modernize, the intensity and nature of individual achievement motivation may change. Chinese people in Taiwan have been exposed to a large-scale importation of Western knowledge, education, religion, and cultural values, and individualist Western concepts and values (such as independence, self-reliance, and individual achievement) have permeated Taiwanese society (see Yang, this volume). IOAM and SOAM are both present in Taiwan and mainland China. In order to measure their different levels, researchers have had to develop appropriate instruments of sufficient reliability and validity.

Within the past ten years, Yu and Yang have developed a scale for students and a scale for adults with a minimum junior high school education. Most preliminary scale items were constructed on the basis of 28 IOAM/SOAM characteristics (A. B. Yu, 1990; A. B. Yu and Yang, 1987). Secondary sources for items included the EPPS (Edwards, 1959), California Psychological Inventory (Gough, 1960), and Academic Achievement Motivation questionnaires (J. H. Chang, 1981; S. Y. Kuo, 1973).

The final student scale was established from responses given by Taipei-area, male and female junior high school students. It encompasses a six-point Likert-type rating scale by which higher total scores reflect stronger SOAM or IOAM. After screening preliminary items in accordance with item selection principles (such as controlling for social desirability and test anxiety), 30 items each were selected from the IOAM and SOAM scales. Examples of SOAM scale items include, 'I try to reach the standards set by teachers when I am doing my homework' and 'If I don't do well in school, I can't face my family and relatives'. Examples of IOAM scale items include, 'I would try to figure out different ways of solving a problem rather than ask for help' and 'I enjoy making progress towards the goals that I've set for myself'.

The final adult scale was established from the responses of 400 adults in Taipei, 80 per cent of whom were between the ages of 21 and 40. Respondents had an average of 14.2 years of formal education. Testing was performed in each subject's home or workplace. After screening preliminary scales items via item selection principles, 29 items were selected from the SOAM scale and 28 items from the IOAM scale. Examples of SOAM scale items include, 'I try my best to meet my parents' expectations so as not to disappoint them' and 'I work hard to reach the standard that my parents have set for me'. Examples of IOAM scale items include, 'I try to do my best if I consider a task to be valuable for me' and 'I evaluate my performance based on my own expectations and standards'.

Reliability and Validity

Internal consistency, test–retest reliability, and construct validity tests were conducted for the SOAM and IOAM scales. For the sake of brevity, reliability indices for the student and adult SOAM/IOAM scales are summarized in Table 15.2; for more detailed information on the factor analysis performed for internal consistency and construct validity, see Chu (1989), Yu (1990), and Yu and Yang (1987). The findings all support the assertion that SOAM and IOAM are independent motivation constructs.

Table 15.2 Reliability Indices for SOAM and IOAM Scales

Subject	Scale	Total # of items	Sample	Cronbach's alpha	Test-retest correlation	Author(s)
Student	SOAM	30	Senior high school students (N=784)	.91		Yu & Yang (1987)
	(IOAM)	(30)		(.87)		
			Senior high school students (N=263)	.88		Yu & Yang (1987)
				(.86)		
			College students (N=299)	.92		Chu (1989)
				(.92)		
			High school and college students (N=827)	.88		Yu (1991)
				(.89)		
			College students (N=185)		.86	Yu & Yang (1987)
					(.80)	
			Senior high school students (N=207)		.84	Yu & Yang (1987)
					(.79)	
Adult	SOAM	29	Employees (N=462)	.89		Yang & Cheng (1987)
	(IOAM)	(28)		(.91)		
			Adults (N=462)	.89		Yu (1990)
				(.89)		
			Elementary school teachers (N=152)	.91		Yu (1990)
				(.91)		
			Elementary school teachers (N=152)		.73	Yu (1990)
					(.68)	

Note (a) total number of items is 28 on the SOAM scale; (b) authors used only 10 items each from A. B. Yu's (1990) original SOAM and IOAM scales; consequently, the Cronbach's alpha values were corrected with the Spearman-Brown formula.

In addition, Yu and Yang (1987) calculated the relationships between the final SOAM and IOAM scales used in their study, as well as the achievement motivation scales developed by Western researchers, including the EPPS *nAch* subscale (Edwards, 1959) and the Sentence Completion Test (SCT)(Rohde, 1957). Their results provide evidence on two points: positively significant correlation coefficients were found between the SOAM and IOAM scales on the one hand, and the EPPS *nAch* subscale on the other, but the difference between these two correlation coefficients revealed statistical significance (the former .16, the latter .53); and a positively significant correlation was found between scores on the SOAM scale and achievement statements from the SCT, but no significant correlation was found between those same SCT statements and the IOAM scale—apparently a reflection of the SOAM and IOAM scales' convergent and discriminant validity.

In a paper discussing the relationship between the Chinese needs for achievement and for 'maintaining face', R. L. Chu (1989) argued that the need to maintain face correlated positively with SOAM but did not correlate significantly with IOAM. In addition, she found that social skills correlated positively with SOAM but negatively with IOAM. Chu therefore asserted that authentic Chinese achievement motivation (SOAM) entails the question of how to act ethically in public, particularly when an individual presents his or her success to an in-group. The close relationship between the need for face, social skills, and SOAM reveals the unique character of Chinese achievement motivation.

Finally, further evidence of the two scales' validity can be found in research conducted by K. S. Yang and Cheng (1987). In the their study, they used two simplified versions of the adult SOAM and IOAM scales to explore relationships between individual achievement motivation, job preference, and organizational behaviour. They found the following: people with strong SOAM consider family interests and welfare first when choosing jobs; job choices that strongly correlate with IOAM help people to improve and develop their personal potential and special skills, and people with strong IOAM prefer these kinds of jobs because they want to work in a harmonious, cooperative environment which emphasizes consideration, equality, and respect; and there is no substantive evidence linking SOAM with organizational commitment or work effectiveness, but IOAM correlates strongly and positively with these two variables. Moreover, the relationship between achievement motivation and intent to leave a job also indicates that IOAM has a higher predictive value than SOAM.

THE SOCIALIZATION OF ACHIEVEMENT MOTIVATION

Previous research on the formation and development of achievement motivation has primarily focused on familial and societal factors, with an emphasis on independence training and achievement (or mastery) training. Several Western researchers in the 1950s found that the more parents emphasized independence training, the higher a child's level of achievement motivation (McClelland and Friedman, 1952; Winterbottom, 1953, 1958). McClelland

(1961) also observed that parental emphasis on achievement or mastery training exerted a positive influence on a child's achievement motivation. In the same work, McClelland argued that in Brazil, Germany, and Japan the relationship between achievement training and a child's achievement motivation is determined by the age at which such training begins. However, other research findings from Germany (Heckhausen and Kemmler, 1957) and the United States (Bartlett and Smith, 1966; Chance, 1961; Smith, 1969) contradict McClelland's assertion.

Olsen (1971) found that when Taiwanese mothers in farming villages discouraged dependence, their sons (but not their daughters) displayed higher levels of achievement motivation. A. K. F. Li's (1974) study of Hong Kong Chinese children revealed that low parental dominance, open communication, and the encouragement of independence led to an increased need for achievement in boys, while parental dominance and limited communication resulted in an increased need for achievement in girls. Ho (1986) also observed that the parents of Hong Kong and Taiwanese girls with high levels of achievement motivation often displayed hostility, sternness, and a lack of affection in child training, and that for boys with high levels of achievement motivation, parents not only expressed caring and forgiveness, but also emphasized independence training. These findings strongly contradict the arguments of several Western researchers who have argued that low achievement motivation in Chinese individuals comes from Chinese parents' inability to promote independence in their children, as well as from their penchant for restricting their children's freedom to explore (see, for example, Kriger and Kroes, 1972; McClelland, 1961, 1963; Scofield and Sun, 1960).

In 1991, Yu attempted to ascertain the relationships between independence, dependence, achievement training, and children's achievement motivation. In undertaking the study, the researcher assumed that achievement training would enhance both the SOAM and IOAM of an individual. Using students from junior high school through college, the research found evidence on three points: the stronger the independence training by parents, the higher the IOAM in a child (with the exception of the effect of maternal independence training on sons), and that parental emphasis on independence training had no effect on SOAM; maternal emphasis on achievement training is one of the key factors in fostering the development of both SOAM and IOAM, but paternal emphasis on achievement training has no effect on either; and paternal dependence training has a direct, positive effect on SOAM, but a negative effect on IOAM in girls and no effect on IOAM in boys (A. B. Yu, 1991).

D. J. Kuo, Zhang, and Yang (1993) used the same parental training scale with the SOAM and IOAM scales to study fourth-, fifth-, and sixth-grade Beijing elementary school students (both sexes analysed together). Using partial correlation analysis, they found the following: paternal and maternal emphasis on independence training correlated significantly with IOAM, but not with SOAM; paternal emphasis on achievement training correlated significantly with both SOAM and IOAM, as did maternal emphasis; and parental emphasis on dependence training did not correlate significantly with either SOAM or IOAM. The researchers used a multiple regression analysis and found that paternal achievement training had the greatest influence on a child's SOAM level (explaining 36.0 per cent of the total variance). They also found that maternal emphasis on independence training was the most important factor for a child's IOAM development, with the second most important factor being maternal emphasis on achievement training. Together, these factors explained 31.4 per cent of the total variance. Most of the findings of the Kuo et al. study are consistent with those of Yu's work, except for the measurement of the effect of parental emphasis on dependence training on children's SOAM. This inconsistency may be due to the fact that certain confounding variables (such as parental emphasis on achievement training) were not controlled in the Kuo et al. study.

Recently, D. Liu (1994) studied junior high school students in northern China and found that parental emphasis on independence training had a direct positive effect on children's IOAM but no effect on children's SOAM, that parental emphasis on dependence training had a positive effect on SOAM but no effect on IOAM, and parental emphasis on achievement training had a direct positive effect on SOAM but no effect on IOAM. Liu's findings are highly consistent with those from Yu's study. However, in the case of the effect of maternal emphasis on achievement training on children's IOAM, results of these two studies are inconsistent.

In a later study explicating the relationships among parental achievement motivation, parental training practice, and a child's achievement motivation, D. Liu (1994) found evidence indicating that the stronger the parental SOAM, the higher the parental emphasis on dependence training and achievement training, whereas the stronger the parental IOAM, the higher the parental emphasis on independence training and achievement training (with the exception of a non-significant correlation between maternal IOAM and maternal emphasis on achievement training). The same study found that the stronger the paternal SOAM, the higher the SOAM of a female child but not a male child, and the stronger the maternal SOAM, the higher the SOAM of both male and female children. The study found that there is no significant relationship between parental IOAM and children's IOAM.

In summary, the results of these three studies presented above mostly show that parental emphasis on independence training and achievement training are critical facilitating factors in the development of children's IOAM. This evidence partially confirms the findings of the Western socialization theories of achievement motivation discussed earlier in this chapter. Additionally, most results of these studies also show that parental emphasis on dependence training and achievement training has a direct positive effect on children's SOAM. According to this evidence, we can confidently assert that the strength and enhancement of children's SOAM and IOAM are positively influenced by different socializing factors in the Chinese family (for the former, parental emphasis on dependence training is the key factor; for the latter, parental emphasis on independence training is the critical variable). However, parental emphasis on achievement training has the same positive effect on children's SOAM and IOAM. Independence and dependence are two opposites in logic and semantics. Yet in terms of psychological and behavioural aspects of individuals, the independence and dependence training emphasized by Chinese parents are orthogonal. Furthermore, Liu's findings provide detailed information for understanding the familial socialization mechanisms of Chinese achievement motivation. These three empirical studies serve as a stepping-stone for constructing a socialization theory of Chinese achievement motivation.

The Sociocultural Context of SOAM Socialization

From the point of view of cultural ecology, the traditional Chinese personality was cultivated through a socialization process determined by the needs of an agricultural society. According to K. S. Yang (1981) and M. C. Yang (1972), people in traditional collectivist and familistic Chinese agrarian society were forced to develop family dependence in order for society to operate smoothly; therefore, traditional Chinese child training placed great emphasis on dependence training (see also Ho, 1981, 1986; F. L. K. Hsu, 1963; Solomon, 1971; Tzeng, 1972; Wolf, 1970, 1972; D. Y. H. Wu, 1966; K. S. Yang, 1965). As a result of this emphasis, pre-industrial society Chinese relied on the assistance, supervision, and encouragement of parents and significant others in their pursuit of achievement. Regarding choice, persistence, extension, and correction of achievement behaviours, such individuals had a greater need for approbation and support from outside, and would not consider lightly actions of which parents or significant others disapproved (C. Hsu, 1972; Scofield and Sun, 1960; D. Y. H. Wu, 1966). Because parents and other family members remain the most significant evaluators of an individual's achievement (Sung, 1989), of primary concern is whether or not a child's achievement performance conforms with the expectations of a family or clan. Simply stated, the goal of parental dependence training is to facilitate and reinforce the development of SOAM in their children (see Ho, this volume; Yang, this volume).

ACHIEVEMENT MOTIVATION AND ACHIEVEMENT-RELATED BEHAVIOUR

Most studies on the relationship between achievement motivation and achievement-related behaviour have either attempted to understand the nature of achievement motivation and its predictive power *vis-à-vis* behaviour, or have tried to establish the predictive or construct validity of achievement motivation measurement instruments. For this reason, before exploring the nature of achievement motivation and its relation to achievement behaviour, one must first determine the motivating force behind the behaviour of people in a particular society. If one accepts IOAM as being but one model of achievement motivation, and one developed by Western-oriented researchers, it follows that previously described relationships between achievement motivation and achievement-related behaviour may well differ from observed relationships between SOAM and achievement-related behaviour.

In one study, Yu (1994) found that high-SOAM individuals who are given social incentives will assertively demand that others give them assistance in order to achieve goals and complete tasks, in contrast to individuals with low levels of SOAM. In addition, the study found no marked change in the tendency of individuals with various levels of IOAM to ask for assistance even when they are given increased social incentives. Furthermore, when examining behaviour persistence, the research failed to find a strong relationship between high IOAM and high levels of persistence—once again attesting to the importance of external social incentives in nurturing SOAM. Finally, Yu noted a higher rate of task completion for high-SOAM individuals when external social incentives were presented, but found no significant variance in task completion rates for individuals with different IOAM levels who were presented with similar incentives. These findings only partially support conclusions reached by Atkinson (1957, 1958), Atkinson and Litwin (1960), Feather (1961, 1962), and Winterbottom (1953, 1958)—all Western researchers working with Western-based models.

AN ATTRIBUTIONAL ANALYSIS OF ACHIEVEMENT MOTIVATION

Using a conceptual scheme resembling Weiner's (1985, 1986) attributional theory of motivation and emotion, K. S. Yang and Yu (1989) and A. B. Yu and Yang (1991) performed attributional analyses of the cognitive, affective, motivational, and behavioural consequences of success or failure according to both SOAM and IOAM.

Consequences of Success

In the case of SOAM, it has been established that success leads to causal attributions that are socially oriented; a successful individual will tend to ascribe his or her success to the intervention of a significant other, the maintenance of good social relations, collective efforts, favourable personal affinity with another person (*yuan*)(K. S. Yang and Ho, 1988), or socially valued personal qualities.

Distinctive dominant attributions elicit distinctive dominant cognitive and affective reactions. Cognitive reactions include an expectancy of future social-oriented success, which may be defined in terms of attaining similar socially defined goals or demonstrating similar socially desirable personal qualities. Affective reactions include positive emotions resulting from socially oriented attributions, including feelings of face-enhancement (social-oriented self-esteem), a sense of shared collective glory (collective pride), gratitude to others, or relaxation (freedom from punishment and shame anxieties). These affects seem to interact with changes in expectations of future success, with future success being seen as the result of different causal attributions or high parental, familial, or other types of social pressure and support, in generating subsequent SOAM and achievement-related behaviour (K. S. Yang and Yu, 1989).

In the case of IOAM, dominant causal attributions are highly individual-oriented; they may emphasize personal ability, effort, luck, ease of task or project, or individually desirable personal qualities or states. Cognitive reactions include increased expectancy of future individual-oriented success and a future demonstration of similar individually desirable personal qualities. This finding is highly significant, since personal pride and individual-oriented self-esteem are positive, affective consequences of individual-oriented success attributions. This type of affect is believed to interact with differential changes in expectations of future success, success as the result of differential causal attributions and low parental, familial, or other types of pressure, and support for better performance in generating subsequent IOAM and achievement-related behaviour.

Consequences of Failure

Unlike success, failure results in feelings of unhappiness as an outcome-dependent, attribution-independent affect, regardless of whether a behavioural outcome is evaluated socially or individually. Following an immediate negative affective reaction, the actor will seek an explanation for his or her failure which may differ greatly depending on what type of achievement motivation characterizes the person who has failed.

In the case of SOAM, the dominant subsequent attributions are social-oriented, and they include a lack of necessary social connections, poor supernatural preconditions such as a bad *ming* (fate), bad *yun* (luck), and bad *yuan* (predestined interpersonal affinity)(K. S. Yang and Ho, 1988), the interference of powerful others, and socially undesirable personal qualities, including lack of modesty, lack of perseverance, or lack of popularity. The researchers believe that people with high SOAM tend to attribute their failure to one or more of these social-oriented causes when making a *post hoc* causal search. Furthermore, social-oriented ascriptions of failure lead to decreased expectations of future success in attaining similar socially defined goals and in demonstrating similar socially desirable qualities. They elicit such social-oriented affects as a sense of shame (equal to a loss of face), social-oriented self-blame, social-oriented guilt, depression, or anxiety (such as punishment and shame anxieties), and anger directed toward others.

The next step in the post-attribution process entails the combined influence of expectancy and affect on achievement motivation. It is assumed here that expectancy and affect interact in a multiplicative rather than additive way to influence achievement motivation. Specifically, decreased expectancy of future social-oriented success interacts with a social-oriented affect or affects to produce a weakened SOAM, which in turn interacts with social pressure for achievement from parents, family, or other membership groups, and which leads to persistent achievement-related behaviour in similar situations. This tendency means that in a collectivist society, weakened SOAM may not result in weakened achievement-related behaviour, since social pressure and subsequent achievement-related behaviour do not accurately reflect SOAM. This last finding would explain why Chinese children usually persist in manifesting considerable levels of achievement-related behaviour even when their achievement motivation (that is, SOAM) is relatively low, especially in the socially privileged realm of academic achievement.

On the other hand, the findings indicate that high levels of IOAM should lead to different effects regarding the content of the causal ascription or ascriptions that an actor uses to explain his or her failure—whether it be low personal ability, insufficient personal effort, job or task difficulty, bad luck, or individually undesirable personal qualities or states such as bad mood, lack of interest, or lack of self-confidence. Individual-oriented ascriptions of failure cause a decreased expectancy of future success in attaining similar socially defined goals and in demonstrating similar socially desirable qualities; they may also induce individual-oriented affects such as lowered individual-oriented self-esteem, self-blame, guilt, depression, anxiety, self-directed anger, and a sense of helplessness. Specifically, the decreased expectancy of success interacts with these affects to produce weakened individual-oriented achievement motivation—an outcome which in turn leads to weakened achievement-related behaviour in similar situations.

R. L. Chu's (1989) study of Taiwanese college students reported that the higher an individual's SOAM, the greater the tendency for the person to make causal ascriptions based on good fortune or luck. In contrast, the higher an individual's IOAM, the greater the tendency to make causal ascriptions to one's ability to concentrate on the project at hand. It appears that, in summary, high-SOAM individuals often ascribe their success or failure to external, unstable, and uncontrollable factors such as fortune or luck, while high-IOAM individuals will more often ascribe success or failure to internal, stable, and controllable factors such as industriousness.

Recently, Shih (1992) adapted Yu and K. S. Yang's (1991) attributional model to look at Beijing University students' causal attributions. The study found that these students' dominant success and failure causal attributions could be divided into three categories: social-oriented ascriptions such as expectations, praise, support, help from significant others, and good or bad learning environment; individual-oriented ascriptions such as psychological properties, adaptability, task difficulty, ability, and effort; and chance ascriptions such as good or bad *ming*. Additionally, Shih reported a positive correlation between social-oriented ascriptions for past success and social-oriented ascriptions for future potential success, and that causal attributional styles were not significantly different between males and females.

Furthermore, when a high IOAM student's performance success is self-evaluated, the degree of individual-oriented, social-oriented, and chance ascriptions for the present is close to that of individual-oriented, social-oriented, and chance ascriptions in the past. However, when a high-IOAM student's performance success is evaluated by others, the degree of individual-oriented ascriptions for the present is significantly lower than that of individual-oriented ascriptions in the past. Meanwhile, the degree of social-oriented ascriptions for the present is also significantly lower than that of social-oriented ascriptions for the past. However, there is no significant difference between the degrees of past and present chance ascriptions. This reflects the finding that high-IOAM persons tend to ignore the information of others' evaluations, and suggests that they should be more humble when their performance success is evaluated by others. These two factors are probably associated with lower individual-oriented and social-oriented ascriptions for high-IOAM persons. It is disappointing that Shih did not investigate the change of degrees of these present and past causal ascriptions by high-SOAM students. We are unable to judge if there is any substantial similarity or difference in any causal ascription strength between high-SOAM and high-IOAM individuals.

CONCLUSION

In this chapter we have primarily addressed two areas of concern. First, we have attempted to elucidate the nature and meaning of Chinese achievement motivation from an indigenous perspective. Through this approach, which takes Chinese culture and history into account, we have presented a sympathetic understanding of the nature of Chinese achievement motivation.

Second, from this indigenous perspective, we have proposed that the dominant achievement motivation of the Chinese can be termed social-oriented achievement motivation (SOAM). An alternative model of achievement motivation, especially as constructed by such Western researchers, as D. C. McClelland and his associates, may be termed individual-oriented achievement motivation (IOAM). Taking into account the characteristics and content of SOAM and IOAM, researchers have designed two kinds of measures for these two motivations, and the reliability and validity of these tools have been validated by empirical research. The findings available thus far indicate that SOAM and IOAM are different motivational constructs, and that most hypotheses that link SOAM and IOAM to individual familial socialization factors, attributional styles and processes, and achievement-related behaviours are supportable.

Chinese achievement motivation aims at complete self-realization (the perfection of the moral self and the familial self), with the Chinese view of self being a social construction which exists between individuals or between an individual and his or her family, clan, society, or state. The true nature of the Chinese self is only revealed when it is placed in the context of affective relationships between an individual, significant others, and the in-groups to which one belongs (A. B. Yu, 1994). From this point of view, Chinese achievement motivation and the Chinese concept of achievement are epistemological ideas that are not only being continuously revised, but also are best understood when placed in the context of the developmental processes of an individual's life history and experience. Future research on ultimate Chinese life concerns, self, and achievement motivation must take place in a hermeneutic, sociocultural context which addresses the meaning of Chinese social life and interaction (Gergen, 1989; C. F. Yang, 1991).

Chapter 16

■

The Role of Beliefs in Chinese Culture

Kwok Leung

Over the years, a large number of studies has examined the psychological characteristics of the Chinese people. Most of these studies, however, have employed a theory of values as their explanatory framework (see Bond, this volume, for a review). Research on beliefs, in contrast, has been haphazard, and a coherent analysis of the beliefs of the Chinese people has yet to be completed. This omission needs to be rectified, as evidence mounts implicating beliefs as major determinants of a variety of social behaviours (see, for example, Jussim, 1990). The primary goal of this chapter is to provide a comprehensive review of the studies that have examined beliefs as they function in Chinese societies. It should be noted that many instruments measuring personality traits, such as the Minnesota Multiphasic Personality Inventory (MMPI), may contain some items that explore belief. However, because these scales also contain a variety of other items, and it is not possible to discuss the belief items in isolation, they are excluded from this review. Interested readers are referred to the chapters by Cheung and Draguns in this volume for such materials.

A THEORETICAL FRAMEWORK

In theorizing about the structure of values, Schwartz (1992) has argued that values represent an attempt to meet three universal requirements of human existence: needs of individual, needs for coordinated social interaction, and needs for the survival and well-being of the group. Leung and Bond (1992) have proposed that this functional framework should be applicable to beliefs, since beliefs also function to help individuals to meet these three requirements of existence. If one follows this framework, then beliefs can be classified into three major types. The first, psychological beliefs, are concerned with characteristics of the individual, which are related to the person's functioning and well-being in society. The second, social beliefs, are concerned with principles that guide individuals in effective interactions with others. The third, environmental beliefs, are concerned with guides that assist individuals in functioning effectively in their physical environment. Following Katz (1960) and Bar-Tal (1990), beliefs can be defined as a proposition about an object or a relation between objects. The proposition can be of any content, and it can be judged with regard to its likelihood of being correct. In the following review, salient beliefs in Chinese societies are organized by reference to these three major types.

A REVIEW OF TRADITIONAL BELIEFS

For an ancient culture such as the Chinese, a great variety of traditional beliefs are readily identifiable in the classical literature and in proverbs from the daily vernacular. Unfortunately, most of these sources have not been explored by psychologists, and it is difficult to evaluate their usefulness in explaining the behaviour of Chinese people. For the sake of comprehensiveness, a few major beliefs identified from sources that are accessible to researchers are briefly reviewed.

Psychological Beliefs

A central assumption of Confucianism is that people are essentially benevolent (Chien, 1979), and this assumption has had a major impact on the social practices and structures of Chinese societies. For instance, the Confucian emphasis on education regardless of social class reflects the belief that all individuals have the potential to be developed. The emphasis on effort by Chinese in educational settings, which will be discussed in a subsequent section, is also related to this Confucian belief of perfectibility. More empirical work is warranted to explore how this belief is linked to various behaviours of the Chinese people.

Social Beliefs

In Confucian thought, individuals are believed to have the ability to develop their moral standards and to abide by them. This assumption provides the foundation for the political and social organization of traditional Chinese societies, which emphasize individual morality and diminish the role of legal regulations (Pye, 1984). This belief in individual morality is often used to explain the lack of an objective, consistent legal system in traditional Chinese societies (Ju, 1947), and it may also be related to the common observation that Chinese do not, as do Westerners, regard the existence of explicit rules as being important to social order. Chinese seem to favour fewer rules and a higher level of flexibility in following what rules are set out. For instance, Pugh and Redding (1985) found that compared to British firms, firms in Hong Kong were less likely to use rules and procedures to regulate work behaviour. If Chinese believe that they can evaluate their own behaviour against their own internal moral standards, it is natural for them to diminish the importance of external regulation by rules. The belief in internal morality may also explain why Chinese who are in positions of power resent the use of objective systems to monitor their behaviour and performance and take offense at challenges to their decisions (Bond and Hwang, 1986). Such external monitoring may be interpreted as evidence of an unnecessary mistrust of their morality, and it is therefore strongly resisted.

In Taoism, the central tenet is that individuals should follow the way of nature and the concept of morality should be abandoned (Sun, 1991). This belief that the natural way is the most effective seems to influence the behaviour of Chinese in a wide variety of contexts. For instance, in Taoist doctrine the most effective government governs through *wuwei* (nonaction)(Pye, 1984). This belief has yet to be empirically explored, and a better understanding of this tenet may provide useful insights about the political behaviour of Chinese people.

Environmental Beliefs

Feng shui is a supernatural belief widely shared by traditional as well as modern Chinese (Pye, 1984). The assumption underlying *feng shui* is that the positions of buildings and furniture relative to each other and in relation to the physical environment can influence the events that occur in the building. To avoid bad luck and to increase the amount of good luck coming to its occupants, the positioning of a building and its furniture should be arranged in a way that takes into account the neighbouring environment. Thus, people often employ a *feng shui* expert to advise them how to decorate homes, shops, factories, and offices. In Hong Kong, these *feng shui* experts may charge up to US$2000 per day for their services. It is unclear to what extent this belief affects the social behaviour of Chinese, and this topic deserves future empirical attention (see Ekblad, this volume).

The beliefs reviewed above are but some of the widespread beliefs in Chinese societies that have escaped the attention of psychologists. Yet, they appear to have important implications for an understanding of the behaviour of Chinese and should be explored in future work. In the following, some beliefs that have been empirically explored are reviewed.

PSYCHOLOGICAL BELIEFS

Locus of Control

Locus of control is probably the most researched belief complex in Chinese societies. When we cite internal control, we refer to the belief that reinforcements are under the control of the individual; external control refers to the belief that reinforcements are under the control of external forces, such as fate, luck, or chance (Rotter, 1966). It is widely agreed in the literature that because of the collectivistic orientation and the Confucianist, Buddhist, and Taoist traditions of Chinese people, they tend to possess a stronger belief in external control than do Westerners (see, for example, Bond, 1986). However, a careful scrutiny of the empirical evidence suggests that this conclusion is not well founded and is only supported unequivocally by two studies.

Based on Rotter's Internal–External Control of Reinforcement (I–E) scale, Hsieh, Shybut, and Lotsof (1969) found that Hong Kong Chinese subjects were more external than were American-born Chinese subjects, who in turn were more external than Anglo-American subjects. Using the same instrument, Hamid (1994) also found that college students in Hong Kong were more external than were college students in New Zealand. The results of another often-cited study are more ambiguous. Also using Rotter's I-E scale, M. S. Tseng (1972) reported that Asians in the United States were more external than were Caucasian Americans. However, it is unclear whether Chinese were included in Tseng's sample, and thus it cannot be established if the results are applicable to Chinese subjects.

One the other hand, at least three studies have cast doubt on the stereotype that Chinese are more external, in our formulation of the concept, than are other ethnic groups. Tsui (1978) found that, based on Rotter's I-E scale, Hong Kong Chinese undergraduates were actually more internal than were American-born Chinese undergraduates in the United States. Hung (1974), also working with Rotter's I-E scale, reported that undergraduates in Taiwan did not differ from the American undergraduates tested by Parsons and Schneider (1974) in internality. Smith, Trompenaars, and Dugan (1993) reported data collected with Rotter's I-E scale from employees of business organizations from 45 countries. The internality of Chinese respondents from China and Hong Kong was similar to that of respondents from a number of Western nations (including the Netherlands, Belgium, and Austria), and was actually higher than that of respondents from several other Western countries (including the United Kingdom and Sweden). Smith, Trompenaars, and Dugan did not perform statistical tests on the national differences observed, but their results make it clear that Chinese are not necessarily more external than are all Westerners. Taken these several studies as a whole, the general conclusion that Chinese exhibit a more external belief system seems to be untenable.

Studies employing a more complex conceptualization of control seem to suggest that the externality of the Chinese is context-specific (see also Crittenden, this volume). According to Levenson (1974), locus of control can be conceptualized as consisting of three components. He uses the term *general internality* to describe the belief that reinforcements are controlled by personal factors; the other two components are the belief that reinforcements are controlled by various powerful others and the belief that reinforcements are controlled by chance factors. In a study comparing undergraduates in Taiwan and the United States, Lao (1977) found that Chinese females were more external than were American females with regard to general internality, but that Chinese subjects of both sexes were more internal with regard to powerful others than were American subjects. There was no difference between the two groups with regard to the chance dimension.

Chan (1989) has administered Rotter's I-E scale to a group of undergraduates in Hong Kong and compared the results with those obtained by Parsons and Schneider's (1974) eight-country study. Parsons and Schneider (1974) classified the I-E items into five content areas: luck–fate, respect, academics, leadership–success, and politics. His evidence indicates that Chan's Hong Kong Chinese subjects were more internal in terms of respect, academics, and leadership–success than were subjects from several Western nations (including the United States, West Germany, Italy, and France), and were only more external than were subjects from these Western nations on the luck–fate dimension. Parsons and Schneider did not report the scores for politics and no comparison on this sub-scale was made by Chan. He further observed that, after comparing the I-E scores of Americans reported in studies in the 1960s and 1970s, Americans seem to be getting more external over time.

Because Lao (1977) and Chan (1989) used different scales to measure locus of control, it is difficult to synthesize their results. Nonetheless, it is now clear that the general conclusion that Chinese are more external than are Westerners is an oversimplification, and that the externality of Chinese is context-specific. A number of such contextual factors are reviewed below.

Externality and the Nature of the Outcome

Many writers have observed that humility is a salient norm in Chinese societies and that this norm originates from Confucianism (see, for example, W. S. Tseng, 1972). In one study, Farh, Dobbins, and Cheung (1991) found that Chinese employees in Taiwan evaluated their performance less positively than did their supervisors, a pattern opposite to that commonly observed in the United States. Farh, Dobbins, and Cheung explained this modesty bias of the Chinese by means of the humility norm in Chinese societies.

Bond, Leung, and Wan (1982) have argued that the humility norm is related to the attributional pattern of the Chinese, who tend to make external attributions for successes and internal attributions for failures. In line with this argument, Bond, Leung, and Wan found that subjects in Hong Kong who followed the humility norm in explaining their success or failure were better liked by observers. Furthermore, Wan and Bond (1982) reported that self-effacement is probably an impression management tactic. Their study showed that Hong Kong Chinese subjects made self-effacing attributions for their performance in public but self-enhancing attributions in private, at least for the attribution category of luck. In line with this finding, Kemp (1994) also found that secondary school children in Hong Kong reported a higher level of self-concept in an anonymous situation than in a situation where they were identifiable.

The salience of the humility norm in Chinese societies suggests that the internality of Chinese people may be qualified by the outcome of their performance. To test this argument, Chiu (1986) administered the Intellectual Achievement Responsibility Questionnaire (IARQ) to children in the sixth to eighth grades in Taiwan and the United States. The IARQ consists of 34 forced-choice items describing either a positive or a negative achievement experience, each of which is followed by two explanations for that experience. One explanation attributes the event to factors controlled by the subject, and the other explanation attributes the event to external factors. American children selected a larger number of internal explanations for successful than for failure situations, whereas Chinese children selected more internal explanations for failures than for successful situations.

Crittenden (1991) administered the Attributional Style Questionnaire (ASQ) to undergraduates in Taiwan and the United States. The ASQ asks respondents to make causal interpretations for six affiliative events involving interpersonal relationships with others and six achievement events as if the events actually happened to them. Half of the events in each type is positive and the other half is negative. Results showed that compared with American undergraduates, Taiwan undergraduates were more external in their attributions for achievement events and were more self-effacing in their attributional pattern. In other words, Taiwanese subjects were more likely to make external attributions for successes and internal attributions for failures than were the American students. With regard to affiliative events, there was no difference in externality between these two groups, but the Taiwanese women were more self-effacing than were their American counterparts.

Lee and Seligman (1993) administered the ASQ to three groups of under-graduates: Americans, Chinese-Americans, and Chinese in mainland China. Their results showed that compared to the two American groups, mainland Chinese were more inclined to make external attributions for both negative as well as positive events. To compare their results with those of Crittenden (1991), their data were transformed to obtain a score to reflect overall internal-ity and another score to reflect self-effacement. Although no statistical tests can be performed on these transformed scores, it was found that, consistent with Crittenden's results (1991), Chinese subjects were more external in their attri-bution and more self-effacing than were the two American groups.

It may now be concluded that the internality of Chinese is qualified by the nature of the outcome. Both Chiu (1986) and Lee and Seligman (1993) found that Chinese were more external for successful events than were Americans. However, Crittenden did not provide any data in this regard. With regard to negative outcomes, the results are less clearly drawn. Chiu (1986) found that Chinese in Taiwan were more internal for negative events, whereas Lee and Seligman (1993) found that mainland Chinese were more external for negative events. Again, Crittenden (1991) provided no relevant data on this issue. This ambiguity involving negative outcomes should be clarified in future research.

Effort and Ability Attributions in Academic Situations

Stevenson and his colleagues have conducted extensive research on the acad-emic achievements of American, Japanese, and Chinese students, and have consistently found that compared with Americans, Chinese believe that acade-mic achievement is more strongly related to effort. In one such study, Stevenson, Lee, Chen, Stigler, Hsu, and Kitamura (1990) found that Chinese parents of primary students in Taiwan put more stress on the importance of hard work, and less on the importance of innate ability, than did American par-ents in explaining their children's academic performance. Watkins and Cheng (in press) found that when college students in Hong Kong were asked to explain their academic performance, over 80 per cent chose effort as the expla-nation. Hess, McDevitt, and Chang (1987) compared mothers' attributions for their children's performance in mathematics in three groups: Caucasian Americans, Chinese-Americans, and mainland Chinese. As expected, in explaining why their children did not do better than they did, Caucasians were most likely to attribute the limitations to ability, followed by Chinese-Americans, and then by mainland Chinese. In a similar vein, mainland Chinese mothers were most likely to attribute academic limitation to a lack of effort, fol-lowed by Chinese-Americans, and then by Caucasian Americans. This pattern of attributions was also found when children were asked to explain their own poor performance.

Chen and Uttal (1988) have suggested that this emphasis on effort is rooted in the belief in human malleability and improvability that is endorsed and advocated by Chinese philosophies such as Confucianism. This philosophical perspective has clearly been imprinted on the minds of the Chinese. Tong, Zhao, and Yang (1985) noted that a favourite adage reported by high school students was 'genius comes from hard work and knowledge depends on accumulation'. Bond (1991) has referred to this emphasis on effort in Chinese societies as the 'cult of effort'. Chen and Uttal concluded that 'according to the Chinese perspective, innate ability may determine the rate at which one acquires knowledge, but the ultimate level is attained through effort' (p. 354).

As effort is an internal attribute, this emphasis on effort in academic settings suggests that Chinese are not neccessarily more external in their belief system than are Westerners. In fact, Munro (1977) has concluded that 'it is accurate to describe the Chinese position as a belief that inner causes (correct thoughts, wishes) can have important effects in changing the material world' (p. 18). We have established that the internality of Chinese is domain-specific, and that Chinese are in fact more internal than are Westerners in failure situations and in the association of effort with academic achievements. It remains to be demonstrated in future research under what circumstances Chinese are more external than are Westerners. Furthermore, initial evidence indicates that under some circumstances, the internal–external distinction is not applicable to Chinese. Luk and Bond (1992) found that when the causes of illnesses provided by college students in Hong Kong were factor-analysed, external and internal items loaded in the same factor. As suggested by Luk and Bond (1992), Chinese may endorse an interactionist perspective in their attribution style, at least with regard to the causes of illnesses, and this possibility should be explored in future work for other domains of behaviour as well.

Control, Psychological Adjustment, and Social Behaviour

A number of studies have shown that similar to results gathered in the United States, Chinese externality in the locus of control is related to poor psychological health. Kuo, Gray, and Lin (1979) found that Chinese-Americans who were more external as measured by the Personal Efficacy Scale showed a higher level of psychiatric impairment and depression, and manifested more problems such as low esteem, apprehension, insomnia, headaches, and other psycho-physiological symptoms. Chien (1984) found that primary school students in Taiwan who were internal as measured by the Nowicki–Strickland Locus of Control Scale were better adjusted personally and socially than were those measured as external. Hwang (1979) reported that primary school pupils in Taiwan who were high in internality as measured by the Nowicki–Strickland scale scored higher in self-acceptance and emotional maturity than did those who measured as low in internality. Chan (1989) found that Chinese undergraduates in Hong Kong who were external as measured by Rotter's I-E scale had a higher level of adjustment problems as measured by the General Health Questionnaire which measures a variety of psychological symptoms. Leung, Salili, and Baber (1986) found that Chinese adolescents in Hong Kong who were external as measured by the Nowicki–Strickland scale reported more adjustment and health problems. Lau and Leung (1992) also found that Chinese adolescents who were external as measured by the Nowicki–Strickland scale reported a lower self-concept, more delinquent behaviours, and poorer relationships with school and parents than did those who were measured as internal. Thus, the negative impact of externality on psychological adjustment and health seems to be generalizable across Chinese societies and the United States.

In contrast, the relationship between control and social behaviour seems to show some cultural variation. Hamid (1994) found that both for college students in Hong Kong and in New Zealand, the relationship between control and the number of social interactions is similar. Externals reported a larger number of social interactions than did internals when their level of self-monitoring was high, but the pattern was the opposite when their level of self-monitoring was low. However, when the level of self-disclosure of these interactions was analysed, cross-cultural differences emerged. Among the New Zealand subjects, internals reported a higher level of self-disclosure than did externals; the opposite was true, however, for the Hong Kong subjects. In the absence of additional data, it is unclear how this result can be interpreted at this time. Further work is needed to explore the relationship between control and social behaviour.

Self-Concept

Many writers have described the Chinese culture as group-oriented, arguing that individuals believe the group rather than the individual is the basic unit in society (see, for example, Hsu, 1981). This group-orientation hypothesis has obvious implications for the conception of the self. Based on an analysis of traditional thought in Chinese culture, Hsu (1971) proposed that social relationships and roles constitute the core of the self in the Chinese culture. In line with this reasoning, Yang (1991) has criticized the use of Western instruments to measure self-concepts in Chinese societies, on the grounds that these instruments fail to capture the social components of the self in Chinese societies.

On the face of it, Hsu and Yang's argument has high validity and is very appealing, but the empirical evidence in its favor is equivocal. Triandis, McCusker, and Hui (1990) found that the collective self was more salient for subjects from China than for American subjects. Specifically, when these subjects were asked to complete 20 statements that began with 'I am...', the number of responses made by the Chinese subjects that fell into the collective category (for example, identifying themselves as the member of a specific group) was almost three times as great as that of the American subjects. However, Chinese subjects from Hong Kong responded at a level similar to the American subjects, making it difficult to conclude whether the difference between the American and mainland Chinese subjects was due to cultural or political and economic differences. Thus, their results only provide some partial support for the analyses of Hsu and Yang. Using a procedure similar to that used by Triandis and his colleagues, Ip and Bond (in press) have provided results that are more consistent with the arguments of Hsu and Yang. They found that in creating self-descriptions, social roles were used more frequently by college students in Hong Kong than by American undergraduates.

In contrast, at least two studies cast some doubt on the conclusion that the self is more social in nature in the Chinese culture than in Western culture. Using a self-description procedure similar to that used by Triandis, McCusker, and Hui (1990), Bond and Cheung (1983) found that Hong Kong Chinese undergraduates reported fewer statements that fell into the collective category than did American undergraduates. Yu, Chang, and Wu (1993) adopted the same procedure as Triandis, McCusker, and Hui (1990) with a sample of college students in Taiwan and found that over 90 per cent of the attributes used for self-description were individual attributions; social attributes were mentioned at a very low frequency. Yu, Chang, and Wu concluded that there seems to be no evidence in support of the position of Yang (1991). Note that both Bond and Cheung (1983) and Yu, Chang, and Wu (1993) used an open-ended format to obtain self-descriptions from subjects; the results do not indicate any bias from individual-oriented instruments. In sum, the proposal that the conception of the self entails more collective elements among Chinese than among Western subjects appears to be an over-simplification. Ip and Bond (in press) have suggested that the nature of the coding scheme may affect the results obtained. This complex issue should be examined systematically in future work.

Structure of Self-concept

It is now widely accepted that the self-concept is multi-dimensional and consists of different facets, including physical abilities, physical appearance, academic ability, relations with peers, relations with parents, and relations with school (see, for example, Marsh, Relich, and Smith, 1983). The complexity of the structure of the self seems to be true for Chinese as well as for other groups, and it has been confirmed with secondary school children from Hong Kong (Leung and Lau, 1989; Kemp, 1994) and from Beijing (Watkins and Dong, 1994). It remains to be demonstrated that the Chinese self entails components that are not observed in the West.

Beliefs about the Self-concept

A number of studies have shown that Chinese hold a less positive view of the self than do Americans. Bond and Cheung (1983) analysed spontaneous statements about the self provided by Hong Kong Chinese and American undergraduates and found that Chinese subjects reported a less positive ratio of statements about the self than did the American subjects. Similar results have also been obtained by Ip and Bond (in press). Stigler, Smith, and Mao (1985) administered the Perceived Competence Scale for Children (PCSC) to primary students in Taiwan and the United States. The PCSC taps three distinct domains of perceived competence—cognitive (or academic), social, and physical—as well as the child's general self-esteem. Stigler, Smith, and Mao found that the factor structure of these four sub-scales was highly similar across the two cultural groups, and thus the cross-cultural validity of the instrument was supported. Furthermore, Stigler, Smith, and Mao found that Chinese children showed lower ratings in three of the four sub-scales: cognitive, physical, and general self-esteem. Turner and Mo (1984) reported that Chinese primary students in Taiwan scored lower on self-image than did American primary school students. White and Chan (1983) found that Chinese-American graduate students and professionals regarded themselves as less active, less attractive, less sharp, and less beautiful than did Caucasian Americans. Paschal and Kuo (1973) found that Chinese undergraduates from Taiwan reported a lower level of self-esteem than did American undergraduates. Huang (1971) found that Chinese undergraduates in the United States reported a lower self-esteem than did American undergraduates.

Two studies of this question involved Australians as the target group for comparison. Kemp (1994) found that Chinese secondary school students in Hong Kong reported a lower level of self-concept than did their Australian counterparts across all the facets of self-concept measured by the self-description questionnaire developed by Marsh et. al. (1983). Finally, Watkins and Dong (1994) reported that secondary school children in Beijing reported a lower general self-concept than did their Australian counterparts. It was also reported, however, that the Chinese children scored higher than did the Australian children in some facets of self-concept, including physical appearance and mathematics. It is clear from the results of these studies that Chinese report a generally lower self-concept than do their counterparts in the West.

Why would Chinese hold a less positive self-concept that do Americans? Bond and Hwang (1986) suggested that the humility norm in Chinese societies may lead to a less positive evaluation of the self, and that 'in the absence of further research, one cannot assume that low self-esteem in the Chinese has the same implications for social functioning as the same level in respondents from some other cultures' (p. 236).

In light of the emphasis on effort in Chinese societies, an alternative explanation can be advanced, which presupposes that Chinese do indeed have a less positive self-concept than do Americans and Australians. Previous research has shown that compared with Americans, Chinese are more likely to attribute failure to a lack of effort rather than to external factors. Research in the United States and Australia shows that effort attributions for failures are related to a lower self-concept (for a review of these findings, see Marsh, 1984; Marsh, Cairns, Relich, Barnes, and Debus, 1984). Consistent with the results obtained in the West, Huang, Hwang, and Ko (1983) found that Chinese undergraduates in Taiwan reported a higher level of depression when they made an internal attribution for failure. Chung and Hwang (1981) found that in Taiwan, the attribution of failures to stable and internal factors was related to poorer self-esteem and a lower level of well-being. It appears that the less positive self-concept of the Chinese is explainable by their greater tendency to attribute negative outcomes to internal factors. A direct test of this proposal should be attempted in future research.

A related explanation would also explain why Chinese report a less positive self-concept than do Americans. In Chinese societies, the indigenous concept of *yuan* (predestined interpersonal affinity) is widely endorsed. *Yuan* refers to the belief that interpersonal outcomes are determined by fate or supernatural forces. Yang (1982) has argued that because *yuan* is an external explanation for interpersonal outcomes, the use of *yuan* attributions by those who enjoy a positive interpersonal relationship will protect the face of others who enjoy less favourable interpersonal outcomes. It should be noted that this argument contrasts sharply with empirical results obtained in the United States, which typically identify a pattern of ego-defensive attributions. In American samples, external causes are more likely to be attributed to failures than to successes (Zuckerman, 1979).

With regard to negative interpersonal outcomes, Yang (1982) and Lee (1982) argue that attributions based on *yuan* function as a defense mechanism that can shield an individual from the negative emotions associated with negative interpersonal outcomes, such as divorce. Thus, the process of attributing *yuan* to negative interpersonal outcomes in Chinese societies is similar to ego-defensive attributions frequently observed in the West. Although *yuan* is used in Chinese societies, and different concepts of an external nature such as bad luck are used in the West, the ego-enhancing function of such external attributions is similar.

To evaluate the ego-defensive function of *yuan* attributions, Huang et al. (1983) divided their undergraduate subjects in Taiwan into a high- and a low-depression group, and found, as expected, that the high-depression group was the less likely to make *yuan* attributions for negative interpersonal outcomes. Huang et al. (1983) also reported both groups of subjects made more *yuan* attributions for positive than for negative interpersonal outcomes. This tendency to make *yuan* attributions for positive outcomes is consistent with Yang's (1992) argument that *yuan* attributions also serve a face-saving function for others.

It is entirely possible that the belief in *yuan* leads Chinese to attribute positive interpersonal outcomes to an external cause, thus weakening their self-esteem. Consistent with this conjecture, Huang et al. (1983) has reported that Chinese subjects who made external attributions for positive interpersonal outcomes showed a higher level of depression. Thus, the belief in *yuan* may be a two-edged sword. It serves as a defense against negative outcomes, but, in the case of one's positive outcomes, its face-saving function for others may be attained at the expense of one's self-esteem. This intriguing possibility should be explored in future research.

Correlates of Self-esteem

Research has shown that in Chinese societies the relationships between self-concept and a wide array of other variables are similar to those identified in American samples. The general pattern found is that a positive self-concept is related to better psychological adjustment. For instance, among Chinese adolescents in Hong Kong, positive self-esteem is related to a lower level of anxiety, social dysfunction, and depression (Chan and Lee, 1993), a higher level of psychological well-being (Leung and Leung, 1992), fewer delinquent behaviours (Leung and Lau, 1989), and better relations with parents and school (Cheung and Lau, 1985; Lau and Leung, 1992). Chang (1982) found that in Taiwan, a positive self-concept is related to more satisfactory interpersonal relationships.

SOCIAL BELIEFS

Collectivist Beliefs

Chinese culture is characterized as collectivistic (see, for example, Bond and Hwang, 1986; Hofstede, 1980; Hsu, 1981), and many empirical studies have supported this description of the Chinese (see Earley, 1989; Leung and Bond, 1984; Li, 1992; Wheeler, Reis, and Bond, 1989). Although no study has yet examined in detail the belief system of Chinese that is related to collectivism, a number of conclusions can be drawn from the studies that have been conducted on the interchange between individualism and collectivism.

The single belief underlying Chinese collectivism is that the futures of individuals from the same in-group are inter-related and that each person's well-being depends upon the results of collective effort. If each person follows the norms of the group and acts in the interests of the group, the group will be harmonious and prosperous. A number of studies has provided results in support of this belief. For instance, Leung and Bond (1984) found that Chinese subjects from Hong Kong allocated a larger share of a group reward to in-group members than did American subjects. Earley (1989) found that Chinese subjects from China displayed less social loafing than did American subjects.

The collectivism of Chinese leads them to believe that an effective way to get things done is often through one's *guanxi*, or interpersonal connections (see, for example, Hwang, 1987). Although this topic has been much discussed (for example, King, 1991), empirical work is needed to clarify the role of this belief in the interpersonal behaviour of Chinese.

Some studies show that Chinese tend to believe that out-group members are less likely to be dependable and trustworthy than are members of the in-group. For instance, Leung (1988) found that Chinese from Hong Kong were more likely to sue a stranger than were American subjects. Li (1992) found that, compared to American subjects, Chinese subjects from Taiwan regarded strangers as less likeable, less likely to be from the same group, and less fair. However, the data provided by Zhang and Bond (1993) are inconsistent with the pattern described above. They found that there was no difference among American, Hong Kong Chinese, and mainland Chinese college students with regard to their trust level towards relatives. But mainland Chinese students showed a higher level of trust towards both friends and strangers than did both American and Hong Kong Chinese students. It is unclear at this point in what types of situations Chinese will demonstrate negative beliefs about out-group members; this issue should be explored in future work.

Leung (1987) argued that in Chinese culture, it is widely believed that it is more effective to resolve disputes through negotiation and compromise rather than through confrontation. Consistent with this argument, Leung found that Chinese subjects from Hong Kong preferred mediation over adjudication in dispute processing, whereas American subjects preferred these two procedures to the same extent. Kirkbride, Tang, and Westwood (1991) found that when Chinese employees in Hong Kong were asked to rank the five conflict resolution styles proposed by Thomas and Kilmann (1974), they ranked compromise first and competition last. In contrast, British managers who worked in Hong Kong ranked competition second and compromise third (Tang and Kirkbride, 1986).

Triandis et al. (1990) found that Chinese from China perceived Chinese as more homogenous than they thought other national groups were, whereas no such results were obtained with Americans. Triandis and his colleagues interpreted this finding as supporting the argument that the collectivistic Chinese believed that the group is the basic unit of analysis, and thus perceived a higher level of homogeneity in their in-group than in out-groups. On the other hand, Lee and Ottati (1993) found that both Americans and mainland Chinese perceived the other group as more homogenous than their own. A careful scrutiny of these two studies suggests that in Triandis et al. (1990), homogeneity refers to behavioural standards and norms, whereas in Lee and Ottati (1993), the measure of homogeneity was broader and included such elements as clothing and physical appearance. Thus, it is hard to reconcile the conflicting results of these two studies.

Triandis et al. (1990) also found that contrary to the common stereotype, Chinese subjects from Hong Kong and China regarded the group as less effective than did American subjects. However, Triandis et al. (1993) reported that for the independence factor, which includes items comparing the effectiveness of the group and the individual, American subjects clearly endorsed independence more strongly than did Chinese subjects from Hong Kong and China. Because the independence factor identified by Triandis and his colleagues contained items concerning friends as well, this result must be interpreted with caution. Again, it is difficult at this point to draw a firm conclusion with regard to the beliefs of Chinese about the effectiveness of the group versus the individual.

Beliefs Related to Power Distance

The social structure in Chinese societies is characterized by many writers as hierarchical (see, for example, Bond and Hwang, 1986; Hsu, 1981; King and Bond, 1985) and exhibits a large power distance (Hofstede, 1980). According to King and Bond (1985), the basic belief underlying this orientation is that the ideal way to organize a collective is through a well-defined hierarchy, with explicit responsibilities for each role in the hierarchy. For instance, the typical leadership pattern in Chinese societies tends to be paternalistic and authoritarian (Bond and Hwang, 1986; Redding and Wong, 1986). This important belief complex should be explored systematically in future work.

ENVIRONMENTAL BELIEFS

Primary and Secondary Control

Rothbaum, Weisz, and Snyder (1982) have reported that in the West, a dominant way to attain one's goals and wishes is to attempt to bring about objective changes in the environment; this type of control is called *primary control*. Weisz, Rothbaum, and Blackburn (1984) further argued that while primary control is the predominant strategy in the West, a different type of control, *secondary control*, is prevalent in the East. Under this strategy, because of the emphasis on interdependence and harmony in groups, people should show a stronger tendency to adjust themselves to fit the environment. Based on this argument, it is possible that Chinese may believe that secondary control is a more effective means to attain their goals than is primary control. Peng and Lachman (1993) administered primary and secondary control scales to 471 American and Chinese-American adults, and they found that American respondents scored higher on primary control and lower on secondary control than did Chinese-American respondents. However, primary control was related to positive psychological adjustment for both groups. Empirical enquiry in this new area may complement the work on locus of control reviewed before.

Beliefs about Uncertain Events

Wright and his associates (1980) have examined the cultural differences in probabilistic thinking between British and three groups of South-east Asian subjects, including Hong Kong Chinese. Their major finding is that British subjects tended to adopt a probabilistic view of uncertainty and were able to assess the likelihood of occurrence of uncertain events more accurately. In contrast, the South-east Asian subjects, including the Hong Kong Chinese subjects, tended to view the world in terms of total certainty or uncertainty, and they were less inclined to make a probabilistic judgement of uncertain events (see also Yates and Lee, this volume).

This conclusion is consistent with the impression of a team of American decision analysts from the University of Michigan who worked with a Chinese team on a project for controlling water pollution in the Huangpu River in mainland China (Pollock and Chen, 1986). They noted that their Chinese counterparts showed a lack of concern for uncertainty and assumed complete certainty for all important information relevant to the decision task. The Chinese found the necessity of assigning probabilities to events strange and unnatural.

In the absence of data, it is not clear how a more undifferentiated view towards uncertainty affects the social behaviour of the Chinese. It is possible that this non-probabilistic world-view may be related to the extensive use of intuition in Chinese culture and in Confucianism, Taoism, and Buddhism (Chou, 1981). A probabilistic view of the world is conducive to a rational approach to decision-making and to the use of facts and figures in coming to a decision, and it is derived from the social logic of low power distance. In contrast, a non-probabilistic world-view would diminish the importance of objective facts and figures, thus making the role of intuition important and arbitrary authority acceptable. A good example to illustrate this argument comes from the business world of Hong Kong, where Chinese tycoons are renowned for their extraordinary 'foresight' (*yanguang*). Major business deals are often based on the intuition of these tycoons rather than on meticulous calculations based on extensive facts and figures. For a succinct description of how Chinese business people rely on intuition in managing their companies, see Redding (1978).

INDIGENOUS BELIEFS IN CHINESE CULTURE

With the exception of *yuan*, the studies reviewed above focus primarily on universal belief elements that can be found both in Chinese as well as in Western societies. In this section, a few indigenous Chinese beliefs are reviewed.

Psychological Beliefs

Beliefs about death

Hui, Chan, and Chan (1989) administered a set of 30 statements about death to Chinese adolescents in Hong Kong and extracted five factors. The first factor,

Buddhist and Taoist belief, is indigenous and pertains to beliefs about reincarnation. The second factor is belief in a just world, which emphasizes the different destinations of the virtuous and the evil-doers. The third factor was labelled naturalistic belief, which suggests that life ends with death. The fourth factor was labelled immortal soul belief, which suggests the soul will persist after death, but does not imply reincarnation. Finally, the fifth factor, Protestant belief, follows Western doctrine that suggests Christians will go to paradise and non-believers will be punished. Hui et al. also reported that this factor pattern was replicated in a different sample of Chinese adolescents in Hong Kong.

It is interesting that an indigenous belief, the Buddhist and Taoist belief, and a Western belief, the Christian belief, are seen to co-exist. This situation leads Hui et al. (1989) to conclude that Chinese in Hong Kong are under the influence of traditional and Western beliefs simultaneously.

Health beliefs

A number of health beliefs can be identified in traditional Chinese thought. The most researched belief in this area is probably the somatization tendency of Chinese who suffer from psycho-pathological problems. A number of studies have shown that Chinese in Taiwan and Hong Kong display a tendency to associate several types of psychosomatic problems with physical causes (for a review, see Cheung, 1986). The belief underlying such a somatization tendency is that some psychosomatic problems are caused by physical factors only (see, for example, Luk and Bond, 1992). It remains unclear, however, where this somatization belief originates, and what role it plays in guiding the behaviour of Chinese.

In some Chinese ancient writings, the semen of men is regarded as a source of strength and energy, and thus frequent intercourse and ejaculation are believed to be associated with a loss of physical strength (Van Gulik, 1961). Menstruation is also regarded as unclean. In a survey of medical students in Hong Kong, Chan (1986) reported that these two traditional beliefs were strongly endorsed. Despite their training in modern medicine, over 90 per cent of the respondents believed that the following statements are to some extent true: frequent ejaculation leads to a loss of physical strength; frequent masturbation is injurious to heath; frequent intercourse is injurious to health; and the healthy vagina is essentially unclean and not bacteria-free. These two beliefs regarding sexual health seem to persist despite the proliferation of modern medical knowledge. It remains to be demonstrated what role they play in the overall belief system and social behaviour of Chinese.

Social Beliefs

Beliefs about reciprocity and retribution

Under the influence of Confucianism and Buddhism, Chinese have developed an indigenous concept of retribution, *bao* (see, for example, Hsu, 1971; Hwang, 1987; Yang, 1957). The concept of *bao* covers both positive and negative events, and thus includes both reciprocity and retribution. With regard to positive outcomes, *bao* requires that individuals should not owe others any favours, either tangible or intangible, and should make an effort to repay what favours they do owe. The belief underlying *bao* is that if individuals do not repay the favours of others, their relationship will become difficult and social harmony will become difficult to sustain (Hsu, 1971).

With regard to negative outcomes, Chinese often believe that retribution to a harm-doer does not necessarily have to be delivered by the victim, and that supernatural forces may punish harm-doers to restore a state of justice. For instance, Chiu (1991) has analysed popular Chinese sayings about inequity and classified them into seven types. One type, clearly indigenous, suggests that retribution may occur to the perpetrators' descendants. These sayings suggest that bad deeds will bring disasters to the descendants of perpetrators or result in the perpetrators having unfilial descendants. The impact of this *bao* belief on social behaviour should be explored in future work.

Belief about morality and social influence

In Confucian thought, morality (*de*) is believed to be able to elicit deference from others and greater authority (Pye, 1984; Yang and Tseng, 1988). This belief, which may be termed the morality power belief, has not been empirically verified, but some indirect evidence hints at its prominence even in contemporary Chinese societies. In a study of leadership behaviour in mainland China, Lin, Chen, and Wang (1987) found that in addition to the two traditional leadership dimensions, namely, performance and maintenance, a third dimension of leadership behaviour was identified. The new dimension was labelled the morality dimension, and includes behaviours manifesting such virtues as honesty, integrity, and commitment. Although this finding does not speak to the morality power belief directly, it suggests that high perceived morality is associated with social influence, and that further work in this area is warranted to attain more firmly based results.

CONCLUSION

As noted in the opening to this chapter, there is a dearth of theorizing and data on the belief systems of Chinese. As seen in this review of the literature, many beliefs that seem to have important bearing on the behaviour of Chinese have remained unexplored. Given the paucity of empirical work, we are a long way from being able to develop a coherent framework for understanding the belief system of Chinese. The tripartite classification of beliefs adopted in this review represents the first step in our effort to develop a framework for understanding the structure and dynamics of beliefs. Many directions for future research have been proposed in the review, and it is hoped that they will stimulate more empirical work in this important area.

Chapter 17

◼

Causal Attribution Processes Among the Chinese

Kathleen S. Crittenden

How do the Chinese make sense of events that occur in their social world? Attribution, the study of how people causally interpret everyday behaviour and events occurring around them, and how they govern themselves in response, has dominated American social psychology for more than two decades. In the years since Bond (1983) noted how little was known about attribution processes in non-Western societies, considerable research has explored attributions among the Chinese. However, no unitary picture of Chinese attribution processes has yet emerged from that research.

In many cases, the empirical yield of attribution research on Chinese people has been hampered by a number of factors, including use of inappropriate instruments for measuring key concepts, inattention to theory testing and development, too little awareness of similar research efforts by scholars in other Chinese societies, a lack of coordination among scholars working on related problems in different settings, little programmatic thrust in the research, and a nearly exclusive reliance on students as research subjects. This chapter reviews the research literature on attributional phenomena and their conse-quences and antecedents among individuals of Chinese ancestry and culture. Phenomena of interest will include attributions concerning the causes of events and behaviour, and enduring attributional styles.

The review covers conceptual issues, strategies for measuring attribution patterns, cross-cultural comparisons of the patterns seen in Chinese samples with those of other groups, and evidence concerning consequences of attribu-tional processes for achievement motivation and behaviour, emotions, mental health, social identities, and strategies for resolving interpersonal conflict. A self-presentational perspective suggests that attributional patterns vary across sociocultural contexts. The review generates more questions than answers, and so it takes the form of a proposal for a research agenda for the future.

CONCEPTUALIZING CAUSAL ATTRIBUTION PATTERNS

This review of causal attribution patterns includes discussion both of *attribu-tions*—causal interpretations for particular events—and *attributional styles*—how individuals habitually tend to attribute events. Attributions vary according to who makes them, the event being explained, and the context in which the explanation is offered. As individual characteristics, attributional styles are assessed by considering causal judgements of multiple events.

To characterize attributional patterns, we will consider the dimensions underlying perceived causes as well as the kinds of events being explained. Causes can be said to vary along four dimensions: by *locus*, the degree to which a person believes the cause is internal or external to the actor; by *stability*, whether the cause is seen as stable or variable over time; by *controllability*, whether the cause is subject to volitional influence; and by *globality*, whether the cause affects a variety of situations or is specific to one event. The type of event may be classified according to the actor, domain, and valence associated with it. A question concerning the actor takes the following form: Does the event happen to the attributor (the self) or to another person (an other)? A question of domain takes this form: Does the event involve an achievement outcome or an affiliation outcome (involving interpersonal relationships)? Finally, a question concerning valence takes this form: Is the outcome good or bad?

Attributional Patterns

Holding the variables of actor and domain constant, we can characterize attributional patterns in terms of two independent components of any dimension. First, we average the values of perceived causes for all events, good and bad, together. Second, we compute the differential, by subtracting the average value for bad events from that of good events.

For the locus dimension, American respondents display regular patterns in both components (Crittenden, 1983). The typical average locus in research on American subjects is termed internal, favoring internal over external causes, particularly for events that happen to others. The typical locus differential is self-enhancing, tending to attribute good events internally and to blame bad events on more external causes. A few studies, however, have found an opposite, self-effacing pattern, in which the subjects attribute good events to external factors and bad events to relatively internal causes. In stability, the typical American differential is optimistic, attributing good outcomes to relatively stable causes and bad outcomes to more variable causes (Weiner, 1986; Abramson, Seligman, and Teasdale, 1978). A pessimistic pattern would attribute good events to relatively variable factors and bad events to more stable causes.

To characterize attributions and attributional styles adequately requires measuring instruments that avoid confounding causal dimensions, actors, or event domains or valences. Correct application of attribution concepts within Chinese culture poses two additional challenges: first, one must identify the causal categories used by the Chinese; and, second, one must assess the dimensions underlying these causes (Fletcher and Ward, 1988).

Causal Categories

What causal categories do the Chinese use? How attributions have been conceptualized and measured has been heavily influenced by Weiner's (1974) original model of the four causes of achievement events: ability, effort, task difficulty, and luck. These four causes have been shown to have some construct validity in Western cultures, but are they equally relevant in a Chinese context (Bond, 1983; Fletcher and Ward, 1988)? Weiner's four causes accounted for fewer than half of the causes offered for achievement events by Taiwan university students (Lin, 1989). Four recent studies have categorized free-response causal explanations from students in Hong Kong, Taiwan, the People's Republic of China (PRC), and Singapore, as well as New Zealand (Hau and Salili, 1990; Lin, 1989; Shi, 1992; and Ng, McClure, and Walkey, 1992). In these studies, effort and ability figure prominently in attributions for achievement events. Chinese students have been shown to offer luck and task characteristics less frequently, and causes involving other people more frequently.

Recommendation 1

The first recommendation of this chapter is that researchers conduct cooperative research that elicits open-ended causal accounts from Chinese in varying locales and circumstances, to generate a set of causal categories with consensual definitions for each domain.

How are the causal categories related to underlying dimensions? Weiner's original taxonomy of four causes for achievement reflected combinations of locus and stability values: ability, internal and stable; effort, internal and variable; task difficulty, external and stable; and luck, external and variable. The fundamental attributional research error, the assumption that researchers can accurately interpret respondents' attributions in terms of subjective causal dimensions (Russell, 1982), is especially serious when Western categories are exported to a non-Western culture. Yet, little attention has been paid to the universality of dimensions across cultures (Fletcher and Ward, 1988).

The dimensional meanings of causes for Chinese respondents are a source of some confusion. Attempting to adapt Weiner's causes for use across domains and cultures, Chandler, Shama, Wolf, and Planchard (1981) have substituted context for task difficulty as an external, stable cause. In Hung and Yang's (1979) Chinese attributional style scale, fate (*mingyun*) is treated as the external, stable cause and luck (*yunqi*) as external and variable. However, Wan and Bond (1982) have interpreted luck as synonymous with fate. Recent research has not established definitively the relationship of causes to underlying dimensions. Factor analyses of causal responses by Chinese students (Hau, 1992; Hau and Salili, 1991; Shi, 1992) yield factors that cut across theoretical dimensions.

Student respondents in Hong Kong, Singapore, and Taiwan have been asked to locate specific causes on conceptual dimensions (Hau and Salili, 1991; Ng et al., 1992; Lin, 1989). How do Weiner's original causes fare in these three studies? Effort, the most important Chinese explanation for achievement, is internal and controllable but has no clear location on the stability dimension. The other three causes are also difficult to locate. Ability is not internal (in Singapore) and not stable. Task characteristics are neither external nor stable (in Hong Kong and Taiwan). Luck, not offered as a cause by Taiwan respondents, is not external (in Hong Kong) and not variable (in Singapore). Fate and context have not been included in the scaling studies. These results cast doubt on the dimensional meanings assumed in Western research for commonly used causes, but they do not offer a compelling set of alternative meanings.

Causes for affiliation events have been little studied. However, some researchers (Yang, 1988, in press; Yang and Ho, 1988) have investigated the concept of *yuan*, an indigenous causal category grounded in traditional, Buddhist beliefs concerning predestination. *Yuan*, determining affinities and repulsions between persons, offers convenient explanations for affiliation outcomes. It is an external cause, with stable and variable forms: *yuanfen* determines long-lasting relationships; *jiyuan* governs chance encounters.

Research in Taiwan and Hong Kong has addressed university students' current understandings of *yuan* and what types of events it can be used to explain (Yang and Ho, 1988; Huang, Hwang, and Ho, 1983). Most of the students expressed some belief in *yuan*, which they characterized as changeable, unpredictable, and uncontrollable, an unexplainable coincidence that contributes to forming a personal relationship. They saw *yuan* as an explanation of friendship or heterosexual love relationships, especially those with good outcomes. These results indicate that the idea of *yuan* remains alive in modern Chinese cultures, but with a lessened religious connotation than in the past. In Taiwan, *yuan* beliefs correlated positively with social orientation and negatively with individual modernity. Strong among university students, these beliefs likely would be even more strongly endorsed in less educated, less modern sectors of Chinese societies.

Recommendation 2

The second recommendation to be made is for collaborative research on indigenous Chinese attributional constructs. A good model for such efforts is the two-country investigation of *yuan*.

Recommendation 3

The third recommendation is to coordinate multi-method, multi-site efforts to ascertain how Chinese respondents understand the dimensional meanings of causal categories.

MEASURING CHINESE ATTRIBUTIONAL PATTERNS

Researchers interested in studying causal attribution patterns among the Chinese have used a variety of measurement strategies, most employed only in a single study. We list them here briefly, along with the countries in which they have been used.

Morris (1993) has coded textual accounts (in Chinese- and English-language newspapers) into causal categories. Investigators have categorized open-ended causal explanations for achievement or affiliation events in Singapore, the PRC, and Taiwan (Ng et al., 1992; Shi, 1992; Huang et al., 1983).

Various studies have asked respondents to rate the importance of a set of causes in determining an achievement outcome. Students in Taiwan, Hong Kong, and the PRC have rated Weiner's four causes (Cheng and Yang, 1977; Chu, 1989; Wan and Bond, 1982; Kuo, 1983; 1984; Liu, 1990). Studies in the

United States, Hong Kong, Singapore, and the PRC (Sun, 1991; Ng et al., 1992; Hau and Salili, 1990; Shi, 1992) have used other sets of causes. Similarly, Chinese in the United States have rated causes for an affiliation event (Morris, 1993).

Other studies have employed summed ratings of causes over multiple events. Chung and Hwang (1981) applied this approach to Weiner's four causes in Taiwan. The Hung and Yang Attribution Scale (HYAS)(Hung and Yang, 1979), used in Taiwan (Chang, 1982; Huang, 1983; Huang and Kuo, 1984; Hung and Yang, 1979; Lin, 1979), substitutes fate (*mingyun*) for task difficulty in the list of four causes for each of 30 scenarios, divided by valence. The Multidimensional–Multiattributional Causality Scale (MMCS)(Lefcourt, von Baeyer, Ware, and Cox, 1979), which replaces task difficulty with context, has been used in Hong Kong and the United States (Bond, 1982; Chan, 1981; Yan and Gaier, 1994). These multi-event instruments yield dimension scales by valence and domain, based on a priori assumptions about dimensional locations of particular causes.

The Intellectual Achievement Responsibility Questionnaire (IARQ) (Crandall, Katkovsky and Crandall, 1965) has been used in Taiwan and the PRC (Chiu, 1988; Liu, 1990). With forced-choice items offering alternative explanations for achievement events, it yields separate dimensional scores by valence.

In the Attributional Style Questionnaire (ASQ)(Peterson et al., 1982), respondents indicate the major cause for hypothetical situations divided by valence and domain, then locate this cause on the dimensions of locus, stability, globality, and (in some cases) controllability. The ASQ permits respondents to supply relevant causal categories, some of which may be unique to the Chinese. By locating these freely offered causes on the dimensional continua, respondents communicate their understanding of the meaning of the causes, and generate etic scale values that can be used in cross-cultural comparisons. Like the MMCS, the ASQ yields dimension scores for domain–valence combinations. The scale has been used in Taiwan, the PRC, and the United States (Crittenden, 1989, 1991; Huang et al., 1983; He, 1991; Lee and Seligman, 1993; Lin, 1989; Zhang and Wang, 1989).

Another approach to achieving dimensional scores is to ask direct questions about dimensions of causes for events, without specifying the causes. Hau and Salili (1989) have used this approach for achievement events in Hong Kong; Liu (1992) employed it in Taiwan and the United States for affiliation events.

For achievement, investigators have also used respondent percentage allocation of influence on an event among several causes (research in Taiwan; Yang, 1982) and Triandis's (1972) antecedent-consequent method (research in Hong Kong; Salili and Mak, 1988). For affiliation, Morris (research in the United States; 1993) has employed counterfactual reasoning to elicit necessary causes for particular affiliation events. Yang and Ho (1988) asked respondents in Hong Kong and Taiwan to indicate whether a specific cause (*yuan*) is operating in a situation, their degree of agreement with popular sayings about the cause, the extent of their belief in this cause, and examples of what it can explain.

To summarize, this review of measurement approaches reveals three problems. First, most standardized instruments for measuring attributional patterns ask respondents to react to a list of potential causes both that includes causes of limited salience to the Chinese and excludes other, more salient causes, and that rests on dubious assumptions about the underlying dimensionality of those causes. Second, although use of multiple measurement strategies enriches a research program, some commonality of measures across studies and groups is essential for the accumulation of findings and valid comparisons. Third, despite the desirability of extending research to non-student Chinese, most available instruments employ scenarios and causes that may limit their applicability to other social groups.

Recommendation 4

The fourth recommendation is that researchers develop and validate measuring instruments that are grounded in research on the salience and dimensionality of causes for Chinese respondents.

Recommendation 5

The fifth recommendation is that we use these valid, consensual, culturally appropriate instruments to elucidate how Chinese attributional patterns vary with social circumstance and locale.

CROSS-CULTURAL COMPARISONS OF CAUSAL ATTRIBUTION PATTERNS

A few studies have included Chinese student samples in cross-cultural comparisons of causal attribution patterns, using several measurement approaches. We review these studies grouped by measurement strategy.

Comparisons Using Lefcourt's Causality Scale

Chandler et al. (1981) and Chandler, Shama, and Wolf (1983) have used Lefcourt's MMCS with students in five countries, and Bond (1982) has administered it to Chinese students in Hong Kong. More recently, Yan and Gaier (1994) have used the MMCS to compare achievement attributions among a mixed group of Chinese students in the United States, three other groups of Asian students in the United States, and domestic American students. With these data taken from all three studies, we can locate the two groups of Chinese students—in Hong Kong and in the United States—with respect to their peers elsewhere.

Achievement

In their achievement attributions, the Hong Kong students and the Chinese students in the United States were similar to other students in how they ranked the importance of causes. In explaining success, students generally rated effort as most important, followed in order by ability, task (or context), and luck (Chandler et al., 1981; Yan and Gaier, 1994); only the Hong Kong students varied from this pattern, rating luck ahead of task. For failure, the Hong Kong students matched the general pattern reported by Chandler and his associates (1981): effort highest, followed by context, luck, and ability. In the Yan and Gaier study (1994), all groups but the Japanese rated ability after effort, but ranked ability ahead of context and luck.

Table 17.1 summarizes average and differential locus and stability in achievement attributions on the MMCS for 11 groups of university students. Both of the Chinese groups ascribed achievement events primarily to internal factors, but the Hong Kong group was less internal than any in the Chandler study, and among the groups studying in the United States, only the Japanese were less internal than were the Chinese. The two Chinese groups saw successes more than failures as internally caused. Their attributions were more self-enhancing than were those of Japanese, Korean, South African, and Yugoslavian students, but less so than were those of the Americans, Indians, and South-east Asians.

Table 17.1   Locus and Stability of Achievement Attributions on the MMCS for 11 Groups of University Students

Study/ Country	Locus		Stability	
	Overall Internality	Differential Self-Enhancement	Overall Stability	Differential Optimism
Chandler et al., 1981:				
India	4.63	7.93	−3.20	3.47
Japan	4.13	−.31	−4.74	0.71
S. Africa	4.23	3.95	−2.37	0.96
United States	5.90	4.76	−1.37	2.64
Yugoslavia	4.42	3.24	−4.06	−1.10
Bond, 1982:				
Hong Kong	3.14	4.41	−2.78	−.06
Yan and Gaier, 1994:				
Mixed Chinese	5.24	1.87	−2.04	3.57
Japan	5.04	.59	−1.72	3.65
Korea	5.37	.38	−2.22	3.24
Mixed SE Asia	5.73	3.94	−1.56	3.72
United States	6.79	4.30	−.71	3.58

On stability, the Hong Kong students shared the overall tendency to attribute achievement events to variable causes. Most non-Chinese groups and Chinese foreign students in the United States exhibited optimistic attributions for achievement; the Hong Kong students did not share this pattern.

Affiliation

Hong Kong students rated ability as the most important cause of affiliation events, followed by effort. Compared with the groups in the Chandler study

(1981), the Hong Kong Chinese emphasized ability and context more, and effort and luck less. Hong Kong students shared a common tendency to ascribe affiliation events to internal causes (Chandler et al., 1981), falling between the most (American) and least internal (Japanese). Their affiliation attributions, although slightly self-enhancing, were less so than the average.

Hong Kong students shared the common tendency to attribute affiliation events to stable causes, less stable than Americans and Indians but more than the Japanese. They also shared a general optimism for affiliation events, more optimistic than the Japanese, but less optimistic than were Chandler's other groups.

Comparisons Using the Attributional Style Questionnaire

Two studies using versions of the ASQ have included Chinese samples in cross-cultural comparisons. Crittenden (1989) has compared college students from Taiwan, Korea, the Philippines, and the United States. Lee and Seligman (1993) have contrasted mainland Chinese, Chinese-American, and domestic American students.

Across domains

In overall attributions across achievement and affiliation events, Taiwan students were the least internal among the groups in the Crittenden study. Mainland Chinese students were less internal than were either American group in the Lee and Seligman study. Overall, the attributional pattern of Taiwan students was slightly self-enhancing, less so than the Americans and Filipinos but more so than the Koreans (Crittenden, 1989). All the Lee and Seligman groups were self-enhancing; mainland Chinese students were the least so, followed by the Chinese-Americans.

All seven groups attributed events to relatively stable causes overall. Taiwan students perceived causes as less stable than did the Koreans, about the same as did the Americans, and more so than did the Filipinos. Both Chinese groups in the Lee and Seligman study attributed events to more stable causes than did the Americans. All seven groups were optimistic: Taiwan students more so than Koreans, similar to Americans, and less so than Filipinos (Crittenden, 1989). Americans were more optimistic than Chinese-Americans or mainland Chinese (Lee and Seligman).

Achievement

Crittenden (1989) has reported attributional patterns separately by domain. For achievement, Taiwan and Filipino students were less internal in locus than were American and Korean students. Taiwan and Korean students were self-effacing, whereas Filipino and American students were self-enhancing. Taiwan students were near the median on stability of perceived causes for achievement events, but they were the least optimistic group.

Affiliation

For affiliation events, the four national groups exhibited a similar, internal pattern, and all were self-enhancing, with Koreans the least so. Again, the Taiwan students were in the middle of the stability distribution. However, they were the most optimistic group concerning affiliation events (Crittenden, 1989).

Cross-cultural Comparisons Using Other Measurement Strategies

Chiu (1988) has used the IARQ to compare high school students in Taiwan and the United States. The Taiwan students were less self-enhancing in their attributions for achievement events than were the Americans.

Ng and others (1992) have compared Chinese students in Singapore with Anglo students in New Zealand on how each rate causes for good or bad achievement events. The Singaporeans rated study techniques more important. Chinese students rated study technique, effort, ability, and interest as the most important causes of success. New Zealanders saw the same four causes as most important, with study technique ranked fourth. To explain failure, Singapore students rated effort as most important, then study technique and difficulty, and then ability. Their New Zealand peers also rated effort first, followed by ability, interest, and difficulty.

Sun (1991) has compared foreign students in the United States from six cultural backgrounds (Chinese, Japanese, Korean, South and South-east Asian, Hispanic-American, and European) on their ratings of the importance of eight causes in determining their passing score on an English-language test. The top five causes—ability, stable effort, mood, task difficulty, and teaching quality—were the same for all six groups. Ability was first or second for each; stable effort was in the top two for all four Asian groups, but fifth for the Americans and Europeans.

In a cross-cultural study of conflict-resolution strategies, Liu (1992) has compared the attributions of marital conflicts by three groups of spouses: Chinese in Taiwan, Chinese in the United States, and Americans. The Chinese groups were less self-serving than were the Americans, but they held their spouses more responsible for negative behaviours.

Morris et al. (1993) and Morris, Nisbett, and Peng (in press) have used three methods to compare how Chinese and American observers attribute the behaviour of an actor toward others. Evaluating accounts of similar mass murders, committed by a Chinese and an American, in Chinese- and English-language newspapers, they have reported that the Chinese accounts emphasized situational causes for each event and the American accounts stressed dispositional (internal) causes. Importance ratings for different causes for these two events by Chinese and American graduate students in the United States showed a similar pattern. The Chinese graduate students also were more likely to view situational causes as necessary causes.

Summary of Cross-cultural Comparisons

Cross-cultural research thus far has used measuring instruments that vary considerably in their choice of causes, and how they relate causes to underlying dimensions. We cautiously offer a few generalizations that seem to hold for more than one measurement strategy.

First, offered a list of causes, and regardless of the domain or valance of the events to be explained, Chinese students do not differ markedly from other students in how they rate the relative importance of those causes in determining events in which they are the actor. Like students around the world, they see effort and ability as potent causes of these events.

Overall, the attributions of Chinese students are internal in locus, but less so than are those of Americans; the attributions of Chinese-Americans fall in between the other two in terms of internality. Chinese students in general are less self-enhancing than are Americans, Indians, and South-east Asians, but more so than are Koreans and Japanese.

The Chinese offer less self-enhancing attributions for achievement than for affiliation events. Their attributions are somewhat optimistic, more so for affiliation than for achievement events. When explaining another person's social behaviour, Chinese students' attributions are more external than are those of American students.

Unfortunately, even studies using the same basic instrument often introduce modifications and procedural idiosyncracies, making valid comparisons across studies difficult. Thus, we cannot characterize variation in attributional patterns among Chinese in different societies or subgroups, and we cannot generalize from one Chinese cultural context to another.

CONSEQUENCES OF CAUSAL ATTRIBUTIONS

Causal Attribution and Achievement

Much attribution research among the Chinese has drawn on Weiner's (1974, 1986) attributional theory of achievement motivation. This theory is concerned with an actor's self-attributions of success and failure, because of their motivational implications for achievement. Weiner began with a simple taxonomy of four causes reflecting the locus and stability dimensions. Based on open-ended causal accounts offered by respondents, however, he has added the third dimension of controllability to his taxonomy. The theory specifies the influence of antecedent conditions on perceived causes, and it links these causal attributions to subsequent behaviour through their influences on affects and goal expectations. Motivation to engage in a particular behaviour is viewed as a function of the value of a goal and the expectation that the behaviour will lead to the goal. The theory has been used to predict emotions, expectations, achievement motivation, and behaviour (persistence, effort, and performance).

In Weiner's theory, the locus of causes influences behaviour through the emotions, especially those related to self-esteem, that affect attraction to the goal. For successes, internal causes lead to feelings of confidence and pride, whereas external causes result in outward-directed emotions such as gratitude. For failures, internal attributions are associated with guilt or self-blame, and external causes, with anger or frustration. The stability of causes influences expectations for future performance. A person approaches an achievement task with expectations about the likelihood of success that increase or decrease in response to the outcome. The stability of perceived causes affects the magnitude of these shifts: an outcome ascribed to stable causes has more influence than does one attributed to variable causes.

A number of studies conducted in the 1980s in Taiwan have correlated attributional patterns of students with achievement-related variables suggested by Weiner (Chang, 1982; Cheng and Yang, 1977; Chung and Hwang, 1981; Hung and Yang, 1979). Taiwanese students of various ages have tended to appear relatively internal and slightly self-effacing in their attributions for achievement events (Cheng and Yang, 1977; Hung and Yang, 1979). Taiwanese students have assigned highest importance to effort as a cause of performance, and have attributed little importance to luck. High-achieving students, those with high self-esteem, and those strongly motivated toward success have tended to be more internal and self-serving in their achievement attributions. Internal attribution of success has been shown to enhance expectations of future success, and ascribing failure to a lack of ability has exacerbated failure expectancies (Chung and Hwang, 1981; Kuo, 1983, 1984).

Empirical studies in the PRC have also related attributions to achievement (Liu, 1990; Shi, 1992). College students have tended to give individual-oriented attributions for success, and social- or chance-oriented attributions for failure. Junior high school students became more self-serving in their achievement attributions when placed in a more competitive situation; their achievement behaviour was enhanced by a tendency to attribute success to internal, stable causes or failure to internal, variable causes.

An ambitious research program by Hau and Salili (Hau, 1992; Hau and Salili, 1989, 1990, 1991) has addressed the role of attributions in achievement among Chinese students in Hong Kong. A variety of instruments developed in this program for measuring achievement attributions would be useful to researchers in other Chinese societies. The research has focused on the achievement goals (learning versus performance) and attributional patterns of students of various ages, relating these to countervailing sociocultural forces: greater emphasis on effort as opposed to ability in traditional Chinese culture, and an emphasis on performance in a modern, highly competitive educational system. The program has produced seven separate but related studies with systematically varied age groups, methodologies and measurement strategies, and research questions.

The studies have reached a number of findings concerning attribution. The first is that students of all ages perceived effort and study skill as the most important causes of performance. Ability usually ranked between third and fifth among 13 causes.

Students' attributions for academic performance were a function of their age, achievement goals, achievement, theories of intelligence, and attitudes toward diligent and intelligent people. Students with stronger learning-achievement goals attributed more to internal and controllable causes, study at home, interest in study, and less to home conditions. Those with stronger performance-achievement goals attributed more to uncontrollable causes, exam difficulty, and intelligence.

Higher achievers tended to attribute performance more to internal, controllable, global, and stable causes. Older high-achievers resembled younger children in their greater perceived and expected attainment, and their attributions. Students who favoured diligent persons more than intelligent ones ascribed performance more to study skills and less to teachers and ability. Those who favoured intelligence attributed more to teachers' help and luck.

Two empirical studies have addressed the affective consequences of attributing achievement outcomes to effort instead of ability. In Taiwan college students associated attributions to effort with being happy and relaxed and attributions stressing ability, with pride; for failure, attributions to effort were linked with self-blame and shame, and emphasis on ability evoked anxiety, loss of confidence, and feelings of incompetence (Yang, 1982). Students in mainland China and the United States equally saw a lack of effort as an antecedent to guilt, but the Americans were more likely to associate effort with feeling pride (Stipek, Weiner, and Li, 1989).

Having reviewed research on achievement motivation in Taiwan, Yang and Yu (1987, 1989; see also Yu, this volume) are developing a model of social-oriented achievement motivation to parallel Weiner's individual-oriented theory. Social-oriented achievement motivation (SOAM) shows a tendency to strive toward an externally determined, challenging goal in a socially selected way; individual-oriented achievement motivation (IOAM) displays a tendency to choose a challenging personal goal and the strategies for attaining it (Yang and Yu, 1989, p. 2). The relative and absolute strengths of SOAM and IOAM for achievement will vary from person to person and across cultures, with higher average SOAM in collectivist, Chinese societies, and higher IOAM in individualist societies. The dominant achievement motive determines a person's causal attributions for the outcomes and the resulting emotional responses, changes in goal expectations, and subsequent behaviour. SOAM attributions involve help or hindrance from others, interpersonal networks (*guanxi*), group effort, fatalistic conditions such as fate (*mingyun*) or luck (*yunqi*), and the social desirability of one's personal qualities. SOAM emotions include enhancement or loss of face (*mianzi*), a sense of collective pride or shame, gratitude, anger, anxiety about punishment, and relaxation due to exemption from negative reinforcements. The relations among attributions, emotions, expectations, and achievement motivation have not yet been articulated for SOAM.

Consistent with SOAM theory, Shi (1992) has found three factors in the ratings of causes for achievement by mainland Chinese students: individual-oriented, social-oriented (but not necessarily external), and chance-oriented. Taking into consideration ratings of Weiner's four causes, Chu (1989) has reported that Taiwan university students with higher SOAM attributed achievement outcomes more to luck, and those with higher IOAM had higher effort ratings. We have found no studies explicitly testing this integrative theory.

Recommendation 6

The sixth recommendation proposed here is that researchers further explicate how cultural context affects achievement within competitive educational systems, by replicating studies from the Hau and Salili research program in other Chinese societies.

Recommendation 7

The seventh recommendation is that researchers coordinate their efforts, based on Yang and Yu's theory, to assess variation in types of achievement motivation and their consequences across and within Chinese societies.

Causal Attribution and Mental Health

Clinical psychologists interested in learned helplessness (Abramson et al., 1978; Peterson and Seligman, 1984) have identified a 'depressive' attributional style that predisposes a person to psychological depression as a response to aversive outcomes. Four dimensions of perceived causes are critical for explaining depression: locus, stability, globality, and controllability. The dimension of locus affects self-esteem, where stability, globality, and controllability are related to the generality of expectations across time and contexts. According to the theory, vulnerability to depression is increased by tendencies to attribute bad outcomes to internal, stable, global, and uncontrollable factors, and good outcomes to external, variable, specific, and uncontrollable causes.

The theory is supported by correlational studies in Taiwan and the PRC. Using the ASQ, with a sample of college students in Taiwan, Huang et al. (1983) have found depression scores to be positively associated with internal, stable, and global attributions for bad events, external causes for good events, variable causes for good achievement events, and uncontrollable causes for good or bad events. They have also reported that attributing bad events to *yuan* may protect against depression, whereas *yuan* attributions for good events may enhance risk. In similar studies of university students in Taiwan (Crittenden and Fugita, 1987) and the PRC (Zhang and Wang, 1989), depression scores were negatively related to the tendencies to see the causes of good events as more stable and global than are those for bad events. The tendency to attribute good events more internally than bad events was negatively correlated with depression in Taiwan, but was not significant in the mainland Chinese sample.

Supporting results also have been found with other instruments in studies of junior high students in Taiwan. Using the HYAS, personal and social adjustment was positively related to a tendency to attribute good events to internal causes, negatively related to attributions of bad events to internal causes, and negatively related to attribution of good or bad events to external causes (Lin, 1979). Using Weiner's four causes, tendency to attribute failures to lack of ability (internal, stable, and uncontrollable) was negatively related, and attribution of successes to internal causes (ability, effort) was positively related to self-esteem and well-being (Chung and Hwang, 1981).

Although studies of attributional patterns and mental health among Chinese students consistently have supported learned helplessness, these studies have not provided rigorous tests of the theory. They were not designed to address the precise causal relationship between attributional style and mental health, nor were they analysed so as to avoid the confounding of causal dimensions.

Recommendation 8

The eighth recommendation to be proposed here suggests that research on attributional style and mental health should involve more rigorous multivariate analyses and longitudinal designs than has been seen in the past.

Identities and Social Functions of Attributions

Evidence indicates that attributions that are communicated have implications for the identities of the persons who offer and receive them (Crittenden, 1989; Crittenden and Bae, 1994).

Personal Identities

In studies of audience reactions to attributional patterns, students in Hong Kong (Bond, Leung, and Wan, 1982) and Taiwan (Crittenden, 1987, 1991) inferred greater social responsibility and likeability from a self-effacing pattern, and greater productivity and competence from a self-serving pattern. An internal pattern implied a more productive and likeable offerer, without detracting from perceived social responsibility (Crittenden, 1987). In Taiwan, male and female students inferred the same traits from particular attributional patterns, but they differed on the gender relevance of these traits (Crittenden, 1991). Women saw social responsibility as feminine, but men saw it as gender-neutral. Both groups associated competence with masculinity. These results suggest that internal attributions may be socially desirable for Chinese students. However, a differential locus for good and bad events represents a choice whether to claim social responsibility, or productivity and competence. It appears that women students must choose between femininity and competence.

In choosing an attributional account, the offerer responds to requirements of the social context. Hong Kong students offered more self-serving attributions for their performance in a competitive game anonymously than they did in public (Wan and Bond, 1982). Students in the PRC completed the ASQ in a more self-serving way when they were instructed to take it as a test to measure competence for a special job position than when they took it ostensibly as a self-test (He, 1991).

Interpersonal Functions

Various scholars (Bond and Hwang, 1986; Hwang, 1987; King and Bond, 1985; Yang, in press) have argued that the Chinese identity or face (*mianzi*) consists primarily of a person's relationships (*guanxi*) with others and group memberships. Thus it is not surprising that the Chinese would use attributions to promote and maintain social harmony and power. Chinese students modify their attributional accounts to influence the audience reactions. Mainland Chinese students indicate that to escape blame and mitigate the anger of the offended party, they would attribute a social breach on their part to uncontrollable, rather than controllable causes (Stipek et al., 1992).

Attributions can exacerbate or ameliorate conflict within a relationship. In a cross-cultural study of married couples in Taiwan and the United States (Liu,

1992), attributional patterns were related to both relationship norms (communal versus exchange-oriented; see Hwang, 1987) and strategies for resolving marital conflicts. Self-serving and spouse-blaming attributional styles were associated with contentious, rather than problem-solving, conflict-resolution strategies. For the Taiwanese couples, attributional style was not directly related to commitment to the relationship. Attributional styles may influence relationship quality less in collectivist cultures that regulate behaviour through norms rather than through individual, cognitive reconstruction processes (Liu, 1992).

Attributions offered by individuals in groups have implications for the identities of other group members. People are socialized to enhance and defend the reputations of the groups to which they belong, so the expectation of modesty for individual attributions is reversed for group-level attributions. Hong Kong students evaluated their partners in a competitive, interdependent task more favourably if they offered group-serving, rather than group-effacing, attributions for the group's performance (Bond, Chiu, and Wan, 1984).

Inter-group Attributions

Attributions also have implications for the social identities that come from group memberships. Tajfel's (1981, 1982) social identity theory posits that individuals define themselves in terms of their social groups and, to enhance their own social identity, use inter-group comparisons that favour the in-group. For example, they tend to give dispositional attributions for negative behaviour by an out-group member, and more external explanations for positive out-group behaviour (Pettigrew, 1979).

Students in competing Hong Kong universities offered attributions that favoured the in-group to explain group differences (Hewstone, Bond, and Wan, 1983). In a study of gender-group comparisons among university students (Bond, Hewstone, Wan, and Chiu, 1985), Hong Kong men and Americans consistently showed in-group–favouring biases in explaining gender-typed behaviour. Hong Kong women, however, did so only for feminine-typed behaviours and only in relative privacy. This Hong Kong result has been interpreted as resulting from gender inequality and a shared commitment to maintaining harmony between men and women. Hewstone and Ward (1985) have considered inter-group attributions among Chinese and Malay university students in Malaysia and Singapore. Attributions by Chinese favored the in-group in neither country, whereas the Malays were in-group–serving in both settings. American reporters gave in-group–serving newspaper reports of mass murders committed by a Chinese or an American, but Chinese reporters did not (Morris, 1993). These results suggest that the Chinese seldom display in-group–serving attributions, but they are more likely to do so in an environment conducive to non-conflictual inter-group competition.

Recommendation 9

The ninth recommendation to be made here suggests more research be conducted on the roles of attribution processes in Chinese social relationships, interactions, and groups.

ANTECEDENTS OF CAUSAL ATTRIBUTION PATTERNS

Virtually all of the research reviewed in this chapter has used Chinese students as subjects. Consequently, we know little about how attribution processes operate in the lives of other Chinese. What we do know suggests that attributional patterns and processes may differ for Chinese in differing social circumstances. All Chinese share a common cultural heritage, but modern Chinese culture is not a unitary whole. Chinese societies vary in socio-political history and circumstances, and thus their cultures have evolved somewhat differently. Within Chinese societies, rapid social and economic change has created generational and sectoral differences in values and perspectives (Yang, 1986, in press).

House (1981) has argued for research specifying proximal social and cultural variables that link individual behaviour and processes to culture. A self-presentational perspective (Crittenden, 1989; Crittenden and Bae, 1994) links attributions to the cultural aspects (norms, values, expectations, and identity structures) of social context (society of residence, location in the social structure, and situation).

Persons must know each other's identities in order to coordinate their conduct in social interaction. An attributional account helps its audience identify and evaluate its author, and the person offering the account often tries to influence the identity inferences drawn. Persons generally want to associate themselves with desirable identities and disclaim undesirable ones. The norms operating in a particular context determine which accounts are socially approved; people tend to conform to these approved accounts in managing their social identities. Attributional norms vary across cultures, and persons tend to display attributional patterns that imply identities that the culture group values and considers appropriate. They do so consciously to gain approval, or unconsciously because they have internalized the cultural norms.

Attributional accounts vary with the information, values, and interests of the audience, the salience of various social roles held by the offerer, and the status and roles of both the offerer and the audience. Accounts may be chosen to influence audience inferences about the offerer's identity, or to nurture the role relationships that underlie the identities. These aspects of sociocultural context indirectly influence attributions, through their influence on the values and expectations of various parties to the interaction. Study of these influences is essential to a general conception of attribution processes among the Chinese.

Attribution research conducted on students contributes to knowledge about academic achievement processes, an important topic in modern Chinese societies. However, the greatest potential yield of attribution research is understanding how varied groups in Chinese societies interpret the events in their diverse lives, and how these interpretations affect their behaviour and well-being. In areas other than school achievement, we cannot generalize from student results to an understanding of attribution processes among all Chinese.

Recommendation 10

The tenth recommendation to be put forward here is to extend research on Chinese attributional patterns and their consequences beyond student populations and school settings.

CONCLUSION

Chinese culture is a gold-mine for developing a comparative social psychology, given its longevity and tradition of diaspora, which have led to the evolution of separate Chinese societies. Because of the variety of circumstances in which Chinese individuals find themselves today, studies of Chinese causal attributional processes are necessarily comparative. Such studies, achieved through development of consensual methodology and cooperative research among Chinese scholars, can expand our understanding of attributional processes and, at the same time, provide a model for cross-cultural psychology in general. This review has attempted to illustrate the difficulty and complexity of the task and to offer helpful suggestions for approaching the coming work.

NOTES

I am indebted to Kwang-Kuo Hwang, Ling-lan Lin, Shu-fen Tseng, Colleen Ward, and Kuo-Shu Yang for help in locating source materials, to Amy Wang and Shu-fen Tseng for translating and explaining Chinese-language texts, and to Kwok Leung and Kelvin Rodolfo for helpful comments.

Chapter 18

Chinese Communication Processes

Ge Gao, Stella Ting-Toomey, and William B. Gudykunst

The academic study of communication began in the United States after the First World War (Littlejohn, 1992). The academic study of communication in Chinese culture, however, is a relatively recent phenomenon. In many respects, the field of communication is predominately Eurocentric. While there has been only a little empirical research conducted on Chinese communication, work in Chinese philosophy, psychology, and sociology provides the foundation for a preliminary discussion of Chinese communication processes. In this chapter, we describe the rules and norms which guide Chinese communication. We begin by defining communication and conceptualizing the process of communication in Chinese culture. Next, we examine the characteristics of Chinese communication: implicit communication, listening-centredness, politeness, the insider effect on communication, and face-directed communication strategies. Finally, we conclude by suggesting directions for future research. Throughout the chapter, we demonstrate the inter-relationship between culture and communication and how Chinese communication processes only can be understood and interpreted in their cultural context.

CONCEPTUALIZING CHINESE COMMUNICATION PROCESSES

Culture influences many facets of human communication. In Chinese culture, communication and its distinctive functions are governed by Chinese cultural orientations. In this section, we present one view of Chinese communication. In addition, we examine some of the premises of Chinese culture and their impact on Chinese communication processes.

Defining Communication

Communication is a foreign concept to the Chinese; no single word in Chinese serves as an adequate translation for the term. Many Chinese equate communication with talk. In Chinese culture, people who have the gift of talking, or *neng shuo*, and are skillful in talking, or *hui shuo*, often are recognized as experts in communication. Communication, therefore, only pertains to a 'privileged' few. This cultural orientation helps explain why communication has not been given a great deal of attention in the Chinese academic domain.

While there is not a single Chinese term that corresponds to the word communication, there are several Chinese translations of the concept. The three most commonly used translations include *jiao liu* (to exchange), *chuan bo* (to disseminate), and *gou tong* (to connect). *Gou tong*, the ability to connect among people, is the closest Chinese equivalent for communication as it is usually used by Western scholars. According to Yan (1987), *gou tong* is the essence of human communication. *Gou tong* emphasizes the interactive nature of the communicative process. In addition, *gou tong* articulates the nature, purpose, and characteristics of communication. The notion of *gou tong* is compatible with a view of communication as 'the process by which we understand others and in turn endeavour to be understood by them. It is dynamic, constantly changing and shifting in response to the total situation' (Littlejohn, 1992, p. 7).

The study of communication focuses on messages. What message is sent, by whom, how, and in what situation, for example, are some of the important issues that are of concern to communication scholars. People are conditioned by their culture and society as to what to say, when to say it, and how to say it. Culture helps define the appropriateness of various communication behaviours such as speaking, listening, politeness, silence, and turn-taking. The culture in which individuals are socialized influences the way communication takes place. Inevitably, the outcome of any communication is affected by how messages are presented and interpreted in a particular cultural context. To achieve effective communication, therefore, requires a working understanding and knowledge of the social and cultural context in which communication takes place.

Chinese Culture and Communication

There are two ways to examine communication in a culture: etic and emic (see, for example, Berry, 1980; Gudykunst and Ting-Toomey, 1988). In the Chinese case, an etic analysis would involve a comparison of Chinese communication with communication in other cultures using culture-general constructs; an emic analysis would involve examination of culture-specific aspects of Chinese communication. To place the analysis in context, we begin with a brief etic analysis and then move on to the specific emic analysis.

The Etic approach

Etic analyses involve comparisons across cultures. For intercultural comparisons, dimensions of cultural variability are needed; the most widely used dimension of cultural variability is individualism–collectivism (Hofstede, 1980; Triandis, 1988). According to Hofstede (1980), people in individualistic cultures tend to emphasize self-actualization, individual initiatives and achievement, and an 'I' identity. The United States, Australia, and Great Britain are commonly given as examples of individualistic cultures. In collectivistic cultures, in contrast, people stress fitting in, belonging to the in-group, and maintaining a 'we' identity (Hofstede, 1980). Korea, Taiwan, Hong Kong, and China are commonly given as examples of collectivistic cultures. In addition, a list of the unique characteristics of collectivistic cultures has been advanced by Triandis (1988). He argues that the in-group (for example, the family, the work unit) is very important in collectivistic cultures. In such a culture, the needs, goals, and beliefs of the in-group often take precedence over those of the individual. As a result, a person in an individualistic culture exists as an independent entity, while a person in a collectivistic culture is defined by his or her in-groups. Within this broad cultural framework, Chinese culture exemplifies the characteristics of collectivism (see also Bond, this volume). The collectivistic aspects of Chinese culture, such as using a 'we' identity, meeting the needs and expectations of others, and being a part of the in-group, shape Chinese communication processes.

Hall's (1976) schema of low- and high-context communication provides another etic framework for cross-cultural comparisons. According to Hall, low-context communication emphasizes directness, explicitness, and verbal expressiveness. High-context communication, on the other hand, involves indirectness, implicitness, and nonverbal expressions. That is, 'most of the information is either in the physical context or internalized in the person, while very little is in the coded, explicit, transmitted part of the message' (Hall, 1976, p. 79). Hall's description of the high-context style of communication provides a characterization of Chinese communication in general.

While individualism–collectivism and communication styles represent two different aspects of a culture, the dimension of individualism–collectivism appears to be linked closely to the preferred mode of communication. According to Gudykunst and Ting-Toomey (1988), people in most individualistic cultures tend to use low-context communication, while high-context communication is utilized by people in most collectivistic cultures. The extent to which one culture is more individualistic than another helps explain holistic differences in many aspects of human behaviour including communication (see, for example, Gudykunst and Ting-Toomey, 1988; Triandis, 1988). The collectivistic orientation of Chinese culture, therefore, can be utilized to interpret Chinese communication processes. Nevertheless, to understand how Chinese communication is affected and guided by certain rules and norms in the culture requires not only a general knowledge of the global position of Chinese culture, but also a specific inquiry into the idiosyncratic nature of the culture itself.

The Emic approach

The core to understanding Chinese communication is the self. Traditionally, the Chinese self is defined by relations with others (Gao, 1994). As Zhuangzi (c. 330–286 BC) wrote, 'When you look at yourself as *part* of the natural scheme of things, you are equal to the most minute insignificant creature in the world, but your existence is great because you are in *unity* with the whole universe' (emphasis added; cited in Dien 1983, p. 282). This quotation suggests that the Chinese make little distinction between themselves and others (Hsu, 1971), because the self would be incomplete if it were separated from others. The self can attain its completeness only through integration with others and with its surroundings. The relational aspects of the self influence all aspects of Chinese communication. As Bond (1991) argues, verbal exchanges in Chinese culture are means of expressing affect and of strengthening relationships, while argumentative and confrontational modes of communication are avoided at all costs. Chinese communication, therefore, serves affective and relational purposes.

The Chinese self is also defined by hierarchy and role relationships. In a hierarchical structure, status is specified clearly and behaviours are guided by the principle of *li* (ritual propriety), that is, doing the proper things with the right people in the appropriate relationships (Bond and Hwang, 1986). In the context of Chinese culture, the sense of 'self' is embedded within multiple prescribed roles. As Cheng (1990) argues, it is the role, not the self, which determines the behaviour. A state of *he* (harmony) can be achieved if one maintains appropriate role relationships, is other-oriented, and accepts the established hierarchy.

Harmony is the foundation of Chinese culture. The Chinese term *he* denotes 'harmony', 'peace', 'unity', 'kindness', and 'amiableness'. *He* permeates many aspects of Chinese personal relationships. The Chinese are inspired to live in harmony with family members, to be on good terms with neighbors, to achieve unity with the surrounding environment, and to make peace with other nations. Seeking harmony thus becomes a primary task in the self's relational development and interpersonal communication. The appropriateness of any communication event, for example, is influenced by the notion of harmony.

In sum, both the etic and emic analyses of Chinese culture suggest that Chinese communication is affectively based and relation-oriented. This cultural tendency leads to a style of communication often characterized as indirect and reserved. Specifically, in Chinese culture, communication is not primarily utilized to affirm self-identity or to achieve individual needs and goals. Rather, the importance of preserving peaceful relations with family, others, and the surrounding environment, as well as acting appropriately with appropriate people in appropriate situations, determines effective communication. The primary functions of communication in Chinese culture are to maintain existing relationships among individuals, to reinforce role and status differences, and to preserve harmony within the group. In the next section, we address the specific characteristics of Chinese communication and their primary functions.

CHARACTERISTICS OF CHINESE COMMUNICATION

The specific functions of Chinese communication dictate a set of communication behaviours that are unique to Chinese culture. There are five major characteristics of the Chinese communication process: *hanxu* (implicit communication), *tinghua* (listening-centredness), *keqi* (politeness), *zijiren* (a focus on insiders), and *mianzi* (face-directed communication strategies). We examine these characteristics and their applications to understanding Chinese communication in this section.

Implicit Communication

The Chinese word *han* may be translated as 'to contain', 'to embody', or 'to reserve'. The term *xu* means 'to store' or 'to save'. Thus, the Chinese phrase *hanxu* refers to a mode of communication (both verbal and nonverbal) which is contained, reserved, implicit, and indirect. *Hanxu* is considered a social rule in Chinese culture (Yu and Gu, 1990). That is, *hanxu* defines appropriate communication in various social and relational contexts. To be *hanxu*, one does not spell out everything, but leaves the 'unspoken' to the listeners.

The practice of *hanxu* (to be implicit) in Chinese communication is compatible with the conceptualization of self in a relational context. An implicit style of communication enables one to negotiate meanings with others in interpersonal relationships, and to help maintain existing relationships among individuals without destroying group harmony. The Chinese say that when there are things left to be said, there is room for 'free advance and retreat'. It is not uncommon for two people to have good feelings toward each other, for example, but never to express them overtly because both fear that direct communication may place them in an unmanageable situation and thus cause damage to their existing relationship.

The value of *hanxu* also explains the importance of nonverbal communication in Chinese culture. Meanings often reside in metamessages: a hand movement, a smile, and a shrug, for example, convey embedded meanings. In addition, nonverbal communication often provides important cues for interpretation of verbal messages. Consistent with Hall's (1976) conceptualization of high-context communication, Chinese communication emphasizes the nonverbal more than the verbal aspects of communicative activity.

Hanxu involves a lack of expressiveness that is apparent in the everyday life of the Chinese. As Hsu (1971) indicates, Chinese are socialized not to openly express their personal emotions, especially strong and negative ones. To a Chinese, extreme emotions often are viewed as sources of various health problems, and moderation in emotional expressions is essential to achieving one's internal balance (Bond, 1993). *The Yellow Emperor's Classic of Internal Medicine* states, 'When joy and anger are without moderation, then cold and heat exceed all measure and life is no longer secure' (cited in Bond 1993, p. 254).

Empirical observations suggest that emotional expressions such as love, anger, joy, and depression are kept covert in Chinese culture. Monitoring overt emotional expression is the basic rule of human interaction. In interpersonal relationships, however, such as social, romantic, or marital relationships, the Chinese rarely verbalize their love, and love often is expressed through caring and helping one another (Potter, 1988). Unspoken actions, not words, are emphasized in Chinese communication. *Hanxu* also influences how joy and anger are expressed. For instance, a Chinese person is rarely seen jumping up and down upon receiving a piece of good news. Chinese insist that a child should not show feelings of anger, disappointment, or vengeance (Smith, 1991). By not showing joy, sadness, or anger, the Chinese avoid imposing their feelings on others and thereby maintain harmony (Bond, 1993; Bond and Hwang, 1986).

Support for the existence of *hanxu* can be found in cross-cultural and clinical research. Studies have shown that Hong Kong Chinese, for example, have more rules about controlling emotional expression than do respondents from individualistic cultures (Argyle, Henderson, Bond, Iizuka, and Contarello, 1986). In a clinical context, Taiwanese informants have been seen to be reluctant to reveal their deep and private ideas and feelings. Requesting or freely expressing such information is seen as 'embarrassing' and 'shameful'

(Kleinman, 1980). According to Kleinman, personal ideas, values, and feelings often are conveyed indirectly through descriptions of situations.

Furthermore, *hanxu* dictates a style of communication that emphasizes nonverbal behaviour and an indirect mode of communication. A Belgian business man, for example, feels that the Chinese with whom he works never tell him directly their intentions or goals (Bi, 1994). Zhang (1994) states, 'I feel Chinese are too *hanxu* (implicit). They always talk in a roundabout way and never get to the point. They rarely show their emotions such as happiness or anger and feelings for their parents, siblings, and friends often are buried deep in their hearts' (p. 99). Chinese also report greater confidence in their ability to predict other people's behaviour based on indirect expressions in romantic relationships than do Caucasian Americans (Gao, 1992). The Chinese rely more on information that is indirect and nonverbal to reduce their uncertainty about others in personal relationships.

Listening-centredness

Two important components of the communication process are the speaker and the listener. (The distinction between the speaker and the listener is artificial, but necessary to make our point clear.) Speakers must be aware what and how they communicate; listeners must be able to understand and interpret the message received. Given that individuals in Chinese culture need to position themselves in the hierarchical structure and to perform their roles accordingly, the role of speakers and listeners is determined by existing status and role relationships.

In Chinese culture, there are conditions associated with speaking, and not everyone is entitled to speak. People only voice their opinions when they are recognized. Recognition often is derived from one's expertise on a subject due to years of experience, education, or a power position. A spoken 'voice', thus is equated with seniority, authority, experience, knowledge, and expertise. As a result, listening becomes a predominant communication activity. The cultural belief that a good child is one who shows listening-centredness (*tinghua*, 'listens talk') can be found not only in the family context, but also in various situations beyond the family. In the Chinese family, children are socialized to take in what their parents say. Obedient children are those who listen but do not voice their own opinions. One often hears parents telling their children to *bie chazui* (don't interrupt) during family conversations. The ability to listen is, therefore, highly emphasized as a major communicative activity for children. The rationale that parents are more experienced and have more authority in the family provides support for the child's passive involvement. Speaking is reserved for the parents.

This observation regarding the relative roles of parents and children is supported by empirical research. Smith (1991) observed clear roles of communication at the dinner table in Taiwan. The eldest men in the family engage in most of the talking, while the children listen and support their elders with occasional comments. The children are to respect but not challenge their elders (Smith, 1991). When a child challenges a parent verbally (*huanzuei*, talks back), it is considered a disobedient behaviour and harmony in the family is disrupted.

In order to maintain the existing status and role relationships, an asymmetrical style of communication is adopted in Chinese societies. The hierarchical structure of the family and its role differentiation are created and reinforced when parents engage in more talking and children in more listening. Similar asymmetrical patterns of communication exist for other relationships as well. For instance, students are expected to listen to their teachers the majority of the time. They are in class to hear what the teachers have to say. Most Chinese schools emphasize listening skills, memorizing skills, writing skills, and reading skills, but rarely give importance to speaking skills. As a result, Chinese children have poor verbal fluency, because assertiveness and eloquence are considered as signs of disrespect (Liu, 1986).

This pattern of superior speaking and inferior listening also extends to work relationships. A good employee is one who practices *tinghua*, does what he or she is told, and has the willingness to meet others' expectations and to accept others' criticism (Zhuang, 1990). In most work situations, communication interaction means learning to listen and, most importantly, learning to listen with full attention. Feedback often is limited, if not entirely absent. King and Bond (1985) suggest that this type of communication is non-reciprocal and passive. It can be argued, however, that Chinese communication appears to be 'passive' in speaking, but it emphasizes 'activeness' in listening. Thus, it is essential for a speaker to have the ability to see if a message is received and/or accepted by listeners through various means, such as detecting nonverbal cues and second-guessing.

The importance of listening supports the non-confrontational way of life in Chinese culture. It is consistent with a common cultural belief that the mouth (*kou*; that is, spoken words) is the root of many misfortunes and calamities in interpersonal interactions, as expressed in the Chinese idiom *huocong koushu* (misfortunes stem from the mouth). That is, when people engage in talk, argumentation or questioning often is an inseparable part of the process. If people focus on listening, however, direct confrontations as such can be avoided. Chinese, as research shows, consider talk as less important than do Americans (Wiemann, Chen, and Giles, 1986). Research on business communication provides further support for this assessment. Chinese managers rank oral communication skills as least important in a prospective employee's preparation for a position (Hildebrandt, 1988). Hildebrandt (1988) attributes this lack of perceived need for oral communication to the Chinese managerial system which promotes acceptance but not assertiveness, argumentation, or debate. Feedback, challenging, questioning, and interrupting others tend to be reduced or absent in Chinese managerial meetings as compared to North American ones (Lindsay and Dempsey, 1985). In addition, given that communication is implicit and indirect in Chinese culture, message interpretation by the listener becomes highly important. As Yum (1991) argues, communication in Asian cultures is receiver-centred.

Politeness

Keqi (politeness) is a basic principle observed by the Chinese in their everyday communication. It is grounded in the Chinese relational concept of the self and concern for others. The ritual of *keqi* applies to all interpersonal interactions and concerns all parties involved. In the host–guest relationship, the host demonstrates *keqi* by doing everything to make the guest 'feel at home', and the guest returns *keqi* by trying not to impose on the host. This process of polite interaction is typical in Chinese culture. A Chinese person's first response to any offer, ranging from a cup of tea to a dinner invitation, often is a ritualized 'no'. 'No' here does not symbolize a rude rejection, as it might be conceptualized in some cultures, or 'self-denial' (Schneider, 1985); rather, it is an expression of politeness. The host, on the other hand, is expected to insist until the offer is accepted. By not accepting the guest's expressed wishes at face value, the host demonstrates the 'sincerity' of his or her offer (Wierzbicka, in press). Chen (1991) observes this type of ongoing exchange of politeness at the Chinese dinner table. The ritual of *keqi* (here a pattern of 'offer-decline-offer-decline-offer-accept') is often seen in Chinese host–guest interactions.

Keqi also embodies the Chinese values of modesty and humbleness. To grow up as a Chinese, one learns not to take credit for one's behaviour or be boastful in any situation. When receiving a compliment, for example, a Chinese will employ the ritual of *keqi* and automatically apologize with a phrase like 'Not really, don't be so polite'. To blatantly accept a compliment is considered impolite. This protocol when applied to interactions with people from other cultures, however, has the potential for cross-cultural misunderstanding. To Caucasian Americans, for example, the cultural norm is to 'accept' compliments (Wierzbicka, in press).

Research findings support this high regard for modesty and humbleness in Chinese culture. In order to be modest, the Chinese are less likely to take pride in their successful endeavours than are North Americans (Stipek, Weiner, and Li, 1989). Hong Kong Chinese, for example, have been documented as liking self-effacing people more than self-enhancing people, even though self-enhancing people are perceived as more competent (Bond, Leung, and Wan, 1982). This finding suggests that liking and competence are two separate issues in Chinese culture, even though a connection between liking and competence clearly exists in the United States (Tetlock, 1980). For the Chinese, observance of *keqi* is not only a self-presentational goal, but a skill essential to any type of interpersonal interaction (see also Gabrenya and Hwang, this volume).

The Insider Effect on Communication

The notion of the in-group is important in Chinese and other collectivistic cultures. In a collectivistic culture, in-groups often serve as the primary and continuing units of socialization for the individual. The needs, goals, and beliefs of the in-group often take precedence over those of the individual (Triandis, 1988).

Zijiren (insider) and *wairen* (outsider) are two important concepts in Chinese culture. The Chinese make clear distinctions between insiders and outsiders, and the distinction between the two helps the Chinese position themselves in established hierarchical and role relationships (Gao, 1994). In the family unit, for example, insiders include members of the family and relatives. Friends and others with whom one has established a special relationship are considered insiders in a social circle. Insiders in organizations may consist of people on the same hierarchical level, such as members of a production group and members of a supervisors' group. The distinction between an outsider and an insider not only places people in different relational circles, but also provides specific rules of interaction in communication. Thus, there is not an open system of communication in Chinese culture (Barnett, 1979).

This closed system of communication creates enormous difficulty for Chinese in their interactions with strangers or outsiders, because most Chinese do not feel comfortable or feel knowledgeable about dealing with strangers. Thus, interactions with strangers often are initiated by a third person (an intermediary) who is known to both parties (King and Bond, 1985). With the help of an intermediary, unpredictability, or even indifference, between outsiders can be reduced. When a dispute needs to be resolved, the intermediary chosen often is a close friend of both parties. A close friend is chosen to be the mediator because an outsider could not persuade each party to accommodate without a loss of face (Bond, 1991). Moreover, 'a *wairen* would not know what has happened. The two in conflict won't talk about their conflict to a *wairen*' (Ma, 1992, p. 274).

The insider effect also influences many other aspects of communication in Chinese culture, creating a communication context in which outsiders are excluded. The Chinese tend to become highly involved in conversations with someone they know, but they rarely speak to strangers. Strangers often do not talk to each other when waiting in a queue, on an airplane, or at a social function. Students from Hong Kong and Taiwan disclose more about themselves to in-group than to out-group members, but no difference in disclosure is found with students from the United States and Australia (Gudykunst et al., 1992). As a result, Chinese are at times perceived as cold and distant to outsiders (Bo, 1992).

Observation of this insider effect suggests that type of relationship is a critical dimension in Chinese communication processes. The nature of the relationship determines what is communicated and how information should be transmitted. One significant cultural expectation among Chinese is that insiders and outsiders should not be treated in the same way, as a recognition that insiders share a sense of unity and interdependence (Wierzbicka, in press; see also Gabrenya and Hwang, this volume). Communication with insiders can be very personal, but with outsiders it can be quite impersonal. In comparison with Americans, Chinese are more likely to pursue a conflict with a stranger than with a friend (Leung, 1988). In close relationships, especially family relationships, imperative requests are more appropriate, but interrogative requests are expected to be used with others (Wierzbicka, in press).

Schneider (1985) notes that the Chinese are more likely to express emotions with close friends than with strangers or acquaintances. Chinese managers tend to deal with problem workers by asking them to have 'heart-to-heart' conversations with their co-workers, friends, and family (Krone, Garrett, and Chen, 1992). These intermediaries are expected to influence the 'difficult' party to be more amenable. Similar processes are reportedly used in many other situations. Research also suggests that Hong Kong Chinese demonstrate more direct resistance to a group insult in an out-group situation than they do in an in-group or private situation. With regard to a personal insult, there is less direct offense in an in-group situation than in an out-group or private situation (Bond and Venus, 1991). It appears that the need to protect the image of the in-group, or the self, is heightened in the presence of an out-group.

Incidentally, one study appears inconsistent with the present argument regarding the insider effect. Ma's (1990) study of discontented responses in North American and Chinese relationships reported that type of relationship (intimate, acquaintance, and stranger) did not have an impact on the discontented responses in the Chinese sample. The small sample size (n = 20) and the use of a Chinese student sample in the United States may help explain this unexpected result. The inconsistent finding warrants further research on the insider effect on communication.

Face-directed Communication Strategies

The notion of face permeates every aspect of interpersonal relationships in Chinese culture because of the culture's overarching relational orientation. In Chinese culture, face is conceptualized in two ways: as *lian* (face) and as *mian* or *mianzi* (image). Hu (1944) defines *lian* as something that 'represents the confidence of society in the integrity of ego's moral character, the loss of which makes it impossible for him [or her] to function properly within the community' (p. 45). *Mian* or *mianzi*, however, 'stands for the kind of prestige that is emphasized in [the United States]: a reputation achieved through getting on in life, through success and ostentation' (Hu, 1944, p. 45). In other words, *mianzi* concerns the projection and the claiming of public image (Ting-Toomey, 1988). Given the relational nature of self in Chinese interpersonal relationships, how face is negotiated, managed, and maintained informs virtually all personal interactions. Face management is essential to maintaining the existing role relationships and preserving interpersonal harmony. Thus, concern for face has significant consequences in many aspects of Chinese communication processes (see, for example, Bond and Lee, 1981; Gao, 1994; Wierzbicka, in press; see also Gabrenya and Hwang, this volume).

One important aspect of Chinese communication processes involves the use of communication strategies in personal interactions. Face concern not only explains but also influences the appropriate use of various communication strategies in Chinese culture. Strategies such as gossiping, conflict management, compliance, and the use of intermediaries exemplify the importance of face in Chinese communication.

Yilun

The Chinese term *yilun* means 'to gossip' or 'to make remarks behind one's back'. Gao (1994) indicates that in Chinese culture public conversations tend to be ritualized to avoid face-threatening situations. Private conversations tend to be substantive. Consistent with this reasoning is Bond and Lee's (1981) finding that more critical comments are given about a speaker in the speaker-uninformed condition than in the speaker-informed and audience-present condition. Responses in the speaker-informed anonymous and speaker-informed face to face conditions fall in the middle. This discrepancy is explained by a

Chinese person's concern for the other's face. In a public conversation, individual views and opinions must yield to the protection of face and the observance of status differences (Bond and Lee, 1981; Yu and Gu, 1990). One way to compensate for this circumspect type of public conversation is to engage in *yilun*. According to Yu and Gu (1990), during *yilun*, Chinese can complain about superiors, parents, teachers, and others who are perceived to have control over them. The Chinese utilize the forum of *yilun* to satisfy their curiosity about others' private lives and the need to speak their true feelings.

The act of *yilun* not only facilitates expressions of true feelings, but also influences how one should behave (Gao, 1994) and relate to others (Bond, 1991). The likelihood of being a target of *yilun* often decreases when one acts appropriately and makes peace with others. *Yilun* provides a forum for public exposure and discussion of private information, and, when exercised as a lever in personal and social control, may force the receiver to take some sort of action. *Yilun* also brings one's face to light for judgement and scrutiny. To the Chinese, concern for one's face makes a person vulnerable not only to what others have said, but also to the anticipation of potential gossip. As Yu (1990) argues, the concern for what others would say usually creates unbearable pressure on a Chinese, and the fear of being criticized and ridiculed by others has a controlling effect on behaviour. Chinese, for example, are reluctant to reveal negative emotions (Cody, Lee, and Chao, 1989; O'Hair, Cody, Wang, and Chao, 1990). Kleinman and Good (1985) suggest that the Chinese conceal 'dysphoria' (depression, sadness, irritability) because it brings shame to self and family.

The communicative consequence of *yilun* can be linked to the role of self-disclosure in Chinese personal relationships. Given that private information can be a potential topic for *yilun*, and thus opens up the possibility of a public loss of face, the fear of exposure of intimate information makes one reluctant to engage in self-disclosure. Personal disclosure of face-threatening information, therefore, is limited to those with whom trust has been established and proven. Chinese students in junior high schools, for example, prefer most to disclose about themselves to their mothers, followed by their best friends, fathers, and ordinary friends regarding topics of general affairs and family. On topics related to sex, their best friends are the most preferred recipients (Yang and Hwang, 1980). This pattern is very different from that seen in other cultures. Caucasian Americans tend to use self-disclosure as a relational strategy to initiate personal relationships. The amount or level of self-disclosure is a part of the process of relationship development. It is not uncommon for a Chinese to know more about a Caucasian American classmate's personal life than that of a close Chinese friend.

Conflict management

As defined by Ting-Toomey (1988), conflict occurs in a problematic situation in which two interdependent parties perceive or have incompatible needs or goals. In Chinese culture, conflict requires active face management. Most Chinese will avoid conflict at all costs because it invites direct confrontation. According to Bond (1991), direct confrontation or initiation of any type of dispute is considered an invitation to *luan* (chaos), which disrupts the harmonious fabric of personal relationships. Smith (1991) observes that conflicts endanger good relationships between relatives, friends, neighbours, and acquaintances. When the parents of two families are involved in a conflict situation, for example, the children of the two families stop playing together.

Conflict management styles are linked closely to one's concern for face. Three face concerns have been identified: *self-face*, *other-face*, and *mutual-face* (Ting-Toomey, 1988). Ting-Toomey argues that people in collectivistic cultures are more concerned with other-face than are those in individualistic cultures. Concern for other-face often leads to a non-confrontational style of conflict management such as avoiding, obliging, and compromising. Mainland Chinese and Taiwanese report a higher degree of obliging and avoiding styles of conflict management than do their counterparts in the United States (Ting-Toomey et al., 1991). The relational self either avoids face-threatening situations or seeks a compromise so as not to make the interdependent parties lose face. This strategy of conflict management not only enables both parties to preserve harmony, but also helps affirm the relational identity of the self. When relationships are intact, the self does not lose since 'one can be serving oneself as one serves others' (Bond, 1993, p. 256).

Compliance strategies

One's concern for face also affects how disagreements or arguments are handled in a relational context. To 'give others face' requires one not to argue or disagree overtly with others in public. Thus, for the Chinese, meanings in messages cannot be negotiated in public. To negotiate conceivable meanings in public is to question authority and threaten interpersonal harmony. In business negotiations, for example, a proposal–counter-proposal style of negotiation is avoided (Hellweg, Samovar, and Skow, 1991). To the Chinese, public disagreement is a face-losing act. Consequently, when one is unavoidably involved in an argument with a friend, it becomes difficult for the two people to remain friends. To protect face and to preserve interpersonal harmony as well as the cohesion of the group, the Chinese tend to adopt an unassertive style of communication in interpersonal interactions. Chinese have learned to be unassertive by articulating their intentions in an indirect manner and leaving room for negotiations in private. This style of communication not only enables them to accomplish their own agenda, but also creates an amicable climate for future cooperation and negotiation. In Chinese culture, assertiveness does not have the positive connotations found in other cultures. Being assertive reflects the bad character of an individual and threatens the harmony and cohesion of interpersonal relationships (Bodde, 1953; Tseng, 1973).

A compliant style of communication may not appear to be compatible with honest or truthful interaction. It can be argued that engaging in face-saving and face-negotiating behaviour is considered more important than is honest and truthful communication. That is, providing the appropriate information at the appropriate time and context with the appropriate persons is a more desirable process than is honest and truthful communication. A basic rule honoured in Chinese culture is 'Honor the hierarchy first, your vision of truth second' (Bond, 1991, p. 83). Consistent with this line of reasoning, most Chinese would sacrifice their credibility to save face. One study has shown that Chinese, in comparison with Canadians, view lying as morally less wrong (McLeod and Carment, 1987).

Using intermediaries

The importance of face further accounts for the frequent use of intermediaries in conflict situations. Through mediation by a third party, the Chinese can avoid direct confrontations which often cause face damage and disruption of interpersonal harmony. As Ting-Toomey et al. (1991) indicate, the Chinese prefer to use a non-confrontational style of management in face-to-face nego-tiations.

The role of an intermediary is to protect the face of each party involved in the interpersonal conflict. Given this designated function, an intermediary often is called a 'go-between', 'mediator', or 'peacemaker' (Ma, 1992). An inter-mediary often is known to both parties to ensure fairness and neutrality. Impartiality and face maintenance for both parties in a conflict are the two key factors in any successful mediation (Ma, 1992; see also Gabrenya and Hwang, this volume). Close friends of both parties and elderly persons respected by both can be unofficial mediators (Ma, 1992), so as to exercise influence on the disputants. Chinese language specialists on a foreign negotiating team often are considered as middle persons between the two teams by the Chinese (Pye, 1982). In traditional marriages matchmakers often assume the role of go-between and are responsible for mediation if a conflict situation should arise.

CONCLUSION

The relational aspect of the self is important not only in the Chinese self-defin-ition, but also in any description of Chinese communication processes. In this chapter, we have argued that the primary functions of communication in Chinese culture are to maintain existing relationships among individuals, to reinforce role and status differences, and to preserve harmony in the group. To accomplish these objectives, several characteristics have been identified to guide a Chinese person's communication with others. Specifically, they are *hanxu*, implicit communication, *tinghua*, listening-centredness, *keqi*, polite-ness, *zijiren*, a focus on insiders, and *mianzi*, face-directed communication strategies.

The research agenda we propose for the future addresses both our concep-tual and our methodological concerns. In order to advance communication theory and research in Chinese culture, we first need to investigate how vari-ous communication events have been conceptually defined by Chinese observers and pinpoint relational properties or dimensions they possess. An understanding of culture-specific meanings of core communication constructs will help us understand and better interpret existing cross-cultural differences and overlaps. Unlike North Americans, Chinese separate disagreement from injury and disappointment, and they also exhibit a lower level of discontent to disagreement than to injury and disappointment (Ma, 1990). This finding can be attributed to how disagreement, injury, and disappointment are viewed differently in the two cultures. We presume that the Chinese would view dis-agreement as less face-threatening to personal relationships than they would injury or disappointment, because disagreement is more task-related in the Chinese interaction context than are injury or disappointment. North Americans, on the other hand, are more likely to conceptualize situations of injury or disappointment as events in which the independent self has been challenged and for which a response is warranted. North Americans tend not to acknowledge that any one message can possess multiple layers of relational meanings and face implications.

Second, we need to focus on how communication differs within Chinese culture. This area of inquiry needs to consider the impact of regional differ-ences, rural and urban contexts, and dialect variations on processes of Chinese communication. In particular, it will be necessary for future investigators to broaden their participant-selection boundaries and factor in how these differ-ences enter into their analyses. Future studies will need also to further examine and correlate various Chinese characteristics presented in this chapter. The insider effect, for example, can be used to study how different types of rela-tionships affect face management in Chinese contexts. Results such as this would advance our understanding of the impact of face on communication.

Finally, the study of Chinese communication processes needs to address some of the methodological concerns that have been highlighted and dis-cussed in the field of communication in general. More than a decade ago, Barnett (1979) argued the need for in-depth interviews, relying on sophisticat-ed content analysis, for the study of Chinese communication systems. More than a decade later, we still argue for the utility and validity of that approach. Furthermore, Chinese communication research needs to examine actual com-municative behaviours in addition to thoughts (Ma, 1990). One of the more illuminating methods involves the use of cultural scripts formulated according to lexical universals in analyzing and explaining communication patterns (Wierzbicka, in press). Wierzbicka's framework of cultural scripts promises to be much more revealing in explicating culture-specific norms and ways of communicating than have been binary labels such as 'direct' and 'indirect'. The study of interpersonal interaction in an experimental setting provides yet another useful alternative. Exploring how Chinese actually respond to a partic-ular structured situation has generated some provocative findings (see, for example, Bond and Venus, 1991; Pierson and Bond, 1982).

In the process of completing this chapter, we have realized how little theo-retical and practical research on Chinese communication has been conducted. The state of scholarship on Chinese communication is aptly summarized in the well-known Chinese phrase, '*lu chang er dao yuan*' (there is a long way to go). We hope that some of the ideas presented here will help direct the first steps in that long journey.

Chapter 19

Chinese Personal Relationships

Robin Goodwin and Catherine So-kum Tang

The field of study addressing personal relationships has expanded rapidly during the last two decades (Duck, 1988), with particular growth evident in the United States. Alongside numerous texts servicing undergraduate and graduate courses on 'personal relationships', the field has spawned two journals (the *Journal of Social and Personal Relationships* and the new *Personal Relationships*) and two rival organizations (the International Network on Personal Relationships and the International Society for the Study of Personal Relationships), each with its own series of established international conferences. This expansion has been accompanied by a growing body of literature in the most prominent of American social psychological journals, reflecting a steady shift towards an emphasis on interpersonal interactions in understanding complex social psychological processes (West, Newsom, and Fenaughty, 1992).

In spite of all this activity there has been very little study of the role and nature of personal relationships in other, non-Western cultures. The Chinese experience, in particular, has been characterized by three types of analysis. One disparate set of studies has taken relatively brief, and rarely representative, snapshots of the society and generated a number of hypotheses about Chinese interactions (see, for example, the controversy surrounding Wheeler's observations on a year in Hong Kong: Lam and Yang, 1989; Wheeler, 1988, 1989). A second set of data has used rather dated anthropological observations that do little to deal with the changing face of modern Chinese societies and the diversity of the Chinese people (compare, for example, the social experiences of rural mainland Chinese to those of entrepreneurs in the Hong Kong stock exchange). A final set of 'imposed etic' research (Berry, 1969) has aimed at comparing Chinese culture to other cultures, often by using cultural variants such as collectivism–individualism or related measures as a means of comparison (see, for example, Gudykunst, Yang, and Nishida, 1985). Such research has frequently relied on established Western scales for its methodology (Feather, 1986). While this latter work provides us with interesting insights into understanding such phenomena as 'culture shock', and illuminates some of the paths leading to cross-cultural misunderstandings, the broad nature of these projects gives only limited insight into the unique and intricate details of Chinese personal relationships.

This chapter uses the available evidence from both comparative Western and indigenous Chinese literature to address six issues. The first section asks 'What is a personal relationship in Chinese society?'. The second considers how intimate relationships are formed and maintained within Chinese societies. The third section asks how relations with close friends may differ from those patterns commonly observed in the West, while the fourth examines the particular significances of relations with kin and close family members. The fifth section considers the changing power relations between the sexes in Chinese relationships, and we conclude in the sixth section by assessing the relevance of a broad etic approach in understanding the specific sphere of Chinese personal relations.

WHAT IS A PERSONAL RELATIONSHIP IN CHINESE CULTURE?

A number of commentators have stressed the significance of personal relationships to the Chinese people (see, for example, Yang, 1992). Personal relations lie at the centre of the marked status differentials evident in Chinese society, and are most clearly seen in the Wu Lun, the five, highly scripted, cardinal relations of traditional Confucian philosophy: the relation between emperor and minister, father and son, husband and wife, brother and brother, and friend and friend (Yang, 1992; see also Gabrenya, this volume). These role relations are complemented by a host of other role relations all of which are marked by differential status. However, these 'unequal' interactions are not one-sided: rather, moral obligations to reciprocate in the appropriate form are evident on both sides, creating a network of role interdependency within Chinese societies (Yang, 1992).

Compare this sense of role obligation with the traditional Western definition of a relationship, defined by Argyle and Henderson (1985) as a 'regular social encounter over a period of time' (p. 4), and by Kelley et al. (1983) as 'an interaction of considerable duration' where the interactions between the people involved are 'strong, frequent and diverse' (p. 38). While, of course, Western conceptions recognize the significance of role relations (see, for example, Peplau, 1983), these are frequently framed in an interpersonal, rather than a macrosocial, context and rely heavily on notions of simple frequency of interaction and negotiated interpersonal roles (Argyle and Henderson, 1985). From the Western perspective, close relationships progress through a number of stages at least initially dependent on interpersonal values and needs (see, for example, Kerckhoff and Davis, 1962). Thus, close relationships in Western societies are more of an interaction between equals, an interaction which deepens in intimacy largely through a process of increasingly personal disclosure (Altman and Taylor, 1973).

We can see a second division between Chinese and Western conceptions in the notion of relationship hierarchy. While there is some evidence for a similarity in the hierarchy of relationships between the British and Chinese (see, for example, Ma, 1985), the distinction between in-group members (*zijiren*, typically kin, the romantic partner, and close friends) and the out-group (*wairen*, all those not in the in-group) appears sharper in Chinese than in other societies (Triandis et al., 1988). Yang (1992) divides Chinese relationships into three groups: *jiajen* (family members), *shoujen* (relatives outside the family, friends, neighbours, classmates, and colleagues), and *shengjen* (strangers). The membership of each group dictates different social interactions in a way quite unfamiliar in Western societies. Thus, in *jiajen* relationships, behaviour is strictly demarcated by role and duty, while in *shoujen* relations there is a more moderate reciprocity and a more conditional sense of independence. In the *shengjen* relationship there is a high degree of reciprocity and no interdependence between actors. This distinction overlaps with Hwang's (1987) concept of the three major exchange rules in Chinese societies. The first is based on the expressive tie, common within the *jiajen* relationship, and involves exchanges based largely on need. The second, the mixed tie, is based on influence and is common in the *shoujen* relationship. Finally, instrumental ties are based heavily on equity principles and are most common with strangers (that is, within *shengjen* relations).

ROMANTIC RELATIONSHIP FORMATION AND MAINTENANCE IN CHINESE SOCIETIES

Relationship Formation

The very study of initial attraction and relationship formation, and in particular the personality correlates associated with these behaviours, may be viewed as a Western phenomenon (Dion and Dion, 1988). The reasons for this cultural emphasis are complex but, as stated above, much probably stems from the individualistic nature of Western social psychological research (see Hogan and Emler, 1978). Furthermore, the significance of romantic relationships in Western societies is likely to reflect wider social variables. Environmental factors such as densely populated cities, easy mobility, and numerous means of communication have encouraged the formation of multiple voluntary relationships. The geographical diversity of the extended family in North America means that for many North Americans their ultimate sense of identity (and a major source of support) depends on an intimate partnership (Moghaddam, Taylor, and Wright, 1993).

To say that intimate romantic relationships are not important in Chinese societies would be misleading, but the dynamics underlying relationship formation do appear to differ from the Western model. A central concept in Chinese intimate relationships, and one discussed by a number of contributors to this volume, is the notion of *yuan*, 'secondary causation'. This concept, which has its origins in Buddhist teachings, stresses the significance of broad, contextual conditions that underlie the progress or failure of a relationship (Chang and Holt, 1991). Thus, individuals are 'passive recipients' of relationships, rather than active creators of them (Yang, 1992, p. 20): 'A relationship is...something which must follow its own development, extending beyond human control' (Chang and Holt, 1991, p. 51). This concept is deeply rooted in all Chinese societies, but the belief in *yuanfen* (predestined affinity) is particularly significant among the more traditional groups in Chinese culture (Yang and Ho, 1988). By emphasizing the significance of contextual factors, the role of simple interpersonal communication between partners is relegated to a less significant position in the evolution of closeness, placing relationship development in the midst of a variety of causes occurring in both this and other lifetimes (Yang and Ho, 1988). The application of this concept helps maintain social harmony by stressing the inevitability of a relationship and the lack of personal causes for relationship difficulties (Yang and Ho, 1988).

However, to 'follow *yuan*' does not necessarily mean to reject the role of the participants in the relationship's success; there is still much that can be done within the restraints of these situational forces. Lee (1985) notes how one can accumulate *yuanfen* through behaviour throughout life, and, as it is necessary to know one's *yuan* with a person early on in the interaction with them, it is important to involve oneself in relationships and search out a suitable partner. Similarly, Yang and Ho's (1988) data suggests that among university students it is the positive aspects of relationships which are attributed the force of *yuan*, with a greater recognition of personal responsibility for relationship failures.

There are other areas in which the process of relationship formation seems to differ between Chinese and Western societies. Physical attractiveness has been shown to be less important in the stereotyping of attributes among Chinese students who are studying in Canada while remaining heavily involved in the Chinese community (Dion, Pak, and Dion, 1990), and attractiveness is rated less highly as a desirable characteristic in a partner in Chinese compared to Western societies (Buss et al., 1990). Less significant, too, in partner selection are abstract personality desiderata such as 'sensitivity', 'humour' (Goodwin and Tang, 1991), and a 'romantic nature' (Chu, 1985) while, consistent with the significance of social achievement in Chinese communities (Yang, 1986), a good money sense was more keenly sought by Chinese students than by their Western counterparts (Goodwin and Tang, 1991). Initial 'mating displays' may also differ between Chinese and non-Chinese societies. In reviewing data from administrations of the Minnesota Multiphasic Personality Inventory, Feather (1986) notes how Chinese respondents often report themselves to be shy and socially withdrawn. Bond and King (1985) asked 100 students to list the primary differences between Chinese and Western societies. One of those areas most frequently cited was in sexual morality, with the Chinese perceiving themselves as less likely to wear sexy clothes and to behave provocatively.

The very nature of romantic love may also differ between Chinese and Western societies. Notions of Western love, with implications of free choice and relatively little influence from outsiders, have been thought to have little effect in Chinese societies. In a rather dramatic example, Hsu (1971, cited in Dion and Dion, 1978, p. 276) claims: 'An American asks, "How does my heart feel?" A Chinese asks "What will other people say?"'

However, more recent work suggests that although there are undoubtedly differences in the number and types of constraints put on love choices, differences between Chinese and Western conceptions of love may not be as significant as is sometimes argued. In a comparative study of American students in the US, and Chinese students from Beijing, Wu and Shaver (1993) report similar conceptions of love among Chinese and American students, with both seeing love as a 'bitter-sweet' affair. The one main difference seems to be that

Chinese are more willing to stress the negative and painful aspects of love, possibly because of the greater Chinese restriction on marital arrangements. This finding may be borne out by ethnographic investigation in the People's Republic of China (PRC). Ruan and Matsumura (1991) talk of the 'misery' of close relationships in Chinese societies, where even holding hands in public can lead to the scorn of others. In the PRC, even the opportunities for romantic contact, through dancehalls and similar institutions, has been dominated by the political whims of the Communist leadership.

There are some areas of relationship formation, however, where we can identify similar processes across Chinese and Western societies. Chang (1976) demonstrated that attitudinal similarity was an important predictor of attraction in a manner similar to that found in Western cultures (Byrne, 1971). In a later research project, Chang (1983) also stressed the significance of physical attractiveness in early relationship formation, a factor widely cited as important in most Western research (see, for example, Walster et al., 1966). Bond and Hwang (1986) suggest that on the basis of such evidence, we should be able to predict a person's desirability from the sum of the desirability of the traits they exhibit. The task for researchers, they claim, is to fill the 'black box' and specify those traits that are desirable, hypothesizing that, in the Chinese case, they are likely to be those that encourage harmonious social relationships.

We can also relate aspects of the concept of *yuan* to the Western love experience. Yang and Ho (1988) point to the significance of *yuan* in the pre-initial meeting situation, where mutual friends or matchmakers may indicate that they expect *yuan* (or no *yuan*) between the parties. The attribution of *yuan* can also improve or inhibit early acquaintances, often by acting as a 'self-fulfilling prophecy'. We suspect that this is not greatly different from the influences of peer groups in the Western, 'pre-meeting' situation, which form part of the 'scripts' that are so influential in early interactions (Sunnafrank and Miller, 1981).

What does all this allow us to say about the formation of Chinese romantic relationships? Certainly, such relationships are more than the disparate personalities and attitudes held by the individuals involved (Chang and Holt, 1991), a view still dominating Western conceptions of relationships. It is possible that, although desirability may be predicted on the basis of a summation of traits, the gulf between wanting and doing may be far more profound in Chinese culture, where both the Buddhist belief in the importance of *yuan*, plus a range of other social strictures restricting relationship formation (such as a Confucian code that restricts inter-sex interaction and, of course, parental prohibitions), may be of greater import. The contrast between desired relationships and the realistic likelihood of achieving these ideals is an important area for future research.

Sexual Behaviour

We have relatively little information about the sexual behaviour of the Chinese, partly because of the reticence of Chinese respondents to freely express themselves on this matter (Tsoi, 1985; Wen, in press), a reticence which probably reflects a wider taboo about sexual matters in traditional Chinese culture (Pan, 1990; Yen, 1990), and partly because the 'closed-door' policy evident in mainland China has made the obtaining of social statistics problematic (Fan, 1990). There is clearly also a great deal of misunderstanding about sexual matters, in particular sexual problems. In the words of Wen (in press), 'It is clear that many Chinese people still hold the folk view that sexual desire and activity need to be carefully regulated, otherwise it would be harmful to your health.' In particular, a great deal of anxiety arises from practicing masturbation, particularly among young males.

There is evidence, however, of an increasing openness in Chinese cultures towards the public discussion of sexual issues (Liu, 1990; Zhou, 1990), although there remain great differences in terms of age, education, and social status in the development of such ideas. In a large comparative study of Taiwanese and mainland Chinese (*China Times Weekly*, 29 October 1993), Taiwanese residents were found to be more sexually active and adventurous than were their Mainland counterparts, while residents from both communities reported satisfaction with their sex life. Nearly half the Taiwanese (but less than a quarter of mainland Chinese) had their first sexual encounter before marriage, and although the Taiwanese reported more sexual experiences than did the mainland residents, the majority of the respondents in both samples reported only having had one sexual partner. The Taiwanese were also more tolerant of premarital and extramarital sex than were the mainland Chinese. In Hong Kong, a Family Planning Association survey (1987) revealed that 38 per cent of men and 24 per cent of women in their mid-twenties had had premarital sex.

Even more dramatically, 86 per cent of respondents in a large Shanghai study approved of premarital sex (Burton, 1990), a finding probably reflected in the recent dramatic rise in abortions (Ruan and Matsumura, 1991). Intriguingly, while there is evidence that young women no longer see premarital chastity as a major goal (see, for example, Shieh, 1990, for Taiwan; Kok, 1990, for Singapore), there is also evidence that they perceive their activities as more restrained than are those of their Western counterparts. Thus, in a study of women college students, Zhou (1990) reported that one-half of the students questioned did not approve of the sexual freedom and emancipation they saw as prevalent in 'the Western world'; the other half did not necessarily endorse such freedom, but took the perspective that this licence may be appropriate for Westerners (although not for Chinese).

Prostitution was well established on the Chinese mainland as early as the seventh century BC, and it was prevalent throughout the state until a clampdown during the 1950s followed the assumption of Communist control (Ruan and Matsumura, 1991). In the mid-1980s, however, there was a strong revival of prostitution, with some commentators claiming that it was now more prevalent than in the years prior to Communist rule (see, for example, Huai, 1989, cited in Ruan and Matsumura, 1991). A growing fear of sexually transmitted disease, however, coupled with strong ideological opposition, led to a second and harsher wave of suppression in the late 1980s (Ruan and Matsumura, 1991), although the long-term efficacy of this attempt has yet to be assessed.

As in most societies, HIV infection is a rising concern in Chinese nations. Liu (1991, 1992) estimates that approximately 5,000 people in Hong Kong are now infected with the HIV virus, but that this number is rising rapidly. Particular factors affect the propensity to engage in sex, including educational level (sexual activity does not usually begin until studying has finished) and occupation, with small business people those most likely to visit prostitutes (Liu, 1991, 1992). In mainland China, officials have claimed an extremely low rate of HIV infection (*People's Daily*, 6 August 1989), although, given the ideological fallout associated with this disease, accurate figures are difficult to obtain. What is clear is that information is still only very limited, and practically nothing is known about the sexual activities of some social groups, such as divorced women.

Married Life

Marriage is a solemn and important event in China (Xintian, 1985), and in Chinese communities throughout the world. Divorce rates are low between Chinese couples, even when the couple is living overseas (Schwertfeger, 1982). Intermarriage is still difficult for many in overseas communities, with data concerning Chinese living in the United States showing that it is most likely to occur among those who are the most unconventional and rebellious (Sung, 1990).

As in other 'Western' societies (Secord, 1982), undoubtedly much of the stability of marriage has to do with perceptions of relationship alternatives. There are considerable structural barriers to the breakup of Chinese relationships, as well as significant personal costs, such as the loss of face (Hsu, 1985). Another factor encouraging harmony is the now-familiar concept of *yuan*. From a Western viewpoint, *yuan* can be seen as a mediator of alternatives: we cannot easily find *yuan* with another, thus our alternatives are automatically reduced. Couples believe that they are together because of *yuan*, and thus their coupling is inevitable. Relationships must be cherished and tolerated (Chang and Holt, 1991), although this does not mean that the couple should not work at the relationship (Yang, 1992). One final reason to expect harmony within Chinese relationships is the need patterns of the Chinese peoples. Given the high affiliative, nurturant, and succorant needs evident among those of a more collectivist orientation (Hui and Villareal, 1989), we might anticipate that dyadic needs play a larger role among the Chinese than among their more individualist counterparts, where the individual needs of autonomy are more evident (Hui and Villareal, 1989). This cultural factor may be seen to provide a further interpersonal bonding that supplements the broader structural forces encouraging relationship commitment.

There is one important caveat to all this, however. Despite the factors promoting harmony, the strong link between politics and sexual matters in the PRC has led to some undermining of Chinese marital relationships (Ruan and Matsumura, 1991). Here, interaction between the partners is largely dictated by the State, which may allocate separate jobs to the partners, an assignment which can mean physical separation for ten years or even longer (Ruan and Matsumura, 1991). This actual interference has led to significant dissatisfaction in many Chinese marital relationships, and an increasing divorce rate.

Homosexuality

There is a small and very selective literature on homosexuality in Chinese societies. Until very recently, homosexuals in mainland China were actively persecuted, often facing charges of 'hooliganism' (Ruan and Matsumura, 1991). This suppression led not only to a fear of penal servitude, but also a feeling of emotional isolation. Contact between gay men was closeted, with meetings occurring in only a few limited places, and contact between lesbians was even further restricted. This was reinforced by a strong publicly held prejudice against lesbians and homosexual men as 'immoral' people (Ruan and Matsumura, 1991).

While there is some evidence of a slowly growing tolerance of homosexuality (Liu, 1991, 1992), few Chinese admit to being homosexual. In a recent survey (*China Times Weekly*, 29 October 1993), most Taiwanese and mainland Chinese had heard of others' homosexual experiences but only 0.3 per cent of Taiwanese and 0.1 per cent of mainland Chinese admitted to personal homosexual experiences. This can compared, for example, with the estimated 5–10 per cent of the US population who are predominantly homosexual (Harry, 1990).

RELATIONS WITH CLOSE FRIENDS

Close friends are important in a range of ways in Chinese cultures. Friendship was the only relationship of possible equality in the Confucian system of relationships, and friendship between males is particularly valued (Won-Doornink, 1991). As Gao (1991) found in her analysis of mainland Chinese, 'You need to be an intimate friend before a Chinese will open up and tell you embedded stories' (Gao, 1991, p. 103), whereas relative strangers in North America are eager to disclose information about their relationships. In a study of Chinese students (Cheung, 1984), friends were sought for help in psychological problems before medical doctors, particularly by women, with medical doctors preferred only for more physiological conditions.

Some evidence suggests that friendship formation in Chinese cultures may take a similar path to that in Western societies. As in most Western cultures, similarity is also important in friendship formation (Cheng, Bond, and Chan, in press), although arguably attitudinal similarity is more important in Chinese societies, where it is important for the maintenance of social harmony. However, given the importance of such harmony in Chinese societies, we suspect that we may be seeing the 'repulsion' factor operating here, with the avoidance of unsuitable others contributing most to the seeking of similar others (cf., Rosenbaum, 1986). Whether, as in Western societies, there are particular areas in which 'uniqueness' (Snyder and Fromkin, 1980) is encouraged is uncertain, although again we suspect that this attraction may occur only in situations when this uniqueness promotes a wider social cohesion.

As in the case of romantic relationship formation, however, there are some areas where cultural practices make the situation more complex. Returning to the issue of disclosure, Wheeler (1988) asserted that Hong Kong Chinese students had fewer interactions than did American students, with most interactions appearing to occur 'by chance'. Other evidence suggests that Chinese friends are less willing than are British friends to disclose in what might be considered taboo areas, despite the fact that there are few cross-national differences in the identification of the taboo subjects (Goodwin and Lee, 1994). Given the corruption widespread in mainland China, one unsurprising area in which mainland Chinese disclosure is limited is in confiding in government institutions (Traver, 1984).

However, to conclude that the Chinese simply disclose less than do Westerners is misleading. As suggested earlier, the demarcation between casual and close friends is very sharp in Chinese societies (Gudykunst and Ting-Toomey, 1988; Triandis et al., 1988), and greater disclosure is evident towards in-group rather than out-group members, a differentiation less evident in Western nations (Gudykunst et al., 1992). We find a similar division in the willingness to trust in Chinese societies (Zhang and Bond, 1993). Thus, although close relationships among Chinese may take some time to mature, they are highly intimate (Hui and Villareal, 1989; Wheeler, Reis and Bond, 1989). The term 'close friend' in the West means something rather less intimate than it does in Chinese cultures, and the apparent sociability of Westerners is perhaps less deep than are the close friendship relationships of the Chinese (Triandis et al., 1988). Much may also depend on the nature of the relationship with the particular individual who is the target of the disclosure. Yang and Hwang (1980) found that disclosure to parents depended on the style of parenting, with, unsurprisingly, more disclosure to loving and accepting, as compared to authoritarian, parents.

A second complexity arises when we consider research on self-monitoring. A number of commentators (see, for example, Hoosain, 1986; Yang, 1992) have pointed to the large degree of self-monitoring in Chinese societies, where people strive to change their behaviour in accordance with the situation in which they find themselves. This avoidance may be attempted largely to avoid criticism and win approval by fitting in with others (Yang). However, some researchers have provided evidence to show that Chinese respondents might be less self-monitoring than are their Western counterparts (Goodwin and Pang, 1994; Gudykunst, Yang, and Nishida, 1987), due to a weaker concern with the self and the greater significance of contextual factors in Chinese societies.

There are a number of interpretations for this apparent contradiction. One stresses the significance of status relationships in Chinese societies, which have the effect that individuals do not simply take on the position of a 'prototypical' respondent in any new situation but have instead to consider role factors relevant to that situation (Gudykunst, Yang, and Nishida, 1987). A further interpretation returns us again to the distinction between the in-group and the out-group so prevalent in Chinese societies. Although Chinese individuals may be keen to conform superficially to a stranger early on in an interaction, they are less likely to conform to casual acquaintances (the targets in Western self-monitoring scales) for more than a very short time, unless some form of *yuan* is established (Triandis et al., 1988). As mentioned above, the distinction between in-group and out-group is less clear in Western societies, and here we might expect a deeper conformity with such acquaintances. Yang (1992) supports this point by noting how the Chinese can be seen as having a public self and private self, with the latter relatively unchanged by external circumstances, although the former is clearly the more visible. Tangential support can be provided for this notion from the work of Goodwin and Pang (1994), who followed Snyder and Simpson's (1987) work on the maladaptive effects of high self-monitoring. In their study of Singaporean Chinese, they found that the effects of high self-monitoring were far more profound (in terms of relationship quality) in British as compared to Chinese subjects. Clearly, further research is needed to clarify the actual extent of self-monitoring in Chinese cultures, and the impact of this self-monitoring on other facets of social life.

FAMILY RELATIONS AND CHILD SOCIALIZATION

At first glance, it seems difficult to overstress the significance of kinship and the family in Chinese societies. In the words of Xiantian (1985), 'the family is still the basic unit of society' (p. 86). This familism has four aspects: a belief in harmony and solidarity, a stress on lineage prolongation and expansion, an emphasis on family prosperity, and a strong sense of sentiment for the family (Yeh, 1990, cited in Yang, 1992). Responsibility towards the family, the interdependence of family members, and respect for parents are still key themes among Chinese populations across the world (Feldman and Rosenthal, 1990; Feldman and Rosenthal, 1991; Ho, this volume; Yang, 1992). Even after migration, many households remain multigenerational (Yu and Wu, 1988; Lum and Char, 1985). The traditional extended family provided not only material security, but also psychological security in terms of ancestral lineage (Chu, 1985). In addition, the family is central to self-identity, with family and individual behaviour difficult to separate (Hsu, 1985). The family may even provide a model for other, non-family organizations, with structural patterns, ethics, role relations, and attitudes learned from family life seeping through into non-familial structures (Yang, 1992).

The Confucian tradition can be seen clearly in the realm of child socialization. This influence is well captured in the Chinese proverb 'strict father, kind mother' (Ho, 1987). Children in Western societies are taught to value independence and individualism, while in Chinese cultures a broader social responsibility is emphasized, with a particular emphasis on socially desirable and culturally approved behaviours, such as the significance of social harmony (King and Bond, 1985; Wu and Tseng, 1985). In Chinese cultures, children are also traditionally taught the inhibition of expression and a general pattern of obedience and piety (Ho, this volume; King and Bond, 1985; Lin and Fu, 1990). Respect is a central tenet of many Chinese relationships. In traditional Chinese societies, a son's respect for his father (filial piety, or *xiao*) may involve a continual display of obedience throughout his life (Hsu, 1983). He may also be obliged to make a financial contribution to his parents even after he has left home (Argyle, 1982).

The tradition of Confucianism and its implications for the close family structure are too well established in Chinese societies to deny their influence (Hsu, 1985). Yet, as many observers note (Anderson, 1992; Chu, 1985; Ho, 1989) to view the modern Chinese family as simply a traditional extended family may be misleading. As early as the late 1940s, Levy observed about Hong Kong, 'The traditional family is being wiped out without being replaced' (Levy, 1949, p. 302); the Chinese family is now in a continuously 'fluid' state, ranging from the traditional conjugal format to the relatively isolated nuclear structure (Lau, 1981; Rosen, 1978). With the nuclear family increasingly the norm (Lau, 1981; Tseng and Wu, 1985), relations are now being built with a wider group of individuals who serve the interests of the family group (King and Bond, 1985). There is increasing evidence of the use of non-kinship, 'pseudo-kin' networks to aid in achieving particular, usually materialistic, goals (Lau, 1981; Lee, 1985; Wu and Tseng, 1985). These new members are 'inducted' into the family group by core (usually blood-related) members (Blau, Ruan, and Ardelt, 1991). Ironically, this adaptation has contributed to a 'new kind of familism', not alien to the Confucian philosophy, with new close non-kinship networks replacing many former family functions (King and Bond, 1985, p. 41). These instrumental networks have tended to be ignored by researchers concerned primarily with the importance of kinship networks in Chinese societies. Yet we might hypothesize that, with the projected decrease in family size, at least in mainland China, such networks are likely to increase in prominence.

The reasons behind these changes are complex, but a number of macrostructural factors have probably been significant. One factor is obviously the greater exposure to alternative, Western models of the family. A second is directly related to the politics of mainland China, where the extended family as an economic unit was challenged by the land reforms of the Communist state (Chu, 1985). The confusion and turmoil of the Cultural Revolution, and its cry for a challenging of traditional authority structures, meant that traditional patterns of social relations based on respect for elders were considerably weakened. It led to a pragmatism and rejection of conservatism and the former authoritarian upbringing (Ho, 1989; Lau et al., 1990; Ho, this volume).

A third force is the increase in market orientation in the Mainland (Pollay, Tse, and Wang, 1990). Here, the severity of the market, and the lack of formal support for those who fail, has led to the development of a 'utilitarianistic familism' where traditional extended family ties are replaced by new ties of economic convenience (Lau, 1981). In some situations, these new formations have superseded family loyalties. To exacerbate matters, a fourth factor, governmental restrictions on family size (Tsoi, 1985), has been reinforced by the increasing availability of contraception to Chinese couples (*South China Morning Post*, 5 November 1993, p. 11), with only 10 per cent of mainland Chinese now using no method of birth control (*China Times Weekly*, 29 October 1993). This restriction on family size is leading to increasingly small family units which can no longer offer the resources of the extended kin network. Urban children themselves, however, may be showing some signs of benefit from these governmental restrictions, with only children (children with no siblings) receiving enhanced attention from their parents. This increased attention may have contributed to their greater educational attainments than were achieved by earlier generations (Poston and Falbo, 1990).

Despite these changes, it would be premature to declare the death of the family in Chinese communities (Hsu, 1985). There is still a persistant loyalty and a sense of commitment that exceeds most Western family obligations (Rosen, 1978). Thus, whether or not the traditional, extended family will eventually exhibit the dramatic decline evident in the West is still far from certain.

CHANGING POWER STRUCTURES IN CHINESE RELATIONSHIPS

In traditional Chinese societies 'males were expected to behave as males, and females as females' (Ho, 1989, p. 154), with sex-role differentiation unambiguous and backed by strong social sanctions. This differentiation began in early childhood and continued into adulthood, and it was most marked in the lower classes (Ho, 1989). We can consider the extent of this differentiation in current Chinese personal relationships by returning to the various issues considered above.

The Development of Romantic Relationships

The man has traditionally been the initiator and dominant presence in romantic relationships, and he has had considerably more sexual freedom prior to marriage. This imbalance is reflected in the choices of partner expressed by the sexes, with men in China particularly valuing chastity (Buss, 1989) and a 'passive' partner, while women idealize the more assertive male, with a high degree of application, intellect, and 'openness to experience' (Cheng et al., in press). This finding contrasts with recent British data, which show that there now appear to be few sex differences in partner preferences in the United Kingdom (Goodwin, 1990).

After marriage there is evidence of a certain double standard in many Chinese societies. For example, in a study conducted by Kok in Singapore (1989, cited in Wen, in press), both young men and women were found to be relatively conservative in their initial sexual experiences, but after marriage more than 15 per cent of men were involved in casual sex, usually with commercial sex partners. While this double standard may be alive and well in many societies around the world (Frayser, 1985), these rates of casual sex among males do appear to be high: in a survey of more than 600 spouses in the United States, 96 per cent claimed they had been monogamous in the previous year (Greeley, Michael, and Smith, 1990).

Close Friendships

Although we have little direct data on this topic, gender differences in friendship choice also appear to reflect enduring Chinese values. Thus, in a study of Chinese school students (aged 17–20 years) ideal female best friends were higher in the communal quality of helpfulness than were ideal male best friends, who in turn were higher on the agentic dimensions of extroversion, application, and assertiveness (Cheng et al., in press). In so far as ideal friendship choice may indicate wider socially approved Chinese behaviours, the authors relate these results to the portrayal of the female as the 'good wife and mother', and the male as more highly achievement-motivated.

Family Power

There is some evidence of changing power relations in the workplace, with Taiwanese women appearing to be leading the way in demanding a more egalitarian role in their society (Chia, Chong, and Cheng, 1986). However, the movement is slow (Hong, 1976; Ho, 1989), with social class, occupation, and location important variables affecting the change. There is evidence that women's employment in Hong Kong is set always in the context of their fami- ly responsibilities, which still play a primary role (Ngo, 1992). At home, as in the West (Argyle and Henderson, 1985; Wiggins, Moody, and Lederer, 1983), men still gain more from their marital relationship than do women (Ying, 1991), particularly from the greater social support offered by their spouse.

In traditional Chinese communities, husbands have wielded considerable power, with older sons inheriting power on the death of the father. The father's unquestioned right to be head of the family has had four features in the home: economic autocracy (all the family's material resources were under his name), thought autocracy (all the family had to accept his standards), strict family rules often reinforced by corporal punishment, and the rigid hierarchical ordering of family members (Yang, 1992). There is some evidence of egalitarianism in more recent family affairs, with both parents now playing a more equal role in a number of key areas of family life. In terms of socialization, it is both parents who now make important family decisions (Yang, 1992). Furthermore, a recent *China Weekly Times* poll revealed that almost 50 per cent of mainland Chinese husbands and 38 per cent of Taiwanese husbands report that they now share in housework.

CONCLUSION:
THE SUITABILITY OF AN ETIC APPROACH FOR STUDYING CHINESE RELATIONSHIPS

In this chapter, we have implied at least three dimensions on which Chinese cultures may vary, although we doubt that these dimensions are orthogonal. One division concerns the dimension of modernity–traditionality; we have fre- quently contrasted 'traditional' Chinese communities with more 'modern' groups. The latter are often characterized by an increased materialism, with the traditional Chinese value of *zhizu* (contentment with one's lot) replaced by the more materialistic greeting of *Gong xi fa cai* (may you make a fortune)(Lee, 1985). Given the economic basis of this change, it is perhaps unsurprising to find that variations across the modernity–traditionality dimension within Chinese societies are correlated with social class (Ho, 1989).

A second division reflects the degree of industrialization and the broader environmental setting (Lee, 1985; see also Ekblad, this volume). In their work on interpersonal trust in Hong Kong, mainland China, and the United States, Zhang and Bond (1993) have argued that it is the degree of industrialization that serves as the critical factor, with persons in Hong Kong and the United States, both highly industrialized societies, showing lower trust towards strangers than did those in the developing PRC. In a review of the literature concerning Taiwan and mainland China, Ho (1989) claims that rural parents are more likely to have kept to traditional patterns of child rearing, although instrumental, utilitarian principles are evident in many traditional family arrangements and may differ from urban arrangements only in degree (Lau, 1981).

A third dimension, individualism–collectivism, is rarely mentioned in any comparative study across different Chinese societies because of the assumption of parity across communities. This dimension, which is discussed by a number of contributors to this book, contrasts the self-focused and individual goal orientation of the individualist culture with a preference for tightly knit social frameworks where one or more primary groups takes central stage (Hui and Villareal, 1989; Triandis et al., 1988). In Hofstede's pioneering research in this area (Hofstede, 1980), Chinese cultures consistently obtained low scores on the individualism scale, whereas Western cultures such as the United States and the United Kingdom scored highly. However, Hofstede's data is now more than 20 years old, and we suspect that the very different trajectories of change that have characterized different Chinese societies may have also contributed to some of the interpersonal differences now evident across Chinese communities (Bond, this volume). Evidence from other cultures undergoing changes on the individualism–collectivism dimension may lead us to expect further changes in socialization and family structures which might serve to reinforce the process of individualization (Goodwin and Emelyanova, in press).

A further variable, that of political ideology, also needs inclusion in any meaningful comparative analysis. Even the oldest relationship practices have been significantly challenged by the dramatic events that have marked the short history of the PRC. Given the consequent rates of migration and persistant cultural connections, these events have, in varying degrees, affected all of the Chinese cultures. In discussing sexual practices Ruan and Matsumura (1991) state, 'We may now be witnessing the most repressive period in all Chinese history' (p. 159). The impact of this repression is difficult to predict at present, but our guess would be that such treatment is likely to leave in its wake a large residue of problems for future generations. There is already evidence of an increase in sex crimes, illegal abortions and unwanted pregnancies, and a growing public resentment towards what many regard as the hypocritical behaviours of many government officials (Ruan and Matsumura, 1991).

One fundamental puzzle that has caused the authors much concern throughout the writing of this chapter is the status of the concept of *yuan*. Such a concept challenges simple communications models of relationship formation and prompts us to focus on multiple other factors that might influence relationship development (Chang and Holt, 1991). This concept seems to have a complex relationship with actual practice: evidence from Hong Kong suggests that there are socio-economic differences in the degree to which individuals in Hong Kong believe in *yuan*, and that for some the belief is more like a ritualistic tradition used, *post hoc*, to explain relationship success or failure (Lee, 1985). Clearly, as Yang and Ho (1988) demonstrate in a rare empirical study of this concept, the notion of *yuan* is still recognized and valued, even among 'modern' university students. Yet, perhaps this concept has more familiarity for those from other cultures than we suspect. Many in Western societies also report themselves to be mystified by the formation of personal relationships and say they would concur with the psychoanalyst Winarick (1985): 'It is as if the whole process of choosing a love involves bumping into the right person and accidentally discovering the right chemistry' (p. 380). This speculation leaves open the question as to whether (and how) this concept may be valuably introduced into Western conceptions of love, and the manner in which a belief in this concept may be a valuable independent variable in future, cross-national research.

This discussion leads us inevitably to conclude this chapter with a familiar line: a call for more research. One obvious deficit in the current body of data is our lack of information concerning mainland China, where government policies have given access to only very limited, often politically controlled, data and where the dramatic changes induced by 40 years of communism have been little explored (Wu and Tseng, 1985). In particular, we know little about ethnic or regional variations on the Mainland, although the scanty evidence available suggests considerable diversity (cf., Ho, 1989, on ethnic variation; Wen, in press, on geographical factors).

Even given the right political climate, getting such data will not be easy. As Gao (1991) notes, there are considerable problems in eliciting intimate disclosure from Chinese respondents. Yet, given the increasing international importance of the Chinese nations, from both academic and commercial perspectives, we urgently need work that will attempt to relate the dramatic changes in the social and political scenery throughout Chinese societies to the individual, everyday lives of the ordinary Chinese citizen. Such work must examine how the fabric of interpersonal support and cohesion which underpin so many of these ancient societies is being stretched to match these new structural realities, and expore the consequences of such adaptations. We also need to go beyond the traditional, rather broad, characterizations of 'the Chinese people' that, while warning us of the dangers of over-generalizing from Western perspectives, often ignore the multiple and complex levels of individual and subgroup variations existing in any society. It is only through such further work that we can obtain real insight into the personal relationships of this vast, complex, and most challenging of peoples.

Chapter 20

Chinese Social Interaction:
Harmony and Hierarchy on the Good
Earth

William K. Gabrenya, Jr, and Kwang-Kuo Hwang

Water and earth—above all, water—set the ecological stage for the emergence of the Chinese ethos several millennia ago. Today, on the good earth and in shining semiconductor factories, a thousand million Chinese interact in ways not unlike those established in ancient times. All under heaven are united in harmony and in chaos, in hierarchy and in rebellion, in stubborn traditionalism and in merciless modernization: all greatly fascinating to the West now as for centuries before.

This brief chapter will attempt to summarize what is known in Western and Chinese social science about the interpersonal behaviour of this vast, ancient, modern, diverse—but surprisingly uniform—segment of the human condition. Readers who find our presentation a too-thin soup should also try the excellent related chapters on communication (Gao, Ting-Toomey, and Gudykunst), intimate relationships (Goodwin and Tang), and achievement (Yu) in this volume.

CONFUCIUS AND CHAOS

The Confucian Ethic and the Regulation of Social Interaction

Any discussion of Chinese behaviour must begin with the pervasive influence of the social philosophy attributed to Confucius (*Kongzi*, 孔子). Confucian concepts are employed both in an analytical, abstract, philosophical sense and as a useful heuristic for describing the professed values of Chinese people. These ideas and ideals are wielded in numerous ways to explain not only the social behaviour of individuals and small groups (see, for example, Bond and Hwang, 1986), but also macroeconomic trends (see, for example, Hwang, 1988, on the Confucian basis for East Asian modernization). Although Chinese social behaviour is often interpreted as a reflection of Confucian ideological beliefs, historical circumstances and current conditions also shape Chinese behaviour in important ways (as historical circumstances shaped Confucianism itself long ago), providing alternate, albeit often concordant, explanations of observed behaviour patterns (see, for example, see Redding, 1990).

The Confucian ethical system regulating social behaviour has three principal ideas: *ren*, *yi*, and *li* (仁、義、禮); benevolence, righteousness or justice, and propriety or courtesy. 'Regulation' is certainly the appropriate term. Confucianism is a thoroughly secular, this–world system developed in a time of chaos to allow China a modicum of harmony in the cool embrace of inescapable hierarchy. In an agrarian society of isolated villages, where relationships are collectivist, involuntary, and permanent, rules regulating social interaction are crucial, as there is essentially no escape from troublesome interpersonal relations (Moghaddam, Taylor, and Wright, 1993). The Confucian system centres on five 'cardinal relations' (the *Wu Lun*/五倫) in which power differentials and responsibilities are prescribed: relations between emperor and minister, father and son, husband and wife, among brothers, and among friends (see Sun, 1993). The most important of these is the father–son relationship, characterized by conformity to the role expectations derived from filial piety (*xiao*/孝), rather than by an affective bond. Hence, for 2,000 years schoolchildren (in the élite class) read the *Xiao Jing* (孝經), which emphasizes duty to established roles. *Xiao* is discussed in detail by Ho (in this volume).

Insecurity

Redding (1990) and others (see, for example, Stover, 1974) maintain that the key to understanding Chinese social behaviour is an appreciation of the extent to which Chinese have experienced insecurity in a bitter sea of tragically endless environmental, political, and economic chaos. The most recent 150 years have been particularly difficult. Data in the Human Relations Area Files document the frequency of uncontrollable disasters such as famine, destructive weather, and pestilence in China. For example, the Mainland received the maximum rating for prevalence of famine in the Standard Ethnographic Sample (Ember and Ember, 1992).

Through most of Chinese history, individuals have been afforded little security by the traditional Chinese state, which was ruled by a distant and thinly scattered political élite unwilling or unable to maintain order through the rule of law. Instead, order was maintained by forcing people to learn their prescribed roles through Confucian education and family socialization, and by enforcing proper role behaviour by threat of punishment.

The kin in-group provided the 'first, last, and only' source of security in traditional China. This security was realized at the expense of a wider sense of community and social responsibility such that families were in various degrees of continual rivalry and competition in what was essentially a zero-sum game. A basic principle of Chinese strategic behaviour is to 'be on guard against everyone and on all occasions'. 'Treat each person like a guest, but guard against him like a thief' (Chiao, 1989). Nepotism has often been the solution to this problem of trust. The absence of a wider sense of community or nation led Sun Yatsen to lament that the Chinese are 'like grains of sand'. Colloquially, Chinese speak of *ren chi ren* (人吃人): 'people eating people'. The levels of threat, insecurity, rival familism, and lack of community have decreased but still remain important features of most Chinese societies' social ecologies.

RELATIONAL PERSONALISM

Social scientists have long sought simple and sovereign conceptions of Chinese social behaviour in a manner reminiscent of the configurationist school of culture and personality (Benedict, 1934). Such ideas include 'situation-centredness' (Hsu 許烺光, 1953), 'personage' (*ren*/人; Hsu, 1971), 'social orientation' (Yang, 1981), 'relation-orientation' (Ho, Chan, and Chiu, 1991), 'collectivism' (Hofstede, 1980; Triandis et al., 1986), and 'personalism' (Redding, 1990). We will follow this tradition by using the term *relation-oriented personalism* or *relational personalism* in this chapter. By this term we intend to emphasize the great extent to which Chinese social interaction is stereotypically 'collectivist' (cooperative or harmonious) in certain social contexts but in others exhibits an 'individualist' (competitive, agonistic) style.

Relationships

Relational personalism begins with a distinction between in-group members or insiders (*zijiren*/自己人) and out-group members or outsiders (*wairen*/外人). In his 'face-and-favour' model of resource allocation, Hwang (黃光國) (1987) divided relationships into three categories: expressive ties, including those with close family members; mixed ties, such as those with friends and other kin; and instrumental ties, those with strangers or out-group members with whom there is no lasting relationship. Social interaction expectations, norms, and behaviours differ for these three kinds of ties in a number of ways presented in later sections of this chapter. Yang (楊國樞) (1992) proposes that Chinese make a fundamental distinction among people who are *sheng* (生; 'raw', outsiders), *shu* (熟; 'cooked', insiders), and *jia* (家; family).

The core idea of Confucianism is *ren*, an insistence that one should practice a hierarchical love tied to intimacy of relationship (Hwang, 1988). The social domain in which one is expected to practice *ren* is the 'greater self' (*da wo*/大我), in juxtaposition to the 'small self' (*xiao wo*/小我). Most Chinese define their *da wo* narrowly as is seen, for example, in their reaction to the idea of public charity: resources given to charity are resources that could have been reserved for the family. The distinction between *xiao wo* and *da wo* is widely used in Chinese daily life. When two or more parties say 'we are *zijiren*' (or *zijiaren*/自家人, persons within the circle of a family), they are trying to create a feeling of *da wo*. Studies of Chinese organizational behaviour have found that Chinese leaders tend to classify their subordinates as either *zijiren* or *wairen* and to treat them accordingly (Hwang, 1990).

Social Networks

Chinese navigate complex networks of *guanxi* (relationships; 關係) which expand, day by day, throughout their lives. Each individual is born into a social network of family members, and as he or she grows up, group memberships involving education, occupation, and residence will provide new opportunities for expanding this network (see, for example, Chang and Holt, 1991). In contrast to the pattern in Western societies, especially the United States, these relationships persist long after the groups are dissolved or no longer have face-to-face interaction, forming lifelong, rich networks of *guanxi*.

The relative permanence of such social networks contributes to the importance and enforceability of the Chinese conception of reciprocity (*bao*/報). Yum (1988) notes that Western societies emphasize short-term, symmetrical reciprocation in exchange relationships while people in Confucian societies recognize that they are 'in it for the long run' and emphasize the extension of the relationship into the unforseeable future. Hence, Chinese friends find it awkward to thank a friend for every little favour, as in 'thanks for giving me a ride'. 'Among the most intimate, gratefulness is not verbalized.' Hwang (1987) has analysed the implications of this long-term reciprocity for people involved in various types of relationships.

Intermediaries are important in the development of networks of *guanxi*. Chang and Holt (1991) used interviews with adults in Taiwan to investigate their perceptions of how one might establish (pull/*la*/拉, manipulate/*gao*/搞, or climb/*pan*/攀) *guanxi* with another. They found four common methods: appealing to kin relations; pointing to a previous association; using in-group connections or mediators; or social interaction requiring social skills such as the ability to play the '*renqing* (favour) game' described by Hwang (1987). Intermediaries are useful in bringing out-group members together into new relationships (Yum, 1988). In a large-scale study of social networks in mainland China and the United States, Blau, Ruan, and Ardelt (1991) found that Chinese kin acted as brokers in aiding their relatives to make contacts with people outside the kinship network, but that American kin did not function in this way.

Face and Social Interaction

In order to gain a comprehensive understanding of Chinese social interaction, the dynamic relationships among the concepts of *mianzi* (面子; face), *renqing* (人情; favour), and *guanxi* must be developed. As the famous writer Lin Yu-Tang (林語堂) put it, 'Here we arrive at the most curious point of Chinese social psychology. Abstract and intangible, it is yet the most delicate standard by which Chinese social intercourse is regulated. ...Not to give a person face is the utmost height of rudeness and is like throwing down a gauntlet to him in the West' (Lin, 1935, p. 201).

Lian and mianzi

In a pioneering paper, Hu (胡先縉) (1944) proposed that there are two basic categories of face in Chinese culture, *lian* (臉) and *mianzi*. An individual's *lian* can be preserved by faithful compliance with ritual or social norms; having *lian* 'represents the confidence of society in the integrity of ego's moral character, the loss of which makes it impossible for him to function properly in the community' (p. 45). In contrast, *mianzi* 'stands for the kind of prestige that is emphasized in this country [the United States]: a reputation achieved through getting on in life, through success and ostentation' (p. 45). She indicated that the Western concept of face corresponds to the Chinese *mianzi* but is wholly lacking in the connotations of *lian*. Both *mianzi* and *lian* are social constructs rather than personological entities resident in the individual (Ho (何友暉), (1976).

In Chinese society, saying an individual *bu yao lian* ('doesn't want face'; 不要臉) means that he or she is nasty, shameless, and immoral; it is a great insult to his or her moral character. However, saying somebody *mei you mianzi* ('has no face'; 沒有面子) simply means that he does not deserve honour or glory. A sense of self-blame, shame or *diulian* (丟臉), is suffered with respect to *lian* as a result of wrong-doing regardless of the presence of an audience (see Bond and Hwang, 1986; Bond and Lee, 1981; King and Meyers, 1977). Chinese students' and adults' emic conceptions of face support Hu's *lian/mianzi* distinction but suggest there are generational or age differences in beliefs about the situations that lead to loss of either kind of face (Cheng 陳之昭, 1988). Redding and Ng (1982) found that Hong Kong Chinese businessmen claim face is a consistently important consideration in their professional interactions, and that fear of losing *lian* formed the basis for the informal system of contracts and agreements that is common in Chinese business.

Shudao and mianzi

King (金耀基) (1988) has argued that the Confucian principle of forgiveness (*shudao*/恕道), which is embodied in the maxim 'Do not do unto others that which you would not wish others to do unto you', includes both self-respect and consideration. For a majority of Chinese, the most frequent practice of *shudao* in daily life is the avoidance of hurting another person's face in social interaction, particularly in public (see, for example, Bond and Lee, 1981). When others are part of the actor's *da wo*, saving one's own face is the same as saving the other's face.

Hierarchy and mianzi

'Harmony within hierarchy' is probably the phrase most commonly used to characterize a wide range of social behaviour in Confucian societies. Chinese tend to be very sensitive to their hierarchical position in social structures and will behave in ways designed to display, enhance, and protect both the image and the reality of this position. To Westerners, these *mianzi*-enhancing behaviours may appear ostentatious (expensive cars) or irrational (for example, the Taiwan baby salamander craze of 1989, in which rare amphibians were smuggled from China as a status symbol). Empirical research has demonstrated the extent to which Chinese use considerations of hierarchy in making socially evaluative judgements (see, for example, Bond, Wan, Leung, and Giacalone, 1985).

The renqing rule

The concept of *renqing* has several implications in Chinese culture (Cheng, 1988; Hwang, 1987). First, *renqing* indicates the emotional or affective responses of an individual confronting various situations or life events. Second, *renqing* means a resource that an individual can present to another as a gift in the course of social interaction. In Chinese society, when one has either happy occasions or difficulties, all one's acquaintances are expected to offer a gift or render some substantial assistance. In such cases, it is said that they send him or her their *renqing*. Henceforth, the recipient will owe *renqing* to the donors. Third, *renqing* connotes the social norms by which one has to abide in order to get along well with other people in Chinese society. The '*renqing* rule' (Hwang, 1987) includes two categories of social behaviour. First, in normal times, one should keep in contact with acquaintances in one's personal network of *guanxi* by greetings, visitations, or exchanging gifts with them from time to time. Second, when a person in one's network gets into trouble or faces a difficult situation in life, one should sympathize with him, help him, and 'do a *renqing*' for that person. Once the recipient has received a *renqing* from other people, he should return it as soon as the opportunity arises.

SOCIAL BEHAVIOUR

Sociability

Chinese patterns of day-to-day social interaction reflect the importance of building lasting personal relationships and extending one's *guanxi*. In a study of university students, Wheeler, Reis, and Bond (1989) found that Hong Kong students had fewer interactions than did Americans, but these interactions were longer and involved more people. In contrast, the picture that emerged of the American students was of the 'social butterfly' engaged in a large number of dyadic interactions with many different people. As Triandis et al. (1988) noted, individualists are not less sociable than are collectivists; indeed, they must work harder to gain entrance to and maintain relationships that are impermanent and subject to change at any time. These findings would seem to support Hsu's (1972) proposal that Americans' feelings of impermanence in their relationships lead to a pervasive sense of individual psychological insecurity (in contrast to the pattern of external insecurity experienced by Chinese; see above). The manner in which Chinese cognitively organize social interactions (Forgas and Bond, 1985), incorporate group memberships as a part of their self-definition (Bond and Hewstone, 1988), and score higher in self-monitoring (Hamid, 1994) underscores the social orientation of the Chinese.

The Chinese valuation of *renao* (熱鬧), roughly translatable as 'bustling atmosphere', also illustrates the social-orientedness and relational personalism of the Chinese (Pan 潘英海, 1993). To be *renao*, an event must feature a high degree of activity and sound, and a large number of people. *Renao* facilitates social interaction somewhat outside of normal social hierarchies and networks, thereby releasing people from the usual constraints inherent in Chinese society. *Renao* is *linruo* (臨若), 'ambiguous' or 'chaotic', producing a situation that promotes social penetration, reorganization of relationships, and emotional expression. Stereotypical *renao* situations include night markets, temple celebrations, and successful dinner parties.

Interaction Style

The concept of *li* permeates both formal social interaction and that of people who feel they are *zijiren*. To a great extent the social interaction of Chinese evidences striking parallels with that of other relational personalist cultures such as the Arabs (Nydell, 1987) and the Japanese (Condon, 1984)(see De Mente, 1989; Hu and Grove, 1991; Kapp, 1983, for detailed discussions of Chinese interaction habits).

Social sensitivity

Attentiveness and sensitivity to the needs of others (see, for example, Markus and Kitayama, 1991) is a key ingredient of *li*. The strong social orientation of the Chinese makes it difficult at times for people to abstract themselves from the interpersonal demands of a situation and, therefore other's actions are given personalistic attributions. For example, interpersonal obligations are sought and perceived in communication:

> Zhang: 'I like your shirt.'
> Li: 'Please take it.'

Chinese expect people to anticipate others' needs or to know their feelings without asking or being told; to do otherwise indicates poor social skills or a characterological deficit. Yum (1988) views this 'anticipatory communication' within the context of a 'receiver-centred', in contrast to the Western 'sender-centred', communication style. (See also Gao, Ting-Toomey, and Gudykunst, this volume.) Friends are not only expected to show high levels of courtesy and warmth to each other, but there is an implicit assumption that when one treats strangers in an overly kindly manner, one is devaluing friendship and has misplaced priorities. Face and hierarchy are maintained in gift-giving rituals, although perhaps not to the carefully articulated extent of the Japanese (Condon, 1984). Direct expressions of gratitude are inappropriate within one's *da wo*, particularly the family; it is future reciprocity that is important.

The dinner party

One of the most important settings in which Chinese maintain and extend their *guanxi* and practice face-work is in the hosted dinner party. 'The Chinese are probably among the peoples of the world most preoccupied with eating' (Chang 張光直, 1977, p. 13; see also Redding, 1990, p. 70). The host can obtain *mianzi* by creating the right kind of *changmian* (場面; literally, 'occasion') through the status of the guests, the quality of the food, the maintenance of a highly boisterous atmosphere, and the appropriate degree of ostentation (*paichang*/排場)(Chen, 1990). Subtle face-saving and face-giving rituals are enacted, in which host and guest must each play their role properly and maintain an appropriate degree of hospitality and gratefulness. 'The interaction at the Chinese dinner invitation can be seen as a highly pre-coded cultural event which engenders group bonding and promotes social harmony' (Chen, 1990, p. 133).

Politeness

Western visitors to China often become fascinated with issues of 'politeness' or 'civil behaviour'. Gu (1990) suggested the Confucian concept of politeness (*limao*/禮貌) has four qualities: respectfulness (concern for the other's face, status, and so forth), modesty (self-denigration), attitudinal warmth (demonstrations of kindness, consideration, and hospitality), and refinement. (See the chapter by Gao, Ting-Toomey, and Gudykunst, this volume.) Conceptions of which specific behaviours Chinese consider polite are highly variable across situations, however, and often diverge from classic Confucian prescriptions (Gabrenya and Shu, 1993).

Tezhifei

The *tezhifei* (特支費; 'special expenses money') system in Taiwan illustrates the adaptation of administrative practices to meet the demands of face and *guanxi*. High officials and administrators in the public sector are given a formal salary supplement to defray the expenses they must incur in carrying out the obligations of their office, including extending their personal and organizational *guanxi* and treating their subordinates appropriately. For example, Chinese etiquette demands that the host or the highest-ranking person pay the bill at a dinner party, avoiding the embarrassment and non-*da wo* atmosphere of individual checks. An administrator gives his subordinates *mianzi* by taking them to dinner, and he or she gains *mianzi* by picking up the tab, which in fact is paid out of the *tezhifei*. At least a portion of the *tezhifei* is not subject to receipts or oversight, giving the administrator great discretion in its use. In line with Chinese valuation of humanism over law, the controls on this money are social rather than legal. *Jiaozhifei* (交際費; 'allowance for social intercourse') is a somewhat more restricted analog to tezhifei in the private sector.

COOPERATION AND CONFLICT

Cooperation

Cooperative behaviour follows essentially the same pattern as the Confucian relational personalist guidelines for benevolence, that is, a strong in-group bias. Studies in the social psychology tradition have been used to assess the extent to which people cooperate or compete on interactive tasks such as the Madsen board, prisoners' dilemma game, and derivative procedures (see Smith and Bond, 1994). This research has found that Chinese in the People's Republic of China (PRC)(Domino, 1992) and Chinese-Americans (Cook and Chi, 1980; Cox, Lobel, and McLeod, 1991) are more cooperative or equalitarian than are Caucasian Americans. 'In more collectivist societies there is a greater reliance on the criteria of equality and need *within* the in-group, but greater use of the equity criterion *outside* the group' (Smith and Bond, 1994, p. 124; italics original). Research on traditional Chinese agriculture suggests that material considerations can also play an important part in guiding patterns of cooperation. Wong (翁紹華, 1970) found that Chinese peasants' cooperative activities and organizations in mainland China prior to the Second World War were rational attempts to make best use of human, land, tool, and animal resources, and to deal with a chaotic ecological and political environment.

Cooperative behaviour can also be observed in the extent to which people work to satisfy group-serving versus self-serving goals. In a line of research that came to be termed 'social loafing', it was found that on moderately intellective tasks Chinese students will perform better as a group than as individuals, whereas American students do the opposite, exhibiting the widely-found social loafing effect (Gabrenya, Latané, and Wang, 1983; Gabrenya, Wang, and Latané, 1985; see also Earley, 1993; Karau and Williams, 1993). Gabrenya (1990) found a relational personalist pattern in a process analysis of the social interactions of Taiwanese and American dyads working on a problem-solving task. Chinese were more polite and cooperative working with friends than with strangers, but Americans showed the opposite effect.

Conflict

Harmony in social relationships is prescribed by the Confucian Doctrine of the Mean (*Zhong Yong*/中庸), while hierarchy and conformity in relationships are demanded by the Wu Lun (Hofstede and Bond, 1988; Westwood, Tang, and Kirkbride, 1992). Aggression against out-groups, however, is energized by the Confucian attachment of moral value and *mianzi* to holding in-group biases (Hwang, 1988). Out-group violence is further exacerbated by the paucity of social norms for out-group interaction, reducing the ability of Chinese groups to peacefully resolve conflict (Bond and Wang, 1983).

Ethnographic information supports this relational personalism pattern. Traditional China ranked at the top of the Human Relations Area Files index for external and civil war, but at the bottom for individual antisocial behaviour (Ember and Ember, 1992). The extent of out-group aggression is also illustrated in several ethnographies (see Bond and Wang, 1983, for a review), of which the story of the Lin family of Wu Feng (Misty Peak) village in central Taiwan (Meskill, 1979) is a case study. The Lins emigrated to Taiwan from mainland China in the early eighteenth century and fought a long series of pitched battles with neighbouring clans. It wasn't until the middle of the nineteenth century that the declining Qing dynasty (1644–1911) succeeded in suppressing this conflict, at which point the Lins became 'gentrified' and entered the Taiwanese élite.

Little comparative research has been reported on interpersonal aggression. Observational studies comparing mainland Chinese and Swedish (Ekblad, 1986, and this volume) and Taiwanese, Japanese, and American (Stevenson, Lee, Chen, Stigler, Hsu, and Kitayama, 1990) schoolchildren found that mainland Chinese children were less aggressive than were Swedish children, but Taiwanese children were more aggressive than were American children. Sampling differences between Taiwan and the PRC may account for these conflicting findings. (The manner in which Chinese socialize children against ingroup aggression is discussed in Ho, 1986.)

Laboratory studies reveal that out-group members are treated more harshly than in-group members (Leung 梁覺, 1988) or fail to constrain verbal aggression (Bond and Venus, 1991). Hierarchical position bestows the right to be aggressive (Bond et al., 1985). Chinese do not evidence the American preference for adversarial judicial systems (Leung and Lind, 1986), but do prefer bargaining and mediation (Leung, 1987).

Conflict in the family

Conflict in the Chinese family has been a rich source of material for Chinese fiction (see the *Dream of the Red Chamber*), a concern of mental health professionals (particularly problems between mothers-in-law and their daughters-in-law), and the focus of anthropological field research (Weller, 1984). In this setting it appears that the idealized systems held as models by Confucians are seriously compromised by the complications of daily life. For example, Cohen (1976) in his *House United, House Divided*, presents a startling description of the processes by which a joint family's sense of *da wo* is sabotaged from within: 'it seems clear that a deliberate effort to force partition is involved when a family's sharing practices are increasingly compromised by the refusal of some individuals to contribute their labor and time, or by the outright embezzlement of family funds' (p. 204).

Face and conflict

Ting-Toomey (1988) proposed that members of collectivist or high-context societies attend more to face-work and look upon conflict from a social rather than a task perspective, avoiding conflict if at all possible. A subsequent scenario study found that Taiwanese students preferred styles of conflict resolution that involved obliging (yielding), avoiding, compromising, and integrating (finding a joint solution) more than did Americans (Trubisky, Ting-Toomey, and Lin, 1991). Ho (1974) noted the importance of saving others' *mianzi* in conflict situations: 'the exercise of caution to prevent hurting people's face is regarded as a hallmark of social skill and experience which presumably mellow with advancing age' (p. 248). As another observer put it, 'Before you hit a dog, you ought to consider the face of its master' (Chiao, 1989). Face must be left for others in conflict (*liu mianzi*/留面子), even defeated adversaries. Ho (1974) pointed out one cost of this strategy: conflicts may not be ultimately resolved, and may be manifested in violence when they again come into the open.

Mediators

Chinese often avoid and resolve conflict and minimize loss of face in real and potential conflict situations by the use of mediators and intermediaries, eschewing the direct approaches favoured in the West (Bond et al., 1985; Bond and Wang, 1983; Cloke, 1987; R. G. Ma, 1992; Wall and Blum, 1991; Yum, 1988). Wall and Blum (1991) interviewed officially designated street mediators in Nanjing, Jiangsu province, during the late 1980s. They found that the mediation system mandated by the government was similar to that used in imperial times. In both imperial and communist China, authorities expected citizens to settle their disputes by referring them to village elders, respected third parties, or, in the present system, to people appointed by the authorities. In neither time was mediation voluntary as it tends to be in the West. Zhang Yimou's film *The Story of Qiu Ju* illustrates the sometimes tragic implications of this system in a humorous way.

Cooperation and Conflict: Negotiation

The small extant cross-cultural literature on negotiation, while largely theoretical and anecdotal, suggests that negotiation norms and practices among the Chinese are consistent with the previous discussions of relational personalism, face-work, cooperation, and conflict. In an interview study cited above, Redding and Ng (1982) found that Hong Kong Chinese managers emphasized the importance of *lian* in commercial contract negotiations but not in more highly bureaucratic interactions involving either government officials or personnel decisions. Shenkar and Ronen (1987) proposed that three categories of norms guide Chinese negotiation. Norms involving communication patterns include emotional restraint and self-control, careful conformity to politeness rituals, and avoidance of aggressive persuasion techniques. The Confucian model follows the form of *xinping qihe*(心平氣和; 'being perfectly calm')(see also Argyle, 1986). Social obligation norms include credibility (信用/*xinyong*), a collective emphasis in which the group's goals are put ahead of those of the individual negotiators, leadership (with deference to the group leader), and a high concern for the encumbrance of indebtedness which requires reciprocity along the lines of the face-and-favour model. Finally, norms about relationships are linked to the powerful in-group/out-group distinction.

Kirkbride, Tang, and Westwood (1991), calling on the earlier work of Pye (1982), suggested that Chinese see conflict as a zero-sum game in which there must be a loser and the relationship is terminated. Conflict is sidestepped by avoidance strategies and by compromise. To Americans and British, compromise may be viewed as necessary but is held to be a sub-optimal solution requiring the making of concessions. In contrast, to the Chinese, compromise is framed as achieving a commonality of purpose that is preferable in that it implies a stronger, longer-term relationship. However, Kirkbride and his colleagues caution that the avoidance of conflict may also delay and complicate its resolution. Empirical support for some of these cultural differences in conflict resolution preferences was found by Tang and Kirkbride (1986) in a comparison of Chinese and British employees of the Hong Kong civil service.

CHINESE SOCIAL INTERACTION: METATHEORETICAL ISSUES

Problems of Theory

We will conclude this chapter by speaking to some concerns we have for the quality and direction of research on Chinese social interaction. We believe that the study of Chinese social interaction shares certain problems with the study of collectivism in general.

The first problem that we would highlight is that the individual and societal levels of analysis are frequently poorly distinguished, and the theoretical links between the levels are not specified.

Second, the distinction between ideology, 'ideal culture', or 'big traditions', and on-the-ground behaviour, real culture, or 'little traditions', is insufficiently drawn, perhaps encouraging an overly enthusiastic, uncritical application of Confucian precepts to modern Chinese life. Empirically, there is a danger that self-report studies fail to penetrate beyond social desirability among Chinese respondents. Yang (in Metzger, 1988, p. 13) and Sun (1993) note that the social scientist must be careful to distinguish between widespread social values and the thought and philosophy of scholars.

Third, the differences between China and the West, such as those related to modernization, may be over-interpreted, since earlier in its development the West resembled China in many respects (K. S. Yang, personal communication, 1989).

Fourth, behaviour is often assumed to be due to internalized values or beliefs, with insufficient attention given to environmental demands. Informal observation of Chinese overseas students and immigrants suggests many of the behaviours discussed in this chapter are as much under situational as intrapsychic control.

Finally, most comparisons in the cross-cultural literature involve Chinese and members of societies, primarily the United States, Great Britain, and Australia, whose origins are British. Such comparisons may exaggerate Sino–Western differences in social behaviour over what might be found if continental European societies were included.

Problems of research

Much of the empirical work in this area is inspired by the methods of American social psychology, despite cross-cultural psychology's attempt to improve on this model (Gabrenya, 1988). Perhaps as a result, the research relies heavily on self-report methods such as scenario studies and value surveys. An examination of 15 years (1979–93) of the *Journal of Cross-Cultural Psychology* (*JCCP*), conducted by the first author, revealed that of 101 articles that reported studies which included Chinese, Japanese, or Korean participants only 26 per cent used behavioural measures.

The research thus far is also overly dependent on college students as respondents. A content analysis of *JCCP* from its founding in 1970 to mid-1993, performed by Öngel and Smith (1994; personal communication, March 29, 1994), found that 50 per cent of studies on Chinese culture used college students as subjects.

Another problem is that the research thus far has been conducted primarily in the *Nanyang* (南洋; 'south ocean'), the area including Hong Kong, Taiwan, and Singapore, or what Fairbank (1987) termed Maritime China, to the near-total exclusion until the late 1980s of the PRC. Öngel and Smith's *JCCP* analysis revealed that only 21 per cent of the 61 studies with Chinese samples included a sample from the PRC. The extent to which mainland and *Nanyang* societies are part of the singular culture of a Greater China (*Da Zhonghua*/大中華) and whether the 'heart' of Chinese culture lies in the centre or the periphery is an actively debated (Gold, 1993; Harding, 1993) and ultimately empirical question with important implications for the generalizability of research.

In addition, research *about* the Chinese, conducted *in* the *Nanyang*, is primarily done *by* Americans. Öngel and Smith examined the authorships of the 61 Chinese studies in their *JCCP* analysis. Only 30 per cent of the first authors were resident in a Chinese society; 56 per cent were in the United States, and none were in the PRC. Of all 120 authors involved in these studies, only one was in the PRC, 10 were in Taiwan, and 32 were in Hong Kong. The effect of this startling authorship bias on the content of research is a highly complex issue that must be considered in the context of the university systems, resources, career paths, language abilities, publication outlets, research agendas, and so forth of cross-cultural psychologists in Chinese and other societies. The Cultural Revolution's suppression of social science and the emerging sinicization movement's (Yang, 1993) encouragement of Chinese-language research outlets must also be considered in interpreting these findings. All such considerations aside, these data beg the question (also discussed in Blowers, this volume), Who ought to study the psychology of the Chinese?

NOTE

We would like to thank Yueh-Ting Lee (黎岳庭) and Geoffrey Blowers for their comments on an earlier draft of this chapter.

Chapter 21

■

Chinese Leadership and Organizational Structures

Peter B. Smith and Zhong-Ming Wang

Research into the processes and dynamics involved in the leadership of organizations has taken a wide variety of perspectives. In this chapter we shall focus primarily upon appointed leaders working within formal organizations. In considering the nature of Chinese organizational leadership, we need to take note of the specific contexts within which it occurs. We shall first briefly examine studies of Chinese organizational structures, as well as some of the historical and contemporary circumstances within which different types of leaders operate. Having established this context, we then shall examine the responses of business leaders or other employees to a variety of questionnaires; these responses allow us to consider how distinctive are the descriptions of Chinese values which can be derived from them. The major part of the chapter then focuses upon Chinese leadership behaviour, noting in particular any evidence for distinctiveness. The practical importance of distinctiveness is underlined in the final section, in which the prospects for the current massive development of commercial joint ventures in mainland China is examined.

ORGANIZATIONAL STRUCTURE

The structure of privately owned Chinese work organizations has been most intensively studied in Hong Kong (Redding and Wong, 1986). Comparison of British and Hong Kong firms showed that the Hong Kong firms were becoming predominantly smaller and that this trend was increasing over time. By 1981, 92 per cent of all companies in Hong Kong employed fewer than 50 persons. The predominance of small size is associated with highly centralized decision-making, concentration upon a single product or market, a lack of role specialization, fewer standardized routines, and a family-based ownership structure. Redding (1990) provides detailed reports of interviews with 72 particularly successful overseas Chinese entrepreneurs, most of them from Hong Kong and Taiwan. He concludes that the culture of their organizations is based upon filial piety, collectivism, and a strong work ethic.

Studies in most countries have shown that as an organization grows, greater specialization and formalization are introduced into it. The studies by Redding and his colleagues indicate that a more frequent pattern among the overseas Chinese is that increasing size threatens the centralized control maintained by the owner, and that sons or other relatives are therefore encouraged to leave and set up their own enterprises.

Hwang (1990, 1991) argues that a fragmentation of Chinese family businesses is by no means the only future that can be imagined. While Confucian family-centred work values may guide small businesses, there are other long-established systems of values upon which managers of expanding businesses may rely. He identifies 'legalism' as such a system, defining it in terms of the rights of the individual and equitable reward for individual effort. In a survey conducted in Taiwan, Hwang showed that among private enterprises which were not family-owned, the perceived clarity and reasonableness of company regulations was as high as that found among a sample of American-owned Taiwanese organizations. Family-owned firms scored much lower on these criteria, while large state-owned enterprises scored lowest of all. Hwang concluded that Chinese organizations become more effective only as they move away from structures reliant upon traditional Confucian values such as paternalism, personalism, and filial piety, and toward structures based upon a more overt rationality, a view markedly different from that of Redding.

State ownership of all organizations on the Mainland until recently provided a setting within which neither schism and fragmentation nor the types of modernization advocated by Hwang could readily occur. Under these circumstances, the centralization of decision-making became focused not upon the family but upon the Communist Party hierarchy. In terms of contemporary patterns of Mainland management structures, there are primarily three kinds of enterprise ownership: State-owned enterprises, with the property belonging to the State and production largely under the State planning system; collectively owned enterprises, where the property belongs to the collective of workers and production is more market-oriented; and joint-venture enterprises, jointly owned and managed by Chinese and foreign partners (Wang 1993).

Current Mainland leadership structures evolved from the 'three-man leadership system' established during the 1930s in the areas of China then under revolutionary Communist control. Under this system, the management team for an enterprise consisted of the factory director, the Party secretary, and the trade union leader. In the 1940s, this system was replaced by the factory committee, which was comprised of the factory director, Party secretary, and trade union leader, plus representatives of technicians and workers. Following the founding of the People's Republic of China in 1949, Soviet-style one-man leadership became the primary model of management for the Chinese. However, this style was inconsistent with the Chinese collectivist tradition, as well as with the need for involvement of the Party leadership in industry. Hence, by the late 1950s and early 1960s the leadership system changed again, toward 'Factory director management under Party committee leadership', a system in which the Party organization, the administrative team, and trade unions were together responsible for the management, although the Party secretary played a decisive role.

Since the nationwide economic reform was launched in 1978, there have been further changes in the leadership structure of Mainland enterprises.

Management power has been greatly decentralized and most industrial enterprises have now adopted the 'management responsibility system' under which managers have much greater authority to run their enterprises (Child, 1994). We discuss current changes in this state of affairs later in this chapter.

LEADERSHIP-RELEVANT VALUES

Several researchers have reported mean scores on various values surveys for samples of Chinese business employees. The results from two particularly large-scale surveys are shown in Table 21.1. Hofstede's (1980) well-known survey did not include samples from the Mainland, but data from three samples, each of which seem to have been comprised largely or wholly of Chinese respondents, are given in the table, which also includes scores from the United States for comparative purposes. It is apparent from the results that the overseas Chinese organization members who provided these responses had a good deal in common. Compared to those in Hofstede's sample of 53 countries, their values were distinctively high on collectivism and power distance and low to moderate on uncertainty avoidance. These data are more fully discussed by Bond (this volume).

Cragin (1986) administered the Hofstede questionnaire to a wide range of Mainland managers. The scores he obtained are also entered (in brackets) in Table 21.1, but their relationship to the other scores is uncertain, since his samples are not directly comparable to those obtained by Hofstede. Nonetheless, Cragin found a similar pattern of relatively high scores on measures of collectivism and power distance. His Mainland sample, however, scored very highly on preference for uncertainty avoidance and on femininity. Additional relevant data are reported by Shenkar and Ronen (1987), who asked 163 male Mainland managers to complete the section of Hofstede's

Table 21.1 Rankings of Chinese Societies on Leadership-relevant Values

	Mainland China	Hong Kong	Singapore	Taiwan	United States
Hofstede (1980)					
Power Distance	(20)	15	13	29	38
Uncertainty Avoidance	(1)	49	53	26	43
Individualism	(23)	37	40	43	1
Masculinity	(54)	18	28	32	15
Trompenaars (1993)					
Achievement	32	20	6	—	2
Universalism	39	38	5	—	7
Internal Control	19	8	14	—	7
Specificity	34	16	19	—	17
Affectivity	41	38	25	—	20

Note Rankings in the table can range from 1 to 54 for the Hofstede data, and from 1 to 46 for the Trompenaars data. Rank 1 refers to the country scoring highest on the dimension named at the left. and rank 54 to the country scoring lowest. Bracketed ranks refer to Cragin's data.

questionnaire which refers to work goals, and from which masculinity–femininity scores can be derived. The Mainland scores obtained by this survey were compared with Hofstede's work goals data for Taiwan, Hong Kong, and Singapore. All four samples agreed in rating cooperation with co-workers rather highly among their goals and relations with their own supervisor somewhat lower on the scale. The balance of evidence suggests that there is not a strong divergence between Mainland and overseas Chinese on masculinity–femininity issues.

Cragin's data do suggest a major difference between the values of Mainland managers and other Chinese samples on uncertainty avoidance. A more recent study contradicts this aspect of Cragin's results as well. Using Hofstede's instrument, Xu and X. C. Wang (1992)(cited in Xu and Z. M. Wang, 1991) found that their Mainland data showed little difference in uncertainty avoidance, masculinity, and power distance between Mainland managers and Hofstede's samples from Taiwan. However, Mainland respondents did show higher scores on the individualism dimension than did subjects from Taiwan.

Redding (1990) has discussed the issue of variations in uncertainty avoidance. He notes that Mainland managers over the past few decades have faced substantial and unpredictable uncertainties. For instance, it has been difficult for them to determine what autonomy they do or do not have, and if they do have autonomy, whether it will last. They also have faced uncertainty about the state of the markets which they wish to supply. This set of conditions could lead Mainland managers to respond positively to the three questions in Hofstede's survey which contribute to his uncertainty avoidance measure, namely, adherence to organizational rules, commitment to stay in one's present employment for a long time, and a denial that one feels tense or stressed.

Overseas Chinese managers have faced substantial uncertainties, and in some cases discrimination as well, but Redding argues that they have succeeded in reducing these uncertainties by relying upon extended family networks to create commercial niches within which they can survive these difficulties. However, since Hofstede's data are taken from employees of a multinational corporation based in the United States, this argument cannot help us to understand why Hofstede's scores for Hong Kong and Singapore are so much lower on the measure of uncertainty avoidance than are the scores for Taiwan.

Trompenaars' (1993) more recent survey included more than 11,000 employees in 46 countries. The previously unpublished scale means given in Table 21.1 indicate that within his samples, some of the values of employees from the Mainland were rather different from those of employees from Hong Kong and Singapore. The mainland Chinese perceived status to be more often ascribed than achieved; they were guided by loyalty to their particular group rather than by universal principles; they viewed relationships in a more global or diffuse manner, rather than specifying different types of role behaviour appropriate to each situation; they saw themselves as less able to control their fate; and they expressed less overt affect. The Trompenaars results provide some of the most extensive comparative data to be collected since Hofstede's work was reported, including good-sized samples from the Mainland, Hong

Kong, and Singapore. The differences reported above may therefore be relatively reliable, in an area where contradictory findings are widespread.

Ralston, Gustafson, Elsacs, Cheung, and Terpstra (1992) and Ralston, Gustafson, Cheung, and Terpstra (1993) compared the values of managers in the United States, Hong Kong, and mainland China. The researchers attempted to overcome one of the possible weaknesses of earlier studies by using both measures which originated in the West and others which had been designed in Hong Kong on the basis of traditional Chinese values (Chinese Culture Connection, 1987). These authors were particularly interested in whether the values of Hong Kong managers were becoming more like those of American managers and less like those of Mainland managers. They found, however, many more differences between mean scores for managers in Hong Kong and the United States than they did between Hong Kong and Mainland managers. The Mainland Chinese managers scored highest on Machiavellianism, belief in an external locus of control, intolerance of ambiguity, and support for Confucian work dynamism. Hong Kong and Mainland managers scored equally high on dogmatism and higher than the American managers on this measure. These findings suggest that despite the political divergences of the past century between Hong Kong and the Mainland, their cultural contexts still retain substantial common elements when compared to non-Chinese samples. It is also possible, however, that some of these results are artefactual, since the researchers had made no correction for differences in response bias between American and Chinese respondents. Chinese respondents may be less willing than are Americans to record their disagreement with positively worded questionnaire items. They may also favour the middle category on rating scales, where Americans are more willing to use the extremes.

The considerable variation in the findings of these different surveys may possibly be accounted for as artefacts of sampling or measurement, or as unrepresentative of the variability in organizational behaviours to be found in each of the four predominantly Chinese societies sampled. At the very least, we can say that Chinese leaders operate within the context of relatively high collectivism and high power distance (see Bond, this volume). Beyond that, the degree of variation recorded in these results provides us with a necessary caution against broad or over-simplified generalizations as to the nature of Chinese leadership.

Political and economic history has ensured that Chinese leadership is enacted within a rich diversity of contexts, many of them currently undergoing rather rapid change. The studies of leadership which we shall now examine give us only isolated glimpses from particular locations and points in time. The portrayal of Chinese values and organizational structures just sketched may lead us to expect that Chinese leaders would favour particular styles of leadership. We consider next whether such distinctiveness has in fact been found to occur.

LEADERSHIP BEHAVIOUR

Several different strands are discernible among studies of Chinese leadership behaviour. Some researchers have taken variables found to be important in

Western studies and tested their endorsement by Chinese managers. Others have focused upon aspects of Chinese leadership thought to be distinctive. A third group has developed extensive projects concerning leadership style whose focus has evolved over time from non-Chinese concepts toward reformulations with greater local relevance. We shall consider these types of study in turn.

Studies Using Imported Concepts

Mintzberg's (1973) well-known observations of how a small group of American managers actually spent their day formed the basis of a study by Boisot and Liang (1992). Six directors of Chinese enterprises in Beijing were each observed over a period of six days in 1987. Substantial similarities were found between the ways in which the two sets of managers spent their time. However, there were also marked differences. The Chinese managers spent much more of their time with their superiors and much less of it with outsiders and peers than did the Americans. They received five times as much written material from their superiors as did the Americans, but they sent up to their superiors less than one-tenth as much as did the Americans. This finding is clearly consistent with the image of Mainland organizations as based upon top-down direction, but recent changes and the small sample size leave some doubt as to whether current practice may have moved some way toward greater autonomy for lower-level managers. This study also makes clear with whom the directors communicated, but it gives a less vivid picture of the focus of their communications. Within the cultural context of high power distance, it is likely that they would give more orders and spend more time checking on their implementation than do Western managers, but no data are available to support or refute this assumption.

Korabik (1992, 1993) interviewed 19 women managers in mainland China. Most of her interviews occurred during 1985. Although her interviewees had experienced many of the difficulties experienced by women managers elsewhere, government policies favouring equality, provision of government-sponsored support services, and extended family networks were all seen as aids to overcoming these difficulties.

Jones, Rozelle, and Chang (1990) compared 60 supervisor behaviours which might be used to reward or punish subordinates in the United States and China. They obtained ratings from 169 managers in southwestern China and 228 in the United States. The overall mean ratings of the 60 behaviours from the two samples correlated at 0.91, so there is a considerable consensus as to the overall difference between supervisor behaviours seen as rewarding and those seen as punishing. However, a number of interesting differences were also found. 'Praises you to others, but not to you directly' was seen as much more rewarding by Chinese supervisors, whereas 'Listens carefully to what you say' was seen as much more rewarding in the United States. A number of other behaviours rated as neutral in China were evaluated in more extreme ways in the United States. For instance, 'Gives you up to an hour off' and 'Publicly acknowledges your contribution to his/her own success' were both rated as rewarding in the United States, but not in China. 'Gives you added work while co-workers sit idle', 'Points out rules, suggesting that you need them specially explained', 'Gives you an average performance rating', and 'Watches over your shoulder while you are working' were all rated as punitive in the United States but not in China. These reported differences are readily interpretable in terms of the greater collectivism of Chinese work groups. As the authors acknowledge, there may be many other differences which the questionnaire failed to detect, since it was designed for use in the United States. A questionnaire designed by Chinese organizational psychologists would be more likely to draw on particular concepts not addressed by Western surveys.

Black and Porter (1991) underline the limitations of the use of Western-designed instruments with Chinese respondents. They asked US managers in the United States, US managers working in Hong Kong, and Chinese managers working in Hong Kong to rate aspects of their own leadership behaviour as managers. Twelve scales were used, deriving from the well-known Ohio State University studies. Each manager was also asked to report what had been the result of their most recent performance evaluation. It was found that for US managers in the United States, scores on eight of the twelve leadership scales were significantly correlated with performance evaluations. For US managers in Hong Kong, there was only one significant correlation, and for Chinese managers in Hong Kong there was none. Valid leadership studies in Chinese cultures thus require either measures which address dimensions of leadership which are ignored by Western measures, or which represent those dimensions in ways that have better local validity. The Jones et al. (1990) study discussed above provides some pointers in this direction, since although it used an instrument designed in the United States, the questions are so specific that they are more likely to detect the meanings put upon specific leader behaviours than are more global ratings.

Studies Identifying Concepts Thought to be Distinctive

Redding and Ng (1983) investigated the degree to which Hong Kong Chinese managers believe that the preservation of face is important in daily business transactions and negotiations. Every one of their 102 respondents asserted strongly that it is. The respondents were then asked to describe recent episodes where face had been an issue. In one instance, a manager responsible for sales seminars described how he gave face to his most important clients by delivering invitations in person, and asked them to give face to him by honouring him with their presence. He telephoned or mailed invitations to less important clients. This strategy worked well until the less important clients became aware of what he was doing and felt that he was not giving them sufficient face. They ceased attending, thereby putting at risk his face, since the important clients saw that they were coming to a meagrely attended seminar. To save his own face, he then had to find a way of giving adequate face to both groups of clients.

A content analysis of these episodes emphasizes the importance of reciprocity in the giving and receiving of face, and the instrumentality of face-concerns as a method of achieving business goals. Hwang (1987) presents an analysis of the use of face as a mechanism for strengthening and exploiting *guanxi*, the granting of favours either directly on the basis of personal relationships or to others to whom one has a special interpersonal linkage. Managers are clearly in a position where they can frequently exercise influence in this way. Numerous commentators concur that *guanxi* is of major importance in determining leadership effectiveness within Chinese cultures, but no data have yet been reported which clarify directly its frequency or effects.

Chang (1985) compared 130 Chinese and 61 American managers, all of whom were working for American-owned firms in Taiwan. Despite the fact that his respondents were all working within the same companies, strong differences were found in the endorsement of items referring to company paternalism. The Taiwanese were much more in favour of life-time employment, company responsibility for employees' welfare, the company's obligation to help with society's problems, and the supervisor's obligation to help subordinates overcome personal problems. Thus, it appears that among the Taiwanese respondents the Confucian value of filial piety found some expression within the workplace, even in cases in which the organization was not family-owned.

Assessment of Leadership Styles

Many American models of leadership style have distinguished two independent dimensions, which concern the task and interpersonal aspects of leadership. A variety of contingency theories have been formulated in an attempt to predict the circumstances under which each dimension of leadership style contributes to group effectiveness.

Task and interpersonal leadership styles

Smith and Tayeb (1988) showed that tests of leadership style theories have yielded rather different results in collectivist cultures than in more individualist Western cultures. In a study which included assembly-line workers and their supervisors in Hong Kong and Japan, as well as in the United Kingdom and the United States, Smith, Misumi, Tayeb, Peterson, and Bond (1989) showed that this outcome may well arise because the distinction between task and interpersonal behaviours is not firmly drawn in all cultures. Data from Hong Kong (as well as from Japan) showed that many 'task' behaviours were seen also as having implications for interpersonal relations within the work group. For instance, 'talking about immediate work problems' was seen in Hong Kong and Japan as relevant to interpersonal relations, whereas in the United States it was not. In a similar way, behaviours thought of as 'interpersonal' in North America were also seen as having implications for task performance. For instance, 'spending time with one's superior socially' was seen in this way by Hong Kong respondents.

Consistent with this finding, studies of effective leadership style in Taiwan have shown that effective leaders are those who are seen as highly ranked on both task and interpersonal aspects of their role. This result has been obtained in studies of female government employees, elementary school teachers, junior high school teachers, factory workers, and accountants (Bond and Hwang, 1986).

'PM' leadership theory

The Institute of Psychology at the Chinese Academy of Sciences in Beijing has conducted a large-scale project which also concerns leadership style (Ling, Chen, and Wang, 1987; Xu, 1989). The researchers' point of departure was the 'PM leadership theory' of Misumi (1985), who has shown that effective leaders in Japan are also those who score highly on both task and social behaviours. Misumi terms these dimensions of leader behaviour performance (P) and maintenance (M). The Beijing group surveyed subordinates' perceptions of the PM styles of their leaders, sampling 53 factories throughout mainland China and obtaining over 16,000 responses. Through the use of cluster analysis, they concluded that to obtain the best predictions of leader effectiveness, a third dimension of leader behaviour had to be introduced into the PM model. The third dimension, which they termed character (C), concerns the perceived moral integrity of the supervisor. Questionnaire items tapping the C dimension refer to qualities such as honesty, integrity, and willingness to listen, as well as commitment to the work team and to the Party (Peterson, 1988).

This revision of a theory originating outside mainland China is one of relatively few to be found in this area of research. Several related studies attest to the plausibility of the amendment, since they also refer to moral questions notably absent from leadership studies conducted elsewhere. We have noted already Chang's (1985) finding that Taiwanese managers believe that companies should contribute to the solution of society's problems. A similar finding is apparent in the comparison by Hunt and Meindl (1991) of the values of 94 managers from northeastern China and 154 managers from the United States. Respondents were asked to rate the importance of 24 work values. There was substantial similarity in the rank order of the responses obtained, with one exception. 'Making a contribution to society' was ranked third by the Chinese respondents and twenty-fourth by the Americans. The identification of a cluster of Chinese values identified as Moral Discipline by the Chinese Culture Connection (1987), discussed by Bond (this volume), most probably also overlaps with the types of values treated by the Beijing researchers as indicators of moral character.

Participative decision-making

Another group of studies that address leadership style has concerned the degree to which Chinese leaders share decision-making with their subordinates. The measure used in most of the studies is based on that devised in the West by Heller and Wilpert (1981). Xia (1987) surveyed managers in four major Chinese cities and found that Chinese managers reported less use of participative methods than had been found in early studies in Europe and North America. However, the most satisfied Chinese managers were those who reported more participation. Jamal and Xie (1991), applying a measure based upon Likert's (1967) theory of leadership to 300 managers and workers in Beijing and Wuhan, also found that respondents who saw their superiors as participative reported more satisfaction, more job involvement, and less role stress.

Wang (1989) described some of the first results from a six-year longitudinal joint research project between Hangzhou University and the Tavistock Institute of Human Relations, which focused on organizational decision-making and new technology. Using Influence Power-sharing as a core variable, he investigated decision-making patterns among 339 Chinese managers (73 top-level managers and 212 middle managers, plus a sample of 54 managers comprising 27 boss–subordinate dyads). The results show that managers at higher levels believed that particular decisions require higher levels of managerial skill than did their subordinates. The higher-level managers also estimated that it took longer for subordinates to learn these skills than did their subordinates. Despite this discrepancy across rank, managers were generally positive toward participation and change, and the main reasons they gave for favouring participation were to improve communication and motivation. Lower-level managers perceived the decision-making styles of higher-level management as less participative than was reported by the higher-level managers with whom they worked, as has also been found in Western studies. Satisfaction was highest among those who reported participative decision-making and high utilization of their skills. These results are relatively similar to those obtained with the same measures in Western countries.

A subsequent study provided a more detailed analysis, differentiating between types of decisions, types of industry, and organizational levels (Wang and Heller, 1993). It was found that the making of short-term decisions involved senior managers much more in mainland China than it did in the United Kingdom. For long-term decisions, the pattern was reversed. There were also substantially different results for manufacturing firms compared to service industries. For instance, in Chinese manufacturing firms, long-term decisions devolved more to junior managers than was the case in the United Kingdom. In service industries the pattern was reversed. These results underline the finding that effective leadership behaviours are not dependent solely on cultural issues, but are driven by an interaction between culture and the logics of each organization's commercial and political environment. Wang and Heller assert that decision-making will occur at more senior levels where uncertainty is greatest. This point is illustrated by the finding that decision-making in China occurred at more senior levels in the newly developing service industries but at lower levels in the more long-established production industries.

Leader event management

A final group of studies of leadership style is concerned with the manner in which managers handle day-to-day events. A model of event management was developed by Smith and Peterson (1988), and data were subsequently collected from managers in more than 20 countries. An initial comparison among Chinese, American, and British managers showed that Chinese managers were much more likely to rely upon their superiors in handing events than were Western managers (Smith, Peterson, and Wang, in press). Subsequent results from 25 countries indicated that managers in China relied more strongly upon widespread beliefs as to what is right than did those in any other sample. Managers in Hong Kong and Macao relied strongly upon their superiors, whereas those in Singapore were guided more by unwritten rules as to how to proceed (Smith and Peterson, 1994).

Wang (1993) surveyed 120 managers from 15 mainland Chinese industrial organizations and found that in making decisions, the managers relied mostly upon their own experience and training, formal rules, and their superior's opinion. In comparison with managers elsewhere, however, as reported above, there was seen a much greater reliance upon beliefs widespread in one's country as to what is the ethically right course of action. Wang's analysis showed that managers from service industries relied more upon subordinates and peers than did managers from manufacturing industries, while joint-venture managers relied more on their own experience and training and less on widespread beliefs in their decision-making than did managers in State-owned companies. This study is closely related to the question of leadership in Chinese–foreign joint-ventures, a topic we shall discuss in a subsequent section.

SELECTION AND ASSESSMENT OF LEADERS

Leadership assessment procedures were developed in mainland Chinese industries in the mid-1980s (Wang, 1988). For a field study conducted in the machine industry in Shanghai in 1982, a three-component assessment system based upon three groups of criteria was developed. Each of the three groups of criteria was given a label: Political Predisposition (political competence, responsibility, modeling, open-mindedness, progressiveness, and so forth), Intellectual Ability (such as abilities in decision-making, creativity, problem-solving, verbal skills, social and interpersonal skills, and coordination with others), and Performance (productivity and social efficiency). More than 2,000 employees took part in this study, which provided personnel information enabling the use of these criteria for leader selection, placement, and training.

Lu (1986) used a management simulation test to evaluate leadership style, assessing four work samples: a document review, involving 15 documents frequently encountered by middle management; a group discussion, based upon a management meeting for personnel placement; a role-played supervisor–subordinate conversation; and planning of a speech concerning a proposal for new production. The results showed that this series of simulation tests was more effective than were traditional paper-and-pencil tests in identifying leaders in terms of such skills as verbal ability, written expression, interpersonal effectiveness, delegation, organization, analytic ability, management creativity, and policy implementation.

In relation to the assessment and selection of managers, a job analysis study was conducted in 60 mainland Chinese factories (Wu, 1986). Seven categories of management functions were identified: general administration, ideological work, production management, technical work, marketing, welfare, and personnel management. An instrument for leadership assessment was devised which included 30 items, tapping four components: political predisposition, knowledge structure, ability level, and work performance. The measures developed by Lu (1986) and Wu (1986) were compared with subsequent ratings by managers and subordinates, which provided some evidence of validity of each of these criteria.

Most of the more recent leadership assessment studies in China have adopted a group approach to evaluation so as to enhance validity and reliability. A 'role set' method of multilevel measurement has been used in many industries and governmental departments (see, for example, Wang, 1988; Xu and Wang, 1994). Each role set involves the leader (or candidate) and his or her supervisor, subordinates, and peers. Each member of the role set assesses the ability and performance of candidates or incumbents for leading positions.

In comparing the development of leadership assessment techniques in mainland China to those in use elsewhere, the most notable feature is the inclusion of criteria such as political predisposition or political competence. Whether such criteria are seen as tapping the same qualities as those defined as 'moral character' by some of the earlier leadership style studies is difficult to determine. Whether this is so or not, one of the most crucial leadership issues in contemporary China concerns the demands put on the exercise of leadership as an ever-growing number of organizations enter into joint-venture partnerships within foreign partners.

LEADERSHIP IN COMMERCIAL JOINT VENTURES

By 1994 about 150,000 joint ventures were in place in mainland China. Research into their functioning is still in its infancy (Kelley and Shenkar, 1993; Child, 1994), but the scale of this development has ensured that researchers are now focusing their attention upon developments within mainland China, rather than upon cross-cultural issues within organizations in other predominantly Chinese societies. That such issues continue to be important is illustrated by the work of Wong and Birnbaum-More (1994), who studied Hong Kong banks. They found that the degree to which banks located in Hong Kong have a centralized and hierarchical structure can be predicted from the Power Distance score assigned by Hofstede (1980) to the nation where ownership of the bank resides.

Studies of Mainland China

Henley and Nyaw (1990) surveyed 34 firms in the Shenzhen special economic zone. About half the firms contacted reported that their joint ventures were functioning effectively. Among those experiencing problems, the most frequently cited difficulty was a lack of clarity between the partners as to which leaders held authority to resolve problematic issues, and what was the nature of that authority. For instance, the right to dismiss workers or to discipline them for rule infractions was not precisely located.

A series of interview-based studies by Child and his colleagues (Child, Ireland, Boisot, Lee, and Watts, 1990; Child and Xu, 1991; Child and Markoczy, 1993; Child, 1994) have studied joint ventures in northern China. They have found that many more difficulties arise than they found in a parallel study of joint ventures in Hungary. The difficulties are most frequent when the partner is an American firm, and they occur most often in the area of human resource management. Typical difficulties follow attempts by US firms to implement systems of selection, appraisal, dismissal, or promotion which local employees see as culturally inappropriate. European partners are somewhat more willing to adjust systems to local conditions, and ventures with Hong Kong-based partners experience the least difficulties.

Wang and Sheng (1990) and Wang (1992) have examined the structures and managerial strategies of 25 joint ventures around Hangzhou, Shanghai, and Tianjing. Their interviews and field surveys indicate a major change in organizational structures, compared to those previously seen in mainland China. The 'general-manager responsibility system of management under the leadership of the board of directors' has been widely adopted; the board of directors makes important and long-term decisions, while the general manager is responsible for daily management tasks. The study found that it is easier for newly created joint ventures to establish positive behavioural norms than it is for previously existing organizations, which often have brought with them old, established working styles and norms. Many of the joint ventures were found to have been organized as 'one company, two management systems', that is, the joint-venture management system concerns production and finance, while the State-owned management system continues to regulate other processes. Variation in management procedures was also seen: some overseas managers have overall charge of the organization, where others are managed on the basis of joint Chinese–foreign responsibility. In contrast to State enterprises, joint-venture managements have full power to run the companies, while trade unions have become relatively independent and serve as representatives of the employees.

A series of detailed case studies (Wang, 1992) further demonstrates that the creation of joint ventures does not automatically lead to the compatibility of management styles between partners. It has been found that overseas managers are usually more task-oriented in style than are local managers, and they tend to take an individualistic approach, making decisions by themselves with implementation mainly through their line managers. However, most Chinese managers are more relationship-oriented than are the foreign managers, and they are accustomed to collective decision-making and consultation with team members before making decisions. Overseas managers are often more outcome-oriented, emphasizing the quality of the outcomes no matter how the task is performed, while Chinese managers are more process-oriented, concerned with the ways in which a task is implemented.

In a more recent field study, Wang and Satow (1994) surveyed the leadership behaviour of 151 Chinese managers from 72 companies (14 Chinese–Japanese joint ventures, 23 other joint ventures, three wholly owned Japanese ventures, and 32 Chinese State-owned companies) in and around Hangzhou, Shanghai, Suzhou, Wuxi, and Shenzhen. Four functional dimensions of leadership style were evaluated: Expectancy (requiring that subordinates would fulfil obligations), Sentiment (supportive behaviours),

Informativeness (communication skills), and Trustworthiness (a general impression of competence). The results indicate a clear factor structure of the constructs and high reliability of the measures. Overall, scores were high on Expectancy but relatively low on Trustworthiness. Among the joint ventures, Japanese leaders were rated higher than were those in other organizations on Sentiment and Informativeness. Managers from Taiwan and Hong Kong were rated much higher on Expectancy, while US managers were rated much lower on Trustworthiness. A comparison of joint ventures with State-owned companies showed the State-owned companies low on most scales, particularly Expectancy.

The managers were also asked to rate the effectiveness of their company on various criteria in comparison to their competitors. Joint ventures and especially Japanese joint ventures were rated the highest. There were also significant links between effectiveness criteria and ratings of the leadership styles, but since all these ratings were completed by the same respondents, the measures may not be independent of one another. However, it does appear from this study that high ratings are achieved in organizations where there is less cultural distance between the partners, but where there is also some foreign involvement, thereby bringing in new procedures, new capital, and other needed resources.

The meaning of these results can be further clarified by the findings of Sonoda (1994), who surveyed 1,034 Chinese middle managers working in 37 Sino–Japanese joint ventures on the Mainland. He found that they evaluate their Japanese superiors positively but are dissatisfied with other aspects of their situation, especially the pay and welfare benefits. Sonoda suggests that this finding is the result of a perception among the managers that each organization is highly successful and they should receive a higher share of the profits from it.

Strategies for Developing Leadership within Joint Ventures

The studies of joint ventures outlined above indicate the need for improved compatibility between managers favouring different values, leadership styles, and corporate cultures. A three-point strategy has been proposed and implemented (Wang, 1990, 1992). The first element is focused upon improving employees' attitudes, interpersonal skills, and decision-making competence, so as to increase compatibility in working styles. This intervention includes two types of training programmes. The first of these programmes provides joint workshops for all managers within a particular venture, focused upon the critical issues in joint-venture management, so as to reach an agreement on appropriate management styles and perspectives. The second intervention uses group attributional analysis techniques, within which managers from both sides discuss and make attributions concerning their performance. This technique has proved very useful in practical settings (Wang, 1988). Each of these training interventions relies upon the two key, culturally-appropriate components of group consultation and team interaction.

The second required element in effective organization development is a systemic strategy for the creation of compatible management structures across organizational levels. This approach can include the establishment of more formal communication channels and networks, restructuring of sub-systems for personnel and performance appraisal, and the setting up of new mechanisms for coordination.

The third element is the enhancement of participation and organizational improvement by emphasizing task commitment and group responsibility. The Wang (1989) study discussed above showed that in mainland Chinese enterprises participation can increase skill utilization and morale, and leads to higher quality decision-making. Attention is therefore given to the locus of decision-making in joint ventures, both laterally and vertically. This targeting can facilitate compatible decision-making and power-sharing and achieve a more positive organizational climate (Wang, 1990).

CONCLUSIONS

Recent research into Chinese leadership shares certain methodological problems noted by the authors of many of the other chapters in this Handbook. Pre-eminent among these is the observation that many of the studies conducted, both those which focus directly upon Chinese subjects and those comparing Chinese and non-Chinese respondents, have used concepts and measures originally designed in Western cultures. Considerable caution is in order until the findings of such studies can be further tested using locally developed measures which have demonstrable validity within Chinese cultural contexts. Shenkar and Von Glinow (1994) identify additional difficulties which we do well to bear in mind. For instance, they point out that Chinese familiarity with questionnaires and rating scales is much lower than in Western countries. Chinese respondents may choose central categories on rating scales in order not to take up extreme positions, and this could well affect the validity of some of the comparisons of the uncorrected mean scores reviewed above. Furthermore, the importance of distinguishing between in-group and out-group in Chinese society may mean that questionnaires will be filled in invalidly or else not completed at all, if insufficient trust has been established between researcher and respondent. Respondents may be concerned that identifiable responses may find their way to out-groups in whom they feel no trust.

With these cautions in mind, what conclusions are permissible from the corpus of research studies so far available? Virtually all the findings we have reviewed are consistent with the position proposed at the opening of this chapter. Chinese societies are somewhat collectivist and rather high on power distance. Effective leadership behaviour is that which works within this premise, but the diversity of current Chinese societies indicates that this prescription is by no means a strait-jacket. There is considerable scope for variations in styles of leadership behaviour depending upon organizational context, as Wang and Heller (1993) have shown, and upon organizational ownership, as Hwang's studies in Taiwan (Bond and Hwang, 1986) have indicated.

A notable feature of the existing studies is that they make little reference to teamwork as an attribute of Chinese organizational life. As in other countries, the qualities of leaders have been analysed largely in terms of relations with subordinates. Peer-oriented collective leadership structures have substantial importance in many Chinese organizations, and little is yet known as to how such leaders work together as teams. It is to be hoped that the next generation of leadership studies can appreciate that Chinese societies are in certain respects different, and so they can move towards specifying more clearly the culturally relevant ways in which leaders can achieve their goals. The results of such studies will have considerable practical importance in defining effective practice within joint ventures. This fine-tuning in the conceptualization of Chinese leadership will require a degree of focus upon the way in which rapidly changing contexts are challenging both mainland and overseas Chinese managers, but it should also include a focus upon such culturally salient aspects as face, paternalism. and moral character.

Chapter 22

Chinese Decision-making

J. Frank Yates and Ju-Whei Lee

A decision-maker's task is to select a course of action that will yield a favourable outcome. Several things distinguish decision problems from more general ones, and make them especially difficult to solve and to study. Perhaps the most significant difference is implicit in the phrase 'favourable outcomes': decision-making centres on people's values. This characteristic complicates matters because of marked differences between the individuals facing the decision. Nearly everyone prefers more money to less. We differ from one another substantially, however, in the degree to which, say, being paid an extra dollar per hour compensates for being required to arrive at work at 5 a.m. rather than at 9 a.m. For some potential outcomes, the reactions of different individuals can be diametrically opposed to each other. Although you consider a certain building design to be truly beautiful, your colleague easily may regard it as unbearably ugly. Thus, in contrast to problems in, say, algebra, solutions to decision problems are not definitively good or bad; their quality is subjective.

As a high-level activity, decision-making is readily influenced by myriad conditions, including the abstract concept dubbed 'culture'. The Chinese experience has been and is distinctive in many ways. It would be surprising indeed if, over time, the Chinese failed to develop at least some decision mechanisms that differ from those of other peoples. The purpose of this chapter is to describe and explain some of the major Chinese versus non-Chinese variations that have been identified. The plan of the chapter is built around several fundamental issues that arise in decision problems and for which Chinese versus non-Chinese differences have been discussed. First, we examine decision considerations: What does the decision maker take into account in deliberating courses of action? Then we consider judgement: What does the decision maker expect would happen if a particular option were selected? Next we discuss the value issue: What decision outcomes and situational features are preferred and by how much? We then examine the participation question: Which people become involved in solving decision problems and what roles do they play? And, finally, we take a broader perspective and consider decision styles and modes: How does the decision maker prefer to approach decision tasks generally? The chapter closes with a discussion of the significance of Chinese versus non-Chinese decision-making differences.

CONSIDERATIONS

A 'representation' is the decision maker's personal characterization of the given situation. It specifies, among other things, what is taken into account and, implicitly, what is ignored. What any decision maker 'sees' as significant can differ markedly from what another regards as pertinent. Research has also indicated that there are systematic differences in the kinds of things that Chinese and non-Chinese include in their decision representations, over and beyond what ordinary individual differences would imply.

By far, the most widely discussed difference in Chinese and Western decision representations concerns social relations. Simply put, the claim is that in many situations a Chinese decision maker's resolution of a decision problem will be affected by social issues that do not even occur to a Western decision maker. This representational difference typically is couched in terms of Chinese collectivism versus Western individualism and related constructs. A study by Gaenslen (1986) provides a good example with a novel projective methodology.

Gaenslen's (1986) data came from representative samples of fiction published in China, Japan, Russia, and the United States. The United States was taken as the prototypical individualistic society; the others were accepted as collectivistic ones. In one analysis, coders identified situations in which there was a conflict between a superior and a subordinate (for example, a teacher and a pupil). Two aspects were noted: whether the conflict occurred in private or in the presence of others, and which of the two persons prevailed. The results showed that the superior usually won in these conflicts, regardless of the origin of the fiction and whether the conflict was public or private. But what is of interest is the 'public–private advantage' of the superior: the percentage of conflicts won by the superior in public minus the percentage of conflicts won by the superior in private. This difference was especially pronounced in the collectivistic societies. For instance, where the public–private advantage of the American subjects was only 6.2 per cent, that of the Chinese was 10.8 per cent.

A significant feature of Chinese collectivism is that publicly acknowledged social status matters a great deal, and behaving in a status-appropriate manner is essential to the image one projects. This facet of Chinese culture seems to be reflected in the high scores of Chinese subjects on the Power Distance dimension identified in Hofstede's (1980) cross-cultural studies of values (see also Bond, this volume). This construct is defined as 'the extent to which the less powerful members of organizations and institutions (like the family) accept and expect that power is distributed unequally' (Hofstede and Bond, 1988, p. 10). Status is seldom completely ignored in individualistic societies, but it is far less important and hence is less likely to be considered when people make decisions, as when the Western subordinates in Gaenslen's (1986) stories chose to either resist or acquiesce to their superiors' demands.

JUDGEMENT

Imagine the following business situation. If a bid for Contract C were success-ful, it would be extremely profitable for your company. But preparing the bid would cost a lot of money, and there is no guarantee that the bid would be accepted. Let us suppose that the problem can be concretized as follows: if you decline to bid on Contract C, you neither gain nor lose anything. If you do offer a bid, there is a 30 per cent chance that you would win the contract, earning your company $500,000. However, if the bid is rejected—a probability of 70 per cent—the company would lose the $200,000 required to prepare the bid. What would you do? What *should* you do?

Much of traditional Western scholarship on decision-making has been con-cerned with circumstances like these. Intuitively, it is clear what kinds of rules make sense. Here, if the chances of the bid being accepted are high enough, then the bid should be submitted; otherwise, it should not. But what is 'high enough?' Is 30 per cent beyond the threshold of success probabilities that war-rant offering the bid? Principles such as expected utility maximization (see, for example, Yates, 1990) provide guidelines for establishing such thresholds.

Consider another issue: What is the origin of decision-relevant likelihood assessments, such as the 30 per cent and 70 per cent probabilities in the bid-ding problem? Interestingly, schemes like expected utility theory are mute on the source of the probabilities used in decision problems. All that matters is that the probabilities be 'probabilities' in the mathematical sense, that they obey the probability theory axioms. Thus, there need be no connection at all between those probabilities and what actually happens in the real world, such as that events assigned high probabilities tend to happen more often than those asso-ciated with low ones. Clearly, however, the material consequences of making real-world decisions on the basis of rules incorporating such assessments depend vitally on their 'accuracy' as predictions of actual events (Yates, 1990). Indeed, the effectiveness of *all* decision procedures that rely on how sure the decision maker is that particular events will occur is inherently limited by the quality of those assessments. This caveat includes formal methods such as expected utility maximization as well as our everyday intuitive approaches.

It sometimes makes sense to speak of 'objective' probabilities and to rely on those in making decisions. Thus, in a game of cards, a player should consider the probability of being dealt a face card in the suit of spades to be 3/52, based on the assumption of random sampling or the observation of lots of hands in the past. However, in comparatively unique situations like our contract bid-ding decision problem—which are the rule rather than the exception—the notion of objective probabilities simply does not apply. There is then no choice but to rely on the assessments of real people, for example, the probability judgements of contracting experts. Such opinions can differ greatly from one person to the next. Suppose that in our example the threshold probability is 25 per cent. One consultant might say there is a 30 per cent chance of a successful bid, implying that the bid should be submitted, while another claims that the bid has only a 20 per cent chance of success, implying that no bid should be offered. Whose opinion should be accepted? Consensus is that decision makers in such circumstances should use the assessments of the consultant whose judgements are usually most accurate.

Variations in Overconfidence

Arguably, the most dramatic and reliable of all variations in the decision-related behaviour of Chinese and non-Chinese occur in probability judgement accuracy and the underlying processes. Inquiry into such variations was initiated by Phillips and Wright (1977). Research by Yates, Zhu, Ronis, Wang, Shinotsuka, and Toda (1989) provide a good illustration of typical findings. In one of those studies, subjects in mainland China and the United States were asked to consider general knowledge items like the following: *Potatoes grow better in (a) warm or (b) cool climates?*

The subject must pick either (a) or (b) as the correct alternative and then state a probability between 50 per cent and 100 per cent that the selected option is in fact correct. Yates et al. calculated two statistics for each subject in their studies. The first was the average probability judgement that his or her chosen answers were correct: AJ = Mean P'(My chosen answer is correct). The second statistic was the proportion of the subject's chosen answers that actually were correct: PC = Proportion of actual correct answers. A third statistic was then derived from these first two: Bias = AJ - PC. The average values of the bias statistic were 13.4 per cent and 7.2 per cent for the Chinese and American subjects, respectively.

Many people, Chinese and non-Chinese alike, find comparisons like these striking and surprising. Why? Probability judgements are said to be 'well-calibrated' to the extent that average probabilities match the corresponding proportions of times the focal events occur. The bias statistic measures a particular form of miscalibration, normally described as 'overconfidence' when the statistic is positive. When bias is positive, this means that the person's average judgement that he or she selected the right answers to various questions outstrips the objective rate at which the person really does pick correct answers. The person appears to believe that his or her knowledge is better than it actually is. For various reasons, people are not terribly surprised that Westerners— particularly Americans—are overconfident in their general knowledge. Those same reasons (to which we return below) suggest that Chinese overconfidence, if it exists at all, should be weaker, not stronger, than Western overconfidence. The data indicate exactly the opposite.

Findings like those of Yates et al. (1989) are not an anomaly; they have been shown to have considerable generality and reliability (see, for example, Wright and Phillips, 1980; Yates, Lee, Levi, and Curley, 1990). One interesting point to note, however, is that the judgement patterns of Yates et al.'s (1989) Japanese subjects were essentially the same as those of their American counterparts, and hence different from those of all other Asian subject groups that have been reported in the literature. Cross-national variations in overconfidence are not restricted to general knowledge or the opinions of lay persons. Yates et al. (1989) had subjects make probability judgements about the future values of various quantities, such as high temperatures in familiar cities. Once again, although virtually all subjects' judgements were overconfident, those of the

Chinese subjects were especially so. Zhang (1992) examined probabilistic predictions of economic indices made by professional forecasters in mainland China. Those judgements evidenced the same extreme overconfidence found in the assessments by the Chinese subjects of Yates et al.

Explanations for Calibration Variations

How can we explain the observed variations in probability judgement calibration? There are likely to be multiple contributors, but first we might consider why people are so surprised to learn that Chinese tend to be more overconfident than Westerners, rather than less so. Implicit in this surprise are two assumptions. The first is that overconfidence has an affective basis, that it reflects a person's ego-driven, inflated opinion of his or her own abilities, a lack of modesty. The second assumption is that Chinese culture pointedly and successfully discourages such immodest opinions, or at least the expression of them. There is good evidence for the latter assumption (see, for example, Bond and Cheung, 1983; Crittendon, this volume; Leung, this volume). This evidence, coupled with findings like those of Yates et al. (1989), therefore casts serious doubt on the validity of the first assumption, for Chinese subjects and perhaps more generally. That is, such overconfidence is unlikely to rest on affect.

Yates, Lee, and Shinotsuka (1992) have proposed and tested a competing cognitive explanation for extreme Chinese overconfidence. This account builds on earlier suggestions about factors that influence overconfidence (for example those of Koriat, Lichtenstein, and Fischhoff, 1980). The proposal is essentially the following: Suppose a person is faced with an issue (such as whether potatoes grow better in warm or cool climates, or whether an economic indicator will exceed a certain point). The person attempts to construct arguments on both sides of the issue (reasons why one should expect potatoes to grow better in warm climates as well as reasons to think they grow poorly in such conditions). The person's judgement of the chances for one particular alternative rests on the number and quality of the generated arguments supporting that option. Because of certain features of the human cognitive system (such as priming mechanisms and limited short-term memory capacity), such 'argument recruitment' is likely to be abbreviated. Specifically, unless extraordinary steps are taken, the process will be limited to a small number of arguments and dominated by the first ones that come to mind. Therefore, the person will see little reason to suspect that the alternative favoured by those initial arguments might be wrong, and hence will have great confidence in its correctness. Yates et al. (1992) submit that, comparatively speaking, argument recruitment should be especially abbreviated for Chinese subjects, at least when they are considering some classes of issues. Recruitment differences are conjectured to reflect certain contrasting 'cognitive customs' in Chinese and non-Chinese communities.

Consider American society. American culture is highly contentious, in some senses 'by design'. In a recent year, for instance, roughly one new lawsuit was filed for every 10 adults in the United States, a rate several times greater than that in Taiwan (President's Council on Competitiveness, 1991; *Zhong Hua Min*

Guo Nian Jian, 1991). In American lawsuits, cases are settled via an adversarial system in which each side makes the best arguments it can for its own position and attacks the arguments of the opposition. Each case is decided by a judge or jury required by law to weigh the relative merits of the competing arguments (the 'evidence') presented to them. A strikingly similar approach to learning is promulgated in American education. 'Critical thinking', in which students question the validity of every idea proposed to them, is actively encouraged and taught (see, for example, Johnson and Johnson, 1993). Clearly, there is a strongly held belief that critical thinking is an effective means of learning as well as an important skill and habit to develop in and of itself.

By contrast, consider corresponding Chinese customs. Chinese civilization is the oldest continuous one in the world today, filled with marvelous achievements extending back well over 3,000 years. That record is a convincing argument for the premium Chinese culture places on its past. For instance, Confucius insisted that he was not personally an originator of important ideas. Instead, he saw himself as merely a transmitter of the principles of 'the Ancients', the heralded kings and dukes of the Zhou dynasty (1027–221 BC) that preceded Confucius's own era (Confucius, 1989, VII, 1-3). Confucius taught that a key to the success of a person and of a society is adherence to the ideals and examples set by those who came before. Implicit in this prescription is a vital principle of learning, in fact, of thinking itself. What one needs to know are facts and procedures that have been accepted as having proved their worth through the empirical test of time: Chinese history. Thus, it would only make sense that the traditional Chinese approach to learning and teaching have at least some different emphases than, say, American approaches.

Given Chinese assumptions, the most reasonable path to knowledge would not be debate over competing ideas but instead activities intended to achieve an understanding of what is already known and accepted as correct, for example, model emulation and practice (cf. Chan, 1967). Indeed, although the meaning has changed over the centuries, Nakamura (1964) maintains that, 'Etymologically, the Chinese word "to learn" has no other meaning but "to imitate"' (p. 214). Different contemporary Chinese societies vary in their emphases on Confucian and other traditional ideas, but it seems naïve to expect that principles that so thoroughly permeated a culture for centuries would be unrecognizable in any of those societies today. Moreover, numerous Chinese and non-Chinese observers of Chinese educational practice maintain that many of those ideas in fact are still very much in evidence (see, for example, Gardner, 1989; Hwu, 1993).

In their experiment, Yates et al. (1992) presented Taiwanese Chinese, Japanese, and American subjects with general knowledge questions of the form described previously. In the Reasons condition of that experiment, before subjects chose what they considered to be the correct answer and wrote down their probability judgements for a given question, they were asked to perform another task: to generate as many reasons as possible favouring and opposing the truth of each of the alternatives, that is, pros and cons. Previous research had shown that this device tends to reduce overconfidence among American subjects, thereby implicating argument recruitment as a factor in the overconfidence phenomenon. Yates et al. (1992) argued that Chinese teaching and learning customs would discourage Chinese subjects from spontaneously generating many pros and cons—particularly cons—for available alternatives, thereby contributing to extreme overconfidence. Thus, these authors expected that the *forced* recruitment of pros and cons would lead to an especially pronounced reduction in overconfidence for their Chinese subjects.

Yates et al. (1992) were surprised that such a reduction did not occur, but an analysis of subjects' reasons generation was most revealing. Consider, for example, the following proportions of reasons subjects generated that argued against the correctness of the answers the subjects eventually chose: Japanese subjects, 47.5 per cent; American subjects, 40.9 per cent; Taiwanese Chinese subjects, 23.6 per cent. The researchers thus discovered that, as suggested by these statistics, even though the Chinese subjects made the attempt, they could produce far fewer reasons that disagreed with the answers they ultimately chose than could their Japanese and American counterparts. The results were consistent with the initial proposal: it appears that the Chinese subjects were more overconfident in their chosen answers because, quite literally, they saw fewer reasons why those answers might be wrong.

The Role of Alternative Forms of Uncertainty

A result by Zhang (1992) seems to have special significance to the issue of Chinese versus non-Chinese probability judgement. Keren (1987) asked Dutch bridge players to report their probability judgements that the final contracts would be made in the games they were playing. Zhang repeated Keren's experiment, but with Chinese bridge players. The results were most interesting. The Chinese players' judgements appeared to be better calibrated than those of the Dutch players. In fact, unlike in any previous comparison between Chinese and Western subjects, the Chinese subjects' judgements were less overconfident, not more.

How can the bridge findings be reconciled with all the previous studies? An especially compelling potential explanation, as noted by Zhang (1992), concerns alternative forms of uncertainty. In card games like bridge, the uncertainty is largely well-defined, frequentistic, and 'aleatory', that is, resting on pure, irreducible chance (see Wright and Ayton, 1994, for discussions of various kinds of uncertainty). One can do best forecasting the outcomes of card games by paying close attention to how similar games turned out in the past or by learning (perhaps inductively) the combinatorial principles involved. But research such as that of Yates et al. (1992) indicates that people do not—in fact, cannot—attack general knowledge and other less well-defined judgement tasks in the same way. Instead, they must adopt strategies such as generating and evaluating arguments for the various possibilities. This suggests an interesting thesis that should be examined in future research: Chinese cognitive customs, which emphasize other skills besides the deliberation of multiple, competing arguments, might not be particularly conducive to good calibration of probability judgements in ill-defined situations. Those same customs, however, might be especially supportive of the judgements demanded in more concrete conditions.

VALUE

In decision-making, the term 'value' refers to the degree of attraction or repulsion people have for specific outcomes that might result from their decisions, and at times to aspects of decision situations themselves. Such affect is strongly shaped by experience. Thus, it would be surprising if there were not myriad differences between the values Chinese and non-Chinese people attach to various entities. Such variations are the subject of the work of market researchers, who seek to identify various market 'segments' in order to make and sell the products that are most appealing to particular populations (consider, say, distinctive Chinese food tastes). Are there general principles that seem to underlie less mundane Chinese versus non-Chinese variations in value assignments? Apparently so. (See also Bond, this volume; Jaccard and Wan, 1986; Ralston, Gustafson, Elsass, Cheung, and Terpstra, 1992.) One particularly significant class of differences in Chinese and non-Chinese value assignments concerns 'risk', the possibility of loss (cf. Yates and Stone, 1992). There have been numerous indications that risk is especially repugnant to Chinese decision makers. Thus, if a decision alternative entails a high degree of risk, some research suggests that Chinese decision makers are relatively more likely to reject that alternative than are their non-Chinese counterparts (see, for example, Clifford, Lan, Chou, and Qi, 1989; Wright, Phillips, and Wisudha, 1983). A study by Hong (1978) involving choice dilemmas is illustrative on this point.

'Choice dilemmas' are vignettes about decision problems entailing risk. One commonly studied dilemma (Kogan and Wallach, 1964) concerns a man who currently has a job that promises a secure but undistinguished future. His problem is whether to relinquish this job in favour of one with a new company. This new job would provide a much more prosperous career, but only if the company succeeds. The subject assumes the role of an advisor: What is the lowest probability of the new company's success the subject would consider acceptable to make it worthwhile for the man to take the new job? All choice dilemmas have this form. One option (for example, the current job) contains little if any risk. The other could entail either a large or small amount of risk, depending on the chances associated with some favourable critical event (for example, the new company's success). The lower the chances, the greater the risk. The higher the subject's stated *acceptable* probability level, the more risk-averse the subject is considered to be.

Hong (1978) presented subjects with a number of choice dilemmas. He found that Chinese subjects from Taiwan were significantly more risk-averse than were American subjects. Research has shown that under many circumstances, Western subjects become less risk-averse when they deliberate choice dilemmas in groups rather than as individuals. Hong's American subjects did indeed display the typical 'risky shifts', but his Chinese subjects did just the opposite, exhibiting 'cautious shifts'. That is, when the Chinese subjects were required to produce consensus risk-taking advice in groups, they were even more risk-averse than when they arrived at their advice alone. Numerous explanations have been proposed for preference shifts in choice dilemmas (see, for example, Bromiley and Curley, 1992; Davis, Kameda, and Stasson,

1992). As Hong notes, his particular findings are highly consistent with the thesis that risk aversion is especially valued in and of itself in Chinese communities.

PARTICIPATION

Most of our discussion has emphasized the perspective of individual decision makers, but many decisions, particularly major ones, involve more than one person. There have been numerous suggestions that Chinese and non-Chinese differ greatly in who participates in collaborative decisions of various kinds and how that collaboration proceeds. One of the most distinctive features of Chinese culture is the significance it places on the family. This emphasis is often traced to China's roots in an agricultural economy whose prosperity depended on strong, stable families (see, for example, Smith, 1973). Thus, since earliest times, the patriarchal family has been the prototype for Chinese organizations of all sorts (Hofstede and Bond, 1988; Yang, 1993). This characteristic is taken as an explanation (see, for example, Hendryx, 1986) for the tendency of Chinese organizational structures to be strong vertically (with respect to relations between superiors and subordinates) but weak horizontally (with respect to relations among equals), as well as an explanation for high Chinese power distance values. Such factors in turn are proposed to account for special characteristics of how the Chinese make decisions involving more than one person.

In situations where decision participants differ in rank, more so than in Western or Japanese organizations, Chinese decisions are made, or at least monitored, centrally. That is, the person with the highest status makes the decision. Or, if the superior's wishes are clear, subordinates decide in accordance with those wishes, essentially as the superior's agents (see, for example, Gaenslen, 1986; Redding and Wong, 1986; Smith and Wang, this volume; Xu and Wang, 1991). A good illustration is provided in a study by Tse, Lee, Vertinsky, and Wehrung (1988). Managers from mainland China, Hong Kong, and Canada were presented with a hypothetical manufacturing decision problem. Using an 'executive in-basket' technique, each subject assumed the role of the decision maker in the problem. The 'vast majority' of the staff in the pertinent organization favoured one particular alternative. However, another option was preferred by 'a couple' of acknowledged experts on the staff. Much more so than did the others, the mainland Chinese managers indicated that they would defer to the wishes of the experts, those in authority. This result seems consistent with the generalization that Chinese decision customs are especially sensitive to status differentials. If we suppose, however, that decision participants have equal status (for example, are members of an executive committee), Chinese decision makers are expected to seek broad and genuine consensus instead of, say, proceeding by simple majority rule after minimal discussion (see, for example, Gaenslen, 1993).

Chinese styles of collaborative decision-making have interesting consequences, most notably concerning speed. Chinese organizations have a reputation for being unusually slow in reaching decisions (see Eiteman, 1990;

Hendryx, 1986). This is typically attributed to either or both of two attributes: the need to have provisional decisions reviewed by superiors and the lengthy process of achieving consensus among peers. There might be cultural values contributing to the slow pace of Chinese decision-making as well. Recalling the Hong (1978) study, in which Chinese subjects were found to exhibit 'cautious shifts' toward less risk taking when they worked in groups rather than as individuals, we might say that a plausible concomitant of the implied shared value on risk aversion might be that in collectives, Chinese decision makers are especially hesitant to decide precipitously. More explicitly, in the Analects of Confucius, we find the following: 'The Master said, "A gentleman covets the reputation of being slow in word but prompt in deed"' (Confucius, IV, 24). This aphorism might be interpreted as advice to weigh decisions carefully but then to execute them immediately and vigorously, consistent with popular characterizations of how Chinese organizations function. In principle, it seems that Chinese organizations have the capacity to decide unusually rapidly also, provided that the decision problem actually reaches the attention of the person highest in authority. This result occurs because this individual has more of a free hand than would his or her counterpart in a non-Chinese organization.

DECISION STYLES

A person's 'decision style' is that individual's characteristically preferred means of making decisions. Consistent with our previous discussion, decision-making entails two major phases: perception of the given situation (essentially, construction of a cognitive representation), and selection of an option on the basis of what is perceived (including, for instance, judging chances, assigning value, and combining various considerations). Decision style researchers maintain that there are stable preferences for how these phases proceed and how they are emphasized. Moreover, these preferences are thought to be especially important for understanding decision-making as it occurs in the chaotic real world (as compared to the carefully controlled laboratory). In fact, there have been several studies indicating reliable relationships between style measures and executives' real-world decision practices (see, for example, Nutt, 1986).

Decision style research is controversial with respect to several issues, such as effect sizes and the quality of the instrumentation (see, for example, Huber, 1983). It is conceivable as well that measurement questions might be especially problematic in cross-cultural comparisons (cf. Jaccard and Wan, 1986). Nevertheless, two recent studies have revealed large differences in the apparent decision styles of Chinese and non-Chinese, differences that warrant attention. In one study, Zhang (1992) made a comparison of university students in mainland China and in the United Kingdom. In the other, by Furnham and Stringfield (1993), the styles of Hong Kong Chinese and European employees of an airline company were contrasted.

It is too early to make a great deal of these initial explorations, but their findings are sufficiently provocative that they should be pursued rigorously in future work. They suggest differences in Chinese versus non-Chinese decision behaviours that have considerable significance if shown to be reliable and generalizable. For instance, they imply a Chinese decision-making stance that is strikingly dispassionate and 'rationalistic', resting heavily on objective, situational facts rather than on considerations of other people's feelings. Some observers, like Zhang (1992), will find this image surprising, in view of prevailing assumptions about Chinese culture's strong collectivism. The observed results might make more sense, however, if one accepts the conclusion of Triandis, Bontempo, Villareal, Asai, and Lucca (1988) that people from collectivistic cultures tend to behave in extremely individualistic ways when dealing with members of out-groups, for example, non-family members (see also Gabrenya and Hwang, this volume; and Yen, Hsu, and Seetoo, 1991). Results on decision styles might thus serve to remind us that concepts like individualism and collectivism are not as simple as they might seem at first.

DECISION MODES

Zhang (1992) suggests an interesting, seemingly radical perspective on Chinese decision-making. It appears that no one (including us) has been able to find in the indigenous Chinese literature a systematic body of scholarship under the rubric of 'decision-making' which proposes principles fundamentally different from those seen in the West. Yet Zhang submits that this state of affairs is deceptive. He implies that, although the term 'decision-making' might not have been used explicitly in all instances, over the centuries the Chinese have developed a quite distinctive approach to decision-making, an approach that permeates the culture itself. Because of its character, that approach would be well described with the expression 'folk precedent matching' (a term coined by us, since Zhang did not adopt one).

The Folk Precedent Matching Concept

The basic idea of folk precedent matching can be described as follows: When confronted with a decision problem, the decision maker searches memory for possible precedents. The precedents are not necessarily or even primarily personal experiences. Instead, for the Chinese, they are often situations in Chinese cultural history, including, presumably, the kinds of stories that largely comprise the classics and folk stories familiar to most Chinese. In such a precedent, a particular path was chosen and—most importantly—was demonstrated to have 'worked'. Thus, if the current situation is deemed parallel to the precedent, the appropriate course of action is obvious: to do what was done before.

The crucial elements of the decision process *per se* are these: First, over the long term, accumulate a large store of precedents and nurture the ability to retrieve them. Then, for a given decision episode, carefully survey the current situation in order to fully appreciate its particulars. And, finally, make a match to the appropriate precedent. As a concrete, even if fictional, example, imagine an executive trying to decide whether to retain a current supplier or replace him with a competitor. In the prototypical prescriptive Western approach, the reasoning of the executive would be dominated by considerations of details like the competitors' costs (financial and otherwise), their chances of making timely deliveries, and how these factors should be weighed against one another. In contrast, the analysis of an executive employing a folk precedent matching strategy would emphasize attempts to identify points of correspondence between the current problem and situations from the collective past: for example, the selection of a public official or of a suitor in a legend.

Folk Precedent Matching as a Decision Mode

From one perspective, Zhang's proposal of folk precedent matching as a decision mode is not quite as radical as it might seem. Decision theorists are coming to acknowledge that decision-making normally proceeds according to three distinct 'modes': analytic, rule-based, and automatic (see related ideas by Hogarth, 1981; Klein, 1993; Marchant, Robinson, Anderson, and Schadewald, 1993). Traditionally, Western scholarship on decision-making has focused almost exclusively on the analytic mode. In those instances, the decision maker examines the details of the given decision situation: identifying the available options, judging the chances of potential outcomes, and assessing values. The decision maker then uses various 'first principles', for example, expected utility maximization, to determine what course of action is most reasonable. Virtually all of the previous discussion in this chapter has been conducted within that framework.

It is unnecessary—and, in fact, impossible—for all decision-making to proceed analytically. After all, analytic decision-making requires effort and is time-consuming. Suppose that the problem currently facing a decision maker is virtually the same as one successfully resolved before. The natural course would be to select the action that corresponds to what was done earlier. Rule-based decision-making rests on this simple idea. Over time, the decision maker builds up (that is, 'learns') a collection of rules for how to proceed in various circumstances, rules that have the form, 'If Condition X holds, then select Action A'. When a new situation arises, the decision maker first tries to match that situation to ones in the 'rule store'. If a match is found, the decision is made according to the prescription of the rule. Analytic decision-making is attempted only if the matching effort fails.

The automatic decision mode is essentially a 'mature' version of the rule-based mode. There, rules that have been used quite often in the past are invoked effortlessly and outside the decision maker's awareness when their preconditions are encountered.

The folk precedent matching proposal thus can be seen as a claim with two important elements. The first is that the Chinese place an especially heavy reliance on rule-based decision-making. The second is that the Chinese, relative to other groups, are more likely to use rules that find their origins and justifications in folk history. There is no rigorously collected direct evidence that folk precedent matching is in fact more common among the Chinese than among other people; compiling and evaluating pertinent evidence should have high priority in future research. But the proposed survey phase of the process, in particular, entails the kind of 'incrementalism' and sensitivity to local conditions that Zhang and others (for example, Redding and Wong, 1986) have claimed are characteristic of Chinese decision behaviour. The folk precedent matching proposal also agrees with common observations about Chinese culture.

One example consists of the indications that cognitive customs contribute to extreme Chinese overconfidence, as was discussed previously in this chapter. Indeed, Nakamura's (1964) more general conclusions about Chinese thought fit almost perfectly: 'The Chinese very often stress precedents, not abstract principles. ...The fruit of the past experiences of people of older times arouses in the Chinese mind a sense of validity' (p. 204). Also consider data implicating the emphasis of mnemonic skill demanded by folk precedent matching. Chen, Braithwaite, and Huang (1983) found that Chinese subjects considered 'information' items on intelligence tests to be much more relevant to the basic intelligence construct than did Australian subjects. Moreover, the Chinese considered memory items to be much easier, perhaps because they were so practiced at them. Finally, there are the customs of the Chinese language. Chinese conversations—including, presumably, discussions about decisions—seem to make especially heavy use of idioms and other references to illustrative stories from the distant past (see, for example, Kiu, 1992; Tan, 1991; Wang, 1993).

SIGNIFICANCE OF CHINESE VERSUS NON-CHINESE VARIATIONS IN DECISION-MAKING

We should be surprised if culturally distinctive features accounted for more than a small fraction of the variability in decision behaviour generally. Thus, Chinese and non-Chinese decision behaviours seem undoubtedly more alike than different. So why should we care about the kinds of variations discussed in this chapter? Such distinctions are significant in their own right as major elements in our understanding of basic cultural variations. They also provide a good, naturalistic test bed for claims about decision principles that at one time were considered 'universal', for example, the foundations of overconfidence. Ultimately, the most important implications of Chinese versus non-Chinese differences in decision-making are likely to be practical ones, relevant to the increased contact between Chinese and non-Chinese societies in a variety of contexts, particularly in business.

In some instances, the parties in these contacts are one another's 'opposites', for example, buyers and sellers. In others, such as in multinational corporations and joint ventures, they are collaborators. In the short run at least, there are bound to be unpleasant misunderstandings as well as genuine conflicts between those subscribing to Chinese and non-Chinese decision customs. It behooves those who anticipate contacts across the traditions to know what to expect, to understand why certain situations will occur, and to try to work around the difficulties (cf. Pollock and Chen, 1986).

In the long run, there surely will be some measure of assimilation of customs, by both Chinese and non-Chinese. For comparison, consider the precedent set by the Japanese. Traditional Japanese managerial styles have several marked differences from Western styles. Because the Japanese have enjoyed such spectacular economic success, however, there have been many concert-

ed attempts to adapt Japanese techniques in Western organizations, with varying degrees of effectiveness (see, for example, Young, 1992). If Chinese economic performance continues its own remarkable course (cf. Hofstede and
Bond, 1988), we can easily envision efforts to emulate Chinese ways of doing
things as well, including Chinese ways of decision-making. The fruitfulness of
these efforts will be enhanced by a deep understanding of the kinds of variations revealed by comparative studies of decision processes.

NOTES

Preparation of this chapter was supported by US National Science Foundation grant
number SES92-10027 to the University of Michigan and by R.O.C. National Science
Council grant number NSC81-0301-H033-02 to Chung Yuan Christian University.
Special thanks are due to LeAnn Franke and Alina Tulchinsky for their bibliographical
assistance. We have benefited greatly from comments made by members of Michigan's
Judgment and Decision Laboratory and its Culture and Cognition Program on various
ideas discussed in this chapter. We also appreciate the helpful suggestions of Peter
Smith and David Kember.

Chapter 23

Understanding Chinese People as Consumers:
Past Findings and Future Propositions

David K. Tse

In past centuries, Chinese emperors were known to live extravagantly, enjoying lifestyles that were 'heavenly' in nature. In the Qing era, for example, the 'emperor's feast' lasted days, with hundreds of different dishes served. In contrast to this history of extravagant consumption, little has been reported in the literature concerning how contemporary Chinese actually behave as consumers. The lack of research activity on this topic may result from the late birth of the study of consumer behaviour as an academic field throughout the world, combined with the—until recently—insignificance of Chinese societies as global markets.

The previous lack of interest does not imply a lack of research opportunities. There are many promising topics for researchers. For example, the current notion of consumption is strongly Western-based, describing how an individual from an individualistic society fulfils his or her needs through a market system that emphasizes individualistic goals. What consumers from a collective society look for in their purchases and how they behave in a market system within a collective society may show fundamental differences that warrant systematic and comprehensive research efforts. This chapter aims to integrate previous work on the subject, and it suggests a set of research propositions that would explore this topic of growing academic and managerial significance.

This chapter traces how consumption is defined in traditional Chinese culture and in contemporary Chinese societies. It also describes the various approaches taken to study cross-cultural consumption behaviour. It then adopts a pan-cultural framework for consumption value, reviews previous research findings on each consumption value, and suggests a collection of research propositions for future studies aimed at understanding Chinese people as consumers.

THE MEANING OF CONSUMPTION IN CHINESE CULTURE

A number of features characterize how Chinese people have regarded consumption as it is represented in traditional literature. Primarily, consumption was not classically regarded as a normative, 'idealistic' goal for the Chinese people. In the Confucian value system, consumption was not included in the six activities that were to be undertaken by gentlemen: practicing manners, appreciating music, shooting, riding, engaging in literary activities, and engaging in scientific activities. Nor was consumption among the personal goals that the Confucian value system emphasizes: building your personality, harmonizing your family, ruling over the country, and bringing peace to the world.

Instead, consumption was regarded in traditional Chinese societies more as a tool to serve higher-order needs than as an activity in its own right. Drinking, for example, would be denounced if one was found to indulge in it privately, but drinking would be appropriate to welcome guests, to express anguish towards unfulfilled personal goals (a Song dynasty poet wrote, 'raise my cup to implore heaven', when his ideas were rejected by his superior), or to enjoy with someone who knows the drinker's 'heart'. In such cases, it was written, a thousand cups would be insufficient.

Similar implications can be drawn if one observes how Chinese people chose their gifts. The gifts they buy often have higher prices than do the objects they normally consume. Such behaviours have been either motivated by *lai* (showing respect for others) or by the need not to 'lose face' (Sun, 1990). No matter the underlying motives, such behaviours have reflected the importance of social relationships and the centrally important way in which Chinese people use consumption activities as tools to foster such relationships. More discussion on how Chinese use consumption to initiate, maintain, and extend social relationships follows later in this chapter.

Consumption tends to carry negative associations in the traditional Chinese value system. In traditional China, excessive consumption, even by noblemen, was heavily criticized. To use drinking again as the example: When emperors indulged in drinking, they would be labelled as playing in 'ponds of wine'. For an individual, a similar negative labelling would emerge, and the drinker would be termed 'someone who indulges in an object', and as one who 'subsequently would lose his or her will in life'. Such anti-hedonic consumption norms may have motivated the Chinese people not to accept consumption as a 'normative' life goal.

As many scholars have noted, traditional Chinese literature is strongly biased towards describing the thoughts and behaviours of those in the society with high social status, or towards establishing an idealized role model for the members of the society to admire and imitate. For ordinary people, it appears, consumption was an acceptable life goal because 'peasants regard eating as important as heaven' (Sun, 1990). To these 'average' people, the need for survival might have justified their consumption activities. In general, however, at all levels of society we can say the enjoyment of consumption was strictly confined within parameters set by the Chinese value system of *lai* and the expectation that one match consumption behaviour with one's social status.

Contrary to any impulse to consume, the Chinese have traditionally been encouraged to save. Their strong urge to save may result from a combination of the lack of a societal security system in most Chinese societies, a long tradition of caring for one's own descendants, and the promotion of saving as a virtue. The importance of looking after one's family members (beyond those of the nuclear family), including both older and younger generations, might also have been a strong motivator. This strong emphasis on savings instead of consumption seems to dominate through time and across Chinese societies of different degrees of wealth. The ratio of the amount of savings relative to gross domestic product, for example, is much higher in Chinese societies. In Singapore it is measured at 48 per cent, in the People's Republic of China (PRC) at 36 per cent, in Hong Kong at 30 per cent, and in Taiwan at 27 per cent, compared with the United States rate of 15 per cent (*Asiaweek* 1994, p. 67).

A number of implications may be drawn from this brief overview of how consumption is defined in traditional Chinese societies. In their relentless pursuit of an idealized self, the traditional Chinese have perceived consumption as a means to serve higher-level, often social, needs. Excessive consumption was denounced, and the strong emphasis on saving restricted consumption to what would be perceived as 'appropriate' in a person's life.

CHANGING VALUES TOWARDS CONSUMPTION

As with other traditional Chinese values, the meaning of consumption is changing quickly among Chinese (see also Yang, this volume). In part, this change may be prompted by the phenomenal economic growth seen in recent years in a number of the predominantly Chinese societies, and seen in particular in Hong Kong, which all other Chinese societies including Singapore, Taiwan, and the Mainland attempt to emulate. By 1994, per capita purchasing power of the Hong Kong Chinese surpassed that of the citizens of many Western European countries, and followed closely behind that seen in Switzerland, the United States, Japan, and Germany (*Asiaweek*, 1994).

In Hong Kong, consumption seems to have been legitimized as a 'daily' goal. Shopping, going to movies, and dining out are some of the territory's favourite leisure activities (Ji, 1986; Lu and Daqiao, 1989). The newly emerging idols in Chinese societies are the rich and famous (Lau and Kuan, 1988): what they wear, what they eat, what they own, and what they do are popular subjects reported in detail in magazines and newspapers. The craze for a luxurious life is also found among the younger generation, who look to popular singers and movie stars as their models. Using Hofstede's concept that a culture can be regarded as core values surrounded by different layers of objects, heros, and rituals (Hofstede, Neuijen, Ohayv, and Sanders, 1990), one might say that the wide acceptance of consumption activities and treatment of the rich and famous as idols implies a fundamtal change in the role of consumption in the Chinese value system.

This transition has also been reflected in more systematic research efforts. Advertisements, potential mirrors of a society, have been used as indicators to reflect a society's value system. Tse, Belk, and Zhou (1989) compared advertisements in the PRC, Taiwan, and Hong Kong and found that Hong Kong advertisements primarily emphasized 'hedonic consumption' (77 per cent of ads expressed this value) and 'price value' (68 per cent of ads expressed this). In contrast, advertisements in the PRC emphasized 'product performance' (78 per cent of the ads) and 'performance assurance' (38 per cent of the ads). The same study revealed that since 1979, hedonic consumption has been increasing in all three of these Chinese societies. Therefore, it is no casual observation when Leung (1991) stressed that 'work hard and play hard' is being accepted as a guiding principle by many people in Hong Kong. In a 1985 survey, Lau and Kuan (1988) found 71.8 per cent of respondents agreed that billionaire industrialists Li Ka-shing and Y. K. Pao should be models for youngsters. Recently, Zheng (1992) also noted that consumption values expressed in advertisements from the PRC have increasingly concentrated on personal values and luxurious lifestyles.

With all these changes, would Chinese people accept consumption as a 'terminal' goal? Or would strong traditional values continue to counteract consumption as a terminal goal for the Chinese? Findings from a cross-cultural comparison of university students (Tse, Hui, and Pan, 1994) provide some insights. One would expect that if consumption were to be accepted as a terminal norm, university students from Hong Kong, a younger and more liberal generation, would be among the first to show it support. Interestingly, the Hong Kong respondents were lukewarm in accepting consumption as a goal in and of itself. In response to two statements, 'Work hard, play hard' and 'One should enjoy as much as one can when the time is good', that measured hedonic lifestyles and instant gratification, their scores were significantly lower (measuring 4.1 and 4.5 on 7-point Likert scales) than were the scores of comparable students in the United States (who measured 5.4 and 5.1). The Hong Kong students' support for consumption as a 'life reward', however, was much stronger. They scored 5.6 (again on 7-point Likert scale) compared to their American counterparts' 5.3 in response to the statement, 'Once a person becomes successful, he or she should enjoy life'. In addition, the Hong Kong students were most ready to use consumption as a source of daily satisfaction. Their scores in response to two statements, 'A beautiful shirt refreshes me' and 'If I find a good purchase I feel happy about it', were as high as those of their American counterparts (5.4 versus 4.8 and 5.8 versus 5.9).

One may argue that these findings suggest a relatively recent transformation in which Chinese people have come increasingly to accept consumption as a normative life goal. Qian (1969), however, in his historical analysis of Chinese values, argued that ordinary Chinese people have adopted a lifestyle embracing wealth as early as the Song dynasty.

A more reasonable and stimulating argument is that these findings suggest some form of a dual value system that operates in the minds of the Chinese when they consider consumption. As first suggested by Yang (1993), the dual value mechanism in Chinese societies may be caused by the interaction between the society's traditional values and changes in the ecological system Chinese now confront. Yang's proposition is most applicable to how Chinese people perceive consumption behaviour. Chinese people may hesitate to openly accept consumption as a terminal goal, but they may readily accept consumption as a legitimate 'life reward' and as 'a source of daily satisfaction'. This effect closely mirrors how contemporary Chinese people regard Confucian virtues: maintaining a high 'moral' standard as an ideal but operating on a more 'down to earth' way in their daily lives. A similar view is shared by Lau and Kuan (1988) who observed that, 'Hong Kong Chinese's view...falls short of the modernization theorists and reflects the imprints of tradition' (p. 45).

In summary, the following four propositions are important to future research in this area. Compared to American consumers (and other representatives of Western culture): Chinese people would be less receptive to consumption as a terminal goal; Chinese would be equally receptive to consumption as a life reward; Chinese would be more receptive to consumption as a source of daily satisfaction; and Chinese would be more receptive to consumption as a tool for building social relationships.

APPROACHES TO UNDERSTANDING THE CHINESE AS CONSUMERS

Previous research has primarily used three methods to study how Chinese values affect Chinese people in their consumption behaviour. Since culture is composed of complex interlocking systems of values and norms, one method used is to unbundle culture into meaningful dimensions. This unbundling may help to isolate the critical aspects of culture's impact without getting lost in the complex interlocking systems of Chinese values and norms. Past studies have identified a list of useful dimensions including Collectivism, Power Distance, Uncertainty Avoidance, Masculinity, and Long-term View (Hofstede et al., 1990). It is important to recognize that these value dimensions largely originate from studies in organizational behaviour (see, for example, Hofstede 1980), and how these dimensions apply to the consumption context is less certain. In addition, there may exist other value dimensions that are specifically related to consumption behaviour.

The second method used to study how cultural values affect consumption is to follow an emic approach, examining how consumers behave in each Chinese society. This method is powerful in capturing all characteristics of consumption, including those that are unique to each of the Chinese societies. For example, Lee and Tse (1994), Leung (1991), and Zheng (1992) have suggested that Hong Kong consumers adopt unique consumption characteristics including a strong liking for named brands, impatience in response to waiting, and pride in being thought of as a Hong Kong person. Results of this approach suggest that there be a developed literature on each of the Chinese societies. To date, there are too few systematic and comprehensive studies on how Chinese people behave as consumers to make this approach viable.

Exceptions are content analysis studies that have investigated advertisements from various Chinese societies. Cheng (1994), for example, compared ads from the PRC in 1982 and 1992. Tse et al. (1989) content-analysed about 1,000 ads from Hong Kong, mainland China, and Taiwan. They found that ads from these three Chinese societies contain 10 major consumption appeals, including appeals based on technology, product performance, performance assurance, image, hedonism, product variety, modernity, ingredients, distribution, and purchase value. These themes were found to be powerful discriminators of the consumption appeals in the three Chinese societies. While such attempts are helpful, researchers have yet to establish a common set of consumption dimensions that would allow meaningful comparison with non-Chinese societies.

The third method used to establish pan-cultural consumption dimensions is to contrast consumers from different cultures so as to understand how Chinese people behave as consumers. 'Consumption value' research (see, for example, Tse and Wong, 1993) adopts such an approach. While this research strategy is in its early stages of development, it has potential to help us understand the underlying motivations of Chinese consumers and the consumers of other cultures. In their cross-cultural survey of five Asian economies (Hong Kong, Japan, Singapore, South Korea, and Taiwan) Tse and Wong found four broad types of consumption values, which they gave the following labels: Utilitarian-related Value (basic performance and higher-level performance), Purchase Value, Aesthetics Value, and Social Value (social acceptance and social distinction). Their classifications were shown to hold across four different product categories (clothing, food, household supplies, and household appliances) and across the five societies they investigated. The following parts of this chapter adopt this pan-cultural approach to summarize previous literature and propose new research questions to understand Chinese people as consumers.

The Utilitarian Dimension

Product performance

Performance attributes comprise a product's (or service's) basic and secondary functional aspects. The basic functional aspects include uses of the product. The secondary functional aspects relate to product quality and long-term performance.

Past studies found that consumers in the PRC place a strong emphasis on the performance dimension in their purchases. For example, Ho and Sin (1986) and Seminik, Zhou, and Moore (1986) reported that PRC advertisers stressed product information in their ads more than did their Hong Kong counterparts. Similar findings were reported in Rice and Lu's comparison of magazine advertisements from the PRC and the United States (1988). Cheng (1994) also found modernity, technology, and quality are important messages in magazine ads produced in the PRC between 1982 and 1992. The problems of false advertising, as noted by Hong (1994), may strongly motivate mainland Chinese to pay attention to the performance of the products. Pollay, Tse, and Wang (1990) judged that consumers from the PRC place strong emphasis on product performance because they are relatively new to the free-market system. With limited financial resources and less experience as consumers, it is likely that PRC buyers need more performance-related information to compare potential purchases than would consumers in other societies. The emphasis on product performance was not restricted to PRC consumers. Tse et al. (1989) found that product performance was the second most frequently used appeal in Taiwanese ads and the fourth most frequently used appeal in Hong Kong ads.

In comparison with consumers in other cultures, Chinese people seem to put less emphasis on product performance than do Japanese and Korean consumers, but more than do their American counterparts. In particular, Tse and Wong (1993) found that Korean and Japanese consumers rate performance dimensions as more important than do Chinese consumers (from Hong Kong, Singapore, and Taiwan). Findings from a study by Tse, Hui, and Pan (1994) also support the salience of product performance when Chinese make purchase decisions. They found that Hong Kong respondents rate comfort and durability as more important than do American respondents. These findings seem to suggest that the strong emphasis contemporary Chinese people place on performance aspects of their purchases may be culturally influenced. The findings imply that consumers from the various Chinese societies differ in their emphasis, but compared to American consumers they place more emphasis on product performance when making a purchase. Compared to Korean and Japanese consumers, however, Chinese consumers place less emphasis on product performance.

Risk-taking

In organizational studies, Chinese managers have been shown to be relatively risk-aversive (see Yates and Lee, this volume). To date, no study has directly linked this cultural dimension to consumption decisions by Chinese consumers.

Results from some studies, however, suggest that Chinese as consumers are not as risk-aversive as they are when playing the role of managers. In particular, Hong Kong consumers are known for their ready acceptance of new products and of ideas from all parts of the world (Lu and Dagian, 1989). New consumption styles, whether from North America, Europe, Japan, or Asia, have been quickly adopted into the society (Zheng 1992). A study by Tse et al. (1994) gave strong indications that as consumers Hong Kong Chinese people are not risk-aversive. They found that there was no significant difference between Hong Kong and American university students in 'their confidence towards products from big companies'.

As suggested in recent literature on risk-taking (Wehrung, Lee, Tse, and Vertinsky, 1990), a person's risk propensity is positively related to his or her perceived control over the decision outcome. Applied to the consumption context, this finding would imply that wealthy consumers would take more risks in their purchases because they have the money to experiment with the purchase, not feeling as much stress if the purchase is unsatisfactory. Accordingly, Hong Kong consumers would likely take more risky decisions compared to Taiwanese and PRC consumers. In summary, the findings suggest that risk-taking in purchase decisions would positively relate to the personal wealth of the consumer, and there would be no difference found between Chinese consumers and American consumers in risk-taking in their purchase decisions.

Purchase Value Dimension

Purchase value refers to how consumers perceive the quality of a product in relation to its price. In the United States, purchase value has attracted strong attention because of the country's weak economy in recent years. In contrast, purchase value has long been a key factor in promoting products and services in some Chinese societies. A study by Tse et al. (1989) confirmed that purchase value was the most important appeal in advertisements from Hong Kong and Taiwan. The salience of purchase value was also supported in a cross-cultural comparison involving five Asian economies. Tse, Wong, and Tan (1989) found that consumers in Chinese economies (including Hong Kong, Singapore, and Taiwan) placed more emphasis on purchase value than did Japanese and Korean consumers in their purchases.

The Chinese people's strong emphasis on purchase value could be the result of a number of factors. As discussed, there is a strong tendency to save among the Chinese. If they have to spend, they are motivated to obtain the same performance at a lower price, thus yielding a higher purchase value. A higher return for their money would be strongly preferred. The lack of an established social pension system (in particular for people in Hong Kong and the PRC) and the common experience of having lived in a poor society may serve to inculcate careful spending habits among the Chinese. Purchase value would naturally be a salient part of their consumption decisions.

It is important not to confuse purchase value with low price. As documented in popular literature, Chinese consumers are willing to spend on name brands. For example, the world's largest fleet of Rolls Royce automobiles is in Hong Kong, and extravagant dinners are popular in Taiwan and southern China. The emphasis is on the product's perceived quality compared to its price, not a straight comparison of the products' prices.

Studies of the behaviour of Hong Kong immigrants to Canada provide another good case. European cars in Hong Kong are sold at a much higher price (because of the marketers' strategy and Hong Kong's high import tax for European cars) than are Japanese cars. In Canada, the price gap is much smaller. As a result, many Hong Kong immigrants in Canada have bought Volvos and other European cars, in part because of the cars' performance, but more because of higher purchase values than they would expect to realize in Hong Kong (Lee and Tse, 1994).

Survey results by Tse et al. (1994) partially confirm the Chinese emphasis on purchase value. Hong Kong students rated the statement 'Export-oriented products are of good price value' more highly than did American students, but they rated the statement 'If I come across something of good purchase value, I shall buy more of it' lower than did the American students. These findings suggest that the following two hypotheses are of significance for future research. First, compared with consumers of other cultures (Western and other Asian), Chinese consumers would be expected to place a stronger emphasis on the purchase value of products and services. Second, Chinese consumers' emphasis on purchase value would be expected to be independent of their wealth.

Aesthetics Dimension

The dimension of aesthetics in consumption decisions is closely related to the hedonic components of a purchase decision. As Chinese societies prosper, it is expected that the aesthetics dimension in purchases will become increasingly important. A study by Tse et al. (1989) revealed that over 65 per cent of advertisements in Hong Kong adopted a hedonic approach in their ads. Taiwanese ads also maintained a strong emphasis on this dimension (42 per cent), while PRC ads lagged behind (32 per cent).

When compared with the aesthetic concerns of consumers in other cultures, the emphasis on aesthetics shown by Chinese consumers has been found to be weak and appears to be product-dependent. Tse and Wong (1993) found that Japanese and Korean consumers both placed stronger emphasis on this dimension in food and appliances purchases. Yet, Chinese consumers from Hong Kong, Singapore, and Taiwan placed a strong emphasis on this dimension when purchasing clothes.

Tse et al. (1994) reported that Hong Kong students rated aesthetics as more important to their clothing purchases than did their American counterparts. They rated the statement 'The most important attribute of clothes is how they look' equally highly and their scores on matching purchases, 'When choosing clothes I try to match them with my shoes', were significantly higher than for American students. Chinese consumers' emphasis on aesthetics does not necessarily imply they have a strong appetite for artistic expression. Instead, their high ratings may be motivated by a need for social status and social identity. In short, we propose first that the emphasis of a product's aesthetic dimension by Chinese consumers would be product-specific. Second, we suggest that strength of a Chinese consumer's emphasis on a product's aesthetic dimension would depend on the consumer's personal wealth.

Social Dimensions

For quite some time, researchers have tried to redefine collectivism so as to explain why Chinese behave differently from members of other cultural groups. A conservative interpretation of collectivism in the consumption context would imply that all Chinese would purchase the same colours of clothes, in the same style, and by the same manufacturer. Of course, this is far from the case.

Yang's recent suggestion (1993) is especially enlightening. She argues that Chinese people are motivated to harmonize (rather than to conform) with their social environment. Accordingly, Chinese have two major social dimensions to maintain: one vertical, the other horizontal. Applied to consumption behaviour, her argument suggests that Chinese people maintain continuously a certain social distance with people of a different social class and at the same time work to reduce the social distance separating them from people in their own social class. In the following, how Chinese people use consumption to balance these two social dimensions and how Chinese people extend their social relationships are discussed.

Name brands and their social values

The need to distinguish oneself from others and one group from other groups is especially strong in Chinese societies. Consumption is a readily available tool to manage such social intricacies. As noted by Lau and Kuan (1988), Hong Kong Chinese have often used material possessions as a primary base for normative judgements. In place of a dichotomous image of social class, they note that 'a finely graded stratification structure, based on the criterion of wealth, was generally held' (p. 65). Thus, Hong Kong Chinese (and, to a lesser extent, Taiwanese and mainland Chinese) use what a person has and the brand names of what a person has to reinforce their social identity. Name brands, especially for visible products, may be used as social tools to increase distance from other social groups and to identify with peers of similar social status.

The recent economic successes of Chinese societies have created strata of people with diverse economic worth. As a result, the motivation to use name-brand products as symbols to underscore social distance from others is most pronounced. The motivation would likely be stronger for the newly wealthy, those who feel their social status to be insecure, and those who do not have other attributes (for example, education, an occupation, and so on) to justify their social status. Hence, it is not coincidental to find that name-brand products command a premium price in Chinese societies (Zheng, 1992). In order to feed the relentless appetite for social distinction, American Express introduced their platinum card in Hong Kong (rather than in the USA), in addition to their gold and regular credit cards. This phenomenon is also confirmed in more systematic investigations. University students in Hong Kong rated name-brand clothes as smarter and name-brand products as higher in value than did American students (Tse et al. 1994). From these findings, we would expect that Chinese consumers would place more emphasis on the social value of brands than American consumers. Moreover, we would expect that Chinese consumers would be more likely to match their social status with a product's brand name than would American consumers. Finally, we would expect that the social value of brands would positively relate to the Chinese consumer's need for social identity.

Yet, within the same social class or reference group, the impulse to behave appropriately (to not deviate from the group) is especially strong in Chinese societies (Sun, 1990; Tan and Farley, 1987). Individuals are well aware of their social roles and obligations, and they know that any deviation would be inappropriate and, at times, lead to a loss of 'face'. These forces form the underlying motivation for an individual to identify with his or her peers. In a survey by Tse et al. (1994), 86.1 per cent of Hong Kong students polled agreed that their consumption choices (particularly in clothing) were affected by their close friends, compared to 71.3 per cent of American students who acknowledged that influence. If their peers acquire a name-brand product, those in the social group are pressured to acquire a product of similar status. A low 43.5 per cent of Hong Kong respondents (compared with 73.6 per cent in the American sample) agreed that they would not mind behaving differently in order to stand out. The strength of the conformity force in Chinese societies is obvious.

From these findings, we expect that within well-defined social groups, Chinese consumers would have more homogeneous consumption patterns than would American consumers. We would also predict that Chinese consumers would place more emphasis on the opinions of their reference group in making purchases than would American consumers. And, we would expect that Chinese consumers would be more likely to use name-brand products to identify with their peers than would American consumers.

Reinforcing social relationships

Let us turn to how consumption activities contribute to the dynamic aspects of social relationships in Chinese societies. Social relationships are most fundamental to life within Chinese societies. For many hundreds of years, Chinese have been known to use products (and services) to initiate, establish, reinforce, and extend relationships in their social circles.

To start a social relationship, for example, and before asking a person for a favour, many Chinese will be likely to present a gift ('for the *lai*') and to ask courteously for a return of the favour on the grounds that a reciprocity obligation has been established (Sun, 1990). In a study by Tse et al. (1994), 83.9 per cent of Hong Kong respondents agreed that asking a person out for a snack would be appropriate to initiate a friendship, compared to 50.8 per cent of American students. This finding reflects the popular use of consumption activities to begin a social relationship in a Chinese society.

Gifts are widely accepted as a tool to reinforce social relations in many cultures. In Chinese societies such behaviour is especially prevalent. In a study by Tse et al. (1994), 78.6 per cent of the Hong Kong respondents reported that they regularly practised gift-giving in the family. In addition, the findings indicate that they tend to pay attention to more than the materialistic aspects of the gifts: 87.6 per cent acknowledged that giving gifts needed to be balanced with the giver's sincerity. In preparing the gifts, 87.5 per cent of the respondents agreed that a gift should reflect their status and not cause them to 'lose face'. These percentages were significantly higher than for their American counterparts. Compared with American consumers, Chinese people appear more likely to use consumption activities to initiate social relationships, and would be more likely to use these activities to maintain and extend social relationships.

SUMMARY AND DISCUSSION

This chapter attempts to integrate previous work that studies Chinese people as consumers. Faced with a profound lack of earlier research on this topic, the author has drawn findings from a variety of disciplines and from work in progress. A number of researchable propositions were presented in the chapter, but a number of warnings are needed.

First, the lack of previous studies in this area prompt speculation and allow only the suggestion of some propositions for future research. It must be emphasized that these research propositions may be premature. Researchers are most welcome to modify, criticize, and formulate alternative paradigms and propositions. A central purpose of this paper is to stimulate more research effort in this area.

Second, the paper attempts to isolate the common thread of Chinese cultural influence that runs through various Chinese societies including Hong Kong, mainland China, Singapore, Taiwan, and other overseas Chinese groups. As pointed out by many researchers (see, for example, Yang, 1993), these societies have each gone through its own specific experiences that may have transformed it into a unique cultural entity. In developing research propositions, we must try to accommodate differences such as income and the society's stage of economic development. Many other sociological and political factors have not been adequately integrated into the research. Researchers are therefore encouraged to fill this gap when conducting their research.

Third, readers may notice that some propositions do not follow directly from previous work in Chinese cultural research. Consumption behaviours are often low-involvement, short-term decisions with fewer and often less severe consequences than other behaviours that have been studied in the past. It is an open question whether the results from studies that investigate how Chinese people function in other roles will apply to their consumption decisions. As a result, we must be selective in developing research propositions.

FUTURE DIRECTIONS FOR RESEARCH

This field of research desperately calls for more work in all areas. The challenge is evident, but so will be the reward.

First, researchers need to look beyond the propositions presented. These propositions are merely catalysts for more creative and innovative thoughts. In focusing on a topic, researchers should assume a programmatic approach in their studies. The lack of previous research efforts suggest that researchers will have to build their research from its foundation.

Second, the paper adopts a more social-psychological approach to reviewing the literature and to developing researchable propositions. Researchers should be aware of developments in other approaches that investigate how Chinese people differ from people of other cultures in their basic behavioural processes. These processes may include categorization, memory retrieval, among others. As the topic emerges into the light, it is highly likely that knowing about work on these basic behavioural processes will become necessary.

Third, this chapter highlights how Chinese people perceive consumption activities, evaluate their purchases, and use consumption as means to foster social relationships. There are other ways to organize the literature to derive insightful propositions. For example, how Chinese people behave before, during, and after their purchase decisions (see Yates and Lee, this volume) may be worth exploring. In the post-choice situation, would Chinese people be more open to extreme evaluations or would they repress their feelings? Would they attribute product successes and failures to external or to internal causes? Would they engage in open complaints or silent exits? Some of these questions are now being pursued by researchers in other contexts. Continuous development would likely further enrich our understanding of Chinese people's consumption behaviour.

Chapter 24

Employee Motivation and Attitudes in the Chinese Workforce

C. Harry Hui and Chen K. Tan

The Chinese workforce is as diverse as is the Chinese race. Fortunately for Western theorists, if a theory concerning the Chinese worker does not receive empirical support in a certain geographical location, it likely will in another. Unfortuately, no theory or set of empirical findings can be generalized with much confidence from one Chinese sample to another. To every 'rule' discovered, there exist many exceptions. This tremendous intragroup heterogeneity must be recognized as we examine the psychology of the Chinese workforce, which is shaped differently in different labour environments.

The environments in which Chinese workers find themselves are different from the ones with which Western researchers and practitioners in organizational behaviour and management science are familiar. These environments are different even among the several major Chinese societies. For example, most members of the workforce in Taiwan and Hong Kong are employed in small- to medium-size companies (Sit and Wong, 1989). Only a small percentage are represented by trade unions, since the latter are primarily organized in the few large enterprises. Contrary to Western practice, the social security system of neither society provides much to those who do not work. There are few if any unemployment benefits. Therefore, people who are not well provided for must work in order to survive.

That is not the situation in the People's Republic of China (PRC). For several decades, every individual's basic survival needs have been taken care of by the State. Everyone has been assigned to work in a 'work unit' (*danwei*) of the State or a State-owned enterprise. Until recently, the system ensured little or no employee turnover by making job changes contingent upon a virtually impossible regimen of interviews and approvals from a hierarchy of bureaucrats.

This labour market is now gradually changing, however, as China moves towards a market economy (or 'socialist market economy'). The emergence of private business enterprises, the establishment of special economic zones, and the opening up of certain cities and towns to foreign investment are creating new employment opportunities. A conservative estimate asserts that three joint ventures with foreign corporations are established in China every two days. There are also changes within State-owned enterprises, with those that continually incur losses being either closed down or merged. Heads of other enterprises have been made accountable for the business performance of their units, a practice unheard of before the mid-1970s. More and more State-owned enterprises are being privatized. All these changes indicate the emergence of a free labour market in mainland China.

Within this context empirical studies of Chinese employees have been conducted. The findings point to factors that have direct or indirect effects on a Chinese employee's work motivation and job satisfaction. Broadly speaking, they can be gathered under three categories which also interact with each other: personal characteristics, organizational characteristics, and cultural values. A heuristic model for organizing the research findings is presented in Figure 24.1.

PERSONAL CHARACTERISTICS

At the individual level are two sub-classes of characteristics: the dispositional (work goals, psychological collectivism, and other personality factors) and the demographic. Both sub-classes have an impact on the person's work motivation and job satisfaction, but the latter also exerts influences through the former.

Work Goals

People work because they see in that activity purposes or the potential for attaining certain goals. In the discrepancy model (Lawler, 1973), the inability to satisfy one's needs is regarded as the primary cause of job dissatisfaction. Therefore, it is important to understand what a Chinese employee wants to attain through work.

Taiwan

The meaning of work to the Chinese in Taiwan has undergone significant changes over the last few decades. Individuals who had obtained their university degrees in 1967 or 1977 saw work as the focus of life (Wang, 1992). It was prized as the main assurance of family livelihood. Thus, activities not related to work were given secondary importance. Those who graduated in 1987, however, saw work as but one element of life. According to these graduates, one's work life can and should be adjusted to fit in with personal interests, needs, family, and leisure. This cohort held that one of the core values of work is 'to do things one likes'. Survival, which once was the concern of post-exile Taiwanese, is no longer the salient reason for one to work.

The Taiwanese want both material satisfaction and social-psychological rewards from their work. A 1992 survey of 401 employees on the island (cited in Huang, 1993) revealed that they valued most highly a high salary, good working conditions, and public recognition for their contribution.

Mainland China

Findings regarding work goals and values isolated in Taiwan can be generalized, with some caution, to workers in mainland China. Shenkar and Ronen (1987) collected ratings on the importance of 14 work goals from 163 male managers in the PRC and compared them with data obtained from Chinese in

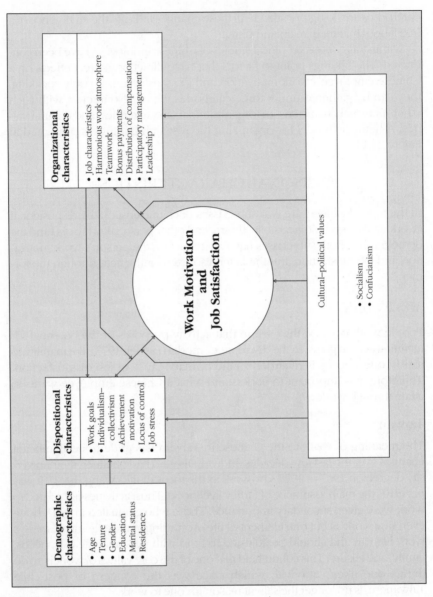

Figure 24.1   A heuristic model linking Chinese employees' work motivation and job satisfaction with personal characteristics, organiational characteristics, and cultural-political values

Hong Kong, Taiwan, and Singapore. Limitations in sample size and representativeness notwithstanding, there was a certain degree of similarity in the rating
patterns seen among the Chinese in the four locations. For example, 'time for
non-work activities' was regarded as least important in all four locations.

However, managers in mainland China regarded 'promotion' as relatively
unimportant, compared with other work goals. This phenomenon, not reported in the other locations, may be explained in terms of the persisting belief
held by many mainland Chinese that career advancement equates with more
responsibility but few extrinsic rewards in the Communist state. Higher status,
more responsibility, and opportunity for growth may not be as attractive as
rewards that can be immediately exchanged for material comforts, especially
in inflation-stricken China (Weldon and Jehn, 1993).

There have been quite remarkable changes in workers' reported values and
work goals over the last decade or so. 'Contribution to nation and community'
was chosen as the most important element in life by only 45 per cent of 15,085
respondents in 1991, as compared to 73.29 per cent in 1986 (Hunan Province
Labour Union, 1991). The proportion of people choosing 'wealth' rose slightly
from 5.82 per cent to 8.2 per cent, and the desire for a 'happy family' rose from
10.27 per cent to 39.2 per cent. These changes represent a shift from a nation-
alist and sacrificial sentiment to a pragmatic and family-centred orientation.
Admittedly, these results may also be seen as a mere reflection of how the
Chinese have become more open and willing to say what had always been
their concerns, as a result of the loosening of ideological control. In any case,
one should note that changes take place rapidly in the present China, and any
survey result can become outdated fairly quickly.

In short, economic reform and modernization have resulted in Chinese
employees' focusing their attention on personal, extrinsic rewards. With the
Mainland being opened more to the outside world, and the increase in trade
and cultural exchanges, a convergence across all Chinese societies in terms of
their work goals may develop in the near future.

Individualism–Collectivism

The individualism–collectivism polarity is a dimension along which both cultures and individuals can be distinguished. Hui (1988) and Hui and Yee (1994)
define collectivism as a syndrome of attitudes and values pertaining to the
belief that the basic unit of survival lies in the group and not the individual. As
readers will see, this construct appears in different forms in different studies.

As a psychological construct, collectivism has important attitudinal and
behavioural correlates (Hui, 1988). Collectivist employees are more satisfied
with various aspects of their work, and are higher in general job satisfaction,
than are individualists (Hui, Eastman, and Yee, 1995).

At least two explanations may clarify these findings. First, collectivists are
unlikely to report negative feelings which may alienate their peers and superiors. Second, collectivists may have lower expectations in terms of individual
rewards and resources. As a result, satisfaction may correspondingly be higher.
More research is needed to evaluate these explanations.

Demographic Variables

Individual characteristics such as age, tenure, geographical location, level of education, and marital status exert considerable influence on the work attitudes of Chinese employees.

Age and tenure

Because of societal and individual modernization, the old and the young in Chinese societies are different in their work goals. A large-scale survey of 2,089 randomly sampled workers identified four groups of instrumental work values: harmony and stability, extrinsic rewards (fame, status, power, and wealth), collective interests (national development, community service, and the pursuit of truth and knowledge), and intrinsic rewards (self-actualization, self esteem, and autonomy). Of the four groups of values, collective interest was found to be most closely related to age. Older people endorsed this value more strongly than did younger ones (Taiwan Work-related Values Research Team, 1993).

The above findings are somewhat consistent with the second part of Wang's (1992) research, which involved a questionnaire survey of 546 individuals. The younger cohort valued personal growth and achievement, as well as extrinsic rewards such as status and income. The older generation, on the contrary, was more concerned about national development and community service.

In all cohorts, entrants to the workforce attached considerable importance to whether the job could provide an opportunity for the individual to utilize his or her skills and would lead to a sense of achievement, personal growth, and self-actualization. The primary concern of these entrants was thus intrinsic rewards. However, within three to five years after joining the workforce, a period when university graduates usually start their families, the concern was seen to shift to living a life of harmony and tranquility. This pattern of development was consistently observed in all three cohorts investigated by Wang (1992).

In short, studies in Taiwan reveal that older workers attach more emphasis to stability and national security, while the younger ones are very similar to their Western counterparts in their outlook on life (that is, striving for achievement, wealth, and self-actualization).

Other empirical findings, on the impact of age on job satisfaction, have generally supported the linearity assumption between the two variables (see, for example, Rodes, 1983; Mottaz, 1987). Older teachers and teachers with longer terms of service are more likely to express greater job satisfaction and job commitment (Huang, 1986; Su and Huang, 1992). This is also true of employees in various other occupations (see, for example, Chen and Huang, 1982; Hsu, 1977; Li and Lu, 1982). Teachers younger in age or with relatively shorter terms of service tend to demonstrate symptoms suggesting emotional and physical exhaustion (Kuo, 1987, 1989, 1990).

Gender

There is some support for gender differences in the attitudes of workers. In general, male workers have a higher level of job satisfaction and job commitment than do female workers (Su and Huang, 1992). They prefer extrinsic rewards to intrinsic rewards (Taiwan Work-related Values Research Team, 1993). On the whole, however, male workers have higher demands for both forms of rewards than do their female counterparts (Wang, 1992). In comparison with female subjects, male workers are more satisfied with opportunities for promotion, but they are less satisfied with their present salary (Huang and Kuo, 1984). Female workers value tolerance, modesty, loyalty, and trustworthiness more than do male workers (Chen and Huang, 1982; Taiwan Work-related Values Research Team; Wang). The latter hold more negative attitudes toward management (Shen, Liu and Huang, 1989), and they are more instrumental in their expectations about job and career (Wang, 1992).

Huang (1984) argues that gender differences in Chinese work attitudes are the results of socially regulated factors such as pay, position, and promotion opportunities. However, indications are that gender inequalities in these aspects are slowly being phased out. Wang (1992), for instance, reported that in Taiwan, younger female workers' work attitudes are becoming increasingly similar to those of their male counterparts.

Marital status

In general, married individuals tend to report higher job satisfaction and job commitment (Chen and Huang, 1982; Huang, 1984; Su and Huang, 1992) than do single workers. Compared with single workers, the married are more satisfied with their opportunities for promotion but less satisfied with their salary (Huang and Kuo, 1984). Consistent with findings in the West, single workers tend to report more job-related stress than do married workers (Hsu and Chen, 1981).

Education

The level of education attained and the individual's work attitudes are related. Huang (1986) found that college graduates tend to be less committed to organizations than do non-graduates. Although the latter are relatively less concerned with personal growth and self-improvement in job settings, they value loyalty more than do the former (Taiwan Work-related Values Research Team, 1993). This phenomenon has been attributed to the high job expectations of college graduates and their high job mobility (Cheng, 1980; Huang, 1986; Chuang, Cheng, and Ren, 1990).

Residence

Work attitudes have been shown to be different between rural and urban workers. Non-city employees tend to feel more satisfied with their current salary, benefits, and job security. They also value modesty, ability, and rationality, as well as loyalty, more than do city workers. The urban employee places a greater emphasis on the self and personal growth than does the rural worker (Taiwan Work-related Values Research Team, 1993).

Other Psychological Characteristics

The list of correlates and antecedents of job satisfaction in Chinese populations are by and large similar to what has been compiled by researchers in the West.

For example, Huang and Kuo (1984) found job satisfaction related to achievement motivation. Wu, Pan, and Ding (1980) found a positive correlation between internal locus of control and job satisfaction. Similar observations have been made in empirical research conducted for theses and dissertations on samples such as law enforcement personnel, female textile workers, female supervisors in private enterprises, employees of a telecommunication company, and company executives.

Summary

Empirical findings generally support Western theorizing on the relationships between job satisfaction and work motivation on one hand, and various psychological and demographic variables on the other. Studies have also shown clearly that there is a trend in which the Chinese are changing to look more like their Western counterparts, presumably as a result of modernization and economic development.

ORGANIZATIONAL CHARACTERISTICS

Job Characteristics

In creating their job-characteristics model, Hackman and Oldham (1976, 1980) argued that job satisfaction and work motivation are functions of several core dimensions of jobs, such as variety, feedback, autonomy, and the possibility that the employee is allowed to complete some identifiable part of the task. This model has been tested on bank employees (Shen, 1978), education administrators (Hong, 1979), managers of small- and medium-sized enterprises (Fu, 1980), employees of financial institutions, auditors, as well as computer personnel of insurance companies, all in Taiwan during the 1970s and 1980s.

A Harmonious Work Atmosphere

Findings indicate that Chinese workers are very concerned about social relationships at work. Cheng (1980) found that young factory workers rated friendship as one of the most important factors to affect their work attitude. Similarly, Wang (1992) reported that Taiwanese industrial workers placed great emphasis on friendship in the work setting. Numerous Master's theses and doctoral dissertations written in Taiwan reported a correlation between organizational climate and job satisfaction (see, for example, Tsui, 1984). Industrial salespersons, as well as high school teachers, have expressed greater satisfaction and performed better in their work when their colleagues were described as friendly and congenial (Huang, 1986; Lo, 1982; Zhong, 1989). The inability to maintain a harmonious relationship between colleagues has been rated as a major reason for work-related stress, burnout, and resignation (Huang, 1986; Kuo, 1989, 1990).

The importance of a harmonious working environment is consistent with the collective feature of interdependence observed often in Chinese culture (Markus and Kitayama, 1991). Chinese believe the self is constituted by personal attributes which are meaningful when defined in a relational context. For example, Chinese consider themselves as part of a family only when they are accorded a relational status, such as being termed a parent or sibling. A breakdown in harmony implies a disregard for interpersonal respect or disagreement in role assignment, thus causing stress and dissatisfaction. However, respect begets respect. When respect is given, Chinese perceive their personal worth as being reinstated in the group. This, in turn, results in high productivity and job satisfaction, as has been recorded by the studies reported above.

As the Chinese become less collectivist and more individualist in their outlook, their desire for a harmonious working environment may to a certain extent diminish. Hui and Yee (1995) studied salespersons of a department store and customer service representatives of a utility company, both in Hong Kong. Among collectivists, as measured with Hui's Individualism-Collectivism Scale, they found a small correlation between employees' job satisfaction and the presence of a congenial work group characterized by mutual support (Hui, 1988). The direction of the correlation was reversed for individualists, as measured on the same scale.

Teamwork

The famous Hawthorne studies (Roethlisberger and Dickson, 1939) documented American workers' reluctance to break their work group's norms in production rates; the studies showed that workers' productivity is largely determined by the group's prevalent norm, which acts either as a motivator or as an inhibitor of effort. Among the Chinese, it appears that employees are equally, if not more, concerned than were the American workers about being ostracized for working too hard or for delaying their work group. Findings indicate that a work group and its members exert an immense force upon each worker, changing the way work is normally done.

Earley (1989) conducted an experiment in which mainland Chinese manager trainees worked on a moderately difficult in-tray task. Half were told that they were part of a ten-person team and that they were to achieve a group goal. The other half of the subjects were told to work by themselves. Results showed that the first group outperformed the second. Furthermore, there was no difference in performance between those subjects who were anonymous and those who could be identified and held accountable. The motivation to work hard was not stifled by being submerged in a group, as the Western social loafing literature has suggested (see, for example, Latane, Williams, and Harkins, 1979).

A similar phenomenon was also found by Wang (1988) in a field experiment which compared the effectiveness and productivity of an individual reward system and a team reward system. A selection of 26 female factory workers in mainland China were assigned to one of two groups to perform similar tasks. Subjects in the control group received rewards on the basis of their individual output. Subjects in the experimental group received rewards on the basis of their team output. During the course of the experiment, which lasted for one month, a weekly, 30-minute training in attribution was given to the experimental group to encourage members to make attributions to their team's collaboration and effort. Results showed that the team-reward system reinforced, by the attribution training, raised each worker's evaluations of the team, her satisfaction with her own work, her satisfaction with interpersonal relationships within the team, her satisfaction with management, and her sense of responsibility. Absenteeism in the experimental group was lower than in the control group, and productivity increased steadily.

These two studies, together with other anecdotes, suggest that Chinese workers' subjective feeling of being members of a group who share in some kind of reward elevates their motivation and enhances productivity. Indeed, in a culture where congenial social relationships are highly valued, people's behaviours are largely intended to expand their social networks and to preserve interpersonal harmony.

It should, however, be noted that just as a person's work motivation can be heightened by being in a group, it can also be dampened if the norm of the group is to reduce production, or if working hard is seen to be counter-productive for the group as a whole. In other words, the group may become an inhibitor counteracting or neutralizing any of the effects an individual incentive scheme is intended to support.

Bonus Payments

In urban areas of mainland China, many employees receive bonuses which account for as much as 40 per cent of their pay package. Bonus payment is usually tied to productivity or profitability, and therefore can be viewed as an incentive. This bonus system can be found in many occupations, such as service personnel in the hotel and catering industries, workers and supervisors in the manufacturing industries, and front-line sales and managers in the retailing industries. Those employed in hospitals and clinics receive a bonus calculated on the number of patients treated. Public security personnel receive a bonus from a pool of money collected as fines. Many regard bonus payment as one of the strongest motivators in the PRC (Yu, 1991).

Bonus payments can be a source of discontent as well. At the macro level, increase in buying power of a portion of the people brings forth adverse effects such as inflation. At the individual level, some recipients may regard the bonus they receive as inequitably small, as compared with that received by other people in the same or other work units. Indeed, in several large-scale surveys involving thousands of workers, 'unfair distribution (of rewards and bonuses)' was cited most frequently (35-40 per cent) as the paramount factor within the organization that dampens employees' work motivation and initiative (Hubei Province Wuhan Muncipal Labour Union, 1991). The sense of unfairness lies in workers' perception that rewards were not distributed on the basis of relative performance (Wu and Cheng, 1992).

Distribution of Compensation

Some researchers of distributive justice note that Chinese prefer to use a more egalitarian approach in distribution of reward. In a series of experimental manipulations, Chinese respondents consistently distributed rewards more equally even when recipients distinctly differed in merit (see, for example, Leung and Bond, 1984). This finding seems particularly true when colleagues are regarded as siblings or comrades. In the traditional Chinese family, cooperation between siblings is necessary for the achievement of harmony in a large extended family household. It is also essential for the maintenance of the widely practised family business (Redding, 1990).

However, the egalitarian approach is not always cherished in family business enterprises and in organizations in the PRC. Yu (1992) asked 845 subjects in 13 Chinese enterprises to indicate on a 5-point scale whether they preferred equal distribution of reward (a rating of 1) or a distribution that would result in a great disparity (a rating of 5). (Note that it was unclear whether or not a rating of 5 meant distribution by proportionality.) The mid-point of the scale was anchored at 'appropriate disparity'. (Again, the meaning is both ambiguous and may lead subjects to acquiesce.) Although the scale suffers from the problems noted, one finding was unmistakable: only 4 per cent of the subjects preferred an equal distribution of rewards. In another, national survey of 2,074 employees of large and medium-size enterprises in 10 Chinese cities, 24.8 per cent of the respondents attributed the present unfair compensation system to 'lip service to the "to each according to their work" principle', a reason that was superseded only by 'corrupt phenomena in the Communist Party' (31 per cent)(China National Labour Union, 1991).

While operatives and front-line production workers in most organizations in non-Communist localities are paid at a per-piece rate, those in the Mainland have a fixed salary. Mainland China has traditionally enforced the equal distribution system in order to be consistent with Communist ideology (Yu, 1992). As can be inferred from the surveys cited above, the effectiveness of this system has been increasingly questioned, as employees begin to express dissent on the neglect of individual contributions in the decision to distribute material rewards (Yu, 1991, 1992; Yang, Zhang, Zhao, and Dang, 1992; Wu, 1992; Wu and Cheng, 1992). Despite putting emphasis on harmony and hierarchy, many Chinese workers believe that application of the equity rule in material reward allocation will boost their work morale (Yu, 1992).

It is wrong, however, to assume that the proportional distribution of bonuses is welcome throughout China. In some organizations, particularly the smaller ones, workers may still prefer to share bonuses on an egalitarian basis. The paradox of egalitarianism accepted as a cultural norm on the one hand and rejected on the other can be explained in several ways.

First, it should be noted that most of the experimental studies that found egalitarianism among the Chinese manipulated low-value rewards such as pencils or a small amount of money. Moreover, respondents in some studies acted as third-party allocators, whose decisions had no real effects on their work or benefits. While this method has its merits and is at times necessary, it divorces respondents from the value of the rewards. The allocation outcome may be so inconsequential that subjects did not find it worthwhile to take the risk of deviating from the widely accepted norm of egalitarianism.

Hui, Triandis, and Yee's (1991) study has some bearing on this hypothesis. In their study, subjects were asked to allocate first an unspecified amount of money, then a specified sum, to a partner with whom they were said to have performed a task. When the amount to be allocated was perceived as unlimited, distribution tended to be egalitarian. However, when a constant sum was to be divided, there was a departure from the equality rule, resulting in an allocation based on each individual's contribution. It appears that when economic resources and rewards are not seen to be sufficient to satisfy everyone involved, the Chinese (especially those in the economically flourishing Greater China) may adopt a more equitable stance when it comes to dividing resources that are highly valued.

A second explanation relates to the size, composition, and cohesiveness of the group. When the proportionality norm is called for, the proponents are usually members of large enterprises where most other workers who would be sharing in the same pool of bonuses are not acquainted with each other. The proponents themselves are also relatively anonymous. Where people reject distribution on the basis of merit, it is usually within a small work group where co-workers know each other fairly well. In such collectivities, one does not want to be different and to alienate other members by receiving a bonus that is bigger than what most colleagues will receive. Neither would one want to be seen as supporting a compensation scheme that might potentially rupture group solidarity. Indeed, Leung and Bond (1984) found that Chinese were more likely to use the proportionality norm when allocating a reward between themselves and a stranger. Similarly, Yang and Hui (1986) found that college students demand proportional distribution of coursework marks in group projects when members involved did not work collectively as a group. In short, Chinese perceive the legitimacy of the equality principle in reward distribution only when used among members of an in-group (Leung and Bond, 1984; Triandis, Bontempo, Villareal, Asai, and Lucca, 1988), and when there is commitment to group stability and welfare. When it comes to dealing with people one does not know, and when maintenance of harmony is not the main concern, the proportionality norm appears to be more favoured.

Participatory Management

Participatory management is motivational in many Western organizations because it supports the culturally espoused values of democracy and individual expression of opinion (see, for example, Erez, 1992). Its effectiveness is, however, debatable in a culture like the Chinese, which traditionally promotes the virtues of submission, humility, tolerance, and hierarchy (see Bond, this volume). 'Empowerment of employees', a concept that has found its way into virtually every management text published in the United States in recent years, surprises many Chinese supervisors and bewilders their subordinates. In Chinese society, leaders are perceived as the parent of the group or organization. A certain amount of autocratic management is therefore accepted, or even expected, by employees, because authoritarian control is a legitimate parental attribute.

Indeed, Chinese workers equate managerial dominance with care for the employees (Hwang, 1983). Although employees welcome relative autonomy and participation in decision-making (Yu, 1991), they interpret managers' non-involvement as evidence of incompetence or inefficiency (cf. Boey, 1991). Predictably, in a study conducted in 53 Hong Kong companies, Redding and Wong (1986) noted that the authority to make decisions is essentially retained by the employer and his or her closest associates. A centralization score of 103.1 was recorded on the Aston questionnaire, in contrast to a rating of 50.1 recorded by Child in the United Kingdom (1972).

Levels of readiness and unreadiness for a participatory management style vary from one Chinese society to another. Documentation of the relative levels, however, in the PRC, Taiwan, and Hong Kong is yet to be established, as is the extent to which centralized decision-making authority is interpreted as a leader's lack of trust in his or her subordinates (Hui, 1990). In light of Hong Kong's relatively frequent and intensive exposure to Western culture, participatory management may be more widely practised there (despite the territory's high centralization score) than it is in Taiwan, where the Confucian philosophy of hierarchical relationship has retained a much stronger hold. One might expect the practice to be least well accepted in the PRC, where four decades of totalitarian rule have instructed the people in the virtue of remaining silent, even when encouraged to differ. It is also possible that while high centralization is looked upon by some in Hong Kong as an untrusting act, most employees in mainland China would simply accept the system. Such data, when gathered, will further corroborate the notion that cultural values play a strong role in determining what constitutes motivational factors.

Leadership

That a supervisor behaves as he or she should and does not deviate too far from the subordinates' expectations is a reason for subordinates to be willing to devote extra effort to their work. This view is shared by Farh, Podsakoff, and Organ (1990), as is evidenced in their study of the relationship between leader fairness and organizational citizenship behaviour.

Chinese employees want their leaders to be considerate and benevolent (Wu, 1986; Zhong, 1989). They do not see such an expectation as incongruous with the acceptance of authoritative supervision. Instead, both characteristics are different but compatible facets of the parental role. Taiwanese teachers reported higher job satisfaction and their schools had a lower staff turnover rate when school principals were perceived to be sensitive and concerned for the teachers' welfare (Huang, 1982, 1984, 1986). Conversely, it has been shown that a supervisor's apathy towards the welfare and concerns of his or her employees adversely affects the employees' work morale (Yu, 1991).

Chinese leaders are also expected to exercise sound moral judgement. A supervisor must be self-restrained, honest towards fellow colleagues and employees, trustworthy, and impartial for subordinates to rate him or her as an effective leader (Ling, Fang, and Khanna, 1991). Indeed, Chinese employees have higher work motivation when their supervisors exhibit personal morality at the workplace (see Smith and Wang, this volume). Congruently, Chinese managers also regard moral character as a requirement of the leadership role, and a precursor of employee satisfaction (Taiwan Work-related Values Research Team, 1993).

Nevertheless, changes are inevitable as a result of modernization. Researchers in Taiwan (see, for example, Huang, 1993) note that the employment relationship is in a state of transition. In the past, the employment relationship was an extension of the family bond; it is now increasingly a contractual agreement. While the relationship used to be socio-emotional, with the employer or superior playing the role of a father, it is now more instrumental. Personal interests, not moral obligations, set the tone for superior–subordinate interactions. That the leader is seen to be 'fair by my standards' and 'willing to do things that benefit me' may soon become the requisites for higher work motivation in Chinese societies.

CULTURAL AND POLITICAL VALUES

Readers should by now appreciate the role Chinese cultural and political values play in shaping individual and organizational characteristics. For instance, the expectation that a leader be a moral person is probably an outgrowth from the Confucian tradition. The emphasis of ideological purity among leaders in the PRC is also a product of socialist values.

Culture and political ideologies also have direct impact on the way workers feel about their job. While studies examining effects of Chinese socialism on workers' motivation and satisfaction could not be found, some work on the relationship between Confucianism and work behaviours may be reported.

Confucianism

The link between economic development and a Confucian or neo-Confucian work ethic has been the topic of discussion of many sociologists and organizational researchers (see, for example, Ng, 1990; Redding, 1990). An employee expends effort at work not only because of the instrumental attractiveness of the job, but also because of his or her moral commitment to fulfill a duty at work and to contribute to the collectivity (Kao and Ng, 1988).

The Confucian view of interpersonal relationships consists of an element of reciprocity (*bao*): in short, the recipient of a favour should repay it (Liu, 1992; Yang, 1957). On the basis of this norm of social exchange is built a strong and extensive social network, which at the workplace ties together superiors, subordinates, clients, and owners. The subordinate, for example, is obliged to reciprocate, by contributing extra effort at work, if the superior has gone out of his or her way to treat the subordinate well.

Findings have linked macro-level productivity to certain aspects of Confucian values. A country's economic growth can be explained in part by the people's long-term orientation, defined as the desire to acquire skills and education, to work hard, to save, and to be thrifty, persevering, and patient. This cluster of values is most enthusiastically embraced by people in the PRC, Hong Kong, Singapore, and Taiwan. These countries also ranked high in national economic growth for the period 1965–87 (Hofstede, 1991; Hofstede and Bond, 1988; Franke, Hofstede, and Bond, 1991).

Unfortunately, no study has been conducted to determine whether a similar relationship exists at the individual level. Furthermore, no data exists to inform us on the extent of employees' acceptance of a Confucian work ethic. It is quite possible, as suggested earlier, that traditional values are waning, at least among certain sectors of the workforce (for example, young college graduates). Thus, whatever was true of the Chinese workforce in previous generations may not be equally applicable to the workforce in future generations.

CONCLUSION

The Changing Face of Chinese Collectivism

Chinese workers exhibit attitudes and motivations which epitomize the very essence of Confucian collectivism. They emphasize the precedence of social relationships and group welfare over individual needs and desires. As a result, their behaviours, relative to the actions of workers in the West, are more likely to strongly reflect social norms and obligations. Personal desires, while also a determinant of behaviours, may play a secondary role (Triandis, 1986). Cooperation is given priority over individual interests (Triandis, Bontempo, Villareal, Asai, and Lucca, 1988; Waterman, 1984), and effort and contribution is directed towards the collective good rather than toward personal benefits and self-recognition (Laaksonen, 1988). Under such circumstances, their attitudes towards work, their occupation, and the organization employing them would be expected to be characterized by passivity, conformity, obedience, altruism, paternalism, and dogmatism (cf. Ng, 1990; Triandis, 1990; Westwood and Chan, 1992).

The present chapter does not deny the validity of findings supporting these hypotheses. The argument champions the notion that collectivism is a unique feature of Chinese organizations, and it suggests that collectivism is more prevalent among individuals in family-controlled organizations in Chinese societies than in non-family organizations (see Redding, 1990, for a discussion of this issue). However, whether this behaviour pattern has been adopted by every member of the Chinese workforce is open to discussion. Reported individual differences indicate enough variation to caution readers against an assumption that the Chinese are homogeneously collectivist. Moreover, the collectivist–familist value appears to be waning as modernization and technological advancement drive societies to develop larger and more complex organizations (Yang, 1988). Instead of accepting 'irregularities' in the name of harmony, individual workers in Chinese companies demand the fulfillment of their own expectations and needs in their work setting. The face of the Chinese workforce is evolving and converging with that seen in other places. Employees in Chinese societies, despite geographical separation, are becoming more and more similar to each other, and more similar to workers in the rest of the world.

Directions for Future Research

In making the above statement we do not intend to give the impression that we know precisely the character of the typical Chinese worker. There are several reasons for qualifying our claims. First, industrial and organizational research is not as fully developed in Chinese communities as it is in the West. Empirical data on the topic are preliminary and not well focused. In these circumstances, it would be presumptuous to generalize from data collected in one geographical location to other locations. Second, of the studies using Chinese workers as subjects, only a few have been published in outlets accessible to the international research community. Because of these limitations, any conclusions drawn from the above review of the literature can at best be treated as tentative hypotheses subject to further research and replication.

More specifically, it should be noted that participants in most studies conducted in Taiwan were primarily literate and employed in large corporations. Similarly, past studies on the PRC workforce have concentrated on the urban areas, and their findings therefore cannot be generalized to people in rural areas, which account for over 80 per cent of the Chinese population. Empirical data are also lacking for individuals employed in the civil service and in State-owned enterprises in the PRC, sectors where a large proportion of the Chinese work. These are the areas where replications are needed.

On a more substantive note, more research is needed to provide a better understanding of people's psychological reactions to the fast-changing economy, especially in mainland China. What effects do political and economic reform have on the motivations of these people? How do Chinese workers, the older ones in particular, cope with the shift from an egalitarian and planned economy to a market economy?

Certain outcomes of job satisfaction and work values have not been fully examined. There has, for example, been little employee turnover in the PRC. As a result, neither theory nor research on this topic could be found. We need to understand the withdrawal behaviour of Chinese workers, which has in the past been chiefly psychological (characterized, for example, by the worker becoming apathetic) but is now becoming more behavioural, in the form of premature resignation.

As one can clearly see, one fundamental motif of this chapter is that the Chinese and their economies are changing rapidly, and so a theory of Chinese work motivation and job satisfaction must be able to take this situation into account. The present chapter has outlined findings which should be useful in this endeavour.

NOTES

A substantial portion of the literature reviewed in this chapter, published and unpublished, was collected while the first author took part in the Overseas Scholars Program sponsored by the National Science Council, Republic of China. The assistance of Professor Ping-Der Huang (Department of Management, National Chengchi University), Professor Kuo-Shu Yang (Department of Psychology, National Taiwan University), and their colleagues is gratefully acknowledged. We thank Professor A. B. Yu for his comments on an earlier version of this chapter, and C. L. Luk for his bibliographic assistance.

Chapter 25

■

Ecological Psychology in Chinese Societies

Solvig Ekblad

This chapter discusses ecological psychology in Chinese societies, with special emphasis on mainland China and the effects the dwelling environment may have upon an individual's psychological health. From the perspective of ecological psychology, we shall focus on factors which distinguish Western and Chinese culture. In Western societies, the prevalent patterns of human functioning may be globally described as 'individual-oriented'; Chinese people in the People's Republic of China (PRC), Hong Kong, Singapore, Taiwan, and the many overseas Chinese societies have been described as 'group-minded' or 'socially oriented' (for a review, see Yang, 1992). The Chinese people have developed cultural norms and values which encourage the maintenance of harmonious relationships among people, and between people and the natural world.

Ecology is the discipline of biology that clarifies the interactive processes among living beings and their surroundings; it is based on the Darwinian view of individuals' development. Ecological psychology is a newly developed school of psychology. The ecological paradigm has been incorporated into several disciplines (for example, economics, public health, psychology, and sociology). If we apply the concept of ecology to humans as human ecology, we must consider the unique features of human beings. People have created culture and civilization during the evolutionary process. They have organized a family and social life with religion, philosophy, art, and other kinds of thinking and performance controls integrated into the human network. The context of people's lives is relevant to understanding the constructive and destructive aspects of their ways of functioning.

The ecosystem is the fundamental unit of ecology, comprising the living organisms and the non-living elements interacting in a defined area. Any ecosystem has limits as well as possibilities. Tensions arise between the environment and the individual when the individual pulls in one direction and the environment pulls in another. Stokols (1992) has reviewed the basic framework for understanding the nature of people's transactions with their physical and sociocultural surroundings.

EAST–WEST APPROACHES TO HUMAN ECOLOGY AND MODERNIZATION

One of the differences between Eastern and Western cultures is in their eco-logical viewpoint. In Chinese philosophy, as interpreted by Song (1990), humans occupy a very small part of the complex world. Human beings are not supposed to fight against the natural environment, but to exist in a harmonious relation with the universe. Traditional Chinese society was based on a mixture of naturalistic approaches to religion, morals, and philosophy. In the doctrine of Taoism, the *dao* (heavenly way) embodied the laws and patterns of nature and society according to which every person was expected to mould his or her thoughts and behaviour. The cosmic elements of yin and yang were female and male, respectively, and both were contained within each person. For this reason, man and woman required each other (Duant, 1954, in Breiner, 1992, pp. 53–4).

Yang (1992) suggested that the interaction of special ecological–environ-mental factors and morphological, physiological, and behavioural traits of the ancient Chinese people are responsible for the formation of both the agricul-tural subsistence economy and the agricultural social structure of traditional Chinese society. Those economic and socio-structural characteristics were combined with specific Chinese socialization practices, and moulded the social-oriented personality of the traditional Chinese.

As an agricultural society is being transformed into an industrial and com-mercial one, the Chinese social orientation is losing its original intensity and changing in its characteristics (see Yang, this volume). Tsai (1986) analysed the modernization process in mainland China, Taiwan, Hong Kong, and Singapore and described a dynamic in which industrialization leads to eco-nomic growth which leads, in turn, to modernization. He drew contrasts between Taiwan's mixture of planning and private enterprise, mainland China's socialism, Singapore's mix of socialism and capitalism, and Hong Kong's market economy. In this analysis, mainland China has experienced faster economic growth but has not succeeded in modernizing itself to the same degree as have the others. While mainland China lags behind the other three political entities, its current modernization campaign may make it one of the leaders among Third World nations. There are empirical data (for a review, see Yang, 1992) which demonstrate that the social orientation has been weak-ening in contemporary Chinese societies. A Chinese version of the individual orientation is gradually being formed as both a new interactional system and a new dispositional pattern for effective social-psychological functioning emerges in the new Chinese societies. In light of these developments, we might ask, How can this knowledge be integrated in an ecological model?

An Ecological Model

The ecological model for assessment and evaluation focuses on three major sub-systems that define a person's complete system: the person, the family, and the community. Within each of these sub-systems, significant variables are organized around three general groupings: physical and manifest features (consitutional or somatic organization); psychological features (the ego or self-concept as an organizing force); and sociocultural features (that is, social, cultural, and ecological determinants, the organizing response to the rules and expectations of society and culture).

According to an ecological approach, the principal difficulties and threats confronting urbanites in Europe may also be confronted in Chinese societies (Dellstra and de Waart, 1989):

(a) large numbers of cars and, as a result, traffic accidents; the lack of accessibility for pedestrians; polluted air, smog, noise, and roadway congestion;

(b) erosion of the built environment, deterioration of old buildings; damage to city trees and greenery from acid rain, smog, and fumes;

(c) an unhealthy climate in both public and private buildings caused by fumes and moisture released from building materials, or by inferior construction and installation;

(d) pollution of soils and surface, drinking, and swimming water;

(e) unhealthy air in public spaces (partly resulting from the lack of shelter, inadequate vegetation and surface water, and the effects of wind on surroundings);

(f) intensive use of energy (in particular by cars, industry, and power stations) causing the 'greenhouse effect' globally and the warming of surface waters and urban 'heat islands' locally;

(g) lack of space for children, the disabled, and the elderly; lack of access to buildings for the handicapped; lack of affordable transport; lack of public meeting places; lack of living spaces for plants and animals; inadequate and unaffordable housing, especially for young people; lack of space for new industry and new initiatives in general; and

(h) crime and vandalism.

Brofenbrenner (1979) has asserted that the social context of individual interactions and experiences determines the development of the individual. There are four basic structures described in his approach, which has been modified by Kobayashi (1993, p. 27, Figure 1) and reproduced here as Figure 25.1. The four structures include, first, the *micro-ecosystem*, the space or world which an individual, especially a child, can access through the sensory system and through interactive processes with other human beings. This is the human network immediately surrounding the individual. Second is the *mini-ecosystem*, the family and the house as the basic unit. It includes not only human relations and culture, but also such physical entities as housing and infrastructure. Between the mini-ecosystem and the largest structure, the macro-ecosystem, is the *meso-ecosystem*, which functions as a connecting link and includes, with respect to children, day-care centres and schools. This system supports the transition of children from the family into society as they grow and develop. At the highest level is the *macro-ecosystem*, the ideological and institutional patterns of a particular culture or subculture.

The degree of influence of these ecosystems on a child changes with age, in other words, with the child's growth and development. Ecological approaches to parenting, education in school, and child development indicate that life stress and social support have a major influence on the quality of mother–child relationships (Leiderman, 1983). Classification of ecofactors for people in a

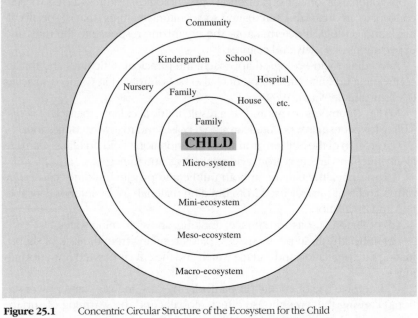

Figure 25.1   Concentric Circular Structure of the Ecosystem for the Child

Source   Reprinted from N. Kobayashi, 'Child ecology: a theoretical basis for solving children's problems in the world', *Childhood*, 1, (1993), by permission of Sage Publications Ltd.

dwelling environment is found in Table 25.1. As is shown by the table, there are qualitative and quantitative differences in ecological factors for each ecosystem.

Table 25.1   Classification of Ecofactors for People

	Relative Importance of Direct Influence for Ecosystem			
	Micro	Mini	Meso	Macro
Natural (weather, land, vegetation)	+–	+	++	+++
Biological (virus, bacteria, parasites, animals, others)	+++	++	+	+
Psychochemical (polluting chemicals radiation heat, others)	+–	++	++	+++
Sociocultural (daily life, nursery, school, work place, hygiene, government, regulations, culture, beliefs and attitudes at home, architecture, design,others)	+++	+++	+++	+++

Source   Revised from Kobayashi, 1993, Table 1, p. 28

Previous Studies of Ecological Impacts on Child Mental Health

Song (1990) illustrated three ecological impacts on child mental health in Taiwan: the children's view of contemporary Taiwan, the impact on child mental health of environmental pollution, and the impact of the school system on the practice of child psychiatry. In the Confucian society of Taiwan, where education is highly valued, children are urged to go to school and are pushed towards higher education (see also Stevenson, this volume). This value orientation (macro-ecosystem), the educational system (mini-ecosystem), and the milieu of school and home (meso-ecosystem), have a tremendous influence on students' mental health and child psychiatric practice. One example of this impact is the high rate (80 per cent) of school phobia precipitated by school-related factors in Taiwan. Some common precipitants of school phobia are school examinations, competition for grades, and corporal punishment by teachers. Effective school mental health programs should, according to Song, include programs within the school, for instance, teaching students to cope with examinations effectively, as well as programs to help parents deal with children under 'school stress'. Additionally, the system of joint entrance examinations could be changed and more educational pathways provided.

From the ecological perspective, health promotion is seen not only in terms of the specific health behaviours of the target group, but also more broadly as a dynamic transaction between individuals and groups and their psychosocial and physical environments. For instance, the social-ecological approach to health promotion requires explicit analysis of the interplay between the environmental resources available in an area and the particular health habits and lifestyles of the people who occupy that area (Lindheim and Syme, 1983).

According to Kobayashi (1993), there are two classes of risk factors which increase the incidence of somatic and psychological disorders in a given group: genetic and non-genetic. The non-genetic risk factors are generally ecological, and we are exposed to them wherever we live. Sociocultural factors, in interaction with other ecological factors, very often play a key role in the causes of such problems. This leads us to the question, What are the characteristics of Chinese social relationships and of their dwelling environments?

CHINESE SOCIAL RELATIONSHIPS AND DWELLING ENVIRONMENTS

System of the Individual, Family, and Community

In Chinese culture the family, rather than the individual, is the major unit of society. The sense of the family's importance, and its contribution to the individual's core identity, has been moulded by cultural norms and values over many centuries. While respect for the past can be seen in ancestor worship, there is simultaneously an emphasis on the future in bearing and raising children to continue the family line. Thus, when a problem effects one individual in a Chinese family, it influences the entire family.

Due to strong cultural norms and associated social and family pressure, marital dissolution has been a rare occurence in mainland China. Traditionally, marriage was not simply regarded as a means of enhancing personal pleasure or the happiness of the married couple, but was seen as a means of promoting the goals of 'familism'. The Chinese family is a close-knit social unit from which its members derive support and security. Divorce is regarded as abnormal and even polluting (Liao and Heaton, 1992, p. 413).

Social and economic development, however, has altered particularly the urban context of marriage in recent years. One important factor contributing to the increased rate of extended family break-up in Singapore, for instance, has been the rapid and massive rehousing of a large number of people in low-cost high-rise buildings (Wong, Oon, and Lun, 1979).

Chinese Dwelling Environments

Many Chinese believe that *feng shui*, the relative position of buildings and furniture in relation to each other and in relation to the physical environment, can influence the events that occur to the occupants of the buildings. To avoid bad influences and to enhance good forces, the layout of the dwelling and its furniture should be arranged in a way that takes into account the neighbouring environment. In Hong Kong, for instance, people often employ *feng shui* experts to advice them how to decorate homes, shops, factories, and offices (see also Leung, this volume).

As reported in Ekblad et al. (1991), Chinese cities, perhaps above all Beijing, have been built up from networks of traditional courtyards over a period of more than a thousand years. Until 1949, the courtyard house was the dominant dwelling in Beijing. In the period immediately thereafter, construction of buildings and the design of residential areas were influenced by Russian mid-rise architecture and planning. Today, however, these courtyard houses are being demolished rapidly and extensively, to be replaced by high-rise buildings. This rapid change will probably lead to significant alterations in the daily life of the city's citizens.

The basic architectural element used in traditional Chinese city planning is the one-storey courtyard house (*ping fang*) surrounded by a wall. The main axis of a typical courtyard house runs from south to north. On each side of the courtyard, buildings or suites of rooms are placed symmetrically. The entrance is at the corner, usually on the south wall, which serves as protection and an enclosure for domestic animals. The organization and form of the courtyard house are the result of a long process in which the form of the house and the social, economic, and cultural needs and habits of the Chinese family were developed interactively. The traditional cultural residence was patrilocal: when a woman married she left her natal home and moved to the house of her husband.

The inner organization of the courtyard likewise reflected the traditional family system based on Confucian patriarchal principles. A single family might include three, four, or even five generations. The head of the family was the father of the oldest generation, and the older generations always had precedence over the younger. This social orgainization was reflected in the design and use of the buildings and courtyards.

Traditionally, the head of the family and his wife lived in the northern house, facing south. The southern exposure receives not only light and warmth, but also yang, the spirit of life. Old Beijing residents had a saying, 'No wealthy people would ever live in rooms facing north or west'. The northern house was the largest and was situated on a platform often three steps above the level of the courtyard. In this building also was the main living room, where the family ate, celebrated, and received their guests. Older children lived in one of the east or west buildings. The platforms of those houses were lower than that of the main building. The south building was occupied by members of the family with the lowest rank, or by servants. This house was also situated on the lowest platform, only one step above the courtyard.

The kitchen, which dominates in many other traditional building cultures, is less important for the organization and design of the traditional Chinese courtyard house. It has no prescribed location and could be set up outdoors on a temporary basis, at the back of the house, or in a side room.

The courtyard was a central part of the traditional Chinese dwelling. It served as a playground for the children, as well as the place for many domestic activities including cooking, repair, storage of coal and cabbage, laundering, and so on. It was the location for social interaction between members of the household and people from different households. It was also an open space where the inhabitants met strangers and other visitors, a private or semi-private zone between the house and the street.

The Russian influence represented a break in the Chinese tradition in many ways. Three- to six-storey residential houses were erected, so called mid-rise buildings. In this new concept of residential planning, the private or semi-private courtyard disappeared and was replaced by open in-between space, an open-ended courtyard, directly connected to the street. The courtyard with its extremely diversified and intensive use, was reduced to a simple passageway. Concurrently, the character of the streets changed from narrow channels between walls to wider streets ornamented with the visual presence of balconies, windows, and views into the spaces between residential buildings. People in the streets became more involved in the lives of the buildings' inhabitants, because the visitors and passing pedestrians could now be watched from windows and open courtyards. At the same time, the open connection with the street and passing pedestrians made the 'courtyard' more public.

These flats were designed to fulfil the needs generated by an extreme housing shortage. Corridor plans were preferred initially because they allowed temporary overcrowding of the building, with one family per room and common use of facilities such as the toilet and kitchen.

By the mid-1970s, the concept, mode, and design of residential buildings had changed again. Design became directly influenced by Western industrial construction systems and high-rise buildings. The change from traditional dwellings to mid-rise and high-rise dwellings, as it is presently carried out in Chinese societies today, results in changes to both the private space and the lifestyle of Chinese families.

The traditional Chinese courtyard had a strong positive influence on privacy, territoriality, activities of children and the elderly, and child rearing, while it has had a negative influence in terms of functionality and accessibility, because

of the surrounding walls and curved narrrow streets. On the other hand, a
modern high-rise home has a strong positive influence in the latter respects but
affects the former negatively, because it provides no space for them. Such spatial constraints shift outside activities indoors and thereby increase the isolation
of the buildings' inhabitants.

Problems with Current Trends in Living Designs

Chinese culture has traditionally viewed people as relational beings, socially
situated and defined within an interactive context (Bond and Hwang, 1986;
Gabrenya and Hwang, this volume). Thus, Chinese societies have historically
functioned as collectivist organisms, in which individual needs and interests
are subordinated to shared goals. Furthermore, Chinese people have traditionally been socialized to function within certain hierarchical relationships in
which individuals must act appropriately according to their status. These functional relationships of traditional China facilitated the Chinese people's acceptance of the Communist mandates of the 1950s and early 1960s. In
contemporary China, individuals still must act with self-abnegation and deference to authority.

Cultural collectivism in China may be a defence against disease, in that it
promotes harmony within a community and between families. This coherence, and the constant support given by caring relatives or friends, act as a
buffer against stress, decreasing the incidence of disease (Bond, 1991). For
instance, the sense of 'we-ness' in Chinatowns may provide security and support to Chinese inhabitants. How strong this support is in fact needs to be
examined in more research.

From the viewpoint of urban development, Hong Kong and Singapore are
fascinating case studies, because their urban policies have been painstakingly
designed and successfully implemented (Yeung, 1987). The two communities'
social policies (for example, the Central Provident Fund in Singapore) are
based on the principles of individual and family responsibility (for more
details, see Asher and Yong, 1993). Against the background of unsuccessful
mass housing in the cities of many developing countries, these city-states' conspicuously effective policy of housing a vast proportion of the population
through the use of public funds has attracted widespread attention. Due to limited land area, the urban ecology of both cities has, by necessity, evolved into
public high-rise, high-density living and ubiquitous, urban, public transporta-
tion.

However, success brings its own challenges and problems, and these
Chinese societies have begun to face the kinds of problems which characterize
cities in developed countries. One change is that the extended family has been
weakened to such an extent that not all aged are looked after by their children,
as they were in the past. In China, according to Wang, Shen, Gu, He, and Ho
(1991), the social, economic, and educational systems, as well as family and
population structures (as in the one child per family policy) are undergoing
remarkable changes as industrialization proceeds. Furthermore, as a consequence of youth's rising expectations, education, training, jobs, recreation, and
crime and drug prevention become the concerns of policy makers. As Chinese
societies become more modern and complex, innovative solutions in lifestyle

and social support networks appropriate for a population with strong Chinese roots must be found for their social and economic problems.

Previous Studies on Chinese Adaptation to High-density Living and Overcrowding

Density is a planning statistic, and crowding is a sociological condition. The density of a city is defined as the overall population divided by the amount of land; crowding refers to the perception of a particular level of density in, for instance, a room or flat, a lift, a bus, or a park. Thus, density is an objective measurement, whereas crowding is a subjective perception. Psychological and cultural factors influence an individual's concept of space. Lo (1976) found that high-density living associated with urbanization in Hong Kong generates a level of emotional strain and psychiatric ill-health that was as high as that seen in New York.

In a preliminary report on a study of the growth, development, and rearing of 782 Chinese children from birth to the age of five years in Hong Kong, Field and Baber (1973, pp. 108–9) found that at the beginning of the survey 59.7 per cent of the families lived in one room only and in 83.5 per cent of these cases the approximate size of the room was 120 square feet or less. They also found that the average number sleeping in each room was from three to six, but that in 14.1 per cent of the cases there were more than six, often with poor ventilation and lighting. The common amenities of bathroom, lavatory, and kitchen were frequently shared with other families.

Infants contracted infections, particularly of the respiratory tract, at an unusually early age, from two to three months, with a peak incidence at seven months of age. Overcrowding was probably the single main factor causing such an early incidence of infection. The impact upon overall health and growth of these infants was particulary great, because these infections occurred frequently.

The importance of taking the child out into the fresh air was not appreciated by the parents. By the fifth month, 50 per cent of the infants were rarely taken out; their constant surroundings were an overcrowded room or the corridor of a resettlement block, where the child could play as she or he grew older. Relatives and friends rarely visted the home, so that the child's experience of people and the things they do was limited. This fact may be related to the excessive shyness noted in some of these children, particularly with respect to strangers. It could also account for the limited willingness to explore noted in some of the performance tests.

These results may give the impression that Chinese families tolerate levels of crowding that would cause serious stress in members of Western societies (Andersson, 1972; Mitchell 1971). Chinese in Hong Kong, however, tolerate intense crowding from next of kin, but they have clear-cut customs for assuring that each family member's space is properly respected. Tolerance and coping among Chinese families in high-density living is, according to Miller (1976), promoted by nine factors: a Chinese tradition which stresses the values of several generations living together, at times in the same dwelling; a definition of privacy which indicates seniority and respect for elders in the family and thus gives them preference for space and social support; an avoidance of negative emotional or social interactions with non-related persons; a habit of using the same living space for various activities (for example, a balcony may be used for cooking, socializing, work, sleeping, and other activities); a sensitivity for time-scheduling of activities in order to use the same area within the flat; the use of compact furniture, appliances, and household items; a cultural acceptance of close physical proximity among individuals, thus building tolerance for the lack of one's own and others' personal space; the custom of entertaining friends and doing business in restaurants; and the availability of hourly hotel rates for intimate relationships.

Studies of social ecology (see, for example, Lai, 1993) use surveys which depend on interviews or self-reports to look into a much wider range of behavioural consequences (such as health status, aggression, family relations, social participation, and alienation, among others) of high-density living. Ward (cited in Lai, 1993) has suggested that the early habituation to frustration and interference, and the inculcation of self-control of aggressive and other emotional behaviours during childhood, contribute to the success of the Chinese in adapting themselves to overcrowded conditions.

One must be circumspect in accepting the belief that Chinese are better adapted to high-density living. The majority of the conclusions supporting that view are based on impressions and not upon structured interviews. These studies, moreover, do not pay much attention to the perceptions of the people themselves. Loo and Ong (1984) showed that Chinese people in San Francisco's Chinatown were not satisfied with a crowded living environment.

In our Swedish–Chinese Housing and Health Study (Ekblad et al., 1991), the primary objective was to use, for the first time to our knowledge, an interactional, interdisciplinary approach to study family functions and quality of life in the three most common types of dwelling in Beijing: the traditional but often primitive courtyard house, which has prevailed for centuries; the Soviet-inspired, four- or five-storey apartment blocks built during the 1950s; and the recently constructed high-rise apartments built under Western influence. The sample consisted of 125 three-generation households with a formal household registration in the Western District of Beijing. The interview questionnaires concerned dwelling as well as social, sanitary, and health conditions. The results show that construction of high-rise apartments was then the top State priority for meeting the tremendous housing demand. The place of employment was typically responsible for providing housing and other essentials. The units were usually designed for the requirements of the nuclear family, and the educational level among the high-rise inhabitants had a tendency to be higher than that of people in the other types of dwellings.

The dwelling situation for all the participants in the study was more crowded than has been observed in developed countries. In the traditional courtyard house, compared to the other two types of dwelling, there was some private space, although the multi-storey dwellings, especially the high-rises, were better equipped both inside for cooking and private hygiene and as regards public and social services. The high-rise dwellers were closest to most of the facilities, but they had reduced social networks and social exchanges compared with those people living in the other two types of housing.

Various types of satisfaction differed according to the type of dwelling. Courtyard respondents reported the least satisfaction with the unmodern, crowded dwellings, but they were most satisfied with the perception of life in the house. Social relationships in the home and neighbourhood played a more important role in relation to health and life compared to physical housing conditions.

Indirect signs of psychosomatic symptoms, including sleeping disturbances from noise and disturbances of privacy, occurred among adult mid-rise dwellers. Adverse behaviours (for example, alcohol consumption) were quite rare, and self-evaluation of health satisfaction was correlated with a lack of family problems and negatively with certain work characteristics (for example, sedentary work, or work that is not psychologically demanding).

Health problems during the year preceding the study were significantly higher among children in multi-storey dwellings. Children with somatic and mental symptoms were very rare. However, children in high-rises spent significantly fewer hours outdoors in winter, as well as in summer, in comparison with children in mid-rise and *ping fang* dwellings.

With age, the stress level caused by crowded living conditions, family work, and economy was found to decrease, while concern for maintaining health and well-being rose. The elderly's physical health was at the average level, but with respect to mental health the number who felt lonely and troubled was lower than in other foreign studies. Modern-type dwellings had a negative influence on their private space.

Finally, gender differences were found in the perceived level of demand from work, and in leisure activities. Women, in general, and the elderly showed a higher evaluation of housing and life satisfaction compared with young and middle-aged men.

In conclusion, we found that the traditional courtyard home satisfies psychosocial needs (privacy, child-rearing patterns, and provision for the welfare of the elderly) and bolsters a supportive and clearly defined social structure, while its physical conditions, lack of modern facilities, and deficient safety features are disadvantages. On the other hand, living in modern high-rise apartment buildings was found to have a negative impact for Beijing residents on health and subjective well-being. Coping with traditional Chinese activities and functions seemed thus to be more difficult for those who lived in modern apartments, which resulted in a diminished social network and fewer social exchanges. These effects were particularly pronounced in the so-called vulnerable groups in the study: children and the elderly. The findings lead us to ask which environmental qualities of Chinese organizational and community settings are buffers, from an ecological point of view, and which are especially health-promoting.

WAYS OF ADJUSTMENT IN DEALING WITH SOCIAL ENVIRONMENTS

The social orientation of both traditional and contemporary Chinese is characterized by specific features which have their origins in traditional Chinese culture. The majority of Chinese people belong to an extended family. In the city these groups become neighbourhoods, districts, and municipalities. Each level of social organization provides mediating groups for dealing with problems of a given degree of complexity and is a means of referring the remaining problems upwards to the next highest level.

CONCLUSION

What Constitutes an Ecologically Healthy Environment for Chinese?

The influence of psychosocial factors on human health has long been recognized in Chinese culture, and somatization as a cultural mode for the expression of emotional distress has received increasing attention in studies of the Chinese by researchers and clinicians (see, for example, Kleinman and Lin, 1981). China's earliest medical text, the Canon of Internal Medicine (*Huangdi Neijing*) of the Warring States period (475-221 BC), deals at length with the relationship between human emotions (joy, anger, melancholy, anxiety, grief, fear, and terror), social factors (such as diet, housing, and income), and the onset of various diseases (Lin and Liang, 1984). Nature in mainland China was and is considered to be closely intertwined with health and illness. Temperature, humidity, nature's symbolic referents such as hot and cold: all are thought to be causes of disease (Louie, 1990). Despite the culture's long-standing sensitivity to the relatedness of various phenomena, basic lessons are in danger of being lost. For example, as the Chinese economy has improved, houses have become Westernized and are now more often equipped with heaters, air-conditioning, carpeting, and other amenities. These elements, unfortunately, in the Chinese climate may contribute to the proliferation of mites.

It should also be stressed to all mothers, and others responsible for the care of children, that it is important to take a child out each day—not only to breathe fresh air but for a change of scenery, to meet other people (young and old), and to gain experience of his or her surroundings as an important part of education at this young age. All of this stimulation may influence intellectual development. Better facilities for parks and playgrounds are required, with easy access from multi-storey buildings, which should be equipped with safety lifts. When constructing new residential buildings, planners should consider the importance of a safe balcony where the infant or toddler can be placed during the day to get fresh air and sunlight.

The concept of health promotion differs from a focus on disease prevention, in that the former places greater emphasis on the role of individuals, groups, and organizations as active agents in shaping health practices and policies. These processes can optimize both individual wellness and collective well-being (for a review, see Stokols, 1992). An important direction for future research on the environmental dimensions of health promotion is identification of the specific mechanisms by which geographic, architectural and technological, and sociocultural factors influence health and illness (Stokols, 1992).

The results of our Swedish–Chinese study (Ekblad et al, 1991, p. 117) indicate that attention to these psychosocial factors could create a new holistic and ecological research approach to city planning, as well as to rural planning. Health interests should be represented in the policy-making process involving housing decisions, and health values should be incorporated into new policies. Municipal authorities and city planners must realize that city planning affects citizens broadly, not just at the clearest interaction points, and they should develop methods and tools to manage it accordingly. Urban planning can contribute to environmental health goals, both by filling a corrective function, assisting in the elimination or modification of present hazards in the environment to aid the health and social well-being of urban residents, and a preventive one, addressing the efficient management of environmental resources of an urban area in such a manner as to promote or enhance health and well being and to avoid hazards.

This proposal fits well with any cultural background as well as all socio-economic levels. For instance, adapting rather than destroying existing housing structures and their surroundings would have a two-fold benefit: reducing material investment and maintaining human well-being with respect to health criteria. There are characteristic factors (for example, regulations and social networks active in Chinese culture) which to some extent counteract the detrimental effects of stress. In Chinese philosophy, the concept of 'optimum health' is often described as a state of balance between the person and the environment, among people, and in the relationships between the person's internal organs, producing a sense of coherence at all levels (Cheng and Williams, 1986).

Sense of Coherence, Coping, and Cultural Collectivism

Antonovsky (1987) has developed the concept of a 'sense of coherence' in discussing the setting of the individual in the environment, and he has published empirical data which supports the contention that this is a health-protective factor. The concept includes a sense of meaningfulness outside the person's personal existence, a capacity to understand current adversity and an experience of the situation's manageability, a recognition that the individual has resources, internal or otherwise, sufficient to solve the problem and to cope with a stressful situation. For instance, a strong commitment to the extended family can give a meaning to life outside the person. Reliance on the kin network may enhance the manageability of a stressful life situation (such as urbanization, crowded situations, high-rise living, modern life-styles, and so on).

The main criterion for assessing the dwelling environment is its suitabilty for individuals, for their psychological and physiological needs, as well as their culture and way of life. If the environment prevents us from satisfying these needs, stress may result. When the fit between the human being and the environment is not optimal, a phenomenon called environmental stress develops.

This poor fit may be expressed as a threat to life, health, and well-being. A person may also perceive a threat to his or her self-esteem. Another threat may be to belongingness, when a person is separated from his or her relatives after living with them for a long time. Still another threat may concern self-realization, as occurs when a person does not have the chance to learn new skills in the dwelling environment. The common feature in all these threats is that the individual has no influence over his or her own situation, he or she suffers from a lack of personal control. Sooner or later the individual will show one or more of the common stress reactions.

Regarding family coping, a study which compared four ethnic groups in Hawaii (Caucasian, Chinese–American, Hawaiian, and Japanese–American), found that the Hawaiian group, in contrast to the three others, tended to seek spiritual support in times of crisis. In comparison, the Chinese-American group preferred to utilize various coping patterns, including mobilizing the resources which exist in the family (Hsu, Tseng, Lum, Lau, Vaccaro, and Brennan, 1988). There are, it seems, certain culture-preferred patterns for families to cope with problems.

It is evident that high population density (and the often-seen result of a feeling of crowding) in itself may have a behavioural and psychological impact. The level of stimulation may exceed what the individual's central nervous system is capable of handling, and so crowding may be a potential source of stress. Two forms of coping, both with important consequences for health and social relationships, are a growing privatization of personal life and a falling back on mind-changing chemical substances (cigarettes, alcohol, and pre-scribed or non-prescribed drugs) to counter the effects of environmentally induced stress (Diekstra, 1988). Chinese cultural collectivism may be a pro-phylaxis, a preventive treatment against disease, in that it promotes harmony within a supportive in-group. This sense of coherence and the availability of caring companions serve as a buffer against stress, decreasing the incidence of disease. Triandis, Bontempo, Villareal, Asai, and Lucca (1988) concluded that 'thus, other things being equal [for example, GNP per capita], the levels of disease in collectivist countries [Chinese societies] should be lower than those in individualistic countries' (p. 328).

Four basic assumptions are suggested by Ekblad and Werne (1990, p. 52) as needing further consideration in ecological research. First, it is believed that rapid changes in the built environment demand considerable mental activity, in the sense that the inhabitants must adapt to the new environment (Korosec-Serfaty, 1976), to learn how to use and live 'together' with it. Individual capa-bility for this kind of adaptation and assimilation is usually high when the individual is young, but becomes very low among the elderly.

Second, it is thought that rapid, radical, and extensive changes to the built environment make many people lose their 'home feeling'. Familial and indi-vidual identities are put at risk and individuals in part lose their connections with the built environment. The cultural heritage and knowledge acquired ear-lier in life concerning the environment become increasingly irrelevant in new, high-rise residential areas.

Third, it is believed that the built environment aids, counteracts, or compli-cates the satisfaction of the physiological, safety, and psychological needs of human beings. Finally, it is assumed that the built environment variously and to a varying degree satisfies the individual's needs with respect to social and commercial services, places of work, cultural and recreational activities, and collective transport facilities. It is hoped that this review will help research to deal more thoughtfully with these considerations in future ecological research with Chinese people.

Chapter 26

∎

The Assessment of Psychopathology in Chinese Societies

Fanny M. Cheung

Clinical psychologists in Chinese societies currently devote much of their professional energies to the task of psychological assessment. In Hong Kong, the amount of time spent by most clinical psychologists on testing and assessment is more than one-third of their total clinical time (Tsoi and Sundberg, 1989). In the People's Republic of China (PRC) and Taiwan, there is not yet a specialized professional division devoted to clinical psychology, as there is in Hong Kong. However, in those countries psychologists and other mental health professionals are employed in psychiatric hospitals, general hospitals, mental health centres, health centres for women and children, rehabilitation services, and forensic institutions, where they are engaged in clinical assessment as a substantial proportion of their work (Dai, Zheng, Ryan, and Paolo, 1993; Ko, 1978). In the PRC in particular, the revival of psychology as a scientific discipline since the 1980s has led to active interest in psychological measurement. Among the major forms of psychological assessment, psychological testing is the method most often used in Chinese societies.

The focus on testing has its roots both in the emerging role of clinical and educational psychologists in contemporary Chinese societies, as well as in the historical development of psychological measurement in ancient and modern China. As in the early stages of development in Western societies, the role of applied psychologists is often relegated by referral agents to that of 'test bashers' who provide an 'objective yardstick' to label a problem. The clinical psychologist often receives referrals with the simple request to administer an IQ test without considering what the psychologist could offer in the consultation. For the young profession of applied psychology, however, its exclusive claim over the domain of psychological testing enhances its scientific status as an independent profession. Psychological tests are scientific tools which psychologists are specially trained to administer. Their role as test bashers may be reinforced until the psychologists themselves feel confident enough to diversify their own professional tasks and functions.

Mental measurement was said to have originated in ancient China (Chan, this volume; DuBois, 1970; Zhang, 1988). As early as 2200 BC, a formal system of examinations was initiated for civil service selection which consisted of a variety of subjects and testing approaches. While early measurement approaches were focused on aptitude and intelligence for the purpose of selection and training, the use of psychological tests for psychodiagnosis in contemporary China after the Cultural Revolution of 1966–76 released clinical psychology from its association with Freudian psychoanalysis. Given its emphasis on empirical research and quantitative techniques, psychological testing fits in well with the process of the Four Modernizations in China's political and economic spheres.

The most commonly used psychological tests in the PRC for cognitive and personality assessment are the Wechsler Adult Intelligence Scale (WAIS), Wechsler Intelligence Scales for Children (WISC), the Wechsler scales for young children, the Eysenck Personality Questionnaire (EPQ) for adults and children, the Minnesota Multiphasic Personality Inventory (MMPI), the Wechsler Memory Scale, and the Draw a Person Test (Dai et al., 1993). The popularity of the intelligence scales is shared in Hong Kong, where the Wechsler intelligence scales are among the psychological tests most frequently used by clinical psychologists across all settings. Other tests with high usage in Hong Kong are the House–Tree–Person test and the Thematic Apperception Test, the Bender Gestalt, and the MMPI (Tsoi and Sundberg, 1989). For many of these tests, local adaptations and norms have been compiled.

The choice of tests is based on the availability of the instruments locally, the training of the test administrator, and the nature of the setting. In most clinical settings, the role of the psychologist is still narrowly prescribed by allied professionals, who have only a limited understanding of the functions of clinical psychologists. Thus, their referral for psychological consultation is typically to request psychological assessment. The most common expectation is in the area of clinical diagnosis, especially in the classification of mental handicap, as is evidenced by the high use of intelligence scales by psychologists in clinical settings. Assigning a number to intellectual functioning in the form of an intelligence quotient (IQ) has lent a scientific guise to the role of the psychologist, a profession that is trying to establish its independent identity in Hong Kong and Taiwan and its legitimacy in the context of the process of the Four Modernizations in the PRC (Zhang, 1988).

ASSESSMENT OF COGNITIVE FUNCTIONING

Given the Chinese emphasis on education, intelligence testing has been readily accepted in Chinese societies. Early intelligence testing was introduced to China together with the Western education system in the early part of the twentieth century (Zhang, 1988). The Binet–Simon Intelligence Scale was translated and modified to accommodate cultural differences in 1922. In the 1930s, the Society of Psychological Testing was founded, signifying an active period in the development of tests on the Mainland. The majority of the tests in use at the time were intelligence and educational achievement tests constructed in China or adopted from abroad; they included the Merrill–Palmer scale and the Draw–a–Person test. Psychological measurement, along with the study of psychology, slowed down during the Sino–Japanese War in the 1930s, and later came to a standstill during the Cultural Revolution in the 1960s (see Blowers, this volume). Currently, the most popular tests of intellectual functioning are the Wechsler scales, including the Wechsler Intelligence Scales for Children (WISC) and the Wechsler Adult Intelligence Scale (WAIS).

Wechsler Intelligence Scales for Children

The translation and adaptation of the WISC was first completed in Taiwan in 1979 at the National Taiwan Normal University (Chen, Hsu, Wu, and Lim, 1988). As is the case with many other psychological tests in Taiwan, little has been reported concerning the quality of the translation or the cultural relevance of the adaptation. The literature on the test usually aims at providing the users with the basic description of the instrument itself. The original American norms are used for test interpretation. It is not clear which parts of the test have been adapted and whether the test is culturally relevant.

As the WISC was one of the most widely used assessment tools among clinical psychologists in Hong Kong in the 1970s, efforts were made by local psychologists to standardize the Cantonese translation and to adapt the items to fit the local situation. A large-scale standardization study was conducted involving 1,100 Cantonese-speaking children from age 5 through 15 years (Special Education Section and Educational Research Establishment, 1986). In addition to adjusting the item order of the subtests of the WISC, items from the revised version, the WISC-R, were included. New items were generated to replace those which had no equivalent form in the Chinese culture or were outside the experience of children in Hong Kong. For the Digit Span subtest, double digits (for example, 12–16–15) were used in the series to replace the single digit series (2–6–5) in order to remove the low ceiling effect. A new vocabulary subtest was constructed, consisting of lexical units of two characters each drawn from textbooks, reading materials, and the everyday environment of children. Factor analysis of the 12 subtests produced three factors for all age groups: Verbal Comprehension, Perceptual Organization, and Freedom from Distractibility (Chan, 1984; Lee, 1984), similar to those found for the Wechsler scales in the West (Kaufman, 1975). The research team concluded that the Hong Kong WISC was a reliable and valid instrument for Hong Kong children.

The revised edition of the WISC (WISC-R) is one of the early tests to be translated and adapted in the PRC after the reinstatement of psychology (Fan, 1979). Fan's national standardization sample for the Chinese revision of the WISC (WISC-CR) consisted of children aged 8, 10, 12, and 14 years. The extracted factors for 8-year-olds were Verbal Comprehension, Perceptual Motor, and Integral Memory; those for the other age groups were Verbal Comprehension and Perceptual Motor. Separate norms for the WISC-CR were developed in Shanghai (Li, Jin, Zhu, and Tang, 1987), on the assumption that economic and cultural development is more advanced in the bigger cities than in the rest of China. It was found that the average scaled scores on the verbal scales for the Shanghai children were generally higher than for American children. In particular, the average scores for Arithmetic and the Digit Span subtests were found to be much higher among the Shanghai children than for the Americans. This pattern was also found in Hong Kong before the changes were made to the Digit Span subtest and new questions were added to the Arithmetic subtest. Lin and Zhang (1986) refined the national standardization study with 2,237 children aged 6 to 16 years. Dai, Lin, and Zhang (1990) ran a principal component analysis on the WISC-CR subtest scores of the national sample and found that the three factors extracted were comparable to those found for American children.

Wechsler Adult Intelligence Scale

A comprehensive effort was made by Gong to revise the Wechsler Adult Intelligence Scale for China (WAIS-RC) in 1982 (Dai, Gong, and Zhong, 1990). Two standardization samples, one urban (N = 2,029) and one rural (N = 992), were used to take into account the huge differences in the subjects' educational and cultural opportunities. The process and results of this revision project have been reported in both Chinese and international journals (Dai and Gong, 1987; Dai, Gong, and Zhong, 1990; Dai, Ryan, Paolo, and Harrington, 1991; Gong and the National WAIS-RC Coordinating Group, 1983; Ryan, Dai, and Paolo, 1992). While the 11 subtests of the WAIS-RC corresponded to those of the WAIS, about 50 per cent of the items were changed to suit the Chinese respondents. The changes included adapting contents of the Information subtest, constructing a new Vocabulary subtest, and extending the maximum of 8 digits in the Digit Span subtest to 12 digits. Special consideration was made to avoid items which depended on educational level, since about one-third of the Chinese population was determined to be illiterate. Factors extracted from the WAIS-RC subtests were similar to those of the WAIS and WAIS-R, with a two-factor model (Verbal Comprehension and Perceptual Organization) more suitable for urban samples, and a three-factor model (adding the Freedom From Distractibility factor) more suitable for rural samples.

While the WAIS-R has been translated into Cantonese and adapted in Hong Kong by the research subcommittee of the division of clinical psychology of the Hong Kong Psychological Society (1989), the standard Cantonese version was meant only for the maintenance of consistency in test administration. Results of a pilot study on 135 adults aged 16 to 74 years were used to readjust the item order of the subtests. No local norms were developed. A Vocabulary subtest was developed by Chang (1992) by modifying the subtest developed by Gong for the WAIS-RC in China. The item difficulty level of the subtest was established among 276 adolescents aged 16 to 19 years. Regional differences between Hong Kong and China were found in terms of the frequency of word usage, familiarity, and conceptualization of word meaning. Using a second group of 69 adolescents, Chang found that the Cantonese version of the Vocabulary subtest was the most reliable and stable measure among the subtests. It correlated significantly with the other subtests of the Cantonese WAIS-R and with public examination results of high school Chinese-language achievement. However, this study was limited to adolescents in Hong Kong whereas in the United States, adults aged between 20 to 34 years were used as the reference group for the development of scaled scores of the WAIS-R subtests.

Raven's Standard Progressive Matrices

In addition to the Wechsler scales, the Raven's Standard Progressive Matrices have been standardized in three Chinese societies (see Chan, this volume). In Taiwan, a preliminary norm was established in 1981, and a revised national norm for Primary 1 to Primary 3 students was established in 1988 (Chen, Hsu, Wu, and Lin, 1988). In Hong Kong, the Standard Progressive Matrices were standardized by the Education Department (1986). Comparison of the mean IQ of 4,858 6-year-old Chinese children in Hong Kong with other Western samples showed that the Chinese children obtained an average score of 116, as compared with a range of 95 to 102 among samples from Australia, Czechoslovakia, West Germany, Romania, the United Kingdom, and the United States (Chan and Lynn, 1989). A similar standardization was conducted in the PRC at the national level in 1986 for the urban cities (Zhang and Wang, 1989). Comparison of the mean IQ of children from ethnic minority areas showed that they scored lower than did children of the majority Han ethnic group (Zheng, 1988).

Other Tests

In attempts at neuro-psychological assessment, cultural differences have been reported in the results with Chinese subjects, with, for example, the Bender Gestalt test in Taiwan (Ko, 1971, 1972; Ko and Hung, 1963) and the Benton Visual Retention Test in the PRC (Tang and Dai, 1992). Revision and standardization projects were also undertaken in the PRC for the Halstead–Reitan Neuropsychological Battery for adults and children (Gong, 1986; Gong and Jie, 1988; Jie and Dai, 1993; Qing, Gong, and Jie, 1992) and the Luria–Nebraska Neuropsychological Battery (Xu, Gong, and Matthews, 1987). However, the utilization of neuro-psychological batteries is relatively low in recent years, due to the amount of time involved in their assessment procedures. Psychologists generally use some of the subtests or other simpler procedures (Dai et al., 1993).

BEHAVIOUR RATINGS

For young children, assessment of social development and behaviour problems is more dependent on parents' or teachers' reports than on clinical assessments. For example, the Vineland Social Maturity Scale, one of the most commonly used assessment instruments for children in Hong Kong (Tsoi and Sundberg, 1989), relies on the parent or caretaker to report on behaviours exhibited by the child. Few studies, however, have been reported on the use of these scales. The only behaviour rating scale studied extensively in Hong Kong has been the Preschool Behaviour Checklist (PBCL), a teacher's questionnaire, which was applied to a random sample of 851 Chinese children aged 36 to 48 months in Hong Kong preschools (Luk, Leung, Bacon-Shone, and Lieh-Mak, 1991). The factor structure of the PBCL was found to be very similar to the original British results. Factor 1 was a combined Hyperactive–Conduct Problems; Factor 2 was concerned with Speech/Withdrawal Problems; Factor 3 referred to Emotional Problems; and Factor 4 represented Sphincter Problems. Boys were rated as having more hyperactive, conduct, and speech problems than were girls. Using the recommended cut-off score, the overall prevalence of behaviour disorders was higher in Hong Kong (27.5 per cent) than in the United Kingdom norms set by the PBCL (21.9 per cent) The authors suggest that the results may reflect the specific cultural demands placed on discipline at school settings in Hong Kong.

A number of studies have been reported in the PRC using the Child Behaviour Checklist (CBCL), which is rated by the child's parents (National 22-cities Survey Coordinating Group, 1993). In several studies conducted by the Coordinating Group, a total of 24,013 children aged 4 to 16 years were studied. The national prevalence rate for behaviour problems was measured at 12.97 per cent. No difference in prevalence was found between children who were an only child and those who came from families of two or more children. The most important factors contributing to the scores on the CBCL were, for the younger age groups, parental socialization methods and the parental relation-ship, and the parent–child relationship and personality for the subjects aged 12 to 16 years. Studies have also shown that the CBCL was able to differentiate among children with different levels of academic achievement (Yang and Li, 1991; Zhu and Wang, 1992) and among children from different family environ-ments (Su, Li and Zhiang, 1991), as well as identifying differences in behaviour problems among ethnic minorities in China (Jin, Jin, Biu, and Cui, 1991).

Cross-cultural comparisons were made between 12-year-old Chinese chil-dren in Beijing and those in other Western countries on a Children's Behaviour Questionnaire (Ekblad, 1990) completed by parents and teachers. The two fac-tors extracted—hyperactive–aggressive and worry–fearfulness—were consis-tent with the results found in similar studies in other developing countries, including Mauritius, Ethiopia, and the Sudan. Chinese boys scored the lowest on aggression but high on psychosomatic symptoms. The children were rated as showing higher frequencies of all behavioural problems by mothers than they were by teachers. Ekblad attributed this defense to the heavy emphasis on social conformity in the home. Girls were rated as better behaved than boys, especially by teachers, who tended to find more sex differences among the children.

PERSONALITY ASSESSMENT

Rorschach Inkblot Test

One of the earliest personality assessment instruments studied in Chinese soci-eties was the Rorschach inkblot test. Due to the nonverbal nature of projective tests, there is less need for test translation than when adapting the instruments to Chinese societies. The test administration procedures for projective tech-niques are relatively simple, thereby encouraging cross-cultural applications in the early days of clinical psychology. A normative study on Rorschach responses of normal Chinese adults was conducted in Taiwan (Yang, Chen, and Hsu, 1965; Yang, Su, Hsu, and Hwang, 1962; Yang, Tsai, and Hwang, 1963; Yang, Tzuo, and Wu, 1963). The normal sample consisted of 347 Chinese adults, regarded as representative of the general Chinese adult population in Taiwan in terms of sex, age, educational level, and occupation. Ten popular responses were established for Chinese adults. Four of these responses were found to be 'universal populars' in other cross-cultural studies (Yang, Tzuo, and Wu, 1963). On the other hand, the P (popular) response of the turtle in card VI was unique to Chinese adults and not found in other cultural groups. Texture responses were also rare among the Chinese. The Chinese adults' total number of responses to the 10 cards was found to be fewer than that reported for normal American adults. Their reaction time prior to the first response and the average time for giving a general response were also longer (Yang, Tsai, and Hwang, 1963). Scoring systems for the evaluation of psychiatric patients were developed with small samples of paranoid schizophrenic patients and other psychotic patients in Taiwan (Ko and Yu, 1966; Yen, 1965; 1983).

However, the use of these projective techniques, especially with adult patients, is limited. In the PRC, none of the projective tests was mentioned among the top 25 frequently used psychological tests (Dai et al., 1993). One of the reasons given was the unpopularity of psychoanalytic theory among Chinese psychologists. The specialized training required for interpreting projective tests also accounted for the limited number of psychologists who could make use of these techniques, especially in the PRC. In Hong Kong, projective techniques used frequently by clinical psychologists are the House–Tree–Person test and the Make-A-Picture-Story test, which are used with children for whom there are few objective personality assessment tools available. The Rorschach is not popular among locally trained psychologists since few of them are formally trained in its interpretation (Tsoi and Sundberg, 1989).

Due to the shortage of adequately translated and standardized objective personality tests available in Hong Kong and the PRC, only a few are frequently used by psychologists in clinical settings. These include the Eysenck Personality Questionnaire (EPQ) and the Minnesota Multiphasic Personality Inventory (MMPI).

The Eysenck Personality Questionnaire

The EPQ has been translated and standardized in Hong Kong by Eysenck and Chan (1982). The 90-item adult version was administered to 270 males and 462 females with a mean age of about 22 years. The 81-item junior version was given to 698 boys and 629 girls aged 7 to 15 years. However, no reference was given to the background or representativeness of these samples. While the EPQ was found to be valid both for Hong Kong adults and children, Hong Kong adults scored higher on Psychoticism and Social Desirability and lower on Extroversion than did adults in the United Kingdom. Based on the factor loadings of the items, one item was omitted from the Psychoticism scale and two items from the Lie scale for the adult form.

Hong Kong children were also found to score lower on Extroversion and Neuroticism but higher on Social Desirability than did children in the United Kingdom. For the junior EPQ, one item each was omitted from the Psychoticism and the Neuroticism scales, while five items were deleted from the Extroversion scale and two from the Lie scale. Given the cultural differences in the stability of some scales, the authors warned about the interpretation of the Psychoticism scales for both the adult and junior forms, the Lie scale for adults and the Extroversion scale for children.

Other cross-cultural research using the EPQ, including studies in Nigeria, Greece, Japan, and Brazil, have identified the Lie scale as the dominant dimension in factor analysis, reflecting the strong tendency towards social desirability among non-British respondents. This dominance, however, was not found among the Chinese adult group. The mean score for the Hong Kong group, although slightly higher than the British samples, is not as pronounced as those found in other cross-cultural samples. The authors surmised that either the items chosen for the Lie Scale were inappropriate for the Hong Kong groups, or the social climate in Hong Kong permits the admission of socially undesirable habits represented in the Lie Scale.

The EPQ has been translated and administered in the PRC by Chen in Beijing (1983), as well as by Dai in Hunan province (1983). Chen translated the 90-item adult form of the EPQ and administered it to a sample consisting of 368 males and 275 females aged 25 to 35 years. The subjects included professionals, teachers, workers, farmers, and students. On the basis of the item analyses, 14 items were deleted, mostly from the Psychoticism scale. A total of 9 new items were added to the four scales, with a total of 85 items remaining in the final form. Chen suggested that with further testing and analysis, the EPQ may be applicable to the Chinese people.

Gong (1984) reported on the administration of Dai's revision of the EPQ to 2,517 adults and 3,901 schoolchildren in 13 Chinese provinces. Comparing those results to the findings of the original use of the EPQ in the United Kingdom, the researchers observed notable cross-cultural differences. Chinese respondents were more likely to endorse items suggestive of pre-psychotic traits. They had higher scores on the Lie scale but lower scores on the Extroversion scale. The three major dimensions of personality were identified. Out of the original sample, 1,000 adults and 1,000 students were chosen to serve as the standardization sample. Dai's revision of the EPQ was tried out on 111 male and 111 female neurotic patients (Han, 1991). The neurotic patients were found to score significantly higher than did the normative sample on the Neuroticism and Psychoticism scales. Although the EPQ is commonly used to assess personality in clinical settings (Dai et al., 1993), there are few published reports on its use with clinical samples.

The EPQ is rarely used by psychologists in Taiwan, and no mention of the test is included in the major references for psychological and educational tests (Chen et al., 1988; Ko, 1978). Instead, personality tests developed in the United States have been translated and adapted for use on the island.

Minnesota Multiphasic Personality Inventory

One of the best researched and standardized personality tests in Chinese societies is the MMPI. The earliest translation and revision was reported by Lu in Taiwan (1967), where the 550-item Chinese version of the group form was tried out on young male subjects. Lu noted that since some of the clinical scales were elevated, it was necessary to rescale the inventory so that the interpretation of scale scores would fit Chinese cultural patterns. The English version of the original MMPI has also been used with Chinese subjects in other societies including the United States (Sue and Sue, 1974) and Singapore (Kadri, 1971). Similar elevations were noted on the F (Infrequency) scale, the Depression scale, and the Schizophrenia scale. However, in these early studies, little attempt was made to investigate the cultural differences, or adapt the test for the Chinese culture.

The most ambitious translation and standardization project using the Chinese MMPI began in Hong Kong in 1976 (Cheung, 1985). The 566-item form R was translated and back-translated to check for linguistic equivalence. Cultural adaptations were made on items where there were no cultural equivalents. The translation equivalence of the Chinese MMPI was ascertained by high correlations between the Chinese and the English versions taken by the same bilingual subjects.

The Hong Kong version of the MMPI was used as the blueprint for the PRC version in 1981. A National MMPI Coordinating Group (1982) was formed under the auspices of the Institute of Psychology of the Chinese Academy of Sciences. Song, Cui, Cheung, and Hong (1987) compared the endorsement patterns of college students in these two Chinese societies with those of college students in the United States. The patterns of responses of the Hong Kong and PRC students were very similar. More discrepancies were found between the Chinese and American students, with the differences most pronounced between the American and the PRC students. These item endorsement discrepancies accounted for some of the overall T-score elevations on a number of clinical scales (the F, Depression, Psychasthenia, and Schizophrenia scales) found among normal Chinese persons when the United States norms were used. If interpreted directly according to the United States norms, there is a tendency to over-identify depressive features, anxiety, bizarre mentation, emotional alienation, and psychological disturbance among Chinese people. Cheung (1985) pointed out that some of the behaviours depicted as clinical features on the MMPI clinical scales were rated as more desirable by Hong Kong college students than by their American counterparts. These behaviours were related to less outgoing and assertive social and interpersonal relationships, attitudes of nonchalance, low arousal and low activity level, modesty, and prudence.

Given the high elevation on the F scale, a new Chinese Infrequency Scale was constructed by selecting those MMPI items which were endorsed by 10 per cent or less of the normal respondents in Hong Kong and the PRC, the same procedure used to derive the original F scale (Cheung, Song, and Butcher, 1991). This new scale provides a better indication of infrequent responses and profile invalidity for the Chinese respondents.

A set of Chinese norms was developed for the MMPI in the PRC from a normative sample of 1,553 males and 1,516 females (National MMPI Coordinating Group, 1985, 1989). The sample was drawn from the six major regions of China and selected to fit the national census characteristics in terms of sex, age, and geographical location. Due to the self-report nature of the MMPI, respondents with less than a primary education were excluded from the study. It was noted that T-scores on the Chinese norms tended to be lower than the United States cut-off point of 70, even among psychiatric patients (Cheung and Song, 1989; Cheung, Zhao, and Wu, 1992). The PRC researchers suggested lowering the cut-off point from a T-score of 70 on the US norms to a T-score of 60 on the PRC norms. In interpreting Chinese MMPI profiles, it is recommended that the overall score elevations on the US norms and the profile pattern of scale elevations on the PRC norms be used at the same time.

Among the Chinese personality tests, the largest number of empirical stud-ies conducted with both normal and clinical samples has used the Chinese MMPI. Clinical validity has been confirmed for schizophrenic patients, neurot-ic patients, psychosomatic patients, and homicide prisoners in the PRC and Hong Kong (Chen and Xu, 1992; Cheung and Song, 1989; Cheung, Zhao, and Wu, 1992; Lee, Cheung, Man and Hsu, 1992; Wu and Zhao, 1991; Zhou and Zhao, 1992). The Chinese MMPI was also adopted and tried in Singapore (Boey, 1985), where different patterns of elevations were found among sub-groups of Chinese people. Using the US norms, the Chinese-educated Singaporean Chinese had similar profiles as the normal samples in Hong Kong, with characteristic elevations on the Depression and Schizophrenia scales (28 codetype). On the other hand, the English-educated Chinese obtained slight elevations on the Schizophrenia and Maturity (89 codetype), although their overall mean profile was more similar to that of the American sample.

Despite cultural differences in the pattern of score elevations, the clinical validity of the MMPI has been confirmed. Chinese clinical samples all score sig-nificantly higher than normal samples on the relevant clinical scales. The code-type patterns derived from the Chinese norms resemble those found for similar diagnostic groups of schizophrenic disorders, neurotic disorders, and manic-depressive disorders in the United States. The factor structure of the clinical scales is also consistent with that found in other cross-national studies of the MMPI, with four factors depicting Psychoticism, Neuroticism, Social Introversion, and Masculinity–Femininity (Butcher and Pancheri, 1976).

The Hong Kong and PRC research teams have continued their collabora-tion on the translation of the MMPI-2, the newly published revision of the MMPI, drawing from their experience in standardizing the original MMPI. A new set of Chinese norms is being developed on a national sample of 1,106 males and 1,108 females (Cheung, Song, and Zhang, in press). Despite changes in the US norms, elevations were still found on similar clinical scales among Chinese normal respondents as in the original Chinese MMPI when the US norms are used. Nevertheless, the few clinical studies conducted so far sup-port the validity of the Chinese MMPI-2 in discriminating between psychiatric patients and normal adults. The factor structure of the Chinese MMPI-2 basic scales was also similar to that found on the MMPI and the MMPI-2.

ASSESSMENT OF MENTAL HEALTH AND PSYCHIATRIC MORBIDITY

To screen for psychiatric morbidity and to detect psychological disturbance in the general population, a few general screening instruments have been trans-lated and applied in Hong Kong, Taiwan, and the PRC. These include self-report measures like the General Health Questionnaire and the Symptom Check List–90, as well as other-ratings like the Brief Psychiatric Rating Scale and the Diagnostic Interview Schedule.

General Health Questionnaire

The General Health Questionnaire (GHQ)(Goldberg, 1978) has been used in a number of large-scale studies to identify mental health problems among normal respondents in Hong Kong. The 30-item GHQ was first tried out in English with a group of 255 university students in Hong Kong (Chan and Chan, 1983). As expected, the endorsement frequencies of all the pathological items were found to be low among the normal respondents. The GHQ was found to have good overall internal consistency as a brief symptom scale. Five factors were extracted from the student data including Anxiety, Inadequate Coping, Depression, Insomnia, and Social Interpersonal Dysfunctioning, comparable to the four factors found in other studies in the United Kingdom. Convergent validity was supported by high correlations with the Chinese MMPI on similar scales. The GHQ was also sensitive in detecting both the 'neurotic' and 'psychotic' cases on the MMPI modal profiles.

The 60-item GHQ was later translated into Chinese (Chan, 1985, 1993). Upon analysis of the results, it was found that a slightly higher number of symptoms may be required as the cut-off score for identifying a probable psychiatric case. Based on the results of factor analysis with 112 general psychiatric patients attending an outpatient clinic, five sub-scales were constructed consisting of four items for each specific symptom area, including dysphoric functioning, health concern, anxious coping, sleep problems, and suicidal ideas. The Chinese GHQ-20 sub-scales were found to correlate highly with the full GHQ-60 scale and were able to discriminate between psychiatric patients and another group of 653 university students. Although the sensitivity of the GHQ-20 was reasonably demonstrated, Chan (1993) raised concerns over the relatively low specificity and high overall misclassification rate. He speculated that one plausible explanation was the use of university students as the non-patient group, who were assumed to be 'non-case' without being interviewed by psychiatrists to determine their mental health status.

The reliability and validity of the Chinese version of the GHQ-30 has been confirmed by Shek (1987, 1989, 1993). The five factors identified by Chan and Chan (1983) were replicated by Shek (1987) on a sample of 2,150 secondary school students. Using the LISREL approach to confirmatory factor analysis, Shek (1993) further found that a higher-order factor model with the original five factors as the primary ones, and a second-order factor of General Psychopathology, would be a more parsimonious model. The GHQ scores also correlated significantly with other measures of anxiety and depression (Shek, 1989).

The GHQ has been used in other clinical studies in Hong Kong to identify adjustment following surgical treatment. Chinese women who underwent tubal ligation and hysterectomy operations were administered the GHQ, the Hs (Hypochondriasis) scale of the Chinese MMPI, and a sex-role inventory (Tsoi and Ho, 1984; Tsoi, Ho, and Poon, 1984). More post-operative symptomatic complaints were found to correlate with preoperational hypochondriasis and stronger expectations of post-operative changes.

In the PRC, two short versions of the GHQ (the GHQ-12 and GHQ-28) have been used to study neurotic disorders among 390 general internal medicine patients in Shanghai (Xiao and Yan, 1993). Using the GHQ as the first-stage screening, 45 patients were identified and later found to satisfy the Chinese classification criteria for neurotic disorders.

The GHQ was also translated in Taiwan and used in conjunction with the Test Anxiety Inventory and the Rosenberg Self-Esteem Scale in a longitudinal study of secondary school students in Taiwan who were taking the joint-universities matriculation examination (Chang, 1987). The GHQ was able to identify students suffering from stress reactions to the matriculation examination.

Symptom Check List–90

In the PRC, the Symptom Check List–90 (SCL-90)(Derogatis, 1977) has been translated by psychiatrists and used to report on the general mental health status of large groups of subjects. A survey of 1,088 secondary school students (Liang, Zhao, and Zheng, 1992) found that the most common disturbances were compulsion, over-sensitivity, depression, and obsession. These problems are mainly associated with stress from strict discipline at home and at school, worries about further studies, and disappointment in love.

A study with earthquake victims (Li, Pang, Yin, Liu, Zhong, Zhiang, Chen, and Liu, 1991) demonstrated post-traumatic stress disorder in a disaster area. The results showed that victims who lost family members and relatives had the poorest level of mental health. Their symptoms included somatization, compulsion, depression, and anxiety.

Brief Psychiatric Rating Scale

In Hong Kong, the Brief Psychiatric Rating Scale (BPRS)(Overall and Gorham, 1962), a broad assessment instrument designed to give a comprehensive description of major symptom characteristics of psychiatric patients by using ratings by psychiatrists, was translated and tried out with 155 Chinese psychiatric patients (Chan and Lai, 1992). The symptom cluster, which was rated as the most severe across the mixed sample of psychiatric patients from the outpatient clinic, was termed Anxious Depression. Although the dimensions of psychopathology for the Chinese patients did not correspond precisely to the clusters originally reported in BPRS studies with non-Chinese patients, common robust symptom dimensions exist for Chinese and non-Chinese patients. The two replicable symptom clusters were Withdrawal Retardation and Anxious Depression, whereas two other distinct clusters, Thinking Disturbance and Hostile Suspiciousness, were invariably associated among Chinese patients.

Diagnostic Interview Schedule

The Diagnostic Interview Schedule (DIS)(Robins, Helzer, Croughan, Williams, and Spitzer, 1981) is the most commonly used second-stage assessment instrument in large-scale adult psychiatric epidemiological studies in Chinese societies. Although other screening instruments such as the Present State

Examination (PSE)(Wing, Cooper, and Sartorius, 1974) have also been used in national surveys of psychiatric morbidity in the PRC, Zhang (1985) and Yan (1985) suggested that the DIS, which corresponds to the Diagnostic and Statistical Manual–III classification system, is more consistent with Chinese clinical diagnoses than is the PSE.

The DIS was translated and modified in Taiwan for the Taiwan Psychiatric Epidemiological Project, which began its work in 1982. Its validity has been established in preliminary studies with clinical patients and community residents designed to examine the diagnostic agreement between the DIS and psychiatrists' clinical diagnosis (Hwu, Yeh, and Chang, 1986; Hwu, Yeh, Chang, and Yeh, 1986). The Taiwan survey included 11,104 adults selected from metropolitan Taipei, small towns, and rural villages between 1982 and 1986. The lifetime prevalence of any psychiatric disorder (excluding tobacco dependency) was 16.3 per cent for Taipei, 28 per cent for the small towns, and 21 per cent for the rural villages (Hwu, Yeh, and Chang, 1989). Four disorders (generalized anxiety disorder, alcohol abuse, tobacco dependence, and cognitive impairment) were more prevalent in the small towns and rural villages than in metropolitan Taipei.

The Cantonese version of the DIS was used in the Shatin Community Mental Health Survey in Hong Kong (Chen, Wong, Lee, Chan-Ho, Lau, and Fung, 1993). From the 7,229 people initially surveyed, 4,173 subjects were identified for the second-stage examination utilizing the DIS. The lifetime prevalence of psychiatric diagnoses, excluding tobacco dependence and pathological gambling, was 19.5 per cent for males and 18.3 per cent for females. When all diagnoses were included, the male prevalence rate rose to 38.8 per cent, while that for females remained around 19.3 per cent. The male-predominant disorders were tobacco dependence, alcohol abuse/dependence, pathological gambling, and antisocial personality. The female-predominant disorders were generalized anxiety disorder, all phobias, dysthymic disorder, major depressive disorder, obsessive–compulsive disorder, and bereavement reactions.

The prevalence rates reported in the Shanghai Psychiatric Epidemiological Survey, which also utilized the Chinese DIS, were much lower than those seen in Hong Kong. The lifetime prevalence rate for all DIS disorders excluding tobacco-related disorders was only 2.8 per cent (Liu et al., cited in Cheung, 1991). Cheung noted that the prevalence rates of neurotic disorders were much lower in the PRC than in Taiwan, Hong Kong, and the West, irrespective of whether the DIS or the PSE system was used.

A modification of the DIS, the Adult Diagnostic Interview Schedule-Present (ADIS-P), which is based on a selection of items adapted from the DIS and the Schedule for Affective Disorders and Schizophrenia, has been examined by Zheng, Yang, Phillips, Dai, and Zheng (1988). A computerized system in Chinese, which provides an immediate psychiatric diagnosis, was developed. The ADIS-P was found to have a concurrent validity as good as that of the DIS.

These diagnostic scales point to growing interest in the clinical utility of simple and comprehensive rating scales in the assessment of general psychopathology among Chinese psychiatric patients, as well as in the general public. Other diagnostic instruments developed at psychiatric settings in the

PRC include the Chinese versions of the Scale for Assessment of Positive Symptoms and the Scale for Assessment of Negative Symptoms, each used in the classification of schizophrenic patients (Phillips, Xiong, Wang, Gao, Wang, Zhang, 1991). The careful development of the Chinese versions of these diagnostic instruments illustrated the importance of culturally sensitive revision and rigorous psychometric evaluation of Western instruments prior to their use in Chinese cultures.

For specific diagnostic assessment, a number of depression scales have been adapted. These include self-report measures like the Beck Depression Inventory, Zung's Self-rating Depression Scale, and the Center for Epidemiological Studies Depression Scale, as well as other similar ratings such as the Hamilton Depression Scale.

Beck Depression Inventory

Studies using the Beck Depression Inventory (BDI)(Beck, Rush, Shaw, and Emery, 1979) have been reported in Taiwan, Hong Kong, and the PRC. In Taiwan, the BDI was used to relate depressive symptoms among university students to their life stresses, attributional styles, and social support (Huang, Hwang, and Ko, 1983). No details were provided concerning the translation or the psychometric properties of the BDI itself.

The Chinese version of the BDI was tested on 2,150 secondary school students in Hong Kong (Shek, 1990, 1991). The scale was found to have high internal consistency and item-total correlations. Two factors, General Depression and Somatic Disturbances, were extracted, supporting the view of depression as a multidimensional construct. The BDI scores correlated strongly with the Depression factor of the Chinese GHQ, and they were shown to be more discriminating as a measure of depression rather than general psychopathology. Chan (1992) used the BDI to identify depressed mood among Chinese medical students in Hong Kong. The coping strategies of depressed students were found to be passive, with greater tendency to avoid and deny problems, and to contain their emotions.

The BDI was found to be less applicable in the PRC. In a study by Zheng, Wei, Gao, Zhang, and Wong (1988) of 329 depressed patients from 24 hospitals across China, many of the items on the Chinese version of the BDI were found to be poorly associated with the intensity of depression measured by the total score of the Chinese version of the Hamilton Depression Scale. The construct validity of the Chinese BDI was questioned on the grounds that three of the six factors extracted by principal component analysis were not explicable in terms of clinical features of depression. The research team suggested developing a culturally sensitive self-report inventory to eliminate the cultural bias of translated instruments. Zheng and Lin (1991) constructed the Chinese Depression Inventory (CDI) on the basis of the responses of the same group of depressed patients. The CDI took into account the Chinese culture, the verbal expression styles of the Chinese patients, as well as the severity of illness among different ethnic groups in China. It was found to have better reliability and validity among the depressed patients than did the Chinese BDI.

Center for Epidemiological Studies Depression Scale

Both the English and Chinese versions of the Center for Epidemiological Studies Depression Scale (CES-D)(Radloff, 1977) have been used in a number of studies to identify depressive symptomology among ethnic Chinese groups in North America. These groups include mainland Chinese students and Taiwanese students residing in the United States (Hong, Chan, Zheng, and Wang, 1992; Ying and Liese, 1991), and Chinese immigrants and Chinese-American adults living in the United States and Canada (Franks and Faux, 1990; Kuo, 1976, 1984; Ying, 1988). The CES-D was used to illustrate changes in emotional well-being related to migration and cultural changes. The pattern of symptoms of other Asian-Americans was similar to that of the Chinese-Americans, who tended to express depression through a combination of mood and somatic descriptors (Kuo, 1984). In one study with a community-based, Chinese-American sample (Ying, 1988), the affective and somatic factor structures were found to be inseparable, a result which may reflect the nature of experience and manifestation of depression in Chinese culture (see Draguns, this volume).

The Chinese CES-D was used in the PRC to survey the prevalence of depression in a normal community sample and among elderly people aged 64 to 92 years (Wu, Yu, and Zhang, 1992; Zhang, 1987). Depressive symptoms were higher among females, and among the 75–84-year-old group.

Zung's Self-rating Depression Scale

The Self-rating Depression Scale (SDS)(Zung, 1965) has been used to identify depressive symptomology among Chinese in the United States. Marsella, Shizuru, Brennan, and Kameoka (1981) compared Chinese-American, Caucasian, and Japanese-American undergraduates in Hawaii. They found that depressives manifested higher levels of body-image dissatisfaction regardless of ethnicity and gender. However, there were ethnic and gender differences with regard to dissatisfaction with specific body parts. Chang (1985) also used the SDS to compare the configurations of depressive symptomology of overseas Chinese college students with African-American and Caucasian college students in the United States. She found different clusters of symptoms for the three groups, with somatic complaints characterizing the overseas Chinese group, a mixture of affective and somatic complaints characterizing the African-American group, and existential and cognitive concerns characterizing the Caucasian group.

Two studies were conducted to validate the SDS in Hong Kong (Lee, 1991). Test results from 265 college students aged 17 to 26 years confirmed the reliability and convergent validity of the SDS. In a study to assess the fakability of the SDS, score patterns of Fake–Bad groups were found to be significantly different from those of the control group. However, there was no difference between the Fake-Good and the control groups. The SDS was also used to assess depression among secondary school students in the PRC (Liu, Kuo, Wang, Yu, and Tien, 1991). A prevalence rate of 25 per cent was found among the 537 students.

Hamilton Depression Rating Scale

A national standardization of the 17-item Hamilton Depression Scale (HDS)(Hamilton, 1967) was conducted by a research team at the Hunan Medical University (Zheng, Zhao, Phillips, Liu, Cai, Sun, and Huang, 1988). Inter-rater reliability and the internal consistency of the scale were good. A high negative correlation between the HDS and the Global Assessment Scale supported its concurrent validity in the assessment of the overall level of disability. Based on the results of 329 depressed patients from 24 clinical units across the country, 5 factors were extracted similar to the original factor structure of the HDS (Zhao and Zheng, 1992). However, some of the individual item loadings on the factors differed from the original HDS factor loadings. The authors suggested there were cultural differences in the expression of depressive symptoms among Chinese patients, who tended to be less direct when discussing symptoms than were patients in the West.

Although all of these depression scales have been tried out in various settings in Chinese societies, it has also been found that the different scales have yielded different levels of depression (Marsella et al., 1975). The differential sensitivity of these measures of depression illustrates the need to consider the frequency, intensity, and duration attributes of symptoms, the use of varying response styles, and other cultural attributes of the respondents in adapting Western-based instruments.

ISSUES RELATED TO ADAPTATION OF WESTERN TESTS

In the early stages of test use in Chinese societies, Western-based instruments have been adopted in an imposed-etic approach (Berry, 1969). The assessed constructs are assumed to be relevant and meaningful in the new culture. Results are directly applied without consideration of cross-cultural differences in terms of the psychometric properties of the instruments or the strategies that must be followed to make interpretations meaningful.

Recent research on the adaptations of assessment instruments has raised concerns about the cross-cultural relevance and validity of these instruments in Chinese culture. Assessment across cultures has been discussed extensively by cross-cultural psychologists (Irvine and Carroll, 1980; Lonner, 1990; Lonner and Ibrahim, 1989). Standard practices in adapting instruments which originate in another culture have been recommended (Cheung, 1985; Hui and Triandis, 1985; Phillips, 1993). However, as seen in the review of many of the tests being used in Chinese societies, these cross-cultural considerations are not always observed.

Phillips, Xiong, Wang, Gao, Wang, and Zhang (1991) noted that the urgent need for clinical assessment tools in mainland China has led to the widespread use of translated instruments from the West. There are duplications of effort when the same test may be translated by different researchers who are not aware of one another's work. The translated instruments are often circulated without following appropriate procedures for obtaining copyright. Especially in the early efforts, instruments may have been directly translated without back-translation or modifications to accommodate the text to the local culture. There is also the danger of direct interpretation of scale scores according to the original norms without taking into account different mean scores among normal respondents from different cultures. Phillips et al. warned that, 'The clinical utility of translated instruments depends on the scientific rigor with which they are evaluated and revised in the target culture' (p. 369). The extent to which the translated instruments have been studied with rigor is not always reported in the literature.

Even when details about the translation process are reported, the sample used to compare the results of the test with the original sample may not be similar. In studies of normal respondents, students are often used as the subjects without commenting on their representativeness *vis-à-vis* the general population. Similarly, in studies of clinical samples, the comparability of the subjects' backgrounds, including diagnostic criteria, types of clinical setting, phase of the illness, and so on, is seldom identified. Generalizations in terms of the score levels and prevalence rates from the conclusions made in these studies are therefore suspect.

Some of the studies have noted cross-cultural differences in the mean scores between the original normative population and the local respondents, such as the score levels of various depression scales and certain scales on the GHQ and the MMPI. This observation needs to be made known to the test users, who may otherwise misclassify the respondents on the basis of the original cut-off criteria. Unfortunately, test users in applied settings are not always familiar with research findings of local applications of the instruments and may rely only on the original test manuals which do not include this culture-specific information.

In a more systematic approach to formalize the application of a translated test, local norms may be developed to provide a more appropriate yardstick for standardizing the test scores. This procedure requires large-scale data collection on a comparable sample and has been taken up with more enthusiasm by PRC research teams with respect to a number of instruments. The representativeness of the normative sample is, however, an issue which deserves attention. Tan (1986) discussed the problems with the normative samples for a number of translated tests in the PRC. He cautioned about the use of college students as the normative sample, especially in tests of intelligence, given the selective opportunity for higher education. Even when a national sample is recruited, the sample may not be representative of the national population in terms of age, education, geographical distribution, and other relevant attributes. In view of the size of the mainland Chinese population and its diverse background, Tan suggested the need for establishing a series of subgroup norms instead of one unified national norm.

A fundamental deficiency in these adaptation methods is the omission of important emic constructs which are important to the Chinese culture. Cheung, Leung, Fan, Song, Zhang, and Zhang (in press) point out that the construction of an instrument which includes the major culture-specific domains is needed if the purpose of assessment is to address the concerns of a particular culture rather than to investigate cultural universals. The issue of construct validity, in determining what constitutes Chinese intelligence, personality, or psychopathology, is a wider concern not only of assessment, but also of the theoretical conceptualization of these constructs themselves.

CONSTRUCTION OF INDIGENOUS ASSESSMENT INSTRUMENTS

Given the effort involved in developing an indigenous instrument, as opposed to adapting an existing Western instrument, only two large-scale projects related to Chinese personality assessment are reported.

Ko's Mental Health Questionnaire

Ko developed Ko's Mental Health Questionnaire (KMHQ) in Taiwan in 1977 partly based on the items of the MMPI (Ko, 1978). From his clinical experience, he found the length of the MMPI a major handicap in testing Chinese patients, and so he tried to construct shorter clinical scales which would be useful in assessing the mental health of Chinese patients. The original questionnaire consisted of 17 scales measuring clinical syndromes and personality styles similar to the clinical scales of the MMPI and the EPQ. In a later revision (Ko, 1981), the number of scales was reduced to 13. Most of the normative studies were conducted using university or secondary school students. The main factor extracted from the KMHQ was Nervousness–Dependence, which accounted for 42 per cent of the total variance (Wu, 1988). Two secondary factors, Sexual Inhibition–Self Confidence and Obsession–Compulsion, accounted for an additional 16 per cent and 11 per cent, respectively. While Ko and his students have been diligent in studying and refining the KMHQ, most of its applications have been confined to students in Taiwan. The results of his studies have been reported in local journals with little accessibility to psychologists from other Chinese societies, thus limiting the recognition and application of his instrument.

The Chinese Personality Assessment Inventory

The Chinese Personality Assessment Inventory (CPAI) was developed in a joint effort by psychologists from Hong Kong and the PRC to provide an omnibus personality inventory covering personality characteristics for normal as well as diagnostic assessment (Cheung and Leung, 1992; Cheung et al., in press; Song, Zhang, Zhang, Cheung, and Leung, 1993). The CPAI combined the emic and etic approaches to personality assessment by including personality constructs which are valid and appropriate cross-culturally, as well as indigenous constructs specific to Chinese culture. Modelled after the scale construction method of the MMPI-2, the CPAI integrates existing methods of personality assessment in the West, folk concepts in Chinese culture, and the experience of local professionals. The constructs in the CPAI were derived from reviews of popular literary works, common Chinese proverbs, and the psychological literature exploring emic and etic constructs among the Chinese people, as well as self-descriptions of people in the street and others' descriptions by professionals. A consensus approach was adopted to select those constructs agreed upon by researchers from Hong Kong and the PRC to be important personality dimensions. References were made to clinical experience and assessment research with Chinese patients.

Items of the CPAI were selected from statements generated in pilot studies, existing instruments addressing the relevant constructs, as well as newly written items. Pre-tests with subjects from different backgrounds were used to ascertain the readability and cultural relevance of the items. Based on the item analysis results from large-scale studies in the PRC and Hong Kong, items which fit the selection criteria for both locations were included in the standardization version of the inventory. The standardization sample in Hong Kong consisted of 441 adults aged 18 to 65 years, drawn from a random list of households generated by the government's Census and Statistics Department. In the PRC, a quota sampling method was used to recruit subjects from urban and rural areas across the nation. Minority ethnic group members who could understand Chinese writing were included in the PRC sample. Comparison of the results from the two national samples showed that with the exception of only three scales, the mean scores for Hong Kong and the PRC were similar, so that a common norm could be constructed for the CPAI. Separate norms were needed for males and females. Subgroup norms on the basis of age, ethnic minority membership, and geographical location would be retained for reference purposes.

The final version of the CPAI consists of 35 scales, of which 22 are normal personality dimensions, 12 (one overlapping with the normal dimensions) are clinical dimensions, and 2 are validity scales. The internal consistency and test–retest reliability of the CPAI were found to be high. Principal components analysis yielded common factors for both Hong Kong and the PRC. For the personality scales, the four factors may be labelled as Dependability, Chinese Tradition, Social Potency, and Individualism. For the clinical scales, two factors were extracted depicting Emotional Problems and Behavioural Problems. The scales which are included in the Chinese Tradition factor include Harmony, *Renqin* (Relationship Orientation), Thrift, Flexibility, and Modernization, illustrating how indigenous and borrowed etic constructs form an important component of the personality structure of the Chinese people. The robust nature of this structure is demonstrated by the similarity between the samples in Hong Kong and the PRC, where the economic and political systems are very different.

The development of the CPAI illustrates a pioneering attempt to expand cross-cultural personality assessment beyond that of test translation and adaptation. Validation studies are underway to try out the inventory in full, as well as its sub-scales, on different groups in clinical and other applied settings. While adopting current advances made in personality assessment methods in the West, the inventory takes into account culturally sensitive approaches in cross-cultural assessment to provide a framework for developing a personality inventory relevant to the Chinese people.

Chapter 27

■

Abnormal Behaviour in Chinese Societies: Clinical, Epidemiological, and Comparative Studies

Juris G. Draguns

What is the interplay between the Chinese culture and the abnormal or mal-adaptive patterns of behaviour and experience that are encountered among the Chinese people? In what ways are these behaviour patterns similar to, and different from, the expressions of maladaptation in other parts of the world? Can culturally distinctive and humanly universal threads of psychological disturbance be discerned in the symptoms and dynamics of Chinese psychiatric patients? And what do the accumulated findings on psychological disturbance in China contribute toward a panoramic view of the psychology of Chinese people?

The scope of the present chapter is vast. It encompasses the available information on the manifestations of maladaptation in the several socio-political settings in which the Chinese people live: mainland China, Taiwan, Hong Kong, Singapore, and the worldwide Chinese diaspora. The available research approaches can be grouped under three general headings: clinical observations that are based on naturalistic descriptions of psychiatric symptoms, often gathered on a case-by-case basis in a treatment context; epidemiological data which involve a psychiatric census of all cases of the disorder in their catchment area; and comparisons of groups or samples of psychiatric patients across two or more culture settings, conducted in the optimal case on appropriate and representative samples with equivalent measures. Although each of these types of studies has its characteristic limitations, taken together they approximate a panoramic view of psychological disturbance within a culture.

EARLY ORIGINS

The first modern observations on the psychopathology of the Chinese go back to the early twentieth century (cf. Pfeiffer, 1994). They pertain to, on the one hand, the symptoms of the Chinese patients hospitalized in the newly established Western-type asylums and, on the other hand, describe psychiatric syndromes allegedly characteristic and unique to China. These two types of reports anticipate the bifurcation of investigation which has not been superceded to this day, toward worldwide similarity and comparability and toward cultural uniqueness or distinctiveness, respectively. These two major points of reference are known as the etic and the emic. The challenge for contemporary students of psychology and culture within Chinese and other cultures is to integrate these two approaches.

Somewhat more recently, four types of studies appeared whose impact reverberates to the present day. Lin (1953) in Taiwan initiated an epidemiological survey of the major varieties of psychiatric disturbance in three settings: urban, suburban, and rural. Yap in Hong Kong (1958, 1958, 1959) undertook a comprehensive study of suicide which uncovered the social factors associated with increased or reduced suicidal risk, thereby providing 'raw material' for generalizations about the interaction of culture and psychopathology. The third type of contribution is represented by the formulation of Tseng and J. Hsu (1970), based on their clinical experience as psychiatrists and life-long participant observers of Chinese culture. Tseng and Hsu opened up the discussion to new issues, for example, the relationship of bodily distress and psychological disturbance. Fourth, F. L. K. Hsu (1949) articulated two influential propositions on the mainsprings of Chinese personality, pertaining, respectively, to the contrast between social, consensual control allegedly predominant in China and the internalization of conventional morality prominent in the West, and relevant to the respective roles of suppression in China and repression in Europe and the United States.

SOMATIZATION IN CHINA: A MAJOR AVENUE FOR EXPERIENCING PSYCHIC DISTRESS?

Tseng and Hsu (1970, p. 11) were among the first observers to report that 'the Chinese are especially concerned with the body and find it relatively easy to somatize. They tend to manifest neurasthenic and hypochondriacal symptoms'. In some cases, this emphasis upon bodily sensations stands in contrast to the sparse and terse communication of mental experience which, from the culture-bound Western perspective, may appear defensive, naïve, and lacking in self-awareness and personal sensitivity.

Tseng (1975) reported that over 70 per cent of psychiatric patients at a Taipei university hospital presented somatic complaints. The interplay of symptom expression and personal experience was intensively studied by Kleinman (1982) with psychiatric outpatients at Hunan Medical College. Many of these patients complained of dizziness, weakness, and chronic pain. This condition was diagnosed by local psychiatrists as neurasthenia, a prominent diagnostic category at one time in North America and Europe, which, however, no longer enjoys this status in the current Diagnostic and Statistical Manual (DSM) version IV of the American Psychiatric Association (American Psychiatric Association, 1994) or in its predecessors (cf. Kleinman, 1982; Kleinman and Kleinman, 1985). On the basis of his earlier observations in Taiwan, Kleinman hypothesized that neurasthenia in Chinese patients represented the culturally indigenous idiom for the expression of depression. To test this hypothesis, Kleinman (1982) collected copious biographical and symptom data on 100 patients diagnosed as neurasthenic. Elaborate precautions were taken to assure the equivalence of the Chinese interview schedules and other instruments to the English-language original versions, and two follow-up interviews were arranged. Kleinman's expectation was supported; out of the 100 cases of neurasthenia, 87 met the DSM-IIIR criteria for major depressive disorder. However, anxiety states were also found in a high proportion of cases (69 out of 100), somatoform disorder was recorded in 25 cases, and chronic pain syndrome in 44. Thus, depressive symptomatology co-existed with somatic distress and psychological discomfort to produce a disorder specific to its space and time.

The origin and meaning of somatic emphasis continues to be a subject of debate and controversy. Is psychological distress transformed into physical discomfort and pain or is the somatic emphasis a culturally prescribed mode of communicating unhappiness and helplessness? Is its source to be found in the Chinese language, the socialization practices in China, the somatopsychic orientation of Chinese medicine, or in the etiquette of patient–physician interaction? Moreover, this intertwining of bodily discomfort and psychological distress is not unknown among Caucasian depressive patients in North America. Is the difference between the two cultures a matter of degree rather than of kind?

All of these explanations have at one time or another been advanced. Thus, the culturally linguistic formulation has capitalized upon the purported imprecision of the Chinese vocabulary of emotional terms, especially as they apply to the expression of personal distress. The supposed preference of the Chinese for inhibitory and suppressive defenses has also been invoked in this connection. Similarly, the alleged absence of a clear-cut Cartesian distinction between body and mind in traditional Chinese systems of thought may also promote the interchangeability of psychic and somatic experiences (cf. Cheung and Lau, 1982). On the cognitive level, Kleinman (1986) and Kirmayer (1984) have proposed that the Chinese may be more perceptive to somatic sensations and may report them more precisely and veridically. Somatization in the West is not highly regarded and is often dismissed by culturally biased, psychodynamically oriented, European and American clinicians as an unsophisticated obstacle to insight and self-awareness.

These explanations, though plausible, have been advanced *post hoc*. They do not shed light on the process that precedes reporting somatic symptoms, nor do they elucidate the subjective experience of such events. In Hong Kong, mildly distressed, problem-burdened persons, mostly university students, have typically presented their complaints in somatic terms (Cheung, 1982, 1984, 1987, 1989; Cheung, Lau, and Wong, 1984). The authors of these reports caution against hasty and excessive generalization of these findings. Data both from Hong Kong and Taiwan (Yeh, Cho, Ko, Ling, and Lee, 1972) suggest that self-awareness and somatic distress are not mutually exclusive. In fact, quite often they co-exist, as Kleinman (1982) also found in Hunan province.

These observations strengthen the case for considering somatic symptom presentation as a culturally shared and context-specific code. It may protect the sufferer from losing face and saves both participants from embarrassment which would be likely to be experienced if the focus of self-presentation shifted from bodily processes to personal, private, and intimate sentiments. Moreover, Cheung et al. (1984), and Cheung, Lee and Chan (1983), suggest that psychological distress is just not recognized, even by many contemporary

Chinese in Hong Kong, Taiwan, and elsewhere, as an appropriate problem for presentation in a health-oriented setting. By contrast, there is no ambiguity or disapproval attached to presenting bodily discomforts, aches, and pains. These sensations may well constitute components of such psychological states as depression or anxiety. Comparisons of Chinese and British patients (Cheng, 1989) have demonstrated that the number of somatic symptoms was approximately equal in the two samples, although the Chinese placed a much greater emphasis on those symptoms. Thus, the phenomenology of physical distress in China may not be as different from the corresponding experience in the West as it might at first appear. However, the importance of somatic components in the total social transaction of seeking and receiving help is divergent in the Chinese and in the European and American cultures.

The diagnostic status of the Chinese neurasthenics remains to be resolved. Are these cases of masked depression or is neurasthenia a distress *sui generis*, qualitatively distinct from the depressive disorder as described in the current diagnostic manuals? In the Hunan project, Kleinman (1982, 1986, 1988) plausibly explained the experience of neurasthenia as a channel for the expression of the distress and suffering endured by many of these patients as a result of socio-political events outside of their control, as exemplified by the extreme stress experienced by many during the Cultural Revolution of 1966–76. Their symptoms came to represent the final pathway in which frustration, personal suffering, and physical malaise coalesced and acquired meaning. In an international comparison by means of vignettes of presenting symptoms (Tseng, Xu, Ebata, Hsu, and Cui, 1986), Chinese psychiatrists exhibited greater readiness to diagnose neurasthenia than did their colleagues in Japan or the United States. In particular, the Chinese diagnosticians were inclined to infer neurasthenia from symptoms of cognitive insufficiency and helplessness.

Kleinman's integration of the social, personal, and somatic components has provoked controversy. His critics (see, for example, Yan, 1989; Young, 1989) contend that the formulation proposed is highly inferential and is based on a sweeping generalization. Moreover, they criticize him for confounding responses of the normal population to traumatic socio-political events with the more complex process of the emergence of psychiatric syndromes. Thus, these proponents of established Chinese diagnostic practice remain skeptical about the weight of depressive factors both in the etiology and the experience of these disorders, and they prefer to consider neurasthenia distinctive.

DEPRESSION IN CHINA: ITS EXPERIENCE AND IMPORTANCE

Depression and somatization in China stand in an apparent compensatory relationship. Tseng and Hsu (1970, p. 11) wrote that 'the Chinese feel embarrassed to express feelings of loneliness and sadness'. Depression then tends to fall through the cracks of the verbally mediated and culturally conceptualized experience.

In Hong Kong, Yap (1965) noted the low frequency and the limited elaboration of depressive experience, as well as the paucity of guilt feelings among his Chinese depressive patients. Upon additional observation, however, Yap (1971) moderated this impression and concluded that guilt was present, though less frequent and less intense, among his Chinese depressed patients by comparison with their Western counterparts. He also came to consider Chinese and European and American expressions of depression as different in degree rather than in kind.

Among the neurasthenics in Hunan, Kleinman (1982) uncovered a great many instances of dysphoria, anhedonia, hopelessness, and loss of self-esteem, but very few verbal expressions of guilt. The depressive symptoms in this investigation were elicited rather than spontaneously expressed, but exemplary care was taken to guard against suggestion effects.

These symptoms were accompanied by the vegetative manifestations of depression, as exemplified by a sense of weakness and fatigue, low energy, and loss of appetite. They have also emerged in a number of multicultural comparisons as the relatively constant expressions of depression (cf. Draguns, 1986; Marsella, 1980; Marsella, Sartorius, Jablensky, and Fenton, 1985; Murphy, Wittkower, and Chance, 1967; World Health Organization, 1983) and possibly as the humanly universal organismic substrate of depressive experience. The affective, cognitive, and interpersonal aspects of depression are both less readily put into words by the sufferer and less quickly noticed by the observer in China than they are in the West. These considerations suggest that depression in the Chinese culture is experienced, albeit in a somewhat somatized guise. But what is the incidence of depression across the entire gamut of its somatopsychic manifestations in China? T. Lin (1985) hypothesized it to be genuinely low. As he pointed out, several plausible antecedents of depression, such as divorce, alcoholism, and drug abuse tend to be low in Chinese cultures. Furthermore, social networks within the family, neighbourhood, or workplace may cushion the impact of depression-producing factors, such as object loss, and lessen the probability of depressive symptom formation. Epidemiological research in Taiwan (T. Lin, 1953; Lin, Rin, Teh, Hsu, and Chu, 1969), Hong Kong (Chen, Wong, Lee, Chan-Ho, Lau, and Fung, 1993; Yap, 1965), and mainland China (P. Cheung, 1991) has produced low rates of depression in light of international trends. These findings, however, cannot be accepted as definitive because of the demonstrated difficulty of eliciting manifestations of depression. Moreover, a study of hospitalized psychiatric patients in Hong Kong (Chan and Lai, 1992) has yielded a mixed picture. About one-third of these patients presented anxious-depressed symptoms, but only 10 per cent exhibited retarded depressive manifestations. Thus, depression may appear in its less pure and characteristic varieties. In the course of collecting norms for the Chinese version of the Minnesota Multiphasic Personality Inventory (MMPI), Song (1981) discovered a higher baseline for the Depression Scale among normal Chinese as compared with their counterparts in Minnesota who were part of the original MMPI validating sample. Two partial explanations can be advanced for this counter-intuitive funding. First, it fits with the trend observed in other MMPI adaptations; norms for the Depression scale across language and cultural lines tend to be higher than in the original version (Butcher and Clark, 1979). Second, the higher Depression scale scores of the Chinese may be consonant with the cultural tendency to regard depression as a private everyday experience, distinct from illness, disorder, or disability. Lin's hypothesis then should be taken seriously and continue to be rigourously and exhaustively tested through epidemiological research, and valid and cross-cultural applicable indicators of depression should be developed.

SUICIDE

Suicide has been a prominent subject of international investigation ever since Durkheim (1951) took up the topic in 1897, perhaps because of the apparent ease with which multinational and worldwide comparisons of suicide rates can be performed. Extensive documentation exists on the suicide rates in Hong Kong, Taiwan, and Singapore, but reception of data from the People's Republic of China (PRC) has been more sporadic.

In Taiwan, the annual suicide rate ranged from 9.8 to 19.5 per 100,000 inhabitants from 1948 to 1988 (Chong, Yeh, and Wen, 1992). In Singapore, over a longer period of time, it fluctuated around 10–11 per 100,000, with the exception of the exceedingly stressful years before and during the Second World War (Peng, 1992; Tsoi, 1985). Data from Hong Kong (Lo, 1992) point to variation between 7.2 to 14.7 per 100,000. Comprehensive national suicide statistics for the PRC have not been released. Through local studies in Shanghai, Beijing, and in rural Jingning County in Yunnan Province (Fan, Li, Wang, and Zhang, 1992) provide useful data. On the basis of the available figures, the estimate of the average annual rate of suicide in Yunnan was 16.4.

Thus, the differences across mainland China, Taiwan, Hong Kong, and Singapore tend to vary over a relatively narrow range. In general, suicide rates of the Chinese fall below the median in the available World Health Organization (1986) statistics, which are based on worldwide, but not comprehensive, data. At the same time, none of the several suicide rates of Chinese populations can be described as extremely low.

Chong et al. (1992) plotted trends in Taiwan for three periods. From 1948 to 1958, suicide rates were on the ascendant, perhaps because of the rapid influx of mainland Chinese and the attendant stress experienced by host and newcomer populations alike. After a peak in 1964, decline of suicide rates set in, as the benefits of industrialization and modernization prevailed over the disruptive and alienating effects of rapid social change. With continuing increase in prosperity and stability, suicide rates then declined to the relatively low level in the range between 10 and 12 per 100,000.

In Hong Kong, suicide rates varied over a lesser span (Lo, 1992) but seemed to reflect the same trends. Attempted suicides, which are generally less comprehensively and reliably recorded, displayed a greater variation in rates, in both Hong Kong and Taiwan, and these trends appeared to reflect the operation of the same social factors: external stress, rapid social change, economic prosperity versus decline (Chong et al., 1992; Yeh, 1985).

In Singapore, suicide rates for the Chinese exceed those of the Malays, but they are somewhat lower than the corresponding figures for the Indian population (Peng, 1992). The direction of the Chinese–Malay difference was corroborated in neighbouring Malaysia (Ong and Leng, 1992). In the multi-ethnic environment of Hawaii, recent data (Tseng, Hsu, Omori, and McLaughlin, 1992) indicate that Chinese had the lowest suicide rates of the five major cultural groups in the islands, even though in past decades Chinese immigrants to Hawaii were found to be at high risk for suicide. Similarly, migrants and refugees from mainland China exceeded substantially the suicide rate of the lifelong residents of Taiwan (Rin, 1975). Compatible trends, on the fluctuations of post-migration suicide rates, were also reported from Singapore (Murphy, 1954).

A distinctive feature of Chinese suicide data is that men exceed women in suicide rates, although not by much (Chong et al., 1992; Peng, 1992). Yap (1958) described a characteristic pattern in Hong Kong which may shed light on Chinese women's relative susceptibility to suicide. In Yap's (1958, pp. 35–6) words:

> 1) Socially the subject is in a subordinate relation to another person (or persons) and is under provocation by the latter; 2) More specifically, the provocateur is a parent (usually the father) or husband; 3) In personality the subject is often aggressive, irritable, and quarrelsome, but on the other hand she may be immature and appear to be unusually meek and yielding; 4) The precipitating cause of the suicidal act is an acute quarrel or scolding, perhaps the culmination of a chronic strife; but in some cases there might only have been a minor reprimand; 5) The suicidal act as a rule comes within a day of the quarrel or reproof; 6) It is mainly to be found among women, especially of the younger age groups.

Such suicidal acts are usually impulsive and they relatively rarely result in death. Yap (1958) attributed their low lethality to defective planning rather than to the absence of a true wish to die.

Among other categories of persons at higher than average risk for suicide are the elderly, the unattached, the isolated, the rejected, those suffering from chronic and painful disorder, and those exposed to major psychological stress. In light of general suicide statistics, in the United States and elsewhere, this listing contains no surprises. However, the upsurge in adolescents' and young adults' suicides, observed in the last two decades in many parts of the world (cf. Jilek-Aal, 1988) has not yet fully crystallized in Hong Kong (Chung, Luk, and Lie-Mak, 1987) or in any of the other Chinese settings. In Hong Kong, there has been a recent rash of media reports of attempted and completed cases of youth suicide. These instances, however, have not been accompanied by a documented substantial increase in the adolescent suicide rate, in light of available statistics (cf. Chong, 1993). On the basis of partial data from mainland China (Fan et al., 1992), an upsurge in adolescent and young suicide rates was observed during and after the Cultural Revolution (cf. Tseng and Peng, 1992). In Taiwan, Hong Kong, and Singapore, suicide rate is correlated with age, and the elderly are at an increased risk for suicide (cf. Chong, 1993). Presumably, they are affected by the increased nuclearization of the traditional extended Chinese family, especially in such high-density urban areas as Hong Kong, Singapore, and Taipei. These trends may result in greater loneliness and isolation for many elderly Chinese and may predispose them to suicide. Paradoxically, loneliness may be more stressful to endure in socially oriented settings, such as the Chinese, than in the individualistic cultures of Western Europe and North America.

Another population segment vulnerable to suicide was composed of middle-class persons during the Cultural Revolution, many of whom experienced painful humiliation, loss of status, and other kinds of trauma and stress. Retrospective examination of age trends for suicide during these years (cf. Fan et al., 1992) reveals an increased suicide rate for middle-aged individuals, especially in Shanghai, but less so in Unang.

Interpersonal reasons for suicide loom large among Chinese patients (Yap, 1958, 1958, 1959), as one might expect in a family-centered culture. Surprisingly, however, the proportion of depressed persons among those who had committed suicide was indeed found to be relatively low in several studies (for example, Peng, 1992; Chong et al., 1992). However, Chiles, Strosahl, Ping, Michael, Hall, Jamelka, Senn, and Reto (1989) reported that, in contrast to American suicidal patients, their Chinese counterparts were less likely to communicate suicidal intentions. In the United States the best predictor of suicidal action was hopelessness, while in China, suicidal acts were most effectively predicted by depression. Moreover, after their suicidal attempts, Chinese patients encountered criticism and condemnation instead of helpfulness and sympathy, quite in contrast to the traditional Chinese attitude which, reportedly, neither condemns nor glamorizes suicide (Rin, 1975). Clearly, these novel results, based on relatively small hospitalized samples, have to be replicated and extended before their meaning and scope can be understood.

ANXIETY: A LITTLE-INVESTIGATED TOPIC

By contrast with the attention lavished upon depression and somatization, little effort has so far been directed toward the investigation of anxiety-related disorders in the several Chinese societies. Yet, as the results of the recent Shatin (Chen, Wong, Lee, Chan-Ho, Lau, Fang, 1993) survey demonstrate, anxiety occupies a prominent place among the complaints voiced by Chinese informants. General conclusions from earlier reviews of psychopathology of Chinese people (F. M. Cheung, 1985; Lin, 1985) point to the paucity of crystallized symptoms, such as obsessions and compulsions, and the prevalence of fragmentary, yet nonspecific, somatopsychic complaints referring to tension, discomfort, and malaise. To judge from these reports, there is less of a cultural barrier against expressing anxiety in a direct and spontaneous manner than there is against the conscious and articulate experience of depression. At the same time, findings on anxiety parallel those on depression in pointing to a high degree of co-morbidity with somatic symptoms and discomfort (cf. Kleinman, 1982). Neurasthenic manifestations accompany, rather then replace, anxiety-related symptoms.

Tseng, Asai, Jieqiu, Wilbulswasd, Suryani, Wen, Brennan, and Heiby (1990) investigated ambulatory psychiatric disorders at five Asian sites: in Shanghai, PRC, Kaohsiung, Taiwan, as well as in Japan, Thailand, and Bali. At each of these locations, diagnosed patients were also compared with normal control subjects. Results revealed generally higher scores in all symptom categories in

Bali than at the two Chinese locations, while the scores of Thai patients were consistently lower than those of the Mainland and Taiwan patients. A subtle and differentiated pattern of scores was found between the Tokyo patients and their Kaohsiung and Shanghai counterparts. Both Chinese samples exceeded the Japanese group in somatic head and chest symptoms while, in Japan, symptom scores were higher in anxiety, phobias, and depression, as compared with either or both Chinese samples.

Tseng et al. (1990) noted the great similarity of the Shanghai and Kaohsiung profiles, which they attributed to the shared Chinese cultural heritage of both groups. At each of the several sites, the symptom profile of the patients represented an exaggeration of the pattern of normal subjects' scores. Tseng et al. (1990, p. 259) concluded that, 'Neurotic manifestation is a magnification of the baseline mental symptoms observed among the normal group, while the baseline among the normal group varies according to the sociocultural and ethnic difference.'

Zhong (1993) and Zhong and Zhang (1993) presented clinical information on 113 anthropophobic patients in Beijing. Their symptoms focused on the fear of being looked at. These patients were described as socially conforming, rigid, and introverted. Zhong and Zhang (1993) pointed to the probable sexual etiology of this disorder, traceable to a punitive parental response to sexual curiosity and exploration. Prince (1991) noted that the onset of social phobia in China was associated with important developmental transitions: personal, occupational, educational, or residential. These syndromes share affinities with *Taijin-Kyofusho* (Tanaka-Matsumi, 1979), the Japanese version of anthropophobia. Their similarities, as well as any possible differences, remain to be explored.

SCHIZOPHRENIA: THE SCOPE OF CULTURAL FACTORS

Schizophrenia has not been found immune to cultural influences. The principal source of information in this regard is the Taiwan cohort of hospitalized schizophrenics which was included in the International Pilot Study of Schizophrenia (IPSS)(World Health Organization, 1973). For political reasons, Taiwan was excluded from this project upon the completion of the initial phase of this research. Thus, follow-up data are limited and the available information on the characteristics of schizophrenics beyond the acute stage of their disorder in Taipei is less than complete.

Perhaps the most important finding of IPSS was the high rate of delusional and other paranoid symptoms within the hospitalized group of Taiwan patients. The prominence of these symptoms in Chinese schizophrenics is corroborated by a number of other clinical studies in Singapore (cf. Tsoi, 1985) and in Taiwan (cf. Lin, 1985). A tricultural comparison of psychotic patients in Taiwan, Japan, and the United States (Rin, Schooler, and Caudill, 1973) confirmed the predominance of ideational and paranoid symptom expression in Taiwan. Moreover, Taiwanese patients directed their symptoms outward in a hostile manner, while their counterparts in Japan focused them inward against themselves. Somatically oriented symptoms were prominent in both Asian countries. Rin et al. (1973) noted that the Chinese tended to complain about bodily problems in the absence of actual or detectable physiological changes, while the Japanese experienced an increase in arousal, sometimes accompanied by affect. Thus, there were subtle culturally patterned differences in modes of somatization.

Lin (1985) reported on the basis of a general synthesis of relevant Taiwan and Hong Kong data, including those of the subsequent phases of IPSS, that the Taiwan schizophrenics tended toward a favourable prognosis, both two and five years after the onset of the illness. In Hong Kong, Lo and Lo (1977) found that two-thirds of the schizophrenics were in remission or showed only mild deterioration upon the ten-year follow-up. In the absence of comparable cross-cultural data, it is difficult to assess the significance of this finding and to pinpoint its possible sources within the family, the hospital, and the community.

In two recent intra-Asian comparisons (Fujimori, Zheng, Kizaki, and Kai, 1988; Kim, Li, Jiang, Cui, Lin, Kang, Chung, and Kim, 1993), cultural differences in delusional content were found which reflected the preoccupations of their respective place and time. Thus, religion loomed larger in the delusions of South Koreans, and political events and activities held greater importance for the delusional mainland Chinese.

Another factor which complicates cross-cultural comparisons, especially of hospitalized psychiatric patients, is the traditional under-utilization of mental health services by the Chinese. Among Chinese Americans, Sue and Zane (1987) traced this tendency to the reluctance of Chinese families to accept mental disorder in members of their families.

EPIDEMIOLOGICAL RESEARCH: A BIRD'S-EYE VIEW OF PSYCHOPATHOLOGY

Population surveys, especially in Taiwan and in Hong Kong, have been a prominent avenue of study for several decades. Lin (1953) pioneered epidemiological research of mental disorders, in a study conducted in three Taiwan communities: a village, a small town, and a section of metropolitan Taipei. This project was replicated in the same three communities 15 years later (Lin, Rin, Yeh, Hsu, and Chu, 1969). Comparisons across time revealed a remarkable constancy in the rates for schizophrenia, while those for neurosis or, in the current terminology, anxiety, somatoform, and dissociative disorders, had increased fivefold. Prevalence of neurosis among the displaced Chinese mainlanders who had fled to the island in 1949 and 1950 was found to be twice as high as among the Taiwanese. Both of these findings highlight the impact of social change upon minor or ambulatory psychopathology and the absence of such an effect upon schizophrenia.

Comparisons of the Chinese majority in Taiwan were also undertaken with four tribes of Taiwan aborigines (Rin and Lin, 1962). These two very different population groups showed differences in schizophrenia, which was higher among the Chinese, as well as alcoholism, personality disorders, and organic psychosis, all of which were found to be more prevalent among the aborigines.

Epidemiological research in Hong Kong began with the Family Life Survey (Mitchell, 1972) and the Biosocial Survey (Millar, 1979). These projects were focused upon stress-related symptoms. Mitchell (1972) compared Langner (1962) scale scores of samples from Hong Kong, Taipei, Singapore, Bangkok, and three major Malaysian cities. Stress levels were higher in Hong Kong than in Taipei and Singapore, but lower than elsewhere in Asia. Millar (1979) investigated the sources of stress in urban living. She found, somewhat surprisingly, that crowding resulted in less of an increase in the number of stress-related symptoms than one might have anticipated on a theoretical or common-sense basis.

Lee (1981, 1985) related this finding to the operation of workable coping mechanisms which permitted Hong Kong residents to mitigate the impact of these stressful conditions. Moreover, in a socially oriented culture, physical proximity may not be experienced as intrinsically unpleasant, and privacy may be redefined to encompass close family and friends. Above all, early and thorough socialization in stoicism and self-control allow many Hong Kong Chinese to endure high residential density with relatively little distress or disruption.

By this time, the 'second generation' of epidemiological studies, more sophisticated in design and grander in scale, have been completed in both Hong Kong (Chen et al., 1993) and Taiwan (Hwu, Yeh, and Chang, 1989). The Taiwan Psychiatric Epidemiological Project (TPEP)(Hwu et al., 1989) confirmed the contrast between the fluctuations of rates of anxiety-related disorders and the stability of such indications for schizophrenics across time and social conditions. The TPEP results were compared *post hoc* with information gathered by means of similar procedures and instruments in the United States (Compton, Helzer, Hwu, Yeh, McEvoy, Topp, and Spitznagel, 1991). This comparison corroborated and strengthened the hitherto suggestive finding that depression is significantly lower in prevalence in Taiwan than in the United States. Antisocial personality disorder and alcohol and drug abuse, however, were more prevalent in the United States.

In the Shatin Community Mental Health Survey (Chen et al., 1993), conducted in Hong Kong, prevalence of several depressive disorders was found to be low. By contrast, general anxiety disorder constituted the most common psychiatric disorder among women and the third most common among men. The discrepancy between these two states of subjective discomfort suggests that the infrequency of depression among the Chinese cannot be ascribed to their reluctance to report internal psychological states.

A surprising amount of epidemiological research has been carried out in mainland China. Between 1958 and 1981, 61 such studies were completed (Liu et al., 1987). In a recent review, P. Cheung (1991) identified and discussed ten more projects which were reported during the 1980s. Over the years, this research has progressed from crude approximations of the numbers of cases of the most disabling disorders to a sophisticated and comprehensive record of the entire range of psychopathology. The conclusions from this body of findings point to rates of schizophrenia that are similar to those in the West. Low rates were found for major depression, bipolar affective disorder, and alcoholism. Neurasthenia emerged as the most common neurotic disorder, followed by hysteria, while personality disorders were rarely encountered or diagnosed. These results from the PRC are surprisingly similar to those for Hong Kong and Taiwan. They suggest that cultural heritage and/or genetic transmission are much more important determinants of psychopathology than are political and economic systems.

ALCOHOLISM: A LIMITED BUT GROWING PROBLEM

The Chinese have a well-deserved reputation for moderate and problem-free consumption of alcohol. This impression is largely confirmed by more systematic studies in Taiwan (Lin, 1953), Hong Kong (Singer, 1972), and the Chinatowns of North America (Wang, 1968). Epidemiological data (as, for example, Hwu, Yeh, and Chang, 1988) are in keeping with this conclusion. The interdependence of the Chinese, their strong controls over behaviour, firm family ties, and a sense of social decorum have been invoked as contributing reasons for this moderation (cf. Lin and Lin, 1982). More generally, it can be said that the traditional Chinese culture has evolved workable methods for permitting and promoting alcohol consumption, yet curbing its excesses. It is as yet unknown whether the demonstrated sensitivity of the Chinese to ethyl alcohol (Wolff, 1972) works as a built-in mechanism of aversion therapy and thereby counteracts immoderate consumption.

Although alcoholism rates have been low among the Chinese, alcohol abuse in Chinese communities does occur. As yet, little is known about the psychological characteristics of Chinese alcoholics. Are they more seriously disturbed than are their counterparts in countries in which alcohol abuse is prevalent? What are the social and biographical pathways toward alcoholism, and how is it overcome?

Within recent decades, investigators (cf. Yeh, 1985) have detected a tendency toward increased alcohol abuse in Taiwan and Hong Kong, although actual rates remain low. If this trend is confirmed and extended, what are its mainsprings? In what manner, if at all, is it related to the dynamics of modernization, Westernization, and economic development?

PSYCHOLOGICAL DISORDERS IN CHILDREN AND ADOLESCENTS: A VARIETY OF LEADS

Systematic study of children's disorders in Chinese societies has been only recently initiated, and the results obtained so far appear fragmentary. Among the epidemiological projects, the large-scale research in Beijing on the behavioural problems of children in grades 1 through 5 stands out (Wang, Shen, Gu, Jia, and Zhang, 1989). The operations of this study were coordinated with Rutter's (1975) measures and procedures. Therefore, *post hoc* cross-cultural comparisons of the Chinese data were possible. Wang et al. concluded that the total percentage of children who were presenting problems was markedly lower in Beijing than in London. Children in Seoul, South Korea, also exhibited problems in a higher proportion than did children in Beijing, while the percentage of behaviour problems was lower in Ciba, Japan, than in mainland China. It is remarkable, however, that the frequency of antisocial behaviour was higher at all three of the Asian sites than in London. Wang et al. traced these counter-intuitive findings to the adult observers' sensitivity to, and lowered thresholds for, antisocial behaviour. Chinese children also exceeded their British, but not their Japanese and Korean, peers in headaches and stomachaches.

Cultural sensitivities are probably also implicated in the frequent, although not entirely consistent, reports of the high incidence of attention deficit–hyperactivity disorder (ADHD) among Chinese children. J. P. Leung (in press) has reviewed this body of findings and concluded that at least some of these estimates are inflated by the perceptions of parents and teachers in a culture which places a high premium on attention, concentration, and suppression of motility, even in young school-age children. Leung calls for comparative studies with identical criteria and operations across several Chinese settings under different levels of Western influences, for example, in the Mainland, Hong Kong, and the Chinese diaspora of Australia or Canada. Pending the implementation of such projects, the contributions of children and their adult observers to the reported prevalence of ADHD are not yet disentangled.

An epidemiological study of preschool children, with appropriate *post hoc* comparisons across cultures, was conducted in Hong Kong by Luk, Leung, Bacon-Shone, Chung, Lee, Cheu, Ne, Lieh-Mak, Ko, Wong, and Yeung (1991). These authors reported a higher frequency of temper tantrums and fearfulness among the Hong Kong children compared with their peers in London. A number of investigators (Ekblad, 1988; Ho, 1986; K. Leung, in press; Shek, in press) are in agreement that aggressive and destructive behaviour is relatively infrequent among the symptoms of Chinese children and adolescents in Hong Kong, Taiwan, and the PRC. This pattern is traceable to Chinese socialization practices which effectively suppress and inhibit direct expressions of aggression, especially in their destructive, violent, and antisocial aspects. The hypothesis may thus be entertained that the symptomatology of both children and adolescents is typically expressed through overcontrolled rather than undercontrolled behaviour (cf. Achenbach and Edelbrock, 1978).

In a unique study, Ney, Lieh-Mak, Cheng, and Collins (1979) observed 14 autistic children in Hong Kong and compared them with their counterparts in the United States. Ney et al. (1979, p. 149) concluded that 'Chinese parents appear to be more involved with their autistic children and the children with them'. This finding requires replication. It is, however, consistent with other observations which point to a greater social interdependence of Chinese psychiatric patients, both child and adult, and their families. As Lin and Lin (1981) have shown, Chinese attitudes toward serious mental illness within their families are compounded of love, denial, and rejection.

A special problem which has only recently been recognized and tackled is that of eating behaviours in adolescents. Lee (1991) presented clinical data on 16 female adolescent cases of anorexia nervosa. Reports of anorexia nervosa, based on information about several patients in each instance, have also appeared in the PRC (Song and Fong, 1990), Taiwan (Tseng, Lee and Lee, 1989), and Singapore (Ong and Tsoi, 1982). The distinctive feature of Chinese symptomatology in anorexia nervosa is the absence of fear of obesity, at least in a substantial proportion of the patients (Lee, 1991; Lee, Ho and Hsu, 1993). Instead of fat phobia, Hong Kong adolescent girls repeatedly invoked such reasons for their self-imposed starvation as 'distaste for food' or 'intolerable fullness' (Lee, Leung, Wing, Chiu, and Chen, 1991).

Compared with the West, incidence of maladaptive eating behaviours, such as bingeing, extreme fasting, and self-induced vomiting is low in Hong Kong (F. Leung, 1994). Leung (1994) found lowered self-esteem, dissatisfaction with body image, fear of negative evaluation, and mood disorder among anorexic adolescents in Hong Kong. However, Leung's subjects were no different from normal controls in a variety of indicators pertaining to intrafamily relationships and interactions. Thus, emic and etic influences are interlaced in the etiology of eating disorders in producing a universal outcome, weight loss and its life-threatening consequences.

EMIC DISORDERS OF THE CHINESE: THE CASE OF *KORO*

Researchers have long been fascinated with culture-bound syndromes or patterns of disturbed behaviour that are distinctive of or unique to a culture or region. In China, the best known culture-bound syndrome is *koro* (Edwards, 1985; Hughes, 1985; Pfeiffer, 1994; Yap, 1965) or *suoyang*. This condition is characterized by a belief in occurrences of genital shrinkage, to which the affected person responds with bouts of dejection and panic. The victim dreads dying of this disease. *Koro* occurs typically in men who are devastated by their conviction that their penis is shrinking. Complaints by women of the retraction of their nipples have been voiced but at a much lower frequency. *Koro* occurs in southern, but not in central, northern, or western China and is also observed throughout Malaysia and Indochina.

Clinically, there has been controversy over the appropriate place for *koro* within the international diagnostic scheme (cf. Yap, 1965). Tseng, Mo, Hsu, Li, Ou, Chen, and Zeng (1988) have contributed to the resolution of this issue by gathering systematic data during a *koro* epidemic in Guangdong province. They found that such outbreaks occur in an atmosphere of widespread social insecurity and may represent displacement of fears of uncontrollable and threatening external events. *Koro* attacks are intense and brief. They typically occur at night and are linked to the fear of spirits, even though in the PRC such apprehensions may not be readily admitted. Only a minority of men, and a much smaller proportion of women, experience attacks of *koro*.

In another study, Tseng, Mo, Li, Ou, and Zeng (1992) obtained symptom, biographical, and psychometric data on 214 *koro* victims from the Leizhou peninsula and Hainan Island. They compared the data with that of two groups, one consisting of persons free of anxiety-related or other symptoms, the other of out-patients treated for conventional anxiety-disorders. Somewhat counter-intuitively, the *koro* patients turned out to be more similar to their normal peers than to the anxiety patients. The *koro* victims were lower than both other groups in intelligence, but they were not different in personality as measured by the Cattell 16-PF Test. The *koro*-sufferers presented anxious and phobic symptoms, similar to the anxiety group, but reported fewer somatic, depressive, and hostile complaints and less interpersonal hypersensitivity. The crucial factor, according to Tseng et al., appears to be their more intense belief in the *suoyang* concept, that is, the reality of genital shrinkage which may have possibly been linked to their greater suggestibility.

Bartholomew (1994) went further and proposed that *koro* not be regarded as an eruption of psychopathological irrationality but as a collective, culturally plausible misperception to which entirely normal individuals, free of disturbance, succumb. Especially where *koro* assumes epidemic proportions, it should best be viewed as a phenomenon of social psychology of a specific place and time, rather than as a culture-bound psychiatric syndrome.

CONCLUSIONS

T. Lin (1985, p. 370) concluded that 'the entire range of psychopathology observed in Western and other cultures in terms of symptoms or syndromes has also been observed in the Chinese', and 'all types of mental disorders, including their subtypes, as discussed in Western literature and textbooks have been observed in the Chinese'. These conclusions are consonant with the findings and observations reviewed in this chapter. However, a cautionary statement must be appended. Many of the disorders within the standard psychiatric nomenclature, for example, borderline personality disorder, have as yet been little studied among the Chinese, let along compared in incidence, nature of manifestations, or etiology across culture lines.

At the same time, these results bring to the fore the distinctiveness in the Chinese patterns and discrete manifestations of abnormal behaviour. Some of these characteristic features include: emphasis upon somatic presentation of distress; difficulties and/or reluctance in expressing the full gamut of depressive manifestations; prominence of paranoid symptoms in schizophrenia and a good prognosis for remission from that disorder; increase in the number of anxiety-related disorders with the complexities of modern living; moderately low suicide rates in international perspective, with several selectively vulnerable segments of the population, such as rejected women in Hong Kong (Yap, 1958, 1958, 1958) and humiliated intellectuals during the Cultural Revolution (Fan et al., 1992); low rates of alcoholism, which may be slowly increasing, especially in the most modernized and cosmopolitan Chinese milieus. Overriding these specific findings, there seems to be a general social emphasis in Chinese symptom experience, which seems to parallel the importance of interpersonal relationships in the Chinese culture.

The findings surveyed have also revealed the complex intertwining of psychopathology and culture. Thus, it would be misleading to conclude that Chinese psychiatric patients simply somatize more or tend less toward depression than do their counterparts in Europe, America, or elsewhere. Kleinman (1988) has emphasized the subtlety of the pathways that transform malaise, helplessness, or confusion into a culturally intelligible and meaningful set of symptoms. In China or elsewhere, it would be a mistake to attribute a person's symptoms exclusively to his or her personal characteristics. The psychiatric observer, the treatment setting, and the community milieu are inevitable participants in this transaction (Draguns, 1973). Future research should incorporate these features of fact-gathering and impression formation within the Chinese culture and, at the same time, should recognize that symptoms and syndromes as recorded represent a process. This progression should be studied both quantitatively and qualitatively; methodological rigour and personal, clinical, and cultural sensitivity should be pursued with equal determination. Concurrently, there is equal need for studies both within and across cultures, for the insider's empathic perspective and for the bird's-eye view of the outsider.

Of necessity, this research enterprise remains unfinished. In particular, it is difficult to generalize findings and conclusions obtained exclusively or primarily in Taiwan, Hong Kong, or a single region within mainland China to the entire range of Chinese cultural experience. Research on psychopathology in the several Chinese political entities has in the past faced insurmountable political obstacles which, by now, may have been reduced or overcome. If that is so, it may be possible to incorporate the several socio-political structures within which the Chinese reside as quasi-experimental conditions created by external circumstances.

There have also been few comparisons of subjects in China and in the diaspora, with the Chinese ethnicity held constant. Moreover, the groups of subjects with whom the Chinese are compared have been typically North American or sometimes European. As yet there have been too few comparative studies with China's Asian neighbours: Japanese, Koreans, Thai, and Indians. However, the number of such studies is increasing. Some of the traits attributed to the Chinese culture may be traceable to more general regional characteristics; apparent commonalities among Asians, for example, in somatic symptom presentation, may turn out to display culturally distinctive nuances. Tseng and Wu (1985) recommended a shift from major to minor psychiatric disorders, and their recommendation is increasingly being implemented.

The resolution of the conceptual, clinical, and practical tangles that beset the field is unthinkable unless the barriers against the simultaneous and coordinated study of normal and abnormal behaviour are broken down. Only then shall we be able to assess the weight of such influences as Chinese social orientations (Yang, 1992) upon the expressions of Chinese psychopathology. Yet, it may be hasty to ascribe all of the differentiating features of Chinese psychopathology to culture. Freedman and Freedman (1969) were able to discern a less reactive and excitable temperament among newborn Chinese infants by comparison with their European and American counterparts. The field is open for disentangling the threads of biological and cultural influence upon psychological disturbance. This challenge, however, has been barely tackled; the empirical and conceptual resolution of this problem is both difficult and indispensable.

Finally, what do the accumulated findings on the psychopathological reactions of the Chinese tell us about the prevalent psychological characteristics of normal and adaptive Chinese individuals? Viewed through the distorting lens of the abnormal behaviour in their midst, the composite sketch of the Chinese personality contains the following features: emphasis upon bodily well-being and comfort; complex, intense, and continuous intertwining of the person with their family and community; a sense of privacy and reluctance to self-disclose; restraint in expression of impulse and feeling; and avoidance of excess.

Undoubtedly, this listing contains distortions and inaccuracies. It is presented here as a source of hypotheses. Once they are tested, inevitable revisions and corrections will be made. At this point, the above conclusions constitute a precarious bridge between the incomplete but growing body of data on Chinese maladaptation and the more substantial store of findings on the development and functioning of the normal Chinese. The integration of these two sources of information will provide a major step toward the formulation of a comprehensive model of Chinese experience.

Chapter 28

Coping in Chinese Communities: The Need for a New Research Agenda

Michael R. Phillips and Veronica Pearson

Coping directly affects the adaptive efficacy of individuals, families, and other social entities, and so the conceptualization of coping influences research and theory in a variety of social, biological, and medical sciences. Cognitive psychologists, who have undertaken most of the research on coping since the late 1970s, consider coping a cognitively mediated *transaction* between the individual and the environment that differs in different situational contexts and that changes over time. The most influential theorist in the field, Richard Lazarus, defines coping as 'a person's constantly changing cognitive and behavioural efforts to manage specific external and/or internal demands that are appraised as taxing or exceeding the person's resources' (1993, p. 237).

Lazarus' model of coping (Lazarus and Folkman, 1984) postulates an ongoing feedback loop of thinking and behaviour: an individual appraises the potential threat of a situation (the primary appraisal), assesses the available resources for dealing with the threat (the secondary appraisal), initiates a coping intervention, and then makes ongoing reassessments of the threatening situation and revisions to the coping intervention until the perceived threat is removed or minimized. The characteristics of the stressor and of the environment in which it occurs are more important determinants of the coping transaction than is the individual's *coping style*, although personality factors, particularly the individual's motivational hierarchy, may influence appraisal of stressors and selection of coping strategies. Folkman and Lazarus (1985) group coping strategies into three broad categories: *problem-focused coping* that aims to solve the problem by changing the person–environment relationship, *emotion-focused coping* that aims to make the individual feel better by changing the emotional response to the stressful situation, and *mixed coping* that has aspects of both problem- and emotion-focused coping (for example, seeking social support). Most current researchers in the field explicitly or implicitly accept this contextual, process-oriented approach to coping, even though the classification of coping strategies as problem-focused or emotion-focused remains controversial (Carver, Scheier, and Weintraub, 1989; Endler and Parker, 1990).

One major limitation of this theory is its dependence on research using urban samples from Western countries. Strictly speaking, this approach to coping only applies to relatively affluent communities that value individualism and pragmatic positivism. The severe, chronic stresses of poverty, disease, famine, and war experienced by large segments of the world's population who have limited, if any, available resources to deal with these stresses may well result in different mechanisms of coping than those seen in the affluent West (Palsane and Lam, in press). The dominant role Western theorists assign to the individual as the primary social unit that engages in coping transactions may not be appropriate in more collectively oriented cultures. Moreover, the Western emphasis on realistic appraisal of stressors, on action-oriented coping, and on the psychological outcomes of different coping strategies reflect values that are not necessarily shared by non-Western cultures.

The culture and socio-economic environment of a community have profound effects on the types of stressors that are experienced in that community, on the resources available for dealing with those stressors, and on the perception of the relative importance of different stressors, coping strategies, and adaptational outcomes. In drawing attention to the role of macro-structural factors and cultural values, cross-national and cross-cultural research on coping could make important contributions to the understanding of the process of coping. This paper discusses the current research on coping in Chinese communities and, based on a critique of this work, suggests an alternative research agenda that, if adopted, could enrich the evolving theory on coping.

CURRENT RESEARCH ON COPING IN CHINESE COMMUNITIES

The traditional philosophies of China—Confucianism, Buddhism, and Taoism—share an approach to the understanding and management of life stresses different from that adopted by Western philosophies. Life's stresses, which these Eastern philosophies often subsume under the rubric 'suffering' (Palsane and Lam, in press), are determined by fate. Patient forbearance of such suffering is highly valued because it repays the debts of previous lives and cultivates the character. Confucian values also emphasize the centrality of the family in the management of life problems and the paramount importance of maintaining harmonious social relationships, even at the cost of increased personal stress.

The influence of these traditional views on the belief systems of modern Chinese communities depends on the extent to which the community has been 'modernized' by urbanization, nuclearization of the family, and contact with Western values. Reports of continued belief in an external locus of control (Hofstede, 1980), frequent use of fatalism as a coping strategy (Hwang, 1977; R. P. L. Lee, 1992), and concern with the proper conduct demanded by a situation rather than with the direct expression of opinions or emotions (Chen, 1988; Hsu, 1953) suggest the ongoing, though attenuated, influence of traditional values (see also Bond, this volume; Leung, this volume).

Relatively little research in Chinese communities specifically addresses the issue of coping, but there is an increasing corpus of work on the related areas of stress, life events, locus of control, and social support networks. Most of this work does not combine or compare results across the different Chinese communities of mainland China, Taiwan, Hong Kong, and the overseas Chinese communities, so we will discuss the work done in each of these locations separately.

Mainland China

Research on stress and coping in mainland China has been quite limited because psychology and other social sciences were actively suppressed as 'bourgeois' during the pre-reform era and have only gradually been re-introduced into academic curricula since 1978 (see Blowers, this volume). Psychology remains an immature field, particularly in the area of theoretical development. Most of the work related to coping is done by psychiatrists who conduct large-scale survey research and retrospective case-control studies focused on the mental health implications of stress.

Recently, research interest has focused on the role of life events in psychiatric and psychosomatic illnesses (Y. Z. Yang, 1991; Y. Zhang, Song, Yao, and Xia, 1992). A nationwide study on the Chinese Life Event Scale (M. Y. Zhang, Fan, Cai, Chi, Wu, and Jin, 1987) determined norms for the relative stressfulness of different types of life events by asking respondents to rate the events (whether or not they had experienced them) compared to the stressfulness of marriage. The pattern of life event stressors identified was different from that found in the West; Chinese respondents place a much heavier emphasis on family problems such as arguments between parents and children, anxiety about children's success at school, conflicts with in-laws, and so forth.

Unfortunately, in assuming the stressfulness of an event will be the same for all individuals, the scale ignores the individual's appraisal of the stressors actually encountered, and so it is of limited usefulness in determining an individual's level of stress or in analyzing the process of coping. Y. P. Zheng (1989) developed more sophisticated life event scales for neurotic patients and medical students that assess the perceived stressfulness and available social support for particular life events actually experienced by the respondents; this approach to life event research, however, is not widely used on the Mainland.

Some of the research on coping in China has been done by Chinese postgraduate students based in Western institutions. Yue (1993) conducted an ethnographic study of stress and coping in 120 university students in Beijing and found that coping strategies based on Confucian self-cultivation and Taoist transcendence were commonly employed. Chen's (1988) study of the role of life events, locus of control, social support networks, self-esteem, and coping strategies on the level of psychological stress has several methodological limitations, but the thesis highlights three important issues. First, the four loci of control identified by Chinese subjects—internal (the self), powerful others, leaders, and chance—differ from those identified by Western subjects. Some of these differences, such as the Chinese belief in fate, are cultural; others, such as the Chinese focus on the role of powerful leaders, are the product of different social systems. These different beliefs about the locus of control result in a preference for different types of coping strategies. Second, the macro-environment (the political and socio-economic context) determines the exposure of individuals to stressful factors and access to supportive resources. For example, the diminished role of friends in the social support network in China compared to other Chinese communities has occurred because friends could not be relied on to maintain confidences in the era of political campaigns and criticism sessions. Third, individuals in different historical cohorts (that is, different age groups) are exposed to different types of stressors. These *cohort vulnerability factors* are particularly important in China, where the political changes between 1949 and 1976 and the economic changes during the reform era from 1978 to the present have resulted in constant changes in the determinants of social status and the opportunity structures of the society—important moderators of stress and of access to social resources.

Some research has focused on family-based coping in China (Pearson and Chan, 1993). Combining data from a multi-centre, cross-sectional study (n = 299) and two longitudinal studies (n = 129), Phillips (1993) assessed coping in families of patients with schizophrenia. Family members play the major roles in the assessment and management of the problems that these disabled individuals must deal with: they coordinate contact with care providers, negotiate on the patient's behalf with employers, and use their social contacts and financial assets to arrange marriages. Confucian values about familial obligations— reinforced by China's Marriage Law—make parents feel obliged to use all the family's resources for the benefit of the ill family member. China's rapid socioeconomic changes are having a dramatic effect on the types of strategies available to these families. For example, the new emphasis on work productivity makes it increasingly difficult for disabled persons to obtain employment and, hence, employment-related social welfare benefits. Thus, both cultural and socio-economic factors influence the selection of family strategies.

Taiwan

The most influential researcher in the area of coping in Taiwan is K. K. Hwang. Based on content analysis of unstructured three-to-six hour interviews that asked 180 married males from Taipei between the ages of 30 and 60 years to discuss 'the beliefs or methods which help you the most to deal with troubles in your life', Hwang (1977, 1978) identified five types of coping strategies: mobilizing personal resources, help-seeking from social resources, appealing to the supernatural, adopting a philosophy of doing nothing, and avoidance. Hwang points out that emotional discharge was not a dominant coping strategy in this group and that forbearance (that is, doing nothing) does not fit into the problem-focused or emotion-focused dichotomy suggested by Lazarus. He found that mobilization of personal resources (a reliance on the self) was the most commonly applied technique, particularly for younger respondents. For those who applied help-seeking methods the order of importance of sources of help was friends, kin, officials, and spouse. Interestingly, this is the reverse of the order specified by 85 married males in Shanghai (Chen, 1988), who identified spouses as the most important social support and work leaders as the second most important social support. Hwang's results have generated considerable interest among Chinese researchers, but it should be remembered that he used a highly selective sample; the results may not apply to females, to persons under 30 or over 60 years of age, and to persons from rural settings.

The longitudinal studies of K. S. Yang (1986) and his colleagues on the changes in motivational, evaluative–attitudinal, and temperamental character-istics of Chinese students over the last 30 years have important implications for the understanding of coping. Social changes in Taiwanese society have been related to a decreased prevalence of the social-oriented values of collectivism, authoritarianism, and submissiveness and to an increased prevalence of the individual-oriented values of individualism, competitiveness, expressiveness, and autonomy. Although coping was not specifically addressed by Yang, this shift in values is likely to result in changes in individuals' methods of appraising stressors and valuing adaptational outcomes. Thus, changes in a community's modal values may well lead to changes in the process of coping.

Yang also reports (1981) that in Taiwan individuals still put considerable weight on the anticipated response of others prior to engaging in a particular behaviour. This suggests that the collectivist tradition persists despite the ongo-ing changes in Taiwanese society and that one of the important determinants of Chinese individuals' selection of coping strategies is the anticipated effects of the strategy on other social actors.

Hong Kong

Much more research on stress, life events, and coping has been done in Hong Kong than in other Chinese communities. Most of these studies address one of three issues: classification of coping responses, determination of the factors that affect the selection of coping strategies, and assessment of the adaptation-al outcomes of coping strategies. The high level of urbanization and Westernization of Hong Kong residents locates them at the extreme 'modern' pole of the traditionality–modernity spectrum defined by K. S. Yang (1986), so the patterns of stress and coping in Hong Kong may be different from those seen in other Chinese communities. Thus, despite the dominant role of studies from Hong Kong in the literature, results from Hong Kong should not be gen-eralized to all persons of Chinese ethnicity.

Classification of Chinese coping strategies

Shek and Mak (1987) developed the Chinese Coping Scale based on a dichotomization of Hwang's five types of coping (1977) into internal strategies (using personal resources, doing nothing, or avoidance) versus external strate-gies (using social resources or appealing to the supernatural). Shek and Cheung (1990) administered this scale to 1,000 working adults in Hong Kong who were asked to report (on a four-point scale) the extent to which they use 16 different methods of coping with four common life problems (marital stress, family-related stress, interpersonal stress, and work-related stress). Assessment of internal consistency and both exploratory and confirmatory factor analysis has demonstrated the independence of the two factors and, hence, the scale's empirical validity. The authors argue that classifying coping strategies as inter-nal or external is more stable, global, and parsimonious than Lazarus' problem-focused versus emotion-focused classification.

Lam and Hong (1992) also question the validity of Lazarus' dichotomous classification of coping strategies for Chinese subjects. Based on their work regarding examination stress in students, they suggest that, 'problem and emotion-focused coping should be viewed not as two discrete categories but as independent dimensions which can both be applied to the description of any coping strategy' (p. 304). All coping strategies have both problem-focused and emotion-focused properties, but they differ in the extent to which they possess these properties.

An elegant three-part study by Hong and Lam (1992) of test anxiety related to university entrance examinations first determined the types of appraisals and coping strategies employed, sorted and cluster-analysed the appraisals and strategies, and finally related the appraisals and strategies to the level of anxiety and guilt experienced. They found that test anxiety was associated with a weak self-efficacy appraisal, cognitive avoidance coping strategies, and the presence of guilt feelings. They emphasize that, given the social and familial pressures for high academic achievement in Hong Kong, 'test anxiety in this context is not just a problem of individual functioning, it is also a sociocultural issue' (p. 286).

In an interesting discussion of the results of the large 1974 Biosocial Survey in Hong Kong, R. P. L. Lee (1985) explains the unexpectedly weak relationship between stress and high-density living and socio-economic disadvantage by postulating three specific coping mechanisms in Chinese culture: behavioural and social norms that ameliorate the stress of high density living, such as placing a positive value on multi-generation households, defining privacy at the familial (not individual) level, and avoiding emotional interactions with non-related persons; active construction and maintenance of instrumental primary networks (with kin and pseudo-kin) that help individuals realize their material aspirations and buffer the effects of economic failure; and continued belief in supernatural explanations of life's vicissitudes (such as *yuanfen*, predestined affinity) and the practice of *fengshui* (geomancy) to manipulate the supernatural forces in one's favour. In a later work Lee (in press) characterizes coping strategies in Hong Kong as 'fatalistic voluntarism', a combination of self-directed approaches to changing conditions and fatalistic acceptance of the way things are. In the West these two types of strategies are viewed as mutually exclusive, but Chinese people often simultaneously employ the 'Confucian strategy' of self-cultivation (active striving to achieve moderation in life) and the 'Taoist strategy' of self-transcendence (detachment from worldly affairs).

Factors that affect the selection of coping strategies

Most of the work on the selection of coping strategies focuses on health-seeking behaviour, the subset of coping related to the stressor of ill health. Cheung, Lee, and Chan (1983) asked 78 Hong Kong university students to list the likely causes and appropriate solutions for five types of health problems: weakness, anxiety, difficulty sleeping, emptiness, and headache. They found that a wide variety of self-help methods (for example, changes in daily habits, psychological endurance, and so forth) were preferred if the problems were mild, but medical treatment from a general physician was preferred if the problems were severe. Psychiatrists and counsellors were not the preferred sources of help even if the perceived cause of the problem was psychological. Thus, the coping strategies adopted depend on the characteristics of the problem (its severity) and on the perceived acceptability of different coping resources, not on the causal attributes of the problem. Cheung (1985) suggests that the emphasis on self-directed coping strategies is related to the Confucian tradition of self-discipline, an ideal expected of persons with high educational and social standing.

Cheung, Lau, and Wong (1984) assessed the previous health-care-seeking patterns of psychiatric patients with various diagnoses at the time of their first visit to a public (n = 226) or private (n = 56) outpatient psychiatric clinic. Compared to public patients, private patients (who have a higher socio-economic status) took longer to seek professional help, were more likely to emphasize the somatic aspects of their problems, were more likely to use Chinese traditional medical practitioners (herbalists and acupuncturists), and were slightly more likely to consult a fortune teller. Studies in developing countries (Li and Phillips, 1990) usually find that non-Western health services are more heavily utilized by persons of lower socio-economic status, so these results from Hong Kong seem counter-intuitive. In Hong Kong, however, public health services provide inexpensive professional care while the services of folk healers and private professionals are relatively expensive. These results highlight the importance of assessing the socio-economic context of health services when evaluating the coping strategies employed to deal with health-related problems.

Adaptational outcomes of coping strategies

The results of research on the adaptational outcomes of coping are mixed, largely due to conceptual and methodological limitations. Based on a study of 94 undergraduate students that used Vaillant's (1976) psychodynamically oriented measure of coping, Chan (1986) attempted to delineate the relationship of life events, coping style, social support, and locus of control with physical and psychological symptoms. He used a sophisticated path-analytic technique to generate a model of the relationships among the various variables. However, the model included several anomalous findings. For example, the relationship between life events and symptoms was not influenced by the type of coping strategy employed; this unexpected result may be due to the problems of using a psychodynamic measure of coping.

Chan (1992) assessed the relationship between depressed mood and coping activities in 95 Hong Kong medical students. Using the 142-item Coping Strategies Scales (Beckham and Adams, 1984) to assess coping strategies, he found that medical students reported that active, problem-focused activities were most beneficial for combating depressive symptoms. Depressed students were more likely than non-depressed students to use the strategies of emotional containment and avoidance or denial, but, given the cross-sectional nature of the data, it was impossible to determine if the coping strategies employed were the cause or the result of the reported depressive symptoms.

H. C. B. Lee, Chan, and Yik (1992) administered a 25-item adolescent coping scale (composed of 10 items from a Western scale and 15 items based on Hwang's categories of coping) and the 60-item General Health Questionnaire

(GHQ) to a representative sample of 832 Hong Kong adolescents. Respondents were asked to state the extent to which they use the 25 coping methods to deal with four problem areas: academic problems, conflicts with elders, conflicts with friends, and concerns about the future. Factor analysis of the results generated four coping strategies: avoidance/blaming, self-reliance/rational problem-solving, religiosity, and emotional regulation. In each of the four problem areas females used emotional regulation more than did males, and the use of avoidance/blaming was associated with higher levels of psychological distress (as measured by the GHQ overall score).

Overseas Chinese Communities

With the exception of Singapore, overseas Chinese communities are minority groups within a dominant culture. The size, cohesiveness, and relative power of the Chinese community, the duration of its residence in the country, and the attitudes of the dominant culture to the assimilation of the Chinese minority all affect the opportunity structures available to the Chinese, the types of stressors experienced by them, and the range of coping strategies available to them. For example, discriminatory regulations in Malaysia have largely limited Chinese citizens to commercial fields. In Vietnam active hatred has lead to large migrations of persons of Chinese ethnicity, and in America a political system that favours equality of opportunity has resulted in relatively quick assimilation. We have been unable to find detailed reports of stress and coping in Chinese communities in other Asian countries, but there is an increasing amount of research on the adaptational problems of the Chinese in Western countries, much of it done by Chinese graduate students.

X. Zheng and Berry (1991) compared coping strategies employed by 68 Chinese sojourners (students from China and Hong Kong) with those of 33 non-Chinese Canadian students and found that the Chinese students were more likely to employ active coping strategies of tension reduction and information-seeking and less likely to employ passive strategies of wishful thinking and self-blame.

Yee (1980) presented first- and second-generation Chinese-Americans with standard vignettes about individuals experiencing physical and psychological symptoms and asked them to describe how they understood and would respond to the problems. These respondents considered the family central to the prevention and management of stressful situations. Stress experienced by the individuals in the vignettes was perceived as occurring within the context of the family system; the appropriate method of managing the stress depended on the individual's role and relationships within the family.

LIMITATIONS OF RESEARCH ON COPING IN CHINESE COMMUNITIES

The preceding sections of this chapter detail the contributions of researchers working in Chinese communities to the study of coping. They have identified differences between Western and Chinese individuals in the relative importance of different stressors and in the types of coping strategies employed. The current work, however, presents a narrow view of culture and how it relates to coping; it does not attempt to explain why coping strategies are different in Chinese communities or to clarify how culture affects the process of coping, the person–environment transaction.

Culture has a profound effect on the motivational and emotional characteristics of individuals, on the inter-relationships between different social entities within communities, and on the macro-structural characteristics of societies. It must, therefore, play a central role in the perception and management of stressors. Researchers in Chinese communities have the opportunity to clarify this role and, thus, make important contributions to the theory on stress and coping, but they have yet to take full advantage of this opportunity. Persistence in using a structuralist approach to coping, the absence of longitudinal studies, the implicit acceptance of many Western assumptions, and the failure to explore the theoretical implications of results seriously undermine the potential value of this work.

Adoption of Structuralist, Cross-sectional, and Hypothetical Approaches to the Study of Coping

Despite paying lip-service to Lazarus' work, most of the research on coping conducted in Chinese communities simply looks for Chinese coping styles or strategies; it does not address the cognitive and transactional aspects of stress and coping. Lazarus' comprehensive review of Western literature (1993) discusses the problems of this structuralist approach to the study of coping: 'Broad coping styles do not adequately explain or predict intraindividual variations in the ways given sources of stress are dealt with in specific contexts' (p. 241). An individual's coping style is only one of several variables that interact during the process of coping.

With the sole exception of Phillips' work on families in China, none of the research on coping is longitudinal, and so it is unable to evaluate the interactive relationship between stresses and coping mechanisms. According to Lazarus, 'to collapse what is happening over time is apt to produce findings that are at best uninterpretable and at worst misleading' (1993, p. 239).

Most of the research asks respondents to describe how they usually act under certain stressful circumstances or how they would act if exposed to a particular stressor, rather than determining how they perceive and respond to specific stressors they actually have experienced. Lazarus comments that when responding to such hypothetical questions 'subjects may be giving nothing more than a vague impression about how they would prefer to cope, perhaps influenced by what they believe is socially desirable or ideal' (1993, p. 242).

To resolve these problems Lazarus recommends an emphasis on naturalistic, longitudinal studies that combine assessment of the motivational and emotional characteristics of individuals with evaluation of the contextual characteristics of stressors and the environments in which they occur. Some researchers in Chinese communities also recommend longitudinal studies that combine qualitative and quantitative data (Shek and Tsang, 1993), but no researcher has, as yet, taken this advice.

Acceptance of Western Cultural Assumptions

Chinese researchers have accepted the Western assumption that the individual is the major actor in the process of evaluating and managing stressors. This is not necessarily the case in the West and most definitely is not the case in the family-centred Chinese culture. Individualism is on the rise in many Chinese communities, particularly in the highly urbanized and Westernized sectors, but the family still acts as the primary arbiter and decision maker for many life transitions and other stressful events. As described by Lin: 'There is a fusion and blending of self and family into a single Chinese social unit...all behaviours and beliefs are developed in reference to the relationship between self and family' (1988, p. 91).

Few of the studies in Chinese communities assess the adaptive effectiveness of coping strategies, and those that do assess effectiveness accept the Western approach that evaluates coping effectiveness in terms of its effect on the individual's psychological health. If social harmony is a more important outcome than individual well-being (Leung and Lee, this volume), individuals and families will tend to select strategies that are likely to maximize their level of social harmony; these are not necessarily the same as the strategies that would maximize personal well-being. Thus, assessment of the effectiveness of a particular strategy in collectivist cultures should focus both on its influence on social harmony and on its influence on the psychological state of the individual.

In the highly urbanized West it is reasonable to generalize results from urban samples; in Chinese communities it is not. In Taiwan and China the socio-economic environment and degree of Westernization is very different between urban and rural communities; Buddhist and Taoist philosophies, Confucian social values, and extended families are much more dominant in the countryside. Virtually all the research on coping in Chinese communities has focused on urban populations, largely because of convenience, but these samples are not representative of all persons of Chinese ethnicity, the majority of whom live in rural areas.

Failure to Address Theoretical Implications of Results

In positivistic Western culture individuals are presumed to be in control of their own destiny, so active, problem-focused coping is highly valued and passive, emotion-focused coping is devalued. In Chinese culture, however, perseverance and Taoist 'wait-and-see' approaches to coping are both common and highly valued, perhaps because of the high perceived social cost (the effect on social harmony) of more active coping strategies. Current research does not assess the relative adaptive value of these fundamentally different approaches to coping, nor does it address the theoretical implications of these cross-cultural differences.

Wheaton (1983), for example, reports that fatalism (defined as belief in an external locus of control) can induce passive coping strategies and lead to mental disorders, possibly because it is associated with low self-esteem and depression. Data from Chinese communities, on the contrary, suggests that fatalistic approaches to managing stress are quite common and are not necessarily related to low self-esteem or psychological dysfunction (see also Leung, this volume). Research in Chinese communities questions the universality of Wheaton's theory, but there is no discussion in the Chinese literature of this contradiction or of why Wheaton's thesis may not apply to Chinese groups.

A NEW RESEARCH AGENDA

The paramount role assigned to the individual in current theories of coping is a product of the Western world-view. Research on the coping of individuals and families in Chinese communities suggests that the experience of stress, the search for the meaning of stressors, and adaptational coping responses occur at multiple levels of social organization, not just at the level of the individual. For example, the chronic illness of an individual affects all the social entities in which the individual plays an important role, so the individual's assessment of the effects of a chronic illness and response to this stressor cannot be fully appreciated unless the assessments and responses of the family, workplace, and other important social entities for the individual are simultaneously considered. Both cultural and socio-economic factors have complex effects on this multi-layered process of coping, and so sociocultural factors must be integrated into the conceptual framework of stress and coping, not—as in Western theories—merely appended as possible moderators of the coping process.

Social psychology, particularly cross-cultural social psychology, currently lacks research strategies and theoretical paradigms that integrate individual and societal levels of analysis (Gabrenya and Hwang, this volume), so evaluation of this 'systems model' of coping will require a new research agenda both in the West and in Chinese communities. At the individual level, we concur with Lazarus' emphasis on the need for longitudinal studies to clarify the dynamic relationship between stress and coping and to delineate the coping patterns individuals develop in responding to a variety of stressors over time. We would, however, add several new questions that highlight the multi-layered, diachronic (historical), and sociocultural aspects of coping.

First, for a particular type of stressful event or circumstance in a particular community, which social entities are primarily responsible for the labelling and management of the stressor? Responsibility is typically apportioned among individuals, families, workplaces, law and order institutions, medical institutions, religious institutions, and so forth. Second, within a particular community, how do the different social entities interact with each other in their search for the meaning of a stressor and in their coping with a stressor? Third, how does this 'apportionment of responsibility' among the various social entities and the interaction among the social entities vary for different stressors within the same community, for the same type of stressor across communities, and for the same stressor within a community over time? Fourth, what are the mediators by which socio-economic and cultural factors affect the process of coping? These will probably include the availability of social resources, the method of attributing social status, the characteristics of social support networks, the relative power of different social entities, and the definition and valuation of norms and ideals. Finally, fifth, how do socio-economic and cultural changes over time alter the process of coping in a community?

This new research agenda presents several challenges for researchers of stress and coping in Chinese communities. They must move beyond the narrow conception of culture as the determinant of different coping styles in Chinese individuals and develop longitudinal, multi-dimensional, and diachronic research strategies that address the following questions: At what points do cultural norms and ideals impinge on the process of coping? What is the role of different social entities—especially the family—in the assessment and management of common stressors such as life transitions, acute and chronic illnesses, social conflicts, and so forth? How do the different social entities (particularly individuals and families) in Chinese communities interact during the assessment and management of stressors? And how do industrialization, Westernization, and changes in the balance between individual and collective values alter the process of coping over time?

Comparison of results in the different Chinese communities could also address important theoretical issues. Clearly, there are major differences in the socio-economic environments of urban and rural China, Taiwan, Hong Kong, and the Chinese communities in Vietnam, Singapore, Malaysia, and Western countries. To what extent do these differences affect the process of coping in the different communities? Are the different patterns of coping solely the result of varying socio-economic environments, or are they partly due to a cultural divergence (differences in values and beliefs) that have developed over time? If there has been cultural divergence, what remains of 'Chinese culture' after Chinese communities have been isolated in distinct socio-economic environments for multiple generations?

SUMMARY

Most research on coping is carried out on Western populations and is focused on individual-level coping. Thus, the role of cultural factors, of macro-structural factors, and of coping at other levels of social organization have not been adequately explored. Moreover, much of the work that has been done in non-Western groups is conceptually limited, so it does not fulfil the promise of expanding the theoretical perspectives adopted by Western researchers. Coping research in Chinese communities, for example, is largely restricted to cross-sectional studies that attempt to identify the coping styles of Chinese individuals; the dynamic, transactional aspects of coping are disregarded, the theoretical implications of the work are rarely discussed, and the role of the family—the primary decision-making unit for a wide variety of stressors in Chinese culture—is largely ignored. To understand the process of coping in Chinese communities and to contribute to international theory-building about coping, researchers in Chinese communities must adopt an alternative research agenda that highlights the dynamic, multi-dimensional, contextual, and cultural aspects of the coping process.

NOTES

This chapter was completed while the first author was supported by a Young Investigator Award from the National Alliance for Research on Schizophrenia and Depression.

Chapter 29

◼

Psychotherapy with the Chinese

Patrick W. L. Leung and Peter W. H. Lee

The term *psychotherapy* has been variably defined in various contexts. In its most restrictive usage, it refers principally to Freudian psychodynamic therapy. A broader and more common usage is to include all types of psychological healing methods developed in the West under the disciplines of psychiatry, psychology, and social work.

However, both definitions have unwittingly ignored a substantive amount of literature in cross-cultural psychiatry and psychology which documents various forms of indigenous psychotherapy in many non-Western cultures. It is more appropriate to define psychotherapy broadly, severing its restrictive link to either a particular school of thought or cultural origin. Key components of such a definition would involve four elements: a healing agent who is designated in the respective culture as an expert in healing; a help-seeker who has difficulty in coping with problems of living; a healing relationship structured covertly or overtly by the healer in such a way as to provide the social context in which the healer induces positive changes in the moods, attitudes, and behaviors of the help-seeker, primarily through words, acts, and rituals; and an ultimate objective of removing distress and enhancing adaptive competence of the help-seeker for his or her own sake (Draguns, 1975; Frank and Frank, 1991). In fact, psychotherapy so defined becomes a universal phenomenon existing since time immemorial. As every culture has its problems of living, each subsequently develops various healing procedures to help its members. From this perspective, Western psychotherapy merely represents one of the many variants in psychotherapeutic procedures offered by cultures to their distressed members.

Guided by the above definition of psychotherapy, we will proceed to review two sets of literature, one pertaining to indigenous Chinese methods of psychotherapy and the other to the application of Western techniques in Chinese culture. They will be discussed in terms of their theoretical foundations, intended outcomes, process components, therapeutic efficacy, and service utilization. One focal point of this review is on the relationship between culture and psychotherapy. Culture is considered as a covert partner in the psychotherapeutic activities of its members (Draguns, 1975; Wachtel, 1978): it helps to shape the definition of problems, the processes of a therapy, and the choice of solutions. In this context, the present review represents part of a broader effort in examining the perennial debate on the cultural specificity or universality of psychotherapy.

One note of caution has to be sounded here. Bond (1993) has questioned the presumption of a Chinese monolith. He cited as a case in point the international study of values by Schwartz in which samples of Chinese from Hong Kong, Taiwan, and China fell into different clusters along various domains of cultural values. Anderson (1992) has also noted subcultural differences between agrarian and fishing communities in China. We shall return to this issue of Chinese heterogeneity later in our discussion.

INDIGENOUS CHINESE PSYCHOTHERAPY

Confucianism, Buddhism, and Taoism

Confucianism, Buddhism, and Taoism provide the main ideological thrusts of Chinese culture, and they also embody psychotherapeutic functions in their philosophies, concerned as they are with self-improvement and humanity (de Bary, 1991; Liu, 1992). Confucianism espouses the virtue of moderation in finding a right balance among life's excesses. Vanity should not be allowed to grow, desire should not be indulged, and pleasure should not be pursued to excess. These restraints are said to lead to tranquillity of the mind. Buddhism and Taoism look for more fundamental changes in attitudes. Each espouses the concept of liberation (Watts, 1961). Buddhism preaches the unreality (nonsignificance) of all worldly affairs. No problem exists for a liberated person! Taoism espouses the concepts of the *dao* (way) and *wuwei* (non-intervention). Mankind is an inseparable part of the cosmos, which has its own *dao* or cosmic course of evolution. Any human intervention will only bring about disharmony and conflicts. Thus, we must practise *wuwei*, to trust and follow our destiny as it is embedded in the *dao*. Our life will take its own course in harmony with the rest of the cosmos, and we will eventually experience fulfillment and peace. A liberated person with a detached attitude and an acceptance of the *dao* will react to any ups and downs in life with moderation. Strong emotions and abrupt behaviours are subdued (see also Bond, 1993).

These orientations are in sharp to contrast to the therapeutic goals of Western psychology which emphasize assertive coping. In the West, efforts are aimed at improving one's mastery skills and in changing the environment. Individuals will not accept things as they are, excelling and conquering if the environment is seen as oppressive or a hinderance to their autonomous longings. In gestalt therapy, the famous assertion is 'I do my thing, and you do your thing. I am not in this world to live up to your expectations and you are not in this world to live up to mine' (Perls, 1969). While both Chinese and Western cultures feel the need to address the problems of living, they espouse for their peoples different orientations and solutions: the former emphasizes collectivism in which a person has to accommodate to the requirements of the system through modification of his or her attitudes and behaviours, while the latter advocates individualism in which, if the two are in conflict, the requirements of the system are subordinate to the individual's fulfillment (Sakei and Borow, 1985).

The Eastern process of achieving moderation and liberation stresses effortful self-cultivation. Teachings are sometimes given in highly abstract and metaphoric terms. In particular, Zen Buddhist monks prefer to impart their teachings by way of koans and riddles, so that their disciples need to think for hours and days to find the answers for themselves. In this sense, Watts (1961) found the process similar to non-directive Rogerian therapy, in which the emphasis is also for the client to find his or her own answers to problems. The art of meditation is another form of self-cultivation, which strives to achieve an altered state of consciousness in which the practitioner can feel more in touch with nature or the *dao*.

For empirical scientists, the above description of the psychotherapeutic orientations of Confucianism, Buddhism, and Taoism is merely hypothetical. While there is no lack of anecdotes concerning men and women of moderation and liberation in history, no empirical data are available either to substantiate their claims or to analyse the process components of self-cultivation. Some data do support the usefulness of meditation as a form of relaxation (Benson, 1975). However, it is not clear whether this relaxation is arrived at through awareness of the *dao*, as is hypothesized by Taoist teachings. It is also unclear what kind of person seeks these kinds of enlightenment and liberation, and who benefits from them. Perhaps the requirement of self-deliberation restricts their appropriateness to people of education, as in the case of Rogerian non-directive therapy which grew out of and came of age on college campuses (Phares, 1992).

However, the prevalent influence of the doctrine of moderation is not to be overlooked. In a survey of attitudes in mainland China, it was rated as a key factor conducive to both physical and mental health (Wang, 1992). Other indigenous Chinese methods of psychotherapy, to be reviewed here, also incorporate this doctrine into their therapeutic regimes.

Psychotherapy by Chinese Medical Practitioners and Herbalists

Traditional Chinese medicine adopts a holistic orientation, in which physical and mental illnesses are not separately considered and in which both physical and psychological etiologies are considered relevant. The principle of the dynamic balancing of polar forces, conceptualized in terms of yin and yang, represents the cornerstone of health in Chinese medicine. If balance cannot be achieved, a situation of dysfunction will follow. In the psychological etiology of illnesses, excess and incongruence of seven kinds of emotions (happiness, anger, sadness, fear, love, hatred, and desire) are regarded as pathogenic (Lin, 1981). Since even positive emotions, such as happiness and love, are included in this list, it is clear that it is the excess, rather than the emotion *per se*, that is the source of the pathology. The remedy for this type of pathology is to balance the excess emotion with an opposing one, an approach that reflects the dominant Chinese value of moderation as described above.

Wu (1982) searched through records of Chinese medical practice and found interventions resembling those of Western psychotherapy. This Chinese method is action-oriented, involving little talk or explanation to the patients. No insight is cultivated, so the need for 'psychological-mindedness' seen in Western psychotherapy can be circumvented. The relationship between doctors and patients is asymmetrical; the former have the unquestioned authority. This form of relating corresponds to the authoritarian nature of social relationships in Chinese culture (Yang, 1993).

In actual practice, deception is sometimes involved. A depressed mood is elicited in a man by fabricating bad news about the health of his parents. This strategy is used to counter-balance the harmful effect of euphoria first evoked by his scholastic success. When a woman falls sick grieving for her deceased mother, a shaman is bribed to tell the woman that her mother, after death, has turned against her and incited her present illness. Upon hearing these remarks, the woman's illness is cured, as her grief turns into anger.

The case records, though intriguing and illustrative, must be viewed as hypothesis-generating at best, to be tested by more systematic research. The strategies are ingenious and the efficacy of the therapy seems magical. All these are reminiscent of the strategic family therapy practised in the West (Haley, 1973, 1976, 1984). In this connection, both forms of therapy arouse equal ethical concerns about their procedures of overt manipulation and reframing, which at times border on dishonesty.

Supernaturally Oriented Folk Psychotherapy

Tseng and McDermott (1975, 1981) traced the development of psychotherapy from supernaturally oriented healing practices, which include shamanism and divination, which are considered folk psychotherapy. Their procedures include such psychotherapeutic universals as inspiration of hope and faith (Calestro, 1972; Frank, 1968), availability of a warm, sensitive and concerned authoritative figure (Kraus, 1970; Lederer, 1959), identification of an explanation for the problems and a prescription for changes (Torrey, 1972; Tseng and McDermott, 1981), and provision of opportunities in the therapy sessions to behave, think and feel differently from day-to-day experience (Draguns, 1975).

In mainland China as recently as the early 1990s, despite shamanism being illegal, up to 70 per cent of rural residents are estimated to have consulted shamans at some point during an illness (Li and Phillips, 1990). Given that 75 per cent of China's population live in the countryside, this percentage represents a very large number of people.

The ability of shamans to put themselves into a trance has raised concerns among orthodox psychiatrists about the stability of their mental state. Furthermore, many Chinese shamans are original help-seekers who contacted senior shamans. Li and Phillips (1990) in mainland China, however, as well as Kleinman and Sung (1979) in Taiwan, failed to find any significant psychopathology in the shamans they studied. It appears that the magical acts of shamans cannot be readily dismissed as the disturbed behaviours of unstable persons.

Cultural considerations are also reflected in these supernaturally oriented healing methods. The Chinese shamans incorporate into their practices Confucian values of familism. Many mental disturbances are interpreted as interruptions caused by an ancestor's spirit (Li, 1972). Consequently, family-related therapeutic activities are prescribed to restore proper family functioning within the confines of Chinese cultural norms (Tseng, 1976, 1978).

However, the shamans are sensitive enough to give prescriptions in symbolic terms with supernatural references, so that the messages are conveyed subtly and acceptably to the clients (Kraus, 1970). In divination, the Chinese draw bamboo sticks which contain fortune-telling messages. These messages invariably reflect Chinese cultural values of moderation and accommodation (Hsu, 1976). They ask the client, for example, to be satisfied and resigned to the role he or she fills, to look forward to the future, to wait for improvement in his or her situation, and not to be aggressive or ambitious or to do things that are incompatible with his or her role and status.

The skilful blending of dominant cultural values into the advice of Chinese folk healing practices makes those practices uniquely appropriate and effective in the Chinese context (Kleinman and Gale, 1982; Kleinman and Sung, 1979). The rate of improved cases was found to be comparable to that treated by Western medicine (Kleinman and Gale, 1982). However, the validity of the comparison is weakened by the recognition that shamans and Western-trained doctors treat somewhat different groups of patients. In the shaman's case-load there is an excess of mild or short-lived (spontaneously remitting) sickness, chronic stable disorders, and somatization cases with depression, anxiety, and hysteria. It is plausible that the above diagnoses and problems are those with which the shamans are most effective. On the other hand, shamanism is often considered ineffective with chronic psychotic cases or severe medical problems (Kleinman and Sung, 1979; Tseng, 1978). Looked at in terms of socio-economic class, the patients of the shamans come predominantly from the lower-middle and lower classes (Kleinman and Gale, 1982; Kleinman and Sung, 1979; Li and Phillips, 1990; Tseng, 1976), similar to the background of their healers. This matching may not be coincidental. Evidence indicates that people of a similar lower-class background are likely to share common cultural beliefs in the supernatural. A shared world-view may partially account for the effectiveness of shamanism (Frank and Frank, 1991). This situation is analogous to that in the West, where most psychotherapists and their clients come from the same middle-class background and share the same values of self-improvement and autonomy embodied in Western psychotherapy.

Kleinman and Sung (1979) approached their study with a skepticism toward the reported efficacy of shamanism, and they questioned the long-term effects of therapeutic universals. The real issue of the client's inept adaptive skills had not been touched upon. However, it can be argued that the psychological support provided in shamanism may serve to mobilize the natural healing forces within a client (Prince, 1980), which in turn enhance his or her adaptive capability. In this sense, the shaman's clients are cured even with regard to their underlying difficulty. The debate on the efficacy of non-specific therapeutic universals underlines the need for long-term follow-up studies in which multiple outcome measures should be used, examining changes in both symptoms and other personal attributes.

Communist Psychotherapy in Mainland China

Mainland China, ruled by a communist government since 1949, has developed a form of psychotherapy, here termed 'communist psychotherapy', which is rooted in a mix of psychotherapeutic universals and the socio-political ideology of communism (Brammer, 1985; Ho, 1974; Karenga, 1978; Li, Xu, and Kuang, 1988; Lu, 1978; Sidel, 1973). First, mental illnesses are considered as reflective of undesirable social elements. In the social context of mainland China, the latter are the legacy left behind by the old political structure before communism took hold. Second, human beings are believed to be capable to excel and remould themselves through therapy. Third, the solutions and strategies for cure are collectively planned by doctors and patients together through 'heart-to-heart' talks in an atmosphere of comradeship. Fourth, therapeutic outcomes are defined in terms of the communist ideology, with self-interests being treated as subservient to those of the group. Fifth, education is seen to represent the primary therapeutic weapon, reinforced by group pressure.

A series of studies have claimed effectiveness for this communist psychotherapy with patients suffering from neurasthenia, chronic schizophrenia, and medical conditions like hypertension or gastric ulcers (Li et al., 1988). Recovery rates in some studies could reach as high as 80–90 per cent in follow-up examinations. Unfortunately, all of these studies have been published by Chinese professionals in rather obscure Chinese journals. In order to verify the results, we need replication studies conducted by independent researchers from a different socio-political culture.

Nonetheless, communist psychotherapy encompasses powerful psychotherapeutic universals. Patients are given definitive explanations of their illnesses that are grounded in the socio-political ideology of the country. The therapy process is construed as a form of self-struggle for the causes of the Communist revolution, generating a sense of 'revolutionary optimism' for the patients (Sidel, 1973). Emphasis on self-involvement leads to procedures like milieu therapy, in which the patient's independence and self-healing capacity are enhanced (Lu, 1978). There is also considerable group support at various levels of the society (Brammer, 1985; Lu, 1978).

However, there are concerns that communist psychotherapy is too closely intermingled with the socio-political culture of mainland China (Brammer, 1985). It is feared that it may be used as a medicalized agent for control of ideological deviance. This is not its problem alone. Psychotherapy in general is considered to be a moral enterprise which reinforces cultural norms and values that are to be met by the client (Draguns, 1981; Nichols and Schwartz, 1991). In fact, it may be argued that what matters most is the way in which the therapy is conducted: Do its practitioners have the ultimate objective of relieving psychological distress in the client? Is the client told explicitly about the values implicit in the therapy? Does the client have the final say as to whether he or she will go into therapy? If therapy is compulsory, what are the safeguards against the potential abuses of unnecessarily enforced changes? These are the ethical and procedural issues to be considered by psychotherapists of all orientations. The form of the therapy itself cannot determine the outcome of these decisions.

With the advent in 1978 of the open-door policy and the reform era in mainland China, there has been an upsurge of interest in Western psychotherapy, making it the standard-bearer of the therapeutic community (Zhong, 1991). This change reflects the overall modernization movement in present-day

China. The shift in the general socio-economical culture has altered ideas pertaining to psychotherapy. However, it is premature to treat communist psychotherapy as merely an historical occurrence. Mainland China remains a communist country, and communism remains the principal socio-political ideology taught in the schools and promulgated in all official media. It is difficult to believe that it has no influence, either overt or covert, on the goals and processes of psychotherapy, when therapists continue to assist their clients in adjusting to the norms and expectations of the society.

WESTERN PSYCHOTHERAPY WITH THE CHINESE

Applicability

The above review has clearly demonstrated the influence of culture on the designs, processes, and aims of indigenous Chinese psychotherapy. It further suggests a range of potent therapeutic universals across different practices. Differences between the Chinese and Western value systems have also been noted, pointing out that each shapes the way problems are construed in psychotherapy in that setting. While most Caucasians define their problems as intrapsychic and individual, most Chinese see theirs as social and relational (Lo, 1993). This finding raises the therapeutic question of whether a Western-trained psychotherapist will treat the relationship problems of a Chinese person by advocating autonomy and independence or accommodation to the system. In fact, conflict between Western and Chinese cultural values in these areas has been the source of psychological distress among many immigrant Chinese-Americans (Bourne, 1975; S. Sue and D. W. Sue, 1971). This being the case, would the imposition of Western psychotherapy produce an exacerbation of the original distress?

Similar cultural incompatibility also poses problems for the training of Chinese psychotherapists (Cheng, 1993). In the Chinese context, the therapist–patient relationship becomes characteristically Chinese: marked by benevolence mixed with omniscience. Transference issues tend to be ignored. Therapists tend to make authoritative decisions for their clients along cultural lines, and they do not aim at establishing or restoring the client's autonomy. All these practices are counter-productive if seen in terms of the goals of Western psychotherapy.

At the level of practice, Chinese clients in therapy exhibit difficulty in expressing their private thoughts and strong emotions (Lih and Lin, 1980; Tseng, 1975). Instead, complaints are often expressed in somatic terms (Cheung, 1987; Lin, 1982), reflecting either a lack of psychological sophistication, an excessive repression, or both of these dynamics (D. W. Sue and D. Sue, 1990). These behaviours run counter to the expectation of openness, introspection, and assertiveness valued in Western psychotherapy (Ching and Prosen, 1980; D. W. Sue and S. Sue, 1972).

Chinese clients also display a lower tolerance for ambiguity, a greater respect for authority, and a stronger preference for practical and immediate solutions to problems (D. W. Sue and Kirk, 1972; D. W. Sue and D. Sue, 1990; Vernon, 1982). They expect the therapy process to be directive and authoritarian (Arkoff, Thaver, and Elkind, 1966; Tan, 1967; Yuen and Tinsley, 1981). These considerations explain why the Chinese least prefer Rogerian non-directive therapy, opting instead for Ellis' directive style of rational–emotive therapy (Waxer, 1989). When asked to act as co-therapists with child therapists in the management of childhood problem behaviours, Chinese parents expect the intervention process to be similarly directive and authoritarian. They prefer to exercise their parental authority directly and to use physical punishment, which they consider to be more effective than non-directive techniques (Lieh-Mak, Lee, and Luk, 1984).

Empirical Studies

In a number of psychotherapy studies in the United States, it has been found that relatively fewer Asian-Americans (including those of Chinese descent) participate in therapy than do Caucasians; if they do participate, Asian-Americans have higher dropout rates, attend fewer sessions, and consider their therapy sessions less helpful and their therapists less competent (Lee and Mixson, 1985, quoted in Leong, 1986; S. Sue and McKinney, 1975). These findings are interpreted as indicative of a pattern of ineffective therapy with Asian-Americans, which results in the technique's unpopularity and poor reputation (Ching and Prosen, 1980; Kaneshige, 1973; D. W. Sue, 1977).

The above conclusion is not entirely negative. After all, Western psychotherapy has been developed to serve Caucasians, and it is thus expected to be more effective with members of that group. A series of case reports and pilot studies is slowly being accumulated that indicates the growing acceptance and applicability of Western psychotherapy in the Chinese communities of Hong Kong, Taiwan, Singapore, and mainland China. For example, in mainland China, clinics and agencies which offer psychological consultation and counselling have been set up in various cities and their popularity is well documented (Chu and Liu, 1991; Ji, Zhang, Zhu, and Yan, 1994; Ni, 1993; Su, Wang, Yan, Chu, Huang, and Huang, 1986; Zhang, Dong, Xu, Ao, Wang, and Gas, 1990; Zhao, Huang, Cai, and Zhang, 1986). While details of the case-loads differ in each context, there are some similarities. The help-seekers tend to be young and better-educated. There is no consistent gender difference. About half suffer from a diagnosable psychiatric disorder, mostly of the neurotic types. The others have interpersonal, marital, family, and health problems.

Studies on the efficacy of Western psychotherapy with Chinese are surprisingly broad-based. These include case reports and empirical studies on psychodynamic or insight-oriented therapy (Dai, 1993; Guo and Cheng, 1991; Jia, 1991; Ko, 1974; Muensterberger, 1984; Tung, 1991; Wu, 1992; Yang, 1983; Zhong, 1988, 1989), non-directive therapy (Cheng and Fan, 1976; Cheng and Lui, 1976; Cheng and Wu, 1977; Ko, 1974; Ng, 1983), behavioural techniques such as cognitive–behavioural therapy, behaviour modification, token economy, systematic desensitization, implosion therapy, thought-stopping, and aversive therapy, among others (Chen, 1991; Cheng, 1975; Cheng and Hsu, 1974; Dong, Li, Tian, and Wen, 1980; Fu, 1993; Huang, Xu, and Zhang, 1989; Leung, 1991; Li and Wang, 1994; Luk, Kwan, Hui, Bacon-Shone, Tsang, Leung, and Tang, 1991; Ong and Leng, 1979; Wang and Cao, 1993; Xu, 1991; Zhao,

Chen, and Yu, 1987; Zheng, 1982), group therapy (Chang, Huang, and Chen, 1993; Chen, 1974, 1984, 1993), family therapy (Chen, Yang, and Zuo, 1993; Gau and Chen, 1993; Ho, Chu, and Yeung, 1993; Kang, Li, and Xie, 1992; Lee, Chan, and Fu, 1993; Wong, 1988, 1990; Zhang, Wang, Li, and Phillips, 1994), and crisis intervention (Ji et al., 1994). Practice of more specialized forms of therapy, such as sex therapy, has also been reported (Li and Yan, 1990; Lieh-Mak and Ng, 1981; Ng, 1988). A review of the above publications leads to the following conclusions.

Efficacy

The reports on efficacy are consistently positive and impressive. Such optimistic results cover the whole range of therapeutic methods and psychiatric disorders, from psychodynamic to behavioural interventions as well as neurotic and psychotic disorders. For example, in some cases improvement rates reach as high as 62 per cent in the treatment of erectile dysfunction by cognitive–behavioural therapy (Li and Yan, 1990), 80–93 per cent in the treatment by family therapy of a wide variety of psychiatric disorders, including childhood problems, psychosomatic illnesses, schizophrenia, and depression (Ho et al., 1993; Chen et al., 1993); 79–87 per cent in the treatment by behavioural techniques of a range of neurotic disorders, such as obsessive–compulsive disorder, phobias, and anxiety disorders (Zhao et al., 1987; Huang et al., 1989), and 82 per cent in the treatment by crisis intervention of suicidal ideation (Ji et al., 1994).

However, caution must be exercised in interpreting these hefty figures. First, there may be publication bias. It is not unusual that positive results will tend to get published more easily than negative findings. Second, many of the studies are methodologically unsophisticated (see review of psychotherapy research methodologies by Kazdin, 1994), a point to be reviewed below. Nonetheless, despite these limitations, we cannot ignore the initial evidence that documentation exists to show the efficacy of the use of Western psychotherapy with Chinese clients.

Outcome criteria

Many studies, particularly those reporting on psychodynamic therapy, still rely on the therapist's opinion as the sole criterion to evaluate effectiveness. This is unsatisfactory in view of the possible personal bias of the therapist. Furthermore, the judgement tends to be global, lacking in specificity. It is preferrable to have multiple, standardized measures which provide perspectives from different sources, and which assess not only improvement in symptomatology but also changes in psychosocial adaptation. The latter is particularly important in a collectivist Chinese society, where the emphasis is on social harmony. Some recent studies have adopted this approach, using such standardized measures as the General Health Questionnaire, the Family Adaptation and Cohesion Evaluation Scales-II, the Minnesota Multiphasic Personality Inventory, and the Symptom Checklist–90, among others (Huang et al., 1989; Li and Yan, 1990; Luk et al., 1991).

Research design

Most of the research designs used are either in the form of single case reports or uncontrolled studies, rendering the interpretations to most findings provisional rather than definitive. Only recently are studies with control groups being reported (Chen, 1993; Ji et al., 1994; Kang et al., 1992; Leung, 1991; Luk et al., 1991; Zhang et al., 1994).

Side-effects

There is no study reporting the harmful side-effects of psychotherapy as applied to the Chinese. Studies in the West suggest a worsening of clinical conditions in about 8 per cent of patients (Lambert and Bergin, 1994). Attention to this neglected area will help to counter-balance the possible over-enthusiasm that would encourage indiscriminate practising of Western psychotherapy with Chinese clients.

Method variables

Almost all the studies of psychotherapy in Chinese contexts have been aimed at testing a single therapeutic method. Among the rare exceptions, one study compared the relative effectiveness of muscle relaxation versus aversive therapy (Cheng, 1975); another studied unstructured versus structured group therapy (Chen, 1993). The results indicate that no one method is consistently better than another. This conclusion also applies in the West (Frank and Frank, 1991). In consequence, researchers have begun looking for common therapeutic ingredients among various forms of psychotherapy (Lambert and Bergin, 1994).

Diagnosis variables

The differential effectiveness of a therapy with various diagnostic problems is seldom explored in studies with the Chinese. Even for those studies in which clients with different diagnoses are involved, data are not separately analysed (Chen et al., 1993; Zhao et al., 1987). One notable exception was a study in group therapy (Chen, 1993), which showed that problems of restlessness and truancy in children improved more from a non-directive form of group therapy. On the other hand, the same study indicated that lying did not show a significant improvement from either directive or non-directive group therapy. Another study (Luk et al., 1991) reported that depression benefitted most from cognitive–behavioural group therapy, while personality disorders benefitted the least.

Client variables

Only occasionally do client data enter into the analysis. Preliminary findings suggest that responders to psychotherapy are younger, better educated, more often successfully married with children, less psychosocially maladjusted, more enlightened about psychotherapy, and quicker in seeking help (Chen et al., 1993; Kang et al., 1992; Li and Yan, 1990; Luk et al., 1991).

Another set of client variables that demand more attention are those relating to help-seeking behaviour. While there are some reports on the demographic background of those seeking counselling, as noted above, their cognitive, emotional, and behavioural processes have not been fully explored. There is some work being done on the Chinese utilization of psychiatric care in general (Cheung, 1987; Cheung, Lau, and Wong, 1984) but, unfortunately, not of psychotherapy in particular.

Therapist variables

There is a general oversight in examining the attributes of the therapist as a potential variable mediating therapeutic outcomes. In those early studies where the effectiveness of psychotherapy with Chinese-Americans was questioned, many of the therapists involved were non-Chinese and did not speak Chinese (Cheng, 1993). It is conceivable that they lacked an understanding of Chinese culture or, even worse, that they might hold certain biased and stereotyped images of the Chinese that would lead to unnecessary misunderstandings. These therapist variables may be partially responsible for the unfavourable outcomes of earlier studies and should be fully explored (Leong, 1986). On the other hand, even when therapists involved are Chinese, no study has yet addressed the concern raised by Cheng (1993) about the potential conflict between therapists' personal values and those inherent in Western psychotherapy. Instead, throughout the studies under review, therapist variables are presumed to be constant and are not entered into the therapeutic formula.

Process variables

Psychotherapy research has been paying increasing attention to the actual processes occurring during a session. This trend is important because the practice of a form of therapy cannot automatically be assumed to be invariable among different therapists in a same study or across different studies (Glover, 1955). Recognition of this problem has prompted researchers to produce operationalized therapy manuals (Lambert and Ogles, 1988; Luborsky and DeRubeis, 1984), so that the processes of a therapy can be more readily standardized and adhered to.

In one study (Luk et al., 1991), a practice manual was written for the therapists conducting cognitive–behavioural therapy. However, no assessment was made to determine how far the practice of the therapy adhered to the written manual. It is still unclear what exactly happens during therapy sessions, and thus it has not been established what processes should account for their efficacy. Another study took a different approach and asked the clients to list the curative factors among therapeutic processes (Chang et al., 1993). In psychodrama, catharsis, an existential factor (responsibility), instillation of hope, and self-understanding were listed, while in group therapy, the curative factors listed were catharsis, interpersonal learning, identification, and altruism. In yet another ongoing study, Cheung and Cheng (1993) have attempted to code and relate an observer's ratings of the therapist's techniques to those of the patients' responses.

Unfortunately, empirical studies of the kind cited above are still relatively rare. Instead, there is a plethora of informed suggestions about how to adapt the processes of Western psychotherapy for the Chinese and address the noted concerns of cultural incompatibility (Cheng, 1991; Chua, 1993; Ho, 1987; Jung, 1984; Ng, 1983, 1985; D. W. Sue and D. Sue, 1990; S. Sue, 1993; S. Sue and Zane, 1987; Tsui and Schultz, 1985; Tung, 1984). Among the issues raised by these suggestions are the following: unfamiliarity with the format and goals of Western psychotherapy can be eliminated by explicit pre-therapy education (role-induction); given that 'passivity' or 'silence' is a cultural expression of the Chinese respect for authority, directive and structured discussion of the client's problem is more productive; in line with the Chinese expectation of the presence of an authority, the therapist should convey expertise and credibility while remaining benevolent; the therapist should model a higher level of personal disclosure and emotional expressiveness than that typical of his or her more reserved Chinese clients; difficulty in expressing anger and hostility can be handled within a framework of psychodynamic therapy by means of labelling negative feelings for the clients or encouraging projection; the therapist should be sensitive to issues of shame and guilt aroused by the considerable stigma attached to mental problems; the therapist should expect a longer time for Chinese clients to confide and should refrain from being too intrusive during initial sessions; resistance to non-directive procedures can be fruitfully interpreted for analytic understanding, leading to more personal disclosure; given the close-knit structure of Chinese families, the therapist may find the assistance of family members invaluable and should consider adopting such approaches as structural family therapy; there are, however, many reservations expressed concerning the use of paradoxical techniques in family therapy, because Chinese clients may not be sophisticated enough to attune to the subtle messages embodied in the paradoxical injunctions; the therapy should be time-limited, focused on concrete problems, and oriented to the present or future; each therapy session should offer some immediate benefits; and, finally, while the therapist may lead and direct the discussion, he or she should create a partnership with the client so that he or she feels involved in the decision process and responsible for any decision that comes out of the therapy.

The above are broad guidelines, but there are other more specific propositions that are also worth highlighting. S. Sue and D. W. Sue (1971) proposed a model of Chinese-American identity development, which was later expanded to become the Racial/Cultural Identity Development Model (Atkinson, Morten, and D. W. Sue, 1993; D. W. Sue and D. Sue, 1990). The model has been found to be useful in generating and depicting hypotheses pertaining to the acculturation processes of Chinese-Americans, the subsequent types of cultural conflicts during each stage of development, and the processes of effective therapy (D. W. Sue, 1993).

The application of psychoanalysis to Chinese clients has been viewed with much skepticism (Blowers, 1994). However, there has recently been a more favourable reception to its major tenets, including such concepts as the id, ego, and superego, as well as unconscious motivation, intrapsychic conflicts, childhood traumas, defense mechanisms, and the therapeutic use of insights (Hu, 1993; Ng, 1983, 1985; Zhong, 1988). The structure of psychoanalysis is not seriously disputed. Instead, disagreement centres around its contents. The excessive reference in orthodox psychoanalysis to sexual conflicts during childhood has been challenged. Childhood traumas in various spheres of life are now to be included as origins of future psychological problems (Zhong, 1988). For example, Hu (1993) has suggested that the Oedipus complex in Chinese people is more concerned with a power struggle than with sexual desire. Chinese analysts are generally well aware of the taboo surrounding sex in Chinese culture and of the resistance its discussion generates. In the therapeutic context, discussion of sex will be obstinately resisted. Furthermore, under the Chinese authoritarian tradition, power issues are more easily understandable as causes of concerns and conflicts.

In the same vein, cultural authoritarianism has also led some Chinese analysts to take a directive approach in psychoanalysis. These analysts explicitly educate their clients about psychoanalysis, and they offer direct interpretations so that insights can be quickly secured and the number of sessions substantively reduced (see, for example, Zhong, 1988). This approach, however, has been criticized for being too rational and educational, leaving the emotional side of the client's experience neglected (Tung, 1991). Nonetheless, Zhong (1988) and others have gradually formulated a Chinese style of psychoanalysis that deserves to be further explored clinically and tested empirically. Guiding such proposed adaptations in Western psychotherapy are the presumed conventions of Chinese culture. Their aim is to make therapy culturally relevant to the Chinese (S. Sue, 1993).

Individualistic versus collectivist outcomes

As noted above, one important concern about the applicability of Western psychotherapy to Chinese culture has been with the value incompatibility between individualism and collectivism. The literature indicates, however, that there are case reports with Chinese clients in which individualism prevails over collectivism. For example, Tung (1991) reported a Chinese man whose year-long depression was lifted when he finally resigned from his successful engineering job, a vocation forced upon him by his family. The man left for another country in pursuit of his own interests. This is a clear example of defiance to the cultural value of filial piety and a striving toward the kind of autonomy and independence implicit in the individualism of Western psychotherapy. In another case (Lo, 1993), a Chinese woman, on the brink of suicide due to the excessive demands of her parents, was helped to assert her autonomy and to say no to them.

Not all favourable outcomes involve achieving autonomy and independence. Tung (1991) has reported another case in which the depression of a Chinese man was lifted abruptly when he decided to stay on with his family business. In retrospect, he admitted that his flirtation with independence from the family was the cause of his depression. In another case (Leung and Sung, 1992), a Chinese woman suffered from a severe low back pain associated with sexual guilt. Her problem was strategically treated by an emphasis on fulfilling her role in the family as wife and mother, a therapeutic prescription in congruence with the traditional family values held by herself and her husband. In both cases, the favourable outcomes represent a return to the familism of collectivist Chinese culture (Yang, 1993).

What is unclear from these case descriptions are the considerations involved in deciding when the therapy should strive for autonomy and when it should instead counsel for adherence to prescribed roles. Leung and Sung (1992) indicate that their therapeutic move was guided by their perception of the traditional family values held by their client and her husband. Is it then the client's degree of exposure to Western values which governs the choice of therapy goals? In other words, as some Chinese are becoming more Westernized in their values (Yang, 1986 and this volume), it may be that the individualistic tendency implicit in Western psychotherapy will generate acceptable solutions. However, for those Chinese still harbouring traditional values, an orientation towards collectivist goals is needed. The above proposition is a re-assertion of the relationship between culture and psychotherapy, punctuated by the client's value orientations.

Summary

The ultimate question in psychotherapy research is usually cited as 'What treatment, by whom, is most effective for this individual with this specific problem, under this set of circumstances?' (Paul, 1967, p. 111). In other words, what is the differential effectiveness of various kinds of psychotherapy in relation to the therapist's and client's attributes, problem categories, and process components? By this standard, most psychotherapy research with Chinese, plagued by unsophisticated research methodology, has only been capable of answering the preliminary question, 'Does psychotherapy produce beneficial changes?' Only a handful of studies displays a more mature methodology. As noted above, there is no shortage of suggestions for how to adapt Western psychotherapy to the Chinese context, but better-designed studies are needed to validate these propositions.

PSYCHOTHERAPY WITH THE CHINESE: THE WAY AHEAD

Most forms of therapy, whether indigenous or Western, claim a fair degree of 'therapeutic success' with the Chinese. Unfortunately, as noted above, unsophisticated research methodology renders those claims of efficacy provisional. Thus, the differential effectiveness of indigenous Chinese versus Western psychotherapy cannot be ascertained. Nonetheless, by contrast with its Western counterpart, indigenous Chinese psychotherapy is a virtually undeveloped empirical discipline. Much work is needed to further document, articulate, and validate the processes and outcomes of its various forms.

Among indigenous Chinese and Western psychotherapies, a wide variety of therapy styles exists, ranging from directive to non-directive procedures, from individualistic to collectivist orientations. The availability of a multitude of diverse but effective therapies is not a phenomenon exclusive to the Chinese. In fact, this is a replica of what has long been a matter of concern for psychotherapy researchers in the West. This debate has led researchers, such as Frank and Frank (1991), to suggest that there are in fact more similarities than differences among superficially diverse forms of psychotherapy. All share common therapeutic universals which account for their effectiveness. The issue is to determine what are the percentages of variance in the therapy out-comes that such universals can account for, and what are the percentages left behind for the other variables to further explain. In relation to the focus of this chapter, how the therapist's and client's cultural orientations affect the choice and success of a therapy will be of particular interest.

The availability of a multitude of diverse therapies may be necessary for modern-day, pluralistic cultures. At the beginning of this chapter, we warned against the assumption of a unified Chinese culture. Instead, it apears that there exists a range of subcultures in terms of education, gender, geographic loca-tion, and economic activities. Given this diversity, it is helpful to remember Pederson's (1978) remark that the practice of all psychotherapy is essentially cross-cultural, given the proliferation of subcultures even within one culture. A multitude of diverse therapies must be developed to cater to the expectations and needs of people from various cultures and subcultures.

As the world gets smaller due to improved communication and transport networks, all cultures will become even more pluralistic, with a range of indigenous and imported cultures and subcultures. Yang (1986, this volume) has documented rapid changes in Taiwan's sociocultural climate. These lead to constant shifts in the cultural make-up of the group of people we collective-ly call 'Chinese'. The end result will be a steady development of a multitude of therapies to meet these changes. Examination of these developments will become an important topic for researchers in the field of culture and psy-chotherapy.

Unfortunately, in many of the studies discussed above, culture is adopted only as a *post hoc*, explanatory variable to account for certain preferences and successes in therapy with the Chinese. Those propositions pertaining to the relationship between culture and psychotherapy have not been empirically tested. In particular, research on this area is impeded by the relative lack of appropriate theoretical constructs and empirical measures to disentangle and categorize such a complex phenomenon as culture (Draguns, 1990). Only a handful of constructs and measures are available, including such formulations as Chinese traditionality versus modernity (Hchu and Yang, 1972; Yang and Hchu, 1974), or the referential versus the indexical self (Landrine, 1992; Markus and Kitayama, 1991). A more comprehensive nosology of culture can be derived from the four cultural dimensions identified by Hofstede (1980)(see also Bond, this volume). Various propositions have been offered pertaining to the relationship between these cultural dimensions and therapeutic processes (for details, see Draguns, 1990). With the availability of these constructs and their empirical measures, culture as a planned variable can be entered into the psychotherapy research equation alongside other variables pertaining to clients, therapists, diagnoses, and process components. This improved research methodology may eventually move us towards better addressing the differential effectiveness of various forms of psychotherapy in the light of the therapist's and client's cultural backgrounds. Of course, the research may ulti-mately demonstrate the universality of human maladjustment and its remedies, despite cultural variations.

Psychotherapy research with the Chinese is a subset of this broader effort in addressing the kinds of relationship between psychotherapy and culture in general. The Chinese cultural context, with its huge diversity and rapid changes, is providing a natural laboratory for this type of research.

Chapter 30

Chinese Adaptation to Foreign Cultures

Kenneth L. Dion and Karen K. Dion

Chinese who have emigrated to other countries were estimated to number between 27 and 28 million people in the 1980s—more than the entire population of Canada and twice that of Australia or the Netherlands (Poston and Yu, 1990). Outside of China itself, Chinese people can be found in virtually every country in the world, constituting a majority in several and a significant minority in many others.

Given the wide distribution of Chinese people throughout the world, the issue of Chinese adaptation to foreign countries is important, for the success and welfare of both the emigrants themselves as well as the host societies. This chapter focuses primarily on Chinese adaptation to countries where English is the primary language, as the available social science literature mostly deals with that case. The chapter is organized into six major sections: discussion of the conceptual and operational definitions of assimilation and acculturation, of Chinese sojourners, of correlates of immigrant status and acculturation, of English as a second language and its modes of assimilation, of the comparative assimilation of Chinese in different societies, and, finally, of Chinese families and cultural adaptation in Westernized societies.

Each section provides a unique, informative perspective on Chinese adaptation to foreign countries. The first section, for example, provides definitions of the terms 'assimilation' and 'acculturation' offered by central theorists and illustrates how acculturation at the individual level (that is, the 'psychological acculturation') of Chinese and others has been (or can be) assessed by social scientists. The second section shows clearly that even living in another country temporarily has evident social-psychological consequences for Chinese 'sojourners'. The third explores the psychological correlates, especially for adjustment, of Chinese immigrants to other countries. For Chinese in English-speaking countries, the immigrants' ability and confidence in the English language is an important determinant of several facets of their adaptation, which provides the focus of the fourth section. As indicated by its title, the fifth section compares assimilation of Chinese within and between different societies. Finally, the sixth section illustrates the importance of the family in the adaptation of Chinese to foreign countries.

ASSIMILATION AND ACCULTURATION: CONCEPTUAL AND OPERATIONAL DEFINITIONS

Conceptual Models

When applied to an immigrant or sojourner to another society, the term 'assimilation' refers to the process of adopting the customs, behaviours, and/or national or collective identity of the host society in preference to, or in place of, those of one's country of origin. Specifically, the concept of assimilation implies that the collective identity, customs, and behaviours acquired in the host society replace those from one's country of origin. American sociologist Milton Gordon (1971) proposed a classic, conceptual model of assimilation in American society that has been influential among social scientists in the West and has been relied upon by several investigators whose research is discussed below.

Gordon's assimilation model

Gordon's (1971) model of assimilation described seven 'variables', or types of assimilation, in order to analyse the assimilation process in a society such as the United States with reference to different 'goal systems' or 'ideal types' (in the Weberian sense), such as the 'melting pot', cultural pluralism, or adaptation to a core society and culture, and to compare different racial, ethnic, religious, and immigrant groups as regards the nature and extent of their incorporation into the society. The model can also be employed as a conceptual framework for devising measures to assess individual differences among members of a given group, such as the Chinese, in regard to different types of assimilation in a given society (see Wong and Cochrane, 1989, on Chinese in Britain).

The seven types of assimilation, with alternate labels (when available) in parentheses are: (1) cultural or behavioural assimilation (also known as acculturation), the adoption of cultural patterns characteristic of the 'core group' or host society; structural assimilation, signifying entrance into the primary group relationships, such as clubs, cliques, and institutions, of the host society; identificational assimilation, the taking of one's sense of 'peoplehood' or collective identity from the host society; marital assimilation (also known as 'amalgamation'), demonstrated by large-scale inter-marriage; attitude-receptional assimilation, characterized by an absence of prejudice; behaviour-receptional assimilation, shown by an absence of discrimination; and civic assimilation, marked by an absence of value and power conflict between or among groups. Each type of assimilation can vary in degree.

Gordon (1971) proposed that cultural-behavioural assimilation (for example, acquiring English language skills and/or behaviour patterns typical of the host society) is the first type to occur once members of an immigrant group arrive in a host society. Acculturation, however, does not necessarily guarantee that any other form of assimilation will occur. By contrast, he saw structural assimilation as very likely to induce all the other forms of assimilation (except for acculturation, which presumably occurred prior to structural assimilation), once it had taken place.

Berry's cross-cultural model of acculturation

Kim and Berry (1986) criticized Gordon's model of assimilation for being 'unicultural' and for assuming a 'linear process of assimilation' whose end goal is the acculturating group's absorption into the dominant, host society. To be sure, Gordon's assimilation model focused on the United States, whose ethic of incorporating immigrants has primarily been that of 'melting' or 'transmuting' the new arrivals into the larger society. By contrast, Berry (1980) has conceptualized a two-dimensional model of acculturation for pluralistic societies with four different options that can result from answering two separate questions either affirmatively or negatively: Is it desirable to maintain one's heritage culture? Is it desirable to maintain positive relations with other groups in the society? Affirmative answers to both questions define the *integration* mode of acculturation. The combination of an affirmative response to the second question and a negative response to the first question describes the *assimilation* mode. The *separation* mode is identified by a combination of a positive response to the first question and a negative answer to the second question. Finally, negative answers to both questions indicate *marginalization*. In Berry's (1980) model of acculturation, then, individuals and groups can adopt several alternative attitudes or orientations to their heritage and host cultures.

To summarize, Gordon's (1971) model of assimilation remains useful for conceptualizing different types of assimilation in a given society and for asking how these different types may relate to one another. However, it is a 'linear' model implicitly, if not explicitly, assuming absorption of immigrant and ethnic groups into the core, dominant society to be the ideal or norm. More recent theories of acculturation proposed by psychologists in the past 10 or 15 years have been 'multiple option' perspectives, assuming that individuals and groups, respectively, have several different orientations or choices regarding maintenance of their heritage culture and contact with other groups. While Berry's (1980) cross-cultural model is one of several multiple option perspectives (see also LaFromboise, Coleman, and Gerton, 1993; Sayegh and Lasry, 1993), it is certainly the most influential one and perhaps the most prominent conceptualization of acculturation in the social science literature today.

Measuring Assimilation and Acculturation

Categories of acculturation.

Researchers interested in Chinese adaptation to foreign cultures have taken several tacks for measuring a respondent's level of assimilation or acculturation to a host society and for comparing groups putatively varying in their acculturation. The most frequent approach has been to rely either upon demographic indicators (for example, length of time in the country of residence, location and years of schooling, age at time of immigration, or generational status in the country) or to compare groups of respondents varying in immigrant status (for example, China- or Hong Kong-born Chinese versus native-born Chinese or native-born members of other ethnic groups), length of immigration (recent versus long-term immigrants), and generational status (first-generation versus second-generation).

Unfortunately, such demographic indicators are not entirely satisfactory or sufficient, in that they probably reflect individual differences in the nature and extent of respondents' psychological acculturation only indirectly and crudely. For example, a Chinese person could have lived much of her or his adult life in the Chinatown of a foreign country's major city and yet be minimally accultur-ated or assimilated to that country. Similarly, demographic indicators such as length of residence or generational status are inevitably confounded with other important variables that can serve as potential rival explanations of any obtained relationships between them and adaptation. Length of residence, for example, is often confounded with citizenship status, and generational status with occupation and education. Fortunately, several measures of psychologi-cal acculturation relevant for Chinese (and other Asian) respondents in the United States (and other countries) currently exist, although they vary in appar-ent adequacy and need further validation.

Measures of Psychological Acculturation

The Suinn-Lew Asian Self-Identity Acculturation Scale

Richard Suinn and his colleagues developed a 21-item measure of accultura-tion, entitled the Suinn-Lew Asian Self-Identity Acculturation (SL-ASIA) scale, which was intended for use with respondents of East Asian background (Chinese, Japanese, and Korean, among others) in the United States (although most of its items are adaptable to other countries)(Suinn, Ahuna, and Khoo, 1992; Suinn, Rickard-Figueroa, Lew, and Vigil, 1987). Its items assess the respondent's reported language abilities and preferences, ethnic self-identity, friendship choices, food preferences, generational status and migration histo-ry, cultural and entertainment preferences, and reported ethnic interactions. Principal component analysis with oblique rotation has indicated that linguis-tic and entertainment preferences account for the majority of the variance (Suinn et al., 1992). Most items incorporate five response options, and all items are keyed in the same 'acculturation' direction. The 21 items are summed together and divided by the number of items to yield a single value from 1 to 5, with higher scores taken as reflecting greater acculturation.

The SL-ASIA scale has yielded good evidence of internal consistency relia-bility (coefficient alphas of .86 or better) with samples of students of Asian eth-nic backgrounds at several universities in the west and midwest of the United States (Atkinson and Gim, 1989; Suinn et al., 1987, 1992; Tata and Leong, 1994). There is also some evidence from these studies of concurrent validity from obtained relationships between SL-ASIA scores and 'criterion' demographic indicators (generational status, years of residence in the United States, English as a first language) or ethnic self-identity categorizations, taken either from the scale itself or measured separately. For example, the greater the number of previous family generations in the United States, the higher was the students' SDL-SIA score (indicating greater acculturation). Similarly, Asian-identified respondents scored lower on the SL-ASIA scale than Western-identified ones.

The SL-ASIA scale has apparent deficiencies as a measure of psychological acculturation. For example, using SL-ASIA scores to define levels of acculturation, as several researchers have done at the recommendation of Suinn and his associates, seems unwise. According to Suinn et al. (1987), the summed and averaged SL-ASIA scores can be taken as indexing three acculturation categories, such that scores of 1, 3, and 5 signify 'Asian identified', 'Bicultural', and 'Western-identified' groups of respondents, respectively. However, as with any summated rating scale, SL-ASIA scores can lack unique meaning. In particular, an average mid-range score of 3 can be attained in a variety of ways (as by strong endorsement of high acculturation options on some items and low acculturation options on other items versus an endorsement of the middle option throughout) that do not always reflect biculturality. Also, the frequency distribution of low, middle, and high acculturation categories from SL-ASIA scores can apparently differ considerably across studies conducted in different geographic regions in the United States (Tata and Leong, 1994). One way to avoid problems with categorizing acculturation levels from SL-ASIA scores is to rely instead on the continuous summary scores resulting from the scale (Tata and Leong, 1994), which has the added benefit of using more of the information inherent in the scale scores than do qualitative categories.

Another problem is the scoring rationale underlying the several ethnic self-identity items, whose scoring and response options are (from 1 to 5): Oriental, Asian, Asian-American, Chinese-American (Japanese-American and Korean-American are also listed), and American. Why is 'Oriental'—a racially oriented and perhaps dated term historically used by some Westerners for referring to 'yellow-skinned' people from the East—indicative of less acculturation than, say, 'Asian'? Similarly, why is 'Asian-American' presumed to reflect less acculturation than is 'Chinese-American'? These problems are probably an inadvertent result of attempting to create a generic 'Asian' identification scale. It may be better to tailor the ethnic self-identity items to specific Asian groups (for example, using 'Chinese' instead of 'Oriental' with respondents of Chinese ethnicity) whenever possible.

The Majority–Minority Relations Survey

In contrast to the unidimensional SL-ASIA scale, Sodowsky, Lai, and Plake (1991) have developed a 43-item multidimensional scale, called the Majority–Minority Relations Survey (MMRS), for assessing the 'acculturation attitudes' of members of American ethnic groups. They administered the MMRS to two groups, Hispanic-Americans and Asian-Americans (including Chinese-Americans), at the University of Nebraska. The instrument yields three factor-based sub-scales—perceived prejudice, acculturation, and language usage—each with acceptable reliabilities. The acculturation sub-scale has 16 items aimed at assessing the respondent's acceptance of American culture and American people. Asian-Americans perceived more prejudice toward them and scored as less acculturated than did Hispanic-Americans. Among Asian-Americans, Vietnamese-Americans were less acculturated than either Japanese-Americans or Korean-Americans, while Chinese-Americans did not differ in acculturation from Japanese-Americans, Korean-Americans, or Asians from the Indian subcontinent. First-generation respondents perceived more prejudice, were less acculturated, and were less likely to use English than were other respondents. Moreover, immigration status was found to be a moderator of acculturation, in that political refugees were less acculturated than were voluntary immigrants. Thus, the MMRS may appeal to researchers interested in assessing acculturation in relation to perceived prejudice and language skills.

Acculturation attitudes

Suinn et al. (1987) has claimed that no 'objective measures' of acculturation usable with Asian-American respondents existed prior to the SL-ASIA scale, which is not, strictly speaking, correct. From 1970 to the present, Canadian cross-cultural psychologist John Berry and his colleagues have reported studies with measures of acculturation attitudes relating to his two dimensional, four-fold typology described above (integration, assimilation, separation, and marginalization). This research has included several aboriginal groups in Australia and multiple samples of 'first nations' peoples (that is, Amerindian respondents) in Canada, as well as a variety of different ethnic groups in Canada: French-Canadians, Portuguese-Canadians, Hungarian-Canadians, and Korean-Canadians (see Berry, Kim, Power, Young, and Bujaki, 1989; Kim and Berry, 1986). Yet other studies have used these measures with Koreans in the process of emigrating to Canada and with non-emigrating Koreans (Kim, 1988) and ethnic Chinese students at the University of Ottawa (Noels, Clement, and Pon, 1992).

While the acculturation attitudes measure is broadly applicable for use with a wide variety of groups in pluralistic societies, tailoring the scales to specific ethnic groups and the particular cultural context is usually required (see Berry et al., 1989). Scale development proceeds by first defining the acculturation issues of concern or interest to the group in a given country and then formulating four statements for each issue that expresses the sentiment of the different acculturation attitudes. For example, in Kim and Berry's (1986) study of Korean-Canadians in Toronto, examples of issues were friendship and Canadian society, respectively. Finally, judges familiar with the underlying theoretical scheme gauge the adequacy of item construction, with high interjudge agreement used as a selection mechanism for constituting the final research instrument.

Internal consistency reliabilities for the four acculturation attitude scales have generally been adequate (coefficient alphas between 0.70 and 0.75), although in some cases this has required deleting items with poor item-total correlations (Berry et al., 1989). The study with Chinese respondents in Canada yielded poor reliability for the acculturation attitudes measures because only a few items defined each scale (Noels et al., 1992). Berry et al. (1989) have also reported considerable evidence of validity for the acculturation attitudes scales, by showing relationships between acculturation attitude scale scores and 'known groups' criteria (for example, membership in ethnic organizations, ethnic identification, language preference, and ethnic newspaper readership) as well as outcome criteria, such as adjustment and acculturative stress. Interscale relationships (for example, negative correlations between assimilation and separation) have also generally conformed to theoretical expectations.

The acculturation attitudes measures assume that members of the same ethnic or immigrant group may experience acculturation in a given society quite differently and with different psychological consequences (Berry et al., 1989). Berry and his colleagues also suggested that they can be profitably used to assess acculturation over time and across generations and to reveal the acculturation issues of particular concern to a given group at different points in time. For example, Kim and Berry (1986) found that the integration option received considerably greater acceptance among Korean-Canadians in Toronto than did the other three acculturation options, which they took as suggesting that the relationship of Korean-Canadians to other Canadians was an overriding issue to that community at that time.

In sum, the acculturation attitudes measure developed by Berry and his associates appears promising for future studies of Chinese adaptation to foreign countries. In Noels et al.'s (1992) study of Chinese university students in Canada, despite disappointing scale reliabilities, theoretically predicted relationships between acculturation attitudes and adjustment measures were nevertheless found (for example, integration scores correlated positively with self-esteem and sense of personal control). If attention is given to defining an appropriate number of issues (for example, between 15 and 20), this measure should prove useful and informative in studies of the psychological acculturation of Chinese in foreign countries.

CHINESE SOJOURNERS

Sojourners live in another culture for a period of time, with the initial, continuous intention of returning to their native land. Chinese sojourners have usually been migrant labourers or students obtaining their education abroad. Psychological research has focused on Chinese university students, especially those studying in the United States or Canada. Sojourning students attending a foreign university have to adapt to a different culture and the stresses of acculturation, in addition to the usual demands of student life. Accordingly, research by psychologists has usually focused on sojourner adjustment and the acculturative stresses confronted by sojourning students while studying in a foreign culture.

Chinese Sojourner Students in the United States

Yung Wing graduated from Yale in 1854, becoming the first Chinese to receive an American undergraduate degree (Bourne, 1975). Upon returning to China, he created an organization to select promising Chinese students for education in the United States, in order to help China modernize. In nineteenth- and early twentieth-century China, an American degree virtually guaranteed an 'iron rice bowl' in the upper ranks of China's socio-political structure. For a century afterwards, Chinese students, whether born in China or the United States, comprised a unique 'minority group' in American universities, one who assiduously resisted assimilation to American culture (Bourne, 1975).

Bourne (1975) reviewed the history of the Chinese student in America and discussed the stresses and psychological problems among Chinese students, in an American university on the west coast, whom he encountered as a psychiatrist in the late 1960s. Then as now (see Dion and Toner, 1988; Pak, Dion, and Dion, 1991), Chinese students felt strong parental pressures to achieve academic excellence and also had a strong sense of being racially discriminated against by majority group members. Other problem areas included interracial dating and maintaining one's Chinese identity in an assimilationist, cultural environment. In a related review of sojourner adjustment literature, Church (1982) noted that students from the Far East experienced the greatest social isolation and most serious adjustment problems among foreign students on American university campuses and also were the least travelled, with the least previous cross-cultural experience.

In addition, some studies focused on the acculturative and stresses for Chinese students on American university campuses. Kang (1972) surveyed Chinese students at the University of Minnesota and found that those who anglicized their names were more acculturated into American society in several regards (more likely to associate with Americans, join non-Chinese student organizations, be familiar with American magazines, and acculturate to American tastes and values) than were those who did not change their Chinese names. For a Chinese, anglicizing one's name was a correlate and possible harbinger of assimilation.

A five-year study by Graham (1983) focused on acculturative stresses in students from nine cultural groups: Polynesian, Asian, and American students on the Hawaii campus of Brigham Young University. In this multicultural, sectarian university setting, Hong Kong Chinese students reported feeling the most exclusion and had the greatest difficulty with Samoan students, owing to opposing cultural norms regarding interpersonal behaviour. However, Chinese students were the most successful academically of the different cultural groups because they gave schoolwork precedence over attending to their personal problems (for example, homesickness, cultural misunderstandings, and financial pressures). Of acculturative stress factors affecting the Chinese and other Asian students, problems with English-language proficiency created the greatest perceived difficulty.

Chinese Sojourners in Canadian Universities

Several studies of Chinese sojourners in Canadian universities have also been reported. Dyal and Chan (1985) found several interesting gender X culture interactions on reported stress and distress that still await fuller explanation. Using the Langner (1962) scale, they compared samples of Chinese students at the University of Hong Kong with Hong Kong Chinese sojourners and 'Euro-Canadian' students at the University of Waterloo (in Ontario) on somatic symptoms of distress and the frequency and impact of stressful life events. Chinese women, whether at the University of Hong Kong or as sojourners in Canada, reported more distress symptoms than did Canadian females or Chinese men. Further, frequency of distress symptoms was differentially related to other dimensions for these student groups. Most notably, the perceived impact of stressful life events correlated positively with distress symptoms for Canadian female students but negatively for Chinese female sojourners. For the latter, the greater the perceived impact of stressful life events, the fewer the somatic distress symptoms reported. Such findings led Dyal and Chan (1985, p. 447) to conclude, 'Female [Hong Kong Chinese] sojourners appear to have a different stress-symptom structure than [do] male sojourners or female Chinese at the University of Hong Kong.'

Similarly, Chataway and Berry (1989) compared stress, anxiety, coping, and appraisal measures for three student groups—Hong Kong Chinese, French-Canadian, and English-Canadian—attending Queen's University in Kingston, Ontario. Chinese sojourner students reported higher trait anxiety, greater racial prejudice toward them, more communication difficulties, more problems with adaptation, and scored higher on an acculturative stress measure, the Cawte (1972) scale, than did native-born, French-Canadian, or English-Canadian students. For Chinese sojourners, perceived social support from friends was the only dimension (of those measured) predictive of lower acculturative stress (ethnicity of friends was unspecified).

Zheng and Berry (1991) extended the preceding research by, first, including additional groups of Chinese university students and scholars (for example, mainland Chinese, Chinese immigrants to Canada, and Chinese-Canadians) and, second, performing a longitudinal study of one group of sojourners whose adaptation was assessed before leaving mainland China and several times after arriving in Canada. Acculturative stress (as Cawte scale scores) increased from pre-departure up to 3–4 months post-arrival and declined slowly for several years thereafter to the pre-departure baseline, forming an inverted U-curve function. Apart from acculturative stress, Chinese sojourners also experienced more problems generally than did either Chinese-Canadian or non-Chinese Canadian students.

The emerging picture for Chinese student sojourners is troubling but consistent. Whether from mainland China or Hong Kong, Chinese students sojourning in US or Canadian universities confront powerful acculturative stresses and challenges in adapting to these cultures with different, if not opposing, values and customs. These acculturative stresses add to other personal and life stresses associated with the university student role, confronting Chinese sojourner students with formidable personal challenges, and making their considerable educational attainments in foreign universities all the more remarkable.

CORRELATES OF IMMIGRANT STATUS AND ACCULTURATION

Researchers in Britain, Canada, and the United States have investigated the psychological correlates of immigrant status, especially adjustment, for Chinese and other East Asian immigrant groups. They have explored different aspects of immigrant status by comparing foreign-born Chinese versus native-born Chinese and/or Caucasians, Chinese immigrants whose length of residence in the host society has varied (for example, recent versus longer-term immigrants), and/or first-generation (for example, Hong Kong- or China-born who emigrated as adults) versus second-generation Chinese (born in the host society or emigrated to it as a child with their parents).

In this research, observed differences in adjustment correlated or associated with Chinese and Asian immigrant status have usually been attributed to acculturation processes by researchers. Unfortunately, acculturation has usually been inferred rather than directly measured. Nevertheless, some evidence suggests a relation between Chinese immigrant status and acculturation in the host society, in the case of immigrant generational status. Specifically, in a study of British Chinese (Wong and Cochrane, 1989), and another of Asian-American (including Chinese) respondents (Sodowsky et al., 1991), first-generation immigrants were found to be less acculturated to the host society than were members of the second generation, using different measures of acculturation, including the SL-ASIA scale (Suinn et al., 1987, 1992) and measures of Gordon's (1971) types of assimilation.

Research on the relation of Chinese (and other Asian) immigrant status to adaptation and other psychological correlates is presented below. The first section presents the correlates of generational status in recent studies of British Chinese. Next, correlates of Chinese immigrant status in the United States and Canada are considered, separately for community and student respondents. Finally, we explore the link between acculturation and counselling for Chinese-American and other Asian-American university students.

Correlates of Generational Status for Chinese in Britain

Chinese constitute a relatively large ethnic minority group in Britain, most having come from Hong Kong. Two studies (Wong and Cochrane, 1989; Furnham and Li, 1993) have explored differences between first-generation (those born in Hong Kong and having immigrated to Britain as young adults or older) and second-generation (British-born or immigrated to Britain as a child) Chinese on measures of psychological adjustment (the Langner inventory of stress symptoms), with community-based samples of 75–80 individuals from several cities in the United Kingdom. Using standard cutoff scores to index psychological maladjustment, both studies indicated that British Chinese were well-adjusted overall, with lower percentages of maladjustment than were demonstrated by native-born English or by several other immigrant groups in the United Kingdom.

On other measures, however, the two studies yielded discrepant findings or explored different correlates of immigrant generational status. Wang and Cochrane (1989) found no generational differences in psychological adjustment. By contrast, Furnham and Li (1993) found a higher incidence of psychological symptomatology in first- than in second-generation Chinese, as well as a different pattern of correlates for mental health in the two generations. They also found that English-language proficiency and personal expectations were correlated with psychological well-being, especially in the second generation. In Wang and Cochrane's study, second-generation Chinese scored higher on several types of assimilation measures.

Generational status, however, was to some extent confounded with occupation in both studies: that is, first-generation respondents predominantly worked in the 'catering trade' (predominantly Chinese restaurants), while the majority of second-generation respondents were students. Thus, effects attributed to Chinese generational status in this research may instead be partly or wholly due to occupation and associated differences. Although perhaps unavoidable in correlational studies with Chinese immigrant communities, such possible confounds must still be kept in mind when interpreting results as potential alternative explanations of generational and immigrant status.

Correlates of Immigrant Status: Community Respondents

Several studies in the United States and Canada have explored depression as a correlate of immigrant status for Chinese and other immigrant groups. The Center for Epidemiological Studies Depression Scale (CES-D)(Radloff, 1977), a 20-item measure developed for use in community research, was one test used to gauge the extent of depression.

Comparisons of foreign-born and native-born Chinese have not always led to the same or even clear conclusions. Kuo (1984) investigated four Asian-American groups in the Seattle area: Chinese, Japanese, Koreans, and Filipinos. By contrast to the other three Asian-American groups, foreign-born Chinese scored lower in depression than did American-born Chinese. However, Ying's (1988) study of Chinese-Americans in San Francisco showed the opposite finding, that US-born respondents scored lower in depression than did their foreign-born counterparts. However, in Ying's (1988) study, this difference disappeared when education and occupation were taken into account as covariates.

Other types of immigrant status comparisons yield apparently clearer conclusions. Kuo (1984) reported that his Asian-American samples indicated more depression symptoms on the CES-D than did Caucasian, native-born counterparts. Similarly, in their study of four groups of immigrant women in London, Ontario, Franks and Faux (1990) found that the percentage of Chinese women presenting high levels of depressive symptomatology on the CES-D exceeded the 'normal' community rate for a national sample in the United States.

For their part, Yeung and Schwartz (1986) explored differences in psychiatric morbidity, as assessed by the General Health Questionnaire (Goldberg, 1978) and a standard, psychiatric interview, in a sample of 124 female, Chinese obstetrical patients, predominantly from New York's Chinatown. Recent immigrants (those in the United States less than one year) scored higher on psychiatric morbidity and were more apt to receive a diagnosis from the Diagnostic and Statistical Manual–III (American Psychiatric Association, 1994) than were longer-term residents. These differences were attributed to the greater emotional distress and acculturative stresses confronting recent immigrants.

Finally, studies in the United States and Canada have explored the nature of the stresses confronting Chinese immigrants and factors that may help buffer or reduce the ill effects of stressors and tendencies toward depression and adjustment difficulties. Kuo and Tsai (1986) reanalysed Kuo's (1984) data, performing separate analyses for each ethnic group. For the Chinese, the most pressing challenges for adaptation were problems with the English language, followed by homesickness and lack of contact with other Chinese. Not surprisingly, stressful life events and greater reported difficulty in adaptation were associated with increased depression. On the other hand, greater hardiness, a personality dimension involving a sense of control and self-esteem, was associated with reduced depression. The buffering effects of hardiness were independently demonstrated in Dion, Dion, and Pak's (1992) study of Chinese community respondents in Toronto. Dion and his colleagues showed that the correlation between stress and perceived discrimination was negligible among Chinese community respondents high in hardiness but substantially positive for those low in hardiness.

In sum, the weight of the evidence suggests that foreign-born Chinese, perhaps especially recent immigrants, are at greater risk for depression and report more somatic complaints than are either their native-born Chinese or Caucasian counterparts. Acculturative stresses are likely a central contributing element to these risks. However, the personality dimension of hardiness may reduce the psychological distresses that Chinese immigrants to North America confront. Precisely how hardiness achieves this buffering effect—whether by reducing felt stresses and strains and/or by enhancing adaptational reserves and coping responses—remains to be determined.

Correlates of Immigrant Status: American Students

Two American studies have focused on Chinese- and other Asian-American students at the University of California at Los Angeles (UCLA). Sue and Zane (1985) compared American-born and foreign-born Chinese students on achievement and socio-emotional adjustment. Chinese students, even recent immigrants to the United States, attained better grades at UCLA than did non-Chinese students. However, recent immigrants (having spent less than six years in the United States) showed greater socio-emotional difficulties on several psychological adjustment measures than did either longer-term Chinese immigrant students or American-born Chinese students. Specifically, recent immigrants were less happy, more anxious, more lonely, more isolated socially, and showed less personal integration on the Omnibus Personality Inventory (OPI)(Heist and Yonge, 1968). By contrast, Chinese immigrant students who had resided in the United States more than six years were quite similar to American-born Chinese, a finding which suggested to the authors a relatively rapid acculturation process for psychological characteristics reflecting socio-emotional adjustment.

A somewhat different conclusion emerged from a study reported several years later by Abe and Zane (1990), who compared Asian-American and Caucasian-American students on two distress indices derived from the OPI personal integration scale. Foreign-born Asian-American students scored as more maladjusted on both intrapersonal and interpersonal distress than did either US-born Asian-Americans or Caucasian-American students. Notably, these differences remained intact even after partialing out potential confounds for response style (for example, social desirability) and personality style (for example, self-consciousness, other directedness, and extraversion) known to differentiate between Asians and non-Asians. Since their foreign-born, Asian-American students had been in the United States for 10 years on average, the authors concluded that the acculturative and other stressors that Asians confront in immigrating to the United States may have a measurable impact for a considerable time after emigration.

Unfortunately, without Asian subgroup analyses we cannot know to what extent Abe and Zane's (1990) conclusions apply to Chinese immigrant students versus Asian-American students of other ethnic and national backgrounds (for example, Vietnamese, Korean, Japanese) at UCLA. The limited size of the native-born and foreign-born Asian-American samples probably precluded subgroup analyses.

Acculturation and Counselling

Atkinson and his colleagues conducted studies at the University of California at Santa Barbara (UCSB) exploring the relation between acculturation, as assessed by the SL-ASIA scale (Suinn et al., 1987), and various aspects of counselling for Chinese-American, as well as other types of Asian-American, students. In their studies considered here, Chinese respondents always predominated in the samples; moreover, the different Asian-American groups constituted levels of an 'ethnicity' variable in the analyses.

Atkinson and Gim (1989) explored ethnicity, acculturation, and gender as correlates of responses to four scales (need, stigma, openness, and confidence) assessing attitudes towards seeking professional help from a counsellor or at a counselling centre. Only acculturation level influenced attitudes toward counselling. Highly acculturated respondents were more likely than those less acculturated to see the need for, and to tolerate the stigma of, seeking professional psychological help, as well as to be willing to discuss their personal problems with a psychologist.

Atkinson, Whiteley, and Gim (1990) investigated the relation of three acculturation types—Western-identified (WI), bicultural (BI), and Asian-identified (AI), as defined by a tertile split on Suinn et al.'s (1987) SL-ASIA scale—to Asian-American student rankings of different help-providers with whom they would be most likely to discuss a personal problem. Here too, acculturation type, but not ethnicity, emerged as significant in the analyses. Asian-identified students rated the oldest person in the community more highly as a potential help-provider than did Western-identified or bicultural respondents. Asian-identified students also rated the counselling psychologist highest as help-provider. These latter findings appear to contradict or to be incompatible with Atkinson and Gim's (1989) previous finding that it is the highly acculturated, or 'Western-identified', respondents who view counselling positively as a means of coping with personal problems.

Atkinson et al. (1990) interpreted their findings as indicating that when they assume they have a personal problem, Asian-identified students are positively inclined toward seeking help from a counsellor or psychologist. Providing some support for this interpretation, Gim, Atkinson, and Whiteley (1990) replicated the finding that when Asian-American students perceive they have a problem, it is the relatively less acculturated who are more likely to seek help from a counsellor. The less acculturated Asian-American students rated financial problems as being the most severe, while the more acculturated saw academic and career problems as being the most severe. Gim, Atkinson, and Kim (1991) compared the reactions of low versus high acculturated students of Asian background to an audiotaped counselling session, in which the counsellor bore either an Asian-American or Caucasian-American name and was either 'culture-sensitive' or 'culture-blind' (that is, recognized the influence and importance of a client's culture and ethnicity or not). Acculturation level interacted in a complex and difficult-to-interpret fashion with the student's gender as well as the two manipulated counsellor dimensions in influencing perceptions of the counsellor's effectiveness. However, that average SL-ASIA scores for the low acculturation group were in the middle range rather than at the low end for this instrument was acknowledged by the authors as a limitation of the study.

Finally, Tata and Leong (1994) assessed acculturation as a predictor of reported attitudes toward seeking professional help with a sample of Chinese-American students at the University of Illinois in Chicago. Using continuous scores on the SL-ASIA scale, rather than defining levels of acculturation, they found that acculturation was a significant predictor, over and above gender, accounting for 3 per cent of the variance in attitudes toward seeking professional help. Highly acculturated students were more positive in their attitudes toward seeking professional help for psychological problems from a counsellor than were less acculturated ones.

Taken together, these studies suggest that acculturation is a relevant psychological dimension among Chinese and other Asian-American students. It potentially influences their attitudes toward mental health services provided by counsellors, their reported desire to seek help from a counselling psychologist and others in confronting a personal problem, the nature and perceived severity of their problems, and the perceived effectiveness of a counsellor, depending on the counsellor's ethnicity and professed culture-sensitivity. The evidence suggests that greater acculturation is related to more positive attitudes to counsellors and counselling for psychological problems (as assessed by an attitude scale) among Chinese-American and other Asian-American university students. However, when they assume that they themselves have a personal problem, it is the less acculturated Asian-American students who are more inclined to seek help from a counsellor.

ENGLISH AS A SECOND LANGUAGE AND MODES OF ASSIMILATION

A central issue for the cultural adaptation of Chinese immigrants or sojourners to English-speaking countries concerns the relation between self-confidence with, and proficiency in, English as a second language and modes of assimilation to 'Anglo' cultural and linguistic contexts. Confidence and proficiency with English can facilitate acculturation or assimilation in some regards, but they also entail costs in psychosocial adjustment and Chinese-language proficiency and identity, as shown by several studies in Canada.

Pak, Dion, and Dion (1985) administered a survey questionnaire in Chinese or English to 174 Chinese students at the University of Toronto—the majority Hong Kong-born. The focal question was whether or not self-confidence with English was associated with cultural assimilation and loss of Chinese cultural heritage, as suggested by prior studies of Canadian francophones learning English (Gardner and Lambert, 1972; Clement, Gardner, and Smythe, 1980). Factor analysis indicated that self-confidence with English among Chinese university students in Toronto was associated with linguistic assimilation (feeling self-assured with English but lacking confidence or proficiency with Chinese-language skills) but not with cultural assimilation (for example, participation in Toronto's Chinese community or loss of Chinese identity). Self-confidence with English was also associated with several indicators of psychosocial adaptation, such as high self-esteem, a greater sense of control over one's life, and greater satisfaction with life in Toronto.

Young and Gardner (1990) later completed a similar study with 102 Hong Kong Chinese students at another Ontario university but using an English-language questionnaire only. Factor analysis yielded a 'linguistic identification' factor very similar to Pak et al.'s (1985) 'linguistic assimilation' factor, in that confidence and proficiency with English were associated with poor proficiency with the Chinese language, but bore no relation to assimilation and integration measures of acculturation attitudes developed from Berry's (1980) four-fold typology.

University student samples alone, however, often yield an incomplete or misleading picture. Dion, Dion, and Pak (1990) explored correlates of self-reported language proficiencies in English and Chinese among 184 members of Toronto's Chinese community, most of whom were born outside Canada but were Canadian citizens or 'landed immigrants' in Canada at the time of the study. For this community sample, self-reported confidence with English related positively to self-esteem but negatively to several aspects of involvement in the Chinese community. Conversely, self-reported confidence in the Chinese language related positively to Chinese community involvement but negatively to aspects of psychosocial adaptation (such as self-esteem, internal control, and reported happiness).

Thus, Dion et al.'s (1990) Chinese community study yielded a quite different picture from that sketched by studies conducted by them and others with Chinese university students in Canada, in that the former suggested that increased confidence and proficiency with English was associated with cultural assimilation. They interpreted the discrepant findings for the two Chinese samples in terms of a majority versus a minority group profile for second-language acquisition (Clement et al., 1980; Clement, 1987).

The Chinese community study yielded findings typifying those for an ethnolinguistic minority in that increasing self-confidence in the second language was associated with assimilation and 'subtractive bilingualism' (a loss of the original or native culture and language skills). By contrast, Chinese university students in Toronto fit a majority group profile in which second-language acquisition is 'additive' (that is, characterized by a feeling of being accepted in the second language community without losing one's cultural identity or ties). Since these Chinese students were more apt to be sojourners in Canada than were members of Toronto's general Chinese community, they may have exhibited a 'sojourner' attitude and adopted a stance similar to that of a majority group member in acquiring English-language skills. The relation of English-language proficiency and confidence to assimilation for Chinese people in Canada, if not elsewhere, may depend upon their status as sojourners versus permanent residents.

COMPARATIVE ASSIMILATION OF CHINESE IN DIFFERENT SOCIETIES

Comparative studies illustrate that structural features of societies powerfully influence different rates and modes of assimilation by Chinese immigrants. Wong (1978) contrasted the Chinese communities of Lima, Peru, and New York City. Chinese immigrants to both cities have similar cultural characteristics and immigration history (the majority of the members of both communities came originally from Guangdong province, spoke a similar Chinese dialect, and immigrated as labourers to the Americas in the nineteenth century for similar economic reasons). Both communities have existed for about 130 years.

Yet, the patterns of assimilation in these two Chinese communities could scarcely be more different. Chinese in Lima are highly assimilated and relatively well integrated into the fabric of Peruvian society, with few apparent limitations to their social and economic mobility and no segregated, Chinese residential or business areas. In terms of Gordon's assimilation model, the Chinese in Lima have obviously attained structural assimilation, if not all the other forms of assimilation. By contrast, New York Chinese 'are highly conservative and nonassimilative', and restricted in their social and economic mobility primarily to the ethnic niche of Chinatown.

Wong (1978) ascribed these striking differences in assimilation to three 'macro-environmental' features: a history of stronger political and legal discrimination against Chinese immigrants in the United States, more economic opportunities in Peru than in the United States, and the Peruvian social institution of *compadrazgo* (godfatherhood), in which Chinese acquire Hispanic-Peruvian godfathers who help integrate them into the social, economic, political, and cultural life of the city.

Similarly, Ward and Hewstone (1985) contrasted Singapore and Malaysia where, due to alternative national policies, inter-group relations among Chinese, Malays, and Indians differ considerably. They styled Singapore's approach as one of tolerant multiculturalism or 'cultural integration', in which citizens can maintain their distinct ethnic identities within a political climate of 'peaceful coexistence' among ethnic and linguistic groups. By contrast, Malaysia's 'potentially assimilationist' policies regarding a single national language (Bahasa Malaysia) and redistribution of wealth in favor of native Malays have created considerable stresses for the Chinese and East Indian minorities there. Ward and Hewstone (1985) linked these different national policies in 'accommodating' ethnic diversity to the social-psychological phenomena of ethnic stereotyping, in-group and out-group attribution, and social distance. For example, the resistance of Singaporeans to stereotyping or differential attri-

butions on the basis of ethnicity may well be due to Singapore's tolerant attitude toward multiculturalism and multilingualism. Likewise, negative in-group
perceptions by Chinese in Malaysia appear to be linked to the oppressive political climate they confront in that society.

Lian (1988) reviewed the history and current position of Chinese in New
Zealand, rejecting assimilation theory as an explanatory framework and
emphasizing instead a socio-political process of identity formation. He suggested that second-generation Chinese in New Zealand have generally adopted a dual identity, similar to the integration option of Berry's (1980) four-fold
typology of acculturation attitudes, in which their relation to the Chinese community and to New Zealand are both retained as elements.

Finally, other studies have investigated the role of different factors in the
adaptation of Chinese into foreign cultures. Kuo and Lin (1977) examined the
assimilation of Chinese-Americans in Washington, DC, during the early 1970s.
They concluded that the pace of assimilation was relatively slow and that
socio-economic attainment had little effect upon the assimilation rate, once
education level was taken into account. Lam (1980) investigated the role of
ethnic media (specifically, Chinese-language newspapers) for Chinese immigrants in Toronto during the 1970s. He concluded that the exposure to ethnic
media had little relation to the subjects' acculturation in Canada, whereas the
network of 'personal communications' among the Chinese immigrants was
important in keeping alive ties to Toronto's Chinese community. Thus, the factors influencing assimilation or acculturation of Chinese in a foreign context
can differ from one country or city to another.

CHINESE FAMILIES AND CULTURAL ADAPTATION IN WESTERNIZED SOCIETIES

Historical Background and Family Structure

In Canada, the United States, and Australia, immigration in the mid- to late
nineteenth century was predominantly male, undertaken in response to the
Gold Rush or for employment opportunities. Wives and children typically
remained in the village of the husbands' family, resulting in the geographical
fragmentation of the family. In Australia, for example, because of restrictive
immigration laws and the importance of maintaining family ties in China, a
'commuting type of migration system' emerged (Choi, 1975, p. 106). Similar
circumstances characterized early Chinese immigration to Canada (Chinese
Canadian National Council, 1992) and the United States (Sung, 1987). After the
Second World War, these policies gradually changed. By the late 1960s, restrictive immigration policies based on specific national origins had been replaced
by individual qualifications related to the labour market (for example, education, occupation, and guaranteed employment) and family re-unification.
Thus, at different phases of the twentieth century, Chinese immigrants have
encountered specific economic and social conditions in the host country
which in turn have had differing impacts on family structure.

Glenn (1983) suggested that three major Chinese family structures have
existed in the United States. The first type, described above, was the 'split

household', which predominated until about 1920. From 1920 to the mid-1960s, the 'small-producer' family prevailed, characterized by a 'work-centred family life' in which all family members worked in labour-intensive, small-scale enterprises. Glenn contended that this structure developed in response to particular social conditions confronting immigrants of Chinese background in the United States, such as restrictions against entering various occupations, as well as the limited financial resources possessed by many immigrant families. Key features of this style of family functioning were cooperation, increased autonomy for the wife, and increased status for children, since their English-language skills were often needed to assist parents. The family structure was close-knit, with children assisting parents in the family business after school.

A third, more recent family structure is the working-class 'dual-earner' family, characterized by the pooling of financial resouces with each spouse working independently. Children were no longer involved in assisting their parents at work after school hours but instead spent after-school time with their peers. According to Glenn, because of the parents' work schedules, there was little shared family activity. In some cases, this set of circumstances made it harder for the family to cope with problems such as language difficulties, low income, or immigration difficulties.

Sung (1987), in her study of the adaptation of children and adolescents in Chinese immigrant families in New York City in the middle-to-late 1970s, similarly noted that frequent parental absence due to work schedules was a salient feature of family life. Nonetheless, a fairly high proportion of the high school students surveyed reported feeling close to their parents. Sung interpreted this pattern as reflecting the persistence of filial piety, since these students were first-generation immigrants. The stresses in family functioning discussed by Glenn (1983) might be more likely to occur in families where the parents were immigrants but their children were born and reared in the host country.

Domains of Acculturation

An important issue to be considered concerns change and continuity in cultural traditions among Chinese families living in Western societies. In a cross-cultural study comparing reported child-rearing practices in Chinese parents from Taiwan, immigrant Chinese parents originally from Taiwan and residing in the United States, and Caucasian-American parents, differences were found on measures of parental control, parental encouragement of the child's independence, and parental emphasis on achievement (Lin and Fu, 1990). As expected, Chinese and immigrant Chinese parents reported greater parental control and parental emphasis on achievement compared to Caucasian-American parents. However, contrary to expectations, Chinese parents and Chinese immigrant fathers indicated greater encouragement of independence in their young children (of kindergarten or early primary school age) than did the Caucasian-American parents. The authors suggested that although interdependence within the family was stressed in Chinese families, independence beyond the family might also be encouraged to facilitate achievement within the larger society.

Rosenthal and Feldman (1990, 1992) studied a sample of first-and second-generation immigrant adolescents (15–18 years old) in Melbourne, Australia, and San Francisco, and compared the results to a sample of Chinese students in Hong Kong, Anglo-Australians (Australian-born Caucasians), and Caucasian-Americans (American-born Caucasians). Adolescents from Westernized societies perceived their families as endorsing autonomy, while Hong Kong teenagers perceived their families as less supportive of autonomy and more self-contained. Chinese immigrant teenagers' view of their families amounted to 'loosening the family boundaries while maintaining conformity to family values' (Rosenthal and Feldman, 1990, p. 511). The adolescents from Chinese immigrant families perceived their families as more controlling and as placing on them more demands for achievement, compared either to non-immigrant Chinese adolescents or to the adolescents from the two Western societies.

Similarly, on a measure of age expectations for autonomy, different domains of behaviour showed different rates of acculturation toward Western norms. The Chinese immigrant adolescents reported greater parental restrictiveness for behaviour pertaining to social relations with the opposite sex when compared to their non-Chinese Australian and American-born peers (Feldman and Rosenthal, 1990). Finally, measures of different components of ethnic identity suggested the need to consider different aspects of ethnic identity when assessing acculturation. The first-generation immigrant adolescents received higher scores on their ethnic knowledge and behaviour than did the second-generation adolescents from immigrant families. However, in the Australian and US samples of immigrant Chinese families, there was no difference recorded between first-generation and second-generation adolescents in their rated importance of knowledge or behaviour pertaining to their ethnic group, or in their evaluation of their ethnic origins (Rosenthal and Feldman, 1992).

In another study of adolescent immigrants, Ho and Hills (1992) compared individual differences in cultural identity among three groups of Hong Kong Chinese youths in three phases of migration to New Zealand: pre-migration, less than two years after migration, and two to four years after migration. Four styles of cultural adaptation were found: assimilation to the host society; integration with the host society while maintaining Chinese identity; retention of the traditional identity (separation); and identification with neither one's native culture nor the host society (marginalization). The proportion of adolescents in the assimilation and integration categories increased with length of time since immigration. However, even after two to four years in New Zealand, about half of the adolescents (52.6 per cent) were categorized as maintaining a predominantly traditional, Chinese cultural identification.

Wolfgang and Josefowitz (1978) explored possible value conflicts for Chinese immigrants in Toronto by assessing Chinese and North American values among 109 high school students, including both foreign-born and Canadian-born Chinese as well as Canadian-born non-Chinese. Marked value similarity among these student groups was found, especially in the domains of family, sex and marriage, nonverbal behaviour, and education. However, non-Chinese Canadian students valued individualism and openness to change more than did the members of the Chinese student groups who, in turn, valued the community more highly than the individual and education as a means to achieve respect. The longer the Chinese students had been in Canada, the more they were concerned with their public self-presentation and the greater was their conservatism in views of family life—for example, opposing premarital sex and emphasizing respect for elders, both of which are traditional Chinese values. However, the greater the length of residence in Canada, the more they also accepted individualistic values (such as standing up for one's own rights and not accepting authority without criticism), which presumably reflected acculturation to Canadian culture over time.

Cultural Conflict and Family Functioning

Another important area of research concerns the stresses related to acculturation resulting from conflicts between Chinese values concerning family relationships and the values encountered in Western societies after migration. In addition, structural changes in some Chinese families in the host society (for example, increased status of young children due to one or both parents' reliance on their children's English-language skills) may result in stress within the family (Yao, 1985).

Several features of traditional Chinese family functioning can be sources of conflict for family members: in particular, the emphasis on parental authority and filial piety, valuing family interests over self-interest, and gender-role expectations (Fong, 1973). Sung (1985) found that Chinese immigrant schoolchildren and adolescents residing in New York City between 1976 and 1979 reported culture-related conflicts concerning perceived parental restrictiveness and the formality of emotional or affective expression in family relationships. In a study of young Chinese immigrant women from Hong Kong residing in Vancouver, Canada, for at least three years, Lee and Cochran (1988) found that these women felt 'polarized and trapped' between opposing cultural values. A central theme emerging from the interviews was the perceived conflict between the pursuit of personal development on the one hand, and the maintainance of family traditions and the security of family relationships on the other.

Cultural conflict related to family issues is also evident in the literature on elderly Chinese immigrants living in the United States. Cheung (1989) reviewed research on the problems confronting some elderly individuals who had emigrated to be with their children in the United States. The older immigrants arrived expecting support, respect, and the continued authority accorded to elder family members, consistent with the tradition of filial piety. However, the nuclear family structure and the more individualistic values of their adult children at times conflicted with these expectations.

Inter-group Marriage

A final area of research on acculturation and family issues concerns the prevalence of inter-group marriage. The repeal of laws prohibiting inter-racial marriage and changing attitudes toward out-group members have contributed to the likelihood of inter-group marriage in the United States (Wong, 1989). The occurrence of exogamous (out-group) marriage in ethnically and racially diverse societies is one important indicator of assimilation. Although assimilation is often assumed to reflect the loss of one's original ethnic identity, other views of assimilation have been proposed. In their study of Asian-American intermarriage, Lee and Yamanaka (1990) contend that 'acceptance of a minority group at all levels does not necessitate any loss of ethnic identity' on the part of minority group members (p. 287, footnote 1). Smith and Bond (1993) have identified personality dimensions and aspects of the social context, which may facilitate retaining one's ethnocultural identity while also fostering integration with the host society.

Research on intermarriage among persons of Chinese ethnicity in the United States has been based on data from the 1980 national census (U.S. Census Public Use Microdata Samples). Census data may underestimate the prevalence of intermarriage for groups containing a large number of immigrants who married while residing in their original country (Hwang and Saenz, 1990; Wong, 1989). In one study using once-married couples only, Wong (1989) found that 23.5 per cent of all Chinese marriages involved one non-Chinese spouse, predominantly (66.5 per cent) to a non-Hispanic Caucasian. In another study, the prevalence of exogamous marriage among Chinese, based on a larger sample of all married couples, yielded a smaller percentage, 15.7 per cent, with most of this group (66.5 per cent) marrying a non-Hispanic Caucasian (Lee and Yamanaka, 1990).

The correlates of intermarriage between Chinese and non-Chinese are also of interest. The findings from these US census data have suggested gender differences, with women of Chinese ethnicity much more likely than their male peers to have an inter-racial marriage, while intermarriage for men of Chinese ethnicity was more likely to involve a spouse from other Asian groups (Wong, 1989). Other important factors related to the prevalence of Chinese/Caucasian marriages were generational status (whether a first- or second-generation immigrant), citizenship status in the United States, reported knowledge of English, and educational level. This type of marriage was more prevalent among US-born citizens of Chinese ethnicity or among those who reported a high level of proficiency with English (Wong, 1989). Since these were census data, however, acculturation was inferred from these factors rather than measured directly.

Complementing these survey data, in a study of intermarriage, Sung (1990) interviewed 50 couples residing in New York City in which the wife was Chinese and the husband was non-Chinese. One salient theme emerging from these interviews was that the couple, particularly the wife, frequently encountered strong objections from her family about her marriage to a non-Chinese. This family disapproval was the most negative aspect of an inter-racial marriage for many of the couples interviewed.

Census data from New York City in 1980, cited by Sung, indicated that the percentage of couples without children among in-group marriages (both spouses Chinese) was 15 per cent, while the percentage of married couples without children was markedly higher for inter-group marriages (49 per cent for non-Chinese wives and 30 per cent for Chinese women married to non-Chinese husbands). As Sung noted, this pattern might reflect other demographic factors such as a higher educational level and socio-economic status, which in turn were related to a smaller family size (in this case, having no children). Alternatively, Sung speculated that the higher percentage of childless couples among intermarried couples in these census data might also reflect the couples' concerns about 'the marginality of the children'. It remains to be seen whether this pattern of findings occurs in US census data from the 1990s, in census data collected from other areas of the United States, and in other countries to which Chinese people have emigrated.

CONCLUSIONS

To understand adaptation to foreign cultures among Chinese sojourners and immigrants, Chinese cultural traditions and the specific social and political conditions prevalent both in the society of origin and the host society must be considered. The process of adaptation is complex, and in some domains, traditional values and behaviour persist. Moreover, some observed differences between Chinese immigrants and non-immigrants may be attributable to selection factors related to the act of immigrating *per se*. Educational and economic opportunities for oneself and one's family are important factors underlying the decision to emigrate to another country. There is some evidence, for example, that greater parental expectations for children's academic and occupational achievement may characterize immigrant families from diverse ethnocultural backgrounds compared to non-immigrant families in the host country (Rosenthal and Feldman, 1990; Marjoribanks, 1991).

In undertaking this branch of study, the impact of factors such as generational status and length of time in residence in a foreign country should be assessed unconfounded by other powerful predictors of adaptation, such as occupational status, educational level, or citizenship status. Moreover, where possible, acculturation should be measured directly, instead of being inferred from variables such as generational status. Developers of acculturation measures should explore and demonstrate the behavioural validity of their scales (their ability to predict actual criterion behaviours) in addition to self-report validity (intercorrelations with other self-report measures). Finally, as is evident from the literature in several sections of this chapter, findings from studies involving university students and community samples of immigrants show some important differences, suggesting the need for caution when attempting to generalize across the two types of respondents.

Despite these challenges and complexities, we believe that this area of research already has yielded substantive and intriguing findings that provide a foundation for even better research on, and more profound insights into, Chinese adaptation to foreign countries in future.

NOTES

Preparation of this paper was facilitated by research grants to the authors from the Social Sciences and Humanities Research Council of Canada, as well as Multiculturalism Canada.

Chapter 31

∎

The Psychological Transformation of the Chinese People as a Result of Societal Modernization

Kuo-Shu Yang

As a global historical movement dating back at least to seventeenth-century England, modernization has manifested itself in three major waves. The first wave, from the seventeenth to the early nineteenth centuries, involved the Christian cultures of Western Europe and North America; the second, from the late nineteenth to the early twentieth centuries, involved other countries in the Christian culture circle (with the exception of Japan); and the third, in the late twentieth century, has involved nations mainly in the Confucian culture circle (with the exception of Turkey and Latin America)(Luo, 1989). Only modernization occurring during the first wave may be considered as endogenous, or primary, in the sense that it originated from natural changes in certain economic, political, and/or sociocultural conditions or features of the society itself. On the other hand, modernization occurring during the second and third waves may be called exogenous, or secondary, in the sense that it emerged as a national response to the challenge and exploitation by countries in which endogenous modernization had tremendously strengthened national wealth and power (Sun, 1991). Exogenous modernization has defensive characteristics and usually provides a strong instrumental value for latecomers to strengthen themselves to ensure a better chance of national existence and prosperity.

As a latecomer in the third wave, China is certainly a case of exogenous or defensive modernization. Under devastating external pressure, mainly from the West, China began to feel a need for modernization as early as the 1840s. However, in the last one-and-a-half centuries, China's efforts at modernization have been repeatedly thwarted by unfavourable factors from both outside and inside. During the 100 years from the mid-nineteenth to the mid-twentieth centuries, China was repeatedly defeated, humiliated, and fragmented by Western and Eastern powers (including Japan) through the signing and enforcement of 'unequal treaties'. As a result, China could no longer consider herself a unified, independent, and autonomous nation. It is against such a historical background that China has been continuously forced to pursue a defensive process of modernization (King, 1977).

At different stages of modernization in recent Chinese history, Chinese intellectuals and government officials have repeatedly initiated and promoted movements of national revitalization. In the late Qing dynasty (1644–1911), there were at least two major national movements of modernization: the Self-strengthening Movement (1860-1894) and the Political Reform Movement

(1906-1911). The first movement set as its goals the initiation and implementation of programmes which involved founding schools, translating books, establishing factories, constructing railroads, and opening mines. The second, while endorsing the efforts of the first, proposed the modernization of the central political system by introducing basic institutional changes.

China switched her central political structure from an imperial to a republican system after the overthrow of the Qing dynasty in 1911 and, as a result, most of the unequal treaties were successively abolished. However, efforts at national reform for modernization were not successful during the early years of the Republican period and a large-scale political protest, later referred to as the May Fourth Movement, occurred in 1919. This protest finally transformed itself into a nationwide cultural reform movement, later labelled the New Culture Movement, which proposed an uncomprising rejection of Chinese traditions (especially those from Confucianism) and advocated a total or whole-hearted Westernization in terms of science and democracy (Sun, 1982). The pervasive influence of the May Fourth Movement has lasted even since China became a divided nation in 1949.

In the past 40 years or so, Taiwan, Hong Kong, and mainland China have each experimented with radically different strategies of modernization and have each experienced strikingly different degrees of success or failure. Taiwan's and Hong Kong's patterns of economic development have been so successful as to create their own economic 'miracles' which have made the social, cultural, and political aspects of these societies change at a speed unprecedented in modern Chinese history. Mainland China, although developing at a much slower tempo, has adjusted its developmental pace and has made impressive progress in economic reform over the past 10 years. This recent development has resulted in conspicuous social and cultural changes on the Mainland, especially in the coastal provinces.

Overall, in the past 100-plus years China has undergone the biggest political, economic, social, and cultural changes of the five millennia of Chinese history. This societal modernization has caused pervasive psychological and behavioural changes. The present chapter attempts to review the major relevant empirical studies so as to generate a valid profile of this psychological transformation for Chinese in Taiwan, Hong Kong, and mainland China. It will also try to clarify some of the relevant theoretical or conceptual issues so that Chinese psychological modernization as a result of societal modernization can be better understood. Systematic knowledge of this transformation, at both empirical and theoretical levels, is a prerequisite for gaining insights into the psychological effects of modernization on the Chinese people, the largest population in the world.

EMPIRICAL RESEARCH ON CHINESE PEOPLE'S PSYCHOLOGICAL CHANGE

In 1986, Yang made the first comprehensive review of empirical studies pertaining to the impact of modernization on the Chinese personality. This work produced a list of three classes of relatively stable traits (motivational, evaluative–attitudinal, and temperamental) that appear to have been changing (decreasing or increasing) in their levels during the process of social change. In another review appearing at about the same time, Yang (1985) extended his list to include a fourth class of psychological characteristics (emotional and patho-logical) that have also been changing as a result of modernization. In the next section we will update that first list of changes, affecting the first three kinds of personality traits, by reviewing relevant empirical studies published since 1985.

Changes in Motivational Characteristics

Few relevant empirical studies on the change of motivational dispositions have been published since 1985. One such study was conducted by C. H. Hwang (1989), in which three comparable samples of students from National Taiwan Normal University (NTNU) were administered the Edwards Personal Preference Schedule in 1963, 1975, and 1987; the results were compared for the purpose of detecting changes in psychogenic needs over a period of more than twenty years. The results obtained indicate that students at NTNU have showed increasing needs across this period on the factors of Exhibition, Autonomy, Intraception, Succourance, Change, and Heterosexuality; they have shown decreasing needs on Deference, Order, Dominance, Nuturance, Edurance, and Aggression.

In another relevant study, conducted by Yu (1990), two scales specifically developed for the measurement of social-oriented achievement motivation (SOAM) and individual-oriented achievement motivation (IOAM), along with the Multidimensional Scale of Chinese Individual Traditionality (MS-CIT) and the Multidimensional Scale of Chinese Individual Modernity (MS-CIM), were administered to a sample of Taiwanese college students. The MS-CIT and the MS-CIM were constructed by Yang and his associates (Yang, 1992; Yang, Yu, and Yeh, 1991) to substitute for the Chinese Individual Traditionality–Modernity Scale (CITMS), originally developed by Yang and Hchu (Hchu, 1971; Yang, 1985; Yang and Hchu, 1974). In Yu's study (1990), SOAM was found to corre-late positively with four of the five components of traditionality and IOAM to correlate negatively with four of the five components of modernity. It may, thus, be inferred that as Chinese traditionality decreases and modernity increases as a result of societal modernization, Chinese people in Taiwan will tend to have a lower need for social-oriented achievement motivation and a higher need for individual-oriented achievement motivation. Although no such empirical research has been conducted in other Chinese societies, com-mon observation seems to indicate that the traditional value of self-content-ment has been replaced by a high level of striving for achievement in Hong Kong (Lee, 1988).

Changes in Evaluative–Attitudinal Characteristics

Since 1985, far more work related to evaluative–attitudinal characteristics has been published than work focused on motivational characteristics. Studies have replicated research published before 1985 by using a sample of the same kind tested in a much later year or in a different Chinese society. Among these studies, two adopted Kluckhohn and Strodtbeck's (1961) conceptual system of value orientations. Liao and Hwang (1992) collected data from a large sample of Taiwanese farmers with the CITMS and a Chinese version of a value orientation questionnaire first used by Yang and Chang (1975), derived from Kluckhohn and Strodtbeck's original instrument. They compared their results with those from a sample of college students reported in Yang and Chang's (1975) investigation and concluded that Taiwanese farmers' value orientations had gradually transformed into a more modern pattern, consisting of individualism (on the relational modality), present emphasis (on the time-perspective modality), and mastery-over-nature (on the man–nature modality). This pattern is similar to, but less modern than, that of Taiwanese college students reported in Yang and Chang (1975).

Another study, using essentially the same measurement tools, was carried out in Xian, Shaanxi province, by Zhang (1990), who essentially provided a replication of Yang and Chang's (1975) study using college students from the Mainland. Zhang's data revealed that more modernized students displayed a stronger tendency to prefer the future orientation and a weaker tendency to prefer the present orientation in the time-perspective sphere, a weaker tendency to prefer the submission-to-nature orientation in the man–nature sphere, and no differential preferences on the activity and relational spheres.

In the years since 1985, there have been several studies using a Chinese version of Allport, Vernon, and Lindzey's (1951) Study of Values (SV) scale. Li (1987) administered the SV scale, the CITMS, and other standardized scales to a sample of college students in Taiwan and found that, while no consistent tendencies were found for male students, more modernized female students tended to place a lower value on the economic sphere and a higher value on the aesthetic sphere. Also using Taiwanese college students, Ho (1990) compared data for two samples collected in 1984 and 1989 with the SV scale, the Rokeach Value Survey, and several other scales. The study found that the 1989 group, compared to the subjects in 1984, put more emphasis on economic and social values and less on aesthetic ones. It was also found that the members of the 1989 group assigned more importance to a comfortable life, a world at peace, and freedom, and less to ambition and obedience.

The directions of change in economic and aesthetic values, as found by Ho, seem inconsistent with the findings of Li's study. As far as the directions of change in these two values are concerned, Li's findings confirm those of Lei and Yang (1986), in which much larger Taiwanese student samples separated by a much longer period (about 20 years) were used. Furthermore, survey data for a large sample of young respondents interviewed in factories, communes, schools, and residential districts in two provinces of southern China revealed an increasingly stronger aesthetic desire for beautiful things (Huang, 1981, cited in Chu, 1985).

Rokeach's Value Survey is another instrument of Western origin that has been adopted as the major questionnaire for value assessment in several large-scale studies conducted before 1985. Recently, local psychologists in Taiwan have constructed partially indigenous value lists with Rokeach's (1973) distinction of instrumental and terminal values as a basic conceptual scheme. Two studies using such a list have provided data relevant to the issue of value change. In one of them, K. K. Hwang (in press) constructed and administered a partially indigenous value list to a sample of Taiwanese males and females ranging in age from approximately 20 to more than 50 years. Each respondent was asked to rate the importance of the values to himself or herself and to his or her father. Factor analyses of respondents' self-rating data identified seven oblique factors. Intergenerational comparisons indicate that the younger generation assigned higher ratings to the value factors Utilitarian (including the values Individualism, Material Enjoyment, and Good-looking), Social (Freedom, Equality, and Intimate Friendship), Knowledge (Scientific Attitudes, Rational Thinking, and Knowledge), and Anti-authoritarian (Democracy, Anti-traditionalism, and Anti-authoritarianism), and lower ratings to the factors Collective (Loyalty, Thrifty, and Seniority), Terminal (Filial Piety, Politeness, and Safety and Security), and Work (Patience, Cautiousness, and Hard Working). These perceived intergenerational differences might partially reflect trends in certain value changes, although they are possibly confounded with normal age trends and with differential biases in the same respondent's ratings for himself or herself and others.

In another study using a Rokeach-type value list, Wang (1994) constructed and administered a partially indigenous list of work values to three cohorts of Taiwanese college graduates with an age interval of ten years. The respondents were asked to rate each value on the list for its importance to himself or herself at the present time and at the time of graduation from university. Results reveal that, on the instrumental values, respondents of younger cohorts rated higher the value factors of Ability and Rationality (including the values Knowledge, Rational Thinking, and Self-assertion) and Modesty and Tolerance (Permissiveness, Politeness, and Modesty), and they rated lower the factors of Righteousness and Principledness (Abstinence, Democracy, and Anti-authoritarianism). On the terminal values, the younger cohorts rated higher the factors of Intrinsic Reward (Sense of Achievement, Effective Use of Personal Expertise, and Self-growth and Progress) and Extrinsic Reward (Reputation and Social Status, Power, and Wealth), and lower the factor of Collective Benefits (Serving the Society, National Development, and Helping Others). These cohort differences might partially reflect trends in certain value changes, although they are potentially confounded with normal age trends and with differential biases in rating the recalled value importance at the time of graduation some years before.

It should be noted that Wang's value factors of Ability and Rationality, Modesty and Tolerance, Righteousness and Principledness, and Collective Benefits more or less correspond to K. K. Hwang's Knowledge, Terminal, Anti-authoritarian, and Collective factors, respectively. Moreover, trends in value changes inferred from the findings of these two studies are similar for the two corresponding sets of value factors.

A fully indigenous value list was constructed by Yang and Cheng (1987) for the purpose of testing Kahn's (1979) and Redding's (1984) post-Confucian hypothesis. In deriving their list of 40 traditional Chinese values, Yang and Cheng relied upon the Chinese Culture Connection's (1987) list of Chinese values, Kahn's (1979) and Redding's (1984) descriptions of the post-Confucian ethic, Lau's (1982) discussion of Chinese utilitarianistic familism, and, most importantly, Yang's life-long experiences as a Chinese and observations for more than 30 years as a student of Chinese personality and social behaviour. A factor analysis of respondents' importance ratings on all of the 40 values for a large sample of employees from nine privately owned companies in Taiwan generated five major value factors: Chinese Familism (including the values Loyalty to Family, Filial Piety, and Mutual Help among Family Members), Modesty and Contentment (Moderation, Non-competition with Others, and Self-sacrifice for Group), Face and Relationship Orientation (Face Protection, Wealth Pursuit, and Relationship Based on Favour), Solidarity and Harmoniousness (Harmony with Others, Spirit of Solidarity, and Honesty and Faithfulness), and Capacity for Hardship and Perseverance (Bearing Risk and Difficulty, Tolerating Hardship, and Accepting the Unavoidable). Yang and Cheng related these five traditional Chinese value factors with the five components of Chinese individual traditionality measured by the MS-CIT and the five components of Chinese individual modernity measured by the MS-CIM. The empirical results reveal complicated patterns of relationships. All five value factors positively correlated with two of the five traditionality components (Submission to Authority and Filial Piety and Ancestral Worship), but failed to correlate substantially with the other three components. The relationships of the five value factors to the five modernity components were inconsistent in that these value factors correlated positively with Optimism and Assertiveness, negatively with Social Isolation and Self-reliance, and insignificantly with the other three components.

Other relevant studies of value change include those by P'ang (1989, cited in C. J. Hwang, 1993), C. J. Hwang (1993), Zhou (1993), and Lan (1994). P'ang compared results between two large-scale studies, completed ten years apart, on a wide range of values judged by college students in Taiwan. He discovered three major trends in value change: increased individualistic consciousness, a higher wish for autonomous social participation, and a stronger utilitarian orientation. C. J. Hwang (1993) collected data on various values from three large samples of young people (ages ranging from 15 to 29 years) in Taipei in 1984, 1988, and 1991. He identified four value types through cluster analysis: Conscientious, Utilitarian, Apathetic, and Conforming. Comparisons of results for the three samples reveal that the proportions of young people endorsing the Utilitarian and Conforming types have been increasing and that endorsing the Conscientious type has been decreasing. Zhou (1993) conducted an empirical study of the generation gap using residents (older than 16 years) in Nanjing, Jiangsu province, as respondents. Comparison of three age groups indicates that younger groups place a higher value on personal achievement and a lower value on a stable social environment and altruistic contribution. Parenthetically, younger groups manifested more favourable attitudes towards competition, premarital sexual behaviour, and divorce, and less favourable attitudes towards fatalistic helplessness and smaller differences in income.

Lan (1994), in a study of factors affecting Taiwanese dual-career couples' ratings of life-role salience, found that Chinese individual traditionality (measured by the MS-CIT) positively correlated with importance ratings of parental, marital, and domestic roles among wives but failed to have a significant linear correlation with ratings of any of those roles among husbands. On the other hand, Chinese individual modernity (measured by the MS-CIM) positively correlated with importance ratings of two of the three family roles (marital and domestic) among husbands but failed to do so with those of all three family roles among wives. Taken together, Lan's results seem to indicate that less traditional wives tend to assign less importance to their family roles and more modernized husbands assign more importance to such roles, revealing a tendency for the traditional division of labour in the family setting between the two sexes to change in the direction of increasing egalitarianism. Lan also found that more modernized wives and husbands placed more importance on their work roles than did their less modernized counterparts.

All of the studies reviewed above concern changes in values. In addition, there has been a disproportionately large number of empirical studies focusing on changes in specific attitudes toward political, economic, social, and cultural matters. Although these studies are too numerous and disorderly to be systematically reviewed here, findings of four such studies will be mentioned for the purpose of illustration.

One such study was conducted by Li (1987), who collected data on changes in Chinese women's femininity–masculinity and social roles in Taiwan. Some of her data suggest that female college students' degree of individual modernity (measured by the CITMS) correlated positively with their masculinity but had no linear relationship with femininity. In another study, Chuang and Yang (1991) re-analysed part of Yang, Yeh, and L. L. Hwang's (1989) indigenous data on filial piety for students and adults in Taiwan. They found that Chinese filial attitudes and behaviour had been changing from a familial to an individualistic orientation, from heteronomous to autonomous concerns, and from mono-beneficial to mutual-beneficial goals, as was theoretically predicted by Yang (1988).

In the third study, Chia, Chong, and Cheng (1986) found scores on the CITMS to be significantly correlated with scores on a Chinese version of Jacobson's (1952) Marriage-role Attitude Scale among college students in Taiwan, with the more modernized individual holding a more egalitarian attitude toward the marriage role. Finally, Wu (1991) correlated traditionality and modernity variables, measured by the MS-CIT and the MS-CIM, with child-care practices, as measured by a revised Chinese version of Baumrind's (1971) items. Results suggest that more modernized or less traditional parents tended to display more authoritative (not authoritarian) parental behaviour.

Changes in Temperamental Characteristics

Relatively little empirical research has examined the changes in temperamental traits since 1985. The two relevant studies to be mentioned here are rather fragmentary or unsystematic. Ying and Zhang (1992) examined the degrees of internality–externality and the strength of norm-abiding or norm-questioning tendencies using a Chinese version of the California Psychological Inventory (Gough, 1987) with a sample of rural and urban residents in Shandong province on China's east coast. They found no consistent patterns of rural–urban differences in the two variables among the young and old groups. Another relevant study, published before 1985 but not covered in Yang's 1986 review, is Yao's (1984) investigation of the relationship between tradition-al–modern cognitive conflict and psychological adjustment. Yang (1985) used Yao's original data to analyse the relationships of scores on the CITMS to a number of variables related to psychological adjustment. It was found that interpersonal sensitivity, hostility, and paranoid tendency tended to correlate positively with individual traditionality and negatively with modernity.

A COMPREHENSIVE PROFILE OF CHINESE PSYCHOLOGICAL TRANSFORMATION

We have now briefly reviewed the major empirical studies related to changes in motivational, evaluative–attitudinal, and temperamental characteristics of Chinese people in Taiwan, mainland China, and Hong Kong since 1985. The directions of psychological changes as a result of societal modernization can be roughly inferred from both diachronic (quasi-longitudinal) and synchronic (cross-sectional) data. In the diachronic case, the direction of psychological change can be observed directly from the trend displayed in the time-series data. The synchronic case is more complicated. Three kinds of cross-sectional variables have been used: observing respondents in communities (for exam-ple, rural versus urban) of varying levels of societal modernization; testing respondents of successive generations; and assessing people showing differ-ent degrees of individual traditionality and modernity (measured by the CITMS, the MS-CIT, or the MS-CIM). While an inference of trends in psycho-logical change from data involving one of the first two kinds of cross-sectional variables is relatively easier to comprehend, that involving the third cross-sec-tional type may present some problems. Hchu (1980) argued that an inference of longitudinal changes in a certain psychological characteristic from cross-sec-tional individual differences in that particular characteristic among people of varying degrees of individual traditionality or modernity committed the indi-vidual fallacy. Yang and L. L. Hwang (1988), however, presented theoretical reasons and empirical evidence for the argument that this may not be the case.

Inferring from both diachronic and synchronic findings reviewed in the above and in Yang's 1986 chapter, an extended list of decreasing and increas-ing psychological characteristics of the Chinese people under the impact of societal modernization may be constructed (see Table 31.1). It may be noted that the substantial expansion of Yang's (1986) list is mainly due to the dispro-portionate increase in the number of evaluative–attitudinal characteristics. As in the case of the 1986 list, the characteristics in the decreasing column in Table 31.1 may be succinctly summarized under the concept of the social-oriented personality and those in the increasing column may be summarized under the concept of the individual-oriented personality.

Recently, Yang (in press) formally and systematically proposed that Chinese social orientation is composed of four major modalities of social psy-chological functioning: the familistic orientation (or more precisely, familistic collectivism), Other orientation (orientation toward the Other), relationship orientation, and authoritarian orientation. He also contended that the four modes of Chinese social interaction would result in four corresponding sets of

Table 31.1 An Extended List of Decreasing and Increasing Psychological Characteristics of Chinese People under the Impact of Societal Modernization

Decreasing	Increasing

Motivational Characteristics (Need for)

MD1. Abasement	MI1. Achievement
MD2. Achievement	(individual-oriented)
(social-oriented)	MI2. Autonomy
MD3. Aggression	MI3. Change
MD4. Deference	MI4. Exhibition
MD5. Endurance	MI5. Heterosexuality
MD6. Nurturance	MI6. Intraception
MD7. Order	MI7. Succourance
MD8. Social approval	

Evaluative-attitudinal Characteristics (Emphasis on)

ED1. Altruistic contributions	EI1. Ability and knowledge
ED2. Capacity for hardship and perseverance	EI2. Achievement (activity)
	EI3. Aesthetic values
ED3. Collectivistic (lineal) relationship	EI4. Autonomous social participation
ED4. Family roles (by wives)	EI5. Comfortable life
ED5. Economic values	EI6. Family roles (by husbands)
ED6. Equality of income	EI7. Freedom
ED7. Face and relationship	EI8. Individualistic consciousness
ED8. Inner development	EI9. Individualistic relationship
ED9. Loyalty to family and family members	EI10. Mastery over nature
ED10. Modesty and contentment	EI11. Present and future time-perspectives
ED11. Obedience	EI12. Scientific and rational thinking
ED12. Patience and hard work	
ED13. Religious values	EI13. Self assertion and growth
ED14. Safety and security	EI14. Self-indulgence and sensuous enjoyment
ED15. Social loyalty and seniority	EI15. Social status, power, and wealth
ED16. Social restraint and self-control	EI16. Tolerance and permissiveness
ED17. Social service and national development	EI17. Utilitarian values
	EI18. Work role
ED18. Social values	EI19. World peace
ED19. Solidarity and harmoniousness	EI20. Autonomous filial attitudes
ED20. Stable social environment	EI21. Competitive attitudes
ED21. Submission to nature	EI22. Democratic attitudes
ED22. Theoretical values	EI23. Individualistic-oriented

Table 31.1   *(Cont'd)*

Decreasing	Increasing
ED23. Authoritarian attitudes	filial attitudes
ED24. External-control beliefs	EI24. Internal-control beliefs
ED25. Familistic-oriented filial attitudes	EI25. Masculinity
ED26. Fatalistic-helplessness attitudes	EI26. Mutual-beneficial filial attitudes
ED27. Femininity	EI27. Positive attitudes toward premarital sexual behaviour
ED28. Heteronomous filial attitudes	
ED29. Mono-beneficial (parents-centered) filial attitudes	
ED30. Negative attitudes toward divorce	

Temperamental Characteristics

TD1. Conscientiousness	TI1. Ascendance and dominance
TD2. Friendliness and harmoniousness	TI2. Emotional stability
	TI3. Flexibility
TD3. Hostility	TI4. Tolerance
TD4. Interpersonal sensitivity	TI5. Sociability and extraversion
TD5. Neuroticism	
TD6. Paranoid tendency	
TD7. Perseverance	
TD8. Self-restraint and cautiousness	

psychological dispositions. As personality traits, these four dispositional orientations are the most basic among the seven orientations or dispositions listed by Yang (1986) as the major aspects of the Chinese social-oriented character. It is important to note that most, if not all, of the characteristics in the decreasing column in Table 31.1 may be reasonably classified into one or more of the four basic social-oriented dispositions as follows:

Familistic orientation: MD2, MD3, MD5, MD6, MD7; ED1, ED2, ED3, ED4, ED5, ED8, ED9, ED10, ED11, ED12, ED13, ED14, ED15, ED16, ED19, ED20, ED24, ED25, ED27, ED28, ED29, ED30; TD1, TD3, TD5, TD6, TD7, TD8.

Other orientation: MD2, MD3, MD8; ED1, ED2, ED6, ED8, ED10, ED14, ED16, ED17, ED18, ED19, ED20; TD6, TD7, TD8.

Relationship orientation: MD1, MD4, MD8; ED4, ED6, ED7, ED8, ED10, ED16, ED18, ED19, ED26; TD2, TD4, TD8.

Authoritarian orientation: MD1, MD4, MD7; ED1, ED3, ED4, ED11, ED14,ED15, ED16, ED23, ED24, ED26, ED27, ED28, ED29; TD3, TD4, TD5, TD8.

Proportionately more characteristics are related in one way or another to the familistic orientation, indicating that this orientation is much more pervasive in its coverage and/or much more influenced by the process of societal modernization than are the other three.

Among the seven orientations or dispositions listed by Yang (1986) as the major aspects of the Chinese individual-oriented character, self orientation, independent (autonomous) orientation, competitive orientation, and egalitarian orientation are the most basic, roughly corresponding to familistic orientation, Other orientation, relationship orientation, and authoritarian orientation as the core of the Chinese social-oriented character. Most, if not all, of the characteristics in the increasing column in Table 31.1 may be properly classified into one or more of these four basic individual-oriented dispositions as follows:

Self orientation: MI1, MI2, MI4, MI5, MI6, MI7; EI1, EI2, EI3, EI4, EI5, EI6, EI7, EI8, EI9, EI10, EI11, EI12, EI13, EI14, EI17, EI18, EI20, EI23, EI24, EI26, EI27; TI1, TI3.

Independent orientation: MI2, MI3; EI4, EI7, EI18, EI19, EI24, EI25; TI3, TI4, TI5.

Competitive orientation: MI1, MI2, MI3, MI4; EI1, EI2, EI14, EI7, EI8, EI21, EI25, EI27; TI1, TI3, TI5.

Egalitarian orientation: EI5, EI6, EI7, EI9, EI16, EI22, EI23, EI26; TI4.

It should be noted that relatively more characteristics are related to self orientation. This suggests that self orientation is much more pervasive in its coverage and/or much more influenced by the process of modernization than are the other three. It should also be pointed out that most, if not all, of the 20 core modern psychological characteristics identified by Yang's (1988) comprehensive review can also be properly assigned to one or more of the four individual-oriented orientations.

COEXISTENCE OF CERTAIN TRADITIONAL AND MODERN PSYCHOLOGICAL CHARACTERISTICS

Based upon the above analysis and the results presented in Table 31.1, it may be said that during the process of societal modernization, the Chinese people's familistic, Other, relationship, and authoritarian orientations have been decreasing in their strength, whereas their self, independent, competitive, and egalitarian orientations have been increasing in strength. More simply, as a result of modernization Chinese people have tended to be less socially oriented and more individually oriented. However, this is not to say that Chinese social orientation will eventually be completely replaced by a form of Chinese individual orientation. Yang (1988, 1992), for example, has already provided some rather direct evidence to the contrary.

Yang's Research Paradigm of Psychological Traditionality and Modernity

Yang's evidence is drawn from a new initiative that has produced systematic studies on Chinese individual traditionality and modernity. Yang and his associates have been conducting research in this area for more than 20 years. Their research at the first stage (roughly from 1969 to 1984) was mainly based upon the classical modernization theory (see, for example, Karsh and Cole, 1968; Kerr, Dunlop, Harbicon, and Myers, 1960; Levy, 1966) and about 20 empirical studies (for reviews, see Yang, 1981, 1985, 1986; Yang and Hchu, 1974) were completed with such a theoretical orientation. During this stage, their major tool (the CITMS) for measuring Chinese individual traditionality–modernity was constructed under the general assumption that psychological traditionalism and modernism are two polar opposites of the same unidimensional continuum with a neutral point at the middle.

Influenced by theoretical criticisms (for example, Bendix, 1967; Gusfield, 1967) of, and scattered fragmentary findings (for example, Trommsdorff, 1983) in opposition to classical modernization theory, they decided in 1984 to switch their research strategy to a new one in which traditionality (T) and modernity (M) are seen as two potentially separate multidimensional psychological syndromes whose components may be different for culturally different peoples. To be more specific, their new approach is different from the previous one in four major respects, as shown in Table 31.2.

Table 31.2   Yang's Previous and New Research Paradigms of Psychological Traditionality and Modernity

Previous approach	*New approach*
1. T-M as a bipolar psychological continuum with two opposite parts	1. T and M as two separate or different psychological syndromes
2. T-M as a unidimensional continuum	2. T and M as multidimensional syndromes, each with more than one component
3. The same person's levels of T-M in various domains of his or her life supposed to be roughly uniform	3. The same person's levels of both T and M supposed to vary substantially across various domains of his or her life
4. The content of T-M supposed to be cross-culturally invariant	4. The components of both T and M supposed to vary substantially across different cultures

By adopting the new approach, two large groups of items were written for the assessment of Chinese traditionality and modernity, separately, guided by two different comprehensive conceptual schemes. Factor analyses of empirical data collected from large samples of Taiwanese students and adults consistently identified five oblique psychological components of Chinese traditionality: Submission to Authority, Filial Piety and Ancestral Worship, Conservatism and Endurance (earlier labelled Passivity and Conservativeness), Fatalism and Defensiveness, and Male Dominance. In addition, the data identified five oblique components of Chinese modernity: Egalitarianism and Open-mindedness, Social Isolation and Self Reliance, Optimism and

Assertiveness, Affective Hedonism, and Sex Equality. In all the samples, the total score of the five traditionality components had only a low negative correlation with that of the five modernity components, confirming the new assumption that traditionalism and modernism are two separate or different psychological syndromes.

Based upon the results of factor analyses and other relevant data, six new scales (the MS-CIT is one) were constructed to measure Chinese traditionality and six (the MS-CIM is one) were constructed to measure Chinese modernity. Some of the six in each set are longer forms and some, shorter ones.

Some scales assess psychological components only, some provide scores for domains of life only, and some cover both components and domains. In the assessment of both traditionality and modernity, separate sub-scale scores can be obtained for ten domains of life: Marriage and Husband–Wife Relationship; Child Training and Parent–Child Relationship; Family and Family Life; Social Life and Interpersonal Relationship; Sex and Man–Woman Relationship; Education and Learning; Occupation and Work; Economic and Consumer Activities; Political and Legal Activities; and Religion and Religious Beliefs.

Yang's Findings of Coexistence of Certain Traditional and Modern Traits

Yang and his associates' new research paradigm enables the researchers to collect systematic data for an empirical test of a puzzling research question: whether or not traditional and modern values or attitudes are able to coexist in a modern society. In one study, Yang (1992) computed partial correlations between each of the five traditionality factors and each of the five modernity factors for large samples of college students in Taiwan. The findings indicate, first, that Submission to Authority, Conservatism and Endurance, and Male Dominance were moderately negatively correlated with Egalitarianism and Open-mindedness; second, Male Dominance was substantially negatively correlated with Sex Equality; third, Filial Piety and Ancestral Worship and Fatalism and Defensiveness were correlated positively with Optimism and Assertiveness and Social Isolation and Self-reliance; and, fourth, all five traditionality factors tended to have a zero or negligible correlation with Affective Hedonism. The first and second findings suggest that, under the impact of societal modernization, Submission to Authority, Conservatism and Endurance, and Male Dominance will be gradually replaced in part by Egalitarianism and Open-mindedness, and Male Dominance will be gradually replaced by Sex Equality. The third and fourth findings reveal that Filial Piety and Ancestral Worship and Fatalism and Defensiveness will be able to coexist with Optimism and Assertiveness, Social Isolation and Self-reliance, and Affective Hedonism during the process of social change. Thus, Yang's research empirically demonstrates that some of the Chinese people's most important traditional attitudes, beliefs, and values need not be replaced by modern ones as some would have expected.

Yang's (1992) findings are supported by Brindley's (1989/90) interview data, which indicate that traditional values such as relationship orientation, moral and self-cultivation, filial piety, and paternalism coexist along with modern values such as scientific thinking, utilitarianism, materialism, and independence among academic, political, and journalistic élites in Taiwan. They are also in agreement with Lee's (1985, 1988) observations that traditional beliefs and practices like *feng shui* (geomancy) and *yuan fen* (predestined affinity) are still alive and well and have important functions for many Chinese residents in Hong Kong to explain away life's vicissitudes and to cope with social and psychological stress generated by modernization (see also Crittendon, this volume; Leung, this volume). Yang's findings are further supported by Chu's (1993) empirical data indicating that certain important traditional values (for example, historical heritage, diligence and frugality, loyalty and devotion to the State) are still endorsed by the majority of Chinese in mainland China, although certain other traditional values (for example, the 'three obediences and four virtues', the way of the golden mean, and differentiation between men and women) are rejected by the majority.

Yang (1988) noted the striking similarity between the 20 core modern psychological traits, derived from his comprehensive review of 1960s-era individual modernity research, and the major aspects of individualism as conceptualized by Hofstede (1980), Hui and Triandis (1986), Triandis (1987), and Waterman (1984). It should be pointed out as well that the five components of Chinese individual modernity, as measured by the MS-CIM, taken as a whole, are conceptually similar to those definitions of individualism, and that the five components of the Chinese individual traditionality, as measured by the MS-CIT, are similar to those definitions of collectivism. Moreover, a careful check of the psychological characteristics listed Table 31.1 reveals that those in the increasing column bear a resemblance to the psychological syndrome of individualism (idiocentrism), and those in the decreasing column resemble the psychological syndrome of collectivism (allocentrism). Given the correspondence of individual traditionality and modernity to collectivism and individualism, Yang's findings of a low correlation between the total score of the multidimensional Chinese traditionality and that of modernity enables us to infer that collectivism and individualism do not necessarily form opposite poles of a single continuum. This inference is consonant with what has been empirically found by, for example, Ho and Chiu (1994), Kagitcibasi (1987), Sinha and Tripathi (1994), and Triandis, Bontempo, Villareal, Asai, and Lucca (1988). It may also be inferred from Yang's (1992) findings of the coexistence of traditionality and modernity traits that some collectivistic and individualistic characteristics may coexist in persons in a modern society, and the former need not be eventually replaced by the latter through the process of societal modernization.

Yang's Revised Theory of Psychological Convergence and Divergence

In examining the effects of increased modernization, a theory is needed to explain which traditional psychological characteristics will be partially or completely replaced by modern ones and which will be able to coexist alongside the modern. Yang (1988) first proposed such a theory; he (Yang, 1992) expanded upon it in a revised theory formulated mainly for the explanation of change and stability of common psychological characteristics that are expressed among the majority of people in a traditional or modern society. His theory is based upon the basic assumption that the formation of the common psychological characteristics of people in a given society is not determined solely by such external factors as ecological, economic, social, and living conditions but instead by the complicated interaction of such factors with the people's common morphological, physiological, and behavioural traits.

The theory began with a distinction between three broad categories of common psychological characteristics. General characteristics are those attitudes, thoughts, values, or behaviours that prevail in all kinds of human societies. Specific characteristics are those attitudes, thoughts, values, or behaviours that prevail in societies of the same type (there are four major types of traditional societies—agrarian, gathering, pastoral, and hunting—and one major type of modern society—industrial). Unique characteristics are those attitudes, thoughts, values, and behaviours that prevail in only one society.

Common psychological characteristics can also be divided into functional and nonfunctional categories. A common functional psychological characteristic is defined as an attitude, thought, value, or behaviour that is helpful or instrumental in the adjustment of a person or group in a society to a certain aspect, condition, or feature of the life environment or the lifestyle in that society. A common nonfunctional characteristic is an attitude, thought, value, or behaviour that does not have such a function for adjustment and is purely stylistic, expressive, or terminal in nature.

The combination of the two classifications yields six subcategories: general–functional, specific–functional, unique–functional, general– nonfunctional, specific–nonfunctional, and unique–nonfunctional. Both traditional and modern psychological characteristics may be classified into these six types. According to Yang's revised theory, only those traditional characteristic that are specific–functional and unique–functional will be most likely to lose their strength and to change in their content during the process of societal modernization. All the other kinds of traditional psychological characteristics (that is, general–functional, general–nonfunctional, specific–nonfunctional, and unique–nonfunctional) will remain unchanged and coexist with the modern ones in people in the same modern society. Among modern characteristics, only those that are specific–functional and unique–functional will be most likely to emerge and increase their strength as a result of societal change. Of the other four types of modern characteristics, only the specific–nonfunctional and unique–nonfunctional will be gradually formed and coexist alongside the traditional characteristics in people in the same modern society; the general–functional and general–nonfunctional characteristics in modern societies are the same as those in traditional societies for the reason that all general characteristics are invariant across all types of societies.

It may be inferred from the above that, under the impact of societal modernization, people in different modern societies will eventually become psychologically similar or convergent in modern characteristics of the specific–functional and specific–nonfunctional types and dissimilar or divergent in modern characteristics of the unique–functional and unique–nonfunctional types as well as in changed traditional characteristics of the specific–functional and unique–nonfunctional types.

Since Yang's revised theory is based upon a functional perspective of cultural–ecological interactionism, it may be properly called a cultural–ecologically interactionistic theory of psychological modernization or transformation. Yang (1992) provided data, collected from college students and adults in Taiwan, for an empirical test of part of his revised theory. A comprehensive test of this theory, however, demands a large-scale cross-societal study, which is feasible only through the international collaboration of a large number of interested researchers.

THE DYNAMIC PROCESS OF ATTITUDE AND VALUE CHANGE DURING SOCIETAL MODERNIZATION: A THEORETICAL ATTEMPT

In this chapter, we have constructed a systematic profile of Chinese psychological transformation as a result of societal change by reviewing the relevant empirical studies conducted in three major Chinese societies. We have provided as well a tentative answer to the thorny question of the coexistence of traditional and modern psychological characteristics in people in a modern society by reviewing previous empirical findings and theoretical formulations. At this point, the reader may naturally come up with the question: What is the dynamic process involved in the psychological transformation of individual persons? Unfortunately, little empirical effort has been made to disclose the specific sequential steps of this process. Empirical research to map out these steps is badly needed, and it should be given a high priority in future research on Chinese individual modernization.

In order for future studies in this area to be systematic, a theoretical scheme of the dynamic process of attitude and value change under societal modernization is to be presented in this section. To save space, the theoretical attempt will be briefly sketched in a skeleton form; the detailed depiction of the theory and its intellectual traditions will have to be presented elsewhere.

As can be seen in Figure 31.1, the theory focuses on intrapersonal processes, states, traits, and types (solid rectangles), with certain social and cultural factors as important determinants (dotted rectangles). The process of psychological change begins with the introduction, importation, and emergence of modern (M) cultural elements (for example, concepts, values, knowledge, ideologies, techniques, and tools) and the coexistence of these elements with persisting traditional (T) ones. If the T and M cultural elements (A and B) are strong enough and exist long enough, both of them will be gradually internalized through various kinds of learning and types of identification (C). As a result, both T and M attitudes and values (D) are formed within the same person, with a greater number of T elements in the early stages, and a greater number of M elements in the later stages of societal change. The coexistence of internalized T and M attitudes and values results in an attitude–value (A–V) system of the primary mixed type (G).

The intensity of a cognitive inconsistency or intentional conflict (F) resulting from the coexistence of contradictory T and M attitudes or values is a function

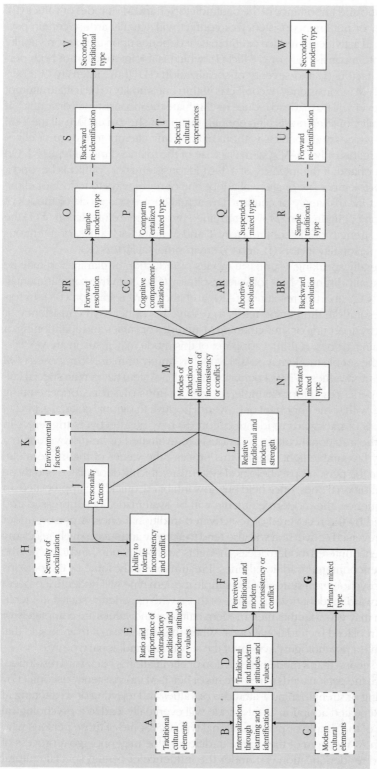

Figure 31.1 The Hypothetical Dynamic Process of Attitude and Value Change under the Impact of Societal Modernization

of the ratio and importance of the contradictory T and M attitudes or values (E). Whether or not an inconsistency or conflict will actually arouse certain psychological activities to reduce or eliminate it depends upon the person's ability to tolerate inconsistency or conflict (I), which is a joint function of both personality factors (J) and severity of socialization (H). If the intensity of a perceived T–M inconsistency or conflict is within one's ability to bear it, no attempt whatsoever will be made to reduce or eliminate the inconsistency or conflict. If one's ability of tolerance is high enough that he or she can endure all the T–M inconsistencies and conflicts without making any attempt to reduce or eliminate them, his or her A–V system is a case of the tolerated mixed type (N). On the other hand, if the intensity of a T–M inconsistency or conflict is beyond a person's tolerance, he or she will adopt one or more ways to reduce or eliminate that inconsistency or conflict. The actual choice of a mode or modes of reduction or elimination (M) is determined by a complex interaction of (1) the relative strength of the contradictory T and M attitudes, values, or intentions (L), (2) personality factors (J), and (3) environmental factors (K).

Generally speaking, four basic modes of reduction or elimination may be conceptually distinguished: forward resolution (FR), cognitive compartmentalization (CC), abortive resolution (AR), and backward resolution (BR). In forward resolution, the person tends to resolve his or her T–M consistency or conflict by accepting or strengthening M attitudes or values and abandoning or weakening T ones. Habitual adoption of this mode may result in an A–V system of the simple modern type (O), which is purely or mainly composed of M attitudes and values. When a person with such a system has certain special cultural experiences (T)(for example, those from unusual, strong, or penetrating contacts with some important or powerful positive traditional cultural aspects), a process of backward re-identification (S) may be effectively triggered, in which the traditional culture is seriously re-evaluated or 're-discovered' in a strongly favourable light. During this process, the values of the modern elements in the person's psychological system are quickly depreciated and those of the traditional ones, once held but now inhibited, quickly re-appreciated. In consequence, the modern elements will be systematically suppressed and replaced by the recovered or re-activated traditional ones. A person under such a reversed conversion will also tend to actively and successively reject any newly encountered modern ideas, thoughts, and behaviours, and to accept the newly encountered traditional ones. Presumably, only some of the persons with a psychological system of the simple modern type will undergo a process of backward re-identification. Some of those who experience such a re-identification may go so far that their modern attitudes and values are completely or mostly replaced by traditional ones. When this is the case, it may be said that they have a psychological system of the secondary traditional type (V).

The second major mode of reduction or elimination is backward resolution, in which the person tends to resolve his or her T–M inconsistency or conflict by accepting or strengthening T attitudes or values and rejecting or weakening M ones. Repeated adoption of this mode will eventually lead to a psychological system of the simple or pure traditional type (R). Some of those persons who have an A–V system of the simple traditional type may undergo a process of forward re-identification (U) under the influence of certain special cultural experiences (for example, those from unusual, strong, or penetrating contacts with some important or powerful positive modern cultural aspects). During this process, the values of the traditional elements in the psychological system are seriously re-evaluated and quickly depreciated and those modern ones, once held but now inhibited, quickly re-appreciated. As a result, the traditional elements will be systematically repressed and replaced by the recovered or re-activated modern ones. A person under such a reversed conversion will also tend to actively and successively reject any newly encountered traditional ideas, thoughts, and behaviours and to accept the newly encountered modern ones. Some of those persons who undergo such a forward re-identification may go so far that their traditional attitudes and values are completely or mostly replaced by modern ones. Such persons may be said to have a psychological system of the secondary modern type (W).

Cognitive compartmentalization is the third major mode of reduction or elimination of inconsistency or conflict, in which the person consciously divides the inconsistent or conflictual attitudes and values into two or more separate compartments or domains of life and thus avoids being aware of attitudes and values in different domains at the same time (for a detailed discussion of this defensive or coping strategy, see Yang, 1994). Repeated adoption of compartmentalization results in a psychological system of the compartmentalized mixed type (P). Such a mixed system consists of traditional attitudes and values in some life domains and modern ones in others. In this case, attitudes and values in different domains tend to remain not uniformly traditional or modernized for long periods.

The fourth major mode is abortive resolution, in which attempts at reducing or eliminating a T–M inconsistency or conflict by adopting any of the above three modes repeatedly fail for one reason or another. In cases of habitual abortive resolution, inconsistencies and conflicts involving the traditional and modern attitudes and values will remain unresolved for a considerable period. This irresolution will result in a psychological system of the suspended mixed type (Q).

What has been presented in this section is a theoretical exposition of the dynamic process involved in the intrapersonal change of attitudes and values under the impact of societal modernization. This theory is potentially applicable not only to the Chinese case but also to cases of the psychological modernization of people in other societies. It is in this sense that the proposed scheme is a general theory of the dynamic process of psychological transformation. It should also be pointed out that the theory is empirically testable for the simple reason that all the psychological and environmental factors and variables in the theory can be operationally defined in one way or another. Indeed, empirical data have been collected and will be analysed for the testing of the last part of the theory, especially the identification of the different types of A–V systems, using Chinese in Taiwan as respondents.

SOME CONCLUDING REMARKS

In the present chapter, I have reviewed empirical studies relevant to changes in motivational, evaluative–attitudinal, and temperamental characteristics of the

Chinese published since 1985. Findings of these studies have been incorporated into those of the studies published before 1985 as reviewed by Yang (1986), to construct a comprehensive list of psychological characteristics that have been increasing and decreasing under the impact of societal modernization. Most, if not all, of the decreasing characteristics can be classified into one or more of the four major dispositions of Chinese social orientation: familistic orientation, Other orientation (orientation toward the Other), relationship orientation, and authoritarian orientation. On the other hand, most, if not all, of the increasing characteristics can be classified into one or more of the four major dispositions of Chinese individual orientation: self orientation, independent orientation, competitive orientation, and egalitarian orientation. There has been empirical evidence indicating that some traditional psychological characteristics may coexist along with certain modern characteristics and that the former need not be replaced by the latter. Yang's revised theory of psychological convergence and divergence has been reviewed to explain why this might be so. Finally, a new theory has been briefly presented for the conceptual analysis of the dynamic process of psychological modernization during societal modernization.

The relevant literature reviewed in this chapter includes studies completed in three major Chinese societies: Taiwan, Hong Kong, and mainland China. Since the number of relevant studies is unevenly distributed across these societies, it is inevitable for the generalizations drawn in this chapter to represent similar phenomena in these different societies to different degrees. Moreover, lack of well-designed comparative research prevents us from inferring psychological and behavioural changes from data collected for the same characteristics in two or more Chinese societies at different stages of societal modernization. Fortunately, thoughtful comparative psychological studies have been planned, and some carried out, by research teams consisting of psychologists and sociologists from both Taiwan and mainland China. Synchronic and diachronic data from such research will clearly contribute to our knowledge about the different psychological effects of societal modernization on Chinese people in different Chinese societies.

Finally, it should be pointed out that the academic movement of indigenization of psychological research in Chinese societies (for reviews, see Yang, 1982, 1993), inaugurated in Taiwan nearly two decades ago, has been energetically and systematically strengthened by Chinese psychologists over the last seven years. The publication since 1988 of a series of books on indigenous Chinese psychology, and the publication of the first issue of the journal *Indigenous Psychological Research in Chinese Societies* in 1993, all in Taiwan, highlight this significant development. With the increasing number of Chinese psychologists with stronger consciousness and more experience of indigenization, research on the psychological effects of modernization on Chinese people will be carried out with theories and methods more closely geared to the social, cultural, and historical conditions of specific Chinese societies. It is to be hoped that through this effort the complexity of the dynamic mechanisms involved in the change of Chinese people's thoughts, sentiments, and actions in the process of societal modernization will be better understood.

Chapter 32

∎

Concluding Remarks:
The End as Beginning

Michael Harris Bond

> Learn, and then you will find your learning inadequate.
>
> *Book of Rites*

Perhaps this is the time and place to reflect on the fruits of the corporate labour which you now hold in your hands. What do we have, what have we missed, and where shall we go in our future work?

What we have, I believe, is a comprehensive integration of almost all the major areas of empirical work in Chinese psychology. Each chapter presents the database and theoretical approaches that social scientists have developed in that line of enquiry. Each provides the intellectual stimulation, suggestions, and references necessary to inspire a host of future studies.

What we have missed is a chapter on political psychology. That is an important but underdeveloped area in psychology generally. Very few psychologists have ventured to study Chinese political psychology, leaving the field instead to political scientists. They have contributed interpretive studies in the main (see, for example, Pye, 1985; Solomon, 1971), but recently careful survey research has begun to appear (for example, Nathan and Shi, 1993). Psychologists studying Chinese political socialization have started contributing their insights as well (see Lee and Zhan, 1991). Sufficient data should soon be available to assess some of the theoretical speculations advanced by the interpretive political scientists.

Regrettably, we have also missed chapters on neurolinguistics and on morality. These were commissioned and indeed presented at the International Conference on Chinese Psychology in May 1994. Their presenters were, however, unable to meet the subsequent schedule for turning their brilliant ideas into polished prose. Interested readers are instead referred to Hoosain (1991) and Geilen (1989), respectively, for earlier insightful work on these two topics.

A number of issues have percolated through the chapters of this Handbook and are worth identifying as future directions for research work into the psychology of Chinese people. First, prior work in this area has typically proceeded by contrasting North Americans with a convenient group of Chinese. The theoretical rationale, if any, for such studies has generally involved some broad-brush distinction, such as individualism versus collectivism. Most results obtained are easily accommodated by such elastic concepts. Outcomes from many such bicultural contrasts then form the empirical core of such compendia as this Handbook.

The resulting intellectual problem is that we are left with no basis for distinguishing among various groups of Chinese in cultural settings as diverse as Beijing, Singapore, and London's Chinatown. Nor are we able to distinguish

Chinese from other cultural groups that are similar in one respect but different in others. Iranians are collectivists, as well, but surely different in their religiosity from Chinese! Such a difference has dramatic consequences for a whole range of political behaviours, for example. Japanese, too, use an idiographic script, but they do not have a tonal language. Surely their cognitive processes differ from those of the Chinese but in ways that we have not yet began to address.

The obvious solution is to conduct careful, multicultural studies (see, for example, Schwartz, 1994). The more cultural groups involved, the more refinement becomes possible in our theoretical understanding of what features make various Chinese groups distinctive among themselves and different from others. The work involved in orchestrating such research is enormous, but the pay-offs are both considerable and necessary to move Chinese psychology to a higher level of sophistication.

Bicultural studies are still useful, but only when the cultural processes involved can be distinguished. This goal can be achieved by selecting two cultural groups which are only different with respect to a given theory of culture in only one respect. So, for example, the mainland Chinese and the Italians are quite similar on Schwartz's (1994) cultural value dimension of conservatism versus openness to change, but they are very different on measures of self-enhancement versus self-transcendence. Differences of behaviour in China and Italy which relate to values can thereby be interpreted unequivocally as connected to different levels of self-transcendence.

Alternatively, the bicultural contrasts may yield value if the underlying psychological processes hypothesized as involved are measured in the study itself and related to the behaviours of interest (see for example, Bond, Leung, and Schwartz, 1992). By using different cultural groups in this way, one can check for both universal and indigenous processes. The universals emerge as main effects in a regression equation including both groups; indigenous processes are revealed from interactions between culture and the mediating variables (see, for example, Singelis, Bond, Lai, and Sharkey, 1995).

Amidst all this scientific activity, we must ensure that Chinese voices are empowered and encouraged to speak. We need more psychologists from Chinese cultural backgrounds, and they must be well trained in the knowledge base and empirical skills required to meet international standards. Whether they communicate in the Chinese language or otherwise, their work must be carefully assessed before publication, so that it can come to receive the respect it deserves. And lest we forget, material support, both in the form of grants and salaries, must be more forthcoming in order to sustain this enterprise.

Only through this development can Chinese psychology shake off the colonial legacy of the discipline's past and present (see Blowers, this volume). For, psychology originated in the West, is dominated at present by Western practitioners, and desperately needs a viable, cultural counterweight to meet charges of intellectual naïvety and imperialism (see, for example, Moghaddam, 1987; Phillips and Pearson, this volume). Contemporary Chinese culture provides just such an opportunity.

The East and the West must unite to provide one another with what is lacking.
Abdu'l-Baha, *Paris Talks*

References

Aaronson, D., and Ferres, S. (1986). 'Sentence processing in Chinese-American bilinguals', *Journal of Memory and Language, 25,* 136-62.

Abbott, K. A. (1970). *Harmony and Individualism.* Taipei: Oriental Cultural Service.

Abe, J. S., and Zane, N. W. S. (1990). 'Psychological maladjustment among Asian and white American college students: Controlling for confounds', *Journal of Counseling Psychology, 37,* 437-44.

Abel, T. M., and Hsu, F. L. K. (1949). 'Some aspects of personality of Chinese as revealed by the Rorschach Test', *Journal of Projective Techniques, 13,* 285-301.

Abramson, L., Seligman, M. E. P., and Teasdale, J. D. (1978). 'Learned helplessness in humans: Critique and reformulation', *Journal of Abnormal Psychology, 87,* 49-74.

Achenbach, T. M., and Edelbrock, C. S. (1978). 'The classification of child psychopathology: A review and analysis of empirical efforts', *Psychological Bulletin, 85,* 1275-1301.

Ahadi, S. A., Rothbart, M. K., and Ye, R. (1992). 'Child temperament in the U.S. and China: Similarities and differences', *European Journal of Personality, 7,* 359-78.

Allport, G. W., Vernon, P. E., and Lindzey, G. (1951). *Study of Values: A Scale for Measuring the Dominant Interests in Personality* (third edition). Boston: Houghton Mifflin.

Altman, I., and Taylor, D. A. (1973). *Social Penetration Processes: The Development of Interpersonal Relationships.* New York: Holt, Rinehart and Winston.

American Chemical Society (1993). *International Chemistry Olympiad Individual Results, 1989-1993.* Washington, DC: American Chemical Society.

American Psychiatric Association (1994). *Diagnostic and Statistical Manual of Mental Disorders.* (fourth edition). Washington, DC: American Psychiatric Association.

Anderson, E. N. (1992). 'Chinese fisher families: Variations on Chinese themes', *Journal of Comparative Family Studies, 23,* 231-47.

Anderson, M. (1992). *Intelligence and Development: A Cognitive Theory.* Cambridge, MA: Blackwell.

Andersson, A., Jr. (1972). 'Some Chinese methods of dealing with crowding', *Urban Antrophology, 1,* 141-50.

Andrews, S. (1982). 'Phonological recoding: Is the regularity effect consistent?' *Memory and Cognition, 10,* 565-75.

Andry, R. (1960). *Delinquency and Parental Pathology* (1970 revision). London: Methuen.

Antonovsky, A. (1987). *Unraveling the Mystery of Health: How People Manage Stress and Stay Well.* London: Jossey-Bass.

Applegate, J. L. (1993). 'Time to bring communication/interaction out of the closet?' *Contemporary Psychology, 38,* 1076-7.

Argyle, M. (1982). 'Inter-cultural communication'. In S. Bochner (Ed.), *Cultures in Contact: Studies in Cross-Cultural Interaction* (pp. 61-79). Oxford: Pergamon.

Argyle, M. (1986). 'Rules for social relationships in four cultures', *Australian Journal of Psychology, 38,* 309-18.

Argyle, M., and Henderson, M. (1985). *The Anatomy of Relationships.* Harmondsworth: Penguin.

Argyle, M., Henderson, M., Bond, M. H., Iizuka, Y., and Contarello, A. (1986). 'Cross-cultural variations in relationship rules', *International Journal of Psychology, 21,* 287-315.

Arkoff, A., Thaver, F., and Elkind, L. (1966). 'Mental health and counseling ideas of Asian and American students', *Journal of Counseling Psychology, 13,* 219-23.

Arnheim, R. (1974). *Art and Visual Perception.* Berkeley: University of California Press.

Asher, M. G., and Yong, P. S. (1993). 'Singapores sociala fondsystem: Implikationer för sparande, boende och socialt skydd' (Singapore's social stock system: Implications for saving, dwelling and social security), *Framtider, 4,* 32-5.

Asiaweek (1994). 'Vital Signs: The bottom line', 26 October, 51.

Atkinson, D. R., and Gim, R. H. (1989). 'Asian-American cultural identity and attitudes toward mental health', *Journal of Counseling Psychology, 36,* 209-12.

Atkinson, D. R., Whiteley, S., and Gim, R. H. (1990). 'Asian-American acculturation and preferences for help-providers', *Journal of College Student Development, 31*, 155-61.

Atkinson, D., Morten, G., and Sue, D. W. (1993). *Counseling American Minorities: A Cross-cultural Perspective.* Dubuque, IA: W. C. Brown Publishers.

Atkinson, J. W. (1957). 'Motivational determinants of risk-taking behaviour', *Psychological Review, 64*, 359-72.

Atkinson, J. W. (Ed.)(1958). *Motives in Fantasy, Action, and Society.* Princeton, NJ: Van Nostrand.

Atkinson, J. W., and Litwin, G. H. (1960). 'Achievement motive and test anxiety conceived as motive to approach success and motive to avoid failure', *Journal of Abnormal and Social Psychology, 60*, 52-63.

Au Yeung, Y. N., Gow, L., Ho, W. F., Lai, C. C., Sivan, A., and Ledesma, J. (in press). 'Survey of attitudes towards external training in the B. Eng. course in Building Services Engineering at Hong Kong Polytechnic', *International Journal of Educational Management.*

Au, T. K. F. (1983). 'Chinese and English counterfactuals: The Sapir-Whorf hypothesis revisited', *Cognition, 15*, 155-87.

Baird, J. R. (1988). 'Quality: What should make higher education "higher"?' *Higher Education Research and Development, 7*(2), 141-52.

Bakan, D. (1966). *The Duality of Human Existence.* Chicago: Rand McNally.

Balla, J. R. (1991). 'A report on student attitudes to language and study at the City Polytechnic of Hong Kong'. Unpublished report, Management Information Office, City Polytechnic of Hong Kong.

Balla, J. R. (1992). 'Language perceptions of students at CPHK: The college perspective'. Unpublished report, Academic Planning Unit, City Polytechnic of Hong Kong.

Balla, J. R., Stokes, M. J., and Stafford, K. J. (1991). 'Using the Study Process Questionnaire to its full potential'. Unpublished technical report, City Polytechnic of Hong Kong.

Balla, J. R., Stokes, M. J., and Stafford, K. J. (1991). 'Changes in student approaches to study at CPHK: A 3-year longitudinal study', *AAIR Conference Refereed Proceedings* (pp. 7-31). Melbourne: Australasian Association for Institutional Research.

Balla, J. R., Stokes, M. J., Stafford, K. J., and Yeung, H. F. (1992). *The Study Process Questionnaire: Norms Derived at the City Polytechnic of Hong Kong.* Unpublished technical report, City Polytechnic of Hong Kong.

Balota, D. A., and Chumbley, J. I. (1984). 'Are lexical decisions a good measure of lexical access? The role of word frequency in the neglected decision stage', *Journal of Experimental Psychology: Human Perception and Performance, 10*, 340-57.

Balota, D. A., and Chumbley, J. I. (1985). 'The locus of word-frequency effects in the pronunciation task: Lexical access and/or production?' *Journal of Memory and Language, 24*, 89-106.

Bar-Tal, D. (1990). *Group Beliefs: A Conception for Analyzing Group Structure, Processes, and Behavior.* New York: Springer-Verlag.

Barnett, A. D. (1979). 'The communication system in China: Some generalizations, hypotheses, and questions for research'. In G. C. Chu and F. L. K. Hsu (Eds.), *Moving a Mountain: Cultural Changes in China* (pp. 386-95). Honolulu: The University Press of Hawaii.

Barnouw, V. (1985). *Culture and Personality* (fourth edition). Belmont, CA: Wadsworth.

Bartholomew, R. T. (1994). 'The social psychology of "epidemic" koro', *International Journal of Social Psychiatry, 40*, 46-60.

Bartlett, E. W., and Smith, C. P. (1966). 'Child rearing practices, birth order, and the development of achievement-related motive', *Psychological Reports, 19*, 1207-16.

Bates, E., and MacWhinney, B. (1982). 'The development of grammar'. In E. Wanner and L. R. Gleitman (Eds.), *Language Acquisition: The State of the Art* (pp. 173-218). New York: Cambridge University Press.

Bates, E., and MacWhinney, B. (1989). 'Functionalism and the competition model'. In B. MacWhinney and E. Bates (Eds.), *The Crosslinguistic Study of Sentence Processing* (pp. 3-73). New York: Cambridge University Press.

Bauer, W., and Hwang, S. C. (1982). *German Impact on Modern Chinese Intellectual History.* Wiesbaden: Franz Steiner Verlag.

Baum, C. L., and Baum, R. (1979). 'Creating the new communist child'. In R. Wilson (Ed.), *Value Change in Chinese Society* (pp. 98-121). New York: Praeger.

Baumrind, D. (1971). 'Current patterns of parental authority', *Developmental Psychology Monographs, 4*, 1-103.

Beach, S. R. H., and Tesser, A. (1988). 'Love in marriage: A cognitive account'. In R. J. Sternberg and

M. L. Barnes (Eds.), *The Psychology of Love* (pp. 330-55). New Haven: Yale University Press.

Beck, A. T., Rush, A. J., Shaw, B. F., and Emery, G. (1979). *Cognitive Therapy of Depression*. New York: Guilford Press.

Becker, C. A. (1976). 'Allocation of attention during visual word recognition', *Journal of Experimental Psychology: Human Perception and Performance, 2,* 556-66.

Becker, C. A. (1980). 'Semantic context effects in visual word recognition', *Memory and Cognition, 8,* 493-512.

Beckman, E. E., and Adams, R. L. (1984). 'Coping behaviour in depression: Report on a new scale', *Behaviour Research and Theory, 22,* 71-5.

Bendix, R. (1967). 'Tradition and modernity reconsidered', *Comparative Studies in Society and History, 9,* 292-346.

Benedict, R. (1934). *Patterns of Culture*. Boston: Houghton Mifflin.

Benson, H. (1975). *The Relaxation Response*. New York: Grove Press.

Berko Gleason, J. (1988). 'Language and socialization'. In F. S. Kessel (Ed.), The *Development of Language and Language Researchers* (pp. 269-80). Hillsdale, NJ: Erlbaum.

Berko Gleason, J., and Weintraub, S. (1976). 'The acquisition of routines in child language', *Language in Society, 5,* 129-36.

Berko Gleason, J., Perlmann, R. Y., and Greif, E. B. (1984). 'What's the magic word: Learning language through routines', *Discourse Processes, 6,* 493-502.

Berlin, B., and Kay, P. (1969). *Basic Color Terms: Their Universality and Evolution*. Berkeley: University of California Press.

Bernstein, B. (1971). *Class, Codes, and Control. Volume I: Theoretical Studies Toward a Sociology of Language*. London: Routledge.

Bernstein, B. (1990). *Class, Codes, and Control. Volume IV: The Structuring of Pedagogic Discourse*. London: Routledge.

Berry, C. (1971). 'Advanced frequency information and verbal response times', *Psychonomic Science, 21,* 151-2.

Berry, J. (1980). 'Introduction to methodology'. In H. Triandis and J. Berry (Eds.), *Handbook of Cross-cultural Psychology* (Vol. 2, pp. 1-28). Boston: Allyn and Bacon.

Berry, J. W. (1969). 'On cross-cultural comparability', *International Journal of Psychology, 4,* 119-28.

Berry, J. W. (1980). 'Acculturation as varieties of adaptation'. In A. Padilla (Ed.), *Acculturation: Theory, Models, and Some New Findings* (pp. 9-25) Boulder: Westview Press.

Berry, J. W., Kim, U., Power, S., Young, M., and Bujaki, M. (1989). 'Acculturation attitudes in plural societies', *Applied Psychology: An International Review, 38,* 185-206.

Berry, M. W. (1989). 'Imposed etics-emics-derived etics: The operationalising of a compelling idea', *International Journal of Psychology, 24,* 721-35.

Bertelson, P., Chen, H. C., Tseng, C. H., Ko, H. W., and de Gelder, B. (in press). 'Explicit speech analysis and orthographic experience in Chinese readers', *Journal of Chinese Linguistics*.

Besner, D., and Hilderbrandt, N. (1987). 'Orthographic and phonological codes in the oral reading of Japanese kana', *Journal of Experimental Psychology: Learning, Memory, and Cognition, 13,* 335-43.

Bi, X. (1994). 'Chinese perfume' [in Chinese]. In Y. Bo (Ed.), *Zhongguoren, Ni Shou Le Shen Me Zhu Zhou?* (pp. 67-73). Taipei: Xingguang Chubanshe.

Bialystok, E. (1991). 'Achieving proficiency in a second language: A processing description'. In R. Phillipson, E. Kellerman, L. Selinker, M. Sharwood Smith, and M. Swain (Eds.), *Foreign/Second Language Pedagogy Research* (pp. 63-78). Clevedon, PA: Multilingual Matters.

Bialystok, E. (Ed.). (1991). *Language Processing in Bilingual Children*. New York: Cambridge University Press.

Biederman, I., and Tsao, Y. C. (1979). 'On processing Chinese ideographs and English words: Some implications from Stroop-test results', *Cognitive Psychology, 11,* 125-32.

Biggs, J. B. (1979). 'Individual differences in study processes and the quality of learning outcomes', *Higher Education, 8,* 381-94.

Biggs, J. B. (1987). *Student Approaches to Learning and Studying*. Hawthorn, Victoria: Australian Council for Educational Research.

Biggs, J. B. (1989). 'Students' approaches to learning in Anglo-Chinese schools', *Educational*

Research Journal, 4, 8-17.

Biggs, J. B. (1990). 'Effects of language medium of instruction on approaches to learning', *Educational Research Journal, 5,* 18-28.

Biggs, J. B. (1991). 'Approaches to learning in secondary and tertiary students in Hong Kong: Some comparative studies', *Educational Research Journal, 6,* 27-39.

Biggs, J. B. (1991). 'Handling change in the language medium of instruction: Effects involving ability, locus of control, and approaches to learning'. In V. Bickley (Ed.), *Where from Here? Issues Relating to the Planning, Management, and Implementation of Language Teaching and Training Programmes in the '90s* (pp. 140-49). Hong Kong: Education Department, Institute of Language in Education.

Biggs, J. B. (1992). *Why and How Do Hong Kong Students Learn? Using the Learning and Study Process Questionnaires* (Education Papers No. 14). Hong Kong: University of Hong Kong.

Biggs, J. B. (1994). 'What are effective schools? Lessons from East and West', *Australian Educational Researcher, 21,* 19-39.

Billing, M. (1994). 'Repopulating the depopulated pages of social psychology', *Theory and Psychology, 4,* 307-35.

Black, J. S., and Porter, L. W. (1991). 'Managerial behaviours and job performance: A successful manager in Los Angeles may not succeed in Hong Kong', *Journal of International Business Studies, 22,* 99-113.

Blau, P. M., Ruan, D. C., and Ardelt, M. (1991). 'Interpersonal choice and networks in China', *Social Forces,* 69, 1037-62.

Blowers, G. H. (1987). 'To know the heart: Psychology in Hong Kong'. In G. H. Blowers and A. M. Turtle (Eds.), *Psychology Moving East: The Status of Western Psychology in Asia and Oceania* (pp. 139-62). Boulder: Westview Press.

Blowers, G. H. (1991). 'The impact of Western psychology in Hong Kong', *International Journal of Psychology, 26*(2), 254-68.

Blowers, G. H. (1994). 'Freud in China: The variable reception of psychoanalysis'. In G. Davidson (Ed.), *Applying Psychology: Lessons from Asia-Oceania* (pp. 35-49). Brisbane: The Australian Psychological Society.

Blowers, G. H. (in press). Gao Juefu: China's Interpreter of Western Psychology'. *World Psychology.*

Blumenthal, E. P. (1976). 'Models in Chinese moral education: Perspectives from children's books'. Unpublished doctoral dissertation, University of Michigan.

Bo, Y. (1992). *The Ugly Chinaman and the Crisis of Chinese Culture* (D. J. Cohn and J. Qing, Eds. and Trans.). Sydney: Allen and Unwin.

Bodde, D. (1953). 'Harmony and conflict in Chinese philosophy'. In A. F. Wright (Ed.), *Studies in Chinese Thought* (pp. 19-80). Chicago: University of Chicago Press.

Boey, K. W. (1976). 'Rigidity and cognitive complexity: An empirical investigation in the interpersonal, physical, and numeric domains under task-oriented and ego-oriented conditions'. Unpublished doctoral dissertation, University of Hong Kong.

Boey, K. W. (1985). 'The MMPI response pattern of Singapore Chinese' [in Chinese], *Acta Psychologica Sinica, 4,* [17(2)] 377-83.

Bohannon, J. N., and Warren-Leubecker, A. (1989). 'Theoretical approaches to language acquisition'. In J. Berko Gleason (Ed.), *The Development of Language* (pp. 167-223). New York: MacMillan.

Boisot, M., and Liang, X. G. (1992). 'The nature of managerial work in the Chinese enterprise reforms: A study of six directors', *Organization Studies, 13,* 161-84.

Bond, M. H. (1979). 'Dimensions of personality used in perceiving peers: Cross-cultural comparisons of Hong Kong, Japanese, American, and Filipino university students', *International Journal of Psychology, 14,* 47-56.

Bond, M. H. (1982). Unpublished data. The Chinese University of Hong Kong.

Bond, M. H. (1983). 'A proposal for cross-cultural studies of attribution'. In M. Hewstone (Ed.), *Attribution Theory: Social and Functional Extensions* (pp. 144-57). Oxford: Basil Blackwell.

Bond, M. H. (Ed.)(1986). *The Psychology of the Chinese People.* Hong Kong: Oxford University Press.

Bond, M. H. (1988). 'Finding universal dimensions of individual variation in multi-cultural studies of values: The Rokeach and Chinese value surveys', *Journal of Personality and Social*

Psychology, 55, 1009-15.

Bond, M. H. (1991). *Beyond the Chinese Face: Insights from Psychology*. Hong Kong: Oxford University Press.

Bond, M. H. (1991). 'Chinese values and health: A cultural-level examination', *Psychology and Health, 5*, 137-52.

Bond, M. H. (1991). 'Cultural influences on modes of impression management: Implications for the culturally diverse organization'. In R. A. Giacalone and P. Rosenfield (Eds.), *Applied Impression Management: How Image-making Affects Managerial Decisions* (pp. 195-218). Newbury Park, CA: Sage.

Bond, M. H. (1993). 'Emotions and their expression in Chinese culture', *Journal of Nonverbal Behavior, 17*(4), 245-62.

Bond, M. H. (1994). 'Trait theory and cross-cultural studies of person perception', *Psychological Inquiry, 5*, 114-7.

Bond, M. H., and Cheung, T. S. (1983). 'The spontaneous self-concept of college students in Hong Kong, Japan, and the United States', *Journal of Cross-Cultural Psychology, 14*, 153-71.

Bond, M. H., Chiu, C. K., and Wan, K. C. (1984). 'When modesty fails: The social impact of group-effacing attributions following success or failure', *European Journal of Social Psychology, 14*, 335-38.

Bond, M. H., and Hewstone, M. (1988). 'Social identity theory and the perception of intergroup relations in Hong Kong', *International Journal of Intercultural Relations, 12*, 153-70.

Bond, M. H., Hewstone, M., Wan, K. C., and Chiu, C. K. (1985). 'Group-serving attributions across intergroup contexts: Cultural differences in the explanation of sex-typed behaviours', *European Journal of Social Psychology, 15*, 435-51.

Bond, M. H., and Hwang, K. K. (1986). 'The social psychology of Chinese people'. In M. H. Bond (Ed.), *The Psychology of the Chinese People* (pp. 213-66). Hong Kong: Oxford University Press.

Bond, M. H., and King, A. Y. C. (1985). 'Coping with the threat of Westernization in Hong Kong', *International Journal of Intercultural Relations, 9*, 351-64.

Bond, M. H., and Lee, P. W. H. (1981). 'Face-saving in Chinese culture: A discussion and experimental study of Hong Kong students'. In A. Y. C. King and R. P. L. Lee (Eds.), *Social Life and Development in Hong Kong* (pp. 288-305). Hong Kong: Chinese University Press.

Bond, M. H., Leung, K., and Schwartz, S. H. (1992). 'Explaining choices in procedural and distributive justice across cultures', *International Journal of Psychology, 27*, 211-25.

Bond, M. H., Leung, K., and Wan, K. C. (1982). 'How does cultural collectivism operate? The impact of task and maintenance contributions on reward allocation', *Journal of Cross-Cultural Psychology, 13*, 186-200.

Bond, M. H., Leung, K., and Wan, K. C. (1982). 'The social impact of self-effacing attributions: The Chinese case', *Journal of Social Psychology, 118*, 157-66.

Bond, M. H., Nakazato, H., and Shiraishi, D. (1975). 'Universality and distinctiveness in dimensions of Japanese person perception', *Journal of Cross-Cultural Psychology, 6*, 346-57.

Bond, M. H., and Venus, C. K. (1991). 'Resistance to group or personal insults in an ingroup or outgroup context', *International Journal of Psychology, 26*, 83-94.

Bond, M. H., and Wang, S. H. (1983). 'China: Aggressive behavior and the problem of maintaining order and harmony'. In A. P. Goldstein, and M. H. Segall (Eds.), *Aggression in Global Perspective* (pp. 58-74). New York: Pergamon.

Bond, M. H., and Yang, K. S. (1982). 'Ethnic affirmation vs. cross-cultural accommodation: The variable impact of questionnaire language', *Journal of Cross-Cultural Psychology, 13*, 169-85.

Bond, M. H., Wan, K. C., Leung, K., and Giacalone, R. A. (1985). 'How are responses to verbal insult related to cultural collectivism and power distance?' *Journal of Cross-Cultural Psychology, 16*, 111-27.

Boring, E. G. (1950). *A History of Experimental Psychology*. New York: Appleton-Century.

Borke, H. (1973). 'The development of empathy in Chinese and American children between three and six years of age: A cross-culture study', *Developmental Psychology, 9*(1), 102-08.

Borke, H., and Su, S. (1972). 'Perception of emotional responses to social interactions by Chinese and American children', *Journal of Cross-Cultural Psychology, 3*, 309-14.

Bornstein, M. H. (1973). 'Color vision and color naming: A psychophysiological hypothesis of cultural difference', *Psychological Bulletin, 80*, 257-85.

Bornstein, M. H. (1973). 'The psychophysiological component of cultural difference in color naming and illusion susceptibility', *Behavior Science Notes, 8*, 41-101.

Boucher, J. D. (1979). 'Culture and emotion'. In A. J. Marsella, R. G. Tharp, and T. V. Ciborowski (Eds.), *Perspectives on Cross-Cultural Psychology* (pp. 159-78). San Diego, CA: Academic Press.

Boucher, J. D., and Brandt, M. E. (1981). 'Judgment of emotion: American and Malay antecedents', *Journal of Cross-Cultural Psychology*, 12, 272-83.

Bourne, P. G. (1975). 'The Chinese student: Acculturation and mental illness', *Psychiatry*, 38, 269-77.

Boynton, R. M. (1979). *Human Color Vision.* New York: Holt, Rinehart and Winston.

Brammer, L. M. (1985). 'Counselling services in the People Republic of China', *International Journal for the Advancement of Counselling, 8*, 125-36.

Breiner, S. J. (1980). 'Early child development in China', *Child Psychiatry and Human Development, 11*(2), 87-95.

Breiner, S. J. (1992). 'Sexuality in traditional China: Its relationship to child abuse', *Child Psychiatry and Human Development, 2*, 3-67.

Brindley, T. A. (1989/90). 'Socio-psychological values in the Republic of China', *Asian Thought and Society, 14*, 98-115, and *15*, 1-15.

Brody, N. (1992). *Intelligence.* San Diego, CA: Academic Press.

Bromiley, P., and Curley, S. P. (1992). 'Individual differences in risk taking'. In J. F. Yates (Ed.), *Risk-Taking Behavior* (pp. 87-132). Chichester, UK: Wiley.

Bronfenbrenner, U. (1979). *The Ecology of Human Development: Experiments by Nature and Design.* Cambridge, MA: Harvard University Press.

Brown, D. E. (1991). *Human Universals.* Philadelphia: Temple University Press.

Brown, L. B. (1981). *Psychology in Contemporary China.* Oxford: Pergamon Press.

Burton, G. M. (1986). 'Values education in Chinese primary schools', *Childhood Education, 62*(4), 250-5.

Burton, S. (1990). 'Straight talk on sex in China'. *Time,* May, 82.

Buss, A. R. (1978). 'Causes and reasons in the attribution theory: A conceptual critique', *Journal of Personality and Social Psychology, 36*, 1311-21.

Buss, D. M (1989). 'Sex differences in human mate preferences: Evolutionary hypotheses tested in 37 cultures', *Behavioural and Brain Sciences, 12*, 1-49.

Buss, D. M. (1991). 'Evolutionary personality psychology', *Annual Review of Psychology*, 42, 459-91.

Buss, D.M., Abbott, M., Angleitner, A., Asherian, A., Biaggio, A., Blanco-Villasenor, A., Bruchon-Schweitzer, M., Ch'u, H., Czapinski, J., Deraad, B., Ekehammar, B., Lohamy, N., Fioravanti, M., Georgas, J., Gjerde, P., Guttman, R., Hazan, F., Iwawaki, S., Janakiramaiah, N., Khosroshani, F., Kreitler, S., Lachenicht, L., Lee, M., Liik, K., Little, B., Mika, S., Moadel-Shahid, M., Moane, G., Montero, M., Mundy-Castle, A., Niit, T., Nsenduluka, E., Pienkowski, R., Pirttila-Backman, A., Leon, J., Rousseau,J., Runco, M., Safir, M., Samuels, C., Sanitioso, R., Serpell, R., Smid, N., Spencer, C., Tadinac, M., Todorova, E., Troland, K., van den Brande, L., Heck, G., Langenhove, L., and Yang, K. (1990). 'International preferences in selecting mates', *Journal of Cross-Cultural Psychology, 21*, 5-47.

Butcher, H. (1968). *Human Intelligence: Its Nature and Assessment.* London: Methuen.

Butcher, J. N., and Clark, L. A. (1979). 'Recent trends in cross-cultural MMPI research'. In J. N. Butcher (Ed.), *New Developments in the Use of the MMPI* (pp. 69-111). Minneapolis: University of Minnesota.

Byrne, D. (1971). *The Attraction Paradigm.* New York: Academic Press.

Calestro, K. M. (1972). 'Psychotherapy, faith healing, and suggestion', *International Journal of Psychiatry, 10*, 83–113.

Campbell, D. T., and Fiske, D. W. (1959). 'Convergent and discriminant validation by the multitrait multimethod matrix', *Psychological Bulletin, 56*, 81–105.

Cao, R. C. (1959). 'Experiences learned from the symposium on psychology' [in Chinese], *Renmin Ribao,* 10 June, 6.

Caprara, G. V., Barbaranelli, C., Borgogni, L., and Perugini, M. (1993). 'The "Big Five Questionnaire": A new questionnaire to assess the Five Factor Model', *Personality and*

Individual Differences, 15, 281–8.

Carey, W. B., and McDevitt, S. C. (1978). 'Revision of the infant temperament questionnaire', *Pediatrics, 61,* 735–9.

Carr, T. H., and Levy, B. A. (Eds.)(1990). *Reading and Its Development: Component Skills Approaches.* New York: Academic Press.

Carr, T. H., and Pollatsek, A. (1985). 'Recognizing printed words: A look at current models'. In D. Besner, T. G. Waller, and E. M. MacKinnon (Eds.), *Reading Research: Advances in Theory and Practice* (Vol. 5, pp. 1–82). San Diego, CA: Academic Press.

Carver C., Scheier, M. F., and Weintraub, J. K. (1989). 'Assessing coping strategies: A theoretically based approach', *Journal of Personality and Social Psychology, 56*(2), 267–83.

Cattell, J. M. (1886). 'The time it takes to see and name objects', *Mind, 11,* 63–5.

Cattell, R. B. (1973). *Personality and Mood by Questionnaire.* San Francisco: Jossey-Bass.

Cawte, J. (1972). *Cruel, Poor and Brutal Nations.* New Brunswick, NJ: Rutgers University Press.

Chalip, L., and Stigler, J. W. (1986). 'The development of achievement and ability among Chinese children: A new contribution to an old controversy', *Journal of Educational Research, 79*(5), 302–7.

Chan, C. (1981). 'A study of acculturative stress and internal-external control on Hong Kong foreign students at the university of Waterloo'. Unpublished Bachelor's honours thesis, University of Waterloo, Ontario.

Chan, D., Leung, R., Gow, L., and Hu, S. (1989). 'Approaches to learning of accountancy students: Some additional evidence'. In *Proceedings of the ASAIHL Seminar on University Education in the 1990s.* Kuala Lumpur: ASAIHL.

Chan, D. W. (1984). 'Factor analysis of the HK-WISC at 11 age levels between 5 and 15 years', *Journal of Consulting and Clinical Psychology, 52,* 482–3.

Chan, D. W. (1985). 'Perception and judgment of facial expressions among the Chinese', *International Journal of Psychology, 20,* 681–92.

Chan, D. W. (1985). 'The Chinese version of the General Health Questionnaire: Does language make a difference?' *Psychological Medicine, 15,* 147–55.

Chan, D. W. (1986). 'Psychosocial mediators in the life event–illness relationships in a Chinese setting', *International Journal of Psychosomatics, 33,* 3–10.

Chan, D. W. (1986). 'Sex misinformation and misconceptions among Chinese medical students in Hong Kong', *Medical Education, 20,* 390–8.

Chan, D. W. (1989). 'Dimensionality and adjustment: Correlates of locus of control among Hong Kong Chinese', *Journal of Personality Assessment, 53,* 145–60.

Chan, D. W. (1990). 'The meaning of depression: Chinese word associations', *Psychologia, 33,* 191–6.

Chan, D. W. (1992). 'Coping with depressed mood among Chinese medical students in Hong Kong', *Journal of Affective Disorders, 24,* 109–16.

Chan, D. W. (1993). 'The Chinese General Health Questionnaire in a psychiatric setting: The development of the Chinese scaled version', *Social Psychiatry and Psychiatric Epidemiology, 28,* 124–9.

Chan, D. W., and Chan, T. S. C. (1983). 'Reliability, validity and the structure of the General Health Questionnaire in a Chinese context', *Psychological Medicine, 13,* 363–71.

Chan, D. W., and Lai, B. (1992). 'Assessing psychopathology in Chinese psychiatric patients in Hong Kong using the Brief Psychiatric Rating Scale', *Acta Psychiatrica Scandinavica, 89,* 1–8.

Chan, D. W., and Lee, B. H. C. (1993). 'Dimensions of self-esteem and psychological symptoms among Chinese adolescents in Hong Kong', *Journal of Youth and Adolescence, 22,* 425–40.

Chan, H. T. I. (1990). 'The relationship between motives, learning strategies, attributions for success and failure, and level of achievement among secondary students in Hong Kong'. Unpublished manuscript, University of Hong Kong.

Chan, J. (1969). 'Experimental studies of certain learning difficulties of A-level biology students in Hong Kong and the implications for teaching'. Unpublished Master's thesis, University of Hong Kong.

Chan, J. (1970). 'The construction and validation of a scholastic aptitude test for Hong Kong sixth form Chinese science students aged 17 to 22'. Unpublished Master's thesis, University of London.

Chan, J. (1972). 'A study of the relation of parent–child interaction and certain psychological attributes of adolescents in Hong Kong'. Unpublished doctoral thesis, University of London.

Chan, J. (1974). 'Intelligence and intelligence tests in Hong Kong', *New Horizons, 15*, 82–8.

Chan, J. (1975). 'Heredity and environment issues of intelligence', *New Horizons, 16*, 78–88.

Chan, J. (1976). 'Problems of psychological testing in two languages in Hong Kong'. In R. Lord (Ed.), *Studies in Bilingual Education* (pp. 110–13). Hong Kong: University of Hong Kong Press.

Chan, J. (1977). 'Family factors and school achievements'. *New Horizons, 18*, 16–18.

Chan, J. (1977). 'Parent–child interaction variables as predictors of academic attainment', *New Horizons, 18*, 60–7.

Chan, J. (1979). 'Effects of parent–child interaction on verbal and other intellectual abilities: An empirical investigation', *New Horizons, 20*, 19–30.

Chan, J. (1980). 'Certain factors affecting academic success of secondary students in Hong Kong: An empirical investigation', *New Horizons, 21*, 65–79.

Chan, J. (1980). 'Two basic concepts in educational psychology: Intelligence and personality' [in Chinese], *New Horizons, 21*, 17–22.

Chan, J. (1981). 'A crossroads in language of instruction', *Journal of Reading, 24*, 411–15.

Chan, J. (1981). 'Correlates in parent–child interaction and certain psychological variables among adolescents in Hong Kong'. In J. L. M. Dawson, G. H. Blowers, and R. Hoosain (Eds.), *Perspectives in Asian Cross-Cultural Psychology* (pp. 112–31). Lisse, the Netherlands: Swets and Zeitlinger B. V.

Chan, J. (1983). 'New norms for Hong Kong'. In J. C. Raven, J. H. Court, and J. Raven (Eds.), *Manual for Raven's Progressive Matrices and Vocabulary Scales*, Section 3 (p. 26). London: H. K. Lewis.

Chan, J. (1984). 'Raven's Progressive Matrices tests in Hong Kong', *New Horizons, 25*, 43–9.

Chan, J. (1985). 'A primer of testing', *New Horizons, 26*, 63–73.

Chan, J. (1985). 'Characteristics of high and low achievers in early childhood'. In *Selected Papers from the First Annual Conference of the Hong Kong Educational Research Association* (pp. 52–61). Hong Kong: Hong Kong Educational Research Association.

Chan, J. (1985). 'Motivation devices, verbal ability, and language achievement', *International Research in Reading, 2*, 5–12.

Chan, J. (1986). 'Cognitive changes in preschool learning', *Journal of the Hong Kong Educational Research Association, 1*, 54–7.

Chan, J. (1986). 'Language testing as an integral part of language teaching'. In *Selected Papers from the First International Conference of the Institute of Language in Education* (pp. 203–10). Hong Kong: Institute of Language in Education.

Chan, J. (1986). 'Sex differences in reading', *International Research in Reading, 3*, 11–16.

Chan, J. (1987). 'Educational and psychological testing in perspective', *New Horizons, 28*, 61–72.

Chan, J. (1987). 'The use of psychological tests in Hong Kong', *Bulletin of the Hong Kong Psychological Society, 18*, 51–60.

Chan, J. (1989). 'Are boys late developers?' *University of Hong Kong Newsletter, 2*, 1–5.

Chan, J. (1989). 'Teacher–pupil interaction: An extended model', *New Horizons, 30*, 116–20.

Chan, J. (1989). 'The use of Raven's Progressive Matrices in Hong Kong: A critical review', *Psychological Test Bulletin, 2*, 40–5. Melbourne: Australian Council for Educational Research.

Chan, J. (1991). 'Are the Western-type mental tests measuring Chinese mental faculties?' *Bulletin of the Hong Kong Psychological Society, 26/27*, 59–70.

Chan, J. (1992). 'Heredity and environment: Implications for teaching', *New Horizons, 33*, 39–44.

Chan, J. (1995). 'The use of Raven's Progressive Matrices Test'. In H. Kao and L. Ou-Yang (Eds.), *The Application of Psychology*, Beijing: World Books Publishing Co., pp. 11-13.

Chan, J. (in press). 'The application of Raven's Progressive Matrices Tests'. Symposium of the Conference of the Shensi Psychological Society.

Chan, J. (in press). 'Measuring intelligence and personality'. In H. Kao (Ed.), *Modern Theories in Psychology*, Hong Kong: The Commercial Press.

Chan, J., and Lynn, R. (1989). 'The intelligence of six-year-olds in Hong Kong', *Journal of Biosocial Science, 21*, 461–4.

Chan, J., and Vernon, P. (1988). 'Individual differences among the peoples of China'. In S. H. Irvine and J. Berry (Eds.), *Human Abilities in Cultural Context* (pp. 340–57). Cambridge:

Cambridge University Press.

Chan, J., Eysenck, H., and Gotz, K. O. (1980). 'A new visual aesthetic sensitivity test: III. Cross-cultural comparison between Hong Kong children and adults, and English and Japanese samples', *Perceptual and Motor Skills, 50*, 1325–6.

Chan, J., Eysenck, H., and Lynn, R. (1991). 'Reaction times and intelligence among Hong Kong children', *Perceptual and Motor Skills, 72*, 427–33.

Chan, J. (Ed.)(1985). *Language, Social Class and Cognitive Style* (Educational and Research Studies, No. 1). Hong Kong: Hong Kong Teachers' Association.

Chan, J. M., and Lee, C. C. (1991). *Mass Media and Political Transition: The Hong Kong Press in China's Orbit.* New York: Guilford Press.

Chan, K. T., and Chen, H. C. (1991). 'Reading sequentially-presented Chinese text: Effects of display format', *Ergonomics, 34*, 1083–94.

Chan, M. C. W. (1992). 'The relationship between mothers' and children's attributions for academic achievement'. Unpublished Master's thesis, University of Hong Kong.

Chan, W. T. (1967). 'Chinese theory and practice, with special reference to humanism'. In C. A. Moore (Ed.), *The Chinese Mind: Essentials of Chinese Philosophy and Culture* (pp. 11–30). Honolulu: East–West Center Press.

Chance, J. R. (1961). 'Independence training and first graders' achievement', *Journal of Consulting Psychology, 25*, 149–54.

Chandler, T. A., Shama, D. D., and Wolf, F. M. (1983). 'Gender differences in achievement and affiliation attributions: A five nation study', *Journal of Cross-cultural Psychology, 14*, 241–56.

Chandler, T. A., Shama, D. D., Wolf, F. M., and Planchard, S. K. (1981). 'Multiattributional causality: A five cross-national samples study', *Journal of Cross-cultural Psychology, 12*, 207–21.

Chandler, T. A., Shama, D. D., Wolf, F. M., and Planchard, S. K. (1981). 'Multiattributional causality for social affiliation across five cross-national samples', *The Journal of Psychology, 107*, 219–29.

Chang, A. S. C. (1989). 'Do students' motives in learning a subject affect their choice of learning strategies?' Paper presented at the annual meeting of the Australian Association for Research in Education, Adelaide, November.

Chang, C. (1987). 'The effect of stress from the joint-universities matriculation examination on adolescents' health' [in Chinese], *Acta Psychologica Taiwanica, 29*(2), 93–112.

Chang, C. F. (1982). 'Interpersonal relations and self concept, attribution traits in college freshmen' [in Chinese], *Journal of Education and Psychology, 5*, 1–46.

Chang, C. H. (1976). 'Sex differences of children in school learning as related to sex differences of teachers' [in Chinese], *Bulletin of Educational Psychology* (Taiwan), *9*, 1–20.

Chang, H., and Holt, G. R. (1991). 'More than relationship: Chinese interaction and the principle of *kuan-hsi*, *Communication Quarterly, 39*, 251–71.

Chang, H., and Holt, G. R. (1991). 'The concept of yuan and Chinese interpersonal relationships'. In S. Ting-Toomey and F. Korzenny (Eds.), *Cross-Cultural Interpersonal Communication* (pp. 28–57). Newbury Park, CA: Sage.

Chang, H. J., Huang, M. G., and Chen, C. C. (1993). 'Cultural implications of psychodramatic treatments in comparison with interview group psychotherapy for Chinese psychiatric patients'. In L. Y. Cheng, F. Cheung, and C. N. Chen (Eds.), *Psychotherapy for the Chinese* (pp. 135–44). Hong Kong: Department of Psychiatry, The Chinese University of Hong Kong.

Chang, H. W. (1992). 'The acquisition of Chinese syntax'. In H. C. Chen and O. J. L. Tzeng (Eds.), *Language Processing in Chinese* (pp. 277–311). Amsterdam: North-Holland.

Chang, J. H. (1981). 'The achievement motive, feminine tendency, occupational choice, and attributional characteristics of college students' [in Chinese]. Unpublished Master's thesis, National Taiwan University.

Chang, K. C. (Ed.)(1977). *Food in Chinese Culture: Anthropological and Historical Perspectives.* New Haven: Yale University Press.

Chang, S. K. C. (1985). 'American and Chinese managers in U.S. companies in Taiwan: A comparison', *California Management Review, 27*, 144–56.

Chang, S. S. (1992). 'Developing a Cantonese version of the Vocabulary subtest of the Wechsler Adult Intelligence Scale-Revised for Chinese adolescents'. Unpublished Master's thesis, Department of Psychology, Chinese University of Hong Kong.

Chang, W. (1976). 'Interpersonal attraction as a function of opinion similarity and opinion presentation sequence', *Bulletin of Educational Psychology, 9*, 73–84.

Chang, W. (1983). 'The prediction of junior high-school student sociometric status from some psycho-social variables'. Unpublished doctoral thesis, University of Oregon.

Chang, W. C. (1985). 'A cross-cultural study of depressive symptomology', *Culture, Medicine and Psychiatry, 9*, 295–317.

Chang, Y., Kohnstamm, G. A., and van der Kamp, L. J. T. (1993). 'Temperament difference in young Chinese children'. Unpublished manuscript, Child Development Center of China.

Chang, Y. G. (1985). 'A study of psychological characteristics of junior high school students from different socio-economic backgrounds' [in Chinese], *Guidance Journal* (Taiwan), *8*, 199–227.

Chang, Y. H. (1979). 'The Chinese language in Singapore'. In T. A. Llamzon (Ed.), *Papers on Southeast Asian Languages* (pp. 191–239). Singapore: Singapore University Press.

Chao, Y. R. (1968). *A Grammar of Spoken Chinese.* Berkeley: University of California Press.

Chao, Y. R. (1976). *Aspects of Chinese Sociolinguistics.* Stanford, CA: Stanford University Press.

Chataway, C. J., and Berry, J. W. (1989). 'Acculturation experiences, appraisal, coping, and adaptation', *Canadian Journal of Behavioural Science, 21*, 295–309.

Chen, C. (1963). 'Some psychological thoughts in the book of Tso Chuen' [in Chinese], *Acta Psychologica Sinica, 2*, 156–64.

Chen, C. (1989). 'A study of Chinese and American children's attitude towards schooling'. Unpublished manuscript, University of Michigan (ERIC Document Reproduction Service No. ED 305 165).

Chen, C., and Stevenson, H. W. (in press). 'Culture and academic achievement: Ethnic and cross-national differences'. In P. Pintrich and M. Maehr (Eds.), *Advances in Motivation and Achievement, Vol. 9: Culture, Race, Ethnicity, and Motivation.*

Chen, C., and Stevenson, H. W. (in press). 'Motivation and mathematics achievement: A comparative study of Asian-American, Caucasian American, and East Asian high school students', *Child Development.*

Chen, C. C. (1974). 'Group therapy with predelinquent schoolchildren in Taipei'. In W. P. Lebra (Ed.), '*Youth, socialization, and mental health* (pp. 178-94). Honolulu, HI: University of Hawaii Press.

Chen, C. C. (1984). 'Group therapy with Chinese schoolchildren', *International Journal of Group Psychotherapy, 34*, 485–501.

Chen, C. C. (1993). 'Application of storytelling and puppet-playing in group therapy with schoolchildren in Taiwan'. In L. Y. Cheng, F. Cheung, and C. N. Chen (Eds.), *Psychotherapy for the Chinese* (pp. 107–20). Hong Kong: Department of Psychiatry, the Chinese University of Hong Kong.

Chen, C. N. (1987). 'Reanalyzing Confucian culture and occupational ethics of the traditional merchants: Confucianism and occupational ideas of the merchants in the Hui state during the Ming and Qing dynasties' [in Chinese], *Contemporary* (Taiwan), *11*, 72-85 [*10*, 54-61?].

Chen, C. N., Wong, J., Lee, N., Chan-Ho, M. W., Lau, J., and Fung, M. (1993). 'The Shatin community mental health survey in Hong Kong: II. Major findings', *Archives of General Psychiatry, 50*, 125–33.

Chen, C. S., and Uttal, D. H. (1988). 'Cultural values, parents' beliefs, and children's achievement in the United States and China', *Human Development, 31*, 351–8.

Chen, F. T. (1991). 'The Confucian view of world order', *Indiana International and Comparative Law Review, 1*, 45–69.

Chen, H. (1988). 'Social and cultural factors and support systems of mental distress in contemporary China'. Unpublished doctoral dissertation, University of Illinois, Chicago (University Microfilm No. 8825109).

Chen, H., Meng, Z., and Lin, J. (1990). 'An experiment on the influence of the pre-elicited emotional experiences on the post-generated emotional processes' [in Chinese], *Acta Psychologica Sinica, 1*, 64–71.

Chen, H. C. (1984). 'Detecting radical components of Chinese characters in visual reading' [in Chinese], *Chinese Journal of Psychology, 26*, 29–34.

Chen, H. C. (1986). 'Component detection in reading Chinese characters'. In H. S. R. Kao and R. Hoosain (Eds.), *Linguistics, Psychology, and the Chinese Language* (pp. 1–10). Hong Kong: University of Hong Kong Press.

Chen, H. C. (1986). 'Effects of reading span and textual coherence on rapid-sequential reading', *Memory and Cognition, 14,* 202–8.

Chen, H. C. (1987). 'Character detection in reading Chinese: Effects of context and display format' [in Chinese], *Chinese Journal of Psychology, 29,* 45–50.

Chen, H. C. (1992). 'Reading comprehension in Chinese: Implications from character reading times'. In H. C. Chen and O. J. L. Tzeng (Eds.), *Language Processing in Chinese* (pp. 175–205). Amsterdam: Elsevier.

Chen, H. C. (1994). 'Parsing in Chinese: Some psychological studies'. Paper presented at the Third International Conference on Chinese Linguistics, Hong Kong, July.

Chen, H. C. (in press). 'Investigating the comprehension processes in reading Chinese text' [in Chinese]. In H. W. Chang, C. W. Hue, J. T. Huang, and O. J. L. Tzeng (Eds.), *Advances in the Study of Chinese Language Processing.* Taipei: National Taiwan University.

Chen, H. C., and Au Yeung, L. H. (1993). 'Reading Chinese text: Effects of spacing and display layout'. Paper presented at International Symposium on Information Processing of the Chinese Language, Beijing, July.

Chen, H. C., and Chan, K. T. (1990). 'Reading computer-displayed moving text with and without self-control over the display rate', *Behaviour and Information Technology, 9,* 467–77.

Chen, H. C., and Chen, M. J. (1988). 'Directional scanning in Chinese reading'. In I. M. Liu, H. C. Chen, and M. J. Chen (Eds.), *Cognitive Aspects of the Chinese Language* (pp. 15–26). Hong Kong: Asian Research Service.

Chen, H. C., and Healy, A. F. (in press). 'Effects of reading efficiency and display size on rapid-sequential reading', *Acta Psychologica.*

Chen, H. C., and Ho, C. (1986). 'Development of Stroop interference in Chinese-English bilinguals', *Journal of Experimental Psychology: Learning, Memory, and Cognition, 12,* 397–401.

Chen, H. C., and Juola, J. F. (1982). 'Dimensions of lexical coding in Chinese and English', *Memory and Cognition, 10,* 216–24.

Chen, H. C., and Tsoi, K. C. (1988). 'Factors affecting the readability of moving text on a computer display', *Human Factors, 30,* 25–33.

Chen, H. C., and Tsoi, K. C. (1990). 'Symbol–word interference in Chinese and English', *Acta Psychologica, 75,* 123–38.

Chen, H. C., and Tzeng, O. J. L. (Eds.). (1992). *Language Processing in Chinese.* Amsterdam: Elsevier.

Chen, H. C., Chan, K. T., and Tsoi, K. C. (1988). 'Reading self-paced moving text on a computer display', *Human Factors, 30,* 285–91.

Chen, H. C., Flores d'Arcais, G. B., and Cheung, S. L. (in press). Orthographic and phonological activation in recognizing Chinese characters. *Psychological Research/Psychologische Forschung.*

Chen, H. C., Healy, A. F., and Bourne, L. E., Jr. (1985). 'Effects of presentation complexity on rapid-sequential reading', *Perception and Psychophysics, 38,* 461–70.

Chen, H. F., and Xu, M. Z. (1992). 'Pre- and post-treatment comparison on the MMPI of schizophrenic patients' [in Chinese], *Chinese Mental Health Journal, 6*(5), 232.

Chen, J. (1991). 'Reports on psychotherapy with seven cases of anorexia nervosa' [in Chinese], *Chinese Journal of Nervous and Mental Diseases, 17,* 53–4.

Chen, L., and Wang, A. S. (1981). 'Hold on to scientific explanation in psychology'. In L. B. Brown (Ed.), *Psychology in Contemporary China* (pp. 151–6). New York: Pergamon.

Chen, L. C. (1980). 'The relationship between teacher's liking toward students and student's social status, achievement motivation, and external-internal control' [in Chinese], *Bulletin of Educational Psychology* (Taiwan), *13,* 187–94.

Chen, L. K., and Carr, H. A. (1926). 'The ability of Chinese students to read in vertical and horizontal directions'. *Journal of Experimental Psychology, 9,* 110–17.

Chen, M. C., Hsu, H. T., Wu, C. S., and Lin, T. Y. (1988). *Glossary of Psychological and Educational Tests in the Republic of China* (Vols. 1 and 2)[in Chinese]. Kaohsiung: Fu Wen Books.

Chen, M. J. (1981). 'Directional scanning of visual display: A study with Chinese subjects', *Journal of Cross-Cultural Psychology, 12,* 252–71.

Chen, M. J., and Chen, H. C. (1988). 'Concepts of intelligence: A comparison of Chinese graduates from Chinese and English schools in Hong Kong', *International Journal of Psychology, 23,* 471–87.

Chen, M. J., Braithwaite, V., and Huang, J. T. (1982). 'Attributes of intelligent behavior: Perceived relevance and difficulty by Australian and Chinese students', *Journal of Cross-cultural*

Psychology, 13, 139–56.

Chen, S. H. (1973). 'Language and literature under communism'. In Y. L. Wu (Ed.), *China: A Handbook* (pp. 705–35). New York: Praeger.

Chen, S. R., and Huang, K. L. (1982). 'The relationship between personality, needs, work nature and job satisfaction' [in Chinese], *Management Review, 1*(1), 18–38.

Chen, V. (1990/91). '*Mien tze* at the Chinese dinner table: A study of the interactional accomplishment of face', *Research on Language and Social Interaction, 24,* 109–40.

Chen, X. Y., Yang, L. L., and Zuo, C. Y. (1993). 'The treatment of psychosis by family therapy' [in Chinese], *Chinese Journal of Clinical Psychology, 1,* 25–8.

Chen, Z. G. (1983). 'Item analysis of Eysenck Personality Questionnaire tested in Beijing district' [in Chinese], *Acta Psychologica Sinica, 15*(2), 211–18.

Cheng, A. S. (1975). 'A comparative study of effectiveness in reducing test anxiety by systematic desensitization and muscle relaxation and electric shock in behavioural counseling' [in Chinese], *Chinese Journal of Psychology, 17,* 39–46.

Cheng, C. H., Cheng, P. Y. L., Ng, C. M. A., and Yip, J. J. F. (1991). 'Validation of the eight-factor model of Chinese personality across instruments'. Unpublished manuscript, Chinese University of Hong Kong.

Cheng, C. H., Bond, M. H., and Chan, S. C. (in press). 'The perception of ideal best friends by Chinese adolescents', *International Journal of Psychology.*

Cheng, C. M. (1981). 'Perception of Chinese characters' [in Chinese], *Acta Psychologica Taiwanica, 23,* 137–53.

Cheng, C. M. (1982). 'Analysis of present-day Mandarin', *Journal of Chinese Linguistics, 10,* 282–358.

Cheng, C. M. (1992). 'Lexical access in Chinese: Evidence from automatic activation of phonological information'. In H. C. Chen and O. J. L. Tzeng (Eds.), *Language Processing in Chinese* (pp. 67–91). Amsterdam: North-Holland.

Cheng, C. M., and Shih, S. I. (1988). 'The nature of lexical access in Chinese: Evidence from experiments on visual and phonological priming in lexical judgment'. In I. M. Liu, H. C. Chen, and M. J. Chen (Eds.), *Cognitive Aspects of the Chinese Language* (pp. 1–14). Hong Kong: Asian Research Service.

Cheng, H. (1994). 'Reflections of cultural values: A content analysis of Chinese magazine advertisements from 1982 and 1992', *International Journal of Advertising, 13,* 167–83.

Cheng, H. H., and Fan, C. M. (1976). 'Comparisons of directive and non-directive counseling methods in vocational counseling' [in Chinese], In H. H. Cheng (Ed.), *Counseling Studies in the Republic of China* (pp. 129–63). Taipei: Young Lion Publishing Co.

Cheng, H. H., and Lui, S. E. (1976). 'Effectiveness of non-directive counseling techniques among high school students'. In H. H. Cheng (Ed.), *Counseling Studies in the Republic of China* (pp. 59–78). Taipei: Young Lion Publishing Co.

Cheng, H. H., and Wu, E. C. (1977). 'Effectiveness of counsel' [in Chinese], *Mental Health Journal, 5,* 38–40.

Cheng, H. L., and Yang, K. S. (1977). 'The effects of attributional process on achievement motivation and scholastic achievement' [in Chinese], *Bulletin of the Institute of Ethnology, Academia Sinica* (Taiwan), *43,* 85–127.

Cheng, K. H. (1980). 'Workers and their job attitudes: Exploratory studies of young factory workers' [in Chinese], *Bulletin of the Institute of Ethnology, Academia Sinica, 26,* 1–170.

Cheng, L. Y. (1991). 'Sino-therapy: Is it necessary? Is it possible?' *Bulletin of the Hong Kong Psychological Society, 26/27,* 71–80.

Cheng, L. Y. (1993). 'Psychotherapy for the Chinese: Where are we going?' In L. Y. Cheng, F. Cheung, and C. N. Chen (Eds.), *Psychotherapy for the Chinese* (pp. iv–viii). Hong Kong: Department of Psychiatry, the Chinese University of Hong Kong.

Cheng, L. Y. (1993). 'Psychotherapy supervision in Hong Kong: A meeting of two cultures', *Australian and New Zealand Journal of Psychiatry, 27,* 127–32.

Cheng, S. H., and Hsu, L. R. (1974). 'The effectiveness of muscle relaxation and systematic desensitization of behavioural counseling in reducing test anxiety of Chinese students', *Acta Psychologica Taiwanica, 16,* 119–34.

Cheng, S. K. (1990). 'Understanding the culture and behavior of East Asians: A Confucian perspective', *Australian and New Zealand Journal of Psychiatry, 24,* 510–15.

Cheng, T. (1977). 'A phenomenological study of emotional experience: A search for cultural differences and similarities in the construction of emotion by a Hong Kong Chinese sample'. Unpublished Master's thesis, University of Hong Kong.

Cheng, T. A. (1989). 'Symptomatology of minor psychiatric morbidity: A cross-cultural comparison', *Psychological Medicine, 19,* 697–708.

Cheng, T. A., and Williams, P. (1986). 'The design and development of a screen questionnaire (CHQ) for use in community studies of mental disorder in Taiwan', *Psychological Medicine, 2,* 415–22.

Cheng, T. C. (1988). 'A theoretical analysis and empirical research on the psychology of face' [in Chinese]. In K. S. Yang (Ed.), *Chinese Psychology* (pp. 155–237). Taipei: Laureate Book Co.

Cheung, F. M. (1982). 'Psychological symptoms among Chinese in urban Hong Kong', *Social Science and Medicine, 16,* 1339–44.

Cheung, F.M. (1984). 'Preferences in help-seeking among Chinese students', *Culture, Medicine and Psychiatry, 8,* 371–80.

Cheung, F. M. (1985). 'An overview of psychopathology in Hong Kong with special reference to somatic presentation'. In W. S. Tseng and D. Y. H. Wu (Eds.), *Chinese Culture and Mental Health* (pp. 287–304). Orlando, FL: Academic Press.

Cheung, F. M (1985). 'Cross-cultural considerations for the translation and adaptation of the Chinese MMPI in Hong Kong'. In J. N. Butcher and C. D. Spielberger (Eds.), *Advances in Personality Assessment* (Vol. 4, pp. 131–58). Hillsdale, NJ: Lawrence Erlbaum Associates.

Cheung, F. M. (1987). 'Conceptualization of psychiatric illness and help-seeking behavior among Chinese', *Culture, Medicine and Psychiatry, 11,* 97–106.

Cheung, F. M. (1989). 'The indigenization of neurasthenia in Hong Kong', *Culture, Medicine, and Psychiatry, 13,* 227–41.

Cheung, F. M., and Cheng, L. Y. (1993). 'Development of a "good moments" instrument in the study of psychotherapy for the the Chinese'. In L. Y. Cheng, F. M.Cheung, and C. N. Chen (Eds.), *Psychotherapy for the Chinese* (pp. 231–46). Hong Kong: Department of Psychiatry, the Chinese University of Hong Kong.

Cheung, F. M., and Lau, B. (1982). 'Situational variations in help-seeking behavior among Chinese patients'. *Comprehensive Psychiatry, 23,* 252–62.

Cheung, F. M., and Leung, K. (1992). 'The construction of the Chinese Multiphasic Personality Inventory in Hong Kong and the PRC' [in Chinese]. Paper presented at the conference on Chinese Psychology and Behavior, Taipei, 23–5 April.

Cheung, F. M., and Song, W. Z. (1989). 'A review of the clinical applications of the Chinese MMPI', *Psychological Assessment: A Journal of Consulting and Clinical Psychology, 1,* 230–37.

Cheung, F. M., Lau, B., and Waldmann, E. (1981). 'Somatization among Chinese depressives in general practice', *International Journal of Psychiatry in Medicine, 10,* 361–74.

Cheung, F. M., Lau, B. W. K., and Wong, S. W. (1984). 'Paths to psychiatric care in Hong Kong', *Culture, Medicine and Psychiatry, 8,* 207–28.

Cheung, F. M., Lee, S. Y., and Chan, Y. Y. (1983). 'Variations in problem conceptualizations and intended solutions among Hong Kong students', *Culture, Medicine and Psychiatry, 7,* 263–78.

Cheung, F. M., Leung, K., Fan, R. M., Song, W. Z., Zhang, J. X., and Zhang, J. P. (in press). Development of the Chinese Personality Assessment Inventory (CPAI). *Journal of Cross-Cultural Psychology.*

Cheung, F. M., Song, W. Z., and Butcher, J. N. (1991). 'An infrequency scale for the Chinese MMPI', *Psychological Assessment: A Journal of Consulting and Clinical Psychology, 3,* 648–53.

Cheung, F. M., Song, W. Z., and Zhang, J. X. (in press). 'The Chinese MMPI-2: Research and applications in Hong Kong and the People's Republic of China'. In J. N. Butcher (Ed.), *International Adaptations of the MMPI-2: A Handbook of Research and Clinical Applications.* Minneapolis: University of Minnesota Press.

Cheung, F. M., Zhao, J. C., and Wu, C. Y. (1992). 'Chinese MMPI profiles among neurotic patients', *Psychological Assessment: A Journal of Consulting and Clinical Psychology, 4,* 214–18.

Cheung, F. M. C. (1986). 'Psychopathology among Chinese people'. In M. H. Bond (Ed.), *The Psychology of the Chinese People* (pp. 171–212). Hong Kong: Oxford University Press.

Cheung, M. (1989). 'Elderly Chinese living in the United States: Assimilation or adjustment?' *Social Work,* 457–61.

Cheung, P. (1991). 'Adult psychiatric epidemiology in China in the 80's', *Culture, Medicine and Psychiatry, 15*, 479–96.

Cheung, P. C., and Lau, S. (1985). 'Self-esteem: Its relationship to the family and school environments among Chinese adolescents', *Youth and Society, 16*, 438–56.

Cheung, P. C., Conger, A. J., Hau, K., Lew, W. J. F., and Lau, S. (1992). 'Development of the Multi-Trait Personality Inventory (MTPI): Comparison among four Chinese populations', *Journal of Personality Assessment, 59*, 528–51.

Chia, R. C., Chong, C. J., and Cheng, B. S. (1986). 'Attitude toward marriage roles among Chinese and American college students', *Journal of Social Psychology, 126*, 31–5.

Chia, R. C., Chong, C. J., and Cheng, B. S. (1986). 'Relationship of modernization and marriage role attitude among Chinese college students', *Journal of Social Psychology, 120*, 599–605.

Chiang, T. (1979). 'Source of interferences of English intonations with Chinese tones', *International Review of Applied Linguistics, 17*, 245–50.

Chiao, C. (1982). '*Kuan-hsi* (relationship): A preliminary analysis' [in Chinese]. In K. S. Yang and I. Wen (Eds.), *The Sinicization of Social and Behavioral Science Research in Chinese Societies.* Taipei: Academia Sinica.

Chiao, C. (1989). 'Chinese strategic behavior: Some general principles'. In R. Bolton (Ed.), *The Content of Culture: Constants and Variants* (pp. 525–37). New Haven: HRAF Press.

Chien, M. (1979). *Chinese National Character and Chinese Culture from the Viewpoint of Chinese History* [in Chinese]. Hong Kong: Chinese University Press.

Chien, M. F. (1984). 'Families' socio-economic status, teachers' expectations, and academic achievement of high school students' [in Chinese], *National Taiwan Normal University Graduate School of Education Research Quarterly, 26*, 1–98.

Chien, M. F. (1984). 'The effect of teacher leadership style on adjustment of elementary school children' [in Chinese], *Bulletin of Educational Psychology, 17*, 99–120.

Chien, Y. C., and Lust, B. (1983). 'Topic-comment structure and grammatical subject in first language acquisition of Mandarin Chinese: A study of equi-constructions', *Papers and Reports of Child Language Development, 22*, 74–82.

Chien, Y. C., and Lust, B. (1985). 'The concepts of topic and subject in first language acquisition of Mandarin Chinese', *Child Development, 56*, 1359–75.

Child, J. (1972). 'Organization structure and strategies of control: A replication of the Aston study'. *Administrative Science Quarterly, 17*, 13–17.

Child, J. (1994). *Management in China During the Age of Reform.* Cambridge: Cambridge University Press.

Child, J., and Markoczy, L. (1993). 'Host country managerial behaviour and learning in Chinese and Hungarian joint ventures', *Journal of Management Studies, 30*, 611–32.

Child, J., and Xu, X. (1991). 'The Communist Party's role in enterprise leadership at the high-water of China's economic reform', *Advances in Chinese Industrial Studies, 2*, 69–95.

Child, J., Boisot, M., Ireland, J., Li, Z., and Watts, J. (1990). *The Management of Equity Joint Ventures in China.* Beijing: China–EC Management Institute.

Chiles, J. A., Strousahl, K. D., Ping, Z. Y., Michael, M. C., Hall, K., Jamelka, R., Senn, B., and Reto, C. (1989). 'Depression, hopelessness and suicidal behavior in Chinese and American psychiatric patients', *American Journal of Psychiatry, 146*, 339–44.

Chin, R., and Chin, A. L. S. (1969). *Psychological Research in Communist China 1949-1966.* Cambridge, MA: MIT Press.

China National Labour Union (1991). 'Survey of employees' political ideology' [in Chinese]. In China National Labour Union (Ed.), *The 1991 Surveys of Chinese Workers' Attitudes* (pp. 1–22). PRC: Jingji Guanli Press.

China National Labour Union (Ed.)(1991). *The 1991 Surveys of Chinese Workers' Attitudes* [in Chinese]. PRC: Jingji Guanli Press.

Chinese Canadian National Council, Women's Book Committee. (1992). *Jin Guo: Voices of Chinese Canadian Women.* Toronto: Women's Press.

Chinese Culture Connection (1987). 'Chinese values and the search for culture-free dimensions of culture', *Journal of Cross-Cultural Psychology, 18*, 143–64.

Ching, C. C. (1980). 'Psychology in the People's Republic of China', *American Psychologist, 35*, 1084–9.

Ching, W., and Prosen, S. S. (1980). 'Asian-Americans in group counseling: A case of cultural dissonance', *Journal of Specialists in Group Work, 5*, 228–32.

Chiu, C. Y. (1991). 'Responses to injustice in popular Chinese sayings and among Hong Kong Chinese students', *Journal of Social Psychology, 131*, 655–65.

Chiu, L. H. (1986). 'Locus of control in intellectual situations in American and Chinese school children', *International Journal of Psychology, 21*, 167–76.

Chiu, L. H. (1987). 'Child-rearing attitudes of Chinese, Chinese-American, and Anglo-American mothers', *International Journal of Psychology, 22*(4), 409–19.

Chiu, L. H. (1988). 'Locus of control differences between American and Chinese adolescents', *Journal of Social Psychology, 128*, 411–13.

Chiu, L. H. (1989). 'Self esteem of American and Chinese children: a cross-cultural comparison'. Paper presented at the annual meeting of the American Psychological Association, August.

Chiu, L. H. (1990). 'Comparison of responses to Edwards Personal Preference Schedule by Chinese and American college students', *Psychological Reports, 67*, 1296–8.

Choi, C. Y. (1975). *Chinese Migration and Settlement in Australia*. Sydney: Sydney University Press.

Chomsky, N. (1986). *Knowledge of Language: Its Nature, Origin, and Use*. New York: Praeger.

Chomsky, N., and Halle, M. (1968). *The Sound Pattern of English*. New York: Harper and Row.

Chong, A. M. (1993). Prevention of suicide in older adults in Hong Kong. *Bulletin of the Hong Kong Psychological Society, 30*, 71–83.

Chong, L. E., Cragin, J. P., and Scherling, S. A. (1983). 'Manager work-related values in a Chinese corporation'. Paper presented to the annual meeting of the Academy of International Business, San Francisco, April.

Chong, M. Y., Yeh, E. K. and Wen, J. K. (1992). 'Suicidal behavior in Taiwan'. In K. L. Peng and W. S. Tseng (Eds.), *Suicidal Behaviour in the Asian-Pacific Region* (pp. 69–82). Singapore: University of Singapore Press.

Chou, E. L. (1958). 'The Task Confronting us in Language and Script Reform' [in Chinese], Beijing: Jenmin Chubanshe.

Chou, S. G. K. (1927). 'The present status of psychology in China', *American Journal of Psychology, 38*, 664–6.

Chou, S. G. K. (1927). 'Trends in Chinese psychological interest since 1922', *American Journal of Psychology, 38*, 487–8.

Chou, S. G. K. (1932). 'Psychological laboratories in China', *American Journal of Psychology, 44*, 372–4.

Chou, Y. S. (Ed.)(1981). *Crisis and Outlook of the Chinese Culture* [in Chinese]. Taipei: Shih Bao Publishing Company.

Chow, R., Gow, L., Kember, D. (1989). 'Factors affecting the ways tertiary students in Hong Kong approach their studies', *New Horizons, 30*, 89–98.

Chow, T. T. (1964). *The May Fourth Movement: Intellectual Revolution in Modern China*. Cambridge, MA: Harvard University Press.

Chu, C. L. (1972). 'On the shame orientation of the Chinese from the interrelationship among society, individual, and culture' [in Chinese]. In I. Y. Lee and K. S. Yang (Eds.), *Symposium on the Character of the Chinese: An Interdisciplinary Approach* (pp. 85–125). Taipei: Institute of Ethnology, Academia Sinica.

Chu, C. M. (1981). 'Concepts of self and friendship among junior high school students' [in Chinese]. Unpublished Master's thesis, National Taiwan Normal University.

Chu, C. P. (1955). 'A modification of TAT adapted to Chinese primary school children'. Unpublished Bachelor's thesis, National Taiwan University.

Chu, C. P. (1968). 'The remodification of TAT adapted to Chinese primary school children: I. Remodification of the pictures and setting up the objective scoring methods' [In Chinese], *Acta Psychologica Taiwanica, 10*, 59–73.

Chu, C. P. (1968). 'The remodification of TAT adapted to Chinese primary school children: II. The application and evaluation of pictures' [In Chinese], *Acta Psychologica Taiwanica, 10*, 74–89.

Chu, C. P., and Liu, X. Y. (1991). 'A report on 1763 cases seeking psychological consultation' [in Chinese]. Paper presented at the first annual conference of the Society on Psychotherapy and Psychological Consultation, Beijing.

Chu, C. P., and Ryback, D. (1973). 'Child-rearing practice in the Republic of China', *Acta*

Psychologica Taiwanica, 15, 6–24.

Chu, G. (1985). 'The changing concept of self in contemporary China'. In A. J. Marsella, G. DeVos, and F. L. K. Hsu (Eds.), *Culture and Self: Asian and Western Perspectives* (pp. 252–77). London: Tavistock.

Chu, G. (1985). 'The emergence of a new Chinese culture'. In W. Tseng and D. Y. H. Wu (Eds.), *Chinese Culture and Mental Health* (pp. 15–27). Orlando, FL: Academic Press.

Chu, G. C. (1993). *The Great Wall in Ruins: Communication and Cultural Change in China*. Albany: State University of New York Press.

Chu, R. L. (1989). 'Face and achievement: The examination of social-oriented motives in Chinese society' [in Chinese]. *Chinese Journal of Psychology* (Taiwan), *31*(2), 79–90.

Chua, L. (1993). 'Clinical experiences in dealing with resistance in expressing anger among Chinese patients in Singapore'. In L. Y. Cheng, F. Cheung, and C. N. Chen (Eds.), *Psychotherapy for the Chinese* (pp. 203–14). Hong Kong: Department of Psychiatry, the Chinese University of Hong Kong.

Chuang, C. J., Cheng, P. S., and Ren, J. G. (1990). 'The relationship amongst employees' career stage, organizational environment, organizational commitment, and job satisfaction: A contingency approach' [in Chinese]. *National Taiwan University Management Research, 1*(1), 105–36.

Chuang, Y. C., and Yang, K. S. (1990). 'Transformation and practice of traditional filial piety: A social psychological investigation' [in Chinese]. In K. S. Yang and K. K. Kwang (Eds.), *Psychology and Behavior of Chinese People: Proceedings of the First Interdisciplinary Conference* (pp. 181–222). Taipei: National Taiwan University, Institute of Psychology.

Chuang, Y. C., and Yang, K. S. (1991). 'The change and fulfillment of traditional filial piety: A social psychological study' [in Chinese]. In K. S. Yang and K. K. Hwang (Eds.), *The Mind and Behaviour of the Chinese: Selected Papers of the 1989 Taipei Conference* (pp. 135–75). Taipei: Laureate Publishing Co.

Chung, S. Y., Luk, S. L., and Lieh-Mak, F. (1987). 'Attempted suicide in children and adolescents in Hong Kong', *Social Psychiatry, 22*, 102–6.

Chung, Y. C., and Hwang, K. K. (1981). 'Attribution of performance and characteristics of learned helplessness in junior high school students' [in Chinese], *Acta Psychologica Taiwanica, 23*, 155–64.

Church, A. T. (1982). 'Sojourner adjustment', *Psychological Bulletin, 91*, 540–72.

Clément, R. (1987). 'Second language proficiency and acculturation: An investigation of the effects of language status and individual characteristics', *Journal of Language and Social Psychology, 5*, 271–90.

Clément, R., Gardner, R. C., and Smythe, P. C. (1980). 'Social and individual factors in second language acquisition', *Canadian Journal of Behavioural Science, 12*, 293–302.

Clifford, M. M., Lan, W. Y., Chou, F. C., and Qi, Y. (1989). 'Academic risk-taking: Developmental and cross-cultural observations', *Journal of Experimental Education, 57*, 321–38.

Cloke, K. (1987). 'Politics and values in mediation: The Chinese experience', *Mediation Quarterly, 17*, 69–82.

Cody, M. J., Lee, W. S., and Chao, E. Y. (1989). 'Telling lies: Correlates of deception among Chinese'. In J. Forgas and M. Innes (Eds.), *Recent Advances in Social Psychology: An International Perspective* (pp. 359–68). Amsterdam: North-Holland.

Cohen, M. L. (1976). *House United, House Divided: The Chinese Family in Taiwan*. New York: Columbia University Press.

Coltheart, M. (1978). 'Lexical access in simple reading tasks'. In G. Underwood (Ed.), *Strategies of Information Processing* (pp. 151–216). London: Academic Press.

Compton, W. M., Helzer, J. E., Hwu, H. G., Yeh, E. K., McEvoy, L., Topp, J. E., and Spitznagel, E. L. (1991). 'New methods in cross-cultural psychiatry in Taiwan and the United States', *American Journal of Psychiatry, 148*, 1697–1704.

Condon, J. C. (1984). *With Respect to the Japanese: A Guide for Americans*. Yarmouth, ME: Intercultural Press.

Confucius (1989). *The Analects of Confucius* (A. Waley, Trans. and Annotation). New York: Vintage.

Conway, M. A., and Gathercole, S. E. (1987). 'Modality and long-term memory', *Journal of Memory and Language, 26*, 341–61.

Cook, H., and Chi, C. (1984). 'Cooperative behavior and locus of control among American and Chinese-American boys', *Journal of Psychology, 118*, 169–77.

Cooper, S. (1980). 'Colonialist fetishism: An answer to the Hong Kong apologists', *Bulletin of the Hong Kong Psychological Society, 4*, 33–43.

Corder, S. P. (1981). *Error Analysis and Interlanguage*. London: Oxford University Press.

Costa, P. T., Jr., and McCrae, R. R. (1992). *Revised NEO Personality Inventory (NEO-PI-R) and NEO Five-Factor Inventory (NEO-FFI) Professional Manual*. Odessa, FL: Psychological Assessment Resources, Inc.

Costa, P. T., Jr., McCrae, R. R., Bond, M. H., and Paunonen, S. V. (1994). 'Evaluating factor replicability with targeted rotation: A Chinese example'. Paper presented at the annual convention of the American Psychological Association, Los Angeles, August.

Cox, T. H., Lobel, S. A., and McLeod, P. L. (1991). 'Effects of ethnic group cultural differences on cooperative and competitive behavior on a group task', *Academy of Management Journal, 34*, 827–47.

Cragin, J. P. (1986). 'Management technology absorption in China'. In S. R. Clegg, D. C. Dunphy, and S. G. Redding (Eds.), *The Enterprise and Management in East Asia* (pp. 327–40). Centre of Asian Studies, University of Hong Kong.

Crandall, V. C., Katkovsky, W., and Crandall, V. J. (1965). 'Children's beliefs in their own control of reinforcements in intellectual-academic achievement situations', *Child Development, 36*, 91–109.

Creel, H. G. (1954). *Chinese Thought from Confucius to Mao Tse Tung*. London: Eyre and Spottiswoode.

Crick, F. H. C., and Koch, C. (1990). 'Some reflections on visual awareness', *Cold Spring Harbor Symposia on Quantitative Biology, 55*, 953–62.

Crissman, L. W. (1991). 'Chinese immigrant families in Australia: A variety of experiences', *Journal of Comparative Family Studies, 22*, 25–37.

Crittenden, K. S. (1983). 'Sociological aspects of attribution', *Annual Review of Sociology, 44*, 425–46.

Crittenden, K. S. (1987). 'The social impact of attributions of good and bad events: Another look at the Chinese case', *Sehui Xuebao, 23*, 107–25.

Crittenden, K. S. (1989). 'Attributional styles of Asian and American students: A four-country study'. Paper presented at the Midwest Sociological Society, St. Louis, April.

Crittenden, K. S. (1989). 'Causal attribution in sociocultural context: Toward a self-presentational theory of attribution processes', *The Sociological Quarterly, 30*, 1–14.

Crittenden, K. S. (1991). 'Asian self-effacement or feminine modesty?: Attributional patterns of women university students in Taiwan', *Gender and Society, 5*, 98–117.

Crittenden, K. S., and Bae, H. (1994). 'Self-effacement and social responsibility: Attribution as impression management in Asian cultures', *American Behavioral Scientist, 37*, 653–71.

Crittenden, K. S., and Fugita, S. S. (1987). 'A cross-cultural study of attributional style and depression'. In W. T. Liu (Ed.), *The Pacific/Asian American Mental Health Research Center: A Decade Review* (pp. 101–7). Chicago: The University of Illinois at Chicago Press.

Cronbach, L. (1969). *Essentials of Psychological Testing*. New York: Harper and Row.

Cronbach, L. J., and Meehl, P. E. (1955). 'Construct validity in psychological testing', *Psychological Bulletin, 52*, 281–302.

Crowder, R. G. (1976). *The Principles of Learning and Memory*. Hillsdale, NJ: Erlbaum.

Crystal, D. S., Chen, C., Fuligni, A. J., Stevenson, H. W., Hsu, C. C., Kitamura, S., and Kimura, S. (1994). 'Psychological maladjustment and academic achievement: A cross-cultural study of Japanese, Chinese, and American high school students', *Child Development, 65*, 738–53.

Cutler, A., and Butterfield, S. (1992). 'Rhythmic cues to speech segmentation: Evidence from juncture misperception', *Journal of Memory and Language, 31*, 218–36.

Cutler, A., Mehler, J., Norris, D., and Segui, J. (1989). 'Limits on bilingualism', *Nature, 340*, 229–30.

D'Andrade, R. G. (1990). 'Some propositions about the relations between culture and human cognition'. In J. W. Stigler, R. A. Shweder, and G. Herdt (Eds.), *Cultural Psychology* (pp. 65–129). Cambridge: Cambridge University Press.

Dai, F. Q. (1993). 'Insight-oriented psychotherapy for two cases of neurosis' [in Chinese], *Chinese Journal of Clinical Psychology, 1*, 114–15.

Dai, G. X. (1983). *Manual of the Revised Eysenck Personality Questionnaire* [in Chinese].

Changsha: Hunan Medical College.

Dai, X., and Lynn, R. (1994). 'Gender differences in intelligence among Chinese children', *The Journal of Social Psychology, 134*, 123–5.

Dai, X. Y., and Gong, Y. X. (1987). 'A comparative study of the factor analysis of the WAIS-RC and the original WAIS-R' [in Chinese], *Acta Psychologica Sinica, 19*(1), 70–8.

Dai, X. Y., Gong, Y. X., and Zhong, L. P. (1990). 'Factor analysis of the mainland Chinese version of the Wechsler Adult Intelligence Scale', *Psychological Assessment: A Journal of Consulting and Clinical Psychology, 2*, 31–4.

Dai, X. Y., Lin, C. D., and Zhang, H. C. (1990). 'Factor analysis of the Wechsler Intelligence Scale for Children-Chinese Revision (WISC-CR)' [in Chinese], *Acta Psychologica Sinica, 22*(4), 377–82.

Dai, X. Y., Ryan, J. J., Paolo, A. M., and Harrington, R. G. (1991). 'Sex differences on the Wechsler Adult Intelligence Scale-Revised for China', *Psychological Assessment: A Journal of Consulting and Clinical Psychology, 3*, 282–4.

Dai, X. Y., Zheng, L. X., Ryan, J. J., and Paolo, A. M. (1993). 'Psychological test usage in Chinese clinical psychology and comparisons with the U.S.' [in Chinese], *Chinese Journal of Clinical Psychology, 1*(1), 47–50.

Dalrymple-Alford, E. C. (1968). 'Interlingual interference in a color-naming task', *Psychonomic Science, 10*, 215–6.

Danks, J. H., and Kurcz, I. (1984). 'A comparison of reading comprehension processes in Polish and English', *International Journal of Psychology, 19*, 245–69.

Danks, J. H., Bohn, L., and Fears, R. (1983). 'Comprehension processes in oral reading'. In G. B. Flores d'Arcais and R. J. Jarvella (Eds.), *The Process of Language Understanding* (pp. 193–223). Chichester, UK: Wiley.

Dardess, J. (1991). 'Childhood in premodern China'. In J. M. Hawes, Joseph M. and N. R. Hiner (Eds.), *Childhood in Historical and Comparative Perspective* (pp. 71–94). New York: Greenwood.

Davidoff (1991). *Cognition through Color.* Cambridge, MA: MIT Press.

Davin, D. (1991). 'The early childhood education of the only child generation in urban China'. In I. Epstein (Ed.), *Chinese Education: Problems, Policies, and Prospects* (pp. 42–65). New York: Garland.

Davis, J. H., Kameda, T., and Stasson, M. F. (1992). 'Group risk taking: Selected topics'. In J. F. Yates (Ed.), *Risk-taking Behavior* (pp. 163–99). Chichester, UK: Wiley.

Davitz, J. R. (1969). *The Language of Emotion.* San Diego, CA: Academic Press.

Dawson, J. L. M., Young, B. M., and Choi, P. P. C. (1973). 'Developmental influences on geometric illusion susceptibility among Hong Kong Chinese children', *Journal of Cross-Cultural Psychology, 4*, 49–74.

De Mente, B. (1989). *Chinese Etiquette and Ethics in Business.* Lincolnwood, IL: NTC Business Books.

De Vos, G. A. (1968). 'Achievement and innovation in culture and personality'. In T. Norbeck, D. Price-Williams, and W. M. McCord (Eds.), *The Study of Personality: An Interdisciplinary Approach* (pp. 348–70). New York: Holt, Rinehart and Winston.

De Vos, G. A. (1973). *Socialization for Achievement: Essays on the Cultural Psychology of the Japanese.* Berkeley: University of California Press.

Deary, I. J., and Matthews, G. (1993). 'Personality traits are alive and well', *The Psychologist,* July, pp. 299–311.

Deelstra, T., and De Waart, J. P. (1989). 'The concept of resourceful cities fit to live: Outline of problems, points of discussion'. In T. Deelstra, H. M. van Emden, W. H. de Hoop, and R. H. G. Jongman (Eds.), *The Resourceful City: Management Approaches to Efficient Cities Fit to Live In* (Proceedings of the MAB-11 workshop, 13-16 September, pp. 13-16). Amsterdam: Royal Netherlands Academy of Arts and Sciences.

DeFrancis, J. (1989). *Visible Speech: The Diverse Oneness of Writing Systems.* Honolulu: University of Hawaii Press.

Derogatis, L. R. (1977). *SCL-90-R: Administration, Scoring, and Procedures Manual I.* Baltimore, MD: Clinical Psychometrics Research.

Diekstra, R. (1988). 'City lifestyles', *World Health Organization,* June, 18–19.

Dien, D. S. F. (1983). 'Big me and little me: A Chinese perspective on self', *Psychiatry, 46*, 281–6.

Digman, J. M. (1990). 'Personality structure: Emergence of the five-factor model', *Annual Review of Psychology, 41,* 417–40.

Ding, Z. (1956). 'Developing a programme in Chinese medical psychology' [in Chinese], *Zhunghua XIenjen Goshu Zashi, 4,* 322–5.

Dion, K. K., Dion, K. L., and Pak, A. W. P. (1990). 'The role of self-reported language proficiencies in the cultural and psychosocial adaptation among members of Toronto, Canada's Chinese community', *Journal of Asian Pacific Communication, 1,* 173–89.

Dion, K. L., and Dion, K. K. (1988). 'Romantic love: individual and cultural perspectives'. In R. Sternberg and M. Barnes (Eds.), *The Psychology of Love* (pp. 264–92). New Haven: Yale University Press.

Dion, K. L., and Toner, B. (1988). 'Ethnic differences in test anxiety', *The Journal of Social Psychology, 128,* 165–72.

Dion, K. L., Dion, K. K., and Pak, A. W. P. (1992). 'Personality-based hardiness as a buffer for discrimination-related stress in members of Toronto's Chinese community', *Canadian Journal of Behavioural Science, 24,* 517–36.

Dion, K. L., Pak, A., and Dion, K. K. (1990). 'Stereotyping physical attractiveness: A sociocultural perspective', *Journal of Cross-Cultural Psychology, 21,* 158–79.

Dixon, R. M. W. (1977). 'Where have all the adjectives gone?' *Studies in Language, 1,* 19–80.

Dockrell, W. (Ed.)(1970). *On Intelligence.* London: Camelot Press.

Domino, G. (1992). 'Cooperation and competition in Chinese and American children', *Journal of Cross-Cultural Psychology, 23,* 456–67.

Domino, G., and Hannah, M. T. (1987). 'A comparative analysis of social values of Chinese and American children', *Journal of Cross-cultural Psychology, 18,* 58–77.

Dong, J. W., Li, X. T., Tian, Z. E., and Wen, Q. R. (1980). 'Behaviour therapy with obsessive-compulsive disorder' [in Chinese], *Chinese Journal of Neurology and Psychiatry, 13,* 161–5.

Draguns, J. G. (1973). 'Comparisons of psychopathology across cultures: Issues, findings, directions', *Journal of Cross-Cultural Psychology, 4,* 9–47.

Draguns, J. G. (1975). 'Resocialization into culture: The complexities of taking a worldwide view of psychotherapy'. In R. W. Brislin, S. Bochner, and W. J. Lonner (Eds.), *Cross-Cultural Perspectives on Learning* (pp. 273–89). New York: John Wiley and Sons.

Draguns, J. G. (1981). 'Cross-cultural counseling and psychotherapy: History, issues, current status'. In A. J. Marsella and P. B. Pedersen (Eds.), *Cross-Cultural Counseling and Psychotherapy* (pp. 3–27). New York: Pergamon Press.

Draguns, J. G. (1986). 'Culture and psychopathology: What is known about their relationship?' *Australian Journal of Psychology, 38,* 329–38.

Draguns, J. G. (1990). 'Applications of cross-cultural psychology in the field of mental health'. In R. W. Brislin (Ed.), *Applied Cross-Cultural Psychology* (pp. 302–24). London: Sage.

DuBois, C. (1944). *The People of Alor.* Minneapolis: University of Minnesota Press.

DuBois, P. H. (1970). *A History of Psychological Testing.* New York: Allyn and Bacon.

Duck, S. (1988). *Relating to Others.* Milton Keynes: Open University Press.

Dunn, J., Zhang, X., and Ripple, R. (1988). 'A study of Chinese and American performance on divergent thinking tasks', *New Horizons, 29,* 7–20.

Durgunoglu, A. Y., and Hancin, B. J. (1992). 'An overview of cross-language transfer in bilingual reading'. In R. J. Harris (Ed.), *Cognitive Processing in Bilinguals* (pp. 391–411). Amsterdam: North-Holland.

Dyal, J. A., and Chan, C. (1985). 'Stress and distress: A study of Hong Kong Chinese and Euro-Canadian students', *Journal of Cross-Cultural Psychology, 16,* 447–66.

Dyer, F. N. (1971). 'Color-naming interference in monolinguals and bilinguals', *Journal of Verbal Learning and Verbal Behavior, 10,* 297–302.

Earley, P. C. (1989) 'Social loafing and collectivism: A comparison of the United States and the People's Republic of China', *Administrative Science Quarterly, 34,* 556–81.

Earley, P. C. (1993). 'East meets west meets mideast: Further explorations on collectivistic and individualistic work groups', *Academy of Management Journal, 36,* 319–48.

Eaves, L. J., Eysenck, H. J., and Martin, N. G. (1989). *Genes, Culture, and Personality: An Empirical Approach.* New York: Academic Press.

Eckman, F. R. (1981). 'On the naturalness of interlanguage phonological rules', *Language*

Learning, 31, 195–216.

Education Department (1986). *Hong Kong Supplement to Guide to the Standard Progressive Matrices.* Hong Kong: Special Education Section, Educational Research Centre, Education Department.

Educational Research Establishment (1964–75). *Hong Kong Ability Tests and Manuals (in Verbal Reasoning and Numerical Reasoning)*(Annuals). Hong Kong: Hong Kong Government.

Educational Research Establishment (1964–94). *Hong Kong Attainment Tests and Manuals (Chinese, English, and Mathematics from Primary 1 to Secondary 3)*(Annuals). Hong Kong: Hong Kong Government.

Educational Research Establishment (1984/5). *Aptitude Tests (Mechanical and Clerical) and Manuals for Prevocational Schools (Blue, Green, and Yellow Versions).* Hong Kong: Hong Kong Government.

Edwards, A. L. (1959). *Manual of the Personal Preference Schedule.* New York: Psychological Corp.

Edwards, J. W. (1985). 'Indigenous *koro*, a genital retraction syndrome of insular Southeast Asia: A critical review'. In R. C. Simon and C. C. Hughes (Eds.), *The Culture-Bound Syndrome: Folk Illnesses of Psychiatric and Anthropological Interest* (pp. 169–92). Dordrecht, the Netherlands: D. Reidel.

Eiteman, D. K. (1990). 'American executives' perceptions of negotiating joint ventures with the People's Republic of China: Lessons learned', *Columbia Journal of World Business, 25*(4), 59–67.

Ekblad, S. (1986). 'Relationships between child-rearing practices and primary school children's functional adjustment in the People's Republic of China', *Scandinavian Journal of Psychology, 27*(3), 220–30.

Ekblad, S. (1986). 'Some determinants of aggression in a sample of Chinese primary school children', *Acta Psychiatrica Scandinavica, 73*, 515–23.

Ekblad, S. (1988). 'Influence of child rearing on aggressive behavior in a transcultural perspective', *Acta Psychiatrica Scandinavica Supplement, 344*, 133–9.

Ekblad, S. (1990). 'The children's behaviour questionnaire for completion by parents and teachers in a Chinese sample', *Journal of Child Psychology and Psychiatry, 31*, 775–91.

Ekblad, S., and Werne, F. (1990). 'Housing and health in Beijing: Implications of high-rise housing on children and the aged', *Journal of Sociology and Social Welfare, 1*, 51–77.

Ekblad, S., Chen, C. H., Li, S. R., Huang, Y. Q., Li, G., Li, Y. T., Zhang, W. X., Liu, M., Xu, L., Wang, Q., Shan, S. W., Ran, W., and Zhang, S. Z. (1991). *Stressors, Chinese City Dwellings and Quality of Life.* Stockholm: Swedish Council for Building Research.

Ekman, P., Friesen, W. V., O'Sullivan, M., Chan, A., Diacoyanni-Tarlatzis, I., Heider, K., Krause, R., Le Compte, W. A., Pitcairn, T., RicciBitti, P. E., Scherer, K., Tomita, M., and Tzavaras, A. (1987). 'Universals and cultural differences in the judgments of facial expressions of emotion', *Journal of Personality and Social Psychology, 53*, 712–17.

Elizur, D., Borg, I., Hunt, R., and Beck, I. M. (1991). 'The structure of work values: A Cross-cultural comparison', *Journal of Organizational Behavior, 12*, 21–38.

Ember, C. R., and Ember, M. (1992). 'Warfare, aggression, and resource problems: cross-cultural codes', *Behavioral Science Research, 26*, 169–226.

Endler, N. S., and Parker, J. D. A. (1990). 'Multidimensional assessment of coping: A critical evaluation', *Journal of Personality and Social Psychology, 58*, 844–54.

Entwistle, N. J. (1968). 'Academic motivation and school achievement', *Journal of Educational Psychology, 38*, 181–8.

Entwistle, N. J., and Percy, K. A. (1971). *Educational Objectives and Student Performance Within the Binary System: Research into Higher Education, 1970.* London: SRHE.

Entwistle, N. J., and Percy, K. A. (1974). 'Critical thinking or conformity? An investigation of the aims and objectives of higher education'. In C. F. Page and J. Gibson (Eds.), *Research into Higher Education, 1973* (pp. 1–30). London: SRHE.

Entwistle, N. J., and Ramsden, P. (1983). *Understanding Student Learning.* London: Croom Helm.

Erez, M. (1992). 'Interpersonal communication patterns in Japanese corporations: Their relationships to cultural values and to productivity and innovation', *Applied Psychology: An International Review, 41*, 43–64.

Erikson, E. H. (1950). *Childhood and Society.* New York: Norton.

Eysenck, H. (1979). 'The family's influence on intelligence', *New Horizons, 20,* 12–18.

Eysenck, H. (1979). *The Structure and Measurement of Intelligence.* New York: Springer-Verlag.

Eysenck, H. (1980). 'Education and intelligence: The biological basis of mental ability', *New Horizons, 21,* 28–40.

Eysenck, H. (1980). 'The structure and measurement of intelligence', *New Horizons, 21,* 41–3.

Eysenck, H. (1982). 'Intelligence: New wine in old bottles', *New Horizons, 23,* 11–19.

Eysenck, H. (1983). 'New light on the nature of intelligence', *New Horizons, 24,* 20–30.

Eysenck, H. (Ed.)(1982). *A Model for Intelligence.* New York: Springer-Verlag.

Eysenck, H. J. (1978). 'Superfactors P, E, and N in a comprehensive factor space', *Multivariate Behavioral Research, 13,* 475–81.

Eysenck, H. J., and Eysenck, S. B. G. (1975). *Manual of the Eysenck Personality Questionnaire.* San Diego: EdITS.

Eysenck, S. B. G., and Chan, J. (1982). 'A comparative study of personality in adults and children: Hong Kong vs. England', *Personality and Individual Differences, 3,* 153–60.

Fairbank, J. K. (1987). *China Watch.* Cambridge, MA: Harvard University Press.

Falbo, T., Poston, D. L., Ji, G., Jiao, S., Jing, Q., Wang, S., Gu, Q., Yin, H., and Liu, Y. (1988). 'Physical, achievement, and personality characteristics of Chinese children', *Texas Population Research Center Papers,* Series 10.

Falbo, T., Poston, D. L., Ji, G., Jiao, S., Jing, Q., Wang, S., Gu, Q., Yin, H., and Liu, Y. (1989). 'Physical, achievement and personality characteristics of Chinese children', *Journal of Biosocial Science, 21,* 483–95.

Family Planning Association of Hong Kong (1987). *The Adolescent Sexuality Study 1986, Household Survey: Summary Findings.* Hong Kong: Family Planning Association.

Fan, D. H. (1979). 'A study of the factor structure of the Revised WISC in China and its short form for Chinese subjects' [in Chinese], *Bulletin of Educational Psychology, 12,* 167–82.

Fan, D. S. (1977). 'The influence of junior high school ability tracking on grades: A factorial analysis' [in Chinese], *Testing and Counseling* (Taiwan), *6*(5), 390–2.

Fan, M. (1990). 'Essence of sex in Chinese culture'. Paper presented at the International Conference on Sexuality in Asia, Hong Kong, May.

Fan, M., Li, C., Wang, J., and Zhang, E. (1992). 'Suicidal behavior in China'. In K. L. Peng and W. S. Tseng (Eds.), *Suicidal Behaviour in the Asia-Pacific Region* (pp. 58–68). Singapore: University of Singapore Press.

Fang, F. X., and Keats, D. (1987). 'A cross-cultural study on the conception of intelligence' [in Chinese], *Acta Psychologica Sinica, 19,* 255–62.

Fang, H., and Heng, J. H. (1983). 'Social changes and changing address norms in China', *Language in Society, 12,* 495–507.

Fang, S. D. (1965). *The History of China's National Language Movement Over the Past Fifty Years* [in Chinese]. Taipei: Guoyu Ribaoshe.

Fang, S. P., Horng, R. Y., and Tzeng, O. J. L. (1986). 'Consistency effects in the Chinese character and pseudo-character naming tasks'. In H. S. R. Kao and R. Hoosain (Eds.), *Linguistics, Psychology, and the Chinese Language* (pp. 11–21). Hong Kong: University of Hong Kong.

Fang, S. P., Tzeng, O. J., and Alva, L. (1981). 'Intralanguage vs. interlanguage Stroop effects in two types of writing systems', *Memory and Cognition, 9,* 609–17.

Farh, J. L., Dobbins, G. H., and Cheng, B. S. (1991). 'Cultural relativity in action: A comparison of self-ratings made by Chinese and U.S. workers', *Personnel Psychology, 44,* 129–47.

Farh, J. L., Podsakoff, P. M., and Organ, D. W. (1990). 'Accounting for organizational citizenship behavior: Leader fairness and task scope versus satisfaction', *Journal of Management, 16,* 705–21.

Farr, R. M., and Moscovici, S. (1984). *Social Representations.* Cambridge: Cambridge University Press.

Farris, C. (1988). 'The gender of child discourse: Sex roles and communicative styles at a Taiwanese kindergarten'. Paper presented at the annual meeting of the Association for Asian Studies.

Fasold, R. (1984). *The Sociolinguistics of Society.* Oxford: Blackwell.

Feather, N. T. (1961). 'The relationship of persistence at a task to expectation of success and achievement-related motives', *Journal of Abnormal and Social Psychology, 63,* 552–61.

Feather, N. T. (1962). 'The study of persistence', *Psychological Bulletin, 59,* 94–115.

Feather, N. T. (1986). 'Value systems across cultures: Australia and China', *International Journal of Psychology, 21*, 697–715.

Feather, N. T. (1988). 'From values to actions: Recent applications of the expectancy-value model', *Australian Journal of Psychology, 40*, 105–24.

Feldman, L. B., and Turvey, M. T. (1983). 'Word recognition in Serbo-Croatian is phonologically analytic', *Journal of Experimental Psychology: Human Perception and Performance, 9*, 288–98.

Feldman, S. S., and Rosenthal, D. A. (1990). 'The acculturation of autonomy expectations in Chinese high schoolers residing in two Western nations', *International Journal of Psychology, 25*, 259–81.

Feldman, S. S., and Rosenthal, D. A. (1991). 'Age expectations of behavioural autonomy in Hong Kong, Australian and American youth: The influence of family variables and adolescents' values', *International Journal of Psychology, 26*(1), 1–23.

Feng, Y. J. (1986). 'A study of Di Zi Zhi' [in Chinese]. *Bulletin of the Taipei Municipal Teachers College, 17*, 41–84.

Feng, Y. L. (1934). *The History of Chinese Philosophy* [in Chinese]. Shanghai: Shan-Wu Book Co.

Ferguson, C. A. (1959). 'Diglossia', *Word, 15*, 325–40.

Fiedler, K. (1978). 'Causal and generalising inferences on the basis of simple sentences', *Zeitschrift für Sozialpsychologie, 9*, 37–49.

Fiedler, K., and Semin, G. R. (1988). 'On the causal information conveyed by different interpersonal verbs: The role of implicit sentence context', *Social Cognition, 6*, 21–39.

Field, C. E., and Baber, F. (1973). *Growing Up in Hong Kong: A Preliminary Report on a Study of the Growth, Development and Rearing of Chinese Children in Hong Kong.* Hong Kong: Hong Kong University Press.

Fincher, B. H. (1973). 'The Chinese language in its new social context', *Journal of Chinese Linguistics, 1*, 171–82.

Fineman, S. (1977). 'The achievement motive construct and its measurement: Where are we now?' *British Journal of Psychology, 68*, 1–22.

Finger, S. (1994). *Origins of Neuroscience: A History of Explorations into Brain Function.* New York: Oxford University Press.

Fiske, A. P. (1991). *Structures of Social Life: The Four Elementary Forms of Human Relations.* New York: Free Press.

Flege, J. E. (1987). 'A critical period for learning to pronounce foreign languages?' *Applied Linguistics, 8*, 162–77.

Flege, J. E., and Fletcher, K. L. (1992). 'Talker and listener effects on degree of perceived foreign accents', *Journal of the Acoustical Society of America, 91*, 370–89.

Flege, J. E., McCutcheon, M. J., and Smith, S. C. (1987). 'The development of skill in producing word-final English stops', *Journal of the Acoustical Society of America, 82*, 433–47.

Fletcher, G. J. O., and Ward, C. (1988). 'Attribution theory and processes: A cross-cultural perspective'. In M. H. Bond (Ed.), *The Cross-Cultural Challenge to Social Psychology* (pp. 230–44). Newbury Park, CA: Sage.

Flores d'Arcais, G. B. (1992). 'Graphemic, phonological, and semantic activation processes during the recognition of Chinese characters'. In H. C. Chen and O. J. L. Tzeng (Eds.), *Language Processing in Chinese* (pp. 37–66). Amsterdam: North-Holland.

Folkman, S., and Lazarus, R. S. (1985). 'If it changes, it must be a process: Study of emotion and coping during three stages of a college examination', *Journal of Personality and Social Psychology, 48*, 150–70.

Fong, S. L. M. (1973). 'Assimilation and changing social roles of Chinese Americans', *Journal of Social Issues, 29*(2), 115–27.

Forgas, J. P., and Bond, M. H. (1985). 'Cultural influences on the perception of interaction episodes', *Personality and Social Psychology Bulletin, 11*, 75–88.

Forster, K. I. (1976). 'Accessing the mental lexicon'. In R. J. Wales and E. C. T. Walker (Eds.), *New Approaches to Language Mechanisms* (pp. 257–87). Amsterdam: North-Holland.

Forster, K. I. (1981). 'Frequency blocking and lexical access: One mental lexicon or two?' *Journal of Verbal Learning and Verbal Behavior, 20*, 190–203.

Forster, K. I., and Chambers, S. M. (1973). 'Lexical access and naming time', *Journal of Verbal Learning and Verbal Behavior, 12*, 627–35.

Frank, J. D. (1968). 'The role of hope in psychotherapy', *International Journal of Psychiatry, 5*, 383–412.

Frank, J. D., and Frank, J. B. (1991). *Persuasion and Healing* (third edition). Baltimore: Johns Hopkins University Press.

Franke, R. H., Hofstede, G., and Bond, M. H. (1991). 'Cultural roots of economic performance: A research note'. *Strategic Management Journal, 12*, 165–73.

Franke, W. (1967). *China and the West*. Oxford: Basil Blackwell.

Franks, F., and Faux, S. A. (1990). 'Depression, stress, mastery, and social resources in four ethno-cultural women's groups', *Research in Nursing and Health, 13*, 282–92.

Frayser, S. (1985). *Varieties of Sexual Experience*. New Haven: Human Relations Area Files.

Frederiksen, J. R. (1981). 'Sources of process interactions in reading'. In A. M. Lesgold and C. A. Perfetti (Eds.), *Interactive Processes in Reading* (pp. 361–86). Hillsdale, NJ: Lawrence Erlbaum.

Frederiksen, J. R. (1982). 'A componential theory of reading skills and their interactions'. In R. J. Sternberg (Ed.), *Advances in the Psychology of Human Intelligence* (Vol. 1, pp. 125–80). Hillsdale, NJ: Lawrence Erlbaum.

Frederiksen, J. R., and Kroll, J. F. (1976). 'Spelling and sound: Approaches to the lexicon', *Journal of Experimental Psychology: Human Perception and Performance, 2*, 361–79.

Freedman, D. G., and Freedman, N. C. (1969). 'Behavioural differences between Chinese-American and European-American newborns', *Nature, 224*, 1227.

Freeman, R. D. (1980). 'Visual acuity is better for letters in rows than in columns', *Nature, 286*, 62–4.

Frost, R., Katz, L., and Bentin, S. (1987). 'Strategies for visual word recognition and orthographical depth: A multilingual comparison', *Journal of Experimental Psychology: Human Perception and Performance, 13*, 104–15.

Fu, D. X. (1980). 'The relationship between job characteristics and job satisfaction in managers of small and medium size enterprises' [in Chinese]. Unpublished Master's thesis, National Chengchi University, Taiwan.

Fu, G. Y. (1993). 'A behaviour modification programme for the problem behaviour of a learning-disabled child' [in Chinese], *Chinese Journal of Clinical Psychology, 1*, 110–11.

Fujimori, H., Zheng, Z. P., Kizaki, Y., and Cai, Z. J. (1988). 'Comparison of content of delusions between Japan and China in schizophrenics: Cross-cultural psychiatric investigation', *Clinical Psychiatry* (Tokyo), *30*, 517–27.

Fujita, I., Tanaka, K., Ito, M., and Cheng, K. (1992). 'Columns for visual features of objects in monkey inferotemporal cortex', *Nature, 360*, 343–6.

Fuligni, A., and Stevenson, H. W. (in press). 'Home environment and school learning'. In T. Husen and N. Postlethwaite (Eds.), *Encyclopedia of Education*. New York: Macmillan.

Fung, H. (1994). 'The socialization of shame in young Chinese children'. Unpublished doctoral dissertation, University of Chicago.

Fung, T. Y. (1983). *The Discussion on Intelligence by Chinese Thinkers* [in Chinese]. Hupeh: Hupeh People's Publishers.

Furnham, A., and Li, Y. H. (1993). 'The psychological adjustment of the Chinese in Britain: A study of two generations', *British Journal of Psychiatry, 162*, 109–13.

Furnham, A., and Stringfield, P. (1993). 'Personality and work performance: Myers-Briggs Type Indicator correlates of managerial performance in two cultures', *Personality and Individual Differences, 14*, 145–53.

Gabrenya, W. K., Jr. (1989). 'Social science and social psychology: The cross-cultural link'. In M. H. Bond (Ed.), *The Cross-Cultural Challenge to Social Psychology* (pp. 48–66). Beverly Hills, CA: Sage.

Gabrenya, W. K., Jr. (1990). 'Dyadic social interaction during task behavior in collectivist and individualist societies'. Paper presented at the Workshop on Individualism and Collectivism, Seoul, Korea, June.

Gabrenya, W. K., Jr., and Shu, Y. M. (1993). 'To Li or not to Li: Politeness-norm learning and adjustment among Chinese students in the United States'. Paper presented to the Society for cross-cultural Research, Washington, DC, February.

Gabrenya, W. K., Jr., Latané, B., and Wang, Y. E. (1983). 'Social loafing in cross-cultural perspective: Chinese in Taiwan', *Journal of Cross-Cultural Psychology, 14*, 368–84.

Gabrenya, W. K., Jr., Wang, Y. E. and Latané, B. (1985). 'Cross-cultural differences in social loafing on an optimizing task: Chinese and Americans', *Journal of Cross-Cultural Psychology, 16,* 223–64.

Gaenslen, F. (1986). 'Culture and decision making in China, Japan, Russia, and the United States', *World Politics, 39,* 78–103.

Gaenslen, F. (1993). 'Decision makers as social beings: Consensual decision making in Russia, China, and Japan'. Paper presented at the 89th annual meeting of the American Political Science Association, Washington, DC, September.

Gao, G. (1991). 'Stability of romantic relationships in China and the United States'. In S. Ting-Toomey and F. Korzenny (Eds.), *Cross-Cultural Interpersonal Communication* (pp. 99–115). Newbury Park: Sage.

Gao, G. (1992). 'A dyadic analysis of communication in romantic relationships in China and the United States'. Paper presented at the annual meeting of the International Communication Association, Miami, May.

Gao, G. (1994). 'An initial analysis of the effects of face and concern for "other" in Chinese interpersonal communication'. Manuscript in preparation.

Gao, G. (1994). 'Self and other: A Chinese perspective on interpersonal relationships'. Paper presented at the annual meeting of the International Communication Association, Sydney, July.

Gao, J. F. (Ed.)(1985). *History of Psychology in China* [in Chinese]. Beijing: Renmin Jiaoyu Chubanshe.

Garden, R. A. (1987). 'The second IEA mathematics study', *Comparative Education Review, 31,* 47–68.

Gardner, H. (1989). 'The key in the slot: Creativity in a Chinese key', *Journal of Aesthetic Education, 23*(1), 141–58.

Gardner, H. (1989). *To Open Minds: Chinese Clues to the Dilemma of Contemporary Education.* New York: Basic Books.

Gardner, R. C., and Lambert, W. (1972). *Attitudes and Motivation in Second Language Learning.* Rowley, MA: Newbury House.

Garner, R. (1990). 'When children and adults do not use learning strategies: Toward a theory of settings', *Review of Educational Research, 60,* 517–29.

Gass, S. M. (1987). 'The resolution of conflicts among competing systems: A bidirectional perspective', *Applied Psycholinguistics, 8,* 329–50.

Gau, S. F., and Chen, C. C. (1993). 'Structured family interviews arranged by psychiatric cases at the National Taiwan University Hospital'. In L. Y. Cheng, F. Cheung, and C. N. Chen (Eds.), *Psychotherapy for the Chinese* (pp. 145–56). Hong Kong: Department of Psychiatry, the Chinese University of Hong Kong.

Geertz, C. (1984). '"From the native's point of view": On the nature of anthropological understanding'. In R. A. Shweder and R. A. LeVine (Eds.), *Culture Theory: Essays on Mind, Self, and Emotion* (pp. 123–36). New York: Cambridge University Press.

Geiger, L. (1880). *Contributions to the History of the Development of the Human Race.* London: Tubner and Company.

Geilen, U. P. (1989). 'Some recent work on moral values, reasoning, and education in Chinese societies'. Paper presented at the 12th annual meeting of the International Society of Political Psychology, Tel Aviv, June.

Gergen, K. J. (1989). 'The possibility of psychological knowledge: A hermeneutic inquiry'. In M. J. Packer and R. B. Addison (Eds.), *Entering the Circle: Hermeneutic Investigation in Psychology* (pp. 239–58). Albany: State University of New York Press.

Gergen, K. J. (1992). 'Towards a postmodern psychology'. In S. Kvale (Ed.), *Psychology and Postmodernism* (pp. 17–30). London: Sage.

Ghuman, P., and Wong, R. (1989). 'Chinese parents and English education', *Educational Research (NFER), 31*(2), 134–40.

Giles, H. A. (1964). *Elementary Chinese* (English translation originally published in 1910). Taipei: Jingwen.

Gim, R. H., Atkinson, D. R., and Kim, S. J. (1991). 'Asian-American acculturation, counselor ethnicity and cultural sensitivity, and ratings of counselors', *Journal of Counseling Psychology, 38,* 57–62.

Gim, R. H., Atkinson, D. R., and Whiteley, S. J. (1990). 'Asian-American acculturation, severity of concerns, and willingness to see a counselor', *Journal of Counseling Psychology, 37*, 281–5.

Gladstone, W. E. (1858). *Studies on Homer and the Homeric Age*. London: Oxford University Press.

Glanzer, M., and Ehrenreich, S. L. (1979). 'Structure and search of the internal lexicon', *Journal of Verbal Learning and Verbal Behavior, 18*, 381–98.

Glenn, E. N. (1983). 'Split household, small producer and dual wage earner: An analysis of Chinese-American family strategies', *Journal of Marriage and the Family, 45*, 35–46.

Glover, E. (1955). *The Techniques of Psychoanalysis*. New York: International Universities Press.

Glushko, R. J. (1979). 'The organization and activation of orthographic knowledge in reading aloud', *Journal of Experimental Psychology: Human Perception and Performance, 5*, 674–91.

Gold, T. B. (1993). 'Go with your feelings: Hong Kong and Taiwan popular culture in greater China', *China Quarterly, 136*, 907–25.

Goldberg, D. P. (1978). *Manual of the General Health Questionnaire*. London: NFER.

Goldberg, L. R. (1993). 'The structure of phenotypic personality traits', *American Psychologist, 48*, 26–34.

Gombrich, E. H. (1969). *Art and Illusion*. Princeton, NJ: Princeton University Press.

Gong, Y. X. (1984). 'Use of the Eysenck Personality Questionnaire in China', *Personality and Individual Differences, 5*(4), 431–8.

Gong, Y. X. (1986). 'Revision of the Halstead–Reitan Neuropsychological Battery for adults in China' [in Chinese], *Acta Psychologica Sinica, 18*(4), 433–42.

Gong, Y. X., and Jie, Y. N. (1988). 'Revision of the Halstead–Reitan Neuropsychological Battery for children in China' [in Chinese], *Acta Psychologica Sinica, 20*(3), 312–19.

Gong, Y. X., and National WAIS-RC Coordinating Group (1983). 'Revision of Wechsler Adult Intelligence Scale in China' [in Chinese], *Acta Psychologica Sinica, 15*(3), 362–70.

Goodwin, R. (1990). 'Sex differences amongst partner preferences: Are the sexes really very similar?' *Sex Roles, 23*, 501–13.

Goodwin, R., and Emelyanova, T. (in press). 'The perestroika of the family? Gender and occupational differences in family values in modern-day Russia', *Sex Roles*.

Goodwin, R., and Lee, I. (1994). 'Taboo topics among Chinese and English friends', *Journal of Cross-Cultural Psychology, 25*, 325–38.

Goodwin, R., and Pang, A. (1994). 'Self-monitoring and relationship adjustment: A cross-cultural analysis', *Journal of Social Psychology, 134*, 35–9.

Goodwin, R., and Tang, D. (1991). 'Preferences for friends and close relationship partners: A Cross-cultural comparison'. *Journal of Social Psychology, 131*, 579–81.

Gordon, I., Zukas, M., and Chan, J. (1982). 'Responses to schematic faces: A cross-cultural study', *Perceptual and Motor Skills, 54*, 201–2.

Gordon, M. M. (1971). 'The nature of assimilation and the theory of the melting pot'. In E. P. Hollander and R. G. Hunt (Eds.), *Current Perspectives in Social Psychology* (third edition)(pp. 102–14). New York: Oxford University Press.

Gough, H. G. (1960). *Manual for the California Psychological Inventory* (revised edition). Palo Alto, CA: Consulting Psychologists Press.

Gough, H. G. (1987). *The California Psychological Inventory Administrator's Guide*. Palo Alto, CA: Consulting Psychologists Press.

Gow, L., and Balla, J. (1994). 'Beyond the Principle of Normalisation to the Principle of Aggregation', *Downs Syndrome Down Under, 6*, 24–38.

Gow, L., and Kember, D. (1990). 'Does higher education promote independent learning?' *Higher Education, 19*, 307–22.

Gow, L., and Kember, D. (1993). 'Conceptions of teaching and their relationship to student learning', *British Journal of Educational Psychology, 63*, 20–33.

Gow, L., Kember, D., and Chow, R. (1991). 'The effects of English language ability on approaches to learning', *RELC, 22*(1), 49–68.

Gow, L., Kember, D., and Cooper, B. (1994). 'The teaching context and approaches to study of accountancy students', *Issues in Accounting Education, 9*(1), 56–74.

Gow, L., Kember, D. and Sivan, A. (1992). 'Lecturers' views of their teaching practices:

Implications for staff development needs', *Higher Education Research and Development*, *11*(2), 135–49.

Graham, M. A. (1983). 'Acculturative stress among Polynesian, Asian and American students on the Brigham Young University-Hawaii campus', *International Journal of Intercultural Relations, 7*, 79–103.

Grant, V. (1976). *Falling in Love*. New York: Springer.

Greeley, A., Michael, R., and Smith, Y. (1990). 'Americans and their sexual partners', *Society*, July, 36–42.

Greenwald, A. G. (1980). 'The totalitarian ego: Fabrication and revision of personal history', *American Psychologist, 35*, 603–18.

Greif, E. B., and Berko Gleason, J. (1980). 'Hi, thanks, and goodbye: More routine information', *Language in Society, 9*, 159–66.

Grieser, D., and Kuhl, P. K. (1988). 'Maternal speech to infants in a tonal language: Support for universal prosodic features in motherese', *Developmental Psychology, 24*, 14–20.

Gu, Y. G. (1990). 'Politeness phenomena in modern Chinese', *Journal of Pragmatics, 14*, 237–57.

Gudykunst, W. B., and Ting-Toomey, S. (1988). *Culture and Interpersonal Communication*. Beverly Hills, CA: Sage.

Gudykunst, W. B., Gao, G., Schmidt, K. L., Nishida, T., Bond, M. H., Leung, K., Wang, G., and Barraclough, R. (1992). 'The influence of individualism-collectivism on communication in ingroup and outgroup relationships', *Journal of Cross-Cultural Psychology, 23*, 196–213.

Gudykunst, W. B., Yang, S., and Nishida, T. (1985). 'A cross-cultural test of uncertainty reduction theory', *Human Communication Research, 11*, 407–54.

Gudykunst, W. B., Yang, S., and Nishida, T. (1987). 'Cultural differences in self-consciousness and self-monitoring', *Human Communication Research, 14*, 7–34.

Guilford, J. P. (1959). *Personality*. New York: McGraw-Hill.

Guo, Q. S., and Cheng, G. P. (1991). 'Psychotherapy on a case of sexual disorder' [in Chinese], *Chinese Mental Health Journal, 5*, 228.

Gusfield, J. R. (1967). 'Tradition and modernity: Misplaced polarities in the study of social change', *American Journal of Sociology, 73*, 351–62.

Guthrie, G. M., and Bennett, A. B. (1971). 'Cultural differences in implicit personality theory', *International Journal of Psychology, 6*, 305–12.

Haas, W. (1982). *Standard Language: Spoken and Written*. Manchester: Manchester University Press.

Haberlandt, K. F., and Graesser, A. C. (1985). 'Component processes in text comprehension and some of their interactions', *Journal of Experimental Psychology: General, 114*, 357–74.

Habermas, J. (1970). 'Towards a theory of communicative competence'. *Inquiry, 13*, 360–75.

Habermas, J. (1987). *Towards a Theory of Communicative Action* (Vol. 2). Boston: Beacon.

Hackman, J. R., and Oldham, G. R. (1976). 'Motivation through the design of work: Test of a theory', *Organizational Behavior and Human Performance, 16*, 250–79.

Hackman, J. R., and Oldham, G. R. (1980). *Work Redesign*. Reading, MA: Addison-Wesley.

Haley, J. (1973). *Uncommon Therapy*. New York: Norton.

Haley, J. (1976). *Problem-Solving Therapy*. Cambridge, MA: Harvard University Press.

Haley, J. (1984). *Ordeal Therapy*. San Francisco: Jossey-Bass.

Hall, E. T. (1976). *Beyond Culture*. New York: Doubleday.

Hama, H., Matsuyama, Y., and Lin, R. Y. (1986). 'Analysis of Chinese emotional words'. Unpublished manuscript, Doshisha University.

Hamers, J. F., and Blanc, M. H. A. (1989). *Bilinguality and Bilingualism*. New York: Cambridge University Press.

Hamid, P. N. (1994). 'Self-monitoring, locus of control, and social encounters of Chinese and New Zealand students', *Journal of Cross-Cultural Psychology, 25*, 353–68.

Hamilton, M. (1967). 'Rating scale for depression', *British Journal of Social and Clinical Psychology, 6*, 278–96.

Han, L. (1991). 'Sex differences on the personality characteristics of neurotic patients' [in Chinese], *Chinese Mental Health Journal, 5*(1), 9–10.

Han, Y. H. (1965). 'Responses of Chinese university students to the Thematic Apperception Test' [in Chinese], *Psychological Testing* (Taiwan), *12*, 52–70.

Han, Y. H. (1967). 'A comparison of the responses of the university students, criminals, and psychiatric patients to the Thematic Apperception Test' [in Chinese]. *Psychological Testing* (Taiwan), *14*, 14–28.

Han, Y. H. (1968). 'A study of personality characteristics and parental image in institutionalized children' [in Chinese], *Psychological Testing* (Taiwan), *15*, 50–69.

Harding, C. (1980). 'East meets West: A conflict of values', *Hong Kong Psychological Society Bulletin, 5*, 35–43.

Harding, H. (1993). 'The concept of Greater China: Themes, variations and reservations', *China Quarterly, 136*, 660–86.

Hare-Mustin, R. T., and Hare, S. E. (1986). 'Family change and the concept of motherhood in China', *Journal of Family Issues, 7*(1), 67–82.

Harr, R. (1987). 'The social construction of selves'. In K. Yardley and T. Honess (Eds.), *Self and Identity: Psychosocial Perspectives* (pp. 41–52). Chichester, UK: John Wiley and Sons.

Harrell, S. (1989). 'Ethnicity and kin terms among two kinds of Yi', *New Asia Academic Bulletin* (Hong Kong), *8*, 190–7.

Harry, J. (1990). 'A probability sample of gay males', *Journal of Homosexuality, 9*, 39–51.

Hartley, J., and Holt, J. (1971). 'Academic motivation and programmed learning', *British Journal of Educational Psychology, 41*, 171–83.

Hartmann, E. (1991). *Boundaries in the Mind: A New Psychology of Personality Differences.* New York: Basic Books.

Hathaway, S. R., and McKinley, J. C. (1983). *The Minnesota Multiphasic Personality Inventory Manual.* New York: Psychological Corporation.

Hatta, T. (1981). 'Differential processing of Kanji and Kana stimuli in Japanese people: Some implications from Stroop-test results', *Neuropsychologia, 19*, 87–93.

Hattie, J., and Watkins, D. (1981). 'Australian and Filipino investigation of the internal structure of Biggs' New Study Process Questionnaire', *British Journal of Educational Psychology, 51*, 241–4.

Hau, K. T. (1992). 'Achievement orientation and academic causal attribution of Chinese students in Hong Kong'. Unpublished doctoral dissertation, University of Hong Kong.

Hau, K. T., and Salili, F. (1989). 'Attribution of examination result: Chinese primary school students in Hong Kong', *Psychologia, 32*, 163–71.

Hau, K. T., and Salili, F. (1990). 'Examination result attribution, expectancy and achievement goals among Chinese students in Hong Kong', *Educational Studies, 16*(1), 17–31.

Hau, K. T., and Salili, F. (1991). 'Structure and semantic differential placement of specific causes: Academic causal attributions by Chinese students in Hong Kong', *International Journal of Psychology, 26*(2), 175–93.

Hchu, H. Y. (1971). 'Chinese individual modernity and personality' [in Chinese]. Unpublished Master's thesis, Department of Psychology, National Taiwan University, Taipei.

Hchu, H. Y. (1980). 'On some psychological indicators of social change' [in Chinese]. In *Proceedings of the First Conference on Social Indicators* (pp. 123–47). Taipei: Institute of People's Three Principles, Academia Sinica.

Hchu, H. Y., and Yang, K. S. (1972). 'Individual modernity and psychogenic needs' [in Chinese]. In Y. Y. Li and K. S. Yang (Eds.), *Symposium on the Character of the Chinese: An Interdisciplinary Approach* (pp. 381–410). Taipei: Institute of Ethnology, Academia Sinica.

He, S. (1991). 'The function of attributions and the study of cross-cultural variance in attributional style'. Unpublished Master's thesis, University of Illinois at Chicago.

Headland, I. T. (1914). *Home Life in China.* London: Methuen.

Healy, A. F. (1976). 'Detection errors on the word *the*: Evidence for reading units larger than letters', *Journal of Experimental Psychology: Human Perception and Performance, 2*, 235–42.

Healy, A. F., and Drewnowski, A. (1983). 'Investigating the boundaries of reading units', *Journal of Experimental Psychology: Human Perception and Performance, 2*, 413–26.

Healy, A. F., Oliver, W. L., and McNamara, T. P. (1987). 'Detecting letters in continuous text: Effects of display size', *Journal of Experimental Psychology: Human Perception and Performance, 13*, 279–90.

Heckhausen, H., and Halisch, F. (1986). '*Operant*' versus '*Respondent*' *Motive Measures: A problem of Validity or of Construct?* Munich: Max-Planck-Institut fur Psychologische Forschung.

Heckhausen, H., and Kemmler, L. (1957). 'Entstehungs bedingungen der kindlichen selbstandigkeit', *Zeitschrift für Experimentelle und Angewante Psychologie, 4,* 603–62.

Heelas, P. (1981). 'Introduction: Indigenous psychologies', In P. Heelas and A. Lock (Eds.), *Indigenous Psychologies: The Anthropology of the Self* (pp. 183–201). London: Academic Press.

Heim, A. (1970). *The Appraisal of Intelligence.* Slough, UK: National Foundation for Educational Research in England and Wales.

Heim, A. (1971). *Intelligence and Personality.* Harmondsworth: Penguin Books.

Heist, P., and Yonge, G. (1968). *Omnibus Personality Inventory.* New York: Psychological Corporation.

Hellweg, S. A., Samovar, L. A., and Skow, L. (1991). 'Cultural variations in negotiation styles'. In L. A. Samovar and R. E. Porter (Eds.), *Intercultural Communication: A Reader* (sixth edition, pp. 185–92). Belmont, CA: Wadsworth.

Helmreich, R. L., and Spence, J. T. (1978). 'The Work and Family Orientation Questionnaire: An objective instrument to assess components of achievement motivation and attitudes toward family and career', *JSAS Catalog of Selected Documents in Psychology, 8,* 35.

Hendryx, S. R. (1986). 'The China trade: Making the deal work', *Harvard Business Review, 64* (July–August), 81–4.

Hess, R. D., Chang, C. M., and McDevitt, T. M. (1987). 'Cultural variations in family beliefs about children's performance in mathematics: Comparisons among People's Republic of China, Chinese-American, and Caucasian-American families', *Journal of Educational Psychology, 79,* 179–88.

Hewstone, M., and Ward, C. (1985). 'Ethnocentrism and causal attribution in Southeast Asia', *Journal of Personality and Social Psychology, 48,* 614–23.

Hewstone, M., Bond, M. H., and Wan, K. C. (1983). 'Social facts and social attributions: The explanation of intergroup differences in Hong Kong', *Social Cognition, 2,* 142–57.

Hildebrandt, H. W. (1988). 'A Chinese managerial view of business communication', *Management Communication Quarterly, 2,* 217–34.

Ho, D. Y. F. (1974). 'Early socialisation in contemporary China'. Abstract in Science Council of Japan, *Proceedings of the Twentieth International Congress of Psychology* (p. 442). Tokyo: University of Tokyo Press.

Ho, D. Y. F. (1974). 'Face, social expectations, and conflict avoidance'. In J. L. M. Dawson and W. J. Lonner (Eds.), *Readings in Cross-Cultural Psychology* (pp. 240–51). Hong Kong: Hong Kong University Press.

Ho, D. Y. F. (1974). 'Prevention and treatment of mental illnesses in the People's Republic of China', *American Journal of Orthopsychiatry, 44,* 620–36.

Ho, D. Y. F. (1976). 'On the concept of face', *American Journal of Sociology, 81,* 867–84.

Ho, D. Y. F. (1981). 'Traditional patterns of socialization in Chinese society', *Acta Psychologica Taiwanica, 23*(2), 81–95.

Ho, D. Y. F. (1986). 'Chinese patterns of socialization: A critical review'. In M. H. Bond (Ed.), *The Psychology of the Chinese People* (pp. 1–37). Hong Kong: Oxford University Press.

Ho, D. Y. F. (1987). 'Fatherhood in Chinese culture'. In M. E. Lamb (Ed.), *The Father's Role: Cross-Cultural Perspectives* (pp. 227–45). Hillsdale, NJ: Erlbaum.

Ho, D. Y. F. (1989). 'Continuity and variation in Chinese patterns of socialization', *Journal of Marriage and the Family, 51*(1), 149–63.

Ho, D. Y. F. (1989). 'Socialisation in contemporary mainland China', *Asian Thought and Society, 14*(41–2), 136–49.

Ho, D. Y. F. (1990). 'Chinese values and behavior: A psychological study'. Unpublished manuscript, University of Hong Kong.

Ho, D. Y. F. (1993). 'Cultural definition of intergenerational relationships: The case of filial piety'. Manuscript submitted for publication.

Ho, D. Y. F. (1994). 'Filial piety, authoritarian moralism, and cognitive conservatism in Chinese societies', *Genetic, Social, and General Psychology Monographs, 120,* 347–65.

Ho, D. Y. F., and Chiu, C. Y. (1994). 'Components of individualism, collectivism, and social organization: An application in the study of Chinese culture'. In U. Kim, H. C. Triandis, C. Kagitcibasi, S. C. Choi, and G. Yoon (Eds.), *Individualism and Collectivism: Theory, Method, and Applications* (pp. 137–56). London: Sage.

Ho, D. Y. F., and Kang, T. K. (1984). 'Intergenerational comparisons of child-rearing attitudes and practices in Hong Kong', *Developmental Psychology, 20*(6), 1004–16.

Ho, D. Y. F., and Lee, L. Y. (1974). 'Authoritarianism and attitude toward filial piety in Chinese teachers', *The Journal of Social Psychology, 92,* 305–6.

Ho, D. Y. F., Chan, S. J., and Chiu, C. (1991). 'Relation-oriented: An inquiry on the methodology of Chinese social psychology' [in Chinese]. In K. S. Yang and K. K. Hwang (Eds.), *Chinese Psychology and Behavior* (pp. 49–66). Taipei: Laureate Book Co.

Ho, D. Y. F., Hong, Y. Y., and Chiu, C. Y. (1989). 'Filial piety and family-matrimonial traditionalism in Chinese societies'. Paper presented at the International Conference on Moral Values and Moral Reasoning in Chinese Societies, Academia Sinica Conference Center, Taipei, May.

Ho, D. Y. F., Spinks, J. A., and Yeung, C. S. H. (Eds.)(1989). *Chinese Patterns of Behavior: A Sourcebook of Psychological and Psychiatric Studies.* New York: Praeger.

Ho, E. K. F. (1994). 'Validating the five-factor model of personality: The Hong Kong case'. Unpublished Bachelor's thesis, Chinese University of Hong Kong.

Ho, E. S., and Hills, M. (1992). 'The challenge of culture change: Hong Kong Chinese adolescent immigrants in New Zealand'. Paper presented at the Asian Conference of Psychology, October.

Ho, M. K. (1987). *Family Therapy with Minorities.* Newbury Park, CA: Sage.

Ho, P. Y. (1966). *The Astronomical Chapters of the Chin Shu.* Paris: Mouton.

Ho, S. C., and Sin, Y. M. (1986). 'Advertising in China: Looking back at looking forward', *International Journal of Advertising, 5*(4), 307–16.

Ho, W. S., Chu, C. K., and Yeung, K. C. (1993). 'Solution-focused therapy with Chinese people'. In L. Y. Cheng, F. Cheung, and C. N. Chen (Eds.), *Psychotherapy for the Chinese* (pp. 97–106). Hong Kong: Department of Psychiatry, the Chinese University of Hong Kong.

Ho, Y. C. (1990). 'The changes of ego identity and subculture of youth over a five-year period: The case of students from two normal universities in Taiwan' [in Chinese], *Bulletin of Educational Psychology* (National Taiwan Normal University), *23,* 119–42.

Hochberg, J., and Brooks, V. (1978). 'The perception of motion pictures'. In E. C. Carterette and M. P. Friedman (Eds.), *Handbook of Perception* (Vol. 10, pp. 259–304). New York: Academic Press.

Hoffman, C., Lau, I., and Johnson, D. R. (1986). 'The linguistic relativity of person cognition', *Journal of Personality and Social Psychology, 51,* 1097–1105.

Hofstede, G. H. (1980). *Culture's Consequences: International Differences in Work-related Values.* Beverly Hills: Sage.

Hofstede, G. H. (1983). 'Dimensions of national cultures in fifty countries and three regions'. In J. B. Deregowski, S. Dziurawiec, and R. C. Annis (Eds.), *Expiscations in Cross-Cultural Psychology* (pp. 335–55). Lisse: Swets and Zeitlinger B. V.

Hofstede, G. H. (1991). *Cultures and Organizations: Software of the Mind.* London: McGraw-Hill.

Hofstede, G. H., and Bond, M. H. (1984). 'Hofstede's culture dimensions: An independent validation using Rokeach's value survey', *Journal of Cross-Cultural Psychology, 15,* 417–33.

Hofstede, G. H., and Bond, M. H. (1988). 'The Confucius connection: From cultural roots to economic growth', *Organizational Dynamics, 16*(4), 4-21.

Hofstede, G. H., Bond, M. H., and Luk, C. L. (1993). 'Individual perceptions of organizational cultures: A methodological treatise on levels of analysis', *Organization Studies, 14,* 483–583.

Hofstede, G. H., Neuijen, B., Ohayv, D., and Sanders, G. (1990). 'Measuring organizational cultures: A qualitative and quantitive study across twenty cases', *Administrative Science Quarterly, 35,* 286–316.

Hogan, R., and Emler, N. (1978). 'The biases of contemporary social psychology', *Social Research, 45,* 478–534.

Hogarth, R. M. (1981). 'Beyond discrete biases: Functional and dysfunctional aspects of judgmental heuristics', *Psychological Bulletin, 90,* 197–217.

Holender, D. (1991). 'Comment: Writing systems and the modularity of language'. In I. G. Mattingly, and M. Studdert-Kennedy (Eds.), *Modularity and the Motor Theory of Speech Perception* (pp. 347–57). Hillsdale, NJ: Lawrence Erlbaum.

Homel, P., Palij, M., and Aaronson, D. (1987). *Childhood Bilingualism: Aspects of Linguistic, Cognitive, and Social Development.* Hillsdale, NJ: Lawrence Erlbaum.

Hong, J. (1994). 'The resurrection of advertising in China', *Asian Survey, 34*(4), 326–42.

Hong Kong Psychological Society (1989). *Manual for Cantonese Administration of the Wechsler*

Adult Intelligence Scale–Revised [in Chinese]. Hong Kong: The Society. Hong kong Psychology.

Hong, L. (1976). 'The role of women in the People's Republic of China: Legacy and change', *Social Problems, 23*, 545–57.

Hong, L. K. (1978). 'Risky shift and cautious shift: Some direct evidence of the culture-value theory', *Social Psychology Quaterly, 41*, 342–6.

Hong, Q. X. (1979). 'The effects of job characteristics on job satisfaction of education administrators' [in Chinese]. Unpublished Master's thesis, National Chengchi University, Taiwan.

Hong, W., Chan, L., Zheng, D. C., and Wang, C. (1992). 'Neurasthenia in Chinese students at UCLA', *Psychiatric Annals, 22*, 199–201.

Hong, Y. Y., and Lam, D. J. (1992). 'Appraisal, coping, and guilt as correlates of test anxiety'. In K. Hagtvet and T. Backer (Eds.), *Advances in Test Anxiety Research* (Vol. 7, pp. 277–87). Lisse, the Netherlands: Swets and Zeitlinger.

Honig, A. S. (1978). 'Comparison of child rearing practices in the People's Republic of China: A personal view', *International Journal of Group Tensions, 8*(1–2), 6–32.

Hoosain, R. (1986). 'Perceptual processes of the Chinese'. In M. H. Bond (Ed.), *The Psychology of the Chinese People* (pp. 38–72). Hong Kong: Oxford University Press.

Hoosain, R. (1991). *Psycholinguistic Implications for Linguistic Relativity: A Case Study of Chinese*. Hillsdale, NJ: Lawrence Erlbaum.

Hoosain, R. (1992). 'Psychological reality of the word in Chinese'. In H. C. Chen and O. J. L. Tzeng (Eds.), *Language Processing in Chinese* (pp. 111–30). Amsterdam: Elsevier.

Hornik, S. (1993). 'How to get that extra edge on health and wealth', *Smithsonian, 24*(5), 70–5.

Houghton, D. (1991). 'Mr. Chong: A case study of a dependent learner of English for academic purposes', *System, 19*(1–2), 75–90.

House, J. S. (1981). 'Social structure and personality'. In M. Rosenberg and R. H. Turner (Eds.), *Social Psychology: Sociological Perspectives* (pp. 525–61). New York: Basic Books.

Hovland, C. I. (1954). 'The effects of mass media on communication'. In G. Lindzey (Ed.), *Handbook of Social Psychology* (pp. 1062–1103). Cambridge, MA: Addison-Wesley.

Hse, C. C. (1971). 'Chinese children's responses on the Coloured Progressive Matrices' [in Chinese], *Journal Formosa Medical Association, 70*, 579–91.

Hsia, J. (1988). *Asian Americans in Higher Education and at Work*. Hillsdale, NJ: Lawrence Erlbaum Associates.

Hsia, S. (1992). 'Developmental knowledge of inter- and intraword boundaries: Evidence from American and Mandarin Chinese speaking beginning readers', *Applied Psycholinguistics, 13*, 341–72.

Hsia, S. (1994). 'The significance of segmental awareness in learning a second language'. Unpublished manuscript, Language Information Sciences Research Centre, City University of Hong Kong.

Hsia, S. (1994). 'Word syllabification strategies among Cantonese adult ESL learners: Implications for word recognition and perception'. Unpublished manuscript, Language Information Sciences Research Centre, City University of Hong Kong.

Hsia, T. T. (1956). *China's Language Reform*. New Haven, NJ: Yale University Press.

Hsieh, N. M. (1982). 'Reading of Chinese characters and words and phonological recoding' [in Chinese]. Unpublished Master's thesis, National Taiwan University.

Hsieh, Y. W., Shybut, J., Lotsof, E. (1969). 'Internal versus external control and ethnic group membership', *Journal of Consulting and Clinical Psychology, 33*, 122–4.

Hsing, Y. T. (1991). 'Person appraisal by body shape and face color in Han dynasty' [in Chinese]. In W. S. Sung, Y. Y. Li, C. W. Hsu, and K. C. Chang (Eds.), *Archeology, History, and Civilization* (pp. 253–65). Taipei: Cheng-Chung.

Hsu, C. (1972). 'Chinese parent-child relationships in children's literature' [in Chinese]. In Y. Y. Li and K. S. Yang (Eds.), *The Character of the Chinese* (pp. 201–18). Taipei: Institute of Ethnology, Academia Sinica.

Hsu, C. C. (1985). 'Characteristics of temperament in Chinese infants and young children'. In W. S. Tseng and D. Y. H. Wu (Eds.), *Chinese Culture and Mental Health* (pp. 135–51). Orlando, FL: Academic Press.

Hsu, C. C., Soong, W. T., Stigler, J. W., Hong, C. C., and Liang, C. C. (1981). 'The temperamental characteristics of Chinese babies', *Child Development, 52*, 337–40.

Hsu, C. K. (1977). 'A research of factory workers' job satisfaction and its correlates' [in Chinese], *Bulletin of the Institute of Ethnology, Academia Sinica, 43,* 23–63.

Hsu, F. G. (1979). 'The formation, evolution, and related historical problems in Chinese filialism' [in Chinese]. In F. G. Hsu, *Collection of History of Chinese Thought* (pp. 155–91). Taipei: Taiwan Student Book Co.

Hsu, F. L. K. (1949). 'Suppression versus repression: A limited psychological interpretation of four cultures', *Psychiatry, 12,* 223–42.

Hsu, F. L. K. (1953). *Americans and Chinese: Two Ways of Life.* New York: Abelard-Schuman.

Hsu, F. L. K. (1963). *Clan, Caste and Club.* Princeton, NJ: Van Nostrand.

Hsu, F. L. K. (1971). 'Eros, affect and *pao'.* In F. L. K. Hsu (Ed.), *Kinship and Culture* (pp. 439–75). Chicago: Aldine.

Hsu, F. L. K. (1971). 'Psycho-social homeostasis and *jen:* Conceptual tools for advancing psychological anthropology', *American Anthropologist, 73,* 23–44.

Hsu, F. L. K. (1972) 'American core value and national character'. In F. L. K. Hsu (Ed.), *Psychological Anthropology* (pp. 241–62). Homewood, IL: Dorsey.

Hsu, F. L. K. (1981). *Americans and Chinese: Passage to Differences* (third edition). Honolulu: University of Hawaii Press.

Hsu, F. L. K. (1983). *Rugged Individualism Reconsidered.* Knoxville: University of Tennessee Press.

Hsu, F. L. K. (1985). 'The self in cross-cultural perspective'. In A. J. Marsella, G. DeVos, and F. L. K. Hsu (Eds.), *Culture and Self: Asian and Western Perspectives* (pp. 24–55). New York: Tavistock.

Hsu, J. (1976). 'Counselling in the Chinese temple: A psychological study of divination by *chien* drawing'. In W. Lebra (Ed.), *Culture-Bound Syndromes, Ethnopsychiatry, and Alternative Therapies* (pp. 211–21). Honolulu: University of Hawaii Press.

Hsu, J. (1985). 'The Chinese family: Relations, problems, and therapy'. In W. Tseng and D. Wu (Eds.), *Chinese Culture and Mental Health* (pp. 95–112). New York: Academic Press.

Hsu, J. S. Z. (1987). 'The history of psychology in Taiwan'. In G. H. Blowers and A. M. Turtle (Eds.), *Psychology Moving East: The Status of Western Psychology in Asia and Oceania* (pp. 127–38). Boulder, CO: Westview Press.

Hsu, J., Tseng, W. S., Lum, K. Y., Lau, L., Vaccaro, J., and Brennan, J. (1988). 'Cross-ethnic study of normal families in Hawaii'. Paper presented at the Asian Family Mental Health Conference Proceedings, Tokyo.

Hsu, M. L., and Chen, S. C. (1981). 'An empirical study of employee's job stress' [in Chinese], *Bulletin of the Institute of Ethnology, Academia Sinica, 51,* 63–88.

Hu, C. T. (1993). 'Some thoughts on psychoanalysis and Confucianism in China'. In L. Y. Cheng, F. Cheung, and C. N. Chen (Eds.), *Psychotherapy for the Chinese* (pp. 63–8). Hong Kong: Department of Psychiatry, the Chinese University of Hong Kong.

Hu, H. C. (1944). 'The Chinese concept of "face"', *American Anthropologist, 46,* 45–64.

Hu, W. Z., and Grove, C. L. (1991). *Encountering the Chinese: A Guide for Americans.* Yarmouth, ME: Intercultural Press.

Huang, F. S. (1974). 'Sources of family influences on high school students' academic achievement' [in Chinese], *National Taiwan Normal University Graduate School of Education Research Quarterly, 16,* 383–486.

Huang, G. Y., and Liu, Y. Y. (1983). 'The impacts of teachers' expectations and socio-economic status on children's academic achievement' [in Chinese], *National Zhengzhi University Research Journal, 47,* 61–95.

Huang, H. C., Hwang, K. K., and Ko, Y. H. (1983). 'Life stress, attribution style, social support and depression among university students' [in Chinese], *Acta Psychologica Taiwanica, 25,* 31–47.

Huang, J. T. (1994). 'Determination of access-route duality and temporal priority of phonological recoding'. Paper presented at the inaugural Asian-Australian Workshop on the Cognitive Processing of Asian Language, Sydney.

Huang, J. T., and Liu, I. M. (1978). 'Paired-associate learning proficiency as a function of frequency count, meaningfulness, and imagery value in Chinese two-character ideograms' [in Chinese], *Acta Psychologica Taiwanica, 20,* 5–17.

Huang, J. T., and Wang, M. Y. (1992). 'From unit to Gestalt: Perceptual dynamics in recognizing Chinese characters'. In H. C. Chen and O. J. L. Tzeng (Eds.), *Language Processing in Chinese* (pp. 3–35). Amsterdam: Elsevier.

Huang, K. H. (1978). 'A comparison of families' socio-economic status between college applicants and those who are admitted' [in Chinese], *National Taiwan Normal University Graduate School of Education Research Quarterly, 20,* 149–326.

Huang, K. L. (1982). 'Leadership styles, job nature, achievement motivation, locus of control, and their influence on Taiwanese teachers'job satisfaction' [in Chinese], *Journal of Education and Psychology, 5,* 47–76.

Huang, K. L. (1983). 'The relationships of stereotype to attribution, dogmatism and demographic variables' [in Chinese], *Jiaoyu Xinli Yanjiu, 6,* 75–98.

Huang, K. L. (1984). 'Employees and job satisfaction in organizational setting: A study in Taiwan' [in Chinese]. In National Taiwan University (Ed.), *Chinese Management Research Seminar* (pp. 1–14). Taiwan: National Taiwan University.

Huang, K. L. (1986). 'Organizational commitment and career commitment among Taiwanese high school teachers' [in Chinese], *National Chengzhi University Bulletin, 53,* 55–84.

Huang, K. L., and Kuo, W. H. (1984). 'Effects of attribution, achievement motivation, dogmatism and demographic variables on college graduates' job satisfaction' [in Chinese], *Journal of Education and Psychology, 7,* 43–61.

Huang, L. J. (1971). 'Sex role stereotypes and self-concepts among American and Chinese students', *Journal of Comparative Family Studies, 2,* 215–34.

Huang, P. D. (1993). 'Labour-management relations in a new era: A new cohort of workforce and the second-generation leaders of family enterprises'. Unpublished manuscript.

Huang, S. F. (1978). 'Historical change of prepositions and the emergence of SOV order', *Journal of Chinese Linguistics, 6,* 212–42.

Huang, S. L., and Huang, J. T. (1994). 'Effects of boundary and binocularity on the emergence of illusory color', *Investigative Ophthalmology and Visual Science, 35*(4), 1665.

Huang, Z. M., Xu, J. M., and Zhang, M. Y. (1989). 'Psychotherapy with 23 cases of phobias' [in Chinese], *Chinese Journal of Nervous and Mental Diseases, 15,* 295–7.

Hubei Province Wuhan Municipal Labour Union (1991). 'Survey on employees' attitudes towards organizational reform' [in Chinese]. In China National Labour Union (Ed.), *The 1991 Surveys of Chinese Workers' Attitude* (pp. 49–65). PRC: Jingji Guanli Press.

Huber, G. P. (1983). 'Cognitive style as a basis for MIS and DSS designs: Much ado about nothing?' *Management Science, 29,* 567–79.

Hue, C. W. (1992). 'Recognition processes in character naming'. In H. C. Chen and O. J. L. Tzeng (Eds.), *Language Processing in Chinese* (pp. 93–107). Amsterdam: North-Holland.

Huey, E. B. (1908). *The Psychology and Pedagogy of Reading.* New York: Macmillan. (Reprinted Cambridge, MA: MIT Press, 1968.)

Hughes, C. C. (1985). 'The genital retraction taxon: Commentary'. In R. C. Simon and C. C. Hughes (Eds.). *The Culture-bound Syndromes: Folk Illnesses of Psychiatric and Anthropological Interest* (pp. 207–10). Dordrecht, the Netherlands: D. Reidel.

Hui, C. H. (1988). 'Measurement of individualism–collectivism', *Journal of Research in Personality, 22,* 17–36.

Hui, C. H. (1990). 'Work attitudes, leadership styles, and managerial behaviors in different cultures'. In R. W. Brislin (ed.), *Applied Cross-cultural Psychology* (pp. 186–208). Newbury Park, CA: Sage.

Hui, C. H., and Triandis, H. C. (1985). 'Measurement in cross-cultural psychology: A review and comparison of strategies'. *Journal of Cross-cultural Psychology, 16,* 131–52.

Hui, C. H., and Triandis, H. C. (1986). 'Individualism–collectivism: A study of cross-cultural researchers', *Journal of Cross-cultural Psychology, 17,* 225–48.

Hui, C. H., and Triandis, H. C. (1989). 'Effects of culture and response format on extreme response style', *Journal of Cross-cultural Psychology, 20,* 296–309.

Hui, C. H., and Yee, C. (1994). 'The shortened Individualism-Collectivism Scale: Its relations with demographic and work-related variables', *Journal of Research in Personality, 28,* 409–24.

Hui, C. H., and Yee, C. (1995). 'The impact of psychological collectivism and workgroup atmosphere on job satisfaction: A test of the interactionist model'. Paper presented at the Inaugural Conference of the Asian Association of Social Psychology, Hong Kong, 1995.

Hui, C. H., Chan, I. S. Y., and Chan, J. (1989). 'Death cognition among Chinese teenagers: Beliefs about consequences of death', *Journal of Research in Personality, 23,* 99–117.

Hui, C. H., Eastman, K. L., and Yee, C. (in press). 'The relationship between individualism-collectivism and satisfaction at the workplace', *Applied Psychology*.

Hui, C. H., Triandis, H. C., and Yee, C. (1991). 'Cultural differences in reward allocation: Is collectivism the explanation?' *British Journal of Social Psychology, 30*, 145–57.

Hui, C., and Villareal, M. (1989). 'Individualism–collectivism and psychological needs: Their relationship in two cultures', *Journal of Cross-Cultural Psychology, 20*, 310–23.

Hunan Province Labour Union (1991). 'Sampling survey of workers in Hunan Province' [in Chinese]. In China National Labour Union (Ed.), *The 1991 Surveys of Chinese Workers' Attitudes* (pp. 325–45). PRC: Jingji Guanli Press.

Hung, D. L., and Tzeng, O. J. L. (1981). 'Orthographic variation and visual information processing', *Psychological Bulletin, 90*, 377–414.

Hung, D. L., Tzeng, O. J. L., and Chen, S. Z. (1993). 'Activation effects of morphology in Chinese lexical processing' [in Chinese]. *World of Chinese Language, 69*, 1–7.

Hung, D. L., Tzeng, O. J. L., and Hung, A. K. Y. (1992). 'Automatic activation of linguistic information in Chinese character recognition'. In R. Frost, and L. Katz (Eds.), *Orthography, Phonology, Morphology, and Meaning* (pp. 119–30). Amsterdam: North-Holland.

Hung, K. Y., and Yang, K. S. (1979). 'Attributional variables as cognitive traits: Measurement and validation' [in Chinese]. *Zhongyang Yanjiuyuan Minzuxue Yanjiusuo Jikan, 48*, 89–154.

Hung, Y. Y. (1974). 'Socio-cultural environment and locus of control' [in Chinese], *Acta Psychologica Taiwanica, 16*, 187–98.

Hung, Y. Y. (1982). 'Psychological characters among the mentally retarded and gifted students in junior high schools' [in Chinese], *Bulletin of Educational Psychology* (Taiwan), *15*, 167–94.

Hunt, E., and Agnoli, F. (1991). 'The Whorfian hypothesis: A cognitive psychology perspective', *Psychological Review, 98*, 377–89.

Hunt, E., Lunneborg, C., and Lewis, J. (1975). 'What does it mean to be highly verbal?' *Cognitive Psychology, 7*, 194–227.

Hunt, J. M. (1961). *Intelligence and Experience*. New York: Ronald Press.

Hunt, R. G., and Meindl, J. R. (1991). 'Chinese political economic reforms and the problem of legitimizing leader roles', *Leadership Quarterly, 2*, 189–204.

Hwang, C. H. (1977). 'Discussing filial piety from a psychological point of view and analying the views of youth toward filial behavior' [in Chinese], *Bulletin of Educational Psychology, 10*, 11–20.

Hwang, C. H. (1979). 'A study of the internal–external control of Chinese school pupils' [in Chinese], *Bulletin of Educational Psychology, 12*, 1–14.

Hwang, C. H. (1982). 'Studies in Chinese personality: A critical review' [In Chinese], *Bulletin of Educational Psychology, 15*, 227–42.

Hwang, C. H. (1989). 'A follow-up study on the psychological needs of Chinese university students' [in Chinese], *Bulletin of Educational Psychology* (National Taiwan Normal University), *22*, 1–21.

Hwang, C. J. (1993). 'An empirical analysis of youth culture in Taipei, Taiwan: Comparison of data collected in 1985, 1988 and 1991' [in Chinese]. Unpublished manuscript, Department of Sociology, Fujen University, Taipei.

Hwang, K. K. (1977). 'The patterns of coping strategies in a Chinese society' [in Chinese], *Acta Psychologica Taiwanica, 19*, 61–73.

Hwang, K. K. (1978). 'The dynamic processes of coping with interpersonal conflicts: A Chinese society', *Proceedings of the National Science Council* (Taiwan), *2*, 198–208.

Hwang, K. K. (1983). 'Business organizational patterns and employee's working morale in Taiwan' [in Chinese], *Bulletin of the Institute of Ethnology, Academia Sinica, 56* (Autumn), 145–93.

Hwang, K. K. (1987). 'Face and favor: The Chinese power game', *American Journal of Sociology, 92*, 944–74.

Hwang, K. K. (1988). *Confucianism and East Asian Modernization* [in Chinese]. Taipei: Chu-Liu Book Co.

Hwang, K. K. (1990). 'Modernization of the Chinese family business', *International Journal of Psychology, 25*, 593–618.

Hwang, K. K. (1991). *The Great Way of the King* [in Chinese]. Taipei: Students Bookstore.

Hwang, K. K. (1992). 'Self-realization and value change in Chinese society' [in Chinese]. In *Proceedings of the International Conference on Values in Chinese Societies: Retrospect and*

534

REFERENCES

Prospect (Vol. 1, pp. 161–200). Taipei: Center for Chinese Studies.

Hwang, K. K. (in press). 'Modern transformation of Confucian values: Theoretical analysis and empirical study' [in Chinese], *Indigenous Psychological Research in Chinese Societies* (National Taiwan University), *3*.

Hwang, S. S., and Saenz, R. (1990). 'The problem posed by immigrants married abroad on inter-marriage research: The case of Asian Americans', *International Migration Review, 24*, 563–76.

Hwu, H. G., Yeh, E. K., and Chang, L. Y. (1986). 'Chinese diagnostic interview schedule: I. Agreement with psychiatrist's diagnosis', *Acta Psychiatrica Scandinavica, 73*, 225–33.

Hwu, H. G., Yeh, E. K., and Chang, L. Y. (1989). 'Prevalence of psychiatric disorders in Taiwan defined by the Chinese Diagnostic Interview Schedule', *Acta Psychiatrica Scandinavica, 79*, 136–47.

Hwu, H. G., Yeh, E. K., Chang, L. Y., and Yeh, Y. L. (1986). 'Chinese diagnostic interview schedule: II. A validity study on estimation of lifetime prevalence', *Acta Psychiatrica Scandinavica, 73*, 348–57.

Hwu, H. G., Yeh, E. K., Yeh, Y. L., and Chang, L. Y. (1988). 'Alcoholism by Chinese diagnostic inter-view schedule: A prevalence and validity study', *Acta Psychiatrica Scandinavica, 77*, 7–13.

Hwu, M. G. (1993). 'Comments on the foundations of rationality and the directions of practice for educational reforms' [in Chinese], *Educational Research, 29*, 21–40.

Hymes, D. (1967). 'Models of the interaction of language and social setting', *Journal of Social Issues, 23*, 8–28.

Hymes, D. (1983). Foreword. In E. Ochs and B. Schieffelin, *Acquiring Conversational Competence*. London: Routledge.

Imada, H. (1989). 'Cross-language comparisons of emotional terms with special reference to the concept of anxiety', *Japanese Psychological Research, 31*, 10–19.

Imada, H., Kujime, Y., and Narita, K. (1994). 'Comparisons of concepts of anxiety, fear, and depres-sion in English and Japanese languages'. Manuscript in preparation, Kwansei Gakuin University, Hyogo, Japan.

Irvine, S., and Carroll, W. K (1980). 'Testing and assessment across cultures: Issues in methodology and theory'. In H. C. Triandis and J. W. Berry (Eds.), *Handbook of Cross-Cultural Psychology* (Vol. 2: Methodology, pp. 181–244). Boston, MA: Allyn and Bacon.

Israel, J. (1966). *The Rise of Student Nationalism, 1927–1937*. Stanford, CA: Stanford University Press.

Izard, C. E. (1977). *Human Emotions*. New York: Plenum Press.

Jaccard, J., and Wan, C. K. (1986). 'Cross-cultural methods for the study of behavioral decision making', *Journal of Cross-Cultural Psychology, 17*, 123–149.

Jackson, D. N. (1974). *Manual for the Personality Research Form*. Goshen, NY: Research Psychology Press.

Jackson, D. N. (1984). *Personality Research Form Manual* (third edition). Port Huron, MI: Research Psychologists Press.

Jacobson, A. H. (1952). 'Conflict of attitudes toward the roles of the husband and the wife in mar-riage', *American Sociology Review, 17*, 146–50.

Jahoda, G. (1977). 'In pursuit of the emic–etic distinction: Can we ever capture it?' In Y. H. Poortinga (Ed.), *Basic Problems in Cross-Cultural Psychology*. Lisse, the Netherlands: Swets and Zeitlinger.

Jahoda, G. (1992). *Crossroads Between Culture and Mind: Continuities and Change in Theories of Human Nature*. London: Harvester/Wheatsheaf.

Jahoda, G. (1994). 'Review of P. B. Smith and M. H. Bond's *Social Psychology across Cultures*', *The Psychologist, 7*(4), 174–5.

Jamal, M., and Xie, J. L. (1991). 'The relationship between managerial style and job involvement, job stress and turnover motivation in China', *International Journal of Management, 8*, 682–94.

James, A. R. (1986). *Suprasegmental Phonology and Segmental Form*. Tubingen: Niemeyer.

James, C. T. (1975). 'The role of semantic information in lexical decisions', *Journal of Experimental Psychology: Human Perception and Performance, 1*, 130–6.

Jankowiak, W. R. (1993). *Sex, Death, and Hierarchy in a Chinese City: An Anthropological Account*. New York: Columbia University Press.

Jensen, A. (1980). 'A critical look at test bias: Fallacies and manifestations', *New Horizons, 21*, 44–64.

Jensen, A. (1981). 'A non-technical guide to the IQ controversy', *New Horizons, 22*, 21–6.

Jensen, A. (1981). *Straight Talk about Mental Tests*. New York: Free Press.

Jensen, A. (1994). 'Review of Nathan Brody's *Intelligence*', *American Journal on Mental Retardation, 98*, 663–7.

Jensen, A., and Whang, P. (1993). 'Reaction times and intelligence: A comparison of Chinese-American and Anglo-American children', *Journal of Biosocial Science, 25*, 397–410.

Jensen, A., and Whang, P. (1994). 'Speed of accessing arithmetic facts in long-term memory: A comparison of Chinese-American and Anglo-American children', *Contemporary Educational Psychology, 19*, 1–12.

Jerath, J. M. (1981). 'The intrinsic and extrinsic components of achievement motivation', *Personality Study and Group Behaviour, 1*(1), 74–81.

Ji, J., Zhang, M., Zhu, Z., and Yan, H. (1994). 'Crisis intervention for suicide-ideators: A hot-line psychological consultation' [in Chinese], *Chinese Journal of Clinical Psychology, 2*, 178–80.

Ji, M. F. (1986). *Today's Women* [in Chinese]. Hong Kong: Publications (Holding) Limited.

Jia, X. L. (1991). 'The treatment of phobia by insight-oriented psychotherapy' [in Chinese], *Chinese Mental Health Journal, 5*, 226–7.

Jiao, S. L., Ji, G. P., and Kong, Q. J. (1986). 'Comparative study of behavioral qualities of only children and sibling children', *Child Development, 57*(2), 357–61.

Jie, Y. N., and Gong, Y. X. (1993). 'Revision and application of the junior Halstead–Reitan Neuropsychological Battery' [in Chinese], *Chinese Mental Health Journal, 7*(2), 49–53.

Jilek-Aal, L. (1988). 'Suicidal behaviour among youth: A cross-cultural comparison', *Transcultural Psychiatric Research Review, 25*, 87–106.

Jin, F. Z., Jin, J. J., Biao, M. Z., and Cui, C. (1991). 'Comparison of Han and Jaoxin tribe children's behaviour problems' [in Chinese], *Chinese Mental Health Journal, 5*(4), 160–2.

John, O. P., Angleitner, A., and Ostendorf, F. (1988). 'The lexical approach to personality: A historical review of trait taxonomic research', *European Journal of Personality, 2*, 171–203.

John, O. P., Goldberg, L. R., and Angleitner, A. (1984). 'Better than the alphabet: Taxonomies of personality-descriptive terms in English, Dutch, and German'. In H. J. C. Bonarius, G. L. M. van Heck, and N. G. Smid (Eds.), *Personality Psychology in Europe: Theoretical and Empirical Developments* (pp. 83–100). Lisse, the Netherlands: Swets and Zeitlinger.

Johnson, D., Nathan, A. J., and Rawski, E. S. (1985). *Popular Culture in Late Imperial China*. Berkeley: University of California Press.

Johnson, D. W., and Johnson, R. T. (1993). 'Creative and critical thinking through academic controversy', *American Behavioral Scientist, 37*(5), 40–53.

Johnson, R. K. (1983). 'Bilingual switching strategies: A study of the modes of teacher-talk in bilingual secondary classrooms in Hong Kong', *Language Learning and Communication, 2*, 276–385.

Johnson-Laird, P. N. (1983). *Mental Models: Towards a Cognitive Science of Language, Inference, and Consciousness*. Cambridge, MA: Harvard University Press.

Jones, A. P., Rozelle, R. M., and Chang, W. C. (1990). 'Perceived punishment and reward values of supervisor actions in a Chinese sample', *Psychological Studies, 35*, 1–10.

Ju, T. Z. (1947). *Chinese Law and Chinese Society* [in Chinese]. China: Min Mian Publishing Company.

Ju, Z. C. (1991). 'The "depreciation" and "appreciation" of some address terms in China', *Language in Society, 20*, 387–90.

Jung, C. G. (1971). *Psychological Types* (H. G. Baynes, Trans., revised by R. F. C. Hull). Princeton, NJ: Princeton University Press. (Originally published in 1923.)

Jung, M. (1984). 'Structural family therapy: Its application to Chinese families', *Family Process, 23*, 365–74.

Juola, J. F. (1988). 'The use of computer displays to improve reading comprehension', *Applied Cognitive Psychology, 2*, 87–95.

Juola, J. F., Ward, N., and McNamara, T. (1982). 'Visual search and reading of rapid, serial presentations of letter strings, words, and text', *Journal of Experimental Psychology: General, 111*, 208–227.

Jussim, L. (1990). 'Social reality and social problems: The role of expectancies', *Journal of Social Issues, 46,* 9–34.

Just, M. A., and Carpenter, P. A. (1980). 'A theory of reading: From eye fixation to comprehension', *Psychological Review, 87,* 329–54.

Just, M. A., Carpenter, P. A., and Woolley, J. D. (1982). 'Paradigms and processes in reading comprehension', *Journal of Experimental Psychology: General, 111,* 228–38.

Kadri, Z. N. (1971). 'The use of the MMPI for personality study of Singapore students', *British Journal of Social and Clinical Psychology, 10,* 90–1.

Kagan, J., Kearsley, R. B., and Zelazo, P. R. (1978). *Infancy: Its Place in Human Development.* Cambridge, MA: Harvard University Press.

Kagitcibasi, C. (1981). 'Individual and group loyalties: Are they compatible?' In C. Kagitcibasi (Ed.), *Growth and Progress in Cross-Cultural Psychology* (pp. 94–104). Lisse, the Netherlands: Swets and Zeitlinger.

Kahn, H. (1979). *World Development: 1979 and Beyond.* London: Croom Helm.

Kaneshige, K. (1973). 'Cultural factors in group counseling and interaction', *Personnel and Guidance Journal, 51,* 407–12.

Kang, M., Li, J., and Xie, J. (1992). 'Rehabilitation of schizophrenic patients by social psychic intervention' [in Chinese], *Chinese Journal of Nervous and Mental Diseases, 18,* 258–60.

Kang, T. S. (1972). 'Name and group identification', *Journal of Social Psychology, 86,* 159–60.

Kang, Y. (1992). *The Origin and Development of Chinese Ideographs* [in Chinese]. Beijing: International Culture Publishing Co.

Kao, H. S. R., and Ng, S. H. (1988). *Organizational Behavior* [in Chinese].Taipei: Sanmin Book Company.

Kapp, R. A. (1983). *Communicating with China.* Yarmouth, ME: Intercultural Press.

Karau, S. J., and Williams, K. D. (1993). 'Social loafing: A meta-analytic review and theoretical integration', *Journal of Personality and Social Psychology, 65,* 681–706.

Karenga, M. R. (1978). 'Chinese psycho-social therapy: A strategic model for mental health', *Psychotherapy: Theory, Research and Practice, 15,* 101–7.

Karsh, B., and Cole, R. E. (1968). 'Industrialization and the convergence hypothesis: Some aspects of contemporary Japan', *Journal of Social Issues, 24,* 45–63.

Katz, B., Juni, S., Shope, C., and Tang, L. (1993). 'The values of Chinese students: At home and abroad', *International Journal of Psychology, 28,* 761–73.

Katz, D. (1960). 'The functional approach to the study of attitudes', *Public Opinion Quarterly, 24,* 163–204.

Katz, L., and Feldman, L. B. (1983). 'Relation between pronunciation and recognition of printed words in deep and shallow orthographies', *Journal of Experimental Psychology: Learning, Memory, and Cognition, 9,* 157–66.

Kaufman, A. S. (1975). 'Factor analysis of the WISC-R at eleven ages between 6 1/2 and 16 1/2 years', *Journal of Consulting and Clinical Psychology, 44,* 739–44.

Kazdin, A. E. (1994). 'Methodology, design, and evaluation in psychotherapy research'. In A. E. Bergin and S. L. Garfield (Eds.), *Handbook of Psychotherapy and Behaviour Change* (fourth edition, pp. 19–71). New York: John Wiley and Sons.

Kellerman, E., and Sharwood Smith, M. (Eds.)(1986). *Crosslinguistic Influence in Second Language Acquisition.* New York: Pergamon Institute of English.

Kelley, H. H., Berscheid, E., Christensen, J., Harvey, T., Huston, T., Levinger, G., McClintock, E., Peplau, A., and Peterson, D. (1983). *Close Relationships.* New York: Freeman.

Kelley, L., and Shenkar, O. (Eds.)(1993). *International Business in China.* London: Routledge.

Kember, D., and Gow, L. (1989). 'A model of student approaches to learning encompassing ways to influence and change approaches', *Instructional Science, 18,* 263–88.

Kember, D., and Gow, L. (1990). 'Cultural specificity of approaches to study', *British Journal of Educational Psychology, 60,* 356–63.

Kember, D., and Gow, L. (1991). 'A challenge to the anecdotal stereotype of the Asian student', *Studies in Higher Education, 16*(2), 117–28.

Kember, D., and Gow, L. (1992). 'Action research as a form of staff development in higher education', *Higher Education, 23*(3), 297–310.

Kember, D., and Gow, L. (1994). 'Orientations to teaching and their effect on the quality of student learning', *Journal of Higher Education. 65*(1), 56–74.

Kember, D., and Kelly, M. (1993). *Improving Teaching Through Action Research* (HERDSA Green Guide No. 14). Sydney: HERDSA.

Kemp, S. (1994). 'An investigation into the self-concept of junior secondary students in Hong Kong'. Unpublished Master's thesis, University of Hong Kong.

Kerckhoff, A., and Davis, K. (1962). 'Value consensus and need complementarity in mate selection', *American Sociological Review, 27*, 295–303.

Keren, G. (1987). 'Facing uncertainty in the game of bridge: A calibration study', *Organizational Behavior and Human Decision Processes, 57*, 226–46.

Kerr, C., Dunlop, J. J., Harbicon, F. H., and Myers, C. A. (1960). *Industrialism and Industrial Man.* Cambridge, MA: Harvard University Press.

Kim, K., Li, D., Jiang, Z., Cui, X., Lin, L., Kang, J. J., Park, K. K., Chung, E. K., and Kim, C. K. (1993). 'Schizophrenic delusion among Koreans, Korean-Chinese and Chinese: A transcultural study', *International Journal of Social Psychiatry, 39*, 190–9.

Kim, U. (1988). 'Acculturation of Korean immigrants to Canada: Psychological, demographic and behavioural profiles of emigrating Koreans, non-emigrating Koreans and Korean-Canadians'. Unpublished doctoral thesis, Department of Psychology, Queen's University, Kingston, Ontario.

Kim, U., and Berry, J. W. (1986). 'Acculturation attitudes of Korean immigrants in Toronto'. In I. Reyes Lagunes and Y. H. Poortinga (Eds.), *From A Different Perspective: Studies of Behavior Across Cultures* (pp. 93–105). Lisse, the Netherlands: Swets and Zeitlinger.

Kim, U., Triandis, H. C., Kagitcibasi, C., Choi, S. C., and Yoon, G. (1994). *Individualism and Collectivism: Theory, Method, and Application.* Thousand Oaks, CA: Sage.

Kimura, Y. (1984). 'Concurrent vocal interference: Its effects on kana and kanji', *Quarterly Journal of Experimental Psychology, 36A*, 117–31.

King, A. Y. C. (1977). *From Tradition to Modernity* [in Chinese]. Taipei: China Times Publishing Co.

King, A. Y. C. (1988). 'Face, shame and the analysis of Chinese behavior' [in Chinese]. In K. S. Yang (Ed.), *Chinese Psychology* (pp. 319–45). Taipei: Laureate Book Co.

King, A. Y. C. (1991). 'Kuan-hsi and network building: A sociological interpretation', *Daedalus, 120*, 63–84.

King, A. Y. C., and Bond, M. H. (1985). 'The Confucian paradigm of man: A sociological view'. In W. S. Tseng and D. Y. H. Wu (Eds.) *Chinese Culture and Mental Health* (pp. 29–46). Orlando, FL: Academic Press.

King, A. Y. C., and Myers, J. T. (1977). *Shame as an Incomplete Conception of Chinese Culture: A Study of Face.* Hong Kong: Social Research Centre, the Chinese University of Hong Kong.

King, B. (1989). 'The conceptual structure of emotional experience in Chinese'. Unpublished doctoral dissertation, Ohio State University, Columbus.

Kipnis, A. (1991). 'Producing guanxi relationships: Relationships, subjectivity and ethnicity in a rural Chinese village'. Unpublished doctoral dissertation, University of North Carolina, Chapel Hill.

Kirkbride, P. S., Tang, S. F. Y., and Westwood, R. I. (1991). 'Chinese conflict preferences and negotiating behaviour: Cultural and psychological influences', *Organizational Studies, 12*, 365–86.

Kirmayer, L. (1984). 'Culture, affect, and somatization' (Parts 1 and 2), *Transcultural Psychiatric Research Review, 21*, 159–88 and 237–62.

Kiu, K. L. (1992). *100 Ancient Chinese Fables.* Hong Kong: Commercial Publishing House.

Klapper, J. T. (1961). *The Effect of Mass Communication.* Glencoe, IL: Free Press.

Klein, G. A. (1993). 'A recognition-primed decision (RPD) model of rapid decision making'. In G. A. Klein, J. Orasanu, R. Calderwood, and C. E. Zsambok (Eds.), *Decision Making in Action: Models and Methods* (pp. 138–47). Norwood, NJ: Ablex.

Kleinman, A. (1977). 'Depression, somatization and the "new cross-cultural" psychiatry', *Social Science and Medicine, 11*, 3–10.

Kleinman, A. (1980). *Patients and Healers in the Context of Culture.* Berkeley: University of California Press.

Kleinman, A. (1982). 'Neurasthenia and depression: A study of somatization and culture in China', *Culture, Medicine, and Psychiatry, 6*, 117–90.

Kleinman, A. (1986). *Social Origins in Distress and Disease.* New Haven: Yale University Press.

Kleinman, A. (1988). *Rethinking Psychiatry: From Cultural Category to Personal Experience.* New

York: Free Press.

Kleinman, A. (1988). *The Illness Narratives: Suffering, Healing, and the Human Condition*. New York: Basic Books.

Kleinman, A., and Gale, J. L. (1982). 'Patients treated by physicans and folk healers: A comparative outcome study by Taiwan', *Culture, Medicine and Psychiatry, 6*, 405–23.

Kleinman, A., and Good, B. (1985). *Culture and Depression: Studies in the Anthropology and Cross-Cultural Psychiatry of Affect and Disorder*. Berkeley: University of California Press.

Kleinman, A., and Kleinman, J. (1985). 'Somatization: The interconnections in Chinese society among culture, depressive experiences, and the meanings of pain'. In A. Kleinman and B. Good (Eds.), *Culture and Depression: Studies in the Anthropology and Cross-Cultural Psychiatry of Affect and Disorder* (pp. 429–90). Berkeley: University of California Press.

Kleinman, A., and Lin, T. Y. (Eds.)(1981). *Normal and Deviant Behavior in Chinese Culture*. Hingham, MA: Reidel.

Kleinman, A., and Sung, L. H. (1979). 'Why do indigenous practitioners successfully heal?' *Social Sciences and Medicine, 13B*, 7–26.

Klineberg, O. (1938). 'Emotional expression in Chinese literature', *Journal of Abnormal and Social Psychology, 33*, 517–20.

Kluckhohn, C. (1951). 'Values and value-orientations in the theory of action: An exploration in definition and classification'. In T. Parsons and E. A. Shils (Eds.), *Toward a General Theory of Action* (pp. 388–433), Cambridge, MA: Harvard University Press.

Kluckhohn, F. R., and Strodtbeck, F. L. (1961). *Variations in Value Orientations*. Evanston, IL: Row, Peterson.

Ko, Y. H. (1971). 'The frequency of eye-movement on the Bender-Gestalt test as a measure of attention breadth', *Acta Psychologica Taiwanica, 13*, 65–74.

Ko, Y. H. (1972). 'The Bender–Gestalt test as a test for visual–verbal coordination', *Acta Psychologica Taiwanica, 14*, 52–66.

Ko, Y. H. (1974). 'A study on the effects of psychotherapy', *Acta Psychologica Taiwanica, 16*, 141–54.

Ko, Y. H. (1978). *Clinical Psychology* (Vol. 1: Psychological Diagnosis)[in Chinese]. Taipei: Dayang Publishers.

Ko, Y. H. (1981). *Ko's Mental Health Questionnaire, KMHQ: Revised Manual* [in Chinese]. Taipei: Chinese Behavioral Science Press.

Ko, Y. H., and Hung, T. P. (1963). 'The localization of brain lesions and the Bender–Gestalt test figure rotation', *Acta Psychologica Taiwanica, 5*, 31–6.

Ko, Y. H., and Yu, W. Y. (1966). 'A scoring system for the evaluation of degree of mental illness through the Rorschach responses', *Acta Psychologica Taiwanica, 8*, 17–28.

Kobayashi, N. (1993). 'Child ecology: A theoretical basis for solving children's problems in the world', *Childhood 1*, 26–38.

Koch, S. (1993). '"Psychology" or "the psychological studies"? *American Psychologist, 48*, 902–3.

Koda, K. (1994). 'Second language reading research: Problems and possibilities', *Applied Psycholinguistics, 15*, 1–28.

Kodama, S. (1991). 'Life and work of Y. K. Yen, the first person to introduce Western psychology to modern China', *Psychologia, 34*, 213–26.

Koestner, R., Weinberger, J., McClelland, D. C., and Healy, J. (1988). 'How motives and values interact with task and social incentives to affect performance'. Unpublished manuscript, Department of Psychology, Boston University.

Kogan, N., and Wallach, M. A. (1964). *Risk Taking: A Study in Cognition and Personality*. New York: Holt, Rinehart and Winston.

Kohn, M. L., Naoi, A., Schoenbach, C., Schooler, C., and Slomczynski, K. M. (1990). 'Position in the class structure and psychological functioning in the United States, Japan and Poland', *American Journal of Sociology, 95*, 964–1008.

Kok, L. (1990). 'Female sexual knowledge and attitudes in Singapore'. Paper presented at the International Conference on Sexuality in Asia, Hong Kong.

Korabik, K. (1992). 'Women hold up half the sky: The status of managerial women in China', *Advances in Chinese Industrial Studies, 3*, 197–211.

Korabik, K. (1993). 'Women managers in the People's Republic of China: Changing roles in changing times', *Applied Psychology: An International Review, 42*, 353–63.

Koriat, A., Lichtenstein, S., and Fischhoff, B. (1980). 'Reasons for confidence', *Journal of Experimental Psychology: Human Learning and Memory*, *6*, 107–18.

Kornadt, H. J., Eckensberger, L. H., and Emminghaus, W. B. (1980). 'Cross-cultural research on motivation and its contribution to a general theory of motivation'. In H. C. Triandis and W. Lonner (Eds.), *Handbook of Cross-Cultural Psychology* (Vol. 3, pp. 223–321). Boston: Allyn and Bacon.

Korosec-Serfaty, P. (1976). 'Appropriation of space'. Paper presented at the Proceedings of the Third International Architectural Psychology Conference, Louis Pasteur University, Strasbourg, France, June.

Kövecses, Z. (in press). 'Language and emotion concepts'. In J. A. Russell, J. M. Fernandez-Dols, A. S. R. Manstead, and J. Wellenkamp (Eds.), *Everyday Conceptions of Emotion*. Dordrect, the Netherlands: Kluwer.

Kövecses, Z. (in press). 'Metaphor and the folk understanding of anger'. In J. A. Russell, J. M. Fernandez-Dols, A. S. R. Manstead, and J. Wellenkamp (Eds.), *Everyday Conceptions of Emotion*. Dordrect, the Netherlands: Kluwer.

Kraus, R. F. (1970). 'A psychoanalytic interpretation of shamanism', *Transcultural Psychiatric Research Review*, *7*, 5–9.

Kriger, S. F., and Kroes, W. H. (1972). 'Child-rearing attitudes of Chinese, Jewish, and Protestant mothers', *Journal of Social Psychology*, *86*, 205–10.

Krone K., Garrett, M., and Chen, L. (1992). 'Managerial communication practices in Chinese factories: A preliminary investigation', *The Journal of Business Communication*, *29*, 229–52.

Kuhn, T. (1970). *The Structure of Scientific Revolutions*. Chicago: University of Chicago Press.

Kuo, D. J., Zhang, G. L., and Yang, S. Z. (1993). 'Impact of parents' training style on child's achievement motivation' [in Chinese], *Journal of Beijing Normal University* (China), *2*, 20–30.

Kuo, E. C. Y. (1979). 'Languages of Singapore: Languages in the Singapore social context'. In T. A. Llamzon (Ed.), *Papers on Southeast Asian Languages* (pp. 159–90). Singapore: Singapore University Press.

Kuo, S. Y. (1973). 'Analysis on psychological characteristics of under-achievement students in public junior high schools' [in Chinese], *Bulletin of Graduate Institute of Education, National Taiwan Normal University* (Taiwan), *15*, 451–534.

Kuo, S. Y. (1975). 'The effect of tremendous discrepancy between parents' expectations and children's actual intelligence on the children's achievement motivation' [in Chinese], *Bulletin of Educational Psychology* (Taiwan), *8*, 61–80.

Kuo, S. Y. (1980). 'Relationships of teacher expectations to teachers' behaviour and students' learning behaviour' [in Chinese], *Bulletin of Educational Psychology* (Taiwan), *13*, 133–52.

Kuo, S. Y. (1982). 'Relationships between teacher expectations and internal–external control in an elementary school children' [in Chinese], *Bulletin of Educational Psychology* (Taiwan), *15*, 139–48.

Kuo, S. Y. (1983). 'Academic achievement and causal attributions of success-oriented and failure-oriented children' [in Chinese], *Jiaoyu Xinli Xuebao*, *16*, 47–59.

Kuo, S. Y. (1984). 'The relationships of causal attributions for success or failure and achievement-related behaviour' [in Chinese], *Bulletin of Educational Psychology* (Taiwan), *17*, 51–72.

Kuo, S. Y. (1987). 'The relationship between teacher burnout and teacher background variables' [in Chinese], *Bulletin of Educational Psychology*, *20*, 37–54.

Kuo, S. Y. (1989). 'Stress and burnout among Taiwanese teachers' [in Chinese], *Bulletin of Educational Psychology*, *23*, 71–98.

Kuo, S. Y. (1990). 'A discriminant analysis of teacher burnout based on teacher stresses and professional attitudes' [in Chinese], *Bulletin of Educational Psychology*, *23*, 71–98.

Kuo, W. H. (1976). 'Theories of migration and mental health: An empirical testing on Chinese-Americans', *Social Science and Medicine*, *10*, 297–306.

Kuo, W. H. (1984). 'Prevalence of depression among Asian-Americans', *Journal of Nervous and Mental Disease*, *172*, 449–57.

Kuo, W. H., and Lin, N. (1977). 'Assimilation of Chinese-Americans in Washington, D. C.', *The Sociological Quarterly*, *18*, 340–52.

Kuo, W. H., and Tsai, Y. M. (1986). 'Social networking, hardiness, and immigrant's mental health', *Journal of Health and Social Behavior*, *27*, 133–49.

Kuo, W. H., Gray, R., and Lin, N. (1979). 'Locus of control and symptoms of psychological distress among Chinese Americans', *International Journal of Social Psychiatry, 25*, 176–87.

Kwok, D. C., and Lytton, H. (1993). 'Perceptions of mathematics ability and mathematics performance: Canadian and Hong Kong Chinese children'. Paper presented at biennial meeting of the Society for Research in Child Development, New Orleans, April.

Kwong, B., and Wong, S. W. (1981). 'Physical presentations of psychological problems among Hong Kong Chinese: Cultural implications', *Journal of Hong Kong Psychiatric Association, 1*, 33-39.

Kwong, J. (1985). 'Changing political culture and changing curriculum: An analysis of language textbooks in the People's Republic of China', *Comparative Education, 21*, (2), 197–208.

Kwong, P. (1987). *The New Chinatown*. New York: Hill.

Laaksonen, O. (1988). *Management in China*. New York: Walter de Gruyter.

LaFromboise, T., Coleman, H. L. K., and Gerton, J. (1993). 'Psychological impact of biculturalism: Evidence and theory', *Psychological Bulletin, 114*, 395–412.

Lai, L. W. C. (1993). 'Hong Kong's density policy towards public housing. A theoretical and empirical review', *Third World Planning Review, 1*, 63–85.

Lakoff, G. (1987). *Women, Fire and Dangerous Things: What Categories Reveal about the Mind*. Chicago: University of Chicago Press.

Lakoff, G., and Kvecses, A. (1987). 'The cognitive model of anger inherent in American English'. In D. Holland and N. Quinn (Eds.), *Cultural Models in Language and Thought* (pp. 195–221). New York: Cambridge University Press.

Lam, A. L., Perfetti, C. A., and Bell, L. (1991). 'Automatic phonetic transfer in bidialectal reading', *Applied Psycholinguistics, 12*, 299–311.

Lam, D. J., and Hong, Y. Y. (1992). 'Strategies and dimensions of coping with examination stress'. In K. Hagtvet and T. Backer (Eds.), *Advances in Test Anxiety Research* (Vol. 7, pp. 304–12). Lisse, the Netherlands: Swets and Zeitlinger.

Lam, D. J., and Yang, C. (1989). 'Social behaviour in real Hong Kong: Comment on Wheeler', *Personality and Social Psychology Bulletin, 15*, 639–44.

Lam, L. (1980). 'The role of ethnic media for immigrants: A case study of Chinese immigrants and their media in Toronto', *Canadian Ethnic Studies, 12*, 74–92.

Lambert, M. J., and Ogles, B. M. (1988). 'Treatment manuals: Problems and promises', *Journal of Integrative and Eclectic Psychotherapy, 7*, 187–204.

Lambert, M. J., and Bergin, A. E. (1994). 'The effectiveness of psychotherapy'. In A. E. Bergin and S. L. Garfield (Eds.), *Handbook of Psychotherapy and Behaviour Change* (fourth edition, pp. 139–90). New York: John Wiley.

Lan, C. J. (1994). 'Factors affecting dual-career Taiwanese couples' ratings of life-role salience' [in Chinese]. Unpublished Master's thesis, Department of Educational Psychology and Guidance, National Taiwan Normal University, Taipei.

Landrine, H. (1992). 'Clinical implications of cultural differences: The referential versus the indexical self', *Clinical Psychology Review, 12*, 224–53.

Langner, T. S. (1962). 'A twenty-two item screening scale of psychiatric symptoms indicating impairment', *Journal of Health and Human Behavior, 3*, 269–76.

Lao, R. C. (1977). 'Levenson's IPC (internal–external control) scale: A comparison of Chinese and American students', *Journal of Cross-Cultural Psychology, 9*, 113–24.

Lapointe, A. E., Meade, N. A., and Askew, J. (1992). *Learning Mathematics*. Princeton, NJ: Educational Testing Service.

Latané, B., Williams, K. D., and Harkins, S. (1979). 'Many hands make light the work: The causes and consequences of social loafing', *Journal of Personality and Social Psychology, 37*, 822–32.

Lau, S. (1981). 'Chinese familism in an urban-industrial setting: The case of Hong Kong', *Journal of Marriage and the Family, 43*, 977–92.

Lau, S. (1988). 'The value orientations of Chinese university students in Hong Kong', *International Journal of Psychology, 23*, 583–96.

Lau, S. (1992). 'Collectivism's individualism: Value preference, personal control, and the desire for freedom among Chinese in Mainland China, Hong Kong, and Singapore', *Personality and Individual Differences, 13*, 361–6.

Lau, S., and Leung, K. (1992). 'Relations with parents and school and Chinese adolescents' self-concept, delinquency, and academic performance', *British Journal of Educational*

Psychology, 62, 193–202.

Lau, S., and Leung, K. (1992). 'Self-concept, delinquency, relations with parents and school and Chinese adolescents' perception of personal control', *Personality and Individual Differences, 13,* 615–22.

Lau, S., Lew, W., Hau, K., Cheung, P., and Berndt, T. (1990). 'Relations among perceived parental control, warmth, indulgence, and family harmony of Chinese in mainland China', *Developmental Psychology, 26,* 674–7.

Lau, S. K. (1982). *Society and Politics in Hong Kong.* Hong Kong: Chinese University Press.

Lau, S. K., and Kuan, H. C. (1988). *The Ethos of the Hong Kong Chinese.* Hong Kong: Chinese University Press.

Lawler, E. E. (1973). *Motivation in Work Organizations.* Monterey, CA: Brooks/Cole.

Lazarus, R. S. (1993). 'Coping theory and research: Past, present, and future', *Psychosomatic Medicine, 55,* 234–47.

Lazarus, R. S., and Folkman, S. (1984). *Stress, Appraisal and Coping.* New York: Springer.

Le Grand, Y. (1975). 'History of research on seeing'. In E. C. Carterette and M. P. Friedman (Eds.), *Handbook of Perception* (Vol. 5, pp. 3–23). New York: Academic Press.

Lederer, W. (1959). 'Primitive psychiatry', *Psychiatry, 22,* 255–65.

Lee, B. (1974). 'A cognitive developmental approach to filiality development'. Unpublished Master's thesis, University of Chicago.

Lee, C. C. (Ed.)(1990). *Voices of China: The Interplay of Politics and Journalism.* New York: Guilford Press.

Lee, C. C., and Cochran, L. R. (1988). 'Migration problems of Chinese women', *Canadian Journal of Counseling, 22,* 202–11.

Lee, C. L., and Zhan, G. Q. (1991). 'Political socialization and parental values in the People's Republic of China', *International Journal of Behavioral Development, 14,* 337–73.

Lee, H. C. B. (1990). 'Reliability, validity and fakability of the Zung Self-rating Depression Scale', *Bulletin of the Hong Kong Psychological Society, 24–5,* 5–15.

Lee, H. C. B., Chan, D. W., and Yik, M. S. N. (1992). 'Coping styles and psychological distress among Chinese adolescents in Hong Kong', *Journal of Adolescent Research, 7,* 494–506.

Lee, H. C. B., Cheung, F. M., Man, H. M. M., and Hsu, S. Y. C. (1992). 'Psychological characteristics of Chinese low back pain patients: An exploratory study', *Psychology and Health: An International Journal, 6,* 119–28.

Lee, H. W., and Petzold, M. (1987). 'Psychology in the People's Republic of China'. In G. H. Blowers and A. M. Turtle (Eds.), *Psychology Moving East: The Status of Western Psychology in Asia and Oceania* (pp. 105–25). Boulder, CO: Westview Press.

Lee, L. M. (1984). Validity studies of the Hong Kong Wechsler Intelligence Scale for Children. Paper presented at the first annual conference of the Hong Kong Educational Research Association, Chinese University of Hong Kong, November.

Lee, R. (1988). 'Chinese coping strategies in rapidly changing Hong Kong' [in Chinese]. In K. C. Hsing (Ed.), *Experiences of Development in Chinese Societies and China's Future* (pp. 29–50). Taipei: Research Center for International Relations, National Chengchi University.

Lee, R. P. L. (1981). 'Sex roles, social status, and psychiatric symptoms in urban Hong Kong'. In A. Kleinman and T. Y. Lin (Eds.), *Normal and Abnormal Behavior in Chinese Culture* (pp. 273–89). Dodrecht, the Netherlands: Reidel.

Lee, R. P. L. (1982). 'Social science and indigenous concepts: With *yuen* in medical care as an example' [in Chinese]. In K. S. Yang and C. I. Wen (Eds.), *The Sinicization of Social and Behavioral Science Research in China* (pp. 361–80). Taipei: Institute of Ethnology, Academia Sinica.

Lee, R. P. L. (1985). 'Social stress and coping behavior in Hong Kong'. In W. S. Tseng and D. Y. H. Wu (Eds.), *Chinese Culture and Mental Health* (pp. 193–214). Orlando, FL: Academic Press.

Lee, R. P. L. (1995). 'Cultural tradition and stress management in modern society: Learning from the Hong Kong experience'. In T. Y. Lin, W. S. Tseng, and E. K. Yeh (Eds.), *Chinese Societies and Mental Health.* Hong Kong: Oxford University Press.

Lee, S. (1991). 'Anorexia nervosa in Hong Kong: A Chinese perspective', *Psychological Medicine.*

Lee, S., Ho, T. P., and Hsu, L. K. G. (1993). 'Fat phobia and nonfat phobia anorexia nervosa, a study of 38 patients', *Psychological Medicine, 23,* 997–1017.

Lee, S., Leung, C. M., Wing, Y. K., Chiu, H. F. K., and Chen, C. N. (1991). 'Acne as a risk factor for anorexia nervosa in Chinese', *Australian and New Zealand Journal of Psychiatry, 25,* 134–7.

Lee, S. M., and Yamanaka, K. (1990). 'Patterns of Asian American intermarriage and marital assimilation', *Journal of Comparative Family Studies, 21,* 287–305.

Lee, S. Y., Stigler, J. W., and Stevenson, H. W. (1986). 'Beginning to read Chinese and English'. In A. Siegel and B. Foorman (Eds.), *Learning to Read: Cognitive Universals and Cultural Restraints* (pp. 123–50). Hillsdale, NJ: Erlbaum.

Lee, S. Y., Uttal, D. H., and Chen, C. (in press). 'Writing systems and reading achievement of Japanese, Chinese, and American first-grade children'. In I. Taylor and D. Olson (Eds.), *Scripts and Literacy: Reading and Learning to Read Alphabets, Syllabaries, and Characters.* Dordrecht, the Netherlands: Kluwer.

Lee, T. H. T. (1991). 'Linearity as a scope principle for Chinese: The evidence from first language acquisition'. In D. J. Napoli and J. A. Kegl (Eds.), *Bridges Between Psychology and Linguistics* (pp. 183–206). Hillsdale, NJ: Erlbaum.

Lee, W., and Tse D. K. (1994). 'Becoming Canadian: Understanding how Hong Kong immigrants change their consumption', *Pacific Affairs, 67*(1), 70–96.

Lee, W. L., Wee, G. C., Tzeng, O. J. L., and Hung, D. L. (1992). 'A study of interlingual and intralingual Stroop effect in three different scripts: Logograph, syllabary, and alphabet'. In R. J. Harris (Ed.), *Cognitive Processing in Bilinguals* (pp. 427–42). Amsterdam: Elsevier Science.

Lee, W. Y., Chan, R., and Fu, A. (1993). 'Structural family therapy for a Chinese family: Children of sleeping beauty and superman'. In L. Y. Cheng, F. Cheung, and C. N. Chen (Eds.), *Psychotherapy for the Chinese* (pp. 157–74). Hong Kong: Department of Psychiatry, the Chinese University of Hong Kong.

Lee, Y. T., and Ottati, V. (1993). 'Determinants of in-group and out-group perceptions of heterogeneity: An investigation of Sino-American stereotypes', *Journal of Cross-Cultural Psychology, 24,* 298–318.

Lee, Y. T., and Seligman, M. E. P. (1993). 'Are Americans more optimistic than mainland Chinese?' Unpublished paper.

Leek, K. J., Weekes, B. S., and Chen, M. J. (in press). 'Visual and phonological pathways to the lexicon: Evidence from Chinese readers', *Memory and Cognition.*

Lefcourt, H. M., von Baeyer, C. S., Ware, E. E., and Cox, D. J. (1979). 'The multidimensional-multiattributional causality scale: The development of a goal specific locus of control scale', *Canadian Journal of Behavioral Science, 11,* 286–304.

Lehmann, W. P. (1975). *Language and Linguistics in the People's Republic of China.* Austin: University of Texas Press.

Lei, T., and Yang, K. S. (1986). 'The change of basic values of Chinese university students in Taiwan: Twenty years later' [in Chinese]. In H. Y. Hchu and E. H. Chang (Eds.), *Social and Cultural Change in Taiwan* (pp. 479–511). Taipei: Institute of Ethnology, Academia Sinica.

Leiderman, P. H. (1983). 'Social ecology and childbirth: The newborn nursery as environmental stressor'. In N. Garmezy and M. Rutter (Eds.), *Stress, Coping and Development in Children* (pp. 133–59). London: McGraw-Hill.

Leong, C. K. (1986). 'What does accessing a morphemic script tell us about reading and reading disorders in an alphabetic script?' *Annals of Dyslexia, 36,* 82–102.

Leong, C. K. (1988). 'A componental approach to understanding reading and its difficulties in preadolescent readers', *Annals of Dyslexia, 38,* 95–119.

Leong, C. K. (1992). 'Cognitive componental modelling of reading in ten- to twelve-year-old readers', *Reading and Writing: An Interdisciplinary Journal, 4,* 327–64.

Leong, F. T. (1986). 'Counseling and psychotherapy with Asian-Americans: Review of the literature', *Journal of Counseling Psychology, 33,* 196–206.

Lesser, G. S., Fifer, G., and Clark, D. H. (1965). 'Mental abilities of children from different social class and cultural groups', *Monographs of the Society for Research in Child Development, 30*(4).

Leung, F. (1994, April). 'Disordered eating behaviors among young Chinese females in Hong Kong: Are they associated with the same psychosocial features observed in the West?' Paper presented at the Sixth International Conference on Eating Disorders, New York.

Leung, J. P. (1991). 'Smoking cessation by auricular acupuncture and behavioural therapy', *Psychologia, 34,* 177–87.

Leung, J. P. (in press). 'Attention deficit-hyperactivity disorder in Chinese children'. In S. Lau (Ed.), *Growing Up the Chinese Way: The Role of Culture in Socialization.* Hong Kong: Chinese University Press.

Leung, J. P., and Leung, K. (1992). 'Life satisfaction, self-concept, and relationship with parents in adolescence', *Journal of Youth and Adolescence, 21*, 653–65.

Leung, K. (1987). 'Some determinants of reactions to procedural models for conflict resolution: A cross-national study', *Journal of Personality and Social Psychology, 53*, 898–908.

Leung, K. (1988). 'Some determinants of conflict avoidance', *Journal of Cross-Cultural Psychology, 19*, 125–36.

Leung, K. (1989). 'Cross-cultural differences: Individual-level vs. cultural-level analysis', *International Journal of Psychology, 24*, 703–19.

Leung, K. (1991). *Consumer Psychology* [in Chinese]. Hong Kong: Publications (Holding) Limited.

Leung, K. (in press). 'Adolescent delinquent behavior in Chinese societies'. In S. Lau (Ed.), *Growing up the Chinese Way: The Role of Culture in Socialization.*

Leung, K., and Bond, M. H. (1984). 'The impact of cultural collectivism on reward allocation', *Journal of Personality and Social Psychology, 25*, 32–9.

Leung, K., and Bond, M. H. (1989). 'On the empirical identification of dimensions for cross-cultural comparisons', *Journal of Cross-Cultural Psychology, 20*, 133–151.

Leung, K., and Bond, M. H. (1992). 'A psychological study of social axioms'. Research grant proposal, the Chinese University of Hong Kong.

Leung, K., and Lau, S. (1989). 'Effects of self-concept and perceived disapproval on delinquent behavior in school children', *Journal of Youth and Adolescence, 18*, 345–59.

Leung, K., and Lind, E. A. (1986). 'Procedural justice and culture: Effects of culture, gender and investigator status on procedural preferences', *Journal of Personality and Social Psychology, 50*, 1134–40.

Leung, K., Bond, M. H., and Schwartz, S. H. (1993). 'Explanatory mechanisms for cross-cultural differences: Values, valences, and expectancies'. Manuscript submitted for publication.

Leung, K., Lau, S., and Lam, W. L. (1994). 'Parenting styles and academic achievement: A cross-cultural study'. Manuscript submitted for publication.

Leung, K. C. (1978). 'The Cantonese student in the Mandarin class: Some special problems', *Journal of the Chinese Language Teachers Association, 13*, 51–5.

Leung, P. W., and Sung, P. (1992). 'Cultural values and choice of strategic moves in family therapy: Reflections on working with a Chinese couple'. Paper presented at the Sixth International Congress on Family Therapy: Divorce and Remarriage, Jerusalem, March.

Leung, P. W., Salili, F., and Baber, F. M. (1986). 'Common adolescent problems in Hong Kong: Their relationship with self-esteem, locus of control, intelligence and family environment', *Psychologia, 29*, 91–101.

Levenson, H. (1974). 'Activism and powerful others: Distinction within the concept of internal-external control', *Journal of Personality Assessment, 38*, 377–83.

Levine, R. A. (1982). *Culture, Behavior and Personality.* New York: Aldine.

Levy, M. (1949). *The Family Revolution in Modern China.* Cambridge, MA: Harvard University Press.

Levy, M. J. (1966). *Modernization and the Structure of Societies.* Princeton, NJ: Princeton University Press.

Levy, R. I. (1973). *Tahitians: Mind and Experience in the Society Islands.* Chicago: University of Chicago Press.

Lew, W. J. F. (1985). 'Traits and dimensions of personality: Chinese intellectuals in Taiwan', *CUHK Education Journal, 13*, 37–48.

Lew, W. J. F., and Hau, K. T. (1987). 'Traits and dimensions of personality: Chinese intellectuals in Hong Kong', *Educational Research Journal, 2*, 6–12.

Li, A. K. F. (1974). 'Parental attitudes, test anxiety, and achievement motivation: A Hong Kong study', *Journal of Social Psychology, 93*, 3–11.

Li, C. N. (1975). 'Synchrony vs. diachrony in language structure', *Language, 51*, 873–86.

Li, C. N., and Thompson, S. A. (1981). *Mandarin Chinese: A Functional Reference Grammar.* Berkeley: University of California Press.

Li, D., Jin, Y., Zhu, Y. M., and Tang, C. H. (1987). 'Report on the norm of Wechsler Intelligence Scale for Children–China Revised (WISC-CR) in Shanghai Proper (WISC-CRs)' [in Chinese], *Acta Psychologica Sinica, 19*(2), 136–44.

Li, F., and Wang, M. (1994). 'A behavioural training programme for chronic schizophrenic patients: A three-month randomised controlled trial in Beijing', *British Journal of Psychiatry, 165*

(Supplement 24), 32–7.

Li, H. D. (1992). *On the Genesis and Evolution of Chinese Orthography* [in Chinese]. Taipei: Lien-Jing.

Li, K. (1986). 'A study of the norms of Hong Kong students of age groups 15 to 18 in the performance of Raven's Advanced Progressive Matrices Test'. Unpublished Master's thesis, the Chinese University of Hong Kong.

Li, M. C. (1981). 'The construction of sex trait inventory and the comparisons of four sex trait categories on achievement motive and attitudes toward marriage, career and sex' [in Chinese], *Acta Psychologica Taiwanica* (Taiwan), *23*(1), 23–37.

Li, M. C. (1987). 'The changes of sex role and sex typing among students in the changing Taiwan' [in Chinese], *Educational and Psychological Research* (National Chungchi University), *10*, 39–59.

Li, M. C. (1992). 'Cultural difference and in-group favoritism: A comparison of Chinese and American college students' [in Chinese], *Bulletin of the Institute of Ethnology, Academia Sinica, 73*, 153–90.

Li, P., Bates, E., and MacWhinney, B. (1993). 'Processing a language without inflection: A reaction time study of sentence interpretation in Chinese', *Journal of Memory and Language, 32*, 169–92.

Li, P., Bates, E., Liu, H., and MacWhinney, B. (1992). 'Cues as functional constraints on sentence processing in Chinese'. In H. C. Chen, and O. J. L. Tzeng (Eds.), *Language Processing in Chinese* (pp. 207–34). Amsterdam: North-Holland.

Li, S. R., Pang, X. X., Yin, C. Y., Liu, S. X., Zhong, Y. S., Zhiang, G. Z., Chen, C. W., and Liu, M. (1991). 'Mental health survey of earthquake victims in Yunan' [in Chinese], *Chinese Mental Health Journal, 5*(1), 11–14.

Li, S. X., and Phillips, M. R. (1990). 'Witchdoctors and mental illness in mainland China: A preliminary study', *American Journal of Psychiatry, 147*, 221–4.

Li, X. Q., and Yan, H. Q. (1990). 'Cognitive-behavioural therapy for erectile disorder: A study from the People's Republic of China', *Sexual and Marital Therapy, 5*, 105–14.

Li, X. T., Xu, S. L., and Kuang, P. Z. (1988). '30 years of Chinese clinical psychology', *International Journal of Mental Health, 16*, 3–21.

Li, Y. Y. (1972). 'Shamanism in Taiwan: An anthropological inquiry'. Paper presented at the Fourth Conference on Culture and Mental Health in Asia and the Pacific, Honolulu, March.

Li, Y. Y., and Lu, Y. X. (1982). 'Research on traditional work attitude and its change' [in Chinese]. In Z. G. Yu (Ed.), *Development of Human Resources in Taiwan* (Vol. 1)(pp. 477–555). Taiwan: Institute of Economics, Academia Sinica.

Lian, K. F. (1988). 'The sociopolitical process of identity formation in an ethnic community: The Chinese in New Zealand', *Ethnic and Racial Studies, 11*, 506–32.

Liang, S. (1993). 'Multilanguage comparability of life satisfaction and happiness measures in mainland Chinese and American students'. Unpublished Master's thesis, University of Illinois at Urbana–Champaign.

Liang, W., Zhao, Q. P., and Zheng, Y. P. (1992). 'Mental health survey of secondary school students' [in Chinese], *Chinese Mental Health Journal, 6*(3), 100–2.

Liao, C., and Heaton, T. B. (1992). 'Divorce trends and differentials in China', *Journal of Comparative Family Studies, 3*, 413–29.

Liao, C. H., and Hwang, C. J. (1992). *The Change of Taiwanese Farmers' Value Orientations in the Post-war Era* [in Chinese]. Taipei: Lianjing Publishing Co.

Liberman, A. M. (1992). 'Plausibility, parsimony, and theories of speech'. In J. Alegria, D. Holender, J. J. de Morais, and M. Radeau (Eds.), *Analytic Approaches to Human Cognition* (pp. 25–40). Amsterdam: North-Holland.

Libet, B., Wright, E. W., Feinstein, B., and Pearl, D. K. (1979). 'Subjective referral of the timing for a conscious sensory experience: A functional role for the somatosensory specific projection system in man', *Brain, 102*, 193–224.

Lieh-Mak, F., and Ng, M. L. (1981). 'Ejaculatory incompetence in Chinese men', *American Journal of Psychiatry, 138*, 685–6.

Lieh-Mak, F., Lee, P. W., and Luk, S. L. (1984). 'Problems encountered in teaching Chinese parents to be behaviour therapists', *Psychologia, 27*, 56–64.

Likert, R. (1967). *The Human Organization*. New York: McGraw Hill.

Lin, B. J. (1971). 'Study of academic achievement and personality traits among junior high school students' [in Chinese], *National Zhengzhi University Research Journal, 23*, 215–43.

Lin, B. S. (1978). 'A study of pre-enrollment expectations and academic performance of high school freshmen in Taipei' [in Chinese], *National Taiwan Normal University Graduate School of Education Research Quarterly, 20*, 487–520.

Lin, C. (1985). 'The intergenerational relationships among Chinese immigrant families: A study of filial piety'. Unpublished doctoral dissertation, University of Illinois at Chicago.

Lin, C. D., and Zhang, H. C. (1986). *Wechsler Intelligence Scale for Children-Chinese* (Revision)[in Chinese]. Beijing: Beijing Normal University.

Lin, C. T. (1980). 'A sketch of the methods of mental testing in ancient China' [in Chinese], *Acta Psychologica Sinica, 1*, 75–80.

Lin, C. Y. C., and Fu, V. R. (1990). 'A comparison of child-rearing practices among Chinese, immigrant Chinese, and Caucasian-American parents', *Child Development, 61*, 429–33.

Lin, J. C., and Liang, H. C. (1984). 'Exploring the social factors affecting health', *China Reconstructs, 25*–7.

Lin, K. M. (1980). 'Traditional Chinese medical beliefs and their relevance for mental illness and psychiatry'. In A. Kleinman, and T. Y. Lin (Eds.), *Normal and Abnormal Behavior in Chinese Culture* (pp. 95–111). Dordrecht, the Netherlands: D. Reidel.

Lin, N. (1988). 'Chinese family structure and Chinese society', *Bulletin of the Institute of Ethnology, Academia Sinica, 65*, 59–129.

Lin, P. C. (1979). 'Relationship between attribution and adjustment in junior high school students' [in Chinese], *Zhonghua Xinli Xuekan, 21*, 61–74.

Lin, T. Y. (1953). 'A study of incidence of mental disorders in Chinese and other cultures', *Psychiatry, 16*, 313–36.

Lin, T. Y. (1981). 'Traditional Chinese medical beliefs and their relevance for mental illness and psychiatry'. In A. Kleinman and T. Y. Lin (Eds.), *Normal and Abnormal Behaviour in Chinese Culture* (pp. 95–111). Dordrecht, the Netherlands: D. Reidel.

Lin, T. Y. (1982). 'Culture and psychiatry: A Chinese perspective', *Australian and New Zealand Journal of Psychiatry, 16*, 235–45.

Lin, T. Y. (1985). 'Mental disorders and psychiatry in Chinese culture: Characteristic features and major issues'. In W. S. Tseng and D. Y. H. Wu (Eds.), *Chinese Culture and Mental Health* (pp. 369–93). Orlando, FL: Academic Press.

Lin, T. Y., and Lin, D. T. C. (1982). 'Alcoholism among the Chinese: Further observations of a low-risk population', *Culture, Medicine and Psychiatry, 6*, 109–16.

Lin, T. Y., and Lin, M. C. (1981). 'Love, denial and rejection: Responses of Chinese families to mental illness'. In A. Kleinman and T. Y. Lin (Eds.), *Normal and Abnormal Behavior in Chinese Culture* (pp. 387–401). Dordrecht, the Netherlands: D. Reidel.

Lin, T. Y., Rin, H., Yeh, E. K., Hsu, C. C., and Chu, H. (1969). 'Mental disorders in Taiwan fifteen years later: A preliminary report'. In W. Caudill and Lin, T. (Eds.), *Mental Health Research in Asia and the Pacific* (pp. 66–91). Honolulu: East–West Center Press.

Lin, W. Q., Chen, L., and Wang, D. (1987). 'The construction of the CPM scale for leadership assessment' [in Chinese], *Acta Psychologica Sinica. 19*, 199–207.

Lin, X. J. (1989). 'How Chinese respondents scale causes of achievement events'. Paper presented at the annual meeting of the Midwest Sociological Society, St. Louis, April.

Lin, Y. H. (1992). 'Transitory life for eternal fame: On Chinese suicide' [in Chinese], *Journal of the Institute of Chinese Literature and Philosophy* (Taiwan), *2*, 423–51.

Lin, Y. T. (1935). *My Country and My people*. New York: John Day.

Lin, Y. Y. (1973). 'Aptitude and academic achievement of junior high school students' [in Chinese], *National Taiwan Normal University Graduate School of Education Research Quarterly* [in Chinese], *15*, 1–128.

Lindheim, R., and Syme, S. L. (1983). 'Environments, people, and health', *Annual Review of Public Health, 4*, 335–54.

Lindsay, C. P., and Dempsey, B. L. (1985). 'Experiences in training Chinese business people to use U.S. management techniques', *Journal of Applied Behavioral Science, 21*, 65–78.

Ling, W. Q., Chen, L., and Wang, D. (1987). 'The construction of the CPM scale for leadership behavior assessment' [in Chinese]. *Acta Psychologica Sinica, 19*, 199–207.

Ling, W. Q., Fang, L. L., and Khanna, A. (1991). 'The study of implicit leadership theory in China' [in

Chinese], *Acta Psychologica Sinica, 3*, 236–42.

Linton, R. (1945). *The Cultural Background of Personality*. New York: Appleton-Century-Crofts.

Liou, S. L. (1992). 'The debate of social being and natural being: The comparison of Confucius's and Lao-Tzu's concepts on art' [in Chinese]. In *Proceedings of the International Conference on Values in Chinese Societies: Retrospect and Prospect* (Vol. 2, pp. 545–72). Taipei: Center for Chinese Studies.

Littlejohn, S. W. (1992). *Theories of Human Communication* (fourth edition). Belmont, CA: Wadsworth Publishing Company.

Liu, C. M. (1992). 'A conceptual analysis of "bao" and its implications for organizational research' [in Chinese]. In *Proceedings of the Interdisciplinary Conference on Chinese Psychology and Behavior*. Taipei: Institute of Ethnology, Academia Sinica.

Liu, D. (1990). 'Present situation of sex culture in China'. Paper presented at the International Conference on Sexuality in Asia, Hong Kong, May.

Liu, D. (1991). *National Sex Civilization Survey* [in Chinese]. Shanghai: Sex Sociological Research Centre.

Liu, D. (1992). *Sexual Behaviour in Modern China: A Report of the Nationwide Sex Civilization Survey of 20,000 Subjects in China* [in Chinese]. Shanghai: SJPC Publishing Company.

Liu, D. (1994). 'The effects of socializing factors on students' achievement motivation in the Chinese family' [in Chinese]. Unpublished Master's thesis, Department of Psychology, Beijing University.

Liu, D. Y. (1994). *Archeology of Art and Ancient Civilization* [in Chinese]. Taipei: Yuan-Chun.

Liu, F. (1987). 'Developmental psychology in China: Some ancient thoughts and recent advances'. Paper presented at ISSBD Workshops of the International Society for the Study of Behavioral Development, Beijing, July.

Liu, F. Y. (1991). 'The generalizability of the NEO Personality Inventory to an university sample in Hong Kong'. Unpublished Bachelor's thesis, the Chinese University of Hong Kong.

Liu, H., Bates, E., and Li, P. (1992). 'Sentence interpretation in bilingual speakers of English and Chinese', *Applied Psycholinguistics, 13*, 451–84.

Liu, I. M. (1986). 'Chinese cognition'. In M. H. Bond (Ed.), *The Psychology of the Chinese People* (pp. 73–105). Hong Kong: Oxford University Press.

Liu, I. M. (1988). 'Context effects on word/character naming: Alphabetic versus logographic languages'. In I. M. Liu, H. C. Chen, and M. J. Chen (Eds.), *Cognitive Aspects of the Chinese Language* (Vol. I, pp. 81–92). Hong Kong: Asian Research Service.

Liu, I. M. (1993). 'Universal versus indigenous psychology: A direction for the future research', *Bulletin of the Hong Kong Psychological Society, 30/31*, 5–14.

Liu, I. M. (1994). Personal communication, 28 March.

Liu, I. M. (1994). 'Script factors that affect literacy: Alphabetic vs. logographic languages'. In I. Taylor and D. R. Olson (Eds.), *Script and Literacy* (pp. 145–62). Dordrecht, the Netherlands: Kluwer.

Liu, I. M., Chou, T. L., and Wu, J. T. (1993). 'Encoding operation and transcoding as the major loci of the frequency effect'. Manuscript submitted for publication.

Liu, I. M., Chuang, C. J., and Wang, S. C. (1975). *Frequency Count of 40,000 Chinese Words*. Taipei: Lucky Books.

Liu, I. M., Zhu, Y., and Wu, J. T. (1992). 'The long-term modality effect: In search of differences in processing logographs and alphabetic words', *Cognition, 43*, 31–66.

Liu, J. (1980). 'An epidemiological investigation of mental disorders in Xuhui district of Shanghai' [in Chinese]. *Chinese Journal of Neurology and Psychiatry, 13*, 1–6.

Liu, J. H. (1985). 'A survey study of junior high school students' expectations for continuing education and the related factors' [in Chinese], *National Taiwan Normal University Graduate School of Education Research Quarterly, 27*, 291–302.

Liu, K. H., Yang, T. T., and Chen, L. C. (1983). 'A research on the EPPS responses of NTNU students' [in Chinese], *Psychological Testing* (Taiwan), *30*, 35–44.

Liu, L. G. (1985). 'Reasoning counterfactually in Chinese: Are there any obstacles?' *Cognition, 21*, 239–70.

Liu, S. H. (1987). 'The ideals of *neisheng waiwang* in Confucianism' [in Chinese]. In S. H. Liu (Ed.), *Proceedings of the Conference on Confucian Ethics* (pp. 218–31). Singapore: The Institute of East Asian Philosophies.

Liu, S. H. (1993). 'The psychotherapeutic function of the Confucian discipline of *hsin* (mind-heart)'. In L. Y. Cheng, F. Cheung, and C. N. Chen (Eds.), *Psychotherapy for the Chinese* (pp. 1–18). Hong Kong: Department of Psychiatry, the Chinese University of Hong Kong.

Liu, S. Q. (1990). 'The effect of competition on student's achievement attribution and achievement behavior' [in Chinese]. *Sehui Xinli Yanjiu, 2,* 48–55.

Liu, W. C. (1992). 'Conflict resolution in close relationships'. Unpublished doctoral dissertation, University of Minnesota, Minneapolis.

Liu, X., Meng, Z., and Lu, W. (1990). 'Is there any consistency of emotionality manifestation among different emotions?' [in Chinese], *Acta Psychologica Sinica, 4,* 406–12.

Liu, X. C., Kuo, C. Q., Wang J. L., Yu, J. C., and Tien, J. (1991). 'Survey of depressive moods and related factors among senior high school students' [in Chinese]. *Chinese Journal of Mental Health, 5*(1), 24–6.

Liu, Y. T. (1992). *The Results and Analyses of the Education Assessment of Middle School Mathematics and Science: A Report from the Second IAEP Study* [in Chinese]. Guangdong: Xinshiji Press.

Liu, Z. H., and Guo, Z. J. (1993). 'Achievement motivation and learning strategies of the middle school students' [in Chinese], *Psychological Science, 4,* 198–204.

Llewellyn, J., Hancock, G., Kirst, M., and Roeloffs, K. (1982). *A Perspective on Education in Hong Kong: Report by a Visiting Panel.* Hong Kong: Hong Kong Government Printer.

Lo, H. T. (1993). 'Psychotherapy for the Chinese Canadians'. In L. Y. Cheng, F. Cheung, and C. N. Chen (Eds.), *Psychotherapy for the Chinese* (pp. 215–24). Hong Kong: Department of Psychiatry, the Chinese University of Hong Kong.

Lo, T. C. (1982). 'The impact of organizational climate and personal characteristics on the industrial salesperson's job satisfaction' [in Chinese]. Unpublished Master's thesis, Tatung Institute of Technology, Taiwan.

Lo, T. W. (1993). 'A study of "A personal Perspective on Mirror Reflection and Image Formation"' [in Chinese]. Unpublished Master's thesis, Department of History, National Tsing-Hua University.

Lo, W. H. (1976). 'Urbanization and psychiatric disorders: The Hong Kong scene', *Acta Psychiatrica Scandinavica, 54,* 174–83.

Lo, W. H. (1992). 'Suicidal behaviour in Hong Kong'. In K. L. Peng and W. S. Tseng (Eds.), *Suicidal Behaviour in the Asia-Pacific Region* (pp. 83–111). Singapore: University of Singapore Press.

Lo, W. H., and Lo, T. (1977). 'A ten-year follow-up study of Chinese schizophrenics in Hong Kong', *British Journal of Psychiatry, 131,* 63–6.

Lock, A. (1981). 'Indigenous psychology and human nature: A psychological perspective'. In P. Heelas and A. Lock (Eds.), *Indigenous Psychologies: The Anthropology of the Self* (pp. 183–201). London: Academic Press.

Lock, A. J. (1980). *The Guided Reinvention of Language.* London: Academic Press.

Locke, J. L. (1983). *Phonological Acquisition and Change.* New York: Academic Press.

Loehlin, J. C. (1992). *Genes and Environment in Personality Development.* Newbury Park, CA: Sage.

Long, F. Y. (1967). 'Psychology in Singapore: Its roots, context and growth'. In G. H. Blowers and A. M. Turtle (Eds.), *Psychology Moving East: The Status of Western Psychology in Asia and Océania* (pp. 223–48). Boulder, CO: Westview Press.

Lonner, W. J. (1990). 'An overview of cross-cultural testing and assessment'. In R. W. Brislin (Ed.), *Applied Cross-Cultural Psychology* (pp. 56–76). Newbury Park, CA: Sage.

Lonner, W. J., and Ibrahim, F. (1989). 'Assessment in cross-cultural counseling'. In P. Pedersen, J. G. Draguns, W. J. Lonner, and J. E. Trimble (Eds.), *Cross-Cultural Counseling* (third edition, pp. 275–303). Honolulu: University of Hawaii Press.

Loo, C., and Ong, P. (1984). 'Crowding perceptions: Attitudes and consequences among the Chinese', *Environmental and Behaviour, 1,* 55–87.

Louie, T. T. T. (1990). 'Explanatory thinking in Chinese Americans'. In P. J. Brink (Ed.), *Transcultural Nursing* (pp. 240–6). Prospect Heights, IL: Waveland Press.

Lu, C. Y. (1967). 'A Chinese revision of MMPI for the Chinese people' [in Chinese], *Psychology and Education, 1,* 20–36.

Lu, D. L., and Daqiao, J. (1989). *City Contact: An Observation of Hong Kong Street Culture* [in Chinese]. Hong Kong: Commercial Press.

Lu, H. J. (1986). 'An application of situational simulation assessment in selection of managerial personnel' [in Chinese], *Information on Psychological Sciences, 2*, 43–8.

Lu, Y. C. (1978). 'The collective approach to psychiatric practice in the People's Republic of China', *Social Problems, 26*, 2–14.

Luborsky, L., and DeRubeis, R. J. (1984). 'The use of psychotherapy treatment manuals: A small revolution in psychotherapy research style', *Clinical Psychology Review, 4*, 5–14.

Luk, C. L., and Bond, M. H. (1992). 'Chinese lay beliefs about the causes and cures of psychological problems', *Journal of Social and Clinical Psychology, 11*, 140–57.

Luk, C. L., and Bond, M. H. (1992). 'Explaining Chinese self-esteem in terms of the self-concept', *Psychologica, 35*, 147–54.

Luk, C. L., and Bond, M. H. (1993). 'Personality variation and values endorsement in Chinese university students', *Personality and Individual Differences, 14*, 429–37.

Luk, S. L., Kwan, C. S., Hui, J. M., Bacon-Shone, J., Tsang, A. K., Leung, A. C., and Tang, K. K. (1991). 'Cognitive-behavioural group therapy for Hong Kong Chinese adults with mental health problems', *Australian and New Zealand Journal of Psychiatry, 25*, 524–34.

Luk, S. L., Leung, P. W. L., Bacon-Shone, J., Chung, S. Y., Lee, P. W. H., Cheu, S., Ng, R., Leih-Mak, F., Ko, L., Wong, V. C. H., and Yeung, C. Y. (1991). 'Behavior disorder in preschool children in Hong Kong: A two-stage epidemiological study', *British Journal of Psychiatry, 158*, 213–21.

Luk, S. L., Leung, P. W., Bacon-Shone, J., and Lieh-Mak, F. (1991). 'The structure and prevalence of behavioral problems in Hong Kong preschool children', *Journal of Abnormal Child Psychology, 19*, 219–32.

Lukatela, G., and Turvey, M. T. (1990). 'Automatic and pre-lexical computation of phonology in visual word identification', *European Journal of Cognitive Psychology, 2*, 325–43.

Lukatela, G., Popadic, D., Ognjenovic, P., and Turvey, M. T. (1980). 'Lexical decision in a phonologically shallow orthography', *Memory and Cognition, 8*, 124–32.

Luke, K. K., and Richards, J. C. (1981). 'English in Hong Kong: Functions and status', *English Worldwide, 3*(1), 46–64.

Lum, K. Y., and Char, W. (1985). 'Chinese adaptation in Hawaii: Some examples'. In W. Tseng and D. Wu (Eds.), *Chinese Culture and Mental Health* (pp. 215–26). New York: Academic Press.

Lummis, M., and Stevenson, H. W. (1990). 'Gender differences in beliefs and achievement: A cross-cultural study', *Developmental Psychology, 26*(2), 254–63.

Luo, G. J. (1987). 'Analysis of traditional moral education of China' [in Chinese], *Educational Research, 3*, 8–11.

Luo, R. Q. (1989). 'Theoretical reflections on tradition and modernization' [in Chinese], *Bulletin of Beijing University* (Special Issue on Philosophy and Social Sciences), *3*, 5–7.

Lust, B., and Chien, Y. C. (1984). 'The structure of co-ordination in first language acquisition of Mandarin Chinese: Evidence for a universal', *Cognition, 7*, 49–83.

Lust, B., Chien, Y. C., Mangione, L. (1983). 'First language acquisition of Mandarin Chinese: Constraints on free and bound null anaphora'. In S. Hattori, K. Inoue, T. Shimomiya, and Y. Nagashima (Eds.), *Proceedings of the XIIIth International Congress of Linguists* (pp. 1127–30). Tokyo: Tokyo Press.

Lutz, C., and White, G. (1986). 'The anthropology of emotions', *Annual Review of Anthropology, 15*, 405–36.

Lynn, R. (1991). 'Educational achievement of Asian Americans', *American Psychologist, 46*, 875–6.

Lynn, R. (1991). 'Intelligence in China', *Social Behavior and Personality, 19*, 1–4.

Lynn, R., Chan, J., and Eysenck, H. (1991). 'Reaction times and intelligence in Chinese and British children', *Perceptual and Motor Skills, 72*, 443–52.

Lynn, R., Pagliari, C., and Chan, J. (1988). 'Intelligence in Hong Kong measured for Spearman's g and the visuo-spatial and verbal primaries', *Intelligence, 12*, 423–33.

Lyons, J. (1968). *An Introduction to Theoretical Linguistics*. Cambridge: Cambridge University Press.

Ma, H. K. (1985). 'Cross-cultural study of the hierarchical structure of human relationships', *Psychological Reports, 57*, 1079–83.

Ma, R. G. (1990). 'An exploratory study of discontented responses in American and Chinese relationships', *The Southern Communication Journal, 55*(3), 305–18.

Ma, R. G. (1992). 'The role of unofficial intermediaries in interpersonal conflicts in Chinese culture', *Communication Quarterly, 40*(3), 269–78.

Ma, X. X. (1985). 'The relationship between family's educational background and academic achievement' [in Chinese], *National Zhengzhi University Research Journal*, *51*, 139–64.

MacNamara, J. (1967). 'The bilingual's linguistic performance', *Journal of Social Issues*, *23*, 58–77.

MacWhinney, B. (1987). 'Applying the competition model to bilingualism', *Applied Psycholinguistics*, *8*, 315–27.

MacWhinney, B. (1989). 'Competition and connectionism'. In B. MacWhinney and E. Bates (Eds.), *The Crosslinguistic Study of Sentence Processing* (pp. 422–57). New York: Cambridge University Press.

MacWhinney, B. (1992). 'Competition and transfer in second language learning'. In R. J. Harris (Ed.), *Cognitive Processing in Bilinguals* (pp. 371–90). Amsterdam: North-Holland.

MacWhinney, B., and Bates, E. (Eds.)(1989). *The Crosslinguistic Study of Sentence Processing*. New York: Cambridge University Press.

Maehr, M. L. (1974). 'Culture and achievement motivation', *American Psychologist*, *29*, 887–96.

Maehr, M. L. (1978). 'Sociocultural origins of achievement motivation'. In D. Bar-tal and L. Sax (Eds.), *Social Psychology of Education: Theory and Research* (pp. 205–27). New York: Wiley.

Maehr, M. L., and Nicholls, J. G. (1980). 'Culture and achievement motivation: A second look' In N. Warren (Ed.), *Studies in Cross-Cultural Psychology* (Vol. 3, pp. 221–67). New York: Academic Press.

Magiste, E. (1984). 'Stroop tasks and dichotic translation: The development of interference patterns in bilinguals', *Journal of Experimental Psychology: Learning, Memory, and Cognition*, *10*, 304–15.

Magiste, E. (1985). 'Development of intra- and interlingual interference in bilinguals', *Journal of Psycholinguistic Research*, *14*, 137–54.

Magliano, J. P., Graesser, A. C., Eymard, L. A., Haberlandt, K., and Gholson, B. (1993). 'Locus of interpretive and inference processes during text comprehension', *Journal of Experimental Psychology: Learning, Memory, and Cognition*, *19*, 704–9.

Marchant, G., Robinson, J., Anderson, U., and Schadewald, M. (1993). 'The use of analogy in legal argument: Problem similarity, precedent, and expertise', *Organizational Behavior and Human Decision Processes*, *55*, 95–119.

Marjoribanks, K. (1991). 'Ethnicity, family environment and social status attainment: A follow-up analysis', *Journal of Comparative Family Studies*, *10*, 5–18.

Markus, H. R., and Kitayama, S. (1991). 'Culture and the self: Implications for cognition, emotion, and motivation', *Psychological Review*, *98*, 224–53.

Marsella, A. J. (1980). 'Depressive experience and disorder across cultures'. In H. C. Triandis and J. G. Draguns (Eds.), *Handbook of Cross-Cultural Psychology* (Vol. 6: Psychopathology, pp. 237-89). Boston: Allyn and Bacon.

Marsella, A. J., Murray, M. D., and Golden, C. (1974). 'Ethnic variations in the phenomenology of emotions: I. Shame', *Journal of Cross-Cultural Psychology*, *5*, 312–28.

Marsella, A. J., Sanborn, K. O., Kameoka, V., Shizuru, L. S., and Brennan, J. M. (1975). 'Cross-validation of self-report measures of depression among normal populations of Japanese, Chinese, and Caucasian ancestry', *Journal of Clinical Psychology*, *31*, 281–7.

Marsella, A. J., Sartorius, N., Jablensky, A., and Fenton, F. R. (1985). 'Cross-cultural studies of depressive disorders'. In A. Kleinman and B. Good (Eds.), *Culture and Depression* (pp. 299–324). Berkeley: University of California Press.

Marsella, A. J., Shizuru, L. S., Brennan, J. M., and Kameoka, V. (1981). 'Depression and body image satisfaction', *Journal of Cross-Cultural Psychology*, *12*, 360–71.

Marsh, H. W. (1984). 'Relations among dimensions of self-attribution, dimensions of self-concept, and academic achievements', *Journal of Educational Psychology*, *76*, 1291–308.

Marsh, H. W., Cairns, L., Relich, J., Barnes, J., and Debus, R. L. (1984). 'The relationship between dimensions of self-attribution and dimensions of self-concept', *Journal of Educational Psychology*, *76*, 3–32.

Marsh, H. W., Relich, J. D., and Smith, I. D. (1983). 'Multidimensional self-concepts: The construct validity of interpretations based upon the SDQ', *Journal of Personality and Social Psychology*, *45*, 173–87.

Marslen-Wilson, W. D. (1987). 'Functional parallelism in spoken word-recognition', *Cognition*, *25*, 71–102.

Marslen-Wilson, W. D., and Tyler, L. K. (1980). 'The temporal structure of spoken language understanding', *Cognition, 8,* 1–71.

Marslen-Wilson, W. D., Tyler, L. K., Waksler, R., and Older, L. (1994). 'Morphology and meaning in the English mental lexicon', *Psychological Review, 101,* 3–33.

Martin, R. (1975). 'The socialisation of children in China and on Taiwan: An analysis of elementary school textbooks', *China Quarterly, 62,* 242–62.

Marton, F., and Saljo, R. (1976). 'On qualitative differences in learning, outcome, and process II', *British Journal of Educational Psychology, 46,* 115–27.

Marton, F., Dall'Alba, G., and Kun, T. L. (1994). 'Memorising and understanding: The keys of the paradox?' In D. Watkins and J. Biggs (Eds.), *The Chinese Learner: Research and Practice* (pp. 89–104). Unpublished manuscript, Hong Kong University.

Mattingly, I. G. (1985). 'Did orthographies evolve?' *Remedial and Special Education, 6,* 18–23.

Mattingly, I. G., and Xu, Y. (1993). 'Word superiority in Chinese'. Paper presented at the Sixth International Symposium on Cognitive Aspects of the Chinese Language, Taipei.

Mauro, R., Sato, K., and Tucker, J. (1992). 'The role of appraisal in human emotions: A cross-cultural study', *Journal of Personality and Social Psychology, 62,* 301–17.

Mazoyer, B. M., Tzourio, N., Frak, V., Syrota, A., Murayama, N., Levrier, Salamon, G., Dehaene, S., Cohen, L., and Mehler, J. (1993). 'The cortical representation of speech', *Journal of Cognitive Neuroscience, 5,* 467–79.

McCann, R. S., and Besner, D. (1987). 'Reading pseudohomophones: Implications for models of pronunciation assembly and the locus of word frequency effects in naming', *Journal of Experimental Psychology: Human Perception and Performance, 13,* 13–24.

McCarthy, T. A. (1973). 'A theory of communicative competence', *Philosophy of the Social Sciences, 3,* 135–56.

McClelland, D. C. (1961). *The Achieving Society.* Princeton, NJ: Van Nostrand.

McClelland, D. C. (1963). 'Motivational patterns in Southeast Asia with special reference to the Chinese case', *Journal of Social Issues, 19*(1), 6–19.

McClelland, D. C. (1965). 'Toward a theory of motive acquisition', *American Psychologist,* 20, 321–33.

McClelland, D. C. (1980). 'Motive dispositions: The merits of operant and respondent measures'. In L. Wheeler (Ed.), *Review of Personality and Social Psychology* (Vol. 1, pp. 10–41). Beverly Hills, CA: Sage.

McClelland, D. C. (1985). 'How motives, skills and values determine what people do', *American Psychologist, 40,* 812–25.

McClelland, D. C. (1985). *Human Motivation.* Glenview, IL: Scott, Foresman and Company.

McClelland, D. C., and Friedman, G. A. (1952). 'A cross-cultural study of the relationship between child-training practices and achievement motivation appearing in folk tales'. In G. E. Swanson, T. M. Newcomb, and E. L. Hartley (Eds.), *Readings in Social Psychology* (pp. 243–9). NY: Holt, Rinehart and Winston.

McClelland, D. C., Atkinson, J. W., Clark, R. A., and Lowell, E. L. (1953). *The Achievement Motive.* NY: Appleton-Century-Crofts.

McClelland, D. C., Atkinson, J. W., Clark, R. A., and Lowell, E. L. (1958). 'A scoring manual for the achievement motive'. In J. W. Atkinson (Ed.), *Motives in Fantasy, Action, and Society* (pp. 179–204). Princeton, NJ: Van Nostrand.

McClelland, D. C., Koestner, R., and Weinberger, J. (1989). 'How do self-attributed and implicit motives differ?' *Psychological Review, 96*(4), 690–702.

McClelland, J. L. (1987). 'The case for interactionism in language processing'. In M. Coltheart (Ed.), *Attention and Performance XII* (pp. 3–36). London: Erlbaum.

McClelland, J. L., and Rumelhart, D. E. (1985). 'Distributed memory and the representation of general and specific information', *Journal of Experimental Psychology: General, 114,* 159–88.

McCrae, R. R. (1989). 'Why I advocate the five-factor model: Joint analyses of the NEO-PI with other instruments'. In D. M. Buss and N. Cantor (Eds.), *Personality Psychology: Recent Trends and Emerging Directions* (pp. 237–45). New York: Springer-Verlag.

McCrae, R. R. (1990). 'Traits and trait names: How well is Openness represented in natural languages?' *European Journal of Personality, 4,* 119–29.

McCrae, R. R. (1994). 'Openness to Experience: Expanding the boundaries of Factor V', *European Journal of Personality, 8,* 251-72.

McCrae, R. R. (Ed.) (1992). 'The Five-Factor Model: Issues and applications', *Journal of Personality,*

60(2)(Special issue).

McCrae, R. R., and Costa, P. T., Jr. (1985). 'Comparison of EPI and Psychoticism scales with measures of the five-factor model of personality', *Personality and Individual Differences, 6,* 587–97.

McCrae, R. R., and Costa, P. T., Jr. (1989). 'The structure of interpersonal traits: Wiggins's circumplex and the five-factor model', *Journal of Personality and Social Psychology, 56,* 586–95.

McCrae, R. R., and Costa, P. T., Jr. (1990). *Personality in Adulthood.* New York: Guilford.

McCrae, R. R., and Costa, P. T., Jr. (in press). 'Conceptions and correlates of Openness to Experience'. In R. Hogan, J. A. Johnson, and S. R. Briggs (Eds.), *Handbook of Personality Psychology.* New York: Academic Press.

McCrae, R. R., and Costa, P. T., Jr. (in press). 'Toward a new generation of personality theories: Theoretical contexts for the five-factor model'. In J. S. Wiggins (Ed.), *The Five-Factor Model of Personality: Theoretical Perspectives.* New York: Guilford.

McCrae, R. R., and John, O. P. (1992). 'An introduction to the five-factor model and its applications', *Journal of Personality, 60,* 175–215.

McDaniel, E. D., and Soong, W. (1981). 'Comparisons of self-concept scores of children in America and Taiwan'. Paper presented at the NATO Conference on Human Assessment and Cultural Factors, Kingston, Ontario.

McGinnies, E. (1965). 'A cross-cultural comparison of printed communication versus spoken communication in persuasion', *Journal of Psychology, 60,* 1–8.

McKay, J., Gow, L., and Kember, D. (1991). 'Action research as a means of improving clinical training', *Research in Radiography, 1*(2), 24–41.

McLeod, B. A., and Carment, D. W. (1987). 'To lie or not to lie: A comparison of Canadian and Chinese attitudes towards deception'. Unpublished manuscript, McMaster University.

McRae, K., Jared, D., and Seidenberg, M. S. (1990). 'On the roles of frequency and lexical access in word naming', *Journal of Memory and Language, 29,* 43–65.

Mehler, J., Dupoux, E., Pallier, C., and Dehaene-Lambertz, G. (1994). 'Cross-linguistics approaches to speech processing', *Current Opinion in Neurobiology, 4,* 171–6.

Mei, J. Y. (1984). *Reading in China: Report of the U.S. Reading Study Team to the People's Republic of China.* Washington, DC: National Committee on U.S.–China Relations.

Meng, Z., and Campos, J. J. (1984). 'The influence of different emotions on mental performance in infancy' [in Chinese], *Acta Psychologica Sinica, 16,* 231–9.

Meng, Z., Wang, L., Liu, X., and Lin, J. (1988). *The Organizational Function of Emotion on Cognitive Task Performance in Infancy* (Annual Report, 1988/9, No. 12). Sapporo, Japan: Research and Clinical Center for Child Development, Faculty of Education, Hokkaido University.

Meng, Z., Yan, J., and Meng, X. (1985). 'A preliminary study on facial expression patterns of infants' [in Chinese], *Acta Psychologica Sinica, 17,* 55-61.

Meskill, J. M. (1979). *A Chinese Pioneer Family: The Lins of Wu-feng, Taiwan, 1729–1895.* Princeton, NJ: Princeton University Press.

Messick, S. (1980). 'Test validity and the ethics of assessment', *American Psychologist, 35,* 1012–27.

Messick, S. (1981). 'Evidence and ethics in the evaluation of tests', *Educational Researcher, 10*(9), 9–20.

Metzger, T. A. (1988). 'Confucian thought and the modern quest for moral autonomy'. Paper prepared for the International Confucius Symposium, St. Augustin, Germany, November.

Meyer, D. E., and Schvaneveldt, R. W. (1971). 'Facilitation in recognizing pairs of words: Evidence of a dependence between retrieval operations', *Journal of Experimental Psychology, 90,* 227–35.

Meyer, J. (1988). 'Moral education in Taiwan', *Comparative Education Review 32*(1), 20–38.

Meyer, J. F., and Parsons, P. (1989). 'Approaches to studying and course perceptions using the Lancaster Inventory: A comparative study', *Studies in Higher Education, 14*(2), 137–53.

Miao, X. C. (1981). 'Word order and semantic strategies in Chinese sentence comprehension', *International Journal of Psycholinguistics, 23,* 109–22.

Miao, X. C., and Zhu, M. S. (1992). 'Language development in Chinese children'. In H. C. Chen and O. J. L. Tzeng (Eds.), *Language Processing in Chinese* (pp. 237–76). Amsterdam: North-Holland.

Millar, S. E. (1979). *The Biosocial Survey in Hong Kong.* Canberra: Australian National University.

Miller, E. S. (1976). 'Health and well-being in relation to high density living in Hong Kong'. Unpublished doctoral dissertation, Australian National University.

Miller, G. A. (1951). *Language and Communication.* New York: McGraw-Hill.

Miller, G. A., and Johnson-Laird, P. N. (1976). *Language and Perception.* Cambridge, MA: Harvard University Press.

Mills, H. (1956). 'Language reform in China: Some recent developments', *The Far Eastern Quarterly, 15,* 517–40.

Milroy, J., and Milroy, L. (1985). *Investigating Language Prescription and Standardisation.* London: Routledge.

Ministry of Education (ROC)(1991). *Education in the Republic of China.* Taipei: Bureau of Statistics, Ministry of Education.

Misumi, J. (1985). *The Behavioral Science of Leadership.* Ann Arbor, MI: University of Michigan Press.

Mitchell, R. E. (1971). 'Some social implications of high density housing', *American Sociological Review, 36,* 18–29.

Mitchell, R. E. (1972). *Family Life in Urban Hong Kong.* Taipei: Oriental Cultural Science.

Moghaddam, F. M. (1987). 'Psychology in the three worlds', *American Psychologist, 42,* 912–20.

Moghaddam, F. M., Taylor, D. M., and Wright, S. C. (1993). *Social Psychology in Cross-Cultural Perspective.* New York: W. H. Freeman.

Monsell, S., Doyle, M. C., and Haggard, P. N. (1989). 'Effects of frequency on visual word recognition tasks: Where are they?' *Journal of Experimental Psychology: General, 118,* 43–71.

Mordkowitz, E. R., and Ginsburg, H. P. (1987). 'Early academic socialisation of successful Asian-American college students', *The Quarterly Newsletter of the Laboratory of Comparative Human Cognition, 9*(2), 85–91.

Morikawa, Y. (1981). 'Stroop phenomena in the Japanese language: The case of ideographic characters (kanji) and syllabic characters (kana)', *Perceptual and Motor Skills, 53,* 67–77.

Morris, C. W. (1956). *Varieties of Human Value.* Chicago: University of Chicago Press.

Morris, M. W. (1993). 'Culture and cause: American and Chinese understandings of physical and social causality'. Unpublished doctoral dissertation, University of Michigan, Ann Arbor.

Morris, M. W., Nisbett, R. E., and Peng, K. (in press). 'Causal attribution across domains and cultures'. In G. Lewis, D. Premack, and D. Sperber (Eds.), *Causal Understandings in Cognition and Culture.* New York: Oxford University Press.

Morris, P. (1983). 'Teachers' perceptions of their pupils: A Hong Kong case study', *Research in Education, 29,* 81–6.

Morton, J. (1969). 'Interaction of information in word recognition', *Psychological Review, 76,* 165–78.

Moscovici, S. (1976). *Social Influence and Social Change.* London: Academic Press.

Moscovici, S. (1988). 'Notes toward a description of social representations', *European Journal of Social Psychology, 18,* 211–50.

Mote, F. (1971). *Intellectual Foundations of China.* New York: Alfred A. Knopf.

Mottaz, C. J. (1987). 'Age and work satisfaction', *Work and Occupation, 14*(3), 387–409.

Mou, T. S. (1985). *On Summum Bonum* [in Chinese]. Taipei: Taiwan Student Book Co.

Munro, D. J. (1969). *The Concept of Man in Early China.* Stanford, CA: Stanford University Press.

Munro, D. J. (1977). *The Concept of Man in Contemporary China.* Ann Arbor: University of Michigan Press.

Munsterberger, W. (1984). 'Transcultural psychoanalysis: The case of a Chinese army officer', *Journal of Psychoanalytic Anthropology, 7,* 3–22.

Murphy, H. B. M. (1954). 'The mental health of Singapore: Part I. Suicide', *Medical Journal of Malaya, 9,* 1–45.

Murphy, H. B. M., Wittkower, E. W., and Chance, N. (1967). 'A cross-cultural inquiry into the symptomatology of depression: A preliminary report', *International Journal of Psychiatry, 3,* 6–15.

Murray, H. A. (1938). *Explorations in Personality.* New York: Oxford University Press.

Murray, H. A. (1943). *Thematic Apperception Test Manual.* Cambridge, MA: Harvard College.

Murstein, B. I. (1963). *Theory and Research in Projective Technique.* New York: Wiley.

Nakamura, H. (1964). *Ways of Thinking of Eastern Peoples: India, China, Tibet, Japan.* Honolulu: East–West Center Press.

Nakayama, K., and Shimojo, S. (1990). 'Toward a neural understanding of visual surface representation', *Cold Spring Harbor Symposium on Quantitative Biology, 55*, 911–24.

Nathan, A. J. (1993). 'Is Chinese culture distinctive? A review article', *Journal of Asian Studies, 52*,
923–36.

Nathan, A. J., and Shi, T. J. (1993). 'Cultural requisites for democracy in China: Findings from a survey', *Daedalus, 122*(2), 95–123.

National MMPI Coordinating Group. (1982). 'The revision, employment and evaluation of MMPI in
China' [in Chinese], *Acta Psychologica Sinica, 17*, 346–55.

Ney, P., Lieh-Mak, F., Cheng, R., and Collins, W. (1979). 'Chinese autistic children', *Social
Psychiatry, 14*, 147–50.

Ng, D., McClure, J., and Walkey, F. (1992). 'New Zealand and Singaporean attributions and
achievement motivation'. Paper presented at the Asian Conference of Psychology,
Singapore, October.

Ng, M. L. (1983). 'Experiences with non-directive psychotherapeutic techniques for Chinese in
Hong Kong', *Journal of Hong Kong Psychiatric Association, 3*, 35–9.

Ng, M. L. (1985). 'Psychoanalysis for the Chinese: Applicable or not applicable?' *International
Review of Psychoanalysis, 12*, 449–60.

Ng, M. L. (1988). 'Sex therapy for the Chinese in Hong Kong', *Sexual and Marital Therapy, 3*,
245–52.

Ng, S. H. (1990). 'The ethos of Chinese at work: Collectivism or Individualism?' *Advances in
Chinese Industrial Studies, 1*, 315–28.

Ng, S. H., Akhtar-Hossain, A. B. M., Ball, P., Bond, M. H., Hayashi, K., Lim, S. P., O'Driscoll, M. P.,
Sinha, D., and Yang, K. S. (1982). 'Values in nine countries'. In R. Rath, H. S. Asthana, and J. B.
H. Sinha (Eds.), *Diversity and Unity in Cross-Cultural Psychology* (pp. 196–205). Lisse, the
Netherlands: Swets and Zeitlinger.

Ngo, H. (1992). 'Employment status of married women in Hong Kong', *Sociological Perspectives,
35*, 475–88.

Ni, J. H. (1993). 'Psychological consultation by phone' [in Chinese], *Chinese Journal of Clinical
Psychology, 1*, 61–2.

Ni, L. (1962). 'Study of the causes of maladjustment of adolescents through the use of projective
test' [in Chinese], *Acta Psychologica Taiwanica* (Taiwan), *4*, 32–52.

Nicholls, J. G. (1984). 'Achievement motivation: Conceptions of ability, subjective experience, task
choice, and performance', *Psychological Review, 91*(3), 328–46.

Nichols, M. P., and Schwartz, R. C. (1991). *Family Therapy* (second edition). Boston: Allyn and
Bacon.

Noels, K., Clément, R., and Pon, G. (1992). 'Language, identity and acculturative stress: The case of
Chinese university students in Ottawa'. Paper presented at the annual meeting of the
Canadian Psychological Association, Quebec City, Quebec, June.

Norman, W. T. (1963). 'Toward an adequate taxonomy of personality attributes: Replicated factor
structure in peer nomination personality ratings', *Journal of Abnormal and Social
Psychology, 66*, 574–83.

Norman, W. T. (1967). *2800 Personality trait descriptors: Normative operating characteristics for a
university population*, Unpublished manusript: University of Michigan.

Nutt, P. C. (1986). 'Decision style and strategic decisions of top executives', *Technological
Forecasting and Social Change, 30*, 39–62.

Nydell, M. K. (1987). *Understanding Arabs: A Guide for Westerners*. Yarmouth, ME: Intercultural
Press.

O'Hair, D., Cody, M., Wang, X. T., and Chao, E. Y. (1990). 'Vocal stress and deception detection
among Chinese', *Communication Quarterly, 38*, 158–69.

O'Neil, M. J., and Child, D. (1984). 'Biggs' SPQ: A British study of its internal structure', *British
Journal of Educational Psychology, 54*, 228–34.

O'Neill, H. B. (1987). *Companion to Chinese History*. New York: Facts on File Publications.

O'Regan, J. K. (1979). 'Eye guidance in reading: Evidence for the linguistic control hypothesis',
Perception and Psychophysics, 25, 501–9.

Ochs, E. (1986). Introduction to B. B. Schieffelin and E. Ochs (Eds.), *Language socialisation across
cultures* (pp. 1–13). Cambridge: Cambridge University Press.

Ochs, E. (1990). 'Indexicality and socialization'. In J. W. Stigler, R. A. Shweder, and G. Herdt (Eds.),

Cultural Psychology (pp. 287–308). Cambridge: Cambridge University Press.

Ochs, E. (1991). 'Misunderstanding children'. In N. Coupland, H. Giles, and J. M. Wiemann (Eds.), *Miscommunication and Problematic Talk* (pp. 44–60). Newbury Park, CA: Sage.

Ochs, E., and Schieffelin, B. B. (1979). *Developmental Pragmatics*. New York: Academic Press.

Olsen, N. J. (1971). 'Sex differences in child training antecedents of achievement motivation among Chinese children', *Journal of Social Psychology, 83*, 303–4.

Ong, S. B., and Leng, Y. K. (1979). 'The treatment of an obsessive–compulsive girl in the context of Malaysian Chinese culture', *Australian and New Zealand Journal of Psychiatry, 13*, 255–9.

Ong, S. B., and Leng, Y. K. (1992). 'Suicidal behaviour in Kuala Lumpur, Malaysia'. In K. L. Peng and W. S. Tseng (Eds.), *Suicidal Behaviour in Singapore* (pp. 176–98). Singapore: University of Singapore Press.

Ong, Y. L., and Tsi, W. F. (1982). 'A clinical and psychosocial study of seven cases of anorexia nervosa in Singapore', *Singapore Medical Journal, 23*, 255–61.

Öngel, Ü., and Smith, P. B. (1994). 'Who are we and where are we going?: *JCCP* approaches its 100th issue', *Journal of Cross-Cultural Psychology, 25*(1), 25–53.

Ostendorf, F. (1990). *Sprache und Persönlichkeitsstruktur: Zur Validität des Fünf-Faktoren-Modells der Persönlichkeit [Language and personality structure: Toward the validation of the five-factor model of personality]*. Regensburg: S. Roderer Verlag.

Ots, T. (1990). 'The angry liver, the anxious heart, and the melancholy spleen: The phenomenology of perceptions in Chinese culture', *Culture, Medicine, and Psychiatry, 14*, 21–58.

Ou, C. H. (1982). 'The influence of value clarification on the achievement motivation and social attitudes of junior high school failed students' [in Chinese]. Unpublished Master's thesis, Graduate School of Educational Psychology and Counseling, National Taiwan Normal University.

Overall, J. E., and Hollister, L. E. (1962). 'The brief psychiatric rating scale', *Psychological Reports, 10*, 799–812.

Paivio, A. (1971). *Imagery and Verbal Processes*. New York: Holt, Rinehart and Winston.

Paivio, A. (1986). *Mental Representations: A Dual Coding Approach*. New York: Oxford University Press.

Pak, A. W. P., Dion, K. L., and Dion, K. K. (1985). 'Correlates of self-confidence with English among Chinese students in Toronto', *Canadian Journal of Behavioural Science, 17*, 369–78.

Pak, A. W. P., Dion, K. L., and Dion, K. K. (1991). 'Social-psychological correlates of experienced discrimination: Test of the double jeopardy hypothesis', *International Journal of Intercultural Relations, 15*, 243–54.

Palsane, M. N., and Lam, D. J. (in press). 'Stress and coping from traditional Indian and Chinese perspectives'. In H. Kao and D. Sinha (Eds.), *Asian Perspectives of Psychology*. Hong Kong: Chinese University Press.

Pan, S. (1980). 'On the investigation of basic theoretical problems of psychology', *Chinese Sociology and Anthropology, 12*, 24–42.

Pan, S., and Gao, J. F. (Eds.)(1983). *The Study of Psychology in Ancient China* [in Chinese]. Nanshong: Jiangxi Renmin Chubanshe.

Pan, S., Chen, L., Wang, J. H., and Chen, D. R. (1980). 'Wilhelm Wundt and Chinese psychology' [in Chinese], *Xinli Xuebao, 12*, 367–76.

Pan, Y. H. (1993). '*Renao:* A Chinese social psychological phenomenon' [in Chinese], *Indigenous Psychological Research in Chinese Societies, 1*, 330–45.

Pan, Z. (1990). 'The traditional Chinese culture: A cause of disability'. Paper presented at the International Conference on Sexuality in Asia, Hong Kong, May.

Papousek, M., Papousek, H., and Symmes, D. (1991). 'The meanings of melodies in motherese in tone and stress', *Infant Behavior and Development, 14*, 415–40.

Parsons, O. A., and Schneider, J. M. (1974). 'Locus of control in university students from Eastern and Western societies', *Journal of Consulting and Clinical Psychology, 42*, 456–61.

Paschal, B. J., and Kuo, Y. Y. (1973). 'Anxiety and self-concept among American and Chinese college students', *College Student Journal, 7*, 7–13.

Pask, G. (1976). 'Styles and strategies of learning', *British Journal of Educational Psychology, 46*, 128–48.

Patberg, J. P., and Yonas, A. (1978). 'The effects of the reader's skill and the difficulty of the text on the perceptual span in reading', *Journal of Experimental Psychology: Human Perception*

REFERENCES

555

and Performance, 4, 545–52.

Patterson, K. E., and Morton, J. (1985). 'From orthography to phonology: An attempt at an old inter-

and Performance, 4, 545–52.

Patterson, K. E., and Morton, J. (1985). 'From orthography to phonology: An attempt at an old interpretation'. In K. E. Patterson, J. C. Marshall, and M. Coltheart (Eds.), *Surface Dyslexia: Neuropsychological and Cognitive Studies of Phonological Reading* (pp. 335–59). Hillsdale, NJ: Erlbaum.

Paul, G. L. (1967). 'Outcome research in psychotherapy', *Journal of Consulting Psychology, 31*, 109–18.

Paunonen, S. V., Jackson, D. N., Trzebinski, J., and Forsterling, F. (1992). 'Personality structure across cultures: A multimethod evaluation', *Journal of Personality and Social Psychology, 62*, 447–56.

Paunonen, S. V., Keinonen, M., Trzebinski, J., Forsterling, F., Grishenko-Roze, N., Kouznetsova, L., and Chan, D. W. (1994). 'The structure of personality in six cultures'. Unpublished manuscript, University of Western Ontario.

Pearson, V. J., and Chan, T. W. L. (1993). 'Relationship between parenting stress and social support in mothers of children with learning disabilities: A Chinese experience', *Social Science and Medicine, 37*(2), 267–74.

Pedersen, P. B. (1978). 'Four dimensions of cross-cultural skill in counselor training', *Personnel and Guidance Journal, 56*, 480–4.

Peng, D. L., and Tan, L. H. (1987). 'Frequency and context in visual recognition of Chinese words' [in Chinese], *Psychology Magazine, 2*, 18–25.

Peng, D. L., Guo, D. J., and Zhang, S. L. (1985). 'The retrieval of information of Chinese characters in making similarity judgment under recognition condition' [in Chinese]. *Acta Psychologica Sinica, 3*, 227–34.

Peng, D. L., Orchard, L. N., and Stern, J. A. (1983). 'Evaluation of eye movement variables of Chinese and American readers', *Pavlovian Journal of Biological Sciences, 18*, 94–102.

Peng, K. L. (1992). 'Suicidal behaviour in Singapore'. In K. L. Peng and W. S. Tseng (Eds.), *Suicidal Behaviour in the Asia-Pacific Region* (pp. 176–98). Singapore: University of Singapore Press.

Peng, Y., and Lachman, M. E. (1993). 'Primary and secondary control: Age and cultural differences'. Paper presented at the 101st annual convention of the American Psychological Association, Toronto, August.

Penney, C. G. (1989). 'Modality effects in delayed recall and recognition: Visual is better than auditory', *Quarterly Journal of Experimental Psychology, 41*, 455–70.

Pennington, M. C., Balla, J., Detaramani, C., Poon, A., and Tam, F. (1992). *Towards a model of language choice among Hong Kong tertiary students* (Research Report No. 18). Hong Kong: Department of English, City Polytechnic of Hong Kong.

Peplau, A. (1983). 'Roles and gender'. In H. H. Kelley, E. Berscheid, J. Christensen, T. Harvey, T. Huston, G. Levinger, E. McClintock, A. Peplau, and D. Peterson (Eds.), *Close Relationships* (pp. 220–64). New York: Freeman.

Pepper, S. (1978). *Civil War in China: The Political Struggle, 1945–1949*. Berkeley: University of California Press.

Percy, K. A., and Salter, F. W. (1976). 'Student and staff perceptions and the pursuit of excellence in British higher education', *Higher Education, 5*, 457–73.

Perfetti, C. A., and Bell, L. (1991). 'Phonemic activation during the first 40 ms of word identification: Evidence from backward masking and masked priming', *Journal of Memory and Language, 30*, 473–85.

Perfetti, C. A., Bell, L., and Delaney, S. (1988). 'Automatic phonetic activation in silent word reading: Evidence from backward masking', *Journal of Memory and Language, 27*, 59–70.

Perfetti, C. A., and Zhang, S. (1991). 'Phonological processes in reading Chinese characters', *Journal of Experimental Psychology: Learning, Memory and Cognition, 17*, 633–43.

Perfetti, C. A., and Zhang, S. (in press). 'Very early phonological activation in Chinese reading', *Journal of Experimental Psychology: Learning, Memory, and Cognition*.

Perfetti, C. A., Zhang, S., and Berent, I. (1992). 'Reading in English and Chinese: Evidence for a "universal" phonological principle'. In R. Frost and L. Katz (Eds.), *Orthography, Phonology, Morphology, and Meaning* (pp. 227–48). Amsterdam: North-Holland.

Perls, F. S. (1969). *Gestalt Therapy Verbatim*. New York: Bantam Books.

Petersen S. E., Fox, P. T., Posner, M. I., Mintun, M., and Raichle, M. E. (1988). 'Positron emission tomographic studies of the cortical anatomy of single-word processing', *Nature, 331*, 585–9.

Petersen, S. E., Fox, P. T., Snyder, P. T., and Raichle, M. E. (1990). 'Activation of extrastriate and frontal areas by visual words and word-like stimuli', *Science, 249*, 1041–4.

Peterson, C., and Seligman, M. E. P. (1984). 'Causal explanations as a risk factor for depression: Theory and evidence', *Psychological Review, 31*, 457–503.

Peterson, C., Semmel, A., Bayer, C., Abramson, L., Metalsky, G., and Seligman, M. E. P. (1982). 'The attributional style questionnaire', *Cognitive Therapy and Research, 6*, 287–300.

Peterson, M. F. (1988). 'Organization development programs in Japan and China based on the Performance–Maintenance (PM) theory of leadership', *Organization Dynamics, 16*, 22–38.

Pettigrew, T. F. (1979). 'The ultimate attribution error: Extending Allport's cognitive analysis of prejudice', *Personality and Social Psychology Bulletin, 5*, 461–76.

Petzold, M. (1984). 'The history of psychology in the People's Republic of China', *ASIEN Serial* (Journal of the German Association for Asian Studies), *12* (July).

Petzold, M. (1987). 'The social history of Chinese psychology'. In M. G. Ash and W. R. Woodward (Eds.), *Psychology in Twentieth Century Thought and Society* (pp. 213–31). Cambridge: Cambridge University Press.

Pfeiffer, W. (1994). *Transkulturelle Psychiatrie* (Transcultural psychiatry)(2nd edition). Stuttgart: Thieme.

Pfister, M. O. (1936). 'Mental and nervous diseases among the Chinese'. *Chinese Medical Journal, 50*, 1627–36.

Phares, E. J. (1992). *Clinical Psychology: Concepts, Methods, and Profession* (fourth edition). Pacific Grove, CA: Brooks/Cole.

Phillips, L. D., and Wright, G. N. (1977). 'Cultural differences in viewing uncertainty and assessing probabilities'. In H. Jungermann and G. de Zeeuw (Eds.), *Decision Making and Change in Human Affairs* (pp. 507–519). Dordrecht, the Netherlands: Reidel.

Phillips, M. R. (1993). 'Evaluation and revision of translated Western scales' [in Chinese]. In X. D. Wang (Ed.) *Rating Scales for Mental Health* (pp. 343–51)(published as a supplement to the *Chinese Journal of Mental Health*).

Phillips, M. R. (1993). 'Strategies used by Chinese families coping with schizophrenia'. In D. Davis and S. Harrell (Eds.), *Chinese Families in the Post-Mao Era* (pp. 277–306). Berkeley and Los Angeles: University of California Press.

Phillips, M. R., Xiong, W., Wang, R. W., Gao, Y. H., Wang, X. Q., and Zhang, N. P. (1991). 'Reliability and validity of the Chinese versions of the Scales for Assessment of Positive and Negative Symptoms', *Acta Psychiatrica Scandinavica, 84*, 364–70.

Phua, S. L. (1976). 'Ability factors and familial psychosocial circumstances: Chinese and Malays of Singapore'. Unpublished doctoral thesis, University of Alberta.

Pick, A. D., and Pick, H. L., Jr. (1978). 'Culture and perception'. In E. C. Carterette and M. P. Friedman (Eds.), *Handbook of Perception* (Vol. 10, pp. 19–39). New York: Academic Press.

Pieke, F. N. (1991). 'Chinese educational achievement and folk theories of success', *Anthropology and Education Quarterly, 22*, 162–80.

Pierson, H. D., and Bond, M. H. (1982). 'How do Chinese bilinguals respond to variations of interviewer language and ethnicity?' *Journal of Language and Social Psychology, 1*, 123–39.

Pirenne, M. H. (1975). 'Vision and art'. In E. C. Carterette and M. P. Friedman (Eds.), *Handbook of Perception* (Vol. 5, pp. 433–90). New York: Academic Press.

Plomin, R. (1988). 'The nature and nurture of cognitive abilities'. In R. J. Sternberg (Ed.), *Advances in the Psychology of Human Intelligence, 4*, 1–33.

Plug, C., and Ross, H. E. (1989). 'Historical review'. In M. Hershenson (Ed.), *The Moon Illusion* (pp. 5–27). Hillsdale, NJ: Erlbaum.

Polit, D. F., and Falbo, T. (1988). 'The intellectual achievement of only children, *Journal of Biosocial Science, 20*, 275–85.

Pollatsek, A., and Rayner, K. (1982). 'Eye movement control in reading: The role of word boundaries', *Journal of Experimental Psychology: Human Perception and Performance, 8*, 817–33.

Pollay R., Tse, D. K., and Wang, Z. (1990). 'Advertising, propaganda and value change in economic development: The new cultural revolution in China and attitudes toward advertising', *Journal of Business Research, 20*, 83–96.

Pollock, S. M., and Chen, K. (1986). 'Strive to conquer the Black Stink: Decision analysis in the People's Republic of China', *Interfaces, 16*(2), 31–7.

Polyak, S. L. (1941). *The Retina.* Chicago: University of Chicago Press.

Poon, P., Yu, W. Y., and Chan, J. (1986). 'A correlation between intelligence and auditory reaction time', *Perceptual and Motor Skills, 63*, 375–8.

Poortinga, Y. (1989). 'Equivalence of cross-cultural data: An overview of basic issues', *International Journal of Psychology, 24*, 737–56.

Poston, D. L., and Falbo, T. (1990). 'Academic performance and personality traits of Chinese children: "Onlies" versus others', *American Journal of Sociology, 96*, 433–51.

Poston, D. L., and Yu, M. Y. (1985). 'Quality of life, intellectual development and behavioural characteristics of single children in China: Evidence from a 1980 survey in Changsha, Hunan Province', *Journal of Biosocial Science, 17*, 127–36.

Poston, D. L., and Yu, M. Y. (1990). 'The distribution of the overseas Chinese in the contemporary world', *International Migration Review, 24*, 480–508.

Potter, S. H. (1988). 'The cultural construction of emotion in rural Chinese social life', *Ethos, 16*, 181–208.

President's Council on Competitiveness. (1991). 'Introduction: Litigation and the American economy'. In *Report from the President's Council on Competitiveness: Agenda for Civil Justice Reform in America* (pp. 1–3). Washington, DC: United States Government Printing Office.

Press, B. K. (1987). 'Observation on early childhood development and education in the People's Republic of China', *Early Child Development and Care, 29*, 375–89.

Preston, M. S., and Lambert, W. E. (1969). 'Interlingual interference in a bilingual version of the Stroop color-word task', *Journal of Verbal Learning and Verbal Behavior, 8*, 295–301.

Prince, R. (1991). 'Social phobias in China', *Transcultural Psychiatric Research Review, 28*, 240–6.

Prince, R. H. (1980). 'Variations in psychotherapeutic procedures'. In H. C. Triandis and J. G. Draguns (Eds.), *Handbook of Cross-Cultural Psychology* (Vol. 6: Psychopathology, pp. 291–349). Boston: Allyn and Bacon.

Prior, M. R., Kyrios, M., and Oberklaid, F. (1986). 'Temperament in Australian, American, Chinese, and Greek infants', *Journal of Cross-Cultural Psychology, 17*, 455–74.

Ptraka, G. A., and Bost, W. (1989). 'Socialization objectives of Chinese primary schools: Results of a comparative textbook analysis', *Studies in Educational Evaluation, 15*, 257–76.

Pugh, D. S., and Redding, S. G. (1985). 'A comparative study of the structure and context of Chinese businesses in Hong Kong'. Paper presented at the Association of Teachers of Management Research Conference, Ashridge, England, January.

Pusey, A. W. (1977). 'A comparative study on achievement motivation between Chinese and Americans'. Unpublished Master's thesis, Bucknell University, Lewisburg, PA.

Pye, L. W. (1978). 'Communications and Chinese political culture', *Asian Survey, 18*, 221–46.

Pye, L. W. (1982). *Chinese Commercial Negotiating Styles.* Cambridge, MA: Oelgeschlager, Gunn and Hain.

Pye, L. W. (1984). *China: An Introduction* (third edition). Boston: Little, Brown and Company.

Pye, L. W. (1985). *Asian Power and Politics: The Cultural Dimensions of Authority.* Cambridge, MA: Harvard University Press.

Pye, L. W. (1992). *The Spirit of Chinese Politics.* (revised edition). Cambridge, MA: Harvard University Press.

Qian, M. (1969). *The Spirit of Chinese History* [in Chinese]. Taipei: Ching Wein.

Qing, D. H., Gong, Y. X., and Jie, Y. N. (1992). 'A neuropsychological study of children with learning difficulties' [in Chinese], *Acta Psychologica Sinica, 9*, 97–101.

Radloff, L. S. (1977). 'The CES-D scale: A self-report depression scale for research in the general population', *Applied Psychological Measurement, 1*, 385–401.

Raichle, M. E. (1994). 'Visualizing the mind', *Scientific American, 270*(4), 36–42.

Ralston, D. A., Gustafson, D. J., Cheung, F. M., and Terpstra, R. H. (1993). 'Differences in managerial values: A study of U.S., Hong Kong and PRC managers', *Journal of International Business Studies, 24*, 233–49.

Ralston, D. A., Gustafson, D. J., Elsacs, P. M., Cheung, F. M., and Terpstra, R. H. (1992). 'Eastern values: A comparison of managers in the United States, Hong Kong and the People's Republic of China', *Journal of Applied Psychology, 77*, 664–71.

Raven, J., and Raven, J. H. (1989). *Manual for Raven's Progressive Matrices and Vocabulary Scales: Research Supplement No. 4.* London: H. K. Lewis.

Rayner, K. (1979). 'Eye guidance in reading: Fixation locations within words', *Perception, 8*, 21–30.

Rayner, K., and Pollatsek, A. (1981). 'Eye movement control in reading: Evidence for direct control', *Quarterly Journal of Experimental Psychology, 33*, 351–73.

Rayner, K., and Pollatsek, A. (1989). *The Psychology of Reading*. Englewood Cliffs, NJ: Prentice Hall.

Redding, S. G. (1978). 'Bridging the culture gap', *Asian Business and Investment, 4*, 45–52.

Redding, S. G. (1984). 'Operationalizing the post-Confucian hypothesis: The overseas Chinese case'. Unpublished manuscript, Department of Management Studies, University of Hong Kong.

Redding, S. G. (1990). *The Spirit of Chinese Capitalism*. New York: Walter de Gruyter.

Redding, S. G., and Ng, M. (1982). 'The role of "face" in the organizational perceptions of Chinese managers', *Organization Studies, 3*, 201–19.

Redding, S. G., and Wong, G. Y. Y. (1986). 'The psychology of Chinese organizational behaviour'. In M. H. Bond (Ed.), *The Psychology of the Chinese People* (pp. 267–95). Hong Kong: Oxford University Press.

Reicher, G. M. (1969). 'Perceptual recognition as a function of the meaningfulness of the stimulus material', *Journal of Experimental Psychology, 81*, 275–80.

Republic of China Yearbook (1991). [In Chinese.] Taipei: Chung Cheng Bookstore.

Reuter-Lorenz, P. A., and Baynes, K. (1992). 'Modes of lexical access in the callosotomized brain', *Journal of Cognitive Neuroscience, 4*, 155–64.

Ribeiro Pedro, E. (1981). *Social Stratification and Classroom Discourse: A Sociolinguistic Analysis of Classroom Practice*. Stockholm: Liber Läromedel Lund.

Richards, J. C., Tung, P., and Ng, P. (1992). 'The culture of the English language teacher: A Hong Kong example', *RELC, 23*(1), 81–102.

Rin, H. (1975). 'Suicide in Taiwan'. In N. L. Farberow (Ed.), *Suicide in Different Cultures* (pp. 239–54). Baltimore: University Park Press.

Rin, H., and Lin, T. Y. (1962). 'Mental illness among Formosan Aborigines as compared with Chinese in Taiwan', *Journal of Mental Science*, 123–46.

Rin, H., Schooler, C., and Caudill, W. (1973). 'Symptomatology and hospitalization: Culture, social structure and psychopathology in Taiwan and Japan', *Journal of Nervous and Mental Disease, 157*, 296–312.

Ripple, R. (1989). 'Ordinary creativity', *Contemporary Educational Psychology, 14*, 189–202.

Roberts, D. (Ed.)(1992). *Hong Kong 1992*. Hong Kong: Government Information Services.

Robertson, P. W. (1967). 'Color words and color vision', *Biology and Human Affairs, 33*, 28–33.

Rodd, W. G. (1959). 'A cross-cultural study of Taiwan's schools', *Journal of Social Psychology, 50*, 3–36.

Rodes, S. R. (1983). 'Age-related differences in work attitudes and behavior: A review and conceptual analysis', *Psychological Bulletin, 93*, 328–67.

Roethlisberger, F. J., and Dickson, W. J. (1939). *Management and the Worker: An Account of a Research Program conducted by the Western Electric Company*, Chicago, Cambridge, MA: Harvard University.

Rohde, A. M. (1957). *The Sentence Completion Method: Its Diagnosis and Clinical Application to Mental Disorders*. New York: The Ronald Press.

Rokeach, M. (1973). *The Nature of Human Values*. New York: Free Press.

Rosch, E. (1978). 'Principles of categorization'. In E. Rosch and B. B. Lloyd (Eds.), *Cognition and Categorization* (pp. 27–48). Hillsdale, NJ: Lawrence Erlbaum.

Rosen, S. (1978). 'Sibling and in-law relationships in Hong Kong: The emergent role of Chinese wives', *Journal of Marriage and the Family, 40*, 621–8.

Rosenbaum, M. (1986). 'The repulsion hypothesis: On the non-development of relationships', *Journal of Personality and Social Psychology, 51*, 1156–66.

Rosenthal, D. A., and Feldman, S. S. (1990). 'The acculturation of Chinese immigrants: Perceived effects on family functioning of length of residence in two cultural contexts', *Journal of Genetic Psychology, 15*, 495–514.

Rosenthal, D. A., and Feldman, S. S. (1991). 'The influence of perceived family and personal factors on self-reported school performance of Chinese and Western high school students', *Journal of Research on Adolescence, 1*, 135–54.

Rosenthal, D. A., and Feldman, S. S. (1992). 'The nature and stability of ethnic identity in Chinese youth: Effects of length of residence in two cultural contexts', *Journal of Cross-Cultural Psychology, 23*, 214–27.

Rothbaum, F., Weisz, J. R., and Snyder, S. S. (1982). 'Changing the world and changing the self: A two-process model of perceived control', *Journal of Personality and Social Psychology, 42,* 5–37.

Rotter, J. B. (1966). 'Generalized expectancies for internal versus external control of reinforcement', *Psychological Monographs, 80*(1), 1–28.

Ruan, F., and Matsumura, M. (1991). *Sex in China: Studies in Sexology in Chinese Culture.* New York: Plenum Press.

Rubenstein, H., Garfield, L., and Millikan, J. A. (1970). 'Homographic entries in the internal lexicon', *Journal of Verbal Learning and Verbal Behavior, 9,* 487–92.

Rubenstein, H., Lewis, S. S., and Rubenstein, M. A. (1971). 'Evidence for phonemic recoding in visual word recognition', *Journal of Verbal Learning and Verbal Behavior, 10,* 645–57.

Russell, D. (1982). 'The causal dimension scale: A measure of how individuals perceive causes', *Journal of Personality and Social Psychology, 42,* 1137–45.

Russell, I. L. (1969). 'Motivation for school achievement: Measurement and validation', *Journal of Educational Research, 62,* 263–6.

Russell, J. A. (1978). 'Evidence of convergent validity on the dimensions of affect', *Journal of Personality and Social Psychology, 36,* 1152–68.

Russell, J. A. (1983). 'Pancultural aspects of the human conceptual organization of emotions', *Journal of Personality and Social Psychology, 45,* 1281–8.

Russell, J. A. (1991). 'Culture and the categorization of emotions', *Psychological Bulletin, 110,* 426–50.

Russell, J. A. (1994). 'Is there universal recognition of emotion from facial expression? A review of the cross-cultural studies', *Psychological Bulletin, 115,* 102–41.

Russell, J. A., and Sato, K. (1995). 'Comparing emotion concepts between languages', *Journal of Cross-Cultural Psychology, 26,* 384-91.

Russell, J. A., Lewicka, M., and Niit, T. (1989). 'A cross-cultural study of a circumplex model of affect', *Journal of Personality and Social Psychology, 57,* 848–56.

Ryan, J. J., Dai, X. Y., and Paolo, A. M. (1992). 'Intersubtest scatter on the mainland Chinese version of the Wechsler Adult Intelligence Scale', *Psychological Assessment, 4,* 60–2.

Sakei, C., and Borow, H. (1985). 'Counseling and psychotherapy: East and West'. In P. B. Pedersen (Ed.), *Handbook of Cross-Cultural Counseling and Therapy* (pp. 221–9). London: Greenwood Press.

Salili, F., and Hau, K. T. (1994). 'The effect of teachers' evaluative feedback on Chinese students' perception of ability: A cultural and situational analysis', *Educational Studies, 20,* 223–36.

Salili, F., and Mak, P. H. T. (1988). 'Subjective meaning of success in high and low achievers', *International Journal of Intercultural Relations, 12,* 125–38.

Sandiford, P., and Kerr, R. (1926). 'Intelligence of Chinese and Japanese children', *Journal of Educational Psychology, 17,* 361–7.

Sapir, E. (1921). *Language: An Introduction to the Study of Speech.* New York: Harcourt, Brace.

Sayegh, L., and Lasry, J. C. (1993). 'Immigrants' adaptation to Canada: Assimilation, acculturation, and orthogonal cultural identification', *Canadian Psychology, 34,* 98–109.

Scarborough, D. L., Cortese, C., and Scarborough, H. (1977). 'Frequency and repetition effects in lexical memory', *Journal of Experimental Psychology: Human Perception and Performance, 7,* 3–12.

Scherer, K. R., Wallbott, H. G., and Summerfield, A. B. (Eds.)(1986). *Experiencing Emotion: A Cross-Cultural Study.* Cambridge: Cambridge University Press.

Scheuch, E. K. (1970). 'Cross-national comparisons using aggregate data'. In A. Etzioni and F. L. Dubow (Eds.), *Comparative Perspectives: Theories and Methods* (pp. 365–86). Boston, MA: Little, Brown and Co.

Schieffelin, B. B. (1987). 'Do different worlds mean different words? An example from Papua New Guinea'. In S. W. Philips, S. Steele, and C. Tanz (Eds.), *Language, Gender and Sex in Comparative Perspective* (pp. 249–60). Cambridge: Cambridge University Press.

Schieffelin, B. B., and Ochs, E. (1986). 'Language socialization', *Annual Review of Anthropology, 15,* 163–91.

Schieffelin, B. B., and Ochs, E. (1986). *Language Socialization Across Cultures.* Cambridge: Cambridge University Press.

Schneider, B., Hieshima, J. A., Lee, S., and Plank, S. (1994). 'East Asian academic success in the

United States: Family, school, and community explanations'. In P. M. Greenfield and R. R. Cocking (Eds.), *Cross-Cultural Roots of Minority Child Development* (pp. 323–50). Hillsdale, NJ: Lawrence Erlbaum.

Schneider, M. J. (1985). 'Verbal and nonverbal indices of the communicative performance and acculturation of Chinese immigrants', *International Journal of Intercultural Relations, 9*, 271–83.

Schwartz, S. H. (1992). 'Universals in the content and structure of values: Theoretical advances and empirical tests in 20 countries'. In M. Zanna (Ed.), *Advances in Experimental Social Psychology* (Vol. 25, pp. 1–65). New York: Academic Press.

Schwartz, S. H. (1994). 'Cultural dimensions of values: Toward an understanding of national differences'. In U. Kim, H. C. Triandis, C. Kagitcibasi, S. C. Choi, and G. Yoon (Eds.), *Individualism and Collectivism: Theory, Method, and Application* (pp. 85–119). Thousand Oaks, CA: Sage.

Schwartz, S. H., and Bilsky, W. (1987). 'Toward a universal psychological structure of human values', *Journal of Personality and Social Psychology, 53*, 550–62.

Schwartz, S. H., and Bilsky, W. (1990). 'Toward a theory of the universal content and structure of values: Extensions and cross-cultural replications', *Journal of Personality and Social Psychology, 58*, 878–91.

Schwertfeger, M. (1982). 'Interethnic marriage and divorce in Hawaii: A panel study of 1968 first marriages', *Marriage and Family Review, 5*, 49–59.

Science Service (1994). *The 53rd Annual Science Talent Search.* Washington, DC: Westinghouse Electric Corporation.

Scofield, R. W., and Sun, C. W. (1960). 'A comparative study of the differential effect upon personality of Chinese and American child training practices', *Journal of Social Psychology, 52*, 221–4.

Scotton, C. M., and Zhu, W. J. (1983). '"Tongzhi" in China: Language change and its conversational consequences', *Language in Society, 12*, 477–94.

Secord, P. (1982). 'The origin and maintenance of social roles: The case of sex roles'. In W. Ickes and E. Knowles (Eds.), *Personality, Roles and Social Behaviour* (pp. 33–53). New York: Springer Verlag.

Segall, M. H., Campbell, D. T., and Herskovits, M. S. (1963). 'Cultural differences in the perception of geometric illusions', *Science, 139*, 769–71.

Segall, M. H., Campbell, D. T., and Herskovits, M. S. (1966). *The Influence of Culture on Visual Perception.* Indianapolis, ID: Bobbs-Merrill.

Seidenberg, M. S. (1985). 'The time course of phonological code activation in two writing systems', *Cognition, 19*, 1–30.

Seidenberg, M. S. (1992). 'Beyond orthographic depth in reading: Equitable division of labor'. In R. Frost and L. Katz (Eds.), *Orthography, Phonology, Morphology, and Meaning* (pp. 85–118). Amsterdam: North-Holland.

Seidenberg, M. S. (1993). 'Connectionist models and cognitive theory', *Psychological Science, 4*, 228–35.

Seidenberg, M. S., and McClelland, J. L. (1989). 'A distributed, developmental model of word recognition and naming', *Psychological Review, 96*, 523–68.

Seidenberg, M. S., Waters, G. S., Barnes, M. A., and Tanenhaus, M. K. (1984). 'When does irregular spelling or pronunciation influence word recognition?' *Journal of Verbal Learning and Verbal Behavior, 23*, 383–404.

Selinker, L. (1972). 'Interlanguage', *International Review of Applied Linguistics, 10*, 209–31.

Semenik, R., Zhou, N. and Moore, W. L. (1986). 'Chinese managers' attitudes toward advertising in China', *Journal of Advertising, 15*(4), 56–62.

Semin, G. R., and Fiedler, K. (1992). *Language, Interaction, and Social Cognition.* Newbury Park, CA: Sage.

Serpell, R. (1976). *Culture's Influence on Behaviour.* London: Methuen.

Shallice, T., Warrington, E. K., and McCarthy, R. (1983). 'Reading without semantics', *Quarterly Journal of Experimental Psychology, 35*, 111–38.

Sharwood Smith, M. (1991). 'Language modules and bilingual processing'. In E. Bialystok (Ed.), *Language Processing in Bilingual Children* (pp. 10–24). New York: Cambridge University Press.

Shaver, P. R., Wu, S., and Schwartz, J. C. (1992). 'Cross-cultural similarities and differences in emotion and its representation: A prototype approach'. In M. S. Clark (Ed.), *Review of Personality and Social Psychology* (Vol. 13: Emotion, pp. 175–212). Newbury Park, CA: Sage.

Shek, D. T. (1987). 'Reliability and factorial structure of the Chinese version of the General Health Questionnaire', *Journal of Clinical Psychology, 43,* 683–91.

Shek, D. T. (1989). 'Validity of the Chinese version of the General Health Questionnaire', *Journal of Clinical Psychology, 45,* 890–7.

Shek, D. T. (1990). 'Reliability and factorial structure of the Chinese version of the Beck Depression Inventory', *Journal of Clinical Psychology, 46,* 35–43.

Shek, D. T. (1991). 'What does the Chinese version of the Beck Depression Inventory measure in Chinese students—general psychopathology or depression?' *Journal of Clinical Psychology, 47,* 381–90.

Shek, D. T. (1993). 'Factor structure of the Chinese version of the General Health Questionnaire (GHQ-30): A confirmatory factor analysis', *Journal of Clinical Psychology, 49,* 678–84.

Shek, D. T. L. (in press). 'Mental health of Chinese adolescents: A critical review'. In S. Lau (Ed.), *Growing Up the Chinese Way: The Role of Culture in Socialization.* Hong Kong: Chinese University Press.

Shek, D. T. L., and Cheung C. H. (1990). 'Locus of coping in a sample of Chinese working parents: Reliance on self or seeking help from others', *Social Behaviour and Personality, 18,* 327–46.

Shek, D. T. L., and Mak, J. W. K. (1987). *Psychological Well-being of Working Parents in Hong Kong: Mental Health, Stress and Coping Responses.* Hong Kong: Hong Kong Christian Service.

Shek, D. T. L., and Tsang, K. M (1993). *Care-givers of Preschool Mentally Handicapped Children in Hong Kong: Their Stress, Coping Resources, and Psychological Well-being.* Hong Kong: Heep Hong Society for Handicapped Children.

Shen, E. (1927). 'An analysis of eye movements in the reading of Chinese', *Journal of Experimental Psychology, 10,* 158–83.

Shen, K. S. (1991). 'A study of S. Y. Nian's Optics' [in Chinese]. In T. H. Yang and I. L. Huang (Eds.), *Treatise on the Contemporary History of Chinese Science and Technology* (pp. 173–93). Taipei: Academia Sinica.

Shen, Q. W., Liu, S. S., and Huang, J. Y. (1989). 'Employees' boycott behavior and attitude towards management control as well as level of satisfaction' [in Chinese], *Management Review, 8,* 159–75.

Shen, W. S. (1978). 'A study of the relationship between job characteristics and job satisfaction: A comparison of experimental and non-experimental banks' [in Chinese]. Unpublished Master's thesis, National Chengchi University, Taiwan.

Shen, Y. (1981). 'Analysis of *Ji jiu pian*' [in Chinese], *History Studies, 3,* 61-87.

Shenkar, O., and Ronen, S. (1987). 'Structure and importance of work goals among managers in the People's Republic of China', *Academy of Management Journal, 30,* 564–76.

Shenkar, O., and Ronen, S. (1987). 'The cultural context of negotiations: The implications of Chinese interpersonal norms', *Journal of Applied Behavioral Science, 23,* 263–75.

Shenkar, O., and von Glinow, M. A. (1994). 'Paradoxes in organizational theory and research: Using the case of China to illustrate national contingency', *Management Science, 40,* 56–71.

Shi, Y. C. (1992). 'The study of academic success and failure attribution of some Chinese college students' [in Chinese]. Unpublished Master's thesis, Beijing University.

Shieh, Y. (1990). 'A survey of female sexuality in Taiwan'. Paper presented at the International Conference on Sexuality in Asia, Hong Kong, May.

Shih, Y. C. (1992). 'The university students' academic achievement attribution in mainland China' [in Chinese]. Unpublished Master's thesis, Beijing University.

Shu, H., and Zhang, H. C. (1987). 'The processing of pronouncing Chinese characters by proficient mature readers' [in Chinese], *Acta Psychologica Sinica, 3,* 282–90.

Shu, S. C. (1979). 'Impact of teachers' expectation on teacher-student interaction and students' personal qualities' [in Chinese], *Bulletin of Educational Psychology* (Taiwan), *12,* 183–94.

Shweder, R. A., and Sullivan, M. A. (1990). 'The semiotic subject of cultural psychology'. In L. A. Pervin (Ed.), *Handbook of Personality: Theory and Research* (pp. 399–416). New York: Guilford.

Shweder, R. A., and Sullivan, M. A. (1993). 'Cultural psychology: Who needs it?' *Annual Review of Psychology, 44,* 497–523.

Sidel, R. (1973). 'The role of revolutionary optimism in the treatment of mental illness in the People's Republic of China', *American Journal of Orthopsychiatry, 43*, 732–6.

Silva, F., Avia, M. D., Sanz, J., and Grana, J. L. (1993). 'The Five-Factor Model in Spain: Contributions to the structure of the NEO-PI'. Paper presented at the sixth meeting of the International Society for the Study of Individual Differences, Baltimore, MD, July.

Simpson, G. B., and Kang, H. (1994). 'The flexible use of phonological information in word recognition in Korean', *Journal of Memory and Language, 33*, 319–31.

Singelis, T. M., Bond, M. H., Lai, S. Y., and Sharkey, W. F. (1995). 'Self construal, self-esteem, and embarrassability in Hong Kong, Hawaii, and Mainland United States'. Manuscript submitted for publication.

Singer, K. (1972). 'Drinking patterns and alcoholism in the Chinese', *British Journal of Addiction, 67*, 3–14.

Singer, M. (1961). 'A survey of culture and personality theory and research'. In B. Kaplan (Ed.), *Studying Personality Cross-Culturally* (pp. 9–90). Evanston, IL: Row, Peterson.

Sinha, D., and Tripathi, R. C. (1994). 'Individualism in a collectivist culture: A case of coexistence of opposites'. In U. Kim, H. C. Triandis, C. Kagistcibasi, S. C. Choi, and G. Yoon (Eds.), *Individualism and Collectivism: Theory, Method, and Applications* (pp. 123–36). London: Sage.

Sit, V. F. S., and Wong, S. L. (1989). *Small and Medium Industries in an Export-Oriented Economy: The Case of Hong Kong.* Hong Kong: Centre of Asian Studies.

Siu, S. F. (1992). *Toward an Understanding of Chinese-American Educational Achievement: A Literature Review.* Boston, MA: Center for Families, Communities, Schools, and Children's Learning.

Sivan, A., Leung, R., Gow, L., and Kember, D. (1991). 'Towards more active forms of teaching and learning in Hospitality Studies', *International Journal of Hospitality Management, 10*(4), 369–79.

Smith, C. P. (1969). 'The origin and expression of achievement-related motives in children'. In C. P. Smith (Ed.), *Achievement-Related Motives in Children* (pp. 102–50). New York: Russell Sage.

Smith, D. C. (1991). 'Children of China: An inquiry into the relationship between Chinese family life and academic achievement in modern Taiwan', *Asian Culture Quarterly, 14*, 1–29.

Smith, D. H. (1973). *Confucius.* London: Temple Smith.

Smith, M. C., and Kirsner, K. (1982). 'Language and orthography as irrelevant features in colour-word and picture-word Stroop interference', *Quarterly Journal of Experimental Psychology: Human Experimental Psychology, 34*, 153–70.

Smith, P. B., and Bond, M. H. (1993). *Social Psychology Across Cultures: Analysis and Perspectives.* Hemel Hempstead, UK: Harvester Wheatsheaf.

Smith, P. B., Dugan, S., and Trompenaars, F. (in press). 'National culture and the values of organizational employees', *Journal of Cross-Cultural Psychology.*

Smith, P. B., Misumi, J., Tayeb, M. H., Peterson, M. F., and Bond, M. H. (1989). 'On the generality of leadership styles across cultures', *Journal of Occupational Psychology, 62*, 97–110.

Smith, P. B., and Peterson, M. F. (1988). *Leadership, Organizations and Culture: An Event Management Model.* London: Sage.

Smith, P. B., and Peterson, M. F. (1994). 'Leadership as event management: A cross-cultural survey based upon managers from 25 nations'. Chairperson's paper presented in symposium conducted at the International Congress of Applied Psychology, Madrid, July.

Smith, P. B., Peterson, M. F., and Wang, Z. M. (in press). 'The management of organizational events in China, USA and Britain', *Journal of International Business Studies.*

Smith, P. B., and Tayeb, M. H. (1988). 'Organizational structure and processes'. In M. H. Bond (Ed.), *The Cross-Cultural Challenge to Social Psychology* (pp. 153–64). Newbury Park, CA: Sage.

Smith, P. B., Trompenaars, F., and Dugan, S. (1993). 'The Rotter locus of control scale in 45 countries: A test of cultural relativity'. Manuscript submitted for publication.

Smith, P. B., and Wang, Z. M. (1994). 'Leadership, decision-making and cultural context: Some studies of joint ventures'. Paper presented in a symposium conducted at the International Congress of Applied Psychology, Madrid, July.

Snook, I. A. (1972). 'Indoctrination and moral responsibility'. In I. A. Snook (Ed.), *Concepts of Indoctrination: Philosophical Essays* (pp. 152–61). London: Routledge and Kegan Paul.

Snow, C. E., and Locke, J. L. (Eds.)(1987). 'The Competition Model and bilingualism', *Applied*

Psycholinguistics (Special Issue), *8*(4).

Snyder, C., and Fromkin, H. (1980). 'The theory of uniqueness'. In C. Snyder and H. Fromkin (Eds.), *Uniqueness: The Human Pursuit of Differences* (pp. 31–55). New York: Plenum Press.

Snyder, M. (1974). 'Self-monitoring of expressive behavior', *Journal of Personality and Social Psychology, 30,* 526–37.

Snyder, M., and Simpson, D. (1987). 'Orientations toward romantic relationships'. In D. Perlman and S. Duck (Eds.), *Intimate Relationships: Development, Dynamics and Deterioration* (pp. 45–62). Newbury Park: Sage.

Sodowsky, G. R., Lai, E. W. M., and Plake, B. S. (1991). 'Moderating effects of sociocultural variables on acculturation attitudes of Hispanics and Asian Americans', *Journal of Counseling and Development, 70,* 194–204.

Solomon, R. H. (1971). *Mao's Revolution and the Chinese Political Culture.* Berkeley: University of California Press.

Sommer, S. (1984). 'Adults evaluating their emotions: A cross-cultural perspective'. In C. Zander Malatesta and C. Izard (Eds.), *Emotion in Adult Development* (pp. 319–38). Beverly Hills, CA: Sage.

Song, W. T. (1990). 'The ecological impact on contemporary child psychiatry in Taiwan'. Paper presented at the 12th congress of the International Association for Child and Adolescent Psychiatry and Allied Professions, Kyoto, July.

Song, W. Z. (1981). 'Application of the Minnesota Multiphasic Personality Inventory in some areas of the People's Republic of China'. Paper presented at the Seventh International Conference on Personality Assessment, Honolulu.

Song, W. Z., Cui, C. Z., Cheung, F. M., and Hong, Y. Y. (1987). 'Comparison of the personality characteristics of Beijing and Hong Kong students: Content analysis on the MMPI item endorsement differences' [in Chinese]. *Acta Psychologica Sinica, 19,* 263–9.

Song, W. Z., Zhang, J. X., Zhang, J. P., Cheung, F. M., and Leung, K. (1993). 'The significance and process of developing Chinese Personality Assessment Inventory (CPAI)' [in Chinese], *Acta Psychologica Sinica, 25*(4), 400–7.

Song, Y. P., and Fong, Y. K. (1990). 'A clinical report of 9 cases of anorexia nervosa', *Chinese Mental Health Journal, 4,* 24–5.

Sonoda, S. (1994). 'Japanese management in Chinese context: A tentative analysis of acculturation process in Sino-Japanese joint ventures'. In Institute of Social Sciences, Chuo University (Ed.), *Market Economy and Social Justice* (pp. 277–91). Tokyo: Chuo University.

Spaai, G. W. G., and Chen, H. C. (1992). 'Beginning reading instruction with the aid of computer speech'. In F. L. Engel, D. G. Bouwhuis, T. Bosser, and G. d'Ydewalle (Eds.), *Cognitive Modelling and Interactive Environments in Language Learning* (pp. 167–73). Berlin: Springer-Verlag.

Special Education Section and Educational Research Establishment (1986). *Technical Report on the Standardization of the Hong Kong Wechsler Intelligence Scale for Children.* Hong Kong: Education Department.

Stanley, J. C. (1989). 'How greatly do Chinese students eclipse ours?' *Journal for the Education of the Gifted, 12*(4), 306–9.

Stanners, R. F., Jastrzembski, J. E., and Westbrook, A. (1975). 'Frequency and visual quality in a word–nonword classification task', *Journal of Verbal Learning and Verbal Behavior, 14,* 259–64.

Stanners, R. F., Neiser, J. J., and Painton, S. (1979). 'Memory representations for prefixed words', *Journal of Verbal Learning and Verbal Behavior, 18,* 733–43.

State Education Commission (PRC)(1992). *Educational Statistics Yearbook of China 1991/1992.* Beijing: People's Education Press.

Stern, K. A. (1978). 'Eye movements, reading, and cognition'. In J. W. Senders, D. F. Fisher, and R. A. Monty (Eds.), *Eye Movements and the Higher Psychological Functions* (pp. 145–55). Hillsdale, NJ: Lawrence Erlbaum.

Sternberg, R. J. (1988). 'A triarchic view of intelligence in cross-cultural perspective'. In S. H. Irvine and J. Berry (Eds.), *Human Abilities in Cultural Context* (pp. 60–85). Cambridge: Cambridge University Press.

Sternberg, R. J., and Gardner, M. K. (1982). 'A componential interpretation of the general factor in human intelligence'. In H. J. Eysenck (Ed.), *A Model for Intelligence* (pp. 231–54). New York:

Springer-Verlag.

Stevenson, H. W. (1987). 'The Asian advantage: The case of mathematics', *American Educator, 11*(2), 26–31, 47.

Stevenson, H. W. (1992). 'Learning from Asian schools', *Scientific American, 267*, 70–6.

Stevenson, H. W., Chen, C., and Lee, S. Y. (1993). 'Mathematics achievement of Chinese, Japanese, and American: Ten years later', *Science, 259*, 53–8.

Stevenson, H. W., Chen, C., and Lee, S. Y. (1993). 'Motivation and achievement of gifted children in East Asia and the United States', *Journal for the Education of the Gifted, 16*(3), 223–50.

Stevenson, H. W., Lee, S. Y., Chen, C. S., Stigler, J. W., Hsu, C. C., and Kitayama, S. (1990). 'Contexts of achievement: A study of American, Chinese, and Japanese children', *Monographs of the Society for Research in Child Development, 55*(1–2)(Serial No. 221).

Stevenson, H. W., and Lee, S. Y. (1990). 'Contexts of achievement: A study of American, Chinese, and Japanese children', *Monographs of the Society for Research in Child Development, 55*(2), 1–116.

Stevenson, H. W., and Lee, S. Y. (in press). The East Asian version of whole-class teaching. *Educational Policy.*

Stevenson, H. W., Lee, S. Y., and Graham, T. (1993). 'Chinese and Japanese kindergartens: Case study in comparative research'. In B. Spodek (Eds.), *Handbook of Research on the Education of Young Children* (pp. 519–35). New York: Macmillan.

Stevenson, H. W., Lee, S. Y., and Stigler, J. W. (1986). 'Mathematics achievement of Chinese, Japanese, and American children', *Science, 231*, 693–9.

Stevenson, H. W., and Stigler, J. W. (1992). *The Learning Gap.* New York: Summit.

Stevenson, H. W., Stigler, J. W., Lee, S. Y., Lucker, G. W., Kitamura, S., and Hsu, C. C. (1985). 'Cognitive performance and academic achievement of Japanese, Chinese, and American children', *Child Development, 56*, 718–34.

Stigler, J. W., Lee, S., and Stevenson, H. W. (1990). *Mathematical Knowledge of Japanese, Chinese, and American Children.* Reston, VA: National Council of Teachers of Mathematics.

Stigler, J. W., Lee, S. Y., Lucker, G. W., and Stevenson, H. W. (1982). 'Curriculum and achievement in mathematics: A study of elementary school children in Japan, Taiwan, and the United States', *Journal of Educational Psychology, 74*, 315–22.

Stigler, J. W., Smith, S., and Mao, L. W. (1985). 'The self-perception of competence by Chinese children', *Child Development, 56*(5), 1259–70.

Stipek, D., Weiner, B., and Li, K. (1989). 'Testing some attribution-emotion relations in the People's Republic of China', *Journal of Personality and Social Psychology, 56*, 109–16.

Stokols, D. (1992). 'Establishing and maintaining healthy environments', *American Psychologist, 1*, 6–21.

Stover, L. E. (1974). *The Cultural Ecology of Chinese Civilization.* New York: New American Library.

Stroop, J. R. (1935). 'Studies of interference in serial verbal reactions', *Journal of Experimental Psychology, 18*, 643–62.

Stump, G. T. (1981). 'The interpretation of frequency adjectives', *Linguistics and Philosophy, 4*, 221–57.

Su, F., Wang, X. D., Yan, H. Q., Chu, Z. M., Huang, Y. X., and Huang, Z. M. (1986). 'Psychological consultation and neuroses' [in Chinese], *Chinese Journal of Neurology and Psychiatry, 19*, 311–13.

Su, L. Y., Li, X. R., and Zhiang, X. A. (1991). 'The influence of family factors on the behaviour of young children' [in Chinese]. *Chinese Journal of Mental Health, 5*(5), 216–18.

Su, S. L., and Huang, K. L. (1992). 'Secondary school teachers' attitudes towards teachers' union participation and strikes' [in Chinese]. *Education and Psychology Research, 15*, 173–214.

Sue, D. W. (1977). 'Counseling the culturally different: A conceptual analysis', *Personnel and Guidance Journal, 55*, 422–5.

Sue, D. W. (1993). 'Psychotherapy with Chinese in the United States: A racial/cultural identity development model'. In L. Y. Cheng, F. Cheung, and C. N. Chen (Eds.), *Psychotherapy with the Chinese* (pp. 187–202). Hong Kong: Department of Psychiatry, the Chinese University of Hong Kong.

Sue, D. W., and Kirk, B. A. (1972). 'Psychological characteristics of Chinese-American students', *Journal of Counseling Psychology, 19*, 471–8.

Sue, D. W., and Sue, D. (1990). *Counseling the Culturally Different* (second edition). New York: John Wiley and Sons.

Sue, D. W., and Sue, S. (1972). 'Counseling Chinese-Americans', *Personnel and Guidance Journal, 50,* 637–44.

Sue, S. (1993). 'Mental health issues confronting Asians in the changing world', *Asian Journal of Counselling, 2,* 61–70.

Sue, S. (1993). 'Psychotherapy with Chinese in the United States: The transmission of Chinese cultural values'. In L. Y. Cheng, F. Cheung, and C. N. Chen (Eds.), *Psychotherapy for the Chinese* (pp. 175–86). Hong Kong: Department of Psychiatry, the Chinese University of Hong Kong.

Sue, S., and McKinney, H. (1975). 'Asian-Americans in the community mental health care system', *American Journal of Orthopsychiatry, 45,* 111–18.

Sue, S., and Okazaki, S. (1990). 'Asian-American educational achievements: A phenomenon in search of an explanation', *American Psychologist, 45,* 913–20.

Sue, S., and Sue, D. W. (1971). 'Chinese-American personality and mental health', *Amerasia Journal, 1,* 36–49.

Sue, S., and Sue, D. W. (1974). 'MMPI comparisons between Asian-American and non-Asian students utilizing a student health psychiatric clinic', *Journal of Counseling Psychology, 21,* 423–7.

Sue, S., and Zane, N. (1987). 'The role of culture and cultural techniques in psychotherapy: A critique and reformulation', *American Psychologist, 42,* 37–45.

Sue, S., and Zane, N. W. S. (1985). 'Academic achievement and socioemotional adjustment among Chinese university students', *Journal of Counseling Psychology, 32,* 570–9.

Suinn, R. M., Ahuna, C., and Khoo, G. (1992). 'The Suinn–Lew Asian Self-identity Acculturation Scale: Concurrent and factorial validation', *Educational and Psychological Measurement, 52,* 1046–51.

Suinn, R. M., and Oskamp, S. (1969). *The Predictive Validity of Projective Measures: A Fifteen Year Evaluative Review of Research.* Springfield, IL: Charles C. Thomas.

Suinn, R. M., Rickard-Figueroa, K., Lew, S., and Vigil, P. (1987). 'The Suinn-Lew Asian Self-Identity Acculturation Scale: An initial report', *Educational and Psychological Measurement, 47,* 401–7.

Sun, C. H. (1993). 'The five interpersonal relationships in the Four Books: A study of Confucian ethics', *National Taiwan University Journal of Sociology, 22,* 1–48.

Sun, C. F., and Givon, T. (1985). 'On the so-called SOV word order in Mandarin Chinese: A quantified text study and its implications', *Language, 61,* 329–51.

Sun, F., Morita, M., and Stark, L. W. (1985). 'Comparative patterns of reading eye movement in Chinese and English', *Perception and Psychophysics, 37,* 502–6.

Sun, K. T. (1982). *The Dispute of Tradition and Westernization in the Late Qing Dynasty* [in Chinese]. Taipei: Shangwu Publishing Co.

Sun, L. J. (1990). *The Deep Structure of the Chinese Culture* (revised edition)[in Chinese]. Taipei: Tong Shan Publishing Company.

Sun, L. K. (1991). 'Contemporary Chinese culture: Structure and emotionality', *The Australian Journal of Chinese Affairs, 26,* 1–41.

Sun, L. P. (1991). 'An analysis of the pattern of Western exogenous modernization' [in Chinese], *Chinese Social Sciences* (PRC), *2,* 213–23.

Sun, Y. M. (1991). 'Analysis of the student's successful exam results: A cross-cultural study of attributional theory' [in Chinese], *Xinli Xuebao, 2,* 178–87.

Sung, B. L. (1985). 'Bicultural conflicts in Chinese immigrant children', *Journal of Comparative Family Studies, 16,* 255–69.

Sung, B. L. (1987). *The Adjustment Experience of Chinese Immigrant Children in New York City.* New York: Center for Migration Studies.

Sung, B. L. (1990). 'Chinese American intermarriage', *Journal of Comparative Family Studies, 21,* 337–52.

Sung, K. Y. (1989). 'Some perspectives on achievement and economical ethics in Ming and Qing family precepts' [in Chinese], *Chinese Studies* (Taiwan), *7*(1), 195–214.

Sung, M. M. Y. (1979). 'Chinese language and culture: A study of homonyms, lucky words and taboos', *Journal of Chinese Linguistics, 7,* 15–28.

Sunnafrank, M., and Miller, G. (1981). 'The role of initial conversations in determining attraction to similar and dissimilar strangers', *Human Communication Research, 8*, 16–25.

T'sou, B. (1989). 'Some language phenomena in Hong Kong and China' [in Chinese], *Chinese University of Hong Kong Chinese Language Bulletin, 4*, 3–9.

Taft, M. (1979). 'Recognition of affixed words and the word frequency effect', *Memory and Cognition, 7*, 263–72.

Taft, M., and Chen, H. C. (1992). 'Judging homophony in Chinese: The influence of tones'. In H. C. Chen and O. J. L. Tzeng (Eds.), *Language Processing in Chinese* (pp. 151–72). Amsterdam: Elsevier.

Taft, M., and Russell, B. (1992). 'Pseudohomophone naming and the word frequency effect', *Quarterly Journal of Experimental Psychology, 45*, 51–71.

Taft, M., Huang, J. S., and Zhu, X. P. (1993). 'The influence of character frequency on word recognition responses in Chinese'. Paper presented at the Sixth International Symposium on Cognitive Aspects of the Chinese Language, Taipei.

Taiwan Work-related Values Research Team (1993). *Taiwan Work-related Values Report.* Taiwan: Faculty of Management, National Taiwan University.

Tajfel, H. (1981). *Human Groups and Social Categories.* Cambridge: Cambridge University Press.

Tajfel, H. (1982). 'Social psychology of intergroup relations', *Annual Review of Psychology, 33*, 1–39.

Tan, C. T., and Farley, J. U. (1987). 'The impact of cultural patterns on cognition and intention in Singapore', *Journal of Consumer Research, 13*(4), 540–4.

Tan, H. (1967). 'Intercultural study of counseling expectancies', *Journal of Counseling Psychology, 41*, 122–30.

Tan, J. L. (1986). 'Problems in the revision of the WAIS and some other psychological tests' [in Chinese], *Acta Psychologica Sinica, 18*, 333–41.

Tan, L. H., and Peng, D. L. (1989). 'Effects of context and frequency on recognition of Chinese words' [in Chinese], *Psychological Science Newsletter, 2*, 1–12.

Tan, L. H., Hoosain, R., and Peng, D. L. (1995). 'The role of early presemantic phonological code in Chinese character identification', *Journal of Experimental Psychology: Learning, Memory, and Cognition, 21*, 43–54.

Tan, S. (1991). *Best Chinese Idioms* (Z. Shuhan and T. Bowen, Trans.). Hong Kong: Hai Feng Publishing Co.

Tanaka, K. (1993). 'Neuronal mechanisms of object recognition', *Science, 262*, 685–8.

Tanaka-Matsumi, J. (1979). '*Taijin–Kyofusho:* Diagnostic and cultural issues in Japanese psychiatry', *Culture, Medicine and Psychiatry, 3*, 231–45.

Tanaka-Matsumi, J., and Marsella, A. J. (1976). 'Cross-cultural variations in the phenomenlogical experience of depression: I. Word association studies', *Journal of Cross-Cultural Psychology, 7*, 379–96.

Tang, K. C. C. (1991). 'Effects of different assessment methods on tertiary students' approaches to studying'. Unpublished doctoral thesis, University of Hong Kong.

Tang, Q. P., and Gong, Y. X. (1992). 'Standardization and testing of the Visual Retention Test' [in Chinese], *Chinese Mental Health Journal, 6*(3), 121–4.

Tang, S. F. Y., and Kirkbride, P. S. (1986). 'Developing conflict management skills in Hong Kong: An analysis of some cross-cultural implications', *Management Education and Development, 17*, 287–301.

Tang, S. P. (1975). 'Address each other and treat each other as comrade' [in Chinese], *The People's Daily*, 2 July.

Tang, T. C. (1988). *Studies on Chinese Morphology and Syntax* [in Chinese]. Taipei: Xue Sheng Shu Ju.

Tang, Y. S., and Sui, Y. L. (Eds.)(1991). *Encyclopedia of Family Education* [in Chinese]. Beijing: Liantian.

Tao, K. T., and Chiu, J. H. (1985). 'The one-child-per-family-policy: Psychological perspective'. In W. S. Tseng and D. Y. H. Wu (Eds.), *Chinese Culture and Mental Health* (pp. 163–6). Orlando, FL: Academic Press.

Taraban, R., and McClelland, J. L. (1987). 'Consistency effects in word recognition', *Journal of Memory and Language, 26*, 608–31.

Tata, S. P., and Leong, F. T. L. (1994). 'Individualism–collectivism, social-network orientation, and acculturation as predictors of attitudes toward seeking professional psychological help among Chinese Americans', *Journal of Counseling, 41*, 280–7.

Taylor, M. J. (1987). *Chinese Pupils in Britain*. Berkshire, UK: NFER-NELSON Publishing Company Ltd.

Tellegen, A. (1991). 'Personality traits: Issues of definition, evidence and assessment'. In W. Grove and D. Cicchetti (Eds.), *Thinking Clearly about Psychology: Essays in Honor of Paul E. Meehl* (Vol. 2, pp. 10–35). Minneapolis: University of Minnesota Press.

Tetlock, P. E. (1980). 'Explaining teacher explanations of pupil performance: A self-presentation interpretation', *Social Psychology Quarterly, 43*, 283–90.

Thomas, A., and Chess, S. (Eds.)(1977). *Temperament and Development*. New York: Brunner/Mazel.

Thomas, E. (1989). 'Filial piety and adolescence in a changing society'. Paper presented at the International Conference on Moral Values and Moral Reasoning in Chinese Societies, Academia Sinica Conference Center, Taipei, May.

Thomas, K. W., and Kilmann, R. H. (1974). *Thomas–Kilmann Conflict MODE Instrument*. Tuxedo, NY: Xicom.

Thomas, L. (1974). *The Lives of a Cell: Notes of a Biology Watcher*. New York: Viking.

Thomson, R. (1966). *The Psychology of Thinking*. Harmondsworth, UK: Penguin Books.

Thorndike, E. L., and Lorge, I. (1944). *The Teacher's Word Book of 30,000 Words*. New York: Bureau of Publications, Teachers College.

Ting-Toomey, S. (1988). 'Intercultural conflict styles: A face-negotiation theory'. In Y. Y. Kim and W. B. Gudykunst (Eds.), *Theories in Intercultural Communication* (pp. 213–35). Beverly Hills, CA: Sage.

Ting-Toomey, S., Gao, G., Trubisky, P., Yang, Z. Z., Kim, H. S., Lin, S. L., and Nishida, T. (1991). 'Culture, face maintenance, and styles of handling interpersonal conflict: A study in five cultures', *International Journal of Conflict Management, 2*, 275–96.

Tong, N., Zhao, R., and Yang, X. (1985). 'An investigation into the current ideology of middle school students' [in Chinese], *Chinese Education, 17*, 6–21.

Tongyong Hanying Cidian [General Chinese-English Dictionary] (1986). Hong Kong: Chung Hwa Book Company.

Torrey, E. F. (1972). *The Mind Game: Witchdoctors and Psychiatrists*. New York: Emerson Hall.

Traver, H. (1984). 'Orientations toward privacy in Hong Kong'. *Perceptual and Motor Skills, 59*, 635–44.

Treiman, R., and Danis, C. (1988). 'Syllabification of intervocalic consonants', *Journal of Memory and Language, 27*, 87–104.

Triandis, H. C. (1986). 'Collectivism vs individualism: A reconceptualization of a basic concept in cross-cultural psychology'. In C. Bagley and G. Berma (Eds.), *Personality, Cognition, and Values: Cross-Cultural Perspectives of Childhood and Adolescence* (pp. 2–42). London: Macmillan.

Triandis, H. C. (1987). Individualism and social psychological theory. In C. Kagitcibasi (Ed.), *Growth and Progress in Cross-Cultural Psychology* (pp.78-83). Lisse, Netherlands: Swets and Zeitlinger.

Triandis, H. C. (1988). 'Cross-cultural contributions to theory in social psychology'. In M. H. Bond (Ed.), *The Cross-Cultural Challenge to Social Psychology* (pp. 122–40). Newbury Park, CA: Sage.

Triandis, H. C. (1990). 'Cross-cultural studies of individualism and collectivism'. In J. Berman (Ed.), *Nebraska Symposium on Motivation, 1989* (pp. 41–133). Lincoln: Nebraska University Press.

Triandis, H. C., Bontempo, R., Betancourt, H., Bond, M. H., Leung, K., Brenes, A., Georgas, J., Hui, H. C., Marin, G., Setiadi, B., Sinha, J. B. P., Verma, J., Spangenberg, J., Touzard, H., and de Montmollin, G. (1986). 'The measurement of the etic aspects of individualism and collectivism across cultures', *Australian Journal of Psychology, 38*, 257–67.

Triandis, H. C., Bontempo, R., Villareal, M. J., Asai, M., and Lucca, N. (1988). 'Individualism and collectivism: Cross-cultural perspectives on self-ingroup relationships', *Journal of Personality and Social Psychology, 54*, 323–38.

Triandis, H. C., Brislin, R., and Hui, C. H. (1988). 'Cross-cultural training across the individualism-collectivism divide', *International Journal of Intercultural Relations, 12*, 269–89.

Triandis, H. C., McCusker, C., and Hui, C. H. (1990). 'Multimethod probes of individualism and collectivism', *Journal of Personality and Social Psychology, 59*, 1006–20.

Triandis, H. C., McCusker, C., Betancourt, H., Iwao, S., Leung, K., Salazar, J. M., Setiadi, B., Sinha, J. B. P., Touzard, H., and Zaleski, Z. (1993). 'An etic–emic analysis of individualism and collectivism', *Journal of Cross-Cultural Psychology, 24*, 366–83.

Trommsdorff, G. (1983). 'Value change in Japan', *International Journal of Intercultural Relations, 7*, 337–60.

Trompenaars, F. (1993). *Riding the Waves of Culture.* London: Nicholas Brealey.

Trubetzkoy, N. S. (1936). 'Essai d'une théorie des oppositions phonologiques', *Journal de Psychologie, 33*, 5–18.

Trubisky, P., Ting-Toomey, S., Lin, S. L. (1991). 'The influence of individualism–collectivism and self-monitoring on conflict styles', *International Journal of Intercultural Relations, 15*, 65–84.

Tsai, W. H. (1986). 'The modernization of four Chinese societies: China, Taiwan, Hong Kong and Singapore', *National Taiwan University Journal of Sociology, 18*, 163–90.

Tsao, Y. C., Wu, M. F., and Feustel, T. (1981). 'Stroop interference: Hemispheric difference in Chinese speakers', *Brain and Language, 13*, 372–8.

Tse, D. K., and Wong, J. K. (1993). 'Are we there yet? Testing and extending Levitt's market globalization paradigm'. Unpublished working paper, Business and Management Department, City University of Hong Kong.

Tse, D. K., Belk, R. W., and Zhou, N. (1989). 'Becoming a consumer society: A longitudinal and cross-cultural content analysis of print ads from People's Republic of China, Hong Kong, and Taiwan', *Journal of Consumer Research, 15*(4), 457–72.

Tse, D. K., Hui, M., and Pan, Y. (1994). 'Cultural values in consumption behaviour: A comparison of Chinese and American consumers'. Unpublished working paper, Business and Management Department, City University of Hong Kong.

Tse, D. K., Lee, K. H., Vertinsky, I., and Wehrung, D. A. (1988). 'Does culture matter? A cross-cultural study of executives' choice, decisiveness, and risk adjustment in international marketing', *Journal of Marketing, 52*, 81–95.

Tse, D. K., Wong, J. K., and Tan, C. (1988). 'Towards some standardized consumption values in Asia Pacific countries'. In Michael J. Houston (Ed.), *Advances in Consumer Research* (Vol. XV, pp. 387–95). Provo, UT: Association for Consumer Research.

Tseng, M. C., Lee, M. B., and Lee, Y. J. (1989). 'A clinical study of Chinese patients with eating disorders', *Chinese Psychiatry, 3*, 17–28.

Tseng, M. S. (1972). 'Attitudes towards the disabled: A cross-cultural study', *Journal of Social Psychology, 87*, 311–12.

Tseng, W. S. (1972). 'On Chinese national character from the viewpoint of personality development' [in Chinese]. In Y. Y. Li and K. S. Yang (Eds.), *The Character of the Chinese: An Interdisciplinary Approach* [in Chinese](pp. 227–50). Taipei: Institute of Ethnology, Academia Sinica.

Tseng, W. S. (1973). 'The concept of personality in Confucian thought', *Psychiatry, 36*, 191–202.

Tseng, W. S. (1975). 'The nature of somatic complaints among psychiatric patients: The Chinese case', *Comprehensive Psychiatry, 16*, 237–45.

Tseng, W. S. (1976). 'Folk psychotherapy in Taiwan'. In W. Lebra (Ed.), *Culture-bound Syndromes, Ethnopsychiatry, and Alternative Therapies* (pp. 164–78). Hawaii: University of Hawaii Press.

Tseng, W. S. (1978). 'Traditional and modern psychiatric care in Taiwan'. In A. Kleinman, P. Kunstadter, E. R. Alexander, and J. L. Gate (Eds.), *Culture and Healing in Asian Societies* (pp. 311–28). Cambridge, MA: Schenkman.

Tseng, W. S., and Jing, H. (1979). 'The Chinese attitude toward parental authority as expressed in Chinese children's stories', *Archives of General Psychiatry, 26*, 28–34.

Tseng, W. S., and McDermott, J. F. (1975). 'Psychotherapy: Historical roots, universal elements, and cultural variations', *American Journal of Psychiatry, 132*, 378–84.

Tseng, W. S., and McDermott, J. F. (1981). *Culture, Mind and Therapy.* New York: Brunner/Mazel.

Tseng, W. S., and Peng, K. L. (1992). 'Conclusion: Comparison of reports from Asia and the Pacific'. In K. L. Peng and W. S. Tseng (Eds.), *Suicidal Behavior in the Asia-Pacific Region* (pp. 249–65). Singapore: University of Singapore Press.

Tseng, W. S., and Wu, D. Y. H. (1985). 'Directions for future study'. In W. S. Tseng and D. Y. H. Wu (Eds.), *Chinese Culture and Mental Health* (pp. 395–406). Orlando, FL: Academic Press.

Tseng, W. S., Asai, M., Jieqiu, L., Wibulswasd, P., Suryani, L. K., Wen, J. K., Brennan, J., and Heiby, E. (1990). 'Multi-cultural study of minor psychiatric disorders in Asia: Sympto-manifestations', *International Journal of Social Psychiatry, 36,* 252–64.

Tseng, W. S., Hsu, J., Omori, A., and McLaughlin, D. G. (1992). 'Suicidal behaviour in Hawaii'. In K. L. Peng and W. S. Tseng (Eds.), *Suicidal Behaviour in the Asia-Pacific Region* (pp. 231–48). Singapore: University of Singapore Press.

Tseng, W. S., Mo, K. M., Hsu, J., Li, L. S., Ou, L. W., Chen, G. Q., and Jiang, D. W. (1988). 'A socio-cultural study of *koro* epidemics in Guangdong, China', *American Journal of Psychiatry, 145,* 1538–43.

Tseng, W. S., Mo, K. W., Li, L. S., Chen, C. Q., Ou, L. W., and Zeng, H. B. (1992). '*Koro* epidemics in Guangdong, China: A questionnaire survey', *Journal of Nervous and Mental Disease, 180,* 117–23.

Tseng, W. S., Xu, N., Ebata, K., Hsu, J., and Cui, Y. (1986). 'Diagnostic pattern for neuroses among China, Japan, and America', *American Journal of Psychiatry, 143,* 1010–14.

Tsoi, M. M., and Ho, P. C. (1984). 'Psychological factors related to adjustment after tubal ligation', *Journal of Reproductive and Infant Psychology, 2,* 1–6.

Tsoi, M. M., Ho, P. C., and Poon, R. S. (1984). 'Pre-operation indicators and post-hysterectomy outcome', *British Journal of Clinical Psychology, 23,* 151–2.

Tsoi, M. M., and Sundberg, N. D. (1989). 'Patterns of psychological test use in Hong Kong', *Professional Psychology: Research and Practice, 20,* 148–50.

Tsoi, W. F. (1985). 'Mental health in Singapore and its relation to Chinese culture'. In W. S. Tseng and D. Y. H. Wu (Eds.), *Chinese Culture and Mental Health* (pp. 229–50). Orlando, FL: Academic Press.

Tsui, A. S. (1984). 'Multiple-constituency framework of managerial reputational effectiveness'. In J. G. Hunt, D. Hosking, C. A. Schrieshiem, and R. Stewart, (Eds.), *Leaders and Managers: International Perspectives on Managerial Behavior and Leadership* (pp.28-44). New York: Pergamon Press.

Tsui, C. L. C. (1978). 'Culture and control orientation: A study of internal-external locus of control in Chinese and American-Chinese women'. (Doctoral dissertation, University of California, Berkeley, 1977). *Dissertation Abstracts International, 39,* 770A.

Tsui, P., and Schultz, G. L. (1985). 'Failure of rapport: Why psychotherapeutic engagement fails in the treatment of Asian clients', *American Journal of Orthopsychiatry, 55,* 561–9.

Tu, W, M. (1985). 'Selfhood and otherness in Confucian thought'. In A. J. Marsella, G. DeVos, and F. L. K. Hsu (Eds.), *Culture and Self: Asian and Western Perspectives* (pp. 231–51). New York: Tavistock.

Tu, W. M. (1985). *Confucian Thought: Selfhood as Creative Transformation.* Albany: State of New York University Press.

Tu, W. M. (1992). 'The development of Mencius' concept of the moral self [in Chinese]. In W. M. Tu (Ed.), *Human Nature and Self-Cultivation* (pp. 79–93). Taipei: Lien-Ching Publishing.

Tung, M. (1984). 'Life values, psychotherapy, and East–West integration', *Psychiatry, 47,* 285–92.

Tung, M. (1991). 'Insight-oriented psychotherapy and the Chinese patient', *American Journal of Orthopsychiatry, 61,* 186–94.

Tupes, E. C., and Christal, R. E. (1992). 'Recurrent personality factors based on trait ratings', *Journal of Personality, 60,* 225–51. (Original work published 1961.)

Turay, A. (1994). 'All homework and no play for HK schoolkids', *South China Morning Post,* 3 April, p. 3.

Turnage, T. W., and McGinnies, E. (1973). 'A cross-cultural comparison of the effects of presentation mode and meaningfulness in short-term recall', *American Journal of Psychology, 86,* 369–81.

Turner, S. M., and Mo, L. (1984). 'Chinese adolescents' self-concept as measured by the Offer Self-Image Questionnaire', *Journal of Youth and Adolescence, 13,* 131–43.

Tzeng, O. J. L., and Hung, D. (in press). *Origin of Cerebral Organization of Language: A Neurolinguistic Perspective* (Cognitive Neuroscience Institute Monograph Series). Cambridge, MA: MIT Press.

Tzeng, O. J. L., and Wang, W. W. S. (1983). 'The first two R's', *American Scientist, 71,* 238–43.

Tzeng, O. J. L., Hung, D. L., and Wang, W. W. Y. (1977). 'Speech recoding in reading Chinese characters', *Journal of Experimental Psychology: Human Learning and Memory, 3,* 621–30.

Tzeng, O. J. L., Hung, D. L., Cotton, B., and Wang, S. Y. (1979). 'Visual lateralization effect in reading Chinese characters', *Nature, 282,* 499–501.

Ungerleider, L. G., and Haxby, J. V. (1994). '"What" and "Where" in the human brain', *Current Opinion in Neurobiology, 4,* 157–65.

Vaillant, G. E. (1976). 'Natural history of male psychological health: V. The relation of choice of ego mechanisms of defense to adult adjustment', *Archives of General Psychiatry, 33,* 535–45.

Van Bezzoijen, R., Otto, S. A., and Heenan, T. A. (1983). 'Recognition of vocal expressions of emotion: A three-national study to identify universal characteristics', *Journal of Cross-Cultural Psychology, 14,* 387–406.

Van Gulik, R. H. (1961). *Sexual Life in Ancient China.* E. J. Leiden: Brill.

Van Orden, G. C. (1987). 'A ROWS is a ROSE: Spelling, sound and reading', *Memory and Cognition, 15,* 181–98.

Van Orden, G. C., Johnston, J. C., and Hale, B. L. (1988). 'Word identification in reading proceeds from spelling to sound to meaning', *Journal of Experimental Psychology: Learning, Memory, and Cognition, 14,* 371–85.

Van Orden, G. C., Pennington, B., and Stone, G. (1990). 'Word identification in reading and the promise of subsymbolic psycholinguistics', *Psychological Review, 97,* 488–522.

Vandenberg, S. G. (1959). 'The primary mental abilities of Chinese students: A comparative study of the stability of a factor structure', *Annals of the New York Academy of Science, 79,* 257–304.

Vandenberg, S. G. (1967). 'The primary mental abilities of South American students', *Multivariate Behavioral Research, 2,* 175–98.

Veith, I. (1972). *Huang Ti Nei Ching Su Wen* [The yellow emperor's classic of internal medicine]. Berkeley: University of California Press.

Verhoeven, L., and Vermeer, A. (1992). 'Modeling communicative second language competence'. In L. Verhoeven and J. H. A. L. De Jong (Eds.), *The Construct of Language Proficiency* (pp. 163–73). Amsterdam: John Benjamins.

Vernon, P. E. (1965). *The Structure of Human Abilities.* London: Methuen.

Vernon, P. E. (1966). *Intelligence and Attainment Tests.* London: University of London Press.

Vernon, P. E. (1969). *Intelligence and Cultural Environment.* London: Methuen.

Vernon, P. E. (1979). *Intelligence: Heredity and Environment.* San Francisco: Freeman.

Vernon, P. E. (1980). 'Chinese immigrants and citizens in Canada', *New Horizons, 21,* 12–25.

Vernon, P. E. (1982). *The Abilities and Achievements of Orientals in North America.* New York: Academic Press.

Vernon, P. E. (1983). 'The right brain: Is it significant for education?' *New Horizons, 24,* 13–19.

Veroff, J. (1969). 'Social comparison and the development of achievement motivation'. In C. P. Smith (Ed.), *Achievement-related Motives in Children* (pp. 46–101). New York: Russell Sage Foundation.

Veroff, J. (1973). 'Wie allgemein ist das leistungsmotiv?' In W. Edelstein and D. Hopf (Eds.), *Bedingungen des Bildungsprozesses* (pp. 94–148). Stuttgart: Klett.

Veroff, J. (1977). 'Process and impact in men's and women's achievement motivation', *Psychology of Women Quarterly, 1*(3), 283–93.

Vogel, E. F. (1965). 'From friendship to comradeship: The change in personal relations in Communist China', *China Quarterly, 54.*

Von Cranach, M., Doise, W., and Mugny, G. (1992). *Social Representations and the Social Bases of Knowledge.* Lewiston, NY: Hogrefe.

Wachtel, P. L. (1977). *Psychoanalysis and Behaviour Therapy: Toward an Integration.* New York: Basic Books.

Waley, C. P. (1978). 'Word-nonword classification time', *Journal of Verbal Learning and Verbal Behavior, 17,* 143–54.

Wall, J. A., Jr., and Blum, M. (1991). Community mediation in the People's Republic of China', *Journal of Conflict Resolution, 35,* 3–20.

Walster, E., Aronson, V., Abraham, D., and Rottman, L. (1966). 'The importance of physical attractiveness in dating behaviour', *Journal of Personality and Social Psychology, 4,* 508–16.

Walters, S., and Balla, J. R. (1992). *English Medium Instruction at City Polytechnic of Hong Kong* (Research Report No. 17). Hong Kong: Department of English, City Polytechnic of Hong Kong.

Wan, K. C., and Bond, M. H. (1982). 'Chinese attributions for success and failure under public and anonymous conditions of rating', *Acta Psychologica Taiwanica, 24*, 23–31.

Wang, B. Z. (1984). 'Critically and selectively adopt ancient moral education' [in Chinese], *Bulletin of the Beijing Normal University, 3*, 63–70.

Wang, C. G. (1992). *The Work Values of College Graduates in a Changing Society* [in Chinese]. Taiwan: Tungwu University.

Wang, H. (1993). 'Measuring college students' achievement motivation with the TAT' [in Chinese], *Social Psychology Research* (China), *1*, 13–18.

Wang, J. (1986). 'Zhuxi's educational philosophy' [in Chinese]. *Educational Research, 9*, 60–8.

Wang, J. K., and Horng, C. H. (1984). *Historical Notes of Ancient Chinese Physical Concepts* [in Chinese]. Taipei: Ming Wen.

Wang, J. S. (1989). *Psychology of Chinese Qigong* [in Chinese]. Beijing: Shehui Kexue Chubanshe.

Wang, K. (1956). *How to Carry Out Writing Reform* [in Chinese] Wuhan: Hubei Renmin Chubanshe.

Wang, L. (1973). *Chinese Phonology* [in Chinese]. Hong Kong: Chung Hwa Publishing.

Wang, L. (1994). 'Analysis of Chinese shame structure'. Unpublished manuscript, Harvard University.

Wang, L., and Meng, Z. (1986). 'A preliminary study of discrimination on facial expressions of adults' [in Chinese], *Acta Psychologica Sinica, 18*, 349–55.

Wang, M. Q. (1992). 'The principle of moderation as a health-promotion measure'. Paper presented at a conference on Chinese psychology and behaviour organized by the Institute of Ethnology, Academia Sinica, Taipei, April.

Wang, P., and Cao, J. H. (1993). 'The treatment of schizophrenic patients by token economy' [in Chinese], *Chinese Journal of Clinical Psychology, 1*, 81–3.

Wang, R. P. (1968). 'A study of alcoholism in Chinatown', *International Journal of Social Psychology, 14*, 260–7.

Wang, T. H., and Xreedon, C. F. (1989). 'Sex role orientations, attributions for achievement, and personal goals of Chinese youth', *Journal of Research, 20*, 473–85.

Wang, T. K. (1994). 'The change of work-related values as a result of social change' [in Chinese], *Indigenous Psychological Research in Chinese Societies* (National Taiwan University), *2*, 206–50.

Wang, W. S. Y. (1973). 'The Chinese language', *Scientific American, 228*, 50–60. (Collected in Scientific American, *Language, Writing, and the Computer*, New York: W. H. Freeman, 1986.)

Wang, W. S. Y. (1981). 'Language structure and optimal orthography'. In O. J. L. Tzeng and H. Singer (Eds.), *Perception of Print: Reading Research in Experimental Psychology* (pp. 223–36). Hillsdale, NJ: Lawrence Erlbaum.

Wang, X. (1993). *Gems of Chinese Wisdom* (L. W. Kam, Trans.). Singapore: Asiapac Books.

Wang, Y. F., Shen, Y. C., Gu, B. M., He, Y., Ho, Y. (1991). 'A comprehensive study of behavioural problems in schoolchildren in urban areas of Beijing', *Integrative Psychiatry, 7*(3–4), 170–83.

Wang, Z. M. (1988). 'The effects of responsibility system reform and group attributional training on performance: A quasi-experiment in a Chinese factory' [in Chinese], *Chinese Journal of Applied Psychology, 3*(3), 7–14.

Wang, Z. M. (1988). *Work and Personnel Psychology* [in Chinese]. Hangzhou: Zhejiang Educational Press.

Wang, Z. M. (1989). 'Participation and skill utilization in organizational decision making in Chinese enterprises'. In B. J. Fallon, H. P. Pfister, and J. Brebner (Eds.), *Advances in Industrial Organizational Psychology* (pp. 19–26). Amsterdam: Elsevier.

Wang, Z. M. (1990). 'Action research and O. D. strategies in Chinese enterprises', *Organization Development Journal, 8*, 66–70.

Wang, Z. M. (1992). 'Managerial psychological strategies for Chinese–foreign joint ventures', *Journal of Managerial Psychology, 7*(3), 10–16.

Wang, Z. M. (1993). 'A comparison of the pattern of management decision-making in joint equity ventures and state-owned enterprises' [in Chinese]. In Z. M. Wang (Ed.), *The Operation of East Asian Enterprises*. Fudan: Fudan University Press.

Wang, Z. M. (1993). 'Culture, economic reform, and the role of industrial/organizational psychology in China'. In H. C. Triandis, M. D. Dunnette, and L. M. Hough (Eds.), *Handbook of Industrial and Organizational Psychology* (second edition, Vol. 4, pp. 689–725). Palo Alto,

CA: Consulting Psychologists Press.

Wang, Z. M., and Heller, F. (1993). 'Patterns of power distribution in managerial decision-making in Chinese and British industrial organisations', *International Journal of Human Resource Management, 4*, 113–28.

Wang, Z. M., and Satow, T. (1994). 'Leadership styles and organizational effectiveness in Chinese–Japanese joint ventures', *Journal of Managerial Psychology, 9*(4), 31–6.

Wang, Z. M., and Sheng J. P. (1990). 'Characteristics of managerial decision-making in Sino-foreign joint ventures and their performance assessment' [in Chinese], *Chinese Journal of Applied Psychology, 5*(4), 29–37.

Ward, C., and Hewstone, M. (1985). 'Ethnicity, language and intergroup relations in Malaysia and Singapore: A social psychological analysis', *Journal of Multilingual and Multicultural Development, 6*, 271–96.

Waterman, A. S. (1981). 'Individualism and interdependence', *American Psychologist, 36*, 762–73.

Waterman, A. S. (1984). *The Psychology of Individualism*. New York: Praeger.

Waters, G. S., and Seidenberg, M. S. (1985). 'Spelling-sound effects in reading: Time course and decision criteria', *Memory and Cognition, 13*, 557–72.

Watkins, D. (1994). 'Hong Kong secondary school learners: A developmental perspective'. Unpublished manuscript, Hong Kong University.

Watkins, D., and Adebowale, A. (1992). 'Assessing the approaches to learning of Nigerian students', *Assessment and Evaluation in Higher Education, 17*(1), 11–20.

Watkins, D., and Cheng, C. (in press). 'The revised causal dimension scale: A confirmatory factor analysis with Hong Kong subjects'. *British Journal of Educational Psychology*.

Watkins, D., and Dong, Q. (1994). 'Assessing the self-esteem of Chinese school children', *Educational Psychology, 14*, 129–37.

Watkins, D., Biggs, J., and Regmi, M. (1991). 'Does confidence in the language of instruction influence a student's approach to learning', *Instructional Science, 20*, 331–9.

Watkins, D., and Hattie, J. (1981). 'The learning processes of Australian university students: Investigation of contextual and personological factors', *British Journal of Educational Psychology, 51*, 384–93.

Watkins, D., and Hattie, J. (1985). 'A longitudinal study of the approaches to learning of Australian tertiary students', *Human Learning, 4*, 127–41.

Watkins, D., Hattie, J., and Astilla, E. (1986). 'Approaches to studying by Filipino students: A longitudinal investigation', *British Journal of Educational Psychology, 56*, 357–62.

Watkins, D., Regmi, M., and Astilla, E. (1991). 'The Asian-learner-as-a-rote-learner stereotype: Myth or reality?' *Educational Psychologist, 11*(1), 21–34.

Watrous, B. C., and Hsu, F. L. E. (1963). 'A thematic apperception test study of Chinese, Hindu, and American college students'. In F. L. K. Hsu (Ed.), *Clan, Caste, and Club* (pp. 263–311). New York: van Nostrand.

Watson, I. (1991). 'Phonological processing in two languages'. In E. Bialystok (Ed.), *Language Processing in Bilingual Children* (pp. 25–48). New York: Cambridge University Press.

Watts, A. W. (1961). *Psychotherapy East and West*. New York: Pantheon Books.

Waxer, P. H. (1989). 'Cantonese versus Canadian evaluation of directive and non-directive therapy', *Canadian Journal of Counseling, 23*, 263–72.

Wegner, D. M. (1986). 'Transactive memory: A contemporary analysis of the group mind'. In B. Mullen and G. R. Goethals (Eds.), *Theories of Group Behaviour* (pp. 185–208). New York: Springer-Verlag.

Wehrung, D. A., Lee, K., Tse, D. K., and Vertinsky, I. (1989). 'Adjusting risky situations: Theory and empirical tests', *Journal of Risk and Uncertainty, 2*, 189–212.

Weiner, B. (1972). *Theories of Motivation: From Mechanism to Cognition*. Chicago: Rand-McNally.

Weiner, B. (1974). *An Achievement Motivation and Attribution Theory*. Morristown, NJ: General Learning Press. Weiner, B. (1980). *Human Motivation*. New York: Holt, Rinehart and Winston.

Weiner, B. (1979). 'A theory of motivation for some classroom experience', *Journal of Educational Psychology, 71*, 3–25.

Weiner, B. (1985). 'An attributional theory of achievement motivation and emotion', *Psychological Review, 92*(4), 548–73.

Weiner, B. (1986). *An Attributional Theory of Motivation and Emotion*. New York: Springer-

Verlag.

Weiner, B., Frieze, I. H., Kukla, A., Reed, L., Rest, S., and Rosenbaum, R. M. (1971). *Perceiving the Causes of Success and Failure.* Morristown, NJ: General Learning Press.

Weiner, B., Heckhausen, H., Meyer, W. V., and Cook, R. E. (1972). 'Causal ascription and achievement behaviour: A conceptual analysis of effort and reanalysis of locus of control', *Journal of Personality and Social Psychology, 21*, 239–48.

Weiner, B., and Kukla, A. (1970). 'An attributional analysis of achievement motivation', *Journal of Personality and Social Psychology, 15*, 1–20.

Weinsten, M. S. (1969). 'Achievement motivation and risk preference', *Journal of Personality and Social Psychology, 13*(2), 153–72.

Weisz, J. R., Rothbaum, F. M., and Blackburn, T. C. (1984). 'Standing out and standing in: The psychology of control in America and Japan', *American Psychologist, 39*, 955–69.

Weldon, E., and Jehn, K. (1993). 'Work goals and work-related beliefs among managers and professionals in the United States and the People's Republic of China', *Asia Pacific Journal of Human Resources, 1* 58–70.

Weller, R. P. (1984). 'Social contradiction and symbolic resolution: Practical and idealized affines in Taiwan', *Ethnology, 23*(4), 249–60.

Wen, C. I. (1972). 'Chinese national character as revealed in value orientations' [in Chinese]. In Y. Y. Li and K. S. Yang (Eds.), *The Character of the Chinese* (pp. 47–84). Taipei: Institute of Ethnology, Academia Sinica.

Wen, C. I. (1989). *Chinese Values* [in Chinese]. Taipei: The Grand-East Book Co.

Wen, J. (1995). 'Sexual beliefs and problems in contemporary Taiwan'. In T. Y. Lin, W. S. Tseng, and E. K. Yeh(Eds.), *Chinese Societies and Mental Health.* Hong Kong: Oxford University Press.

Weng, B. K. (1991). 'Differential relationship of work stress to mental ill-health and job dissatisfaction among nursing professionals', *Chinese Journal of Psychology, 33*, 77–86.

Werker, J. F., Pegg, J. E., and McLeod, P. J. (in press). 'A cross-language investigation of infant preference for infant-directed communication', *Infant Behavior and Development.*

West, S., Newsom, J., and Fenaughty, A. (1992). 'Publication trends in JPSP: Stability and change in topics, methods, and theories across two decades', *Personality and Social Psychology Bulletin, 18*, 475–84.

Westwood, R. I., and Chan, A. (1992). 'Headship and leadership'. In R. I. Westwood (Ed.), *Organizational Behavior: Southeast Asian Perspectives.* Hong Kong: Longman.

Westwood, R. I., Tang, S. F., and Kirkbride, P. S. (1992). 'Chinese conflict behavior: Cultural antecedents and behavioral consequences', *Organization Development Journal, 10*(2), 13–19.

Wheaton, B. (1983). 'Stress, personal coping resources, and psychiatric symptoms: An investigation of interactive models', *Journal of Health and Social Behaviour, 24*, 208–29.

Wheeler, L. (1988). 'My year in Hong Kong: Some observations about social behaviour', *Personality and Social Psychology Bulletin, 14*, 410–20.

Wheeler, L. (1989). 'A reply to Lam and Yang', *Personality and Social Psychology Bulletin, 15*, 644–47.

Wheeler, L., Reis, H. T., and Bond, M. H. (1989). 'Collectivism–individualism in everyday social life: The Middle Kingdom and the melting pot', *Journal of Personality and Social Psychology, 57*, 79–86.

White, W. G., and Chan, E. (1983). 'A comparison of self-concept of Chinese and White graduate students and professionals', *Journal of Non-White Concerns in Personnel and Guidance, 11*, 138–41.

Whiting, J. W. M., and Child, I. L. (1953). *Child Training and Personality: A Cross-Cultural Study.* New Haven: Yale University Press.

Whorf, B. L. (1956). 'Science and linguistics'. In J. B. Carroll (Ed.), *Language, Thought and Reality: Selected Writings of Benjamin Lee Whorf* (pp. 207–19). Cambridge, MA: MIT Press.

Wiemann, J., Chen, V., and Giles, H. (1986). 'Beliefs about talk and silence in a cultural context'. Paper presented to a meeting of the Speech Communication Association, Chicago, November.

Wierzbicka, A. (1986). 'Human emotions: Universal or culture-specific?' *American Anthropologist, 88*, 584–94.

Wierzbicka, A. (in press). 'Contrastive sociolinguistics and the theory of "cultural scripts": Chinese vs. English'. In M. Hellinger and U. Ammon (Eds.), *Contrastive sociolinguistics*, The Hague: Mouton.

Wiesel, T. N., and Gilbert, C. D. (1989). 'Neural mechanisms of visual perception'. In D. M. K. Lam and C. D. Gilbert (Eds.), *Neural Mechanisms of Visual Perception: Proceedings of the Retina Research Foundation Symposia* (Vol. 2, pp. 7–33). Woodlands, TX: Portfolio.

Wiggins, J., Moody, A., and Lederer, D. (1983). 'Personality typologies related to marital satisfaction', *American Mental Health Counsellors Association Journal, 5*, 169–78. Wiggins, J. S. (1992). 'Have model, will travel', *Journal of Personality, 60*, 527–32.

Wilson, R. W. (1970). *Learning to be Chinese: The Political Socialization of Children in Taiwan*. Cambridge, MA: MIT Press.

Wilson, R. W. (1974). *The Moral State: A Study of the Political Socialization of Chinese and American Children*. New York: The Free Press.

Wilson, R. W. (1980). 'Conformity and deviance regarding moral rules in Chinese society: A socialization perspective'. In A. Kleinman and T. Y. Lin (Eds.), *Normal and Abnormal Behavior in Chinese Culture* (pp. 117–136). Dordrecht, the Netherlands: D. Reidel.

Wilson, R. W. (1981). 'Moral behavior in Chinese society: A theoretical perspective'. In R. W. Wilson, S. L. Greenblatt, and A. A. Wilson (Eds.), *Moral Behavior in Chinese Society* (pp. 1–20). New York: Praeger Publishers.

Wilson, R. W., and Pusey, A. W. (1982). 'Achievement motivation and small-business relationship patterns in Chinese society'. In S. L. Greenblatt, R. W. Wilson, and A. A. Wilson (Eds.), *Social Interaction in Chinese Society* (pp. 195–208). New York: Praeger Publishers.

Winarick, K. (1985). 'The "chemistry" of personal attraction', *The American Journal of Psychoanalysis, 45*, 380–8.

Wing, J. K., Cooper, J. E., and Sartorius, N. (1974). *The Measurement and Classification of Psychiatric Symptoms*. Cambridge: Cambridge University Press.

Winner, E. (1989). 'How can Chinese children draw so well?' *Journal of Aesthetic Education, 23*(1), 41–63.

Winterbottom, M. R. (1953). 'The relation of childhood training in independence to achievement motivation'. Unpublished doctoral dissertation, University of Michigan.

Winterbottom, M. R. (1958). 'The relation of need for achievement to learning experiences in independence and mastery'. In J. W. Atkinson (Ed.), *Motives in Fantasy, Action, and Society* (pp. 453–78). Princeton, NJ: Van Nostrand.

Wiseman, S. (Ed.)(1967). *Intelligence and Ability*. Harmondsworth: Penguin Books.

Wolf, M. (1970). 'Child training and Chinese family'. In M. Freedman (Ed.), *Family and Kinship in Chinese Society* (pp. 37–62). Stanford, CA: Stanford University Press.

Wolf, M. (1972). *Women and the Family in Rural Taiwan*. Stanford, CA: Stanford University Press.

Wolff, P. H. (1972). 'Ethnic difference in alcohol sensitivity', *Science, 175*, 449–50.

Wolfgang, A., and Josefowitz, N. (1978). 'Chinese immigrant value changes with length of time in Canada and value differences compared to Canadian students', *Canadian Ethnic Studies, 2*, 130–5.

Won-Doornink, M. (1991). 'Self-disclosure and reciprocity in South Korean and U.S. male dyads'. In S. Ting-Toomey and F. Korzenny (Eds.), *Cross-Cultural Interpersonal Communication* (pp. 116–31). Newbury Park, CA: Sage.

Wong, B. (1978). 'A comparative study of assimilation of the Chinese in New York City and Lima, Peru', *Comparative Studies in Society and History, 20*, 335–58.

Wong, C. K. (1988). 'The unseen tears of children: A Chinese boy who vomited for 14 months', *Canadian Journal of Psychiatry, 33*, 751–3.

Wong, C. K. (1990). 'Too shameful to remember: A 17-year-old Chinese boy with psychogenic amnesia', *Australian and New Zealand Journal of Psychiatry, 24*, 570–4.

Wong, G., and Cochrane, R. (1989). 'Generation and assimilation as predictors of psychological well-being in British-Chinese', *Social Behavior, 4*, 1–14.

Wong, G. Y. Y., and Birnbaum-More, M. (1994). 'Culture, context and structure: A test on Hong Kong banks', *Organization Studies, 15*, 99–123.

Wong, J. (1970). 'Peasant economic behaviour: The case of traditional agricultural co-operation in China', *The Developing Economies, 9*, 332–49.

Wong, M. (1990). 'The education of White, Chinese, Filipino, and Japanese students: A look at "high school and beyond"', *Sociological Perspectives, 33*, 355–74.

REFERENCES															575

Wong, M. G. (1989). 'A look at intermarriage among the Chinese in the United States in 1980',
    Sociological Perspectives, 32, 87–107.
Wong, S. L. (1968). *A Chinese Syllabary Pronounced According to the Dialect of Canton* [in
    Chinese]. Hong Kong: Chung Hwa Publishing.
Wong, S. T., Oon, D., and Lun, K. C. (1979). 'Survey on child rearing patterns of families of low
    socio-economic status living in high-rise flats in Singapore: A preliminary report', *Annals
    Academy of Medicine, 3*, 227–36.
Woods, A. H. (1929). 'The nervous diseases of the Chinese', *Archives of Neurology and Psychiatry,
    21*, 542–70.
World Health Organization (1973). *Report of the International Pilot Study of Schizophrenia.*
    Geneva: World Health Organization.
World Health Organization (1979). *Schizophrenia: An International Follow-up Study.* Geneva:
    World Health Organization.
World Health Organization (1983). *Depressive Disorders in Different Cultures: Report on the WHO
    Collaborative Study on Standardized Assessment of Depressive Disorders.* Geneva: World
    Health Organization.
World Health Organization (1986). *World Health Statistics Annual.* Geneva: World Health
    Organization.
Wright, G., and Ayton, P. (Eds.)(1994). *Subjective Probability.* Chichester, UK: Wiley.
Wright, G. N., and Phillips, L. D. (1980). 'Cultural variation in probabilistic thinking: Alternative
    ways of dealing with uncertainty', *International Journal of Psychology, 15*, 239–57.
Wright, G. N., Phillips, L. D., and Wisudha, A. (1983). 'Cultural comparison on decision-making
    under uncertainty'. In J. B. Deregowski, S. Dziurawiec, and R. C. Annis (Eds.), *Expiscations in
    Cross-Cultural Psychology* (pp. 387–402). Lisse, the Netherlands: Swets and Zeitlinger.
Wright, G. N., Phillips, L. D., Whalley, P. C., Choo, G. T., Ng, K. O., Tan, I., and Wisudha, A. (1978).
    'Cultural differences in probabilistic thinking: Alternate ways of dealing with uncertainty',
    International Journal of Psychology, 15, 239–57.
Wu, C. H. (1986). 'Young children's comprehension of the Chinese passives'. In H. S. R. Kao and R.
    Hoosain (Eds.), *Linguistics, Psychology and the Chinese Language* (pp. 115–24). Hong
    Kong: University of Hong Kong.
Wu, C. H. (1991). 'Parental socialization practices and the child's ability of self-control' [in Chinese].
    In K. S. Yang and K. K. Hwang (Eds.), *The Mind and Behaviour of the Chinese: Selected
    Papers of the 1989 Taipei Conference* (pp. 383–449). Taipei: Laureate Publishing Co.
Wu, C. Y., and Zhao, J. C. (1991). 'A study of MMPI profile characteristics of neurotic patients' [in
    Chinese], *Acta Psychologica Sinica, 23*(2), 207–15.
Wu, D. Y. H. (1966). 'Looking at problems in Chinese child-rearing from an anthropological per-
    spective' [in Chinese], *Thought and Word* (Taiwan), *3*(6), 741–5.
Wu, D. Y. H. (1982). 'Psychotherapy and emotion in traditional Chinese medicine'. In A. J. Marsella
    and G. M. White (Eds.), *Cultural Conceptions of Mental Health and Therapy* (pp. 285–301).
    Dordrecht, the Netherlands: D. Reidel.
Wu, D. Y. H. (1985). 'Child training in Chinese culture'. In W. S. Tseng and D. Y. H. Wu (Eds.),
    Chinese Culture and Mental Health (pp. 113–34). Orlando, FL: Academic Press.
Wu, D. Y. H. (1985). 'Modernization, changing family, and the issues concerning Chinese child
    rearing' [in Chinese]. In C. Chiao (Ed.), *Proceedings of the First Conference on Modernization
    and Chinese Culture* (pp. 31–9). Hong Kong: New Asia College, Chinese University of Hong
    Kong.
Wu, D. Y. H. (1991). 'China's population policy and the rearing of single-children' [in Chinese]. In
    C. Chiao (Ed.), *Chinese Family and Change* (pp. 277–85). Hong Kong: Chinese University of
    Hong Kong.
Wu, D. Y. H. (1994). 'Self and collectivity: Socialization in Chinese preschools'. In R. T. Ames, W.
    Dissayanake, and T. P. Kasulis (Eds.), *Self as Person in Asian Theory and Practice* (pp.
    235–49). Albany: State University of New York Press.
Wu, D. Y. H. (1995). 'Parental control: Psychocultural interpretations of Chinese patterns of social-
    ization'. In S. Lau (Ed.), *Youth and Child Development in Chinese Societies.* Hong Kong:
    Chinese University Press.
Wu, D. Y. H., and Tseng, W. S. (1985). 'Introduction: The characteristics of Chinese culture'. In W.
    S. Tseng and D. Y. H. Wu (Eds.), *Chinese Culture and Mental Health* (pp. 3–13). New York:

Academic Press.

Wu, D. Y. H., and Xue, S. Z. (Eds.)(1995). *Socialization of Chinese Children* [in Chinese]. Shanghai: Educational Literature Press.

Wu, E. C. (1988). 'On the factor structure of Ko's Mental Health Questionnaire—from the viewpoint of need theory' [in Chinese], *Chinese Journal of Mental Health* (Taiwan), *4*(2), 73–84.

Wu, J. (1992). 'Masochism and fear of success in Asian women: Psychoanalytic mechanisms and problems in therapy', *American Journal of Psychoanalysis, 52,* 1–12.

Wu, J. J., and Cheng, B. L. (1992). 'A correlational study of academic motivation, learning strategies and academic performance of elementary and junior high school students' [in Chinese]. *National Zhengzhi University Research Journal, 66,* 13–38.

Wu, J. J., Lin, X. J., and Lai, X. F. (1978). 'Revisions of the Work and Family Orientation Scale' [in Chinese]. Unpublished manuscript.

Wu, J. J., Pan, Y. Y., and Ding, X. X. (1980). 'The relationships among locus of control, job satisfaction, and efficiency', *National Chengchi University Journal, 41,* 61–74.

Wu, J. T., and Liu, I. M. (1988). 'A data base system about the psychological features of Chinese characters and words'. In I. M. Liu, H. C. Chen, and M. J. Chen (Eds.), *Cognitive Aspects of the Chinese Language* (pp. 171–86). Hong Kong: Asian Research Service.

Wu, J. T., Chou, T. L., and Liu, I. M. (1993). 'The locus of the character/word frequency effect'. Paper presented at the Sixth International Symposium on Cognitive Aspects of the Chinese Language, Taipei.

Wu, L. L. (1986). 'An analysis of management dynamics in Chinese enterprises' [in Chinese], *Chinese Journal of Applied Psychology, 1*(3), 12–16.

Wu, L. L. (1992). 'A research on bonus distribution methods and its motivating effects' [in Chinese]. In *Proceedings of the Annual Conference of Industrial Psychology, Committee of the Chinese Psychological Society and Cognitive Ergonomics Society* (pp. 11–16). Shanghai: East China Normal University.

Wu, L. L., and Cheng, Z. G. (1992). 'The methods and efficiency of material rewards in enterprises' [in Chinese]. *Chinese Journal of Applied Psychology, 7*(4), 34–41.

Wu, S., and Shaver, P. R. (1993). 'American and Chinese love conceptions: Variations on a universal theme'. Poster presentation at the 101st meeting of the American Psychological Association, Toronto, August.

Wu, W. T., and Chen, H. J. (1978). 'Teacher leadership behaviour as related to students' expectation, achievement, and adjustment' [in Chinese], *Bulletin of Educational Psychology* (Taiwan), *11,* 87–104.

Wu, W. Y., Yu, Q. F., and Zhang, M. Y. (1992). 'Factors affecting the depressive symptomology of the elderly' [in Chinese], *Chinese Mental Health Journal, 6*(6), 256–7.

Wu, Y. F. (1981). 'The study of personality characteristics and social adjustment of children in different achievement motivation levels' [in Chinese], *Educational Review* (Taiwan), *3,* 111–60.

Wydell, N., Patterson, K. E., and Humphreys, G. W. (1993). 'Phonologically mediated access to meaning for Kanji: Is a *Rows* still a *Rose* in Japanese Kanji?' *Journal of Experimental Psychology: Learning, Memory, and Cognition, 19,* 491–514.

Xia, R. J. (1987). 'Participative decision-making behaviour in industrial organizations' [in Chinese]. Unpublished Master's thesis, Institute of Psychology, Academy of Sciences, Beijing.

Xiantian, L. (1985). 'The effect of family on the mental health of the Chinese people'. In W. S. Tseng and D. Wu (Eds.), *Chinese Culture and Mental Health* (pp. 85–93). New York: Academic Press.

Xiao, S. F., and Yan, H. Q. (1993). 'A survey of psychological disorders in general internal medical outpatients' [in Chinese], *Chinese Mental Health Journal, 7*(4), 154–7.

Xie, K. D. (1992). 'The conditions and strategies to achieve the historical commission of eliminating illiteracy' [in Chinese]. In China National Institute of Educational Studies (Ed.), *Selection of Research Results* (pp. 214–8). Beijing: Jiaoyu Kexue Press.

Xu, J. M. (1991). 'The treatment of depression by cognitive-behavioural therapy' [in Chinese], *Chinese Mental Health Journal, 5,* 221–3.

Xu, L. C. (1989). 'Comparative study of leadership between Chinese and Japanese managers based upon PM theory'. In B. J. Fallon, H. P. Pfister, and J. Brebner (Eds.), *Advances in Organizational Psychology* (pp. 42–9). Amsterdam: Elsevier.

Xu, L. C., and Wang, Z. M. (1991). 'New developments in organisational psychology in China',

Applied Psychology: An International Review, 40, 3–14.

Yamamoto, J. (1985). 'Are American psychiatric outpatients more depressed than Chinese outpatients?' *American Journal of Psychiatry, 142,* 1347–51.

Yamauchi, H., and Li, Y. (1993). 'Achievement-related motives and work-related attitudes of Japanese and Chinese students', *Psychological Reports, 73,* 755–67.

Yan, H. Q. (1989). 'The necessity of retaining the diagnostic concept of neurasthenia', *Culture, Medicine and Psychiatry, 13,* 139–46.

Yan, J. J. (1987). 'On establishing the field of Chinese communication' [in Chinese], *Xing Wen Xue Kan, 10,* 50–3.

Yan, W., and Gaier, E. L. (1994). 'Causal attributions for college success and failure: An Asian American comparison', *Journal of Cross-Cultural Psychology, 25,* 146–58.

Yan, X. Y. (1985). 'Folklore and moral education' [in Chinese], *Educational Research, 2,* 39–44.

Yang, C. F. (1991). 'A review of studies on self in Hong Kong and Taiwan: Reflections and future prospects' [in Chinese]. In C. F. Yang and H. S. R. Kao (Eds.), *Chinese and Chinese Heart* [in Chinese] (pp. 15-92). Taipei: Yuan Liu Publishing Company.

Yang, C. F., and Chiu, C. Y. (1988). 'The significance of frequency words in the MMPI lie test'. In I. M. Liu, H. C. Chen, and M. J. Chen (Eds.), *Cognitive Aspects of the Chinese Language* (pp. 69–79). Hong Kong: Asian Research Service.

Yang, C. F., and Hui, C. H. (1986). 'Reward allocation behavior and feeling of unfairness', *Chinese Journal of Psychology, 28,* 59–78.

Yang, E. L. (1993). 'What kinds of special talents are needed in Taiwan?' [in Chinese], *Commonwealth,* March, 20–65.

Yang, H., Zhang, L. H., Zhao, J. W., and Dang, J. (1992). 'A research on the equity differential threshold of salary and bonus distribution in the enterprises and colleges' [in Chinese]. In *Proceedings of the Annual Conference of Industrial Psychology Committee of the Chinese Psychological Society and Cognitive Ergonomics Society* (pp. 17-24). Shanghai: East China Normal University.

Yang, H. Y. (1983). 'Psychotherapy for phobias' [in Chinese], *Chinese Journal of Nervous and Mental Diseases, 9,* 102–3.

Yang, K. S. (1965). 'Psychological studies on Chinese national character: A literature review' [in Chinese], *Thought and Word* (Taiwan), *2,* 3–19.

Yang, K. S. (1972). 'Expressed values of Chinese college students' [in Chinese]. In Y. Y. Li and K. S. Yang (Eds.), *Symposium on the Character of the Chinese: An Interdisciplinary Approach* (pp. 257–312). Taipei: Institute of Ethnology, Academia Sinica.

Yang, K. S. (1981). 'Social orientation and individual modernity among Chinese students in Taiwan', *Journal of Social Psychology, 113,* 159–70.

Yang, K. S. (1981). 'The formation and change of Chinese personality: A cultural-ecological perspective' [in Chinese], *Acta Psychologica Taiwanica, 23,* 39–56.

Yang, K. S. (1982). 'Causal attributions of academic success and failure and their affective consequences' [in Chinese], *Acta Psychologica Taiwanica, 24*(2), 65–83.

Yang, K. S. (1982). 'Sinicization of psychological research in Chinese society: Directions and issues' [in Chinese]. In K. S. Yang and C. I. Wen (Eds.), *The Sinicization of Social and Behavioural Science Research in Chinese Societies* (pp. 153–87). Taipei: Institute of Ethnology, Academia Sinica.

Yang, K. S. (1982). '*Yuan* and its functions in modern Chinese life' [in Chinese]. In *Proceedings of the Conference on Traditional Culture and Modern Life* (pp. 103–28). Taipei: Committee on the Renaissance of Chinese Culture.

Yang, K. S. (1985). 'The change of personality and behaviour among the Chinese people in Taiwan' [in Chinese]. In *Proceedings of the Conference on Modernization and Its Problems in Taiwan* (pp. 75–100). Taipei: Institute of Three People's Principles, Academia Sinica.

Yang, K. S. (1986). 'Chinese personality and its change'. In M. H. Bond (Ed.), *The Psychology of the Chinese People* (pp. 106–70). Hong Kong: Oxford University Press.

Yang, K. S. (1988). 'Chinese filial piety: A conceptual analysis' [in Chinese]. In K. S. Yang, *The Metamorphosis of the Chinese People* (pp. 31–64). Taipei: Laureate Publishing Co.

Yang, K. S. (1988). 'The Chinese concept of *yuan* and its function' [in Chinese]. In *Zhongguoren De Tuibian* (pp. 1–30). Taipei: Gue Guan.

Yang, K. S. (1988). 'Will societal modernization eventually eliminate cross-cultural psychological differences?' In M. H. Bond (Ed.), *The Cross-Cultural Challenge to Social Psychology* (pp. 67–85). Beverly Hills, CA: Sage.

Yang, K. S. (1992). 'Do traditional and modern values coexist in a modern Chinese society?' [in Chinese]. In *Proceedings of the Conference on Chinese Perspectives on Values* (pp. 117–58). Taipei: Center for Sinological Studies.

Yang, K. S. (1993). 'Can traditional and modern values coexist?' [in Chinese]. In K. S. Yang (Ed.), *Chinese Value: A Social Science Viewpoint* (pp. 65–120). Taipei: Kwai Kuan.

Yang, K. S. (1993). 'Chinese social orientation: An integrative analysis'. In W. L. Y. C. Cheng, F. M. C. Cheung, and C. N. Chen (Eds.), *Psychotherapy for the Chinese* (pp. 19–56). Hong Kong: Department of Psychiatry, Chinese University of Hong Kong.

Yang, K. S. (1993). 'Why do we need an indigenous Chinese psychology?' [in Chinese], *Indigenous Psychological Research in Chinese Societies* (Taiwan), *1*, 6–88.

Yang, K. S. (1994). 'Chinese response to modernization: A psychological perspective'. Unpublished manuscript, Department of Psychology, National Taiwan University, Taipei.

Yang, K. S. (1995). 'Chinese social orientation: An integrative analysis'. In W. S. Tseng, T. Y. Lin, and Y. K. Yeh (Eds.), *Chinese Societies and Mental Health*. Hong Kong: Oxford University Press.

Yang, K. S. (in press). 'Theories and research in Chinese personality: An indigenous approach'. In H. S. R. Kao and D. Sinha (Eds.), *Asian Psychology*. Thousand Oaks, CA: Sage.

Yang, K. S. (Ed.)(1993). *Indigenous Psychological Research in Chinese Societies* (Vol. 1)[in Chinese]. Taipei: Gueiguan.

Yang, K. S., and Bond, M. H. (1985). 'Dimensions of Chinese person perception: An emic approach'. In C. Chiao (Ed.), *Proceedings of the Conference on Modernization and Chinese Culture* (pp. 309–25). Hong Kong: Institute of Social Studies, the Chinese University of Hong Kong.

Yang, K. S., and Bond, M. H. (1990). 'Exploring implicit personality theories with indigenous or imported constructs: The Chinese case', *Journal of Personality and Social Psychology, 58*, 1087–95.

Yang, K. S., and Chang, F. L. (1975). 'Chinese value orientations and their change: The case of university students' [in Chinese]. Unpublished manuscript, Department of Psychology, National Taiwan University, Taipei.

Yang, K. S., and Cheng, B. S. (1987). 'Confucianized values, individual modernity, and organizational behaviour: An empirical test of the post-Confucian hypothesis' [in Chinese], *Bulletin of the Institute of Ethnology, Academia Sinica* (Taiwan), *64*, 1–49.

Yang, K. S., and Hchu, H. Y. (1974). 'Determinants, correlates, and consequences of Chinese individual modernity' [in Chinese], *Bulletin of the Institute of Ethnology, Academia Sinica, 37*, 1–38.

Yang, K. S., and Ho, D. Y. F. (1988). 'The role of *yuan* in Chinese social life: A conceptual and empirical analysis'. In A. C. Paranjpe, D. Y. F. Ho, and R. W. Rieber (Eds.), *Asian Contributions to Psychology* (pp. 263–81). New York: Praeger Publishers.

Yang, K. S., and Hwang, L. L. (1988). 'The change of preferences for ways to live of Chinese university students in Taiwan: Twenty years later' [in Chinese]. In H. Y. Hchu and E. H. Chang (Eds.), *Social and Cultural Change in Taiwan* (pp. 443–8). Taipei: Institute of Ethnology, Academia Sinica.

Yang, K. S., and Lee, P. H. (1971). 'Likeability, meaningfulness and familiarity of 557 Chinese adjectives for personality trait description' [in Chinese], *Acta Psychologica Taiwanica, 13*, 36–7.

Yang, K. S., and Liang, W. H. (1973). 'Some correlates of achievement motivation among Chinese high school boys', *Acta Psychologica Taiwanica, 15*, 59–67.

Yang, K. S., and Tseng, S. C. (Eds.)(1988). *Management Theories of the Chinese People* [in Chinese]. Taipei: Guei Guen Publishing Company.

Yang, K. S., and Wen, C. I. (Eds.)(1982). 'The sinicization of social and behavioural science research in China', *Institute of Ethnology Academia Sinica Monograph Series*, B, 10.

Yang, K. S., and Yu, A. B. (1988). 'Social-oriented and individual-oriented achievement motivation: Conceptualization and measurement'. Paper presented at the symposium on Chinese personality and social psychology, 24th International Congress of Psychology, Sydney.

Yang, K. S., and Yu, A. B. (1989). 'Social- and individual-oriented achievement motivation: An attributional analysis of their cognitive, affective, motivational, and behavioral consequences'. Paper presented at the 10th biennial meeting of the International Society for the

Study of Behavioral Development, Jyväskylä, Finland, July.

Yang, K. S., Chen, W. Y., and Hsu, C. Y. (1965). 'Rorschach responses of normal Chinese adults: IV. The speed of production', *Acta Psychologica Taiwanica*, *7*, 34–51.

Yang, K. S., Ko, Y. H., and Yang, L. P. H. (1973). 'Personality correlates of scholastic achievement among Chinese junior high school students' [in Chinese], *Bulletin of the Institute of Ethnology, Academia Sinica* (Taiwan), *35*, 41–86.

Yang, K. S., Su, C., Hsu, H. H., and Hwang, C. H. (1962). 'Rorschach responses of normal Chinese adults: I. The normal details', *Acta Psychologica Taiwanica*, *4*, 78–103.

Yang, K. S., Tsai, S. G., and Hwang, M. L. (1963). 'Rorschach responses of normal Chinese adults: III. The number of responses and number of refusals', *Psychological Testing* (Taiwan), *10*, 127–36.

Yang, K. S., Tzuo, H. Y., and Wu, C. Y. (1963). 'Rorschach responses of normal Chinese adults: II. The popular responses', *Journal of Social Psychology*, *60*, 175–86.

Yang, K. S., Yeh, K. H., and Hwang, L. L. (1989). 'The social attitudes and behaviour of filial piety conceptualization and measurement' [in Chinese], *Bulletin of the Institute of Ethnology, Academia Sinica* (Taiwan), *65*, 171–227.

Yang, K. S., Yu, A. B., and Yeh, M. H. (1991). 'Chinese individual traditionality and modernity: Conceptualization and measurement' [in Chinese]. In K. S. Yang and K. K. Hwang (Eds.), *The Mind and Behaviour of the Chinese: Selected Papers of the 1989 Taipei Conference* (pp. 241–306). Taipei: Laureate Publishing Co.

Yang, L. S. (1957). 'The concept of *pao* as a basis for social relations in China'. In J. K. Fairbank (Ed.), *Chinese Thought and Institutions* (pp. 291–309). Chicago: University of Chicago Press.

Yang, M. C. (1972). 'Chinese familism and national character' [in Chinese]. In Y. Y. Li and K. S. Yang (Eds.), *The Character of the Chinese* (pp. 127–74). Taipei: Institute of Ethnology, Academia Sinica.

Yang, M. J., and Hwang, K. K. (1980). 'Interrelations of models of self-disclosure' [in Chinese], *Acta Psychologica Taiwanica*, *22*, 51–70.

Yang, Y. Z. (1991). 'Investigation of life events of first-episode rural schizophrenics' [in Chinese], *Chinese Mental Health Journal*, *5*, 172–3.

Yang, Z. W., and Li, X. R. (1991). 'Comparative studies of the IQ level, social adjustment, and behavior problems of children aged 9 to 11 with learning difficulties' [in Chinese], *Chinese Mental Health Journal*, *5*(4), 155–9.

Yao, E. L. (1985). 'Adjustment needs of Asian immigrant children', *Elementary School Guidance and Counseling*, *19*, 222–7.

Yao, T. T. (1984). 'The relationship of traditional–modern cognitive conflict to physiopsychological adjustment: The case of female students' [in Chinese]. Unpublished Master's thesis, Department of Psychology, National Taiwan University.

Yap, P. M. (1958). 'Hypereridism and attempted suicide in Chinese', *Journal of Nervous and Mental Disease*, *127*, 34–41.

Yap, P. M. (1958). 'Suicide in Hong Kong', *Journal of Mental Science*, *104*, 266–301.

Yap, P. M. (1959). *Suicide in Hong Kong*. London: Oxford University Press.

Yap, P. M. (1965). 'Koro: A culture-bound depersonalization syndrome', *British Journal of Psychiatry*, *111*, 43–50.

Yap, P. M. (1965). 'Phenomenology of affective disorders in Chinese and other cultures'. In A De Reuck and R. Porter (Eds.), *Transcultural Psychiatry* (pp. 84–114). Boston: Little, Brown.

Yap, P. M. (1971). 'Guilt and shame, depression and culture: A psychiatric cliche re-examined', *Community Contemporary Psychiatry*, *1*(2), 35.

Yates, J. F. (1990). *Judgment and Decision Making*. Englewood Cliffs, NJ: Prentice Hall.

Yates, J. F., and Stone, E. R. (1992). 'The risk construct'. In J. F. Yates (Ed.), *Risk-Taking Behavior* (pp. 1–25). Chichester, UK: Wiley.

Yates, J. F., Lee, J. W., Levi, K. R., and Curley, S. P. (1990). 'Measuring and analyzing probability judgment accuracy in medicine', *Philippine Journal of Internal Medicine*, *28* (Supplement 1), 21–32.

Yates, J. F., Lee, J. W., and Shinotsuka, H. (1992). 'Cross-national variation in probability judgment'. Paper presented at the annual meeting of the Psychonomic Society, St. Louis, November.

Yates, J. F., Zhu, Y., Ronis, D. L., Wang, D. F., Shinotsuka, H., and Toda, M. (1989). 'Probability judgment accuracy: China, Japan, and the United States', *Organizational Behavior and Human*

Decision Processes, 43, 147–71.

Ye, G. A. (1978). 'The socio-economic status, achievement motivation, aspirations, and academic achievement of Taiwanese normal college and university students' [in Chinese]. Unpublished Master's thesis, National Taiwan Normal University.

Yee, T. N. J. T (1980). 'Chinese American conceptualization of physical and mental well-being', *Dissertation Abstracts International, 42,* 706-B.

Yeh, E. K. (1985). 'Sociocultural changes and prevalence of mental disorders in Taiwan'. In W. S. Tseng and D. Y. H. Wu (Eds.), *Chinese Culture and Mental Health* (pp. 265–86). New York: Academic Press.

Yeh, E. K., Chu, H. M., Ko, Y. H., Lin, T. Y., and Lee, S. P. (1972). 'Student mental health: An epidemiological study in Taiwan', *Acta Psychologica Taiwanica, 14,* 1–26.

Yeh, J. S., and Liu, I. M. (1972). 'Factors affecting recognition thresholds of Chinese characters' [in Chinese], *Acta Psychologica Taiwanica, 14,* 113–17.

Yeh, K. H., and Yang, K. S. (1989). 'Cognitive structure and development of filial piety: Concepts and measurement' [in Chinese], *Bulletin of the Institute of Ethnology, 56,* 131–69.

Yeh, K. H., and Yang, K. S. (1990). 'An analysis of the typology of cognitive structures of filial piety' [in Chinese]. In K. S. Yang and K. K. Hwang (Eds.), *Psychology and Behavior of Chinese People: Proceedings of the First Interdisciplinary Conference* (pp. 141–79). Taipei: National Taiwan University, Institute of Psychology.

Yen, C. F., Hsu, S. C., and Seetoo, D. H. (1991). 'An investigation of negotiation decision behavior: Effects of potential value of social transaction and potential value of economic transaction' [in Chinese], *Management Review, 10,* 215–42.

Yen, H. (1990). 'A review of sex education in the last ten years in the Taiwan area'. Paper presented at the International Conference on Sexuality in Asia, Hong Kong, May.

Yen, Y. S. (1965). 'The diagnostic indications of the delusion of the paranoid schizophrenia in the Rorschach test', *Acta Psychologica Taiwanica, 7,* 63–70.

Yen, Y. S. (1983). 'Diagnostic indications of cognitive distortions of schizophrenics in the Rorschach test' [in Chinese], *Acta Psychologica Taiwanica, 25,* 13–23.

Yeung, S. (1989). 'The dynamics of family care for the elderly in Hong Kong'. Unpublished doctoral dissertation, University of Hong Kong.

Yeung, W. H., and Schwartz, M. A. (1986). 'Emotional disturbance in Chinese obstetrical patients: A pilot study', *General Hospital Psychiatry, 8,* 258–62.

Yeung, Z. F. (1993). 'Are Chinese really "collective"?' [in Chinese]. In K. S. Yang (Ed.), *Chinese Values: A Social Science Viewpoint* (pp. 321–434). Taipei: Kwai Kuan.

Yik, M. S. M. (1993). 'Self- and peer ratings of personality traits: Evidence of convergent and discriminant validity among Hong Kong university students'. Unpublished Master's thesis, Chinese University of Hong Kong.

Yik, M. S. M., and Bond, M. H. (1993). 'Exploring the dimensions of Chinese person perception with indigenous and imported constructs: Creating a culturally balanced scale', *International Journal of Psychology, 28,* 75–95.

Yik, M. S. M., Meng, Z., and Russell, J. A. (1994). 'Freely produced emotion labels for spontaneous facial expressions: A cross-cultural comparison' [in Chinese]. Unpublished manuscript.

Ying, Y. W. (1988). 'Depressive symptomatology among Chinese-Americans as measured by the CES-D', *Journal of Clinical Psychology, 44,* 739–46.

Ying, Y. W. (1991). 'Marital satisfaction among San Francisco Chinese-Americans', *International Journal of Social Psychiatry, 37,* 201–13.

Ying, Y. W., and Liese, L. H. (1991). 'Emotional well-being of Taiwan students in the U.S.: An examination of pre- to post-arrival differential', *International Journal of Intercultural Relations, 15,* 345–66.

Ying, Y. W., and Zhang, X. (1992). 'Personality structure in rural and urban Chinese people', *Bulletin of the Hong Kong Psychological Society, 28/29,* 81–93.

Young, D. (1989). 'Neurasthenia and related problems', *Culture, Medicine and Psychiatry, 13,* 131–8.

Young, L. W. L. (1994). *Crosstalk and Culture in Sino-American Communication.* Cambridge: Cambridge University Press.

Young, M. Y., and Gardner, R. C. (1990). 'Modes of acculturation and second language proficiency', *Canadian Journal of Behavioural Science, 22,* 59–71.

Young, S. M. (1992). 'A framework for successful adoption and performance of Japanese manu-facturing practices in the United States', *Academy of Management Review, 17*, 677–700.

Yu, A. B. (1990). 'The construct validity of social-oriented and individual-oriented achievement motivation' [in Chinese]. Unpublished doctoral dissertation, Department of Psychology, National Taiwan University.

Yu, A. B. (1991). 'Socializational factors of an individual's achievement motivation in the family' [in Chinese], *Bulletin of the Institute of Ethnology, Academia Sinica* (Taiwan), *71*, 87–132.

Yu, A. B. (1994). 'An exploration of new directions in cultural psychology: An analysis of Taiwanese folk sayings' [in Chinese]. In Y. H. Chang, Y. C. Fu, and H. Y. Chiu (Eds.), *Exploration and Foresight in Social Science Research Method* (Vol. 2). Taipei: Institute of Ethnology, Academia Sinica.

Yu, A. B. (1994). 'Is social-oriented achievement motivation (SOAM) different from individual-oriented achievement motivation (IOAM)? Further discussions of the relationship between motivation and behaviour' [in Chinese], *Bulletin of the Institute of Ethnology, Academia Sinica* (Taiwan), *76*, 197–224.

Yu, A. B. (1994). 'The self and life goals of traditional Chinese: A philosophical and psychological analysis'. In A. M. Bouvy, F. J. R. Van de Vijver, P. Boski, and P. Schmitz (Eds.), *Journeys into Cross-Cultural Psychology* (pp. 50–67). Lisse, the Netherlands: Swets and Zeitlinger.

Yu, A. B., Chang, Y. J., and Wu, C. W. (1993). 'The content and categorization of the self-concept of college students in Taiwan: A cognitive viewpoint' [in Chinese]. In Y. K. Huang (Ed.), *Humanhood, Meaning, and Societies* (pp. 261–304). Taipei: Institute of Ethnology, Academia Sinica.

Yu, A. B., and Yang, K. S. (1987). 'Social-oriented and individual-oriented achievement motivation: A conceptual and empirical analysis' [in Chinese], *Bulletin of the Institute of Ethnology, Academia Sinica* (Taiwan), *64*, 51–98.

Yu, A. B., and Yang, K. S. (1991). 'Reflections on the indigenization of Chinese achievement motivation' [in Chinese]. In C. F. Yang and H. S. R. Kao (Eds.), *Chinese People Chinese Mind: Perspective on Personality and Society* (pp. 201–90). Taipei: Yuan-Liou Publishing Co.

Yu, A. B., and Yang, K. S. (1994). 'The nature of achievement motivation in collectivist societies'. In U. Kim, H. C. Triandis, C. Kagitcibasi, S. C. Choi, and G. Yoon (Eds.), *Individualism and Collectivism: Theory, Method, and Applications* (pp. 239–50). Thousand Oaks, CA: Sage.

Yu, B., Zhang, W., Jing, Q., Peng, R., Zhang, G., and Simon, H. A. (1985). 'STM capacity for Chinese and English language materials', *Memory and Cognition, 13*, 202–7.

Yu, D. H. (1990). 'The hidden stories of Chinese' [in Chinese]. In *Zhong guo ren de xin li* (Vol. 3. *Zhongguo Ren De Mian Ju Xing Ge: Ren Qing Yu Mian Zi*, pp. 63–107). Taipei: Zhanglaoshi chubanshe.

Yu, E. S. H. (1974). 'Achievement motive, familism, and *hsiao*: A replication of McClelland–Winterbottom studies'. Unpublished doctoral dissertation, University of Notre Dame.

Yu, E. S. H. (1980). 'Chinese collective orientation and need for achievement', *International Journal of Social Psychiatry, 26*, 184–9.

Yu, J. (1994). 'Free-listing study of emotion-related words in China'. Unpublished data, Nanjing Normal University, China.

Yu, L., and Wu, S. (1988). 'Effects of length of stay in the United States on how the Chinese fulfilled their filial obligations'. In L. Adler (Ed.), *Cross-Cultural Research in Human Development* (pp. 121–30). New York: Praeger.

Yu, L. C. (1983). 'Patterns of filial belief and behavior within the contemporary Chinese American family', *International Journal of Sociology of the Family, 13*, 17–36.

Yu, W. Z. (1991). 'Motivational and demotivational factors in enterprises' [in Chinese], *Chinese Journal of Applied Psychology, 6*(1), 6–14.

Yu, W. Z. (1992). 'Motivational mechanism of the allocation system reform' [in Chinese]. In *Proceedings of the Annual Conference of Industrial Psychology Committee of the Chinese Psychological Society and Cognitive Society* (pp. 1–10). Shanghai: East China Normal University.

Yue, X. D. (1993) 'Coping with psychological stress through Confucian self-cultivation and Taoist self-transcendence'. Unpublished doctoral dissertation, Harvard University, Cambridge, MA.

Yuen, R. K., and Tinsley, H. E. (1981). 'International and American students' expectations about counseling', *Journal of Counseling Psychology, 28*, 66–9.

Yueng, Y. M. (1987). 'Cities that work: Hong Kong and Singapore'. In R. J. Fuchs, G. W. Jones, and E. M. Pernia (Eds.), *Urbanization and Urban Policies in Pacific Asia* (pp. 257–76). London: Westview Press.

Yum, J. O. (1988). 'The impact of Confucianism on interpersonal relationships and communication patterns in East Asia', *Communication Monographs, 55,* 374–88.

Yum, J. O. (1991). 'The impact of Confucianism on interpersonal relationships and communication patterns in East Asia'. In L. A. Samovar and R. E. Porter (Eds.), *Intercultural Communication: A Reader* (sixth edition, pp. 66–78). Belmont, CA: Wadsworth.

Zeki, S. (1993). *A Vision of the Brain.* Oxford: Blackwell.

Zhang, B. (1992). 'Cultural conditionality in decision making: A prospect of probabilistic thinking'. Unpublished doctoral dissertation, Department of Information Systems, London School of Economics and Political Science, University of London.

Zhang, B., and Peng, D. (1992). 'Decomposed storage in the Chinese lexicon'. In H. C. Chen and O. J. L. Tzeng (Eds.), *Language Processing in Chinese* (pp. 131–49). Amsterdam: North-Holland.

Zhang, B. Y., Dong, J. W., Xu, X. R., Ao, M., Wang, P., and Gao, L. (1990). 'Psychological consultation by telephone: "hotline of hope"' [in Chinese], *Chinese Mental Health Journal, 4,* 178–80.

Zhang, C. S. (Ed.)(1993). *The Treasure of Chinese Family Teaching* [in Chinese]. Changchun: Jilin Renmin Publishers.

Zhang, H. C. (1988). 'Psychological measurement in China', *International Journal of Psychology, 23,* 101–24.

Zhang, H. C. (1988). 'Psychological testing and China's modernization', *International Test Commission Bulletin, 27,* 23–31.

Zhang, H. C. (1992). 'Views of intelligence and mental testing in China'. In *Proceedings of the Second Asian–African Psychological Conference* (pp. 842–7). Beijing: Beijing University Press.

Zhang, H. C., and Shu, H. (1989). 'Phonetic similar and graphic similar priming effects in pronouncing Chinese characters' [in Chinese], *Acta Psychologica Sinica, 3,* 284–9.

Zhang, H. C., and Wang, X. P. (1989). 'Revision of Raven's Standard Progressive Matrices in China' [in Chinese], *Acta Psychologica Sinica, 21*(2), 113–21.

Zhang, J., and Zhong, Y. (1993). 'Discussion on psychopathological nature and pathogeny of anthropophobia' [in Chinese], *Chinese Journal of Neurology and Psychiatry, 19,* 269–71.

Zhang, J. X., and Bond, M. H. (1993). 'Target-based interpersonal trust: Cross-cultural comparison and its cognitive model' [in Chinese], *Acta Psychologica Sinica, 2,* 164–72.

Zhang, K. C. (1990). 'The value orientations of Chinese students in China mainland' [in Chinese]. Unpublished Master's thesis, Department of Education, Shanxi Normal University, Xi'an.

Zhang, M., Wang, M., Li, J., and Phillips, M. R. (1994). 'Randomised-control trial of family intervention for 78 first-episode male schizophrenic patients: An 18-month study in Suzhou, Jiangsu', *British Journal of Psychiatry, 165* (Supplement 24), 96–102.

Zhang, M. H. (1978). 'Familial factors that influence the opportunity to enter college in our country' [in Chinese], *National Taiwan Normal University Graduate School of Education Research Quarterly, 20,* 589–602.

Zhang, M. Y. (1987). 'Application of the CES-D in the survey of depression in a normal sample' [in Chinese], *Chinese Journal of Neuropsychiatry,* 20–2.

Zhang, M. Y., Fan, B., Cai, G. J., Chi, Y. F., Wu, W. Y., and Jin, H. (1987). 'Life events scale: Norms' [in Chinese], *Chinese Journal of Nervous and Mental Diseases, 13,* 70–3.

Zhang, S. Y. (1994). 'Reading *The Ugly Chinese*' [in Chinese]. In Y. Bo (Ed.), *Zhongguo Ren, Ni Shou Le Shen Me Zhu Zhou?* (pp. 95–102). Taipei: Xingguang Chuban She.

Zhang, Y. (1991). 'The measurement of experimentally induced affects' [in Chinese], *Acta Psychologica Sinica, 1,* 99–106.

Zhang, Y., Song, W. Z., Yao, L., and Xia, C. Y. (1992). 'Investigation of the effects of life events and personality on various psychosomatic illnesses' [in Chinese], *Acta Psychologica Sinica, 24,* 35–42.

Zhang, Y., Yang, W., Phillips, M. R., Dai, C., and Zheng, H. (1988). 'Reliability and validity of a Chinese computerized diagnostic instrument', *Acta Psychiatrica Scandinavica, 77,* 32–7.

Zhang, Y. X., and Wang, Y. (1989). 'Attributional style and depression' [in Chinese], *Xinlin Xuebao, 21,* 141–8.

Zhao, G. Y., Chen, Y. P., and Yu, L. F. (1987). 'The effectiveness of psychotherapy with 214 cases of obsessive–compulsive disorder, phobia, and anxiety disorder' [in Chinese], *Chinese Journal of Nervous and Mental Diseases*, *13*, 84–6.

Zhao, G. Y., Huang, D. X., Cai, X. S., and Zhang, J. B. (1986). 'A report on 1000 cases of outpatient psychological consultation and 500 cases of consultation by mail' [in Chinese], *Chinese Journal of Neurology and Psychiatry*, *19*, 325–8.

Zhao, J. P., and Zheng, Y. P. (1992). 'Reliability and validity of the Hamilton Depression Rating Scale' [in Chinese], *Chinese Mental Health Journal*, *6*(5), 214–16.

Zhao, L. R. (1983). 'Pneumatology: A Chinese translation of Joseph Haven's "Mental Philosophy"' [in Chinese], *Xinli Xuebao*, *15*, 380–8.

Zhao, L. R., Lin F., and Zhang, S. Y. (1989). *History of Psychology* [in Chinese]. Beijing: Tungyi Chubanshe.

Zheng, D. L. (1992). *The Hong Kong Miracle: Economic Success as a Cultural Motivation* [in Chinese]. Hong Kong: Commercial Press.

Zheng, L. X. (1952). 'The problems of Chinese script reform' [in Chinese]. Beijing: Xin Jianshe Zazhishe.

Zheng, X., and Berry, J. W. (1991). 'Psychological adaptation of Chinese sojourners in Canada', *International Journal of Psychology*, *26*(4), 451–70.

Zheng, Y. (1988). 'Cross-cultural study of the differences in the intellectual development of primary and secondary children of Li and Han ethnic background in Hainan Island' [in Chinese], *Acta Psychologica Sinica*, *20*(2), 179–85.

Zheng, Y. M. (1982). 'Psychotherapy with a girl suffering from psychogenic vomiting and 23-year follow-up' [in Chinese], *Chinese Journal of Neurology and Psychiatry*, *15*, 46–8.

Zheng, Y. P. (1989). *Handbook for Clinical Scales* (second edition) [in Chinese]. Changsha: Biometrics Department, Mental Health Research Institute of Hunan Medical College.

Zheng, Y. P., and Lin, K. M. (1991). 'Comparison of the Chinese Depression Inventory and the Chinese version of the Beck Depression Inventory', *Acta Psychiatrica Scandinavica*, *84*, 531–6.

Zheng, Y. P., Wei, L. A., Goa, L. G., Zhang, G. C., and Wong, C. G. (1988). 'Applicability of the Chinese Beck Depression Inventory', *Comprehensive Psychiatry*, *29*, 484–9.

Zheng, Y. P., Xu, L. Y., and Shen, Q. J. (1986). 'Styles of verbal expression of emotional and physical experiences: A study of depressed patients and normal controls in China', *Culture, Medicine and Psychiatry*, *10*, 231–43.

Zheng, Y. P., Zhao, J. P., Phillips, M. Liu, J. B., Cai, M. F., Sun, S. Q., and Huang, M . F. (1988). 'Validity and reliability of the Chinese Hamilton Depression Rating Scale', *British Journal of Psychiatry*, *152*, 660–4.

Zhong, Y. (1993). 'Treatment of anthropophobia' [in Chinese]. In *Cognitive-Insight Therapy* (pp. 68-105). Guiyang: Guizhou Press of Science and Technology and Guizhou Educational Press.

Zhong, Y. B. (1988). *Chinese Psychoanalysis* [in Chinese]. Shenyang: Liaoning People's Publishing Co.

Zhong, Y. B. (1989). 'Resistance in psychotherapy with obsessive-compulsive patients' [in Chinese], *Chinese Journal of Nervous and Mental Diseases*, *15*, 65–7.

Zhong, Y. B. (1991). 'Psychotherapy and psychological consultation in mainland China' [in Chinese]. *Chinese Mental Health Journal*, *5*, 38–40.

Zhong, Y. Y. (1989). 'Overall analysis of Taiwan job satisfaction research' [in Chinese], *National Central University Management School Report*, *19*, 135–79.

Zhou, M. (1990). 'Sex viewpoint of women college students in continental China today'. Paper presented at the International Conference on Sexuality in Asia, Hong Kong, May.

Zhou, R. (1993). 'A sociological analysis of the generation-gap phenomenon among Chinese in mainland China' [in Chinese]. Unpublished Master's thesis, Department of Sociology, Nanjing University.

Zhou, Y. G. (1978). 'To what degree are the "phonetics" of present-day Chinese characters still phonetic?' [in Chinese], *Zhongguo Yuwen*, *146*, 172–7.

Zhou, Y. Z., and Zhao, C. Y. (1992). 'A study of clinical diagnostic validity of MMPI' [in Chinese], *Chinese Mental Health Journal*, *6*(5), 211–13.

Zhu, G. L., and Wang, X. (1992). 'Study and analysis of the behaviour problems of 220 Form 1 students in an elite urban secondary school' [in Chinese], *Chinese Mental Health Journal*, 6(3), 103–4.

Zhu, Y., Liu, I. M, Shieh, Y. T., and Fan, C. (1992). 'Visual and auditory frequency differences and the visual presentation superiority effect' [in Chinese]. In P. Z. Kuan and C. T. Chang (Eds.), *Proceedings of the Fifth International Conference on Cognitive Aspects of the Chinese Language* (pp. 83–7). Beijing: Science Publisher.

Zhuang, H. Q. (1990). 'Defeating the internal enemy' [in Chinese]. In *Zhongguo ren de xin li* (Vol. 3. *Zhong Guo Ren De Mian Ju Xing Ge: Ren Qing Yu Mian Zi*, pp. 109-119). Taipei: Zhang Laoshi Chubanshe.

Zou, Y., Zhao, C., and Jiang, C. (1989). 'Analysis of the structure validity of the Chinese version of MMPI' [in Chinese], *Acta Psychologica Sinica, 3,* 266–73.

Zuckerman, M. (1979). 'Attribution of success and failure revisited, or the motivational bias is alive and well in attribution theory', *Journal of Personality, 47,* 245–87.

Zuckerman, M. (1979). *Sensation Seeking: Beyond the Optimal Level of Arousal.* Hillsdale, NJ: Lawrence Erlbaum Associates.

Zung, W. W. K. (1965). 'A self-rating depressive scale', *Archives of General Psychiatry, 12,* 371–9.

Index